For Our
Beloved
Country

For Our Beloved Country

American War Diaries from the
Revolution to the Persian Gulf

Edited by Speer Morgan
and Greg Michalson

THE ATLANTIC MONTHLY PRESS
NEW YORK

The journal of George Sargent originally appeared in slightly different form in *The Missouri Review,* Volume XII, Number 3, 1989, by permission of The Huntington Library.
The diary of Amy Wingreen originally appeared in *The Missouri Review,* Volume XV, Number 3, 1993, by permission of The Newberry Library.
Selected footnotes from *Private Yankee Doodle* by Joseph Plumb Martin, edited and annotated by George Scheer © 1962, 1990, reprinted by permission of Little, Brown and Company.
The diary of Duane Lee Smith by permission of the author.
The diary of Joseph Abodeely by permission of the author.
The diary of Everett Fulton by permission of the author.
The diary of Charles Ponton by permission of Mrs. Lucille Ponton Weting and The Bentley Historical Library.

Published simultaneously in Canada
Printed in the United States of America

FIRST EDITION

Library of Congress Cataloging-in-Publication Data

For our beloved country: American war diaries from the Revolution to the Persian Gulf / [compiled by] Speer Morgan and Greg Michalson.
Includes bibliographical references
ISBN 0-87113-549-3
1. United States—History, Military—Sources. 2. Soldiers—United States—Diaries. 3. United States—Armed Forces—Diaries.
4. Soldiers' writings, American. I. Morgan, Speer, 1949–   .
II. Michalson, Greg.
E181.F67   1994   973—dc20   93-2495

Design by Laura Hough
Maps created by Jeanne Peters-Baker

The Atlantic Monthly Press
841 Broadway
New York, NY 10003

FIRST PRINTING

Contents

Acknowledgments

We would like to thank the hundreds of veterans and relatives of veterans who sent in their diaries for consideration for use in this book, as well as the dozens of librarians and curators who helped us track down material. Particularly generous were Gary Yarrington, Curator of the Lyndon Baines Johnson Library; Diana Haskell, Margaret Kulis, and Patrick Morris at the Newberry Library; David Keough, Curator of the U.S. Army Military History Research Collection at Carlisle Barracks; Nancy Bartlett of the Bentley Historical Library of the University of Michigan; and Harriet McLoone of the Huntington Library. We want to thank Charlotte Overby and Jodee Stanley for research help on the Revolution and the Spanish-American War; Sam Stowers for help with the Gulf War; historian Tom Alexander for guidance regarding the Civil War; Major William McCormick for fact checking and editing suggestions regarding the Gulf War; Andrew Dyer of the National Archives for help with George Sargent's records; and the people at the U.S. Park Service who were gracious about answering many questions.

Many thanks to George Scheer for his fine scholarship and his cooperation regarding the Joseph Plumb Martin diary. Many of the footnotes in this diary are his and are marked with his initials, G.S.

Thanks to Marilynn Keil for handling the difficult job of turning handwritten scripts into type. And very special thanks indeed to Dedra Veach, without whom this book could not exist.

Finally, our thanks to Everett Fulton, Joseph Abodeely, and Duane Lee Smith for their cooperation and assistance with their diaries, and to Mrs. Lucille Ponton Weting for help with her father's diary.

For Our
Beloved
Country

Introduction

Americans don't think of themselves as a war-like people. The radically democratic founders of this country were deeply suspicious of standing or professional armies. They feared that such armies could too easily become forces of corruption and tyranny—essentially, kept bureaucracies looking for trouble. Throughout our history we have encouraged the notion that this nation is always dragged reluctantly into war. Yet the country has fought at least nine wars and several other conflicts in as many generations. In the two hundred some years of its existence, the United States has involved itself more times in bloody conflicts than perhaps any other major military power. We have repeatedly armed and disarmed. The United States is a nation born from war that was stimulated by the engines of war and that reached greatness in the eyes of the world in no small part through the display of military power. In this century America has won two world wars and become stronger for it, while the other leading nations were mostly either defeated or diminished by the experience. America's military history has helped define our national identity, created many of our myths, helped shape our view of the world and our influence in it, and shown us our limits.

This book brings the individual's voice to that history with seven personal accounts from seven wars, from the Revolution to the recent Gulf War. These are the crucial conflicts in U.S. military history seen through the experiences, language, and sensibilities of people who fought in them. Taken together, they provide an inside look into what has changed and what has remained surprisingly constant about the soldier's world.

America's war diaries and memoirs describe widely different circumstances, and yet there are striking similarities among them. American soldiers seem to have spent much of their time just surviving in the field. Their days have been taken up surprisingly often with worries about whether they have enough to eat, whether their rations are edible, whether they are too hot or cold or wet or receiving mail from home. Their enemies are boredom, discouragement, a sense of abandonment, and disease. Their allies include ingenuity, a sense of purpose, adaptability, and mail. For most soldiers, fear comes in short bursts of action. In their descriptions of battle, there is a surprisingly widespread tendency in American diaries toward understatement and euphemism.

Yet each story is different. In these accounts:

• A young man joins the Continental Army in 1776 because it calls to his restless spirit. He soon finds himself in a hungry army, where officers treat soldiers with condescension, cruelty, and floggings. His memoir of the War of Independence is garrulous, but lively and literate—one of the little-known prizes of the American revolutionary period. It is also comprehensive, covering much of the eight-year conflict, from the New York campaigns to Yorktown, as experienced by the core Continental Army. In colorful but straightforward fashion, uncontaminated by sentimentality, it describes the daily life of a soldier in a ragtag army.

• An eighteen-year-old from Charlestown, Massachusetts, signs up to be a bugler with the First New England Cavalry in the Civil War. He marches with an army that is on the receiving end of one of the most celebrated campaigns in military history—the baffling Shenandoah Valley campaign of Stonewall Jackson; later in the war he is at the battles of Fredericksburg, the second Bull Run, Petersburg, and several others, including the dramatic last encounters of the war. Among other things, he describes a Union Army that to a surprising degree is left to shift for itself. Observant, increasingly sensitive over time, he has a sense of wonder and of history, and a plainspoken urge to understand the unimaginable.

• A young nurse from Chicago, trained at Cook County Hospital as "an expert in cases of yellow fever," answers her country's appeal to work in the hospital camps in Cuba during the Spanish-American

War. She is among the very first group of women ever to be officially recruited by the army for service in a war zone. She sees the chance to go to Cuba as her opportunity for adventure as well as a patriotic act. Her romantic idealism at the beginning of the journey may be naive, but it is this same quality that lends her strength to keep working under the most appalling conditions. Surrounded by death, exhausted, and herself coming down with fever, she refuses to lose heart or give up tending to "my brave boys."

• A high-school teacher from Kalamazoo joins the American ambulance corp in World War I and is among the first large group of Americans to arrive in France. After a submarine-haunted crossing, his corp is stationed with the French army at Verdun, near Fort Douaumont, the geographical epicenter of World War I. His diary describes the bizarre world at and just behind the front lines, where drivers desperately try to keep their Ford ambulances running on bomb-rained roads, where German aviators are falling out of the sky, and censors are continually looking over their shoulders for signs of "pacifism." At the end of the war he undertakes a tortured love affair, in which a young woman teaches him some of the essential differences between the French and Americans.

• A Texas farm boy raised during the Depression, who as a teenager in the 1930s learns to fly sixty-mile-an-hour biplanes, joins the navy, at first for the purpose of receiving an education. At the outbreak of World War II he reenlists to become a navy carrier pilot and eventually serves in one of the most hazardous theaters of war in American military history—the American retaking of the Pacific. From Saipan to Leyte, he flies against the Imperial Fleet and air force, losing seven roommates in as many months, winning the Distinguished Flying Cross for his part in the battle of the Philippine Sea. His diary provides a detailed, steady-handed account of the terrifying world of the Pacific skies.

• A twenty-four-year-old college graduate and ROTC officer volunteers for Vietnam because he is moved by stories of U.S. military "advisors" being killed in action. His initial motives are a sense of patriotism and a desire for adventure. He serves through one of the bloodiest years of the war during the infamous Tet Offensive, heading a platoon that leads the relief of the marines besieged at Khe Sanh, alternately air-assaulting and walking for days in the jungles of the A Shau Valley on search-and-destroy sweeps, supervising the building of an R&R Center in Camp Evans, fraternizing with the Vietnamese while learning their language. After having served in five campaigns, he leaves Vietnam a more thoughtful person, thankful to have gotten out alive and to have kept his men alive.

• A young man from Missouri, the first of his family to finish college, enters the ROTC program to help finance his education. After serving several assignments as a liaison and logistics officer, he finds himself in the desert in Saudi Arabia, leading a unit whose job it will be to collect and ensure the humane treatment of thousands of Iraqi prisoners of war, many of whom are starving and shell shocked. Providing adequate food, shelter, and necessary medical attention becomes a daunting humanitarian challenge.

In more than one sense, these diarists are like the epic adventurers of imaginative literature. They travel to distant, exotic settings where they are challenged, sometimes to the limit of human ability. Those who write about combat describe it as one of the most memorable experiences of a lifetime. Operating at the height of their animal powers, living at the existential edge, they are asked to do things that are at times inexpressibly strange, and surprisingly often they make the noblest choice that life offers, to die for others.

Yet while the endeavor and setting may be epic, the substance and tone of most true war accounts tend toward realism, irony, and absurdism. In war, what is supposed to happen seldom does. The ridiculous, the sublime, and the tragic intermingle. The diarist is concerned not about writing something that is "unified" but about telling his story as he has seen it. The diary is a soldier's companion and counsellor. Sometimes he chats with it, and sometimes he tells it things that he can't tell anybody else. The diarist's need to tell and our need to listen are finally the most persuasive kinship between these accounts and literature.

* * *

Introduction

For historians, diaries have both the advantages and disadvantages of having been written on the spot. Unrevised diaries have an immediacy and detail that are unblemished by later reinterpretations. Their weakness is their myopia, which can sometimes be particularly apparent in war diaries, where soldiers are often not able to see the larger picture.

Historians used to make rigid distinctions regarding the usefulness of different kinds of personal accounts, more or less automatically assigning a higher value to the most immediate, least amended, and least source-influenced diaries. One of the ill effects of this assumption was that some of the best personal accounts were banished from serious historical consideration because they were "polluted" by emendation or outside sources. In the current era of radical skepticism regarding historical records, however, there is less concern about the precise genre of a piece (pure diary, amended diary, memoir, etc.) than about the individual quality of information that it contains. So-called "objective" sources are not necessarily either objective or very valuable, while presumably highly subjective documents may in fact be rich with valuable information. As historians have become more skeptical about all primary sources, paradoxically they are opening themselves up to a wider variety of them, including everything from previously obscure data to novels.

This approach is helpful in the field of war memoirs and diaries since in the confusion of war very few accounts are made on a daily basis, and many of the best are some composite of memoir and diary. Joseph Plumb Martin's Revolutionary War memoir was written when he was an old man, at a time when one might expect an old soldier's memory to be shot through with all kinds of misrememberings. On every matter that can be checked against records, however, Martin is either accurate or so close to it that his account, although written at a considerable distance in years, retains the immediacy and quality of detail of a diary. George Sargent's Civil War diary was written in the field, but Sargent apparently later added some explanatory passages to it. It is an expanded diary with a high quality of detail.

No individual's experience of any war speaks for another's. There are as many different versions of every war as there are people who fought in them. None of the selections presented here is "typical." Each is one person's record of managing to cope, understand, and survive under fast-changing conditions. Yet certain characteristics of the different wars do emerge from these and other personal accounts.

Most Revolutionary War diaries are pocket notebooks with briefly scribbled entries, consisting mainly of travel and weather records. *The sky is finally clear. We march to Morrisville.* Such briefness is not surprising since few Continental and militia soldiers either were fluent enough at writing or had sufficient basic conditions of comfort in which to write long meditations. There was plenty of time in this long war, but common soldiers were usually operating at the edge of survival. Of necessity, weather was something they cared about since much of the time the sky was their shelter. A majority of them were farmers, bred to care about the weather. Travel was noteworthy to them because few had done much of it prior to their service. Before joining, many had not traveled over five or ten miles from their birthplaces, and tramping all around New York, New Jersey, Pennsylvania, Maryland, Virginia, even going as far as South Carolina, was a fairly remarkable experience. It is a truism in war that soldiers' morale picks up when they are on the move, and this was particularly the case during the Revolution, a war that involved so much waiting. Movement implied danger, but it also relieved the characteristic boredom of spending months at a time in the wretched shantytown winter camps.

Many Revolutionary War diaries and memoirs describe only one campaign or a brief period of service. For the first couple of years of the war, the American army was trying to operate on six-month enlistments, a system that proved unworkable. Also, American soldiers were seldom paid and infrequently fed, and for many of them enthusiasm faded and diary-keeping became more infrequent. On the other hand, there is an amazing number of extant diaries from the enthusiastic moments, like Benedict Arnold's quixotic expedition to capture Quebec, when a thousand men marched across nearly four hundred miles of wilderness to attack the British stronghold. Many soldiers died of starvation, three companies turned back, but over five hundred made it to Quebec, earning praise for themselves and Arnold despite their defeat. The number of men on the Quebec expedition, many scarcely literate, who wrote such accounts testifies both to the excitement of that first year of the war and of travel; but almost none of the Quebec accounts goes beyond this expedition. After that brief involvement, the men either quit the army at the end of their enlistments or lost interest in diary-keeping. This was the challenge in the War of Independence—keeping an army in the field, sustaining morale in a conflict that for at least five of its eight years was questionable and, among many colonials, unpopular.

The experience of the American Revolution is often obscured in a numinous fog of national mythology and the dazzling eloquence of the founding documents. *That all Men are created equal, that they are endowed by their Creator with certain unalienable Rights*—it is hard to imagine America's Revolution as anything but grand and dignified. Even the low points in one fashion or another have been mythologized—Washington crossing the Delaware all dressed up at the prow of an oarboat. In fact, the Revolution was a desperate and ragged venture, from the start well beyond the finish. Its diaries and memoirs convey a strong sense of just how speculative an undertaking the creation of the United States was.

The connection between enthusiasm, morale, and how many diaries are kept is reflected by America's other long and relatively unpopular war. In any war, the percentage of soldiers who keep diaries is small, but in Vietnam the number was apparently minuscule. This has partly to do with the fact that many soldiers were young conscripts with a low educational level. Also, a popular method of correspondence for American soldiers in Vietnam was by means of tape recorders. Finally, there was an often expressed belief, encouraged by command, that keeping diaries risked compromising one's unit and might even be grounds for court-martial.

On the other hand, a plethora of accounts has already surfaced from America's most recent, brief conflict—the Gulf War. Some of them are voluminous, complete with tables of contents and indexes. The army and guard units were all-volunteer, and the encounter was not long or costly enough to become unpopular. Many U.S. soldiers had access to portable computers, they had much time on their hands, and their basic needs for shelter, food, and mail were taken care of. They went with a sense of participating in history, and wanting to record the event for their children and grandchildren. The language of these accounts, often written or rewritten on computers, can be heavily salted with technologese, and many of them speak directly about the paradox of high technology screaming across the ancient emptiness of the desert. Most of the killing in the Gulf War was done at the far end of screens, keyboards, control sticks, and computers. Pilots in billion-dollar jets unleashed unprecedented killing power, tank battalions fought battles for the first time without ever seeing their enemy (a reminder of what happened for the first time in naval battles during World War II), while on the ground soldiers were typically coping less with combat than with an enemy who could not surrender fast enough.

Support services in Desert Storm were lavish at times almost to a point of bewilderment. An incident, verbally recalled by a National Guard soldier:

> We're travelling in a convoy through the desert. There's nothing here but the desert, just like in movies about deserts. Days and days we've been out here. We see a tent on the horizon. We're directly approaching it, wondering why the lieutenant isn't being more careful. He obviously knows what it is. We make out a satellite dish in front of it. We finally roll up near the place and he tells us that we have an hour to make telephone calls. We walk into this big tent, and it's all set up with cubicles and telephones that accept credit cards. I'm thinking this is weird. Finally, what the hey, I get out my plastic and call my mom and dad back in Arkansas.

The Civil War, though, is the clear winner of the documentation prize. It was the most written about of all U.S. wars, both during and after. Because of railroads, letters were delivered with enough frequency to encourage soldiers to write, and food was available often enough that soldiers were not ceaselessly having to worry about the next meal. Tin cans of vegetables and condensed milk provided a great advance in rationing in the Civil War; however, descriptions in Union as well as Confederate diaries habitually speak of the lack of available supplies that made it necessary to live off the land. As in the Revolution, the armies were a plague of hungry locusts wherever they went.

Field conditions in the Civil War were often reminiscent of conditions during the Revolution. The quality of medical support on the Union side was possibly better than the average medical care of the time. However, that isn't saying much, since few medical procedures helped wounded or sick soldiers, and many finished them off. Hospital tents were considered to be little more than places to die or be dismembered. Shock was not understood (it only began to be understood during World War I), transfusion wasn't used, and amputations, the stock-in-trade of the Civil War "sawbones," were made without sterilization. A soldier who was wounded was ten times more likely to die than a soldier in World War I. As many died in the Civil War (620,000) as in all other U.S. wars combined, and twice as many soldiers died of disease as died of wounds. The volunteer Sanitary Commission, staffed by unpaid women volunteers with paid men officers, provided Union camps with latrines, water supplies, cooking, and other advantages and aids to health, but they could not follow the armies everywhere.

The diaries, letters, and memoirs, much more than the histories of the Civil War—as in fact of all wars—speak of hunger and of soldiers being left to fend for themselves in varying states of confusion. High-ranking officers of both sides included a number who had gained some experience in the brief war with Mexico and in Indian conflicts; some had a modicum of training in the state militias, and several had attended the U.S. Military Academy. The war with Mexico, however, had consisted primarily of one extended raid, lessons gained from Indian fighting were without much applicability, and the state militias, prior to war, were not real military organizations. At the time, the U.S. Military Academy was an excellent training ground for habits of discipline and the liberal arts, but its curriculum was only marginally concerned with war-making. The result was that, as in the Revolution, most officers got their training in the havoc that these great clashing armies soon provided.

Historical accounts of wars suggest a false chess-like rationality about the nature of the experience. We read of certain numbers of men moving from certain locations over a certain period, lining up in this or that pattern over the conveniently provided map, displaying a certain degree of aggressiveness or lack of it, and doing a certain degree of damage to each other. In fact, a soldier or even a general in the field may have experienced very little that relates to these lucid and quantified patterns.

World War II is a particular case in point, since it was the largest, most dramatic, and best-managed of the major U.S. wars. Viewed through the safe spyglass of time, the whole course of World War II might seem a fast-moving, almost swashbuckling spectacle—as if all narrated in the stately rhetoric of Winston Churchill. Soldiers' accounts of this war, however, are often grim. There was little of the cheerful naivete of World War I and little of the sense of glory of other wars. Irony and gallows humor interlace many of their accounts, but so does an uncommon attitude of tenacity. They had a job to do, and there was no thought of shirking it. The completeness of the U.S. commitment in World War II was reflected in the fact that only one-third of one percent of those signing up for selective service identified themselves as conscientious objectors.

In *Goodbye, Darkness,* William Manchester tells about the sergeant talking to his people before the invasion of Saipan. " 'Saipan is covered with dense jungle, quicksand, steep hills and cliffs hiding batteries of huge coastal guns, and strongholds of reinforced concrete. Insects bear lethal poisons. Crocodiles and snakes infest the streams. The waters around it are thick with sharks. The population will be hostile toward us.' There was a long silence. Then a corporal said, 'Sarge, why don't we just let the Japs keep it?' "

The soldiers best fit to make it through the experience of war psychologically whole are those who either know or figure out what they are fighting for, who in some way make the war their own or put it into their own terms. One of the few allies of the soldiers of the American Revolution was an understanding of the importance of their efforts, despite the nearly unbearable circumstances of serving in a long war in an army that was little funded, under "gentlemen" officers who typically cared nothing about them as individuals. In the Civil War, many Northern soldiers fought to uphold the sacred Union, and some increasingly became convinced that they were also fighting for emancipation. The soldiers of World War II had a very plain and practical motive—to stop Hitler and Japan. In every war, though, one of the primary motives of continued involvement—the cohesive glue of a fighting force—is one's fellow soldiers. A soldier's messmates become his family, and in combat, even when little else makes sense, he seldom forgets that a friend is on his flank.

The onset of wars often have an eerily festive quality. There is a strange excitement in the air. Almost everyone feels it. People talk who otherwise would never speak to each other. Young warriors are admired by families, friends, and acquaintances. It's a time of spontaneous gatherings, of romance, and of making commitments. There is a mental anaesthesia that goes along with the euphoria.

During the American Revolution this period of excitement was called the *rage militaire,* and something like it has happened with almost all American wars. Teddy Roosevelt and other New York bluebloods formed volunteer units that were virtual social clubs for the rousing adventure of the Spanish-American War. A popular World War I song asked the question, "How will you keep them down on the farm?" Many Americans experienced something of the power of mobilization fever during the Gulf War. When the drums begin to beat, the majority of citizens and the media typically respond to the government line and readily cooperate.

While mobilization for wars is romantic, real wars are not. Governments typically try to pump up morale among their own troops, discourage the enemy, and maintain support for the war effort at home. The distortions of propaganda can cause serious morale problems if a war becomes complicated, lengthy, expensive, or if it is questionably ended. It can also have the unintended effect of confusing one's own side, as it did for the Japanese at crucial moments during World War II, when the delusions of "honor" and invincibility interfered with the most basic fact gathering. During the Revolution, newspaper and pamphlet exaggerations of American military strength and of British weakness and corruption led to wildly unrealistic expectations of an easy American victory, which in turn eventually triggered such disillusionment that by 1779 the American effort came to the verge of collapse.

Diaries by American soldiers of all wars sometimes show feelings of isolation from or abandonment by the citizenry. The angry or embittered Vietnam veteran is not a new species. Soldiers on furlough may go into the "normal world" only to discover that it has become a strange place. During the war at times they may feel a greater sense of identity with the enemy, who after all are living the same life they are, than with the people merrily going about their business back home. Truly some of the greatest burdens of war come afterward—integrating back into civilian life, picking up the pieces, trying to get beyond it—and many soldiers and their families continue to pay a high personal price.

Incidents of fraternization in the Civil War were widespread and, though not surprising, they were dramatic because of the overall spectacle of one nation, cleaved, tearing at itself in battles of mind-stunning horror. Sometimes during lulls in the fighting, soldiers would meet in the night, trading coffee for tobacco and sharing news. But some fraternization has occurred in all wars of any length. A common element in many war diaries is curiosity about the enemy, a desire to look at them, assess them, talk to them, find out how this experience affects them.

War diarists and writers of memoirs often describe incidents in which the enemy seems disturbingly "human," more like themselves than like any propaganda image. World War II was unusual in this regard. While there were occurrences of such feelings toward individual German and Italian soldiers, diaries show fewer of them overall than in most wars, and they show very few indeed between Americans and Japanese, where on both sides there was racism, wide language barriers, and different codes of conduct.

The Vietnam Memorial, "the Wall," is this generation's most moving memorial to those who have died in service to their country. The memorial's power has something to do with its simplicity. It merely gives the names, no frills, no extras, just the names of those who fell in the least glorious of our major wars. For the living, who come to find and perhaps to touch a name, the memorial makes them work a little. One must look up a name in a directory, find which panel it is located on, then go searching. The Wall is organized by date of casualty, although dates do not appear on the memorial itself. The first casualty, from 1959, is at the apex of one of the two highest panels, in the center of the Wall, and then the list of names moves through time, day by day, downward and eastward until reaching the last panel on the east end. The names of the dead continue on the far western end of the Wall, moving back toward the center, where the last of the approximately 58,200 to have died—on 15 May 1975—is physically next to the first.

In a salutary sense, the Wall is austere and "disorganized," a little like war. When looking for a name, one must search for it among so many others. One can see the variety of names of this immigrant nation present on all one hundred forty panels. Yet finally they are all together in one construction, which is not rectilinear but conforms to the hill, not heroic or impressive in any obvious way. The Wall does not bear ranks or service records or any of the other accoutrements of the military. One of the things that makes the Vietnam Memorial so powerful is that it allows the dead to be solemnly remembered, but as human beings rather than as militarized martyrs.

By reading the accounts in this book, one touches the inner lives of people serving as soldiers. These are not the important commanders, not the generals, but the hands and feet of America's wars. They write about the mud, weather, boredom, friendships, and empty stomachs, the repulsion, the terror, and the spiritual struggles that someone faces where the lines have been drawn.

These diaries, written over the course of two hundred years, have presented a variety of editing challenges. In general, we have quietly made minor corrections in grammar and punctuation, and on a few occasions in syntax, for the sake of clarity and readability. Here and there, phrases or passages have been deleted and paragraphing added, as well. In some of the diaries, consistent usages, like adjectives in place of adverbs, have been left, but where it seemed appropriate we have standardized or Americanized spellings while at the same time trying to respect the original text. Some of the diaries have been excerpted for reasons of economy. Our decisions regarding what to cut were based on interest level.

1

The War of American Independence

The American Revolution was in some ways an ancestor to the Vietnam War, but with the sides reversed. Like Vietnam, the American colonies in the 1770s were a comparatively primitive country with uncertain political authority. Americans finally won independence less by their own military muscle than by keeping an army in the field and cultivating a powerful ally while the attrition of a long war in an undeveloped, vast country eventually defeated the better equipped and supported invading forces.

General Washington played a defensive, elusive, harassing role from early in the war until the battle of Yorktown. Until that opportunity arrived, six long years into the conflict, his main hope was to hang on, evade, and survive. It was a role that Washington bitterly disliked. His main military accomplishment may have been to recognize and accept what he hated doing. Washington wanted to command an army that could defend the capital and meet the enemy in the field. At various times throughout the war the strategy of avoiding decisive conflict resulted in intrigues and cabals against Washington, as well as public discussion that he should be replaced as commander by someone more aggressive. More than once his generals had to close ranks and defend his so-called "Fabian" strategy, named after Quintus Fabius Maximus, who defeated Hannibal by avoiding direct conflict.

Through the whole course of it, the American Revolution was fought in a land of divided loyalties, where civilian sympathies ebbed and flowed in both directions, depending on the current status of the war and local clashes between civilians and armies. While both the American and British sides caused great physical destruction to the country, the mindless

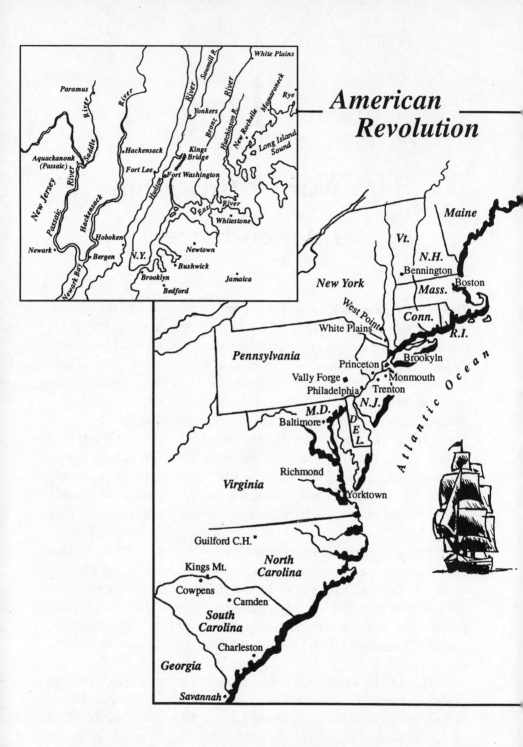

American Revolution

Maine

Vt.

N.H.
Bennington

Mass.
Boston

Conn.

R.I.

New York

West Point

White Plains

Brookyln

Pennsylvania

Princeton

Vally Forge

Monmouth

Philadelphia

Trenton

N.J.

M.D.

Baltimore

D E L.

Richmond

Yorktown

Virginia

Guilford C.H.

Kings Mt.

North
Carolina

Cowpens

Camden

South
Carolina

Charleston

Georgia

Savannah

A t l a n t i c   O c e a n

Inset map:

Paramus

White Plains

Sawmill R.

River

River

River

Bronx

River

Yonkers

Rye

Mamaroneck

New Rochelle

Hutchinson R.

Hackensack

Kings
Bridge

Long Island
Sound

Aquackanonk
(Passaic)

River

Fort Lee

Fort Washington

River

Saddle

Hudson

New Jersey

Passaic

River

Hackensack

Hoboken

N.Y.

East

River

Whitestone

Newark

Bergen

Brooklyn

Bushwick

Newtown

Jamaica

Newark Bay

Bedford

wholesale devastation caused by British forces in places like New Jersey and South Carolina eventually served to excite civilian resentment against the British among civilians who previously either hadn't cared much about the conflict or who had favored the British.

The British Crown was never fully committed in the colonial war. North America did not have the immediate value of the Caribbean basin, which was the richest trading area in the world. The mercantile British feared losing the annual high revenues of the sugar trade more than losing rule over the colonies. Just as the U.S. in the 1960s was less concerned about Vietnam than about her benefactors Russia and China, so the British were less worried about preindustrial North America than about France, her global and industrial rival and competitor in trade. If the former colonies won their independence it would be an embarrassment and would have "implications," but such one-step-removed concerns lost urgency when the war became an expensive quagmire. For the British, the American Revolution was never a total war, never—despite efforts to make it so—a gut issue.

Although the British were as sick of the war as anybody, they were essentially winning in 1781. They had virtually shut down the American effort. Clinton controlled New York and Cornwallis was having his way in Virginia. The bankrupt Continental Congress had just made a last desperate effort to finance the war by appointing a financial czar in the person of Robert Morris. This would turn out to be a providential choice, but it was done barely in time.

The battle of Yorktown, too, came along just in time, and the French made it possible. The two countries shared an enthusiasm for democratic theory, but France allied with the Continentals largely for reasons of *Realpolitik:* They were struggling with the British for maritime dominance in the Caribbean and elsewhere. After years of cultivation by Benjamin Franklin in Paris, the French sent five thousand troops to Rhode Island, at first for the purpose of joining with Washington to attack Clinton's army in New York. Meanwhile, a British army first under the traitor Benedict Arnold, then under Cornwallis, was ravaging Virginia.

Assuming that, as usual, he could call up the navy for reinforcements or evacuation, Cornwallis rested from his campaign in the tobacco port of Williamsburg, at the head of the Chesapeake Bay. Washington and Rochambeau were biding their time in the north, both feeling uneasy about attacking Clinton in New York. They were amazed when word came that a lull in military needs in the Caribbean allowed the French to cut loose a fleet of twenty-eight ships of the line plus dozens of support vessels under Admiral de Grasse.

This allowed them to plan going after Cornwallis in the south in the way Washington had long yearned for, in a full-blown, modern, European-style battle, complete with entrenchments, lines, cannons, sea support, and calculable odds. Their plan depended upon Admiral de Grasse arriving in time to seal off the Chesapeake Bay, and he did, turning away the British fleet. Washington was so exhilarated at Yorktown that he happily turned over field command to the French.

But after it was over, it wasn't over. As with most wars, the victor was left with her problems, and any of several of them could have fatally compromised the adolescent nation. Whether the United States would remain sovereign, whether it could pay its debts, whether it would remain united, whether it could defend its borders—such questions remained up in the air through the 1790s, through the War of 1812, indeed, through the Civil War.

Like a lot of men later contemplating their reasons for having gone off to war as a young man, the elder Joseph Plumb Martin looked upon himself as a sixteen-year-old with some amusement. His immediate reasons for signing up in the army had more to do with the call to adventure than with political commitment. Yet Martin had grown up listening to stories of disputes and skirmishes between the colonies and Britain. The conflict erupting over the Stamp Act, in which the colonies had faced down Britain, had occurred when he was only five years old; the Boston Massacre, in which five colonials were shot after eruptions over the Townshend Acts, when he was ten; and the Boston Tea Party when he was thirteen. These anecdotes of resistance had long been part of his life, calling to the restive spirit of a young man bored by farming. When the final break with the mother country was made and war was evident, it seemed to some extent a natural outcome of what he had heard about for years. War promised adventure to Joseph Martin; it offered something other than farming, something other than being under the thumb of the grandparents who raised him.

As was later the case in the Civil War, draft-age men in this country had several choices—of joining either side, buying their way out of the draft, or simply disappearing from the local area. While in different parts of the country significant numbers of young men chose either to go with the British or not to be involved, the scene as Martin describes it clearly shows that the revolutionaries were dominant in the area around Milford, Connecticut, as indeed they were in most parts of New England.

The immediate appetizer for this sixteen-year-old, and for most young men, was the bounty incentive which was created by a combination of congressional, state, and local pools. Three pounds looked very tasty indeed to a young man who'd lived his whole life in a cash-thin economy. Later, as the war dragged on and soldiers on leave came home and described conditions in the army, the bounty incentive became even more important in keeping up the army's rolls, and the bounties themselves had to become considerably larger. Soldiers discovered that monthly pay was rare, low, and increasingly depreciated, with the script that usually constituted pay being worth only a fraction of its face amount. Men sought their main pay in the bounty. Draftees got a bounty even when they hired a substitute, whom they usually paid more than the official bounty. All of this resulted in considerable fraud, with some soldiers repeatedly disappearing from their companies and signing up elsewhere to collect multiple bounties, and enlistment officers faking the rolls and stealing from the bounty pools.

Why Martin first signed up is less to the point than why he and other young men remained in the army and even signed up again. The frenzied *rage militaire* that had burned through the rebels in 1775 was already dying down when Martin first joined, and the loss of it was lamented by politicians, newspapers, and generals for several years afterwards. By summer, 1776, close to the Declaration of Independence, the excitement following the skirmishes around Boston had already blown away like a thin cloud. Martin later rejoined during one of the longest periods of stalemate and defeat in American military history and probably the worst period in terms of overall conditions—and he had already had more than a taste of it.

General Washington yearned for a well supplied, well disciplined force capable of matching the British like a respectable European army. Instead, he commanded a shabby, wretched, ill supplied, often ill disciplined band of men who were made sport of by nonpartisans and by enemies. The American revolutionary effort was starting from ground zero in many departments, and it took on increasing problems as fast as it accomplished solutions, with wavering civilian support, little effective or realistic financing until six years into the war, and a high level of corruption among suppliers.

The survival of the American forces is all the more remarkable considering the fact that despite the confederation there was no true union between the colonies, nor any executive authority in government until Superintendent of Finance Morris became a de facto executive in 1781. Martin freely describes some of the consequences of these deficiencies in the lives of soldiers: little food, little supply, almost no pay, and, for the most part, a poor system of leadership in the field, connected to an ineffective but slowly improving army discipline.

British soldiers feared the buckskin-wearing Western militia—who tended to be good marksmen with their groove-barreled rifles—more than the Continental Army. The popular American view later latched onto this fact and fancied the Revolution as an encounter between stiff, proper, well dressed dummies and canny fringed frontiersmen intelligently hiding behind trees and mowing down the Redcoats. The advantages of good marksmanship, however, go only so far. Above all, an army has to remain intact, go where it is told to go, and do what it is told to do. The Western riflemen too often melted away, leaving the Continentals and state militias with the problems of maintaining, supplying, training, and disciplining a band of men. Washington would have lost the war if he'd had only riflemen.

The colonies had to invent whole armies, and for lack of any other way to quickly distinguish officers from soldiers they resorted to class status to decide who would lead. Unlike the Confederates in the Civil War, the Continental government and the states had no extensive history of military training or substantial class of proven officers, therefore officers were chosen from the class of "gentlemen" and soldiers from among commoners. Being a gentleman in the late eighteenth century supposedly required the cultivation of sensibility, the appreciation of women and of scenic beauty, friendship with other gentlemen, loyalty to nation, self sacrifice, and a certain theoretical compassion for the unfortunate, as well as some wealth or discernible kinship to wealth.

There weren't enough gentlemen who were also able to lead men in war, and strife arose from the socially retrograde, class-based system. Over time, changes did occur in some areas, but the American army remained the most antiquated of the four army cultures involved in the American Revolution. Officers treated soldiers with condescension, cruelty, elaborate displays of class status, and floggings, all of which was thought to keep soldiers in awe of officers and in their places.

Officers in the army included non-line and support staff, creating an expanding population of officers working ever harder to demonstrate their gentlemanly rank. Field-grade officers surrounded themselves with aides and honor guards in an effort to avoid the lower orders of company-grade officers. Among junior grades many had no military skills at all. Officers frequently fell into squabbling, jealousies, and disputes. The class and pseudo-class divisions and general behavior of American officers surprised the French when they arrived late in the war. They surprised even the British, who prided themselves on relaxed relations between officers and soldiers.

Martin's reactions to many officers is similar to other soldiers' accounts: outrage, puzzlement, resentfulness, indignity, and sarcasm. The decency that he sees in certain officers is noteworthy, as if it were a rare commodity. For the most part, he regards them as distant, unfriendly, and uninvolved.

The lack of effective leadership worsened camp conditions and exacerbated discipline problems. Camps were debilitating places without order or sanitation, blanketed by smoke from green wood and odors from animal carcasses and scattered sewage. Guns were constantly popping off and accidentally wounding or killing soldiers. "Seldom a day passes but some persons are shot by friends," Washington wrote in 1776. Discipline improved somewhat after Valley Forge, but as late as 1781, American soldiers were still amazed by the order and cleanliness of the French soldiers.

The disciplinary system employed flogging and courts-martial in which men were frequently condemned to death. The majority of death sentences were commuted at the last minute—supposedly due to the noble generosity of officers—but this mercy act increasingly lost effectiveness over time, as Martin's account implies.

Martin doesn't write about floggings, although it was an ongoing and widely discussed issue. While flogging was also used by the British, the French were amazed at how much of it went on in the American army. In 1776, the Congress allowed the number of lashes to be raised from thirty-nine to one hundred. Officers sometimes exceeded this limit. Men were either whipped with cat-o'-nine tails or made to run the gauntlet. The hundred lashes could be spread over four days with salt rubs to make it worse. It took no more than fifty lashes to completely flay the skin off the back. A few of the better generals did not regularly use whipping, but Washington, who continuously fretted about the lack of discipline in American camps, attempted to get Congress to raise the limit to match the British five hundred lashes, and to its credit the Congress did not go along with him.

While Joseph Martin's description of Valley Forge is limited, and his mention of Baron von Steuben is brief, his account of succeeding years confirms that after that winter, there was a somewhat higher level of professionalism in certain parts of the army. The baron's "Prussian system" was important not just because it involved soldiers in the "continual drill" that Martin notes, but because it involved officers in drill, as well. Von Steuben's main contribution was helping some officers recognize that in order to lead men they had to drill with them and regularly demonstrate that they cared about them. From this and other diaries, however, one gets the impression that historians may exaggerate the Prussian's influence if they suggest that after Valley Forge there was a steadily increasing overall competency building up to Yorktown.

The dominant theme in Martin's account is hunger. Even looking back on the experience forty years later he vividly remembers instance after instance of the continuing battle with starvation. While he does sometimes feel the sense of abandonment expressed by many soldiers, more remarkable is his clear sense of sympathy for civilians whose lives were disrupted by the armies. Both armies were destructive to civilians. When an army was on the march, civilians desperately tried to hide food and bury their valuables. In later years there were many tales of the discovery of Revolutionary War hoards. In one of many wonderful moments in his diary, when Martin is describing a woman trying to protect her soup pot, he shows a clear-eyed but unsentimental sympathy for civilians. Many soldiers must have become cynical, predatory, and corrupted.

While viewing his overall experience as a soldier with good humor, Martin's picture is of a hard, hungry, and little rewarded ordeal. Clearly he does also regard it as a definitive experience for himself and his nation, but he doesn't indulge much, even retrospectively, in discussing the ideals of the Revolution. One of the great strengths of the revolutionary cause, however, was that Americans had a clearly articulated purpose. Revolutionary Americans knew precisely what they wanted to achieve. It could be stated in a single word: Independence.

Revolutionary Americans saw England as corrupt, and many believed that America had been chosen to represent self-government for the world. If they did not resist England they would be enslaved by her. That meant alien armies and court systems, indiscriminate taxes and officials, expropriation of property, and pervasive corruption. While these fears were by no means universally held, they were widely discussed in newspapers, pamphlets, and government decrees. Most Americans believed in the fundamental democratic ideals of equality at birth and a government acquiring its authority from the governed. Democratic political ideas, in turn, were backed by de facto economic transitions going on in western economies and by emergent capitalistic theory.

The American endeavor was further aided both by the isolation of the colonies and the fact that they were not yet "worth" an all-out effort by England to squelch it. It was sometimes recognized in England that independent colonies might be worth as much or even more to the empire as a trading partner, as indeed soon would prove to be the case despite ongoing political strife between the two nations after the war. The colonies' small population (two and a half million) and lack of capital development relative to older nations was compensated by a widespread belief in the future growth of the nation. Americans knew that they were sitting on sizable economic potential. They had something promising to fight for.

The Continental government was at least a step in the direction of union but it was the very model of an unworkable system. Representatives to the Continental Congress were appointed by the state assemblies rather than elected by the people, and their ultimate obligation was to the states. Most of their attempts to create and collect taxes was shot down by the states. When the Congress passed an amendment, like the impost amendment in the later phase of the war—a time when mounting debts were threatening to swamp the American effort—it had to be passed by every state legislature, which predictably proved to be impossible. The Continental Congress had no executive until Robert Morris was appointed Superintendent of Finance in 1781. The canny, rich Philadelphia merchant managed to create money for the war effort by using his own resources, by financial legerdemain, and by fearless harassment of the states. The details of Morris's superintendency during the last years of the war vividly demonstrate just how much of a bootstrap operation the Continental government and the war effort were. It also demonstrates that at the end of the war the United States faced what in the future they would always face after major wars, threateningly large debts.

Joseph Martin's memoir was first published anonymously in Hallowell, Maine, in 1830, as *A Narrative of Some of the Adventures, Dangers, and Sufferings of a Revolutionary Soldier, Interspersed with Anecdotes of Incidents That Occurred Within His Own Observation*. The book is physically small (octavo) with a calf spine and wooden-board covers. Its author was a seventy-year-old resident of Prospect, Maine. There are perhaps a half-dozen known, extant copies of it, making this odd little locally published memoir one of the rarest and most valuable books in America.

Martin's memoir is garrulous, informal, but lively and literate, and it is comprehensive, covering much of the war from New York to Yorktown as experienced by the core Continental Army. In colorful but straightforward fashion, uncontaminated by sentimentality, it describes the daily life of a soldier in the ragtag Continental Army. After Martin's death, a Maine historian eulogized him by praising his narrative but regretted the fact that he had not "submitted it to some judicious friend for revisal." In fact, had the book been subjected to current editorial taste and practices, it would have lost much of its vernacular charm and power. Obscure local publication prevented Martin's voice from being lost.

The anonymously published memoir was briefly rediscovered by historians in the later nineteenth century, although its author was incorrectly identified as James Sullivan Martin, Joseph's son and the copyright holder. In more recent years, D. S. Freeman's biography *George Washington* (New York, Scribners and Sons, 1947–57) referred to it. Francis S. Ronalds, Superintendent of the Morristown National Historical Park, discovered it in the private collection of Lloyd W. Smith of Morristown and offered his friend George Scheer the opportunity to edit a new edition of it. Scheer's edition of 1962 (*Private Yankee Doodle*, Little Brown, 1962) is the best introduced and annotated version of the entire book.

George Scheer collected the facts about Martin's life outside the army. He was the son of Ebenezer Martin, a Yale graduate and Congregational minister, and Susanna Plumb of Milford, Connecticut. Apparently due to financial and personal problems, Ebenezer Martin lost two pastorates and barely escaped being thrown into debtors' prison in Connecticut. At the age of seven, Joseph was sent off to live with his mother's family on their prosperous farm near New Haven.

Joseph Martin was too young to join the army when war first broke out, but in 1776, at sixteen, he signed up for a short term, then later reenlisted until the end of the war. After the war he traveled to Frankfort, a town of about one hundred people near the mouth of the Penobscot River in frontier Maine, where he lived the rest of his life as a farmer, laborer, and town clerk. Martin first built a cabin on the headland of Cape Jellison, then some years later was able to move into a frame house in town. At the age of thirty-four Martin married Lucy Clewley, in the same year that the town's name was changed from Frankfort to Prospect. Martin read extensively and amused himself with drawing and versification. Several of his sketches of wild birds, drawn between 1838 and 1841, survive in the hands of a descendant, along with a book of his verses.

In 1818 Congress passed a bill for needy veterans and Joseph Martin applied for and received a pension of eight dollars a month. His application shows that he had five children and limited financial means. He received the ninety-six-dollars-per-year pension, supplementing his income as an occasional laborer and, until 1843, town clerk. Martin died in 1850 at the age of ninety and was buried in Sandy Point Cemetery with the epitaph "A Soldier of the Revolution." The adventure that he had entered upon as a naive young man had proved to be the adventure of a lifetime.

The Diary of Joseph Plumb Martin

I lived with my parents until I was upwards of seven years old, when I went to live with this good old grandsire; for good he was, particularly to me. He was wealthy, and I had everything that was necessary for life and as many superfluities as was consistent with my age and station. There were none belonging to the family, as constant residents, except the old gentleman, lady, and myself. It is true my grandsire kept me pretty busily employed, but he was kind to me in every respect, always gave me a playday when convenient, and was indulgent to me almost to a fault.

I remember the stir in the country occasioned by the Stamp Act, but I was so young that I did not understand the meaning of it; I likewise remember the disturbances that followed the repeal of the Stamp Act, until the destruction of the tea at Boston and elsewhere. I was then thirteen or fourteen years old and began to understand something of the works going on. I used, about this time, to inquire a deal about the French War, as it was called, which had not been long ended; my grandsire would talk with me about it while working in the fields, perhaps as much to beguile his own time as to gratify my curiosity. I thought then, nothing should induce me to get caught in the toils of an army. "I am well, so I'll keep," was my motto then, and it would have been well for me if I had ever retained it.

The winter of this year passed off without any very frightening alarms and the spring of 1775 arrived. Expectation of some fatal event seemed to fill the minds of most of the considerate people throughout the country. I was ploughing in the field about half a mile from home, about the twenty-first day of April, when all of a sudden the bells fell to ringing and three guns were repeatedly fired in succession down in the village; what the cause was we could not conjecture. I had some fearful forebodings that something more than the sound of a carriage wheel was in the wind. I set off to see what the cause of the commotion was. I found most of the male kind of the people together; soldiers for Boston were in requisition. A dollar deposited upon the drumhead was taken up by someone as soon as placed there, and the holder's name taken, and he enrolled with orders to equip himself as quick as possible. My spirits began to revive at the sight of the money offered. O, thought I, if I were but old enough to put myself forward, I would be the possessor of one dollar, the dangers of war to the contrary notwithstanding; but I durst not put myself up for a soldier for fear of being refused, and that would have quite upset all the courage I had drawn forth.

Soldiers were at this time enlisting for a year's service. I did not like that; it was too long a time for me at the first trial; I wished only to take a priming before I took upon me the whole coat of paint for a soldier. However the time soon arrived that gratified all my wishes. In the month of June, this year, orders came out for enlisting men for six months from the twenty-fifth of this month. The troops were styled new levies. They were to go to New York. And notwithstanding I was told that the British army at that place was reinforced by fifteen thousand men, it made no alteration in my mind; I did not care if there had been fifteen times fifteen thousand, I should have gone just as soon as if there had been but fifteen hundred. I never spent a thought about numbers; the Americans were invincible in my opinion. If anything affected me, it was a stronger desire to see them.

I was now what I had long wished to be, a soldier.[1] I had obtained my heart's desire; it was now my business to prove myself equal to my profession. Well, to be short, I went with several others of the company on board a sloop bound to New York; had a pleasant though protracted passage; passed through the straight called Hell Gate; arrived at New York; marched up into the city, and joined the rest of the regiment there.[2]

And now I had left my good old grandsire's house, as a constant resident, forever, and had to commence exercising my function. I was called out every morning at reveille beating, which was at daybreak, to go to our regimental parade in Broad Street,[3] and there practice the manual exercise, which was the most that was known in our new levies, if they knew even that.[4]

Soon after my arrival in New York, a forty-four-gun ship (the *Phoenix*) and a small frigate (the *Rose*, I think) came down the North or Hudson River (they had been some time in the river) and passed the city in fine style, amidst a cannonade from all our fortifications in and near the city. I went into what was then called the Grand Battery, where I had a complete view of the whole affair.[5] Here I first heard the muttering of cannon shot, but they did not disturb my feelings so much as I apprehended they would before I had heard them; I rather thought the sound was musical, or at least grand. I heard enough of them afterwards to form what ideas I pleased of them, whether musical, grand, or doleful, and perhaps I have formed each of those ideas upon different occasions.

I remained in New York two or three months when, sometime in the latter part of the month of August, I was ordered upon a fatigue party. We had scarcely reached the grand parade when I saw our sergeant major directing his course up Broadway, towards us, in rather unusual step for him. He soon arrived and informed us and then the commanding officer of the party that he had orders to take off all belonging to our regiment and march us to our quarters, as the regiment was ordered to Long Island, the British having landed in force there.[6] Although this was not unexpected to me, yet it gave me rather a disagreeable feeling, as I was pretty well assured I should have to snuff a little gunpowder. However, I kept my cogitations to myself, went to my quarters, packed up my clothes, and got myself in readiness for the expedition as soon as possible. I then went to the top of the house where I had a full view of that part of the Island; I distinctly saw the smoke of the field artillery, but the distance and the unfavorableness of the wind prevented my hearing their report, at least but faintly. The horrors of battle then presented themselves to my mind in all their hideousness; I must come to it now, thought I. Well, I will endeavor to do my duty as well as I am able and leave the event with Providence. We were soon ordered to our regimental parade, from which, as soon as the regiment was formed, we were marched off for the ferry.[7]

We soon landed at Brooklyn, upon the Island, marched up the ascent from the ferry to the plain. While resting here, which was not more than twenty minutes or half an hour, the Americans and British were warmly engaged within sight of us. What were the feelings of most or all the young soldiers at this time, I know not, but I saw a lieutenant who appeared to have feelings not very enviable; whether he was actuated by fear or the canteen I cannot determine now. I thought it fear at the time, for he ran round among the men of his company, sniveling and blubbering, praying each one if he had aught against him, or if he had injured anyone that they would forgive him, declaring at the same time that he, from his heart, forgave them if they had offended him, and I gave him full credit for his assertion; for had he been at the gallows with a halter about his neck, he could not have shown more fear or penitence. A fine soldier you are, I thought, a fine officer, an exemplary man for young soldiers! I would have then suffered anything short of death rather than have made such an exhibition of myself. [8]

Our regiment was alone, no other troops being near where we were lying. [9] We were upon a rising ground, covered with a young growth of trees; we felled a fence of trees around us to prevent the approach of the enemies' horse. We lay there a day longer. In the latter part of the afternoon there fell a very heavy shower of rain which wet us all to the skin and much damaged our ammunition. About sunset, when the shower had passed over, we were ordered to parade and discharge our pieces. We attempted to fire by platoons for improvement, but we made blundering work of it; it was more like a running fire than firing by divisions.

We marched off in the same way that we had come on to the Island, until we arrived at the ferry, where we immediately embarked on board the bateaux and were conveyed safely to New York, where we were landed about three o'clock in the morning, nothing against our inclinations. [10]

We stayed several days longer in the city, when one morning we discovered that a small frigate had advanced up and was lying above Governors Island, close under the Long Island shore. Several other ships had come up and were lying just below the town. [11] They seemed to portend evil. In the evening, just at dark, our regiment was ordered to march to Turtle Bay, [12] a place about four miles distant on the East River, where were a large warehouse or two, called then the King's stores, built for the storing of marine stores belonging to the government before the war. There was at this time about twenty-five hundred barrels of flour in those storehouses, and it was conjectured that the design of the forementioned frigate was to seize on this flour. We were, therefore, ordered to secure it before the British would have an opportunity to lay their unhallowed hands upon it. We continued here some days to guard the flour. We were forbidden by our officers to use any of it, except our daily allowance. We used, however, to purloin some of it to eat and exchange with the inhabitants for milk, sauce, and such small matters as we could get for it of them.

One evening while lying here, we heard a heavy cannonade at the city, and before dark saw four of the enemy's ships that had passed the town and were coming up the East River. They anchored just below us. These ships were the *Phoenix* of forty-four guns; the *Roebuck* of forty-four; the *Rose* of thirty-two; and another, the name of which I have forgotten. Half of our regiment was sent off under the command of our major to man something that was called "lines," although they were nothing more than a ditch dug along on the bank of the river with the dirt thrown out towards the water. They stayed in these lines during the night and returned to the camp in the morning unmolested. [13]

It was on a Sabbath morning, [14] the day in which the British were always employed about their deviltry if possible, because, they said, they had the prayers of the church on that day. We lay very quiet in our ditch waiting their motions, till the sun was an hour or two high. We heard a cannonade at the city, but our attention was drawn toward our own guests. [15] But they being a little dilatory in their operations, I stepped into an old warehouse which stood close by me with the door open inviting me in and sat down upon a stool. The floor was strewed with papers which had in some former period been used in the concerns of the house but were then lying in "woeful confusion." I was very demurely perusing these papers when all of a sudden there came such a peal of thunder from the British shipping that I thought my head would go with the sound. I made a frog's leap for the ditch and lay as still as I possibly could and began to consider which part of my carcass was to go first. The British played their parts well; indeed they had nothing to hinder them. We kept the lines till they were almost leveled upon us, when our officers, seeing we could make no resistance and no orders coming from any superior officer and that we must soon be entirely exposed to the rake of their guns, gave the order to leave the lines. [16]

In retreating we had to cross a level, clear spot of ground forty or fifty rods wide, exposed to the whole of the enemy's fire, and they gave it to us in prime order. The grapeshot and langrage flew merrily, which served to quicken our motions. When I had gotten a little out of the reach of their combustibles, I found myself in company with one who was a neighbor of mine when at home and one other man belonging to our regiment. Where the rest of them were I knew not. We went into a house by the highway in which were two women and some small children, all crying most bitterly. We asked the women if they had any spirits in the house. They placed a case bottle of rum upon the table and bid us help ourselves. We each of us drank a glass and bidding them good-by betook ourselves to the highway again.

We had not gone far before we saw a party of men, apparently hurrying on the same direction with ourselves. We endeavored hard to overtake them, but on approaching them we found that they were not of our way of thinking: they were Hessians. We immediately altered our course and took the main road leading to King's Bridge. [17] We had not long been on this road before we saw another party, just ahead of us, whom we knew to be Americans. Just as we overtook these, they were fired upon by a party of British from a cornfield and all was immediately in confusion again. I believe the enemy's party was small, but our people were all militia, and the demons of fear and disorder seemed to take full possession of all and everything on that day. [18] When I came to the spot where the militia were fired upon, the ground was literally covered with arms, knapsacks, staves, coats, hats, and old oil flasks. All I picked up of the plunder was a block-tin syringe, which afterwards helped to procure me a Thanksgiving dinner. Myself and the man whom I mentioned as belonging to our company were all who were in company at this time, the other man having gone on with those who were fired upon.

We had to advance slowly, for my comrade having been for some time unwell was now so overcome by heat, hunger, and fatigue that he became suddenly and violently sick. I took his musket and endeavored to encourage him on. He was, as I before observed, a neighbor of mine when at home and I was loath to leave him behind, although I was anxious to find the main part of the regiment if possible before night, for I thought that that part of it which was not in the lines was in a body somewhere. We soon came in sight of a large party of Americans ahead of us who appeared to have come into this road by some other route. We were within sight of them when they were fired upon by another party of the enemy. They returned but a very few shots and then scampered off as fast as their legs would carry them. When we came to the ground they had occupied, the same display of lumber presented itself as at the other place. We here found a wounded man and some of his comrades endeavoring to get him off. I stopped to assist them in constructing a sort of litter to lay him upon, when my sick companion growing impatient moved on, and as soon as we had placed the wounded man upon the litter I followed him.

While I was here, one or two of our regiment came up and we went on together. We had proceeded but a short distance, however, before we found our retreat cut off by a party of the enemy stretched across the island. I immediately quitted the road and went into the fields, where there happened to be a small spot of boggy land covered with low bushes and

34

weeds. Into these I ran and squatting down concealed myself from their sight. Several of the British came so near to me that I could see the buttons on their clothes. They, however, soon withdrew and left the coast clear for me again. I then came out of my covert and went on, but what had become of my sick comrade or the rest of my companions I knew not. I still kept the sick man's musket. I was unwilling to leave it, for it was his own property and I knew he valued it highly and I had a great esteem for him.

I went on and directly came to a foul place in the road, where the soldiers had taken down the fence to pass into the fields. I passed across the corner of one field and through a gap in a cross fence into another. Here I found a number of men resting under the trees and bushes in the fences. Almost the first I saw, after passing the gap in the fence, was my sick friend. I was exceeding glad to find him, for I had but little hope of ever seeing him again. He was sitting near the fence with his head between his knees. I tapped him upon the shoulder and asked him to get up and go on with me. "No," said he, at the same time regarding me with a most pitiful look, "I must die here." I endeavored to argue the case with him, but all to no purpose; he insisted upon dying there. I told him he should not die there nor anywhere else that day if I could help it, and at length with more persuasion and some force I succeeded in getting him upon his feet again and to moving on.

After proceeding about half a mile we came to a place where our people had begun to make a stand. A number, say two or three hundred, had collected here, having been stopped by the artillery officers; they had two or three fieldpieces fixed and fitted for action, in case the British came on, which was momentarily expected. I and my comrades were stopped here, a sentinel being placed in the road to prevent our going any further. I felt very much chagrined to be thus hindered from proceeding, as I felt confident that our regiment or some considerable part of it was not far ahead, unless they had been more unlucky than I had. I remonstrated with the officer who detained us. I told him that our regiment was just ahead. He asked me how I knew that. I could not tell him, but I told him I had a sick man with me who was wet and would die if exposed all night to the damp cold air, hoping by this to move his compassion, but it would not do. He was inexorable. I shall not soon forget the answer he gave me when I made the last-mentioned observation respecting the sick man. "Well," said he, "if he dies the country will be rid of one who can do it no good."

Pretty fellow! thought I, a very compassionate gentleman! When a man has got his bane in his country's cause, let him die like an old horse or dog, because he can do no more! The *only wish* I would wish such men would be to let them have exactly the same treatment which they give to others. [19]

I saw but little chance of escaping from this very humane gentleman by fair means, so I told my two comrades to stick by me and keep together and we would get from them by some means or other during the evening. It was now almost sundown and the air quite chilly after the shower, and we were as wet as water could make us. I was really afraid my sick man would die in earnest. I had not stayed there long, waiting for an opportunity to escape, before one offered. There came to the sentinel I suppose an old acquaintance of his, with a canteen containing some sort of spirits. After drinking himself, he gave it to the sentinel who took a large pull upon it. They then fell into conversation together, but soon taking a hare from the same hound, it put them into quite a talkative mood. I kept my eyes upon them and when I thought I saw a chance of getting from them, I gave my companions a wink and we passed by the sentinel without his noticing us at all.

We went on a little distance when we overtook another man belonging to our company. He had just been refreshing himself with some bread and dry salt fish and was putting the fragments into his knapsack. I longed for a bit, but I felt too bashful to ask him and he was too thoughtless or stingy to offer it. We still proceeded, but had not gone far when we came up with the regiment, resting themselves on the cold ground after the fatigues of the day. Our company all *appeared* to rejoice to see us, thinking we were killed or prisoners. I was *sincerely* glad to see them, for I was once more among friends or at least acquaintances. Several of the regiment were missing, among whom was our major. He was a fine man and his loss was much regretted by the men of the regiment. We were the last who came up, all the others who were missing were either killed or taken prisoners. [20]

Another affair which transpired during and after the above-mentioned engagement deserves to be recorded by me, as no one else has, to my knowledge, ever mentioned it. A sergeant belonging to the Connecticut forces, being sent by his officers in the heat of the action to procure ammunition, was met by a superior officer, an aide-de-camp to some general officer, I believe, who accused him of deserting his post in time of action. He remonstrated with the officer and informed him of the absolute necessity there was of his obeying the orders of his own officers, that the failure of his procuring a supply of ammunition might endanger the success of the day. But all to no purpose. The officer would not allow himself to believe him, but drew his sword and threatened to take his life on the spot if he did not immediately return to his corps. The sergeant, fired with just indignation at hearing and seeing his life threatened, cocked his musket, and stood in his own defense. He was, however, taken, confined and tried for mutiny, and condemned to be shot.

The sentence of the court-martial was approved by the Commander in Chief, and the day for his execution set. When it arrived, an embankment was thrown up to prevent the shot fired at him from doing other damage, and all things requisite on such occasions were in readiness. The Connecticut troops were then drawn out and formed in a square and the prisoner brought forth. After being blind-folded and pinioned, he knelt upon the ground. The corporal with his six executioners were then brought up before him, ready at the fatal word of command to send a brave soldier into the eternal world because he persisted in doing his duty and obeying the lawful and urgent orders of his superior officers, the failure of which might, for aught the officer who stopped him knew, have caused the loss of hundreds of lives. But the sergeant was reprieved, and I believe it was well that he was, for his blood would not have been the only blood that would have been spilt: the troops were greatly exasperated, and they showed what their feelings were by their lively and repeated cheerings after the reprieve, but more so by their secret and open threats before it.

The reprieve was read by one of the chaplains of the army after a long harangue to the soldiers setting forth the enormity of the crime charged upon the prisoner, repeatedly using this sentence, "crimes for which men ought to die," which did much to further the resentment of the troops already raised to a high pitch. But, as I said before, it was well that it ended as it did, both on account of the honor of the soldiers and the safety of some others. I was informed that this same sergeant was honored the year following, by those who better knew his merits, with a captain's commission. [21]

Sometime in October, the British landed at Frog's Neck, or Point, and by their motions seemed to threaten to cut off our retreat to York

Island.[22] We were thereupon ordered to leave the island. We crossed King's Bridge and directed our course toward the White Plains. We saw parties of the enemies foraging in the country, but they were generally too alert for us. We encamped on the heights called Valentine's Hill,[23] where we continued some days, keeping up the old system of starving. A sheep's head which I begged of the butchers who were killing some for the "gentlemen officers" was all the provisions I had for two or three days.

We marched from Valentine's Hill for the White Plains in the night. There were but three of our men present. We had our cooking utensils (at the time the most useless things in the army) to carry in our hands. They were made of cast iron and consequently heavy. I was so beat out before morning with hunger and fatigue that I could hardly move one foot before the other. I told my messmates that I could not carry our kettle any further. They said they would not carry it any further. Of what use was it? They had nothing to cook and did not want anything to cook with. We were sitting down on the ascent of a hill when this discourse happened. We got up to proceed when I took up the kettle, which held nearly a common pailful. I could not carry it. My arms were almost dislocated. I sat it down in the road and one of the others gave it a shove with his foot and it rolled down against the fence, and that was the last I ever saw of it. When we got through the night's march, we found our mess was not the only one that was rid of their iron bondage.

We arrived at the White Plains just at dawn of day, tired and faint, encamped on the plains a few days and then removed to the hills in the rear of the plains.[24] Nothing remarkable transpired while lying here for some time, [but] the British were advancing upon us. Before we were ready to march, the battle had begun. Our regiment then marched off, crossed a considerable stream of water which crosses the plain, and formed behind a stone wall in company of several other regiments and waited the approach of the enemy.[25]

They were not far distant, at least that part of them with which we were quickly after engaged. They, however, soon made their appearance in our neighborhood. There was in our front, about ten rods distant, an orchard of apple trees. The ground on which the orchard stood was lower than the ground that we occupied but was level from our post on the verge of the orchard, when it fell off so abruptly that we could not see the lower parts of the trees. A party of Hessian troops and some English soon took possession of this ground, fired, and fell back and reloaded their muskets. Our chance upon them was, as soon as they showed themselves above the level ground, or when they fired, to aim at the flashes of their guns; their position was as advantageous to them as a breastwork. We were engaged in this manner for some time, when finding ourselves flanked and in danger of being surrounded, we were compelled to make a hasty retreat from the stone wall. We lost, comparatively speaking, very few at the fence, but when forced to retreat we lost in killed and wounded a considerable number. One man who belonged to our company, when we marched from the parade, said, "Now I am going out to the field to be killed," and he said more than once afterwards that he should be killed, and he was. He was shot dead on the field. I never saw a man so prepossessed with the idea of any mishap as he was. We fell back a little distance and made a stand, detached parties engaging in almost every direction.[26]

During the night we remained in our new-made trenches, the ground of which was in many parts springy. In that part where I happened to be stationed, the water before morning was nearly over shoes, which caused many of us to take violent colds by being exposed upon the wet ground after a profuse perspiration. I was one who felt the effects of it and was the next day sent back to the baggage to get well again, if I could, for it was left to my own exertions to do it and no other assistance was afforded me. I was not alone in misery; there were a number in the same circumstances. When I arrived at the baggage, which was not more than a mile or two, I had the canopy of heaven for my hospital and the ground for my hammock. I found a spot where the dry leaves had collected between the knolls. I made up a bed of these and nestled in it, having no other friend present but the sun to smile upon me. I had nothing to eat or drink, not even water, and was unable to go after any myself, for I was sick indeed. In the evening, one of my messmates found me out and soon after brought me some boiled hog's flesh (it was not pork) and turnips, without either bread or salt. I could not eat it, but I felt obliged to him notwithstanding. He did all he could do. He gave me the best he had to give, and had to steal that, poor fellow.

The British, soon after this, left the White Plains and passed the Hudson into New Jersey. We likewise fell back to New Castle and Wright's Mills.[27] Here a number of our sick were sent off to Norwalk in Connecticut to recruit. I was sent with them as a nurse. We were billeted among the inhabitants. I had in my ward seven or eight sick soldiers who were (at least, soon after their arrival there) as well in health as I was. All they wanted was a cook and something for a cook to exercise his functions upon. The inhabitants here were almost entirely what were in those days termed Tories. An old lady, of whom I often procured milk, used always when I went to her house to give me a lecture on my opposition to our good King George. She had always said, she told me, that the regulars would make us fly like pigeons.[28] My patients would not use any of the milk I had of her for fear, as they said, of poison. I told them I was not afraid of her poisoning the milk; she had not wit enough to think of such a thing, nor resolution enough to do it if she did think of it.

Our surgeon came amongst us soon after this and packed us all off to camp, save two or three who were discharged. I arrived at camp with the rest, where we remained, moving from place to place as occasion required, undergoing hunger, cold, and fatigue until the twenty-fifth day of December, 1776, when I was discharged, my term of service having expired, at Philipse Manor in the state of New York near Hudson's River.[29]

Campaign of 1777

The spring of 1777 arrived. I had got recruited during the winter,[30] and begun to think again about the army. In the month of April, as the weather warmed, the young men began to enlist. Orders were out for enlisting men for three years, or during the war. The general opinion of the people was that the war would not continue three years longer; what reasons they had for making such conjectures I cannot imagine, but so it was. Perhaps it was their wish that it *might* be so, induced them to think that it *would* be so.

The inhabitants of the town were about this time put into what were called squads, according to their ratable property. Of some of the most opulent, one formed a squad; of others, two or three, and of the lower sort of the people, several formed a squad. Each of these squads were to furnish a man for the army, either by hiring or by sending one of their own number.

One of the above-mentioned squads, wanting to procure a man, the lieutenant told them that he thought they might persuade me to go for them, and they accordingly attacked me, front, rear, and flank. I thought, as I must go, I might as well endeavor to get as much for my skin as I could. Accordingly, I told them that I would go for them, and fixed upon a day when I would meet them and clinch the bargain. The day, which was a muster day of the militia of the town, arrived. I went to the parade, where all was liveliness, as it generally is upon such occasions; but poor *I* felt miserably; my execution day was come. I kept wandering about till the afternoon, among the crowd, when I saw the lieutenant, who went with me into a house where the men of the squad were, and there I put my name to enlisting indentures for the last time. [31]

Just at this time the British landed in Connecticut, and marched twenty miles into the country, where they burnt the town of Danbury with all the public stores it contained, which were considerable, among which was all the clothing of our regiment. The militia were generally turned out and sent to settle the account with them. The newly enlisted soldiers went with the militia. The enemy had, however, executed his commission, and made considerable progress on his return before we came up. We had some pretty severe scratches with them; killed some, wounded some, and took some prisoners. The remainder reached their shipping, embarked, and cleared out for New York, where they arrived soon after, I suppose, much gratified with the mischief they had done. We likewise returned home, with the loss of three men belonging to the town, one of whom was an enlisted soldier. Major General David Wooster, of New Haven, an old and experienced officer, likewise fell in this expedition. General [Benedict] Arnold had a very close rub, but escaped. [32]

Soon after the above transaction, we had orders to join our regiment, at Newton, the residence of our colonel [John Chandler]. We stayed but a short time here, but went on to Danbury, where I had an ample opportunity to see the devastation caused there by the British. The town had been laid in ashes, a number of the inhabitants murdered and cast into their burning houses, because they presumed to defend their persons and property, or to be avenged on a cruel, vindictive invading enemy. I saw the inhabitants, after the fire was out, endeavoring to find the burnt bones of their relatives amongst the rubbish of their demolished houses. The streets, in many places, were literally flooded by the fat which ran from the piles of barrels of pork burnt by the enemy. They fully executed their design.

We stayed here but a short time, and then marched to Peekskill, on the Hudson River, and encamped in the edge of the Highlands, at a place called Old Orchard. [33] Here we were tormented by the whippoorwills. A potent enemy! says the reader. Well, a potent enemy they were, particularly to our rest at night. They would begin their imposing music in the twilight and continue it till ten or eleven o'clock, and commence again before the dawn, when they would be in a continual roar. No man, unless he were stupefied, could get a wink of sleep during the serenade, which, in the short nights in the month of May, was almost the whole of the night.

I was soon after this transaction ordered off, in company with about four hundred others of the Connecticut forces, to a set of old barracks, a mile or two distant in the Highlands, to be inoculated with the smallpox. We arrived at and cleaned out the barracks, and after two or three days received the infection, which was on the last day of May. We had a guard of Massachusetts troops to attend us. Our hospital stores were deposited in a farmer's barn in the vicinity of our quarters. [34]

I had the smallpox favorably as did the rest, generally. I left the hospital on the sixteenth day after I was inoculated, and soon after joined the regiment, when I was attacked with a severe turn of the dysentery, and immediately after recovering from that, I broke out all over with boils. Good old Job could scarcely have been worse handled by them than I was. I had eleven at one time upon my arm, each as big as half a hen's egg, and the rest of my carcass was much in the same condition. I attributed it to my not having been properly physicked after the smallpox, in consequence of our hospital stores being in about the same state as the commissary's.

In the latter part of the month of June, or the beginning of July, I was ordered off in a detachment of about a hundred men, under the command of a captain, to the lines near King's Bridge, to join two regiments of New York troops which belonged to our brigade. Upon the march (which was very fatiguing, it being exceeding hot weather) we halted to rest.

We arrived upon the lines and joined the other corps which was already there. No one who has never been upon such duty as those advanced parties have to perform can form any adequate idea of the trouble, fatigue and dangers which they have to encounter. Their whole time is spent in marches, especially night marches, watching, starving, and in cold weather, freezing and sickness. If they get any chance to rest, it must be in the woods or fields, under the side of a fence, in an orchard or in any other place but a comfortable one, lying down on the cold and often wet ground, and, perhaps, before the eyes can be closed with a moment's sleep, alarmed and compelled to stand under arms an hour or two, or to receive an attack from the enemy; and when permitted again to endeavor to rest, called upon immediately to remove some four or five miles to seek some other place, to go through the same maneuvering as before. For it was dangerous to remain any length of time in one place for fear of being informed of by some Tory inhabitant (for there were plenty of this sort of savage beast during the Revolutionary War) and ten thousand other causes to harass, fatigue and perplex, which time and room will not permit me to enumerate.

Our troops, not long after this, marched to join the main army in Pennsylvania.[35] The heavy baggage was left to come on after them, and I, being an invalid, was left as one of the guard to conduct it. The baggage soon followed the troops, and I underwent not a little trouble on the march in consequence of my lame foot. When I joined the regiment the baggage was immediately sent back to Bethlehem, nearly fifty miles in the country, and I was again sent with it as a guard. It was much against my inclination to go on this business, for I had for some time past been under the command of other officers than my own, and now I must continue longer under them. Soldiers always like to be under the command of their own officers; they are generally bad enough, but strangers are worse. I was obliged to obey my officers' orders and go on this duty, but when I was away they could not hinder me from coming back again. I was resolved not to stay at Bethlehem, and as soon as we arrived there I contrived to get the permission of the officers of the guard to return to camp again immediately. I arrived at camp the second day after leaving the baggage. My officers inquired of me why I had returned? If I was able to do hard duty, they said they were glad that I had joined the command again; if not, they were sorry. I endeavored to appear to be as well as possible, for I had no notion of being sent away from my officers and old messmates again, if I could avoid it.

When I arrived at camp it was just dark, the troops were all preparing for a march. Their provisions (what they had) were all cooked, and their arms and ammunition strictly inspected and all deficiencies supplied. Early in the evening we marched in the direction of Philadelphia. We naturally concluded there was something serious in the wind. We marched slowly all night. In the morning there was a low vapor lying on the land which made it very difficult to distinguish objects at any considerable distance.

About daybreak our advanced guard and the British outposts came in contact. The curs began to bark first and then the bulldogs. Our brigade moved off to the right into the fields. We saw a body of the enemy drawn up behind a rail fence on our right flank; we immediately formed in line and advanced upon them. Our orders were not to fire till we could see the buttons upon their clothes, but they were so coy that they would not give us an opportunity to be so curious, for they hid their clothes in fire and smoke before we had either time or leisure to examine their buttons. They soon fell back and we advanced, when the action became general. The enemy were driven quite through their camp. They left their kettles, in which they were cooking their breakfasts, on the fires, and some of their garments were lying on the ground, which the owners had not time to put on.

Affairs went on well for some time. The enemy were retreating before us, until the first division that was engaged had expended their ammunition. Some of the men unadvisedly calling out that their ammunition was spent, the enemy were so near that they overheard them, when they first made a stand and then returned upon our people, who, for want of ammunition and reinforcements, were obliged in their turn to retreat, which ultimately resulted in the rout of the whole army. [36]

I had now to travel the rest of the day, after marching all the day and night before and fighting all the morning. [37] I had eaten nothing since the noon of the preceding day, nor did I eat a morsel till the forenoon of the next day, and I needed rest as much as victuals. I could have procured that if I had had time to seek it, but victuals was not to be found.

After the army had collected again and recovered from their panic, we were kept marching and countermarching, starving and freezing, nothing else happening, although that was enough, until we encamped at a place called the White Marsh, about twelve miles to the northward of Philadelphia. [38] While we lay here, there was a spell of soft still weather, there not being wind enough for several days to dispel the smoke caused by the fires in camp. My eyes were so affected by it that I was not able to open them for hours together. The ground, which was soft and loamy, was converted into mortar, and so dirty was it that any hogsty was preferable to our tents to sleep in; and to cap the climax of our misery, we had nothing to eat, nor scarcely anything to wear.

Being pinched with hunger, I one day strolled to a place, where sometime before some cattle had been slaughtered. Here I had the good luck (or rather bad luck, as it turned out in the end) to find an ox's milt, which had escaped the hogs and dogs. With this prize I steered off to my tent, threw it upon the fire and broiled it, and then sat down to eat it, without either bread or salt. I had not had it long in my stomach before it began to make strong remonstrances and to manifest a great inclination to be set at liberty again. I was very willing to listen to its requests, and with eyes overflowing with tears at parting with what I had thought to be a friend, I gave it a discharge. But the very thoughts of it would for some time after almost make me think that I had another milt in my stomach.

About this time information was received at headquarters that a considerable body of British troops were advanced and encamped on the western side of the river Schuylkill, near the lower bridge, two or three miles from Philadelphia. Forces were immediately put in requisition to rout them from thence. Our brigade was ordered off, with some detachments from other parts of the army. We marched from camp just before night as light troops, light in everything, especially in eatables. We marched to a place called Barren Hill, about twelve or fifteen miles from the city. From here, about ten o'clock in the evening, we forded the Schuylkill where the river, including a bare gravelly island, or flat which we crossed, was about forty rods wide, as near as I could judge, and the water about to the waist. It was quite a cool night, in the month of October; the water which spattered on to our clothes froze as we passed the river. Many of the young and small soldiers fell while in the water and were completely drenched. We, however, got over and marched two or three miles on a dreary road, for that part of the country, surrounded by high hills and thick woods. All of a sudden we were ordered to halt. We were, to appearance, in an unfrequented road, cold and wet to our middles, and half starved. We were sorry to be stopped from traveling, as exercise kept us warm in some degree. We endeavored to kindle fires, but were ordered by the officers immediately to extinguish them, which was done by all except one, which having been kindled in a hollow tree could not be put out. I got so near to this that I could just see it between the men's legs, which was all the benefit that I derived from it.

The intention of the quartermaster sergeants was to give each man a gill of liquor,[39] but as measuring it out by gills was tedious, it was dealt out to us in pint measures, with directions to divide a pint between four men. But as it was dark and the actions of the men could not be well seen by those who served out the liquor, each one drank as much as he pleased; some, perhaps, half a gill, some a gill, and as many as chose it drained the pint.

We again moved on for the camp, distant about five miles. We had not proceeded far before we entered a lane fenced on either side with rails, in which was a water plash, or puddle. The fence was taken down on one side of the road to enable us to pass round the water. It was what is called a five-rail fence, only the two upper rails of which were taken out; here was fun. We had been on the march since we had drank the whiskey just long enough for the liquor to assume its height of operation; our stomachs being empty the whiskey took rank hold and the poor brain fared accordingly. When the men came to the fence, not being able, many or most of them, to keep a regular balance between head and heels, they would pile themselves up on each side of the fence, swearing and hallooing, some losing their arms, some their hats, some their shoes, and some themselves. Had the enemy come upon us at this time, there would have been an action worth recording.

Soon after this affair our two Connecticut regiments [Durkee's Fourth and Chandler's Eighth] (they being the only troops of that state then with the main army) were ordered off to defend the forts on the Delaware River, below the city.[40] We marched about dark, hungry and cold, and kept on till we could proceed no further, from sheer hunger and fatigue. We halted about one o'clock at night, in a village, and were put into houses of the inhabitants, much, I suppose, to their contentment, especially at that time of night. Sleep took such strong hold of me and most of the others, that we soon forgot our wants. Not so with some five or six of our company, who were determined not to die of hunger that night, if any means could be devised to prevent it. They, therefore, as soon as all was still, sallied out on an expedition. They could not find anything eatable but the contents of a beehive, which they took the liberty to remove from the beehouse to a place which they thought more convenient.

We crossed the Delaware, between the town of Bristol, in Pennsylvania, and the city of Burlington, in New Jersey. We halted for the night at the latter place, where we procured some carrion beef, for it was not better. We cooked it and ate some, and carried the remainder away with us.

We arrived at Woodbury, New Jersey, which was the end of our present journey. We encamped near the village, planted our artillery in the road at each end of it, placed our guards and prepared to go into Fort Mifflin, on Mud Island. [41]

Immediately after our arrival at Woodbury, I was ordered upon an advanced guard, about half a mile in advance of a bridge which lay across a large creek, into which the tide flowed. The enemy's shipping lay in the river a little below us. They had also a fortification on the shore opposite to their shipping, at a place called Billingsport. There was a guard of the Jersey militia in advance of us. We used to make excursions in parties of three or four, from our guard, into the neighborhood of the enemy, and often picked up stragglers from their post and shipping.

I was soon relieved from this guard, and with those who were able, of our two regiments, sent to reinforce those in the fort, which was then besieged by the British. Here I endured hardships sufficient to kill half a dozen horses. In the cold month of November, without provisions, without clothing, not a scrap of either shoes or stockings to my feet or legs, and in this condition to endure a siege in such a place as that was appalling in the highest degree.

In confirmation of what I have here said, I will give the reader a short description of the pen that I was confined in. Confined I was, for it was next to impossible to have got away from it, if I had been so disposed. Well, the island, as it is called, is nothing more than a mud flat in the Delaware, lying upon the west side of the channel. It is diked around the fort, with sluices so constructed that the fort can be laid under water at pleasure.

On the western side of the fortification was a row of barracks, extending from the northern part of the works to about half the length of the fort. On the northern end was another block of barracks which reached nearly across the fort from east to west. In front of these was a large square two-story house, for the accommodation of the officers of the garrison. Neither this house nor the barracks were of much use at this time, for it was as much as a man's life was worth to enter them, the enemy often directing their shot at them in particular. In front of the barracks and other necessary places were parades and walks; the rest of the ground was soft mud. I have seen the enemy's shells fall upon it and sink so low that their report could not be heard when they burst, and I could only feel a tremulous motion of the earth at the time. At other times, when they burst near the surface of the ground, they would throw the mud fifty feet in the air.

The British had erected five batteries with six heavy guns in each and a bomb battery with three long mortars in it on the opposite side of the water, which separated the island from the main on the west, and which was but a short distance across.

Our batteries were nothing more than old spars and timber laid up in parallel lines and filled between with mud and dirt. The British batteries in the course of the day would nearly level our works, and we were, like the beaver, obliged to repair our dams in the night. During the whole night, at intervals of a quarter or half an hour, the enemy would let off all their pieces, and although we had sentinels to watch them and at every flash of their guns to cry, "a shot," upon hearing which everyone endeavored to take care of himself, yet they would ever and anon, in spite of all our precautions, cut up some of us.

The engineer in the fort was a French officer by the name of [François Louis de] Fleury, the same who struck the British flag at the storming of Stony Point. He was a very austere man and kept us constantly employed day and night; there was no chance of escaping from his vigilance.

What little provisions we had was cooked by the invalids in our camp and brought to the island in old flour barrels; it was mostly corned beef and hard bread, but it was not much trouble to cook or fetch what we had.

We continued here, suffering cold, hunger and other miseries, till the fourteenth day of November. On that day, at the dawn, we discovered six ships of the line, all sixty-fours, a frigate of thirty-six guns, and a galley in a line just below the chevaux-de-frise; a twenty-four-gun ship (being an old ship cut down) her guns said to be all brass twenty-four pounders, and a sloop of six guns in company with her, both within pistol shot of the fort, on the western side. We immediately opened our batteries upon them, but they appeared to take very little notice of us. We heated some shot, but by mistake twenty-four-pound shot were heated instead of eighteen, which was the caliber of the guns in that part of the fort. The enemy soon began their firing upon us and there was music indeed. The soldiers were all ordered to take their posts at the palisadoes, which they were ordered to defend to the last extremity, as it was expected the British would land under the fire of their cannon and attempt to storm the fort. The cannonade was severe, as well it might be, six sixty-four-gun ships, a thirty-six-gun frigate, a twenty-four-gun ship, a galley and a sloop of six guns, together with six batteries of six guns each and a bomb battery of three mortars, all playing at once upon our poor little fort, if fort it might be called. [42]

About the middle of the day some of our galleys and floating batteries, with a frigate, fell down and engaged the British with their long guns, which in some measure took off the enemy's fire from the fort. The cannonade continued without interruption on the side of the British throughout the day. Nearly every gun in the fort was silenced by midday. Our men were cut up like cornstalks. I do not know the exact number of the killed and wounded but can say it was not small, considering the numbers in the fort, which were only the able part of the Fourth and Eighth Connecticut regiments, with a company or two of artillery, perhaps less than five hundred in all.

The cannonade continued, directed mostly at the fort, till the dusk of the evening. As soon as it was dark we began to make preparations for evacuating the fort and endeavoring to escape to the Jersey shore. [43] When the firing had in some measure subsided and I could look about me, I found the fort exhibited a picture of desolation. The whole area of the fort was as completely ploughed as a field. The buildings of every kind [were] hanging in broken fragments, and the guns all dismounted, and how many of the garrison sent to the world of spirits, I knew not. If ever destruction was complete, it was here. The surviving part of the garrison were now drawn off and such of the stores as could conveniently be taken away were carried to the Jersey shore.

I happened to be left with a party of seventy or eighty men to destroy and burn all that was left in the place. We proceeded to set fire to everything that would burn, and then repaired immediately to the wharf where three bateaux were waiting to convey us across the river. And now came on another trial. Before we could embark the buildings in the fort were completely in flames, and they threw such a light upon the water that we were as plainly seen by the British as though it had been broad day. Almost their whole fire was directed at us, but by the assistance of a kind Providence we escaped without any further injury and landed, a little after midnight, on the Jersey shore.

We marched a little back into some pitch-pine woods, where we found the rest of the troops that had arrived before us. They had made up some comfortable fires and were enjoying the warmth, and that was all the comfort they had to partake of, except rest, for victuals was out of the question. I wrapped myself up in my blanket and lay down upon the leaves and soon fell asleep and continued so till past noon, when I awoke from the first sound sleep I had had for a fortnight. Indeed, I had not laid down in all that time. The little sleep I had obtained was in cat naps, sitting up and leaning against the wall, and I thought myself fortunate if I could do that much. When I awoke I was as crazy as a goose shot through the head.

Here ends the account of as hard and fatiguing a job, for the time it lasted, as occurred during the Revolutionary War. Thomas Paine, in one of his political essays, speaking of the siege and defense of this port, says, "They had nothing but their bravery and good conduct to cover them." He spoke the truth. I was at the siege and capture of Lord Cornwallis, and the hardships of that were no more to be compared with this than the sting of a bee is to the bite of a rattlesnake. But there has been but little notice taken of it, the reason of which is, there was no Washington, Putnam, or Wayne there. Had there been, the affair would have been extolled to the skies. No, it was only a few officers and soldiers who accomplished it in a remote quarter of the army. Such circumstances and such troops generally get but little notice taken of them, do what they will. Great men get great praise; little men, nothing. But it always was so and always will be. [44]

We marched from hence and crossed the Delaware again between Burlington and Bristol. Here we procured a day's ration of southern salt pork (three fourths of a pound) and a pound of sea bread. We marched a little distance and stopped "to refresh ourselves." We kindled some fires in the road, and some broiled their meat; as for myself, I ate mine raw. We quickly started on and marched till evening, when we went into a wood for the night. We did not pitch our tents, and about midnight it began to rain very hard, which soon put out all our fires and we had to lie "and weather it out." The troops marched again before day.

We continued our march until sometime after dark, when we arrived

50

in the vicinity of the main army. We again turned into a wood for the night. The leaves and ground were as wet as water could make them. It was then foggy and the water dropping from the trees like a shower. We endeavored to get fire by flashing powder on the leaves, but this and every other expedient that we could employ failing, we were forced by our old master, Necessity, to lay down and sleep if we could, with three others of our constant companions, Fatigue, Hunger, and Cold.

Next morning we joined the grand army near Philadelphia, and the heavy baggage being sent back to the rear of he army, we were obliged to put us up huts by laying up poles and covering them with leaves, a capital shelter from winter storms. Here we continued to fast; indeed we kept a continual Lent as faithfully as ever any of the most rigorous of the Roman Catholics did.

While we lay there, there happened very remarkable northern lights. At one time the whole visible heavens appeared for some time as if covered with crimson velvet. Some of the soldiers prognosticated a bloody battle about to be fought, but time, which always speaks the truth, proved them to be false prophets.

While we lay here there was a Continental Thanksgiving ordered by Congress; and as the army had all the cause in the world to be particularly thankful, if not for being well off, at least that it was no worse, we were ordered to participate in it. We had nothing to eat for two or three days previous, except what the trees of the fields and forests afforded us. But we must now have what Congress said, a sumptuous Thanksgiving to close the year of high living we had now nearly seen brought to a close. Well, to add something extraordinary to our present stock of provisions, our country, ever mindful of its suffering army, opened her sympathizing heart so wide, upon this occasion, as to give us something to make the world stare. And what do you think it was, reader? Guess. You cannot guess, be you as much of a Yankee as you will. I will tell you; it gave each and every man half a gill of rice and a tablespoon of vinegar! [45]

The army was now not only starved but naked. The greatest part were not only shirtless and barefoot, but destitute of all other clothing, especially blankets. I procured a small piece of raw cowhide and made myself a pair of moccasins, which kept my feet (while they lasted) from the frozen ground, although, as I well remember, the hard edges so galled my ankles, while on a march, that it was with much difficulty and pain that I could wear them afterwards; but the only alternative I had was to endure this inconvenience or to go barefoot, as hundreds of my companions had to, till they might be tracked by their blood upon the rough frozen ground.

We arrived at Valley Forge in the evening [December 18]. It was dark; there was no water to be found and I was perishing with thirst. I searched for water till I was weary and came to my tent without finding any. Fatigue and thirst, joined with hunger, almost made me desperate. I felt at that instant as if I would have taken victuals or drink from the best friend I had on earth by force. I am not writing fiction, all are sober realities. Just after I arrived at my tent, two soldiers, whom I did not know, passed by. They had some water in their canteens which they told me they had found a good distance off, but could not direct me to the place as it was very dark. I tried to beg a draught of water from them but they were as rigid as Arabs. At length I persuaded them to sell me a drink for three pence, Pennsylvania currency, which was every cent I could then call my own, so great was the necessity I was then reduced to.

The second evening after our arrival here I was warned to be ready for a two days command. I never heard a summons to duty with so much disgust before or since as I did that. How I could endure two days more fatigue without nourishment of some sort I could not tell, for I heard nothing said about "provisions." However, in the morning at roll call, I was obliged to comply. I went to the parade where I found a considerable number, ordered upon the same business, whatever it was. We were ordered to go to the quartermaster general and receive from him our final orders. We accordingly repaired to his quarters, which was about three miles from camp. Here we understood that our destiny was to go into the country on a foraging expedition, which was nothing more nor less than to procure provisions from the inhabitants for the men in the army and forage for the poor perishing cattle belonging to it, at the point of the bayonet. [46] We stayed at the quartermaster general's quarters till sometime in the afternoon, during which time a beef creature was butchered for us. I well remember what fine stuff it was, it was quite transparent. I thought at that time what an excellent lantern it would make. I was, notwithstanding, very glad to get some of it, bad as it looked. We were then divided into several parties and sent off upon our expedition.

Our party consisted of a lieutenant, a sergeant, a corporal and eighteen privates. We marched till night when we halted and took up our quarters at a large farmhouse. The lieutenant, attended by his waiter, took up his quarters for the night in the hall with the people of the house. We were put into the kitchen. We had a snug room and a comfortable fire, and we began to think about cooking some of our fat beef. One of the men proposed to the landlady to sell her a shirt for some sauce. She very readily took the shirt, which was worth a dollar at least. After we had received the sauce, we went to work to cook our supper. By the time it was eatable the family had gone to rest. We saw where the woman went into the cellar, and, she having left us a candle, we took it into our heads that a little good cider would not make our supper relish any the worse; so some of the men took the water pail and drew it full of excellent cider, which did not fail to raise our spirits considerably. Before we lay down the man who sold the shirt, having observed that the landlady had flung it into a closet, took a notion to repossess it again. We marched off early in the morning before the people of the house were stirring, consequently did not know or see the woman's chagrin at having been overreached by the soldiers.

This day we arrived at Milltown, or Downingstown, a small village halfway between Philadelphia and Lancaster, which was to be our quarters for the winter. It was dark when we had finished our day's march. There was a commissary and a wagon master general stationed here, the commissary to take into custody the provisions and forage that we collected, and the wagon master general to regulate the conduct of the wagoners and direct their motions. The next day after our arrival at this place we were put into a small house in which was only one room, in the center of the village. We were immediately furnished with rations of good and wholesome beef and flour, built us up some berths to sleep in, and filled them with straw, and felt as happy as any other pigs that were no better off than ourselves. And now having got into winter quarters and ready to commence our foraging business, I shall here end my account of my second campaign.

Campaign of 1778

I do not remember that during the time I was employed in this business, which was from Christmas to the latter part of April, even to have met with the least resistance from the inhabitants, take what we would from their barns, mills, corncribs, or stalls, but when we came to their stables, then look out for the women. Take what horse you would, it was one or the other's "pony" and they had no other to ride to church. And when we had got possession of a horse we were sure to have half a dozen or more women pressing upon us, until by some means or other, if possible, they would slip the bridle from the horse's head, and then we might catch him again if we could. They would take no more notice of a charged bayonet than a blind horse would of a cocked pistol. It would answer no purpose to threaten to kill them with the bayonet or musket; they knew as well as we did that we would not put our threats in execution, and when they had thus liberated a horse (which happened but seldom) they would laugh at us and ask us why we did not do as we threatened, kill them, and then they would generally ask us into their houses and treat us with as much kindness as though nothing had happened.

The women of Pennsylvania, taken in general, are certainly very worthy characters. I was always well treated both by them and the men, especially the Friends or Quakers,[47] in every part of the state through which I passed, and that was the greater part of what was then inhabited. But the southern ladies had a queer idea of the Yankees (as they always called the New Englanders); they seemed to think that they were a people quite different from themselves, as indeed they were in many respects.[48]

I happened once to be with some wagons, one of which was detached from the party. I went with this team as its guard. We stopped at a house, the mistress of which and the wagoner were acquainted. (These foraging teams all belonged in the neighborhood of our quarters.) She had a pretty female child about four years old. The teamster was praising the child, extolling its gentleness and quietness, when the mother observed that it had been quite cross and crying all day. "I have been threatening," said she, "to give her to the Yankees." "Take care," said the wagoner, "how you speak of the Yankees, I have one of them here with me." "La!" said the woman. "Is he a Yankee? I thought he was a Pennsylvanian. I don't see any difference between him and other people."

I have before said that I should not narrate all the little affairs which transpired while I was on this foraging party. But if I pass them all over in silence the reader may perhaps think that I had nothing to do all winter, or at least, that I *did* nothing, when in truth it was quite the reverse. Our duty was hard, but generally not altogether unpleasant.[49] I had to travel far and near, in cold and in storms, by day and by night, and at all times to run the *risk* of abuse, if not of injury, from the inhabitants when *plundering* them of their property, for I could not, while in the very act of taking their cattle, hay, corn and grain from them against their wills, consider it a whit better than plundering—sheer privateering. But I will give them the credit of never receiving the least abuse or injury from an individual during the whole time I was employed in this business. I doubt whether the people of New England would have borne it as patiently, their "steady habits" to the contrary notwithstanding.

After I had joined my regiment I was kept constantly, when off other duty, engaged in learning the Baron de Steuben's new Prussian exercise. It was a continual drill. [50]

About this time I was sent off from camp in a detachment consisting of about three thousand men, with four fieldpieces, under the command of the young General Lafayette. [51] We marched to Barren Hill, about twelve miles from Philadelphia. We halted here, placed our guards, sent off our scouting parties, and waited for—I know not what. [52] A company of about a hundred Indians, from some northern tribe, joined us here. There were three or four young Frenchmen with them. The Indians were stout-looking fellows and remarkably neat for that race of mortals, but they were Indians. [53] There was upon the hill, and just where we were lying, an old church built of stone, entirely divested of all its entrails. The Indians were amusing themselves and the soldiers by shooting with their bows, in and about the church. I observed something in a corner of the roof which did not appear to belong to the building, and desired an Indian who was standing near me to shoot an arrow at it. He did so and it proved to be a cluster of bats; I should think there were nearly a bushel of them, all hanging upon one another. The house was immediately alive with them, and it was likewise instantly full of Indians and soldiers. The poor bats fared hard; it was sport for all hands. They killed I know not how many, but there was a great slaughter among them. I never saw so many bats before nor since, nor indeed in my whole life put all together.

Just at the dawn of day the officers' waiters came, almost breathless, after the horses. Upon inquiring for the cause of the unusual hurry, we were told that the British were advancing upon us in our rear. How they could get there was to us a mystery, but they were there. We helped the waiters to catch their horses and immediately returned to the main body of the detachment. We found the troops all under arms and in motion, preparing for an onset. Those of the troops belonging to our brigade were put into the churchyard, which was enclosed by a wall of stone and lime about breast high, a good defense against musketry but poor against artillery. I began to think I should soon have some better sport than killing bats. But our commander found that the enemy was too strong to be engaged in the position we then occupied. He therefore wisely ordered a retreat from this place to the Schuylkill, where we might choose any position that we pleased, having ragged woody hills in our rear and the river in front.

It was about three miles to the river. The weather was exceeding warm, and I was in the rear platoon of the detachment except two platoons of General Washington's Guards. The quick motion in front kept the rear on a constant trot. Two pieces of artillery were in front and two in the rear. The enemy had nearly surrounded us by the time our retreat commenced, but the road we were in was very favorable for us, it being for the most part through small woods and copses. When I was about halfway to the river, I saw the right wing of the enemy through a lawn about half a mile distant, but they were too late. Besides, they made a blunder here. They saw our rear guard with the two fieldpieces in its front, and thinking it the front of the detachment, they closed in to secure their prey, but when they had sprung their net they found that they had not a single bird in it.

We crossed the Schuylkill in good order, very near the spot where I had crossed it four times in the month of October the preceding autumn. As fast as the troops crossed they formed and prepared for action, and waited for them to attack us; but we saw no more of them that time, for before we had reached the river the alarm guns were fired in our camp and the whole army was immediately in motion. The British, fearing that they should be outnumbered in their turn, directly set their faces for Philadelphia and set off in as much or more haste than they had left Barren Hill. They had, during the night, left the city with such silence and secrecy, and by taking what was called the New York road, that they escaped detection by all our parties, and the first knowledge they obtained of the enemy's movements was that he was upon their backs, between them and us on the hill. The Indians, with all their alertness, had like to have "bought the rabbit." They kept coming in all the afternoon, in parties of four or five, whooping and hallooing like wild beasts. After they had got collected they vanished; I never saw any more of them. Our scouting parties all came in safe, but I was afterwards informed by a British deserter that several of the enemy perished by the heat and their exertions to get away from a retreating enemy.

Soon after this affair we left our winter cantonments, crossed the Schuylkill and encamped of the left bank of that river, just opposite to our winter quarters. We had lain here but a few days when we heard that the British army had left Philadelphia and were proceeding to New York, through the Jerseys. We marched immediately in pursuit. We crossed the Delaware at Carroll's Ferry, above Trenton,[54] and encamped a day or two between that town and Princeton. Here again I was detached with a party of one thousand men, as light troops, to get into the enemy's route and follow him close, to favor desertion and pick up stragglers.[55]

We passed through Princeton and encamped on the open fields for the night, the canopy of heaven for our tent. Early the next morning we marched again and came up with the rear of the British army. We followed them several days, arriving upon their camping ground within an hour after their departure from it. We had ample opportunity to see the devastation they made in their rout; cattle killed and lying about the fields and pastures, some just in the position they were in when shot down, others with a small spot of skin taken off their hind quarters and a mess of steak taken out; household furniture hacked and broken to pieces; wells filled up and mechanics' and farmers' tools destroyed. It was in the height of the season of cherries; the innocent industrious creatures could not climb the trees for the fruit, but universally cut them down. Such conduct did not give the Americans any more agreeable feelings toward them than they entertained before.[56]

It was extremely hot weather, and the sandy plains of that part of New Jersey did not cool the air to any great degree, but we still kept close to the rear of the British army. Deserters were almost hourly coming over to us, but of stragglers we took only a few.

The next morning, as soon as the enemy began their march, we were again in motion and came to their last night's encamping ground just after sunrise. Here we halted an hour or two, as we often had to do, to give the enemy time to advance, our orders being not to attack them unless in self-defense. We were marching on as usual, when, about ten or eleven o'clock, we were ordered to halt and then to face to the right about. As this order was given by the officers in rather a different way than usual, we began to think something was out of joint somewhere, but what or where our united wisdom could not explain.

We were early in the morning mustered out and ordered to leave all our baggage under the care of a guard (our baggage was trifling), taking only our blankets and provisions (our provisions were less), and prepare for immediate march and action. [57]

The officer who commanded the platoon that I belonged to was a captain, belonging to the Rhode Island troops, and a fine brave man he was; he feared nobody nor nothing. When we were paraded, "Now," said he to us, "you have been wishing for some days past to come up with the British, you have been wanting to fight. Now you shall have fighting enough before night."

After all things were put in order, we marched, but halted a few minutes in the village, where we were joined by a few other troops, and then proceeded on. We now heard a few reports of cannon ahead. We went in a road running through a deep narrow valley, which was for a considerable way covered with thick wood; we were some time in passing this defile.

It was ten or eleven o'clock before we got through these woods and came into the open fields. The first cleared land we came to was an Indian cornfield, surrounded on the east, west and north sides by thick tall trees. The sun shining full upon the field, the soil of which was sandy, the mouth of a heated oven seemed to me to be but a trifle hotter than this ploughed field; it was almost impossible to breathe. We had to fall back again as soon as we could, into the woods. By the time we had got under the shade of the trees and had taken breath, of which we had been almost deprived, we received orders to retreat, as all the left wing of the army, that part being under the command of General [Charles] Lee, were retreating. Grating as this order was to our feelings, we were obliged to comply.

We had not retreated far before we came to a defile, a muddy, sloughy brook. While the artillery were passing this place, we sat down by the roadside. In a few minutes the Commander-in-Chief and suite crossed the road just where we were sitting. I heard him ask our officers "by whose order the troops were retreating," and being answered, "by General Lee's," he said something, but as he was moving forward all the time this was passing, he was too far off for me to hear it distinctly. Those that were nearer to him said that his words were "d--n him." Whether he did thus express himself or not I do not know. It was certainly very unlike him, but he seemed at the instant to be in a great passion; his looks if not his words seemed to indicate as much. After passing us, he rode on to the plain field and took an observation of the advancing enemy. He remained there some time upon his old English charger, while the shot from the British artillery were rending up the earth all around him. [58] After he had taken a view of the enemy, he returned and ordered the two Connecticut brigades to make a stand at a fence, in order to keep the enemy in check while the artillery and other troops crossed the before-mentioned defile.

Our detachment formed directly in front of the artillery, as a covering party, so far below on the declivity of the hill that the pieces could play over our heads. And here we waited the approach of the enemy, should he see fit to attack us.

By this time the British had come in contact with the New England forces at the fence, when a sharp conflict ensued. These troops maintained their ground, till the whole force of the enemy that could be brought to bear had charged upon them through the fence, and after being overpowered by numbers and the platoon officers had given orders for their several platoons to leave the fence, they had to force them to retreat, so eager were they to be revenged on the invaders of their country and their rights.

As soon as the troops had left this ground the British planted their cannon upon the place and began a violent attack upon the artillery and our detachment, but neither could be routed. The cannonade continued for some time without intermission, when the British pieces being mostly disabled, they reluctantly crawled back from the height which they had occupied and hid themselves from our sight.

Before the cannonade had commenced, a part of the right wing of the British army had advanced across a low meadow and brook and occupied an orchard on our left. The weather was almost too hot to live in, and the British troops in the orchard were forced by the heat to shelter themselves from it under the trees.

We were immediately ordered from our old detachment and joined another, the whole composing a corps of about five hundred men. We instantly marched towards the enemy's right wing, which was in the orchard, and kept concealed from them as long as possible by keeping behind the bushes. When we could no longer keep ourselves concealed, we marched into the open fields and formed our line. The British immediately formed and began to retreat to the main body of their army. Colonel Cilly, finding that we were not likely to overtake the enemy before they reached the main body of the army, on account of fences and other obstructions, ordered three or four platoons from the right of our corps to pursue and attack them, and thus keep them in play till the rest of the detachment could come up. I was in this party; we pursued without order.

As I passed through the orchard I saw a number of the enemy lying under the trees, killed by our fieldpiece, mentioned before. We overtook the enemy just as they were entering upon the meadow, which was rather bushy. When within about five rods of the rear of the retreating foe, I could distinguish everything about them. They were retreating in line, though in some disorder. I singled out a man and took my aim directly between his shoulders. (They were divested of their packs.) He was a good mark, being a broad-shouldered fellow. What became of him, I know not; the fire and smoke hid him from my sight. One thing I know, that is, I took as deliberate aim at him as ever I did at any game in my life. But after all, I hope I did not kill him, although I intended to at the time.

One little incident happened during the heat of the cannonade, which I was eyewitness to, and which I think would be unpardonable not to mention. A woman whose husband belonged to the artillery and who was then attached to a piece in the engagement, attended with her husband at the piece the whole time. While in the act of reaching a cartridge and having one of her feet as far before the other as she could step, a cannon shot from the enemy passed directly between her legs without doing any other damage than carrying away all the lower part of her petticoat. Looking at it with apparent unconcern, she observed that it was lucky it did not pass a little higher, for in that case it might have carried away something else, and continued her occupation. [59]

The next day after the action each man received a gill of rum, but nothing to eat. We then joined our regiments in the line and marched for Hudson's River. We marched by what was called "easy marches," that is, we struck our tents at three o'clock in the morning, marched ten miles and then encamped, which would be about one or two o'clock in the afternoon. Every third day we rested all day. In this way we went to King's Ferry, where we crossed the Hudson.

From King's Ferry the army proceeded to Tarrytown, and from thence to the White Plains. [60] Here we drew some small supplies of summer clothing of which we stood in great need. While we lay here, I, with some of my comrades who were in the battle of the White Plains in the year '76, one day took a ramble on the ground where we were then engaged with the British and took a survey of the place. We saw a number of the graves of those who fell in that battle. Some of the bodies had been so slightly buried that the dogs or hogs, or both, had dug them out of the ground. The skulls and other bones and hair were scattered about the place. Here were Hessian skulls as thick as a bombshell. Poor fellows! They were left unburied in a foreign land. They had, perhaps, as near and dear friends to lament their sad destiny as the Americans who lay buried near them. But they should have kept at home; we should then never have gone after them to kill them in their own country. But, the reader will say, they were forced to come and be killed here, forced by their rulers who have absolute power of life and death over their subjects. Well then, reader, bless a kind Providence that has made such a distinction between your condition and theirs. And be careful, too, that you do not allow yourself ever to be brought to such an abject, servile and debased condition.

We lay at the White Plains some time. While here I was transferred to the Light Infantry, when I was immediately marched down to the lines. There were three regiments of Light Infantry,[61] composed of men from the whole main army. It was a motley group—Yankees, Irishmen, Buckskins and what not. The regiment that I belonged to was made up of about one half New Englanders and the remainder were chiefly Pennsylvanians— two sets of people as opposite in manners and customs as light and darkness. Consequently, there was not much cordiality subsisting between us, for to tell the sober truth, I had in those days as lief have been incorporated with a tribe of western Indians as with any of the southern troops, especially of those which consisted mostly, as the Pennsylvanians did, of foreigners. But I was among them and in the same regiment too, and under their officers (but the officers, in general, were gentlemen) and had to do duty with them. To make a bad matter worse, I was often, when on duty, the only Yankee that happened to be on the same tour for several days together. "The bloody Yankee," or "the d--d Yankee," was the mildest epithets that they would bestow upon me at such times. It often made me think of home, or at least of my regiment of fellow Yankees.

We lay at Bedford till the close of the season. Late in the autumn, the main army lay at New Milford, in the northwestern part of Connecticut;[62] while there, the Connecticut troops drew some winter clothing. The men belonging to that state, who were in the Light Infantry, had none sent them; they therefore, thought themselves hardly dealt by. Many of them, fearing they should lose their share of the clothing (of which they stood in great need), absconded from the camp at Bedford and went to New Milford. This caused our officers to keep patrolling parties around the camp during the night to prevent their going off. In consequence of this, I had one evening nearly obtained a final discharge from the army.

I had been, in the afternoon, at a small brook in the rear of the camp, where the troops mostly got their water, to wash some clothes. Among the rest was a handkerchief, which I laid upon a stone or stump, and when I went to my tent I forgot to take it with me. Missing it after roll call, I went to the place to get it. It was almost dark, and quite so in the bushes, when I got there. I was puzzled for some time to find the place, and longer before I could find the handkerchief. After finding it I did not hurry back, but loitered till the patrols were out, for I did not once think of them. It had now become quite dark and I had to pass through a place where the soldiers had cut firewood. It was a young growth of wood, and the ground was covered with brush and the stumps about knee-high, quite thick. Just as I entered upon this spot I heard somebody challenge with "Who comes there?" I had no idea of being the person hailed, and kept very orderly on my way, blundering through the brush. I, however, received a second and third invitation to declare myself, but paid no attention to the request.

The next compliment I received was a shot from them. The pall passed very near to me but I still kept advancing, when instantly I had another salute. I then thought that since I had been the cause of so much noise and alarm, it would be best for me to get off if possible, for I knew that if I was brought before our hotspur of a general I should "buy the rabbit." Accordingly, I put my best foot foremost. The patrol, which consisted of twelve or fifteen men, all had a hack at me, some of the balls passing very near me indeed. One in particular passed so near my head as to cause my ear to ring for sometime after. I now sprang to it for dear life, and I was in those days tolerable "light of foot"; but I had not made many leaps before I ran my knee with all my force against a white oak stump, which brought me up so short that I went heels over head over the stumps. I hardly knew whether I was dead or alive. However, I got up and blundered on till I reached my tent, into which I pitched and lay as still as the pain in my knee would allow me. My messmates were all asleep and knew nothing of the affair then, nor did I ever let them or anyone else know of it till after the close of the campaign, when I had joined my regiment in the line and was clear of the southern officers. But my knee was in a fine pickle; the next morning it was swelled as big as my head, and lame enough. However, it did not long remain so. When I was questioned by the officers or any of the men how I came by my wound, I told them I fell down, and thus far I told the truth; but when anyone asked me how I came to fall down, I was compelled to equivocate a little.

We arrived at Reading about Christmas or a little before, and prepared to build huts for our winter quarters. And now came on the time again between grass and hay, that is, the winter campaign of starving. We had not long been under the command of General Putnam, [63] before the old gentleman heard, or fancied he heard, that a party of the enemy were somewhere "down below." We were alarmed about midnight, and as cold a night as need be, and marched off to find the enemy, if he could be found. We marched all the remaining part of the night and all forenoon of the next day, and when we came where they were, they were not there at all at all, as the Irishman said. We now had nothing more to do but to return as we came, which we immediately set about.

We marched back to Bedford, near the encamping ground I had just left. We were conducted into our bedroom, a large wood, by our landlords, the officers, and left to our repose, while the officers stowed themselves away snugly in the houses of the village, about half a mile distant. We struck us up fires and lay down to rest our weary bones, all but our jawbones, they had nothing to weary them. About midnight it began to rain, which soon put out all our fires, and by three or four o'clock it came down in torrents. There we were, but where our careful officers were, or what had become of them, we knew not, nor did we much care. The men began to squib off their pieces of derision of the officers, supposing they were somewhere amongst us, and careless of our condition; but none of them appearing, the men began firing louder and louder, till they had brought it to almost a running fire. At the dawn, the officers, having, I suppose, heard the firing, came running from their warm, dry beds, almost out of breath, exclaiming, "Poor fellows! Are you not almost dead?" We might have been for aught they knew or cared. However, they marched us off to the village, wet as drowned rats, put us into the houses, where we remained till the afternoon and dried ourselves.[64]

Campaign of 1779

We got settled in our winter quarters at the commencement of the new year and went on in our old Continental line of starving and freezing. We now and then got a little bad bread and salt beef (I believe chiefly horse-beef, for it was generally thought to be such at the time). The month of January was very stormy, a good deal of snow fell, and in such weather it was a mere chance if we got anything at all to eat.[65] Our condition, at length, became insupportable. We concluded that we *could* not or *would* not bear it any longer. We were now in our own state and were determined that if our officers would not see some of our grievances redressed, the state should. Accordingly, one evening after roll calling, the men generally turned out, but without their arms, and paraded in front of their huts. We had no need of informing the officers; we well knew that they would hear of our muster without our troubling ourselves to inform them.

We had hardly got paraded, before all our officers, with the colonel at their head, came in front of the regiment, expressing a deal of sorrow for the hardships we were compelled to undergo, but much more for what they were pleased to call our mutinous conduct. This latter expression of their sorrow only served to exasperate the men, which the officers observing, changed their tone and endeavored to soothe the Yankee temper they had excited, and, with an abundance of fair promises, persuaded us to return to our quarters again. But hunger was not to be so easily pacified, and would not suffer many of us to sleep. We were therefore determined that none others should sleep. Martial law was very strict against firing muskets in camp. Nothing could, therefore, raise the officers' lofty ideas sooner, or more, than to fire in camp; but it was beyond the power or vigilance of all the officers to prevent the men from making void the law on that night. Finding they were watched by the officers, they got an old gun barrel which they placed in a hut that was unfinished. This they loaded a third part full and putting a slow match to it, would then escape to their own huts, when the old barrel would speak for itself, with a voice that would be heard. The officers would then muster out, and some running and scolding would ensue; but none knew who made the noise, or where it came from. This farce was carried on the greater part of the night; but at length the officers getting tired of running so often to catch Mr. Nobody, without finding him, that they soon gave up the chase, and the men seeing they could no longer gull the officers, gave up the business likewise.

We fared a little better for a few days after this memento to the officers, but it soon became an old story and the old system commenced again as regular as fair weather to foul. We endeavored to bear it with our usual fortitude, until it again became intolerable, and the soldiers determined to try once more to raise some provision, if not, at least to raise another dust.

Accordingly, one evening, after dark, we all turned out again with our arms, appointed a commander and were determined that time, if we could not be better accommodated, to march into the center of the state and disperse to our homes, in presence of as many of our fellow citizens as chose to be spectators. After we had organized ourselves and regulated the plan for our future operations, it was the design of our regiment to have marched to our field officers' quarters, and through them to demand of our country better usage. But before we had got all our little matters of etiquette settled, our adjutant came up (he having been over at the village on some errand best known to himself) and seeing us in arms upon the parade at that time of night, mistrusted something was in the wind. He passed us without saying a word and went directly and informed the other officers, all of whom were soon upon the parade.

Our major was the first that arrived; he was a fine, bold-looking man, and made a fine appearance. He came on to the right of the regiment, and soon after the colonel and other officers came in front. The commanding sergeant ordered the men to shoulder arms and then to present (which is a token of respect) and then to order them again. The major then addressed the sergeant thus: "Well, Sergeant—you have got a larger regiment than we had this evening at roll call, but I should think it would be more agreeable for the men to be asleep in their huts this cold night, than to be standing on the parade, for I remember that they were very impatient at roll call on account of the cold."

"Yes, sir," said the sergeant, "Solomon says that 'the abundance of the rich will not suffer him to sleep,' and we find that the abundance of poverty will not suffer us to sleep." By this time the colonel had come to where the major and sergeant were arguing the case, and the old mode of flattery and promising was resorted to and produced the usual effect. We all once more returned to our huts and fires, and there spent the remainder of the night, muttering over our forlorn condition.

We went by easy marches and nothing of consequence occurred until we arrived at New London. [66] Here we were put into houses, and here, too, we almost starved to death, and I believed should have quite starved, had we not found some clams, which kept us from absolutely dying. We had nothing to eat except now and then a little miserable beef or a little fresh fish and a very little bread, baked by a baker belonging to the town, which had some villainous drug incorporated with it that took all the skin off our mouths. I sincerely believe it was done on purpose to prevent our eating. I was not free from a sore mouth the whole time I stayed there.

Just before we left this place a privateer brig arrived from a cruise. She was hauled up and dismantled. One day I went on board her, and in the bread room I found one or two bushels of sea biscuit. At night I again went on board and filled my knapsack, which was a relief to my hungry stomach. But this bread had nearly as much flesh as bread, being as full of worms as ever the dry sapwood of a white ash pole was. Consequently, it required a great deal of circumspection in eating it. However, it was better than snowballs. The other men in my room, likewise, used to avail themselves of the opportunity to procure some, after I had told them where it might be obtained.

We stayed here, starving, until the first of May, when we received orders to march to camp and join our regiments. The troops belonging to New Hampshire marched sometime before we did. While on our march, we halted in a village. Here I went into a house, with several other soldiers, which happened to be a deacon's. While there some of the men chanced to swear (a circumstance extremely uncommon with the soldiers), upon which the good woman of the house checked them. "Is there any harm in it?" said one of them. "Yes," said she. "Well," said he, "may I not say swamp it?" "No," said she, "nor maple log roll over me, neither." She then turned to me and said, "I do not like you soldiers." I asked her why. "Because," said she, "there came some along here the other day and they stole every morsel of my dinner from the pot, while it was boiling over the fire, pudding bag and all." I told her that her case was, upon the whole, a rather calamitous one, but, said I, "I suppose the soldiers thought your pot could be easier replenished than their kettles." She made me no answer, whatever she thought.

In the night we heard the cannon at Stony Point, and early next morning had information of the taking of that place by the Light Infantry of our army under the command of General [Anthony] Wayne. [67] Our officers were all on tiptoe to show their abilities in executing some extraordinary exploit. Verplanck's Point was the word. [68] "Shall the Light Infantry get all the honor, and we do nothing!" said they. Accordingly, we set off, full tilt, to take Verplanck's Point; we marched directly for the Peekskill and arrived near there early in the day. We there received information that the British at Verplanck's Point were reinforced and advancing to attack us. We were quite knocked on the head by this news. However, we put ourselves in as good a condition as our circumstances would admit and waited their approach. They were afraid of us, or we of them, or both, for we did not come in contact that time. And thus ended the taking of Verplanck's Point and our honorable expectations.

While lying at, or near, the Peekskill, a man belonging to the cavalry was executed for desertion to the enemy, and as none of the corps to which he belonged were there, no troops were paraded, as was customary on such occasions, except a small guard. [69] The ground on which the gallows was erected was literally covered with pebble stones. A brigade major attended the execution, his duty on these occasions being the same as the high sheriff's in civil matters. He had, somewhere, procured a ragamuffin fellow for an executioner, to preserve his own immaculate reputation from defilement. After the culprit had hung the time prescribed by law, or custom, the hangman began stripping the corpse, the clothes being his perquisite. He began by trying to pull off his boots, but for want of a bootjack he could not readily accomplish his aim. He kept pulling and hauling at them, like a dog at a root, until the spectators, who were very numerous, the guard having gone off, growing disgusted, began to make use of the stones, by tossing several at his pretty carcass. The brigade major interfering in behalf of his aide-de-camp, shared the same usage; they were both quickly obliged to quit the field. As they retreated the stones flew merrily. They were obliged to keep at a proper distance until the soldiers took their own time to disperse, when they returned and completed their honorable business.

We remained at and near Peekskill till sometime in the month of December. About the middle of this month (December) we crossed the Hudson, at King's Ferry, and proceeded into New Jersey, for winter quarters. The snow had fallen nearly a foot deep. Now I request the reader to consider what must have been our situation at this time, naked, fatigued and starved, forced to march many a weary mile in winter, through cold and snow, to seek a situation in some (to us, unknown) wood to build us habitations to starve and suffer in. I do not know how the hearers of this recital may feel, but I know how I felt at the time and I know how I yet feel at the recollection of it; but there was no remedy, we must go through with it, and we did go through it, and I am yet alive. [70]

Campaign of 1780

Sometime in the month of January there happened a spell of remarkably cold weather. In the height of the cold, a large detachment from the army was sent off on an expedition against some fortifications held by the British on Staten Island. The detachment was commanded by Major General John Sullivan. It was supposed by our officers that the bay before New York was frozen sufficiently to prevent any succors being sent to the garrison in their works. It was therefore determined to endeavor to surprise them and get possession of their fortifications before they could obtain help. Accordingly, our troops were all conveyed in sleighs and other carriages, but the enemy got intelligence of our approach (doubtless by some Tory) before our arrival on the island. When we arrived we found Johnny Bull prepared for our reception. He was always complaisant, especially when his own honor or credit was concerned. We accordingly found them all waiting for us, so that we could not surprise them, and to take their works by storm looked too hazardous; to besiege them in regular form was out of the question, as the bay was not frozen so much as we expected. There was an armed brig lying in the ice not far from the shore; she received a few shots from our fieldpieces for a morning's salutation. We then fell back a little distance and took up our abode for the night upon a bare bleak hill, in full rake of the northwest wind, with no other covering or shelter than the canopy of the heavens, and no fuel but some old rotten rails which we dug up through the snow, which was two or three feet deep. The weather was cold enough to cut a man in two.

We lay on this accommodating spot till morning when we began our retreat from the island. The British were quickly in pursuit; they attacked our rear guard and made several of them prisoners, among whom was one of my particular associates. Poor young fellow! I have never seen or heard anything from him since. We arrived at camp after a tedious and cold march of many hours, some with frozen toes, some with frozen fingers and ears, and half-starved into the bargain. Thus ended our Staten Island expedition. [71]

Soon after this there came on several severe snowstorms. At one time it snowed the greater part of four days successively, and there fell nearly as many feet deep of snow, and here was the keystone of the arch of starvation. [72] We were absolutely, literally starved. I do solemnly declare that I did not put a single morsel of victuals into my mouth for four days and as many nights, except a little black birch bark which I gnawed off a stick of wood, if that can be called victuals. I saw several men roast their old shoes and eat them, and I was afterwards informed by one of the officers' waiters, that some of the officers killed and ate a favorite little dog that belonged to one of them.

We left Westfield about the twenty-fifth of May and went to Basking Ridge to our old winter cantonments. We did not reoccupy the huts which we built, but some others that the troops had left, upon what account I have forgotten. Here, the monster Hunger, still attended us. He was not to be shaken off by any efforts we could use, for here was the old story of starving, as rife as ever. We had entertained some hopes that when we had left the lines and joined the main army, we should fare a little better, but we found that there was no betterment in the case. For several days after we rejoined the army, we got a little musty bread and a little beef, about every other day, but this lasted only a short time and then we got nothing at all. The men were now exasperated beyond endurance; they could not stand it any longer. They saw no other alternative but to starve to death, or break up the army, give all up and go home. This was a hard matter for the soldiers to think upon. They were truly patriotic, they loved their country, and they had already suffered everything short of death in its cause; and now, after such extreme hardships to give up all was too much, but to starve to death was too much also. What was to be done? Here was the army starved and naked, and there their country sitting still and expecting the army to do notable things while fainting from sheer starvation. All things considered, the army was not to be blamed. Reader, suffer what we did and you will say so, too.

We had borne as long as human nature could endure, and to bear longer we considered folly. Accordingly, one pleasant day, the men spent the most of their time upon the parade, growling like soreheaded dogs. At evening roll call they began to show their dissatisfaction by snapping at the officers and acting contrary to their orders. After their dismissal from the parade, the officers went, as usual, to their quarters, except the adjutant, who happened to remain, giving details for the next day's duty to the orderly sergeant, or some other business, when the men, none of whom had left the parade began to make him sensible that they had something in train. He said something that did not altogether accord with the soldiers' ideas of propriety, one of the men retorted; the adjutant called him a mutinous rascal, or some such epithet, and then left the parade. This man, then stamping the butt of his musket upon the ground, as much as to say, I am in a passion, called out, "Who will parade with me?" The whole regiment immediately fell in and formed.

We had made no plans for our future operations, but while we were consulting how to proceed, the Fourth Regiment, which lay on our left, formed, and came and paraded with us. We now concluded to go in a body to the other two regiments [the Third and Sixth] that belonged to our brigade and induce them to join with us. These regiments lay forty or fifty rods in front of us, with a brook and bushes between. We did not wish to have anyone in particular to command, lest he might be singled out for a court-martial to exercise its clemency upon. We therefore gave directions to the drummers to give certain signals on the drums; at the first signal we shouldered our arms, at the second we faced, at the third we began our march to join with the other two regiments, and went off with music playing.

By this time our officers had obtained knowledge of our military maneuvering and some of them had run across the brook, by a nearer way than we had taken, it being now quite dark, and informed the officers of those regiments of our approach and supposed intentions. The officers ordered their men to parade as quick as possible without arms. When that was done, they stationed a camp guard, that happened to be near at hand, between the men and their huts, which prevented them from entering and taking their arms, which they were very anxious to do. Colonel [Return Jonathan] Meigs, of the Sixth Regiment, exerted himself to prevent his men from obtaining their arms until he received a severe wound in his side by a bayonet in the scuffle, which cooled his courage at the time. He said he had always considered himself the soldier's friend and thought the soldiers regarded him as such, but had reason now to conclude he might be mistaken. Colonel Meigs was truly an excellent man and a brave officer. The man, whoever he was, that wounded him, doubtless had no particular grudge against him; it was dark and the wound was given, it is probable, altogether unintentionally.

When we found the officers had been too crafty for us we returned with grumbling instead of music, the officers following in the rear growling in concert. One of the men in the rear calling out, "Halt in front," the officers seized upon him like wolves on a sheep and dragged him out of the ranks, intending to make an example of him for being a "mutinous rascal," but the bayonets of the men pointing at their breasts as thick as hatchel teeth, compelled them quickly to relinquish their hold of him. We marched back to our own parade and then formed again. The officers now began to coax us to disperse to our quarters, but that had no more effect upon us than their threats. One of them slipped away into the bushes, and after a short time returned, counterfeiting to have come directly from headquarters. Said he, "There is good news for you, boys, there has just arrived a large drove of cattle for the army." But this piece of finesse would not avail. All the answer he received for his labor was, "Go and butcher them," or some such slight expression. The lieutenant colonel of the Fourth Regiment [John Sumner] now came on to the parade. He could persuade his men, he said, to go peaceably to their quarters. After a good deal of palaver, he ordered them to shoulder their arms, but the men taking no notice of him or his order, he fell into a violent passion, threatening them with the bitterest punishment if they did not immediately obey his orders. After spending a whole quiver of the arrows of his rhetoric, he again ordered them to shoulder arms, but he met with the same success that he did at the first trial. He therefore gave up the contest as hopeless and left us and walked off to his quarters, chewing the cud of resentment all the way, and how much longer I neither knew nor cared. The rest of the officers, after they found that they were likely to meet with no better success than the colonel, walked off likewise to their huts.

While we were under arms, the Pennsylvania troops, who lay not far from us, were ordered under arms and marched off their parades upon, as they were told, a secret expedition. They had surrounded us, unknown to either us or themselves (except the officers). At length, getting an item of what was going forward, they inquired of some of the stragglers what was going on among the Yankees. Being informed that they had mutinied on account of the scarcity of provisions, "Let us join them," said they. "Let us join the Yankees; they are good fellows, and have no notions of lying here like fools and starving." Their officers needed no further hinting. The troops were quickly ordered back to their quarters, from fear that they would join the Yankees. We knew nothing of all this for some time afterwards.[73]

After our officers had left us to our own option, we dispersed to our huts and laid by our arms of our own accord, but the worm of hunger gnawing so keen kept us from being entirely quiet. We therefore still kept upon the parade in groups, venting our spleen at our country and government, then at our officers, and then at ourselves for our imbecility in staying there and starving in detail for an ungrateful people who did not care what became of us, so they could enjoy themselves while we were keeping a cruel enemy from them. While we were thus venting our gall against we knew not who, Colonel [Walter] Stewart of the Pennsylvania Line, with two or three other officers of that Line, came to us and questioned us respecting our unsoldierlike conduct (as he termed it). We told him he needed not to be informed of the cause of our present conduct, but that we had borne till we considered further forbearance pusillanimity; that the times, instead of mending, were growing worse; and finally, that we were determined not to bear or forbear much longer. We were unwilling to desert the cause of our country, when in distress; that we knew her cause involved our own, but what signified our perishing in the act of saving her, when that act would inevitably destroy us, and she must finally perish with us.

"Why do you not go to your officers," said he, "and complain in a regular manner?" We told him we had repeatedly complained to them, but they would not hear us. "Your officers," said he, "are gentlemen, they will attend to you. I know them; they cannot refuse to hear you. But," said he, "your officers suffer as much as you do. We all suffer. The officers have no money to purchase supplies with any more than the private men have, and if there is nothing in the public store we must fare as hard as you. I have no other resources than you have to depend upon. I had not a sixpence to purchase a partridge that was offered me the other day. Besides," said he, "you know not how much you injure your own characters by such conduct. You Connecticut troops have won immortal honor to yourselves the winter past, by your perseverance, patience, and bravery, and now you are shaking it off at your heels. But I will go and see your officers, and talk with them myself." He went, but what the result was, I never knew. This Colonel Stewart was an excellent officer, much beloved and respected by the troops of the line he belonged to. He possessed great personal beauty; the Philadelphia ladies styled him the *Irish Beauty*.

Our stir did us some good in the end, for we had provisions directly after so we had no great cause for complaint for some time. [74]

And now there was to be a material change in my circumstances, which, in the long run, was much in my favor. There was a small corps to be raised by enlistments, and in case of the failure of that, by drafts from the line. These men were called "Sappers and Miners," to be attached to the engineer's department. [75] The captain was personally acquainted with our major and told him he would like to have him furnish him with a man from the regiment that he knew was qualified for a noncommissioned officer. The major then pitched upon me. How far he was to be justified in his choice the reader may, perhaps, be enabled to judge by the construction of this present work; I give him my free consent to exercise his judgment upon it.

I was accordingly transferred to this corps and bid a farewell forever to my old comrades, as it respected any further associating with them, or sharing in their sufferings or pleasures. I immediately went off with this (now my) captain and the other men drafted from our brigade, and joined the corps in an old meetinghouse at the Peekskill. It was after dark when we arrived there. I had now got among a new set, who were, to a man, entire strangers to me. I had, of course, to form new acquaintances, but I was not long in doing that. I had a pretty free use of my tongue, and was sometimes apt to use it when there was no occasion for it. However, I soon found myself at home with them. We were all young men and therefore easy to get acquainted.

* * *

Soon after this journey, one night, the British brig came down the river with her precious cargo—Arnold—on board. There were several shots discharged at her as she passed the blockhouse, but she went by without paying us much attention. The next day it was reported that General Arnold had deserted. I should as soon have thought West Point had deserted as he, but I was soon convinced that it was true. Had I possessed the power of foreknowledge, I might twice have put Arnold asleep without anyone knowing it and saved the life of, perhaps, a better man, and my country much trouble and disgrace. [76]

The first time was at the Peekskill in a barn, just before Andre came to his quarters and while their clandestine negotiation was in progress. I was upon a guard, "There are men," says Shakespeare, "who in their sleep, mutter all their conceits." Such a one was Arnold, and therefore afraid to sleep near anyone lest he should "babble his conceits" in his sleep. He ordered me and my guard out of the barn, that he might have his bed upon the floor. I was so put out of my bias at the time, that had I known what plans he had in his head, I should have needed but little persuasion to have had a reckoning with him.

The other time was but three or four days before his desertion. I met him upon the road a little distance from Dobbs Ferry; he was then taking his observations and examining the roads. I thought that he was upon some deviltry. We met at a notch of the roads and I observed he stopped, and sitting upon his horse, seemed minutely to examine each road. I could not help taking notice of him, and thought it strange to see him quite alone in such a lone place. He looked guilty, and well he might, for Satan was in as full possession of him at that instant as ever he was of Judas; it only wanted a musket ball to have driven him out.

Campaign of 1781

We now expected soon to lay close siege to New York. [77] Our Sappers and Miners were constantly employed with the engineers in front of the army, making preparations for the siege. One day I was sent down towards the enemy with a corporal and twelve men, upon a reconnoitering expedition, the engineers having heard that there was a party of Refugees, or Cowboys, [78] somewhere not far from their premises. My orders were to go to a certain place and if I did not see or hear anything of the enemy to return; or if I did find them to return as soon as possible and bring word to the officers, unless I thought we were able to cope with them ourselves.

We set off upon our expedition early in the afternoon and went as far as directed by our officers, but saw no enemy. We stopped here a while and rested ourselves. When we had refreshed ourselves, we thought it a pity to return with our fingers in our mouths and report that we had seen nothing. We therefore agreed *unanimously* to stretch our orders a trifle and go a little further. We were in the fields; about a mile ahead were three or four houses at which I and some others of our party had been before. Between us and the houses there was a narrow wood, mostly of young growth and quite thick. We concluded to go as far as the houses, and if we could not hear anything of the Cowboys there, to return contented to camp.

Agreeably to our plan we set out, and had but just entered the wood when we found ourselves flanked by thirty or forty Cowboys, who gave us a hearty welcome to their assumed territories and we returned the compliment, but a kind Providence protected every man of us from injury although we were within ten rods of the enemy. They immediately rushed from their covert, before we had time to reload our pieces; consequently, we had no other alternative but to get off as well and as fast as we could. They did not fire upon us again, but gave us a chase, for what reason I know not. I was soon in the rear of my party, which had to cross a fence composed of old posts and rails with trees plashed down upon it.

When I arrived at the fence, the foremost of the enemy was not more than six or eight rods distant, all running after us helter-skelter, without any order. My men had all crossed the fence in safety, I alone was to suffer. I endeavored to get over the fence across two or three of the trees that were plashed down. Somehow or other, I blundered and fell over, and caught my right foot in a place where a tree had split partly from the stump. Here I hung as fast as though my foot had been in the stocks, my ham lying across the butt of another tree, while my body hung down perpendicularly. I could barely reach the ground with my hands, and, of course, could make but little exertion to clear myself from the limbs.

The commander of the enemy came to the fence and the first compliment I received from him was a stroke with his hanger across my leg, just under or below the kneepan, which laid the bone bare. I could see him through the fence and knew him. He was, when we were boys, one of my most familiar playmates, was with me, a messmate, in the campaign of 1776, had enlisted during the war in 1777, but sometime before this, had deserted to the enemy, having been coaxed off by an old harridan, to whose daughter he had taken a fancy. The old hag of a mother, living in the vicinity of the British, easily inveigled him away. He was a smart active fellow and soon got command of a gang of Refugee Cowboy plunderers. When he had had his hack at my shins, I began to think it was "neck or nothing," and making one desperate effort, I cleared my foot by leaving my shoe behind, before he could have the second stroke at me. He knew me as well as I did him, for as soon as he saw me clear of the fence and out of the reach of his sword, he called me by name, and told me to surrender myself and he would give me good quarters. Thought I, you will wait until I ask them of you. I sprang up and run till I came to my party, who were about a hundred rods ahead, waiting to see how I should come off.

The enemy never fired a shot at me all the time I was running from them, although nearly the whole of their party was standing on the other side of the fence when I started from it. Whether his conscience smote him and he prevented them from firing at me, or whether they were unprepared, not having had time to reload their pieces in pursuit of us, or from what other cause, I know not, but they never interfered with me while I was running across the field, fifty or sixty rods, in open sight of them. Thus I escaped, and this was the only time the enemy drew blood from me during the whole war.

The first of August, I think it was the first day of the month, we all of a sudden marched from this ground and directed our course towards King's Ferry, near the Highlands, crossed the Hudson and lay there a few days, till the baggage, artillery, &c. had crossed, and then proceeded into New Jersey. We went down to Chatham, where were ovens built for the accommodation of the French troops. We then expected we were to attack New York in that quarter, but after staying here a day or two, we again moved off and arrived at Trenton by rapid marches. It was about sunset when we arrived here and instead of encamping for the night, as we expected, we were ordered immediately on board a vessel then lying at the landing place, and a little after sunrise found ourselves at Philadelphia.[79]

We, that is, the Sappers and Miners, stayed here some days, proving and packing off shells, shot, and other military stores. While we stayed here we drew a few articles of clothing, consisting of a few tow shirts, some overalls and a few pairs of silk-and-oakum stockings. And here, or soon after, we each of us received a month's pay, in specie, borrowed, as I was informed, by our French officers from the officers in the French army. This was the first that could be called money, which we had received as wages since the year '76, or that we ever did receive till the close of the war, or indeed, even after, as wages. [80]

When we had finished our business at Philadelphia, we (the Miners) left the city. A part of our men, with myself, went down the Delaware in a schooner which had her hold nearly full of gunpowder. We passed Mud Island, where I had experienced such hardships in Nov. '77. It had quite a different appearance to what it had then, much like a fine, fair, warm and sunny day succeeding a cold, dark, stormy night. Just after passing Mud Island, in the afternoon, we had a smart thundershower. I did not feel very agreeably, I confess, during its continuance, with such a quantity of powder under my feet. I was not quite sure that a stroke of the electric fluid might not compel me to leave the vessel sooner than I wished—but no accident happened, and we proceeded down the river to the mouth of Christiana Creek, up which we were bound.

We were compelled to anchor here on account of wind and tide. Here we passed an uneasy night from fear of British cruisers, several of which were in the bay. In the morning we got under weigh, the wind serving, and proceeded up the creek fourteen miles, the creek passing, the most of its course, through a marsh, as crooked as a snake in motion. There was one place in particular near the village of Newport [Delaware] where you sail four miles to gain about forty rods. We went on till the vessel grounded for lack of water. We then lightened her by taking out a part of her cargo, and when the tide came in we got up to the wharves and left her at the disposal of the artillerists.

We then crossed over land to the head of the Elk, or the head, or rather bottom, of Chesapeake Bay. Here we found a *large* fleet of *small* vessels waiting to convey us and other troops, stores, &c. down the bay. We soon embarked, that is, such of us as went by water, the greater part of the army having gone on by land.

We passed down the bay, making a grand appearance with our mosquito fleet, to Annapolis, which I had left about five months before for West Point. Here we stopped, fearing to proceed any further at present, not knowing exactly how matters were going on down the bay. A French cutter was dispatched to procure intelligence. She returned in the course of three or four days, bringing word that the passage was clear. We then proceeded and soon arrived at the mouth of James River, where were a number of armed French vessels and two or three fifty-gun ships. We passed in sight of the French fleet, then lying in Lynnhaven Bay; they resembled a swamp of dry pine trees. We had passed several of their men-of-war higher up the bay. [81]

After landing we marched to Williamsburg, where we joined General Lafayette, [82] and very soon after, our whole army arriving, we prepared to move down and pay our old acquaintance, the British, at Yorktown, a visit.

We marched from Williamsburg September the twenty-eighth. When we had proceeded about halfway to Yorktown we halted and rested two or three hours. Here, or about this time, we had orders from the Commander-in-Chief that, in case the enemy should come out to meet us, we should exchange but one round with them and then decide the conflict with the bayonet, as they valued themselves at that instrument. The French forces could play their part at it, and the Americans were never backward at trying its virtue. The British, however, did not think fit at that time to give us an opportunity to soil our bayonets in their carcasses, but why they did not we could never conjecture; we as much expected it as we expected to find them there. We went on and soon arrived and encamped in their neighborhood, without let or molestation.

We now began to make preparations for laying close siege to the enemy. We had holed him and nothing remained but to dig him out. Accordingly, after taking every precaution to prevent his escape, [we] settled our guards, provided fascines and gabions, made platforms for the batteries, to be laid down when needed, brought on our battering pieces, ammunition, &c. On the fifth of October we began to put our plans into execution. [83]

One-third part of all the troops were put in requisition to be employed in opening the trenches. A third part of our Sappers and Miners were ordered out this night to assist the engineers in laying out the works. It was a very dark and rainy night. However, we repaired to the place and began by following the engineers and laying laths of pine wood end-to-end upon the line marked out by the officers for the trenches. We had not proceeded far in the business before the engineers ordered us to desist and remain where we were and be sure not to straggle a foot from the spot while they were absent from us. In a few minutes after their departure, there came a man alone to us, having on a surtout, as we conjectured, it being exceeding dark, and inquired for the engineers. We now began to be a little jealous for our safety, being alone and without arms, and within forty rods of the British trenches. The stranger inquired what troops we were, talked familiarly with us a few minutes, when, being informed which way the officers had gone, he went off in the same direction, after strictly charging us, in case we should be taken prisoners, not to discover to the enemy what troops we were. We were obliged to him for his kind advice, but we considered ourselves as standing in no great need of it, for we knew as well as he did that Sappers and Miners were allowed no quarters, at least, are entitled to none, by the laws of warfare, and of course should take care, if taken, and the enemy did not find us out, not to betray our own secret.

In a short time the engineers returned and the aforementioned stranger with them. They discoursed together some time when, by the officers often calling him "Your Excellency," we discovered that it was General Washington. Had we dared, we might have cautioned him for exposing himself too carelessly to danger at such a time, and doubtless he would have taken it in good part if we had. But nothing ill happened to either him or ourselves. [84]

It coming on to rain hard, we were ordered back to our tents, and nothing more was done that night. The next night, which was the sixth of October, the same men were ordered to the lines that had been there the night before. We this night completed laying out the works. The troops of the line were there ready with entrenching tools and began to entrench, after General Washington had struck a few blows with a pickax, a mere ceremony, that it might be said "General Washington with his own hands first broke ground at the siege of Yorktown." The ground was sandy and soft, and the men employed that night eat no "idle bread" (and I question if they eat any other), so that by daylight they had covered themselves from danger from the enemy's shot, who, it appeared, never mistrusted that we were so near them the whole night, their attention being directed to another quarter. There was upon the right of their works a marsh. Our people had sent to the western side of this marsh a detachment to make a number of fires, by which, and our men often passing before the fires, the

British were led to imagine that we were about some secret mischief there, and consequently directed their whole fire to that quarter, while we were entrenching literally under their noses.

As soon as it was day they perceived their mistake and began to fire where they ought to have done sooner. They brought out a fieldpiece or two without their trenches, and discharged several shots at the men who were at work erecting a bomb battery, but their shot had no effect and they soon gave it over. They had a large bulldog and every time they fired he would follow their shots across our trenches. Our officers wished to catch him and oblige him to carry a message from them into the town to his masters, but he looked too formidable for any of us to encounter.

I do not remember, exactly, the number of days we were employed before we got our batteries in readiness to open upon the enemy, but think it was not more than two or three. The French, who were upon our left, had completed their batteries a few hours before us, but were not allowed to discharge their pieces till the American batteries were ready. Our commanding battery was on the near bank of the [York] river and contained ten heavy guns; the next was a bomb battery of three large mortants; and so on through the whole line. The whole number, American and French, was ninety-two cannon, mortars and howitzers. Our flagstaff was in the ten-gun battery, upon the right of the whole. I was in the trenches the day that the batteries were to be opened. All were upon the tiptoe of expectation and impatience to see the signal given to open the whole line of batteries, which was to be the hoisting of the American flag in the ten-gun battery. About noon the much-wished-for signal went up. I confess I felt a secret pride swell my heart when I saw the "star-spangled banner" waving majestically in the very faces of our implacable adversaries. It appeared like an omen of success to our enterprise, and so it proved in reality. A simultaneous discharge of all the guns in the line followed, the French troops accompanying it with "Huzza for the Americans!" It was said that the first shell sent from our batteries entered an elegant house formerly owned or occupied by the Secretary of State under the British government, and burned directly over a table surrounded by a large party of British officers at dinner, killing and wounding a number of them.[85] This was a warm day to the British.

The siege was carried on warmly for several days, when most of the guns in the enemy's works were silenced. We now began our second parallel, about halfway between our works and theirs. There were two strong redoubts held by the British, on their left. It was necessary for us to possess those redoubts before we could complete our trenches. One afternoon, I, with the rest of our corps that had been on duty in the trenches but one before, were ordered to the lines. I mistrusted something extraordinary, serious or comical, was going forward, but what I could not easily conjecture.

We arrived at the trenches a little before sunset. I saw several officers fixing bayonets on long staves. I then concluded we were about to make a general assault upon the enemy's works, but before dark I was informed of the whole plan, which was to storm the redoubts, the one by Americans and the other by the French.[86] The Sappers and Miners were furnished with axes and were to proceed in front and cut a passage for the troops through the abatis, which are composed of the tops of trees, the small branches cut off with a slanting stroke which renders them as sharp as spikes. These trees are then laid at a small distance from the trench or ditch, pointing outwards, and the butts fastened to the ground in such a manner that they cannot be removed by those on the outside of them. It is almost impossible to get through them. Through these we were to cut a passage before we or the other assailants could enter.

At dark the detachment was formed and advanced beyond the trenches and lay down on the ground to await the signal for advancing to the attack, which was to be three shells from a certain battery near where we were lying. All the batteries in our line were silent, and we lay anxiously waiting for the signal. The two brilliant planets, Jupiter and Venus, were in close contact in the western hemisphere, the same direction that the signal was to be made in. When I happened to cast my eyes to that quarter, which was often, and I caught a glance of them, I was ready to spring on my feet, thinking they were the signal for starting. Our watchword was "Rochambeau," the commander of the French forces' name, a good watchword, for being pronounced *Ro-sham-bow,* it sounded, when pronounced quick, like rush-on-boys.

We had not lain here long before the expected signal was given, for us and the French, who were to storm the other redoubt, by the three shells with their fiery trains mounting the air in quick succession. The word *up, up,* was then reiterated through the detachment. We immediately moved silently on toward the redoubt we were to attack, with unloaded muskets. Just as we arrived at the abatis, the enemy discovered us and directly opened a sharp fire upon us. We were now at a place where many of our large shells had burst in the ground, making holes sufficient to bury an ox in. The men, having their eyes fixed upon what was transacting before them, were every now and then falling into these holes. I thought the British were killing us off at a great rate. At length, one of the holes happening to pick me up, I found out the mystery of the huge slaughter.

As soon as the firing began, our people began to cry, "The fort's our own!" and it was "Rush on boys." The Sappers and Miners soon cleared a passage for the infantry, who entered it rapidly. Our Miners were ordered not to enter the fort, but there was no stopping them. I could not pass at the entrance we had made, it was so crowded. I therefore forced a passage at a place where I saw our shot had cut away some of the abatis; several others entered at the same place. While passing, a man at my side received a ball in his head and fell under my feet, crying out bitterly. While crossing the trench, the enemy threw hand grenades (small shells) into it. They were so thick that I at first thought them cartridge papers on fire, but was soon undeceived by their cracking. As I mounted the breastwork, I met an old associate hitching himself down into the trench. I knew him by the light of the enemy's musketry, it was so vivid. The fort was taken and all quiet in a very short time. Immediately after the firing ceased, I went out to see what had become of my wounded friend and the other that fell into the passage. They were both dead. In the heat of the action I saw a British soldier jump over the walls of the fort next the river and go down the bank, which was almost perpendicular and twenty or thirty feet high. When he came to the beach he made off for the town, and if he did not make good use of his legs I never saw a man that did.

All that were in the action of storming the redoubt were exempted from further duty that night. We laid down upon the ground and rested the remainder of the night as well as a constant discharge of grape and canister shot would permit us to do, while those who were on duty for the day completed the second parallel by including the captured redoubts within it. We returned to camp early in the morning, all safe and sound, except one of our lieutenants, who had received a slight wound on the top of a shoulder by a musket shot. Seven or eight men belonging to the infantry were killed, and a number wounded.

In the morning, while the relieves were coming into the trenches, I was sitting on the side of the trench, when some of the New York troops coming in, one of the sergeants stepped up to the breastwork to look about him. The enemy threw a small shell which fell upon the outside of the works; the man turned to look at it. At that instant a shot from the enemy, which doubtless was aimed for him in particular as none others were in sight of them, passed just by his face without touching him at all. He fell dead into the trench. I put my hand on his forehead and found his skull was shattered all in pieces and the blood flowing from his nose and mouth, but not a particle of skin was broken. I never saw an instance like this among all the men I saw killed during the whole war.

After we had finished our second line of trenches there was but little firing on either side. After Lord Cornwallis had failed to get off, upon the seventeenth day of October (a rather unlucky day for the British) he requested a cessation of hostilities for, I think, twenty-four hours, when commissioners from both armies met at a house between the lines to agree upon articles of capitulation. [87] We waited with anxiety the termination of the armistice and as the time drew nearer our anxiety increased. The time at length arrived—it passed, and all remained quiet. And now we concluded that we had obtained what we had taken so much pains for, for which we had encountered so many dangers, and had so anxiously wished. Before night we were informed that the British had surrendered and that the siege was ended.

The next day we were ordered to put ourselves in as good order as our circumstances would admit, to see (what was the completion of our present wishes) the British army march out and stack their arms. The trenches, where they crossed the road leading to the town, were leveled and all things put in order for this grand exhibition. After breakfast, on the nineteenth, we were marched onto the ground and paraded on the right-hand side of the road, and the French forces on the left. We waited two or three hours before the British made their appearance. They were not always so dilatory, but they were compelled at last, by necessary, to appear, all armed, with bayonets fixed, drums beating, and faces lengthening. They were led by General [Charles] O'Hara, with the American General Lincoln on his right, [88] the Americans and French beating a march as they passed out between them. It was a noble sight to us, and the more so, as it seemed to promise a speedy conclusion to the contest. The British did not make so good an appearance as the German forces, but there was certainly some allowance to be made in their favor. The English felt their honor wounded, the Germans did not greatly care whose hands they were in. The British paid the Americans, seemingly, but little attention as they passed them, but they eyed the French with considerable malice depicted in their countenances. They marched to the place appointed and stacked their arms; they then returned to the town in the same manner they had marched out, except being divested of their arms. After the prisoners were marched off into the country, our army separated, the French remaining where they were and the Americans marching for the Hudson.

Campaign of 1782 [89]

Soon after this came on my trouble, and that of several others of the men belonging to our corps. Sometime in the month of January two of our men were taken down with a species of yellow fever; one recovered and the other died. Directly after, one belonging to our room was seized with it and removed to the hospital, where he recovered. Next I was attacked with it. This was in February; it took hold of me in good earnest. I bled violently at the nose, and was so reduced in flesh and strength in a few days that I was as helpless as an infant. [90] O! how much I suffered, although I had as good attendance as circumstances would admit. The disorder continued to take hold of our people till there were more than twenty sick with it. Our officers made a hospital in an upper room in one of the wings of the house, and as soon as the men fell sick they were lodged there.

About the first of March I began to mend, and recovered what little reason I ever possessed, of which I had been entirely deprived from nearly the first attack of the fever. As soon as I could bear it, I was removed from my room to the hospital among those that were recently taken. For what reason I was put with the sick and dying, I did not know, nor did I ask. I did not care much what they did with me, but nothing ill resulted from it that I know of. The doctor belonging to the artillery regiment (who attended upon us, we having no doctor in our corps) went home on furlough, and it was a happy circumstance for us, for he was not the best of physicians. Besides, he was badly provided to do with. The apothecary's stores in the Revolutionary army were as ill furnished as any others.

Eight men died at this time, the rest recovered, though the most of them very slowly. Some were as crazy as coots for weeks after they had gained strength to walk about. My hair came off my head and I was as bald as an eagle, but after I began to gain strength I soon got about. But it was a grievous sickness to me, the sorest I had ever undergone. Although death is much nearer to me now than it was then, yet I never had thought myself so near death as I did then.

Campaign of 1783

The great chain that barred the river at West Point had been regularly taken up every autumn and put down every spring ever since it had been in use (that chain which the soldiers used to denominate General Washington's watch chain; every four links of which weighed a ton),[91] but we heard nothing of its being put down this spring, although some idle fellow would report that it was going to be put down immediately. These simple stories would keep the men in agitation, often for days together (for the putting down or the keeping up of the chain was the criterion by which we were to judge of war or peace), when they would get some other piece of information by the ears, which would entirely put the boot on the other leg. The political atmosphere was, at this time, as full of reports as ever the natural was of smoke, and of about as much consequence.

Time thus passed on to the nineteenth of April [1783], when we had general orders read which satisfied the most skeptical, that the war was over and the prize won for which we had been contending through eight tedious years.[92] But the soldiers said but very little about it; their chief thoughts were more closely fixed upon their situation as it respected the figure they were to exhibit upon their leaving the army and becoming citizens. Starved, ragged and meager, not a cent to help themselves with, and no means or method in view to remedy or alleviate their condition. This was appalling in the extreme. All that they could do was to make a virtue of necessity and face the threatening evils with the same resolution and fortitude that they had for so long a time faced the enemy in the field.

At length the eleventh day of June, 1783, arrived. "The old man," our captain, came into our room, with his hands full of papers, and first ordered us to empty all our cartridge boxes upon the floor (this was the last order he ever gave us) and then told us that if we needed them we might take some of them again. They were all immediately gathered up and returned to our boxes. Government had given us our arms and we considered the ammunition as belonging to them, and he had neither right nor orders to take them from us. He then handed us our discharges, or rather furloughs, for they were in appearance no other than furloughs, permission to return home, but to return to the army again if required. This was policy in government; to discharge us absolutely in our present pitiful, forlorn condition, it was feared, might cause some difficulties which might be too hard for government to get easily over. [93]

The powder in our cartridges was soon burnt. Some saluted the officers with large charges; others only squibbed them, just as each one's mind was affected toward them. Our "old man" had a number of these last-mentioned symbols of honor and affection presented him. Some of the men were not half so liberal in the use of powder as they were when they would have given him a canteenful at once.

I confess, after all, that my anticipation of the happiness I should experience upon such a day as this was not realized; I can assure the reader that there was as much sorrow as joy transfused on the occasion. We had lived together as a family of brothers for several years, setting aside some little family squabbles, like most other families, had shared with each other the hardships, dangers, and suffering incident to a soldier's life. In short, the soldiers, each in his particular circle of acquaintance, were as strict a band of brotherhood as Masons and, I believe, as faithful to each other. And now we were to be, the greater part of us, parted forever; as unconditionally separated as though the grave lay between us. I question if there was a corps in the army that parted with more regret than ours did, the New Englanders in particular. Ah! it was a serious time.

I now bid a final farewell to the service. I had obtained my settlement certificates and sold some of them and purchased some decent clothing, and then set off from West Point. I went into the Highlands, where I accidentally came across an old messmate who had been at work there ever since he had left the army in June last, and, as it appeared, was on a courting expedition. I stopped a few days with him and worked at the farming business. I got acquainted with the people here, who were chiefly Dutch, and as winter was approaching and my friend recommended me to them, I agreed to teach a school amongst them. A fit person! I knew but little and they less, if possible. "Like people, like priest." However, they had a school of from twenty to thirty pupils, and probably I gave them satisfaction. If I did not, it was all one; I never heard anything to the contrary. Anyhow, they wished me to stay and settle with them.

When the spring opened I bid my Dutch friends adieu and set my face to the eastward, and made no material halt till I arrived in the, now, state of Maine, in the year 1784, where I have remained ever since, and where I expect to remain so long as I remain in existence, and here at last to rest my warworn limbs. And here I would make an end of my tedious narrative, but that I deem it necessary to make a few short observations relative to what I have said, or a sort of recapitulation of some of the things which I have mentioned.

When those who engaged to serve during the war enlisted, they were promised a hundred acres of land, each, which was to be in their own or the adjoining states. When the country had drained the last drop of service it could screw out of the poor soldiers, they were turned adrift like old worn-out horses, and nothing said about land to pasture them upon. Congress did, indeed, appropriate lands under the denomination of "Soldier's lands," in Ohio state, or some state, or a future state, but no care was taken that the soldiers should get them. No agents were appointed to see that the poor fellows ever got possession of their lands; no one ever took the least care about it, except a pack of speculators, who were driving about the country like so many evil spirits, endeavoring to pluck the last feather from the soldiers.[94] The soldiers were ignorant of the ways and means to obtain their bounty lands, and there was no one appointed to inform them. The truth was, none cared for them; the country was served, and faithfully served, and that was all that was deemed necessary. It was, soldiers, look to yourselves; we want no more of you. I hope I shall one day find land enough to lay my bones in. If I chance to die in a civilized country, none will deny me that. A dead body never begs a grave—thanks for that.

Almost every one has heard of the soldiers of the Revolution being tracked by the blood of their feet on the frozen ground. This is literally true, and the thousandth part of their sufferings has not, nor ever will be told. That the country was young and poor, at that time, I am willing to allow, but young people are generally modest, especially females. Now, I think the country (although of the feminine gender, for we say "she" and "her" of it) showed but little modesty at the time alluded to, for she appeared to think her soldiers had no private parts. For on our march from

87

the Valley Forge, through the Jerseys, and at the boasted Battle of Monmouth, a fourth part of the troops had not a scrip of anything but their ragged shirt flaps to cover their nakedness, and were obliged to remain so long after. I had picked up a few articles of light clothing during the past winter, while among the Pennsylvania farmers, or I should have been in the same predicament. "Rub and go" was always the Revolutionary soldier's motto.

We were, also, promised six dollars and two thirds a month, to be paid us monthly, and how did we fare in this particular? Why, as we did in every other. I received the six dollars and two thirds, till (if I remember rightly) the month of August, 1777, when paying ceased. And what was six dollars and sixty-seven cents of this "Continental currency," as it was called, worth? It was scarcely enough to procure a man a dinner. Government was ashamed to tantalize the soldiers any longer with such trash, and wisely gave it up for its own credit. I received one month's pay in specie while on the march to Virginia, in the year 1781, and except that, I never received any pay worth the name while I belonged to the army. Had I been paid as I was promised to be at my engaging in the service, I needed not to have suffered as I did, nor would I have done it; there was enough in the country and money would have procured it if I had had it. It is provoking to think of it. The country was rigorous in exacting my compliance to my engagements to a punctilio, but equally careless in performing her contracts with me, and why so? One reason was because she had all the power in her own hands and I had none. Such things ought not to be.

Notes

1. Martin enlisted July 6, 1776, in Samuel Peck's Third Company, William Douglas's Fifth Battalion, James Wadsworth Jr.'s Brigade of new levies. In a manuscript of accounts of Douglas's Regiment, in the Revolutionary War Records at the National Archive, Martin is shown as having received an enlistment bounty of three pounds, a bounty for "gun, bayonet, cartouche box, and blanket," and pay for a total of five months, nine days, for his service in 1776.–GS

2. The British high command, having relinquished Boston to General Washington's besieging Continentals in March, 1776, decided now to attack New York City, to which Washington had hurried his army. British General Sir William Howe landed nine thousand men on undefended Staten Island and later reinforcements swelled his force to over a third more fighting men than Washington's twenty-three thousand.–GS

3. Broad Street, east of and paralleling Broadway, ran from the Exchange at Dock Street to Wall. New York City at the time occupied only the southern tip of Manhattan Island, an area about a mile square. Its northern boundary ran roughly from today's Grand Street on the East River to Vestry Street on the Hudson. Northward lay farmlands, woods, and marshes.

4. The most popular treatise used during the early years of the war was Lewis Nicola's *Treatise of Military Exercise*. Americans believed that the essentials of drill were all that were necessary; even Washington was personally uninterested in drill practice, although at the same time he continually fretted at the lack of discipline and orderliness of his army.

5. The *Phoenix*, the *Rose*, an accompanying schooner, and two tenders had sailed up the Hudson past an American cannonade, July 12, and anchored in the Tappan Sea, severing river communication between New York and Albany. On August 17, they had been attacked by American fire-rafts, which burned the schooner, and on the eighteenth the surviving vessels ran down the river and rejoined their fleet in the lower harbor. The Grand Battery was the fortification at the southern tip of Manhattan.–GS

6. The date was August 27. Howe had landed his forces near Gravesend, Long Island, August 22. To defend New York, Washington had scattered his five divisions, placing one under Putnam on Long Island, where Brooklyn Heights commanded New York. Putnam had placed half his nine thousand men behind a line of thickly wooded hills about a mile and a half advanced from his Brooklyn works.

During the night of August 26, Howe moved up to attack. At daylight, his left began playing on the American right with cannon fire, while he successfully commanded a turning column behind the American left.–GS

7. The Manhattan terminus of the Long Island ferry was at the foot of Maiden Lane.

8. It is possible that the poor lieutenant is displaying not only fear but "sensibility." During the Revolution, men claiming to be gentlemen—which included virtually all of the lieutenant rank and above—affected the cult of sensibility as one of the distinctions of their class. Martin seems to be as disgusted by the lieutenant's "sissy" manners as by his fearfulness.

9. Martin's regiment was in Brooklyn at this point, after the collapse and retreat of the Americans on Long Island.

10. The northeaster that blew sporadically from the afternoon of August 28th prevented Howe's fleet from coming up East River and cutting the rebels off from New York. Washington successfully withdrew to Manhattan on the night of the twenty-ninth.–GS

11. On the night of September 3, the *Rose,* with twenty flatboats, went up East River and anchored under Blackwell's (present-day Welfare) Island.

12. Turtle Bay was an indentation in the East River shoreline of Manhattan Island at about present day 46th and 47th streets.–GS

13. The lines were at Kip's Bay, a cove that reached to between present-day First and Second Avenues from 32nd Street to about 38th. It was an especially likely enemy landing place because it was easily navigable and from its shore rose a large, open, V-shaped meadow, an excellent beachhead and assembly area.–GS

14. September 15th. They had been at Kip's Bay for ten days.

15. Using social euphemisms for "enemy" and for various kinds of fighting was commonplace, particularly during the Revolutionary and Civil Wars.

16. A few days earlier, when Washington thought Howe was preparing to land in the vicinity of King's Bridge to cut off his exit from New York, he had begun to evacuate the city. From the mainland King's Bridge crossed Spuyten Duyvil into the Bronx near what is now West 230th Street and Marble Hill Avenue. Washington planned to mass most of his strength on the rocky plateau called Harlem Heights, north of present day 125th Street, which he felt he could defend. Only about half of his force was behind the bluffs at Harlem when Howe struck; the rest were still in the city on the East River lines.–GS

17. This was the principal evacuation route, the Post Road from New York to Boston. It followed roughly the course of present-day Lexington Avenue, turned east toward Kip's Bay, and ran across Harlem Heights to King's Bridge.–GS

18. The American forces consisted of the national or Continental Army and the state militias.

19. With no military tradition and a great deal of uncertainty regarding how to establish lines of authority, the Continental Armies and militias tried to maintain discipline on the basis of class division between "gentlemen" officers and "commoner" soldiers. There were more officers' positions than there were true gentlemen ready to fill them, and the policy backfired. While the British armies of the day tried to maintain easy relations between officers and men, the Americans tried to segregate them. Consequently, soldiers regarded officers with resentment, dismay, perplexity, apathy, and sometimes revolt.

20. After landing unopposed at Kip's Bay Howe failed to drive across the waist of the island, which allowed some three thousand American troops to escape along the Bloomingdale Road up the west side of the island. All but some four hundred of the defenders of the East River shore also reached Harlem Heights. The missing major of Martin's regiment was Phineas Porter, who had been captured.–GS

21. The officer was Colonel Joseph Reed, and the soldier was Ebenezer Leffingwell, who was court-martialed on September 22. Courts-martial with death sentences and last-minute stays of execution were used so commonly, particularly during the early years of the Revolution, that they lost whatever effectiveness they might have had.

22. Frog's (Throckmorton's) Neck was the point of land on the north shore where the East River joins Long Island Sound (present-day Fort Schuyler in the Bronx). Howe landed on October 22.–GS

23. To meet Howe's move on his flank and rear, Washington set up a succession of posts west of the Bronx River. The position at Valentine's Hill was east of Harlem River, some two or three miles from King's Bridge.–GS

24. Martin's regiment marched to White Plains on the evening of October 20. Evidently, when Martin returned from detached duty he marched with Heath's Division, which marched all night the twenty-first and arrived at White Plains early the next morning.–GS

25. On the morning of October 28, American militia was entrenching on Chatterton Hill, beyond the Bronx River, about a mile from White Plains, slightly in advance of Washington's right wing. Continentals were moving to support the militia when Howe attacked. A force under General Joseph Spencer, including Martin's regiment, marched to meet the enemy in front.–GS

26. After driving back Spencer's Division, Howe concentrated on Chatterton Hill until he possessed it. Then he made no further aggressive movement.–GS

27. Washington, on November 1, withdrew from his lines at White Plains to strong defensive positions to the north, eventually encamping at North Castle

beyond Croton River, thirteen miles away. Wright's Mills, later the village of Kensico and now Kensico Reservoir, was some four miles north of White Plains. Undoubtedly Martin meant North Castle for New Castle.—GS

28. Borrowing from the British, Americans called the civilian revolutionists "Whigs" and the Loyalists "Tories." Sentiments on both sides were in constant ebb and flow, with Loyalists and Whigs generally living in the state of uneasy peace represented in this anecdote. Late in the war, however, the two sides terrorized each other in some parts of the South, particularly in South Carolina. The old lady's term "regulars" was the generally used word for British soldiers.

29. Although Martin recalled being discharged on Christmas, records in the National Archives indicate he was discharged ten days before.—GS

30. Martin is using the term "recruited" for resting and restoring his strength.—GS

31. Washington's army had shrunk to about three thousand men during the winter of '76–'77, and he feared that if the recruitments of '77 failed, "the game will be pretty well up." The short-term enlistments of early in the war had proved to be an unmanageable headache with soldiers constantly leaving and green soldiers constantly arriving. By the time of Martin's reenlistment, Continentals were enlisting men for three years or for the duration, with some states offering up to a twenty-dollar bounty for the duration, substantially higher than the bounties for short-term enlistment offered early in the war. Martin reenlisted for the duration in Captain David Smith's Company, Colonel John Chandler's Eighth Connecticut Regiment of Continentals.

32. General William Tyron raided Danbury on April 26, 1777. The hastily assembled American troops attacked him on his withdrawal to his transports on the twenty-seventh and twenty-eighth. Arnold's horse was shot, and he narrowly escaped capture.—GS

33. Absent from the army from Christmas until April, 1777, Martin had participated neither in Washington's disheartening retreat into New Jersey after the loss of New York nor in his brilliant actions at Trenton and Princeton. Following these engagements, Washington had gone into winter quarters at Morristown, New Jersey, with what was left of his army, diminished to almost nothing by the expiration of short-term enlistments, to await spring and new forces. Noting enemy operations from both the headwaters and the mouth of the Hudson, he concentrated the incoming New Englanders at Peekskill to reinforce the troops already guarding the Hudson Highlands.—GS

34. When a smallpox epidemic threatened his army in the winter of 1776, Washington, realizing "we should have more to dread from it, than from the Sword of the Enemy," determined that all troops should be inoculated. Inoculation usually induced typical smallpox and was naturally greatly feared. Patients were quaran-

tined under guard in inoculation hospitals. To conceal from the enemy the weakening of his army by mass inoculation, Washington cautioned his physician in chief to keep "the matter as secret as possible."–GS

35. The Connecticut Line had remained at Peekskill for some months, with occasional expeditions toward King's Bridge, while Washington met Howe at Brandywine on September 11, 1777, was outflanked, and lost Philadelphia to the enemy. When Washington then planned to attack Howe's main body, which were encamped five miles northwest of Philadelphia at Germantown, he ordered Putnam, in command in the Highlands, to send reinforcements. Martin's regiment was one of four forwarded under General Alexander McDougall, who was assigned to General Nathaniel Greene's Division on the left flank of the army.–GS

36. This was the Battle of Germantown, October 4, 1777, the loss of which provoked severe criticism of American military leadership.

37. Following the battle, Washington marched his men back twenty-four miles to Pennypacker's Mill before encamping.–GS

38. Washington moved in to White Marsh after he learned, on October 15, that Howe had withdrawn his whole force into Philadelphia.–GS

39. One gill was four ounces, the official daily ration of rum, when it was available. Liquor was generally thought to enhance the fighting spirit, and wine—as many as four bottles a day—was thought to prevent "putrid fevers."

40. The Americans had originally built three forts and chevaux-de-frise (spiked walls) in the Delaware River to protect the capital city. Now that Philadelphia was lost, they intended to use the forts to harass Howe and prevent his communication and resupply, but he had taken possession of one of the forts, at Billingsport, twelve miles below Camden, on September 9.

41. Fort Mifflin was on Port Island in the river, within hailing distance of Fort Mercer at Red Bank. In contemporary accounts, Mud Island often was confused with Port Island, a few hundred yards downstream.–GS

42. Artillery was a well established military science by the late eighteenth century. British orderly books from the Revolution show detailed calculations of weight, angle, and distance of shots in order to try to achieve accuracy.

43. The fort was evacuated during the night of November 15–16.–GS

44. Martin was right about this. In histories of the Revolution, the dramatic losses of the Delaware River forts are mostly consigned to a phrase.

45. The Congress, now in York, Pennsylvania, after being run out of Philadelphia by Howe's army, was in a bad state. Because it had no executive structure, all issues had to be hammered out in legislative and committee session. Delegates

were suffering from overwork and rising censure from the public. The money that they were printing was locked into an inflationary spiral. Thorny state legislatures would not comply with the Congress. With losses now at Brandywine, Germantown and the Delaware forts, and Philadelphia abandoned, there was a growing sense that General Washington was weak and that Gates should be put in his place.

46. The Pennsylvania legislature approached the Congress protesting the winter encampment of the army, because local farms, already being crowded by Philadelphia refugees, were now being pillaged by the army.

47. Soldiers' diaries in most major American wars note the extraordinary kindness of Philadelphians to soldiers.

48. The term "South" is generally used by New England diarists in reference to Philadelphia and all points southward.

49. The army's experience at the winter camp at Valley Forge—a small city of log shacks located twenty miles outside Philadelphia—was not as bad as the later winter of '79–'80. It gained popular renown after the war partly because it was the first winter that many of the new three-year recruits had suffered, and partly because it marked the beginning of a new spirit of professionalism in the army. As Martin indicates, the camp was fairly active with drills, foraging parties, and soldiers coming and going on furlough. Some officers wives were there, including Lady Washington. Personal calls for help by furloughing soldiers brought some shipments of supplies.

50. The Baron von Steuben was one of the many whom Franklin, in Paris, encouraged to go and join the war. At almost fifty, von Steuben was a bankrupt who had fled Prussia incognito with another bankrupt, a prince who'd given him the baron's title before the crisis of their financial troubles. Franklin encouraged him to "promote" himself to former lieutenant general from the lowly title of captain, so that he would make a bigger impression on the American army. He came to the army at Valley Forge as a volunteer training officer and provided the invaluable service of making the American army more disciplined, involving both the soldiers and "gentlemen" officers in drill and exercise, which until then Washington—and consequently most officers below him—had regarded as a "disagreeable necessity." Von Steuben taught soldiers a simplified Prussian system of maneuvers. He placed emphasis on action and movement, partly for the purpose of keeping discontent down. His maneuvers were extremely useful at Yorktown where for the first and last time Americans fought a European-style battle. Von Steuben's pamphlet *Regulations,* which came to be called the Blue Book, went through seventy editions. The baron was also committed to caring for muskets and equipment, and from that point forward the loss and breakage of muskets markedly decreased. Valley Forge marked the beginning of the professionalism

that Washington had yearned for but not yet accomplished. Valley Forge is remembered as the crucible of the American army partly because of von Steuben's presence and influence.

51. The Marquis de Lafayette was a tall, thin nineteen-year-old French reserves captain whose genuine interest in the American cause prompted Congress in 1777 to promote him to lieutenant general. Lafayette had marched out of Philadelphia at Washington's side toward the disaster at Brandywine. He became fiercely loyal to Washington and proved to be a good leader.

52. Washington had heard that Howe was evacuating Philadelphia and he sent Lafayette to reconnoiter.–GS

53. Washington, believing Indians "mixed with our own parties" should be valuable as scouts and light troops, had been authorized to raise four hundred. The first of them, Iroquois, arrived at Valley Forge on May 13. By then, with the military situation altered, Washington had changed his mind and suggested that no more be sent to camp. The Iroquois joined Lafayette's movement.–GS

54. Coryell's Ferry, between New Hope, Pennsylvania, and Lambertville, New Jersey.

55. The British army, now under General Sir Henry Clinton, evacuated Philadelphia on June 18. As Clinton moved sluggishly through New Jersey toward New York, Washington was presented with a commander's dream, the chance to strike a strung out, hot, and tired army—ten thousand men with 1,500 wagons moving through difficult terrain. Washington sent out a Jersey militia and Daniel Morgan's riflemen to observe the enemy, and he called a counsel of his generals, as he customarily did—counsels that Alexander Hamilton likened to "a gaggle of midwives." A ten-day dispute followed, at first dominated by the more senior Charles Lee, who insisted that the main force should sit tight at Valley Forge. Anthony Wayne, Lafayette, and others finally carried the opinion to seriously engage the enemy. Martin marched with the major detachment sent off on the twenty-fourth.

56. Martin's comments are astute. The wholesale devastation of the countryside by the British and their German auxiliaries made the American populace increasingly hostile to them.

57. According to the seniority etiquette under which Washington operated, the sour and defeatist Charles Lee had to be offered command of the major striking force. He at first refused it as too unimportant for him, and the relieved Washington happily sent out Lafayette in charge, but when Lee found out how many troops were involved he stormed and raged and convinced Washington to put him in charge. Martin's regiment, in General James M. Varnum's Brigade (now commanded by Colonel John Durkee in Varnum's absence on leave), was in the front. The confused battle of Monmouth ensued, in which General Lee scattered

his men, marching and countermarching in total confusion, while offering no help to Wayne and his six hundred Pennsylvanians at the front.

58. Washington rode out of Englishtown and made appearances all over the field, calming the general retreat and ordering cover for them. For Lafayette, it was one of the grand moments of the war. He said that Washington rode "all along the lines amid the shouts of the soldiers, cheering them by his voice and example and restoring to our standard the fortunes of the fight. I thought then, as now, that never had I beheld so superb a man." The rest of the day, attacks and counterattacks continued, with hard fighting all over the field.

59. Although this account sounds a little fanciful, Mary Ludwig Hayes, wife of a Pennsylvania private whom she followed to war, does seem to have been assigned to a gun battery. A woman of no education who smoked, chewed tobacco, and "swore like a trooper," she won immortal fame as Molly Pitcher.

60. Following Monmouth, with Clinton finally in New York, active operations came to an end for more than a year. Washington observed that after two years, "both armies are brought back to the very point they set out from."–GS

61. Washington formed his first Light Infantry Corps in August, 1777, by drawing off picked men from the brigades. The chosen men were young, agile, and good shots. The corps proved so useful that Washington obtained authority to organize in every regiment a Light Company; during a campaign the companies were formed in a separate corps. The corps brought together after Monmouth was commanded by Colonel David Henley.–GS

62. Washington remained in the "grand camp" at White Plains and Fredericksburg until almost the end of the year before transferring his main body to Middlebrook, New Jersey. On October 22, the Connecticut Division under McDougall (not the "main army") set out to winter at Redding, Connecticut. On the twenty-fifth it reached New Milford and encamped until November nineteenth.

63. Major General Israel Putnam, veteran of the French Wars, had been among the active generals from the first of the war.

64. Although this episode describes an angry cry for help, the casual firing off of muskets in American camps was a continuing problem. Camps were often enveloped in the smoke of fires, the smell of offal and sewage, and the casual popping off of muskets. Although neatness tended to increase in the last years of the war, American soldiers were amazed by the cleanness and order of French troops and camps.

65. Soldiers were angry about their conditions, but they were particularly angry at the public, who seemed to nonchalantly sit at a distance expecting them to perform miracles while they starved. At times, the army seemed to have declined to an outlaw band. Washington was seriously concerned that they would disband.

66. Martin was sent in a detachment of four hundred, under Israel Putnam, to guard New London against a possible maritime raid. So far, the winter had been quiet.

67. "Mad" Anthony Wayne was one of the Washington stalwarts and among the few unquestionably good fighting generals among the inner circle.

68. The British had taken this fortification on the eastern side of the Hudson on June 1.

69. Josiah Edwards of Sheldon's Second Continental Dragoons, was executed on November 12, 1779.–GS

70. The winter of 1779–80 was the worst in forty years. Roads were often impassable. Soldiers hadn't been paid at all for months, and the discounted value of government scrip was declining at dizzying rates. The public seemed to have abandoned the Revolution, with little notice of the army or the war even appearing in newspapers. The public was tired of the war and the army was tired of their insouciance.

71. This daring but poorly managed raid was mounted during the night of January 14, 1780, under command of Major General William Alexander, not, as Martin recalled, under General Sullivan.–GS

72. One contemporary recorded twenty-eight snowfalls, including the great storm of January 2–4, 1780.–GS

73. The fear of the Pennsylvania officers proved to be more than justified. The Pennsylvania troops—here used to quell Connecticut soldiers—eight months later would undertake the most serious mutiny of the war.

74. Martin's narrative of this mutiny of May 25, 1780, is the most complete and dramatic account of an event which Washington told Congress "has given me infinitely more concern than any thing that has ever happened."–GS

75. In July, 1780, Washington directed that one man be drawn from each regiment to compose the sappers and miners. They were to work with mines and saps, the approach trenches to enemy works. Their training and duties broadened to include choosing, laying out, and fortifying camps, opening or repairing roads before the army, reconnoitering, and other tasks. A listing of the corps in the National Archives, Revolutionary War Rolls, cites Martin as a corporal who enlisted January 1, 1781.–GS

76. Benedict Arnold, one of the most talented generals in the Continental Army, had always sought the most rigorous assignments, but he fretted at having too little money. After being put in charge of the command at Philadelphia, he was court-martialled in 1779 for graft. He then secretly negotiated with the British for over a year, agreeing to sell them the "invulnerable" West Point for twenty thou-

sand pounds. He also sent them several articles of intelligence as signs of good faith. His British contact, Major Andre, was captured, and Arnold fled to the *Vulture* on September 25, 1780. The brig slipped down river to safety the morning of the twenty-sixth, and his treason was announced to the army. Arnold quickly became the archetypal traitor in the Revolution, burned in effigy everywhere. Paid six thousand pounds instead of twenty, he ended up in London, where he became something of a social outcast.

77. Clinton, revived by his decisive victory in South Carolina a year before, was now back in New York. He had captured Charleston, forcing Benjamin Lincoln to surrender his entire command of 5,500 men unconditionally, the most severe disaster of the war for the Americans. Now, in May, 1781, Washington with the French allies who had come in force to Rhode Island, planned a joint attack on New York City, hoping to force Clinton to recall Cornwallis, whom he'd left in charge of the South. The attack was planned for July 2. Washington's forces were to descend both banks of the Hudson and meet the French at the point of attack as they closed in from Westchester. An unintended skirmish near Old Fort Independence, northeast of King's Bridge, alerted the British and wrecked the scheme.

78. "Refugees" and "Cowboys" were freebooters with Tory sympathies operating in the countryside around New York. Another group, calling themselves "Skinners," were freebooters with rebel sympathies. The term cowboy had been used in England for at least a century to mean "one who tends livestock." These American "cowboys" may have been named for the fact that they stole livestock.

79. The great march of combined American and French forces for Yorktown began August 19, 1781. To deceive the enemy, Washington made as if to assail New York through Staten Island. The troops intended for Virginia were moved into New Jersey, and parties were sent about inquiring freely for boats. To create the impression that the French were settling in for a siege of New York, word was spread that the breadbaking ovens they built at Chatham were but the first of many to be constructed. The ruse worked long enough to get the armies safely on their way. The Americans and French marched through Philadelphia on September 2–4.–GS

80. For several months now, merchant and politician Robert Morris had been serving in the newly created role of Superintendent of Finance for the Continental Congress—its first true executive office—and he had managed to come up with stopgap funds for food, clothing, and even some pay.

81. Over the previous two years the French fleet had been engaged in furious marine warfare with the British fleet in the Caribbean, but on August 14, 1781, word had reached Washington that Comte François Joseph Paul de Grasse had left the West Indies with twenty-eight ships of the line and a swarm of transports carrying three regiments under General the Comte de St. Simon. Immediately,

Washington began to plan a combined effort against Cornwallis in the South. The "several" men-of-war noted by Martin were a key to the strategy, since the whole venture was contingent upon the French ships being able to control the Bay and prevent Cornwallis from being reinforced or taken to safety.

82. Lafayette and Anthony Wayne were sparring in Virginia with Cornwallis, who'd been left in charge of the British in the South.

83. Siege warfare in the eighteenth century adhered to a century-old set of rules for building lines to protect the besieger, bombardments, and the opening of a series of parallel encircling trenches. The first parallel usually was dug six hundred yards from the besieged fortress, out of range of small-arms fire and grape and canister. The earth excavated from the parallels was thrown over fascines in front of the parallels to form parapets. Earthen artillery batteries were constructed, connected to the parallels by communication trenches. Saps, or smaller trenches, were dug, zigzagging toward the fortress. At three hundred yards from the fortress a second parallel was dug. If necessary, a third was finally dug close enough for breaching the fortress walls by an infantry attack. Yorktown was the first and only siege conducted by the Continental Army—and the last in history of its kind.–GS

84. Washington was uncommonly expansive at Yorktown—and understandably so. As a commander in chief, he finally faced a major battle in which the odds allowed him to throw off the defensive strategy that he had employed during most of the war. By the time all French and American troops had massed, he had sixteen thousand men against Cornwallis's six thousand bottled-up British, Hessians, and Tories. As a battlefield general, Washington finally had his European-style engagement, in which the sappers and miners played a key role. (For the battlefield area commander, he readily accepted the Marquis de Choisy, who had distinguished himself at the siege of Cracow in Poland.) Personally, Washington had also just visited his home in Mount Vernon for the first time since 1776.

85. The house of Thomas Nelson, onetime Secretary of the Virginia Council, which had been occupied by Lord Cornwallis as headquarters.–GS

86. On the night of October 14, the Americans prepared to assault redoubts anchoring the left of the Yorktown lines. Alexander Hamilton led the Americans in the assault.

87. On the windy night of October 16, Cornwallis made a desperate effort to save his army by crossing the York River to Glocester Point, intending to go from there to the sea, but the weather was against him and de Choisy had pushed the lines so close to the British works that any kind of movement was difficult.

88. General Charles O'Hara of the Guards had been sent out by Cornwallis. He rode up first to Rochambeau, and Rochambeau indicated that he should present himself to Washington. He did so, Washington asked him where Cornwallis was,

and O'Hara explained that he was ill and had deputized him to make the surrender. Washington indicated that deputy should surrender to deputy, and he indicated General Lincoln, who previously had been so humiliated at Charleston. Lincoln rode up and touched O'Hara's sword in token acceptance and told him how the British were to march out and stack their arms before returning to Yorktown to await further orders.

89. Despite the obvious importance of Yorktown, it did not necessarily spell the end of the war. Powerful forces remained at Charleston and New York. However, in March, 1782, the House of Commons passed a resolution against any further prosecution of the war. North's ministry fell, and Sir Guy Carleton was appointed commanding general in America with the clear mandate to wind things up. Peace negotiators labored in Paris through the fall of the year. Martin's unit was stationed in Trenton, then Burlington.

90. Yellow fever struck seaport areas repeatedly in the eighteenth and nineteenth centuries, often killing thousands of people. Mosquitoes had yet to be identified as the carrier, and there was no known cause or cure. The fever ran a rampant course, lasting between twelve hours to four days. Most patients died on the third or fourth day.

91. This great chain was one of the obstructions laid at various times across the Hudson. In fact each link weighed 180 pounds and the whole was five hundred yards long. Some of its original links are preserved at the United States Military Academy.–GS

92. Congress approved a provisional treaty of peace on April 15, 1783, and it was formally announced to the army on April 29.

93. Washington endeavored to get at least three months' back pay for the troops, but Congress could not grant even that much. To reduce the cost of maintaining the men, it directed Washington to grant furloughs and offered the troops certificates for their overdue pay. The furlough paper would automatically become a discharge upon the ratification of a final peace treaty. Congress voted the men their arms as a farewell gift, but many were obliged to sell them on their way home for travel money.–GS

94. Martin is probably referring to the speculation mania early in the 1790s, when Revolutionary War scrip suddenly rose in value from fifteen to thirty cents on the dollar (much had traded as low as 12.5 cents) to near par price. This happened after Alexander Hamilton, Secretary of the Treasury, proposed his funding program. Hamilton proposed a total assumption of the country's debt as the best way to solidify the union—the germ of which Robert Morris had set forth near the end of the war. The funding program called for all of the country's war debts, including the debts of the states, to be paid, funded by taxes and bonds. This aggressive assumption plan made all of the old debt scrip paid to soldiers and to

suppliers, which had been floating around at severely discounted prices, suddenly jump in value. A second element of the Hamiltonian Funding Program, the establishment of a national bank, made the war scrip even more valuable, since the plan called for shares of the new bank's stock to be issued, buyable partly with Revolutionary War scrip. The many who wanted to acquire a stake in National Bank stock were faced with an artificial shortage of debt scrip and they bid up the prices even higher. Henry Lee, traveling from Philadelphia to Virginia in 1791, wrote that the whole country had become "one continued scene of stock gambling." All of this was of little use to the vast majority of soldiers who had been forced to sell their scrip at fractional prices well before its rise in value.

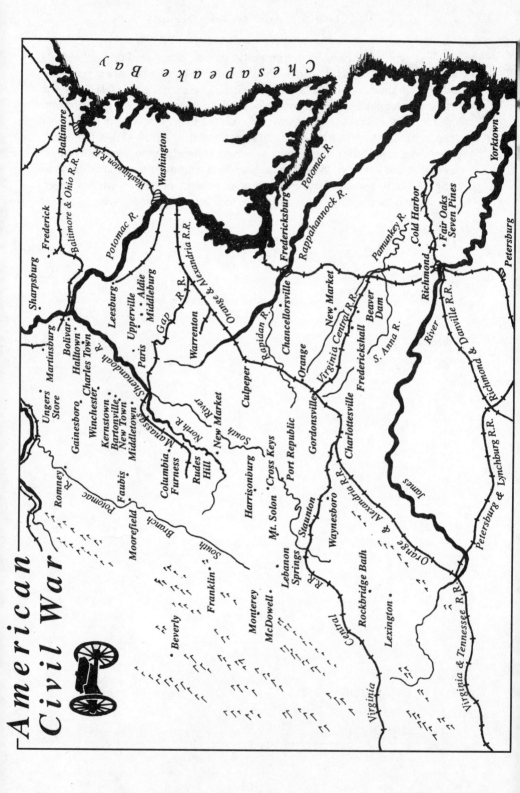

American Civil War

2

The Civil War

During the American Revolution, the diaries and memoirs of New England soldiers who were sent to the American South contain an often repeated theme: The "South" for many Yankee soldiers began at Philadelphia, but the deep South of Virginia and the Carolinas was a truly exotic zone inhabited by strange people with even stranger social arrangements. New England diarists often relate lurid images of "naked" male slaves casually standing beside frilly, prettified, insouciant Southern ladies. Such sightings have a tone of titillated disbelief about them, as if what the diarist witnessed in the South stretched the limits of the imagination. To the New England soldiers of the Revolution, fellow soldiers from the South were strange enough, but Southern civilians in their element were anthropological curiosities. Similarly, to Southern soldiers, the North is already a strange place, and Yankees are already "damn Yankees."

Diarists from both sections suggest that the 170 years of American settlement leading up to the Revolution had spawned two civilizations, and that the root of the difference between them was the institution of slavery. Northerners and Southerners were different breeds, separated not just by climate, crops, and economics but also by morals, religion, and social behavior.

If the two civilizations managed to live with each other for so long, what finally caused the situation to erupt in the most destructive war in U.S. history? What caused the North and South to stop tolerating each other? While this question cannot be answered in a word, it had a great deal to do with the growth and expansion of the United States and the consequent threat to the previous political equilibrium. The addition of the Missouri Territory, the territory from the Mexican War, and Western states like Kansas and Nebraska reignited the issue of slavery, adding to the tension, with both sides fearing loss of parity in the federal government.

When the Southern-dominated Supreme Court passed the Dred Scott Decision allowing slavery in all U.S. territories, the friction between proslavery and antislavery settlers on the border of Kansas and Missouri broke into a shooting war. Lincoln's election clearly indicated to Southerners that they had become a minority in the federal government, and secession began. But if slavery and the two civilizations were the Civil War's root causes, secession undoubtedly was the immediate cause. How the issue of slavery should be resolved was still unclear, as Lincoln's well known uncertainty about the issue demonstrated. But the otherwise careful Mr. Lincoln was very definite about the Union.

This seemingly weak president had arrived in office without a single electoral vote from the slave states, yet somehow he had the courage to insist that the Southern states could not drop out of the Union. In world politics 130 years later, dropping out of national governments has become almost an everyday event. Lincoln could insist otherwise in 1860 because by then the Union had achieved almost the status of a religious principle. The Union might have been man-made but it was also consecrated. Schoolteachers and ministers all over the country, including the South, had taught and preached for years that the Constitution and the Union of states that it defined were one of the most important achievements in the history of humankind. It must not be broken.

As in the Revolution, the Civil War began with a flurry of patriotism and powerful sentiments on both sides. Reporters in both Massachusetts and South Carolina were astonished at the level of emotion expressed in crowds. Young men rushed to sign up for the adventure of war. The early weeks were a vortex into which tens of thousands of men were drawn, as if by some easy and inevitable magnetism.

Among them was an eighteen-year-old from Charlestown, Massachusetts, named George Sargent. Rejected by a doctor for service in a Massachusetts regiment because he was too skinny, he went elsewhere and eventually signed up to be a bugler with the First New England Cavalry.

Sargent would serve two years, reenlist, and stay through the end of the war.

During his training period, he began to take diary notes and continued to do so throughout the war. Some time afterwards—there is no clear indication when—he recopied his diaries into a single journal, adding further details and anecdotes. At the beginning and end of this final copy, and in various passages throughout, Sargent includes comments that were certainly added at this later time, yet the bulk of the document was composed in the field. The result is a diary-based account covering a remarkable span of events, picturing a branch of Civil War service that may nowhere else be this closely detailed—the life of a field musician in the cavalry.

Sargent's regiments (he was later switched to a New Hampshire unit) served in the area west of Washington, near Bull Run and throughout the Shenandoah Valley. They slogged along month after month, decimated by illness and casualties, afflicted by what at first was a better-led, superior army. Sargent was assigned to the cavalry band, which he appreciated because a musician was a little less likely to be killed in battle. In an age before radio, the military band provided entertainment in the camps, music for marching, and occasionally music in battle. Band members also worked in field hospitals, carried food to men in trenches, and helped around headquarters. Because they spent so much time in Virginia—the seat of the war—Sargent's band played music for Southerners as well as for their own side, often as a mild kind of psychological warfare, marching through little Virginia towns playing "Yankee Doodle" or the "Star-Spangled Banner." Yet "Dixie" was also in their repertoire, and at times they played it and other Southern songs for everyone's enjoyment.

The frequent episodes of friendliness between the two sides in the Civil War was not strange, after all, given the shared language and history of the two sides. Almost everybody had relatives, friends, or acquaintances who joined the other side. Friendly incidents with enemy soldiers and enemy civilians of the kind that Martin reports were not unique to the Civil War, but it did seem bizarre in the context of the war's terrible slaughters.

Sargent was present at the battles of Fredericksburg, the second Bull Run, Petersburg, and several others, as well as at the dramatic treeing of

Lee's army in 1865, by which time Sargent had been reassigned to the job of bugler serving within the Provost Guard of General Philip Sheridan's Cavalry Corps.

In the beginning, Sargent's diary depicts an army that seemed unsure of itself. A politically divided command structure, lack of regular supplies in the field, friction between officers and "laborers" (as Sargent calls enlisted men), and uncertain movements in battle partly reflected the period of befuddlement in Washington, when Lincoln was unable to find effective leadership for the Eastern theatre. Equally, though, they resulted from the fact that the military planners of both the North and the South had to do what never had been done in terms of numbers of men, rapidity of movements, supplies, zone of conflict, and communications. The Crimean War provided the only case of anything like contemporary warfare, and its lessons were sketchy and insufficient in an era of telegraphy and advanced rail transport.

Overall Northern strategy evolved with the transition between generals and with evolving technology. Northerners began the war with a strategy in some ways similar to the British strategy at the beginning of the Revolution, attempting to defeat the insurrectionists and retake territory for the Union. This evolved toward a policy of more concentrated warfare, as Grant's early attempts at tactical adroitness were roundly repulsed. Like General Washington, Grant finally had to do not what he wanted but what he had to do, which was to give up outfoxing the Confederates and simply try to destroy them. The Confederates had one-third the manpower of the unionists, and far less wealth and manufacturing potential. Lee was forced to retreat into a rigorously defensive strategy. Taking advantage of rifled guns and better trench-making ability, he inflicted terrible losses on the attacking Union soldiers, and the war finally devolved into an even more terrible stage, a total war against civilians and resources as well as armies, with Sherman's destruction of Georgia and South Carolina.

In the early stages, Sargent's unit was engaged in undramatic work, sweeping back and forth in the area west of Washington, engaging in feints, scrapes with guerillas, and small dogfights. Sometimes they headed through one of the gaps into the Shenandoah Valley. In their first battle, they had the bad luck to encounter Stonewall Jackson, who was at the moment making a place for himself in military history in his remarkable Shenandoah Valley campaign of 1862. The second noteworthy period of

Sargent's cavalry service was again in the Shenandoah Valley, when he served in General Philip Sheridan's expedition of 1864.

Sheridan's campaign was in some ways the opposite of Stonewall Jackson's campaign two years before, which had been a marvel of military field strategy and tactics, of fooling the enemy and engaging him where he least expected it. Sheridan, too, was tactically nimble, yet his assignment was aimed not primarily at the Confederate army but the resources that supported it—cropland, livestock, and railroads. This and Sherman's march to the sea in Georgia in 1864, were early instances of what we have come to call "modern warfare," directly attacking the resources and political will of the opponent, as well as its armies. In his diary, George Sargent questioned some of the incidents in Sheridan's campaign, as it seemed to spin out of control and become a succession of ugly acts of revenge on both sides.

Throughout his account, Sargent describes the lives of soldiers in the field, who were often left to build their own shelters, find their own food, and survive or not on their own. While supplies were certainly more frequent than in the Revolution, in order to feed themselves soldiers were again regularly required to go on official and unofficial foraging expeditions. Conditions did not significantly change with the fortunes of the war. The soldiers' most persistent enemies were exposure, freezing, exhaustion, starvation, illness, "the blues," and the inability to find drinkable water. Someone has said that the Civil War was a modern war fought in medieval conditions, and, while this enlisted man's diary confirms that summation, he seemed to hold almost no grudges about it.

Temperamentally unsuited to complaining, George Sargent preferred to dwell in loving detail on the few occasions of pleasure—nights spent in a warm bed, good fruit to steal and eat, a watermelon or cup of cider given him by some kind soul, moments of peaceful contemplation. Such things he loved to describe at length, while preferring to dispatch the preponderant unpleasantness of life in the field with understatement. As in the Revolution, Sargent and other Civil War enlisted men often describe combat obliquely, with understatement and the euphemisms of social interaction and games. In the most gruesome war of American history, in which the combined forces of transportation, technology, and population growth eventually combined to mass huge numbers of men under the most devastating firepower, Sargent and many other humble diarists are likely to describe combat with awesomely undramatic phrases like "We gave them a warm welcome."

It is often assumed that less educated, less privileged Americans tend toward the purple end of the rhetorical spectrum, that vividness, embellishment, and exaggeration are the verbal predilections of unsophisticated Americans. Reading the diaries of soldiers, however, one wonders if understatement is not more common in the voice of plain Americans. George Sargent, at any rate, did not feel that it was necessary to exaggerate what was already almost incomprehensibly terrible.

As the early command structure of the army fell away, the Union Army gained in self-confidence and ability, and so did Sargent. At twenty-one, the three-year veteran had grown up. He looked at things more critically. He decided, for example, that patriotism of the kind delivered by pious speechmakers was "humbug." At the same time, he was more capable of identifying with the good or the essential in the Northern cause, and his evolution in this regard was to some extent representative of an overall shift in emphasis as the war progressed.

While slavery was the key motive in the political crisis building up to the war, the breaking of the Union was the acute cause. It was the thing the government and the young men of the North were ready to risk extinction to prevent. Pride in America's political system, pride in the Union, had been extremely high in the decade before the war. The issue of slavery was far less clear. At the beginning of the war, a vast majority of Northerners were opposed to abolition of the radical sort that Lincoln eventually set forth. Many were opposed to abolition in any form. Active racism was rampant in the North among certain ethnic and political groups, as well as being part of the overall cultural conditioning of whites. However, the issue of slavery, the war's root cause, eventually came back to the forefront as the war wore on, partly due to the leadership of radicals in Congress and finally of Lincoln himself, and partly as a result of the widespread feeling that Southern whites had forfeited their right to slavery by their act of rebellion.

George Sargent's diary confirms this picture. His primary motive for joining, at first, was to prevent the country from being divided. The enemy was identified as secessionists or "secesh." He and fellow soldiers were fighting, as he put it, "for our beloved country." That he retained this faith in the Union is particularly meaningful when seen through the details of his experience in the field, years of managing to stay alive in enemy territory, among people who hated him, insulted him, and would have killed him if they could.

Our young diarist was of humble beginnings and education, but he was from the Boston area, one of the most radical places in the country on the issue of slavery, and he had certainly been exposed to zealous abolitionism; yet he uses the word "nigger" several times in the diary, often in reference to one of the many huts or shacks ("nigger hut") where soldiers were forced to find shelter. The word was almost universally used, in newspaper headlines of major city papers as well as in general parlance, and it was less indicative of an attitude than it is today. What is interesting, though, is that Sargent occasionally begins to use the words "negro" or "colored individual," and, as time goes on, more frequently expresses support for blacks, both for fellow soldiers and civilians.

His final note about Lincoln, after his assassination had been announced to the troops, is "the country loses a great, good, and honorable man, the colored man a firm protector." This statement represents a position not apparent at the start of his diary. At the end of the war, on the day of Lee's surrender, he reports that he and other white soldiers lined the sides of the road, "cheering and encouraging" black soldiers on. " 'Give it to them, boys, we've got them in a tight place! Show them what the colored soldiers can do.' " In short, his feeling that the war was being fought for emancipation, and for the Negro, increased over time.

Temperamentally, Sargent was a realist or a cheerful fatalist, and this was one of his main allies in getting through the war. Another of the survival attributes of this young man, who was at first too skinny to be admitted to the army, was his simple physical appetite. Something good to eat was a glorious thing, and a good Thanksgiving dinner inspired his most loving descriptions. He was also a person of deep curiosity, observing the countryside, feeling its mood, talking to captured enemies and finding out about their lives. He had a sense of wonder and a sense of history, and a plain spoken urge always to make sense of things.

Sargent grew up in the most terrible war for Americans, yet his document speaks to us, over time, of the best in our history, of a justifiable pride in our political institutions, our ability to transcend cultural conditioning, our resiliency and fortitude, and our capacity to fight for ideals without bitterness.

George Sargent was 5′9″ tall, of light complexion, brown hair, and black eyes. His official record of cavalry service confirms the facts given in his diary/reminiscence.

Nine years after the end of the war, in 1874, he married Josephine Nichols, and they had two children: Marion Nichols Sargent, in 1876, and Albert Edwin Sargent, in 1882. In one of his pension applications late in life, he listed his occupation as "druggist." He apparently outlived his wife, since she made no pension applications after his death in 1928 in Reading, Massachusetts.

Sargent's name is spelled "Sargeant" in about half of his official army and pension records. We have chosen "Sargent" because in his one reference to his name in the diary he uses that spelling. His diary is handwritten. It is difficult to read in places, especially where the lines get so close together that they are virtually superimposed, and we have doubtless made some mistakes in deciphering it. His writing style was quite good for his probable level of education, particularly in syntax, yet such matters as capitalization, parallel phrasing, consistency of verb tense, and punctuation are erratic. He uses commas and periods almost in a random way, often with the comma serving as the full stop and the period the briefer pause.

The Diary of George Sargent

In the fall of 1861 I caught the disease called war fever, which was spreading very rapidly about that time, [1] and if once fairly seated it is hard to be cured, no matter how much doctoring you have done. In November I applied at the recruiting office of the 24th Massachusetts Volunteers to make one of that regiment. I signed my name to the roll, then was told to make the surgeon a visit for inspection. I found him all ready to receive visitors, so I pulled off my dry goods and he made an examination. "Now" said he, "I advise you not to enlist. You may make a good soldier as far as discipline is concerned, but you had ought to be put out to pasture in order to fatten up a little. Your bones are too prominent. I will give you until tomorrow to think of it, and if you make up your mind to go, come in and see me." I thanked him for his good advice and left.

In looking over the *Herald* a few days afterwards, my eyes happened to alight on an advertisement that attracted my attention. "Wanted 24 young men to enlist in the 1st New England Cavalry and learn to play the bugle. Apply to music store." On the 30th November '61, I called again and signed my name to serve Uncle Samuel an apprenticeship of three years. Me and my valise together with three other blowers started from the store to take the 11:00 train for Providence. We arrived about 12:30, jumped out of the cars, and went in search of the surgeon. After walking through about half the city and asking numerous questions, we spied his name on the corner of a street, and all four of us bolted in. We found him attending to important business (eating his dinner), but he said he would attend to our cases in a few moments. After he got through, we were all inspected and pronounced sound in limb and wind. We went to the colonel's office to be sworn in, but when he learnt that we had not partaken of our noontide meal, he postponed it until after that event, thinking, no doubt, as we had a bad job to perform, we could stand it better on a full stomach.

After dinner we were sworn in, holding up our right hands, while the officer read off a long string of articles, signifying that we should do all in our power to aid and help the government, obey all our superior officers, and be good boys generally. Oh! thinks I, after this was over, I'm done for now, stuck for three years sure. However I'll grin and make the best of it.

It happened to be a great day in Rhode Island. All the militia in the state were to parade that afternoon, in all about three thousand. While I was standing on the sidewalk seeing them pass by, thinks I, this is all very good fun, playing soldier.

Early Monday morning we took the omnibus for camp, which was about three miles from the city. We reported to the chief bugler, and in the course of the forenoon we were supplied with uniforms. When I got it on, I felt like a cat in a strange garret, as though I didn't belong there. Next came dinner: We all had to fall in line with our tin plates, dippers and iron spoons, march up to the cook house and receive our rations *a la* Oliver Twist.

In the afternoon we got our bugles and went down to a pond about half a mile distant to practice. I have heard it remarked that music hath charms to split a rock, but I think the music that afternoon was enough to split a whole stone quarry. It was the first time I ever undertook to blow a wind instrument, but before night I felt competent to act as clerk to a fish peddler, that is I could do the blowing part. This pond was once a good place to fish, but after we had been there, the boys all swore that there was not a fish in it.

We were furnished with two blankets apiece, and a large bag, which we filled with straw, to answer for a mattress. I retired at nine, but with the cold and the strange situation, I could not get to sleep. About midnight I crawled out of the tent to thaw out beside the log fire. Next morning, we all turned out at reveille (sunrise). Soap and towel in hand, we started for the pond, broke the ice and performed our toilet. Come to look for my boots, I found I was a pair of governments out.

I thought it pretty tough living out in tents in the winter, but soon learnt that we were going to a new camp in Pawtucket, as soon as they got the barracks completed. In the meantime we were kept busy learning the art of handling the sabre, practicing on the bugle, and foot-drilling.

On Sunday, December 8th, we left Camp Hallett for our new one in Pawtucket, passing through Providence while the bells were ringing for church. It was a walk of about six miles, and we arrived there with a good appetite just before dinner. Our camp was situated on the race course about one and a half miles from the centre of the town. They selected that place I suppose, because it had a high fence around it and would probably keep the boys in.

All the musicians stopped together in one house. It had twelve bunks and accommodations for twenty-four. We had about the same routine of duty to go through every day, and when not on duty we were either playing cards, checkers, writing letters, reading, kicking football, or skylarking someway or other. The boys are a jolly crowd, and we enjoyed ourselves hugely. We had one minister among us, a Methodist. Another was an organist, and others were mostly clerks and mechanics.

About the middle of December, fourteen of the best musicians were picked out of the regiment for the purpose of forming a band, the instruments arrived a few days after, and, as we all understood music, after a little practice we played pretty smart. Besides the brass pieces, we had a full set of quadrille instruments, consisting of harp, violins, clarinets, piccolo, guitar, and bass viol. Most every evening, we would have music, and sometimes dancing; the only thing we lacked was partners of the female persuasion, but we had gay times for all that. Sometimes we had spectators from outside, and it wasn't long before we had invitations to play for parties in Providence and Pawtucket.

About the middle of January, four companies from New Hampshire joined our regiment, forming one battalion. They came all mounted and equipped.

About the latter part of January, a piece came out in the papers, saying that no more cavalry regiments were wanted, there being seventy in the field then. Every few days a new story would be circulated around camp. Either we were going to be disbanded, turned into infantry, or sent to the forts to guard prisoners. The boys began to be afraid that they would not have a chance to take a part in the mess, but some of the wiser ones said that we should see all the fun we would want.

One day while we were all in barracks, a man came in to sell some patriotic songs, composed, he said, by himself. He said he had been round to the different camps through the states and had sold quite a number. He wanted to sell us some and have our leader arrange it for the band. He would go out on the parade, mount a barrel or box and sing his song, then he would peddle them out at five cents apiece. A few evenings after, about half a dozen of us went to a prayer meeting in town and saw him there; he got up, made a few remarks, and prayed for the restoration of our beloved country. When we got to Virginia, this same codger came round our camp selling writing paper and postage stamps. In July, '63, just after the battle of Gettysburg, he might be seen by anyone travelling that way, hanging by the neck to the limb of a tree. He was caught a few days before, endeavoring to put our wagon train on the wrong road, so as to have it fall into the hands of the Rebs. He was searched, the documents found on his person proving that he was a Rebel spy. He was strung up to the nearest tree, without a trial, by General Buford just outside of Hagerstown.

On the 9th of March Governor Sprague received a dispatch from Washington wanting this regiment to be sent on as soon as possible to join the Army of the Potomac. As soon as the boys heard of this, there was great excitement in camp, the band was ordered out to play patriotic airs, the boys gathered in groups and let out some of the enthusiasm that had been corked up all winter, and everybody was highly elated at the prospect of soon seeing active service. All were anxious to get a pass to visit home once more. Some got it and some didn't, and some of those that did not took one on their own responsibility. I got one to go to town but extended it, myself, as far as Boston. I got back at noon on the twelfth and started that afternoon for Washington.

We reached Groton about midnight and took the steamer *Commonwealth* for New York, arriving at seven the next morning, and here we got 190 of our horses. We left the city at two in the afternoon in the steamer *Transport.*

The day was warm and pleasant, so I stopped on deck and enjoyed the fine scenery. Landed at four, took the cars for Camden, crossed in a ferry boat from there to Philadelphia, marched to the Cooper Shop Soldiers' Dining Saloon, and had supper at 10:00 that night. Left for Baltimore at midnight, crossed the Susquehanna, and arrived next morning at the same depot where the 6th Massachusetts was attached.

On the whole route, as the cars were going by, men and women would run out of their houses and wave a flag or a handkerchief or their hats. At Perryville one young lady, more patriotic than the rest, had on an apron made of stars and stripes, which she took off and waved as we slowly passed by the station. "Hurrah," cries out one of the boys, "that's the flag we're going to fight under." "Well," says she, "you can't fight under this one!"

All along from Baltimore to Washington, the road was well guarded, probably to keep the Rebs from making a raid on it, as the secession element is well represented here. [2]

We arrived in Washington in the afternoon of the fourteenth and put up at night in a building called the soldiers' retreat, erected for the accommodation of regiments arriving. That evening we got treated to our first meal of salt junk and hardtack. Thinks I, if this is the kind of grub we've got to live on for the next three years, I might as well go to some blacksmith's shop and have my teeth ground down to an edge.

A New York Zouave regiment had just arrived from somewhere and were waiting to be sent home, and they were the nastiest, dirtiest, ruggedest looking human beings that ever I laid eyes on. I wondered to myself if I should ever be as dirty. The 96th New York arrived the same night as ourselves. Troops were at that time pouring into the city at an average of half a dozen regiments a day.

The next day I visited the Capitol, went into the House of Representatives, Senate Chamber, saw those beautiful paintings by Turnbull, and went into the dome. From here you can see the city of Alexandria, and the country for miles around, and camps innumerable.

Saturday night we started for our camp, which was situated two miles east of the Capitol. It was raining hard, and the mud was ankle deep. We found barracks which were larger and better than those we had just left at Camp Arnold, one barrack large enough to accommodate a whole company. We are on the same ground where that large review of seventy thousand troops took place a short time ago. From where we are we can look in every direction and see encampments. There are at least fifty thousand troops in and around the city.

March 19th. Yesterday I took a stroll around the country, visited the congressional burying ground where there is a monument erected for every member who has died, saw the Potomac and the remains of a bridge that was burnt by the Rebs, also visited a fortification on a branch of the Potomac.

Last night we had retired as usual, but had not been to bed more than two hours when the captain rushed into the barrack and said that every man must be ready to march in a quarter of an hour. We thought we were to be initiated into the art of fighting that night sure, as we had heard firing all day. There was great excitement for a few moments, some looking for one thing and some another, and some couldn't find anything they wanted. "Whar's my sabre?" "Who's hooked my revolver?" "Who'll give me some cartridges for my carbine?" "I guess we will smell gun powder tonight," and similar remarks might be heard, but when the captain came in and said, "Boys you needn't take your arms," they cooled down a little. The question was where we were going this time of night. We were all in line at the appointed time, then started for the city. When we got almost there the captain told us that we were going to the depot to get our horses, which had just arrived. The mystery being solved, some of the boys felt easier. We led them out one by one and started back for camp, some riding bareback. We hitched them up in the stables and turned in again about 2:00. So much for our first scare.

The other day, one of our companies went to Bull Run battlefield with an ambulance to bring back the remains of the late Colonel Slocum, and other officers of the 2nd Rhode Island.[3] The same day, I had the misfortune to upset my rations of hot coffee on my arm, making it feel very uncomfortable. I called on the doctor and he gave me some laudanum, which relieved some of the pain.

We have the privilege of going to the city when we can get a pass, but some take the privilege without one. If they are caught by the patrol, they are given free lodgings in the guard house.

My first experience at horseback riding was rather a laughable one, or at least I thought it would have been to anyone who could have looked on and seen me, but I was pretty well scared at the time. We all had to go down to a brook about half a mile distant to water our horses. We had to go together, in line, walking them. My horse was exceedingly thirsty and was nearly the last to leave the brook. In order to catch up to the rest, I touched him up with a switch I had. He didn't like the feeling of it and started off a little faster than I wanted him to. In order to keep from tumbling off, I clasped my legs round under him, which made him shoot off like a streak of lightning. When I came up to the others, I sang out, "Whoa! Whoa! Whoa!" but he couldn't see it, and kept going faster the tighter I held on. When he came to the feed trough, he stopped all of a sudden, and over his head I went into the feed box among the oats. Come to look down at my feet, I found that I had both spurs on, the cause of all the trouble.

April 3rd. Today we had orders to be ready to start for the front early next morning.

April 4th. Reveille sounded at three, ate breakfast, cleaned, fed, and saddled my horse, but we didn't get started until eight. Passed through Pennsylvania Avenue, by the White House, crossed the long bridge onto the sacred soil of Virginia. About noon we reached Voailey's crossroads, where we stopped for lunch and fed our horses.

Every little distance, we passed an unoccupied house with the doors and windows missing, and sometimes nothing but the chimneys left standing. Everything looked sad and desolate, reminding one that it was time of war. We arrived at Fairfax Court House just before dark, where we stopped for the night. This is an inferior looking town, the houses old and dilapidated, and nearly all unoccupied.

There was but one shop open in town that was occupied by a Yankee as a sutler's establishment. He soon had plenty of hungry customers for gingerbread and root beer. I bought some bread and ham for my supper, then made preparations for a night's sleep. Some of the boys slept in the Court House and others outside. I made up my couch in a peach orchard, beside a fence, and hitched my horse to a peach tree. I spread my blankets on the ground, wrapped myself in them, and slept very well till morning, considering it was my first night in the open air.

We started early next morning and reached Autreville heights about eleven. This was a very strongly fortified place, there being about a dozen forts in a row on the top of the hill, and the space in front about a mile of smooth ground. It was impossible to capture from the front, but it could easily be flanked. The barracks were all standing just as the Rebels left them. The town is a small, dirty-looking place. We forded the Bull Run stream about four, going close to the battlefield, and arrived at Manassas, the once-celebrated stronghold of the Rebs, at six.

Next morning before starting off, we got the order to load our carbines and revolvers, and be ready to use them. After dark, we had to pass through a large piece of woods said to be full of Reb scouts, so we went through on the run. One of our captains saw, or thought he saw, two men crawling on their hands and knees, so he fired two shots, but I guess he didn't hurt anybody. Instead of sleeping on the ground that night, our company was fortunate enough to get into an old church. I occupied a front seat in the gallery. We arrived at our destination (Warrenton Junction) about noon on the 7th. It commenced to rain that forenoon and continued all day.

The roads were in an awful state; you can judge their condition by the time it took us (three and a half days). The distance from Washington is only about fifty miles. Sometimes it would take two or three hours to go a couple of miles, a wagon would get stuck fast, a dozen or twenty men would jump off their horses, get a rail from the fence side of the road, and pry it out. So it was, all day long.

We had to sit in our saddles two long hours in the rain, while the officers were looking out a suitable camping ground, and a detail of men to cut posts, sink them into the ground and stretch ropes across, to hitch our horses. By this time we got wet through to the skin, besides having our blankets soaked.

We were then told to erect for ourselves some kind of shelter, as each man had nothing but a piece of rubber cloth, about five feet by six. We didn't make out very well. We cut poles in the woods and made huts of all shapes and sizes, looking more like a band of travelling Gypsies than a military encampment.

Instead of putting us into the woods, as we had ought to have been, the Colonel put us into an open field on ploughed ground. The soil was soft, and, due to its being continually walked over, the mud began to resemble pudding.

Next morning there were several horses found dead at the picket line. They lay down to rest and got stuck in the mud, and, being weak from exposure, couldn't get up. In some places the mud was up to their knees. It continued raining, hailing, and snowing the next three days, and, not having a dry stitch of clothing during that time, nor even a fire, I began to think that a soldier's life was not always gay, and that this was a rather rough commencement. No doubt many of the boys wished themselves in their fathers' barns or some other dry place, but we thought if we lived through this we shall be pretty well broke in.

The water here was very bad, containing a great deal of sulfur. For two or three days after a rain, it would be about the color of coffee. It made us all sick, more or less, sending some to the hospital, where a few died.

Two of our band boys got their discharge on the strength of it, and one of them died after being at home some time.

April 10th. Today we were put into Abercrombie's Brigade, Bank's Division, together with the 12th and 13th Massachusetts. [4]

On the night of the twelfth we started off on our first night expedition. Word came that afternoon that Ashby's black-horse cavalry were in Warrenton ten miles distant. Our regiment, together with the 1st Maine, started about ten to try and capture them. Instead of taking the main road, we went across fields, through woods, over fences and ditches, and struck the road about half a mile this side of the town. We had got but a few miles from camp when my saddle turned. I dismounted, unbuckled the girt, buckled it up again, and found that I should have to make another hole in the strap before I could get it tight enough. I happened to have a knife in my pocket. By this time the column had got about a mile ahead. I began to feel pretty scared there all alone in a strange country. I was in such a hurry to mount my horse and catch up with the column that I forgot my knife and left it on the ground. I was very sorry in losing it because it was made a present to me before leaving home.

I went ahead some distance and, not hearing or seeing anything of them, began to think I had lost my way. I dismounted to see if I could find any tracks, leading my horse until I found the trail, then mounted and went in search of them. I found them after some trouble, then rode up and took my place in the line. "Halloa bugler," said the captain, "I don't want you to get lost. We may need your services tonight. Ashby's whole force is in town, and I guess we will have warm work." [5] I took a look at my revolver to see if it was all right. There were six charges in it, but when I came to cock it, I couldn't stir the hammer. I'd be in a pretty scrape if I had occasion to use it. It probably got rusted when it was exposed to the rain. Within half a mile of town, we halted, and the 1st Maine went a roundabout way to the opposite side of the town. When we had given them sufficient time to get there, we got the order to draw sabre and then charged on the full run into town. The clock was striking the hour of midnight as we passed through the streets. We found the town empty, the Rebs having got wind of our coming and left twenty minutes before we entered.

May ?. [6] The dead were brought in and the wounded attended to. While I was looking at the dead bodies lying side by side on the floor, I began to realize some of the stern realities of war, and to think what sorrow it will cause their families and friends when the sad news reaches them in their quiet homes among the granite hills. It almost made me sick, but such is the fate of war.

May 31st. Preparations were made for the funeral coffins, headboards were made of rough pine boards, and, when everything was ready, they were carefully lifted into the ambulance, followed by the men with reversed arms. We reached the graves, the chaplain read passages from the scriptures, and with uncovered heads we listened to a prayer. Then we saw the last remains of our dead comrades laid beneath the sacred soil of Virginia, buried there with a single slab of wood for a tombstone, to be soon forgotten except by those loving ones at home who have been waiting patiently for their safe return. From dust thou art to dust thou shalt return.

June 1st. The remainder of our regiment, the other two battalions, arrived, and we were ordered to join them. We camped in a grassy field near the banks of the Shenandoah. We stopped here two weeks, where nothing of any note happened. We went bathing occasionally in the river and foraging several times after cherries.

June 14th. Broke camp and started for Manassas Junction, passing through the towns of Salem, New Market, and White Plains. Salem is quite a neat little town containing three churches and two taverns.

June 16th. Reached the Junction about noon and camped in a large clover field near the Bull Run stream. In the afternoon we were reviewed and drilled by General McDowell. [7] I guess we were not quite to the standard, for we were kept busy drilling two hours, twice a day, for a month afterwards. A few days later we got a lot of "A" tents. The camp was laid out in streets, and we had orders to build stables for the horses. So many men from each company were detailed each day to cut timber and another lot to collect pine bows to cover the roof to protect the horses from the sun. Indications showed that we should stop here some time, so we fixed up a little ourselves. We planted young trees in front of our tents, made tables of cracker boxes, foraged boards from neighboring farmers to make ourselves bunks, and made ourselves comfortable generally. The regiment has diminished in numbers greatly, being only about half as large as when it left Rhode Island. Late marches used up the weaker sisters, sending them to the hospital. The 13th Massachusetts are but a mile from us, and I visit them quite often.

July 1st. We were visited by Governor Sprague, and on the second he reviewed us, and, notwithstanding rain, we were drilled two hours in his presence. When we got through, we formed in a hollow square and he made a speech, complimenting our battalion very highly for their conduct in the late fight. While at Camp Mud, our Colonel was taken sick and shortly after resigned. Now a new Colonel has just been appointed, his name Duffie (pronounced "Doof-yea"). He is a Frenchman and a Lieutenant in the French Hussars, in this country on furlough during the war. He was appointed Lieutenant in the Ira Harris Cavalry from New York, and held a Major's commission in the same regiment, at the time of his promotion to our regiment. It did not suit our Lieutenant Colonel to have an officer of an inferior rank taken from another regiment and placed over him, so he resigned, together with a major, chaplain and other officers. The Lieutenant Colonel's and Major's resignations were accepted, the others were not. It was not a great loss to the regiment; although they were good men, they did not know much about the military.

The whole regiment was down on Duffie at first. He could not speak English very plain, and at the first dress parade when he gave the order to draw sabres, the boys laughed and hooted. He rode up to the regiment shaking his sabre saying, "You think me one jackass, but I teach you, I make soldiers of you," and he did. I'll venture to say that a month afterwards there was not a better drilled regiment in the service. We perceived a vast difference after he took command: The officers had to study their tactics and recite to him every day, and he would go round inspecting the camp looking into the cookhouses to see if we had our full rations and looking to the welfare of his men generally. His first night in camp the band serenaded him, which pleased him much, and from that time forth the band began to prosper. A trust fund was established: Each commanding officer was to contribute so much each month, the chaplain had charge of it, and when a certain sum was collected it was to be divided among the band.

Before he came, the officers took no interest in the band, and of course the band took no interest in the regiment. I have seen them on dress parade with not more than half a dozen pieces with the bass drum, while the rest would be skylarking round the country at the neighboring farmers, or after cherries; now every man had to be on hand when duty called, or give a sufficient reason.

July 4th. Awoke this morning at five as usual (not by fire crackers), blew reveille, fed and cleaned my horse, dined on salt junk, soft bread, and coffee (whenever we stopped in a camp any length of time we were supplied with soft bread from the government bakeries in Washington, but on the march we always got hardtack) and at nine, four of us saddled up to pay a visit to Bull Run battlefield about four miles distant. We first visited a stone house occupied by an old man. In his yard there were fourteen of our soldiers buried in one grave. There were several holes in the old man's house made by shells or solid shot. The graves in some places were very thick; bones or a remnant of clothing sticking out, and in some instances the bodies would not be buried at all—merely a little dirt thrown over them as they lay on the field, the skull and feet exposed to view. We then went to where the famous Black Horse Cavalry made their charge, and there were several carcasses still lying on the field where they fell. We called on one of the farmers and got a lunch. On our way home we filled up with cherries.

July 5th. I received a box from home containing some of the good things that Uncle Sam don't furnish his laborers. It is needless to say that they were relished, after living on salt junk and hardtack for three or four months. The weather is extremely hot, the thermometer ranging some days as high as 104 in the shade; it is so hot in my tent that a tallow candle will melt. We have an excellent chance to bathe in Bull Run stream and improve the opportunity most every day. Blackberries.

July 20th. Today I joined the band, the leader thinking that cymbals would improve it. The Colonel objected to it at first, as we had but a few buglers, but the leader got his consent after making up some kind of a story. He started that day for Washington to buy a pair. I was well pleased with the change for several reasons: I was very fond of music, besides my duty would be lighter; and in case of a fight I would not be in so much danger. All we had to do besides taking care of our horses was to play at Grand Mounting in the morning, dress parade in the afternoon, and before the Colonel's quarters in the evening.

August 1st. We broke camp today after six weeks rest. We enjoyed ourselves while here, and this camp will be often thought of with pleasing recollection. Stopped for the night at Bristow Station.

August 2nd. Arrived at Rappahannock town this afternoon. The Colonel read to us the order from General Pope to live on the country. [8] As soon as camp was established, five of the band went out foraging for the whole band, bringing in corn and hay for the horses and turkeys and chickens for ourselves. Coming back, I had a race with the fastest horse in the regiment.

August 4th. Today four of us went out on a tour of observation, travelling about a mile when we came to a large house, probably a wealthy planter. We walked round the house without seeing anyone, then we spied a nigger. "Who lives here?" "My massa." "What's his name?" "Massa Bowen." "Is he secesh?" "I reckon he is, sah." "Has he got any sons in the Rebel army?" "One, sah." We knocked at the door and the old man himself came out. "We would like to be supplied with dinner for four of us." "I really don't know," said he. "I'll go and see my wife. Won't you step in?"

We went into the parlor, which was furnished very well, and presently the lady of the house came, followed by her daughter of sixteen or eighteen, who I suppose wanted to see some live Yankees. The lady commenced the conversation by saying that times were mightily hard, food high, money scarce, they had to bring all their provisions from Richmond, but, finally, she thought she might scrape up something. So she set one of the niggers at work getting it. Someone suggested that the young lady should play on the piano. No, she didn't play much, was out of practice, got a cold or something or other. So one of our boys sits down and plays a few pieces, mixed in with "Yankee Doodle" and "Star Spangled Banner." I looked at the lady and her daughter to see how that hit them, and it evidently did not sit very well on their crops. We sat down to a table with boiled ham, potatoes, corn bread, honey, and iced milk. The man and woman sat down with us but did not eat. We gave the meal ample justice, and they probably wondered if all Yankees had such appetites. When we got through, we expressed our thanks and said such a dinner as that needs no apology. We paid the old man in secesh scrip manufactured in Philadelphia, and then wended our way towards camp, thinking this was one of the bright spots in a soldier's life.

August 8th. We started this morning with the expectation of having a fight before night. We arrived near the foot of Cedar Mountain late in the afternoon. It was too late to commence work, and we laid on our armor with a prospect of a fight on the morrow. The Rebs occupied the mountain and its immediate vicinity. We could see dim objects moving to and fro, and in the evening could see their camp fires plain.

August 9th. We were up at five and in line of battle at six, the first regiment on the field, and for some time the only one. Finally we were joined by Maine, New York, Pennsylvania, and New Jersey cavalry regiments, and a battery was planted on a knoll near us. About the middle of the forenoon the Rebs threw a few shells as feelers to find out where our batteries were. But we kept silent. It seemed to me that both parties were afraid to commence, but I suppose we had not got ready. At noon there was a lively shelling from both sides for about half an hour, then everything was quiet until the middle of the afternoon.

We (the band) were lying in a piece of woods, our horses hitched to the trees, when someone sings out, "Here comes the Rebs." We were on to our horses in a half shake, in the excitement I left my sabre behind, I went back after it and hadn't been gone but a few minutes when they poured a volley into our regiment, which was in a field on the opposite side of the road. They had got around on our right flank, where we were little expecting them. We started back for the rear and met the infantry advancing in the line of battle. I was standing on a rail fence watching proceedings when a shell came whiz-z-z-z not more than ten feet over my head, then the teams, niggers, and lead horses began to skedaddle. The Provost Marshall ordered all non-combatants to the rear, and we went back out of the reach of the shells and halted.

By this time the engagement became general, the roaring of cannon and rattling of musketry was terrible. This was my first battle, and I had an idea that it must be a great one for the great amount of noise, but learnt afterward that it was merely a skirmish compared to some. Pretty soon a regiment came along, and, having been relieved, we joined and started back towards Culpeper. We met McDowell's division going to the front, I saw the 13th Massachusetts, and one of my friends wants to know if there is any fun going on up there? Yes, says I, much as you'll want to see. We camped that night in a barnyard three or four miles from the battlefield.

August 10th. Was up early trying to find out who got licked, but nobody seemed to know. Saw some officers on top of the barn looking through a field glass, went up there and learnt that the Rebs had left the field. Both parties claim the victory, but the Rebs crawled away during the night, so the victory can be chalked down on our side with safety.[9] We camped near Pony Mountain where we stopped one week, parties were sent out every day foraging. One day our crowd brought in a beehive, and trying to smoke the bees out some of the boys got stung.

August 18th. Arrived at the Rapidan River. This is the advance part of the Union Army. We found two regiments guarding the river, the Harris Light Cavalry and the 14th Brooklyn (Red Legs); but soon after dark they left, leaving us the only regiment in the face of a large force of the enemy, the force from the peninsula.[10] We had strict orders not to make any noise or to build any fires. Our regiment picketed this side of the river, the Rebs the other, firing at each other all night.

August 19th. At 3:00 this morning the chaplain went round waking the men, telling them to saddle up immediately, no bugle allowed to be blown. We stole off quietly, being followed close by the Rebs. We were rear guard. Passed through Culpeper playing "Yankee Doodle," while the Rebs were entering the other end of the town. Camped for the night at Brandy Station.

August 20th. This morning one of our boys killed a hen that he had been carrying some time in his feed bag when on the march. She laid an egg regular every morning, but he got hard up for grub and killed her. We saddled up early so as to be all ready to start as soon as the Rebs should make their appearance. We had waited an hour or two, when the Colonel wanted some music, and we had got all ready to play when three or four of the regiment who had been down the road to water their horses came rushing back saying the Rebs were coming. Their statement was verified by the popping of musketry. We left, the Rebs following at our heels all the way until we crossed the Rappahannock. Here we found our army had made a stand, the opposite bank bristling with cannon. As there was nothing but their cavalry following us up close, our whole cavalry force re-crossed the river, gave them a good thrashing then came back satisfied.

August 21st. Today about one hundred recruits joined our regiment from Rhode Island. Heavy artillery firing. Prospect of a fight. The whole army wagon train and non-combatants ordered to the rear to Cattlett's Station. The recruits went with us, as they had no horses or arms. We arrived at the station about dark, having been wet through on the way by a thunderstorm. We had got unsaddled and were making some coffee when we were startled by a volley of musketry and a yell. We were wondering what this could mean, when two or three infantry men rushed up to where we were and said their camp had been fired into by guerillas. We grabbed our revolvers and stood in readiness. "Put out your fires," says the quartermaster. "The Rebs are right on to us."

Two of our boys started off to ascertain what was the trouble; they didn't come back that night, and it was concluded they got taken prisoners. Every few minutes we would hear a volley and a yell, they charging on some part of the wagon train, destroying it, then firing up in the woods where we were. We kept quiet so that they would not discover our situation. It was the longest, most tedious, wearisome night I ever spent. I did not get a wink of sleep, it rained pitchforks, and was dark as Egypt. The situation was not a very pleasant one, surrounded by Rebs all night, expecting every minute to have them pounce in upon you. Towards morning they went off.

August 22nd. About daylight our two band fellows made their appearance covered with mud and water. We had given them up for lost. When they left us they went down toward the station, and, seeing a lot of dismounted men, went to find out who they were. It was so dark that you couldn't tell a Reb from a Yank, but they commenced to fire up into the woods and our men came to a hasty conclusion that they must be Rebs, so they stole quietly away, crossed to the other side of the track, and hid themselves in a ditch all night. I went down to the station to see what damage had been done.

The wagon train which had been parked round there had partly been destroyed, several sutlers' teams had been cleaned out. They stole about five hundred mules and several horses. Several bodies of both parties lay round the station. One Union soldier was shot on the platform of the station while crawling on his hands and knees and must have died instantly, for his knees were drawn up and his arms stretched out while he layed on his back. Another was shot for refusing to surrender his musket, which was still in his hands. Out of our regiment several were taken prisoners: one captain (the one who arrived from Rhode Island that day with the recruits), the wagon master, one or two blacksmiths, and one cook.

The recruits thought this was rather a rough initiation. Some were so scared that they climbed the trees and roosted there all night. All the fighting force we had was a few companies of Pennsylvania Rifles who had been guarding a bridge in the vicinity. The Reb force was the whole of Stuart's cavalry.[11] They had travelled around our army and struck us in the rear. The wagon train was destroyed, and it was said that they captured a large amount of specie. About noon, the head of McClellan's army passed here in the cars on their way to the front from the peninsula.

August 24th. Left for Warrenton, camped within half a mile of the city, dined with one of the inhabitants, a strong secessionist. He was confident of gaining their independence. This is the prettiest place I've seen in Virginia: The houses are neat and pretty, mostly of wood except on the main street, the sidewalks are brick, and it reminds one more of a New England town than any I've seen before.

August 27th. Left Warrenton and camped for the night near New Baltimore in a farmer's front yard, tying our horses to his fence. We made ourselves perfectly familiar with his cornfield and made the acquaintance of a barrel of cider which he had stored away in his barn.

August 28th. Arrived in the vicinity of the old battlefield of Bull Run. Our forces were massed in the area, and it was evident there was to be a fight. Our regiment went up to the front, leaving us behind. We remained here a couple of hours, then went up towards the front to see what was to be seen. We came to an open lot and were looking round, not thinking that any enemy was near, when a masked battery opened on us not more than an eighth of a mile off, the shell bursting over our heads. We took the hint and left, followed by more shells. Went back about half a mile. Did not know what direction to take. The firing seemed to be all around us, and we didn't know how our lines were situated. We thought if we could find our ambulances we would be all right.

After groping round in the dark about three hours, we found them and learnt that our regiment was three miles off. Started off to find them if possible, had to cross part of the battlefield, and the sights I saw then will always be fresh in memory. There lay the dead and wounded of both sides, the wounded groaning and screaming, men with candles, and stretchers looking for them, and carrying them to the rear; poor fellows too weak to stand alone were leaning against trees, having their arms or legs dressed or their heads bandaged. Others too feeble to stand were lying on the ground, the surgeons amputating their limbs; a gun dismounted, the cannoneers lying dead or wounded around it. Those are the sights I saw that night.

Presently, we were halted and told we couldn't go much farther without running into the enemy. We concluded we had got on the wrong road and turned back. On returning, we found the different regiments in line, and some officer calling the roll. After midnight we lay down to get a little rest, and had hardly got to sleep when the order came for us to fall back, as the enemy were advancing; we were woke up quietly, not a drum or bugle was heard, and started for the Junction which we reached at daylight. This was the battle of Groveton. [12]

August 29th. Left for Centreville, short of rations. We called on one of our neighbors, who we used to visit while we camped at Manassas. He furnished our crowd with meals and at night gave us a room which we all occupied, put our horses up in his barn, and took turns standing guard, for fear the infantry would steal them.

August 30th. Heavy fighting on the old Bull Run battlefield. Although three or four miles from the contest, we could hear the musketry very plain and see the bursting shells. The wounded came pouring into Centreville in streams, enquiring the way to the hospital. Part of Fitz-John Porter's corps passed through town, and for some reason that I'm not aware of, halted and did not take part in the fight. Towards night, our left wing gave way and the town was soon full of troops. The whole army fell back behind the fortifications at Autreville. It was one of the grandest sights I ever saw—between seventy-five and one hundred thousand men drawn up in line of battle. [13]

September 1st. Left for Alexandria. On the way my horse stumbled over something while galloping, turned a somersault, and threw me headlong into the road dust about three inches deep. I got up looking like a sugar-coated hill. Arrived there before dark. It commenced raining that afternoon and continued all night. As we couldn't get any poles to erect our shelter tents, the prospect looked good for our lying out in the rain. After considerable coaxing, we managed to borrow an "A" tent from one of the teams. These tents are made to accommodate two or three, but seven of us managed to pile in by laying heads at points. The rest thought they were fortunate in securing the dry spot under the wagons.

September 2nd. It turned cold during the night and in the morning groups of unfortunates could be seen shivering over miserable little fires.

September 4th. . . . Camped in the vicinity of Fort Corcoran. Here we are in a civilized country again, in sight of Washington, women and girls come round peddling pies, cakes, fruit (but not a red in my pocket). Is there anything more aggravating to half-starved men than having these good things placed before his eyes and not being able to obtain them?

September 19th. Broke camp and passed through Georgetown and Washington. It seemed good to get into a city again after living in the woods so long, to see the stores open, the horsecars running, children going to school. Camped that night at Brookville about seventeen miles from Washington.

September 21st. (Tuesday) Passed through Jamestown and arrived at Poolesville, playing a quickstep for the people to march out of church by. We arrived here ragged and dirty after a long campaign. We went into camp in a pleasant grove just outside of the town, and, as there was a prospect of our remaining here some time, we all drew a new uniform, coming out in bright colors. We stopped in this camp about two weeks, then went to a higher piece of ground the other side of the town. We enjoyed ourselves here hugely: nothing to do but play three times, take care of our horses, and cook our grub. Our rations were good and plenty of them, fresh beef, salt pork, potatoes, beans, dried apple, soft bread, coffee and sugar.

We had the favorite New England dish, baked beans, every few days, and cooked them as follows: parboil them first over a fire, dig a round hole in the ground, make a fire of hardwood, let it burn to coals, take out a shovel-full, put the camp kettle in, scatter the coals round the side, put a piece of tin or sheet iron over the hole, and cover the whole over with dirt, letting them stay overnight. Take the kettle out in the morning, and the beans would be smoking hot for breakfast.

The worst trouble we had was for the want of fuel. There were no woods very near, but there was a rail fence, and the way those rails disappeared after dark was amazing. Fruit here is plentiful, especially peaches, at about seventy-five cents a bushel. We went serenading some Union citizens in town several times, the population being about half Union and half Secesh.

Near the middle of October, Stuart's cavalry made a dash into Pennsylvania after horses and grub. On their way back they camped one night within two miles of us. A dispatch was sent to the force here intending to reach here at 2:00 in the morning so as to surprise us, but for some reason or other it did not get here till ten. Ours, together with three or four infantry regiments and a battery, started after them, but we were too late. They managed to get over the Monxsy River all safe with five hundred stolen horses. Then they planted their guns on the other side as if to defy us to come across. We came back with tails drooping.

Another lot of recruits.

The following is an address the Colonel made us recently on dress parade.

Head Quarters 1st R. I. Cav
Poolesville, Md. Oct 5th 1862

Special Order
In calling the attention of the regiment to the late campaign from the Potomac to the Rapidan and back, your commander wishes to

assure you of the high encomiums, which have been passed upon by officers high in rank and military attainments, upon the admirable manner in which you performed your part in that ever memorable retreat from the Rapidan to the Potomac. The last federal soldiers to leave the Rapidan, the last to leave the Rappahannock, the last to leave Warrenton and vicinity. In several of the severest battles, under fire many times, at all other times in outpost or other hazardous duty, and on almost every march the rear guard of the Grand Army of Virginia. You never faltered, you never once hurried, but steadily and in good order, as upon a parade, you retired when obliged reluctantly to turn from the superior numbers of the foes. Upon the 30th of August at Bull Run, it is especially true that when thousands around in direst confusion were escaping as best and as fast as they might, your evolutions were more steadily and perfectly performed than I have ever seen them at any other time. That is so true that you have by your beautiful appearance attracted the confidence of your brothers without commands, and soon behind your ranks were eight hundred seeming to implore your protection. Generals of divisions have been anxious for your services, and many applications have been made for them. You have endured fatigue and privations without murmuring. You are known and appreciated in the proper quarters. Soldiers, your record is a proud one, see that it is not blotted.

A.N. Duffie, Colonel Com.
1st Rhode Island Cavalry[14]

October 26th. A severe northeast storm, wind blowing very hard, got the order to be ready to march early next.

October 27th. Order countermanded, would be impossible to ford the river on account of the storm. Continued storming all night and part of the day, our horses which were out in the whole of it, were shivering, chilled through. The whole regiment was ordered out to exercise them. The Colonel took us on a jaunt of eight miles trotting all the way. Arrived back pretty well shaken up.

October 28th. The Colonel with one squadron went over first to reconnoiter; finding no enemy in town, sent for the rest. We first passed through a subterranean passage under the canal, then forded the river near Ball's

Bluff. [15] When we saw some of those ahead of us have their horses taken off their feet by the current, we began to shake in our boots, but the thing had to be done. It was almost deep enough in some places for the horses to swim, the current very swift, the bottom covered with big rocks. If your horse happened to stumble he was a goner, the rider making his way ashore best way he could. There were a few horses lost, but no men. I arrived safe on the opposite shore, my boots full of water (not a very pleasant sensation on an October morning).

We arrived in Leesburg, the regiment was divided into squads and sent in all directions to ascertain if the enemy were in the vicinity. We halted in the middle of the town, where a man came to us and wanted us to play "Star Spangled Banner." He said he was the only Union resident in town. The town is quite large and pretty, looks like a flourishing place in times of peace—paved streets, brick sidewalks. The women are very bitter. A school-teacher got her scholars out on the sidewalk and made them cheer three times for Jeff Davis. A scouting party was going out one day, and a young lady who was standing on the sidewalk expressed the wish that every one of them would be killed.

A couple of our boys were scouting around town and heard of some knapsacks that were stowed away in a barn. We went and helped ourselves, as we considered them captured property. They belonged to the 50th Georgia Volunteers. While here, fifty-seven of our regiment were taken prisoners while on picket. An old traitor living in the vicinity of the reserve pickets informed Stuart of our whereabouts and the exact position. His cavalry got in between the pickets and the reserves and made a charge capturing fifty-seven and killing one captain.

November 3rd. Left Leesburg and stopped one day near Montville. The regiment went out scouting, leaving us behind, and the farmer on whose place we stopped gave us half a bushel of potatoes, some meal, and bacon. Next went to Upperville, Little Washington, and Waterloo, stopping only a day or two in each place. The day we arrived at Little Washington it had been snowing all day. At night we cut corn stalks, laid them on the ground, and spread our blankets on them, sleeping quite comfortable. A few days previous, an order had been issued against foraging, but our mouths began to water when we saw a litter of young pigs. We went to the Colonel to see if we couldn't have them. He thought a minute and said, "Don't you let me hear them squeal." We chased them off about half a mile, and had fresh pork for breakfast next morning. We then camped in the vicinity of Warrenton for about a week. Heard of the removal of General McClellan. [16] Both officers and men felt indignant at first, but it soon blew over. Persimmons are very plentiful in this region. They are delicious when perfectly ripe, but get an unripe one and your mouth would feel as though it was tied in a knot.

November 23rd. Arrived near Falmouth, the Reb army are encamped at the opposite, their pickets can be seen pacing back and forth on the bank of the river, and their campfires by night. [17] They occupy a naturally strong position on the heights of Fredricksburg and are entrenching themselves. Our army is camped on this side in the vicinity of Falmouth in fields and woods. Drums and bugles can be heard from reveille in the morning till tattoo at night for miles around.

November 24th. Thanksgiving day. Have faint recollections of roast turkey, plum pudding and pies, but no such food for us. Those who have plenty of hardtack consider themselves lucky. I dined off of two dry hardtack. For three or four days we lived on almost nothing, owing to the difficulty in transportation. The railroad, which was torn up by the Rebs, is being relaid and will be finished in a few days. [18]

December 1st. We moved back two or three miles near Potomac Creek.

December 3rd. Received a box from home containing clothing, the eatable part being spoiled. As it was supposed we could stop here all winter, we went to work as busy as bees erecting for ourselves a log hut. After a few days labor we got it completed.

December 10th. Got the order to march at daylight.

December 11th. Were awakened from our slumbers before daylight by the booming of cannon. We knew by that, that our forces had commenced crossing the river. Got within eight miles of Fredricksburg when our brigade halted and dismounted. We played lively airs as the infantry were marching by on their way to battle. Remained there all day; at night tied our horses in a piece of woods and rested.

December 12th. Fighting at the front all day. Rumors that the Reb cavalry are in our rear. Ours go after them and are gone two days. No damage done except a few sutlers captured.

December 13th. Today was the heaviest fighting, such a roaring of cannon and rattling of musketry I never heard before, cheers could be heard occasionally; I suppose when they were charging their breastworks. [19] Professor Lowe made several ascensions in his balloon during the day. The Rebs fired at him, and once just as he was about to ascend a solid shot came very near hitting it.

December 14th. The troops began to recross the river, and next day we had orders to go to our old camps. Thus ended the first battle of Fredricksburg, another disaster for our side. Although we lay four days within sight of the town, our brigade did not fire a shot, and it was said that not more than half of the army were engaged.

We got orders to go into camp for the winter. As we were placed on different ground and had to build another hut, we commenced work immediately to make ourselves as comfortable as possible for the winter. After working like beavers four or five days, got it completed. At home it would be called a good pigsty, but out here it is a palace. It is about 12-by-25 feet made of logs notched together, the cracks filled with mud. The roof is made of small poles laid close together and covered with turf or sods. We have a fireplace in one corner and a chimney outside made of stones and mud topped with a barrel to make it draw well.

Inside, we have two bunks made of poles covered with hay, one above the other, two occupying each. Over the fireplace is a mantelpiece on which may be found the ornaments peculiar to the cavalry service. Our door was made from a cracker box covered with a rubber talmar and hinges made from an old boot leg. The side of the door was a window sash, which one of the boys foraged from an empty house in the vicinity. In one corner may be seen the cover of an old medicine chest stuck on four sticks that are driven into the ground. This was our table. Although our stock of furniture and cooking utensils was rather small at first to commence housekeeping, we made additions occasionally by Yankee ingenuity and from the sutler. Knives and forks were a scarce article, and, as fingers were invented before them, they had to perform the duty. Such dishes as we got up could not be found in any cook book: fried pork, boiled pork, broiled pork (on a stick), hardtack fried whole, hardtack broken up, soaked in water, and fried hardtack pounded up fine, soaked, molded by the hands in the shape of doughnuts, pork and hardtack à la frigage, ... "George, what would you like for dinner today?" "I was thinking of going over to the market and ordering some fish, as it is Friday, so as to accommodate our help. Matilda dear, I will stop on my way downtown and order some steak for dinner. I will be at home at 12:00 precisely. . . ." Dinner time arrives and our dreams vanish rapidly, rapidly, at the sight of hardtack and pork.

But after the paymaster made us a visit and the greenbacks began to roll in, our larder increased and we had the satisfaction of sitting down to more than one good square meal. With a good solid smoke by the way of dessert, we felt happy as clams at high water. After a while, when camp finally got established, our rations grew better. Soft bread and fresh beef were issued two or three times a week, but such meat? The animals looked as though they had travelled the roads of Virginia from the commencement of the war, and been fattened on army bread. We most always had to make soup of it, for if fried it was like so much shoe leather.

Washing day came round about once a fortnight. Sometimes we would be fortunate enough to hire some nigger to do it for us. I don't envy the job anytime. We would drive two crotched sticks into the ground with a pole across, on which a camp kettle would hang, build a fire underneath and let them boil a short time, put them into the tub (half a pork barrel), and scrub till every bone in our bodies ached and we wished it was the custom to follow the fashion of our first parents, Adam and Eve, and wear nothing but the fig leaf. I often thought that I should like to have some civilized folks look in upon us when we were either cooking, darning stockings, cleaning house, or washing. I guess they would enjoy a hearty laugh.

Sometime in the fall, the order was issued from the War Department allowing but one chief bugler to a regiment. Two was the number until then; our leader held that position and he was the lucky one to get his discharge. As the band had improved lately, the officers did not want it broken up, so they secured the services of a leader from Rhode Island.

December 31st. Our new leader arrived this afternoon. He proposed that we should commence the year by playing the old one out and the new one in. So we sat up past 12:00, commencing with "Old Hundred" and ending with "America." He plays the key bugle and is called one of the best players in this part of the country. Shortly after we got our extra pay from the post fund, it was proposed we should buy some new instruments. The old ones were all shapes and patterns and considerably the worse for wear. After much talk and arguing, it was finally agreed to get a full set of German silver instruments made by D.C. Hall of Boston.

In about two weeks they arrived, shining like a new silver dollar just out of the mint. They cost between $700 and $800. We got some new numbers, lots of new music, and by practicing every day we got the reputation of being one of the best bands in the corps.

We have the same routine of duty to go through every day, Sunday being the busiest one. Guard mounting at 8:00; inspection at 9:00; church services at 11:00; brigade review at 2:00; play before the Colonel's quarters at sundown, and sometimes go serenading after that. Dress parades are most always mounted; we have all grey horses, making quite a show up and down the line. We got a few new horses while here, and for the first few times playing on them they acted rather wild, but soon got used to it, going as steady as old veterans. They got so attached to each other and so accustomed to being together that it was almost impossible to go off alone, especially on my horse. If she was out of sight of the others, she would make a terrible fuss, or if we should all leave camp and one horse be left behind, there would be considerable neighing and stamping of feet, and if the halter was not very strong the animal would be pretty sure to get loose. Let a dark horse go in among ours and you would see heels flying in all directions.

When we were at Manassas our snare drummer was sick and did not go at guard mounting with us. His horse was loose, nibbling grass round the tents. As soon as he saw us start off, he followed on after; we tried to drive him back but 'twas no go. We took our position and he came and took his accustomed place in the rear rank. He marched up and down the line and wheeled just as if somebody was on his back. When we got through, he followed us back to camp and commenced eating grass again.

Sometime in January we had a new standard presented to us by the ladies of Rhode Island. It is a splendid silk one with the state seals of Rhode Island and New Hampshire, one on each side worked with worsted.

March 16th. Our whole division started on some kind of an expedition, played several lively pieces for our regiment to cheer them up while they were marching out of camp. Next day we heard the rumbling of guns in the distance, so we supposed they had run into something. On the afternoon of the eighteenth they came back, and looked as though they had seen rough usage, some with bandaged heads, and many empty saddles, the riders either killed or taken prisoner. When they got unsaddled, groups of men could be seen here and there relating their adventures, telling how many Rebs they shot, the hand-to-hand conflicts they had. Our regiment was the first to cross the river, and had to do it under the fire of sharpshooters, and lost in the fight forty-two. One lieutenant had his head blown off by a solid shot. A few of the wounded died afterwards. This was the first cavalry fight of any consequence and was called the battle of Kelley's Ford. The Reb cavalry were mostly young men who have been accustomed to ride horseback almost from their infancy and considered themselves superior to ours, but we soon found men with strong arms who knew how to handle the sabre and ride horses, even if they were northern mechanics.

April 2nd. We went off on a serenading expedition, first to General Hooker's Army Command, then to General Sterieman, our Corps Commander, where we were treated to a collation, next to the 2nd Rhode Island Infantry where we were well entertained. When we got through, one of the officers apologized for not being better prepared, and thanked us for the kind favor we had shown them. The whole regiment was standing round while we played, and as we were leaving the adjutant proposed three cheers for the 1st Rhode Island Cavalry Band, which was given with a will. Arrived back to our camp in the evening just as the buglers were blowing tattoo, rather tired but well pleased with our day's proceedings. When Hooker took command of the army the cavalry were formed into a separate corps.

April 6th. Today all the cavalry belonging to the Army of the Potomac was reviewed by the President. The force was between fifteen and twenty thousand strong, making a grand show, a sight not to be seen outside of the army. We were put into the place assigned us, waited an hour or two, heard music in the distance, and presently he came galloping along followed by two or three hundred officers of all rank. We struck up "Hail to the Chief," playing until the next band on our left commenced then. I must say he is the most awkward looking figure on horseback I ever saw, long legs, dangling down most to the ground, his body bent forward, looking as though he was about to pitch headlong, and an old stovepipe hat many years behind the fashion. We then formed in platoons and marched by him in review. As we got opposite him, we wheeled out and played until our brigade got by, then followed on behind. As we stood in front of him, I could not help but notice how pale, haggard, and careworn he looked, as though there was a heap of trouble on the old man's mind.[20] As each brigade passed, they took the nearest route to their several camps.

April 13th. . . . During the last part of our stay in winter quarters, wood became very scarce. When we first came here the camp was in a thick forest, but now hardly a tree was to be seen. The boys would go round chopping down the old stumps. When that supply gave out, we had to hire a team to go off a few miles for a dollar a load. The winter was a very mild one, there being but a few days that an overcoat was needed. We had a few snow storms, but it would not lie on the ground any length of time.

April 14th. All those left behind in camp were ordered to be ready to march early next morning for Dumfries. The idea of leaving our comfortable log huts where we had enjoyed ourselves hugely for four long months to enter upon another long, dreary campaign, exposed to all kinds of weather, was not a very pleasant one. During such a long stop in one place, many articles would collect which would be handy and useful in the future, but, as our travelling accommodations were not on a very extensive scale, we could take nothing but what was actually necessary. All clothing that you could possibly do without, all extra cooking utensils, blankets, and rations had to be left behind in order to make the load for your horse as light as possible.

April 15th. Was up early, attended to my horse, got breakfast, horse saddled and packed by daylight, but did not start for an hour or so after. Before we left, we had orders to burn our houses and everything we could not carry. While witnessing it burning, I thought of the good times we had together under its roof, and the shelter it afforded us from the number of storms. It seemed like losing an old friend.

Our old Colonel started on a twenty-day furlough.

We started off in a rain storm, and it continued all morning. Passed through Stafford Courthouse. In the afternoon we came to a stream that was too deep and swift to ford and had to wait until the next morning. Started in search of some old building where we could find shelter and make a fire to dry ourselves. Found an old saw mill where we stopped a short time. I emptied about a half a pint of water out of each boot, and thought a fire would not feel bad. Presently one of the boys discovered an old building, formerly a nigger hut, where there was a fireplace. The lower floor was occupied by some infantry, who were encamped in the vicinity, as a cookhouse. They said we could stop upstairs, providing we slept on those rafters. Some party had torn the floor up, probably for firewood. An old blacksmith's shop was not long in coming down, the boards serving to make us a floor. The party downstairs generously furnished us with a supper of fried ham, cakes, cheese and hot coffee. We made a roaring fire, dried ourselves, and went to bed, thinking we were lucky dogs to fall into such company.

April 16th. Left at 7:00 this morning and after halting about a dozen times for the teams that got stuck in the mud, arrived in Dumfries at 3:00 in the afternoon. As there was an empty house in town, we took possession of it. It is a large structure on the main street and is at least one century old. We sleep upstairs, use the parlor for a rehearsal room, hire a nigger to do our cooking, and live in grand style. Our horses are hitched in the yard, and we take turns standing guard over them at night.

The town is a little, low, dirty, nasty, muddy hole, situated on a stream from the Potomac—not a sidewalk or even a curb stone to be seen. The houses are old and dilapidated and haven't seen paint for at least half a century. It is said that it was once a large and flourishing place. It was the first tobacco port in Virginia, and contained the courthouse where Patrick Henry made his celebrated speech, but it is now torn down, the soldiers using the bricks to make chimneys for their winter huts. It also contains the house where Washington spent his early days at school. Our next-door neighbor was a New Hampshire Yankee who makes his living by catching shad in the Potomac, and we were well supplied in the fish line.

April 20th. All the infantry that were quartered here during the winter left for the front. We went out in front of the house and played while they passed by. One Colonel was so pleased at the idea that he gave the order to "left into line, wheel," then said, "Boys give nine cheers and a tiger for that band," and they did give it. Although such little acts were not in our line of duty, we were always ready to perform them because it put the soldiers in good spirits and left a good feeling behind.

April 29th. The General Commander of this post and officers took a trip down the Potomac to inspect the shores, and, as they wanted some music, they invited us to go along with them. The steamer was a small one about the size of a large tug boat, and we enjoyed the trip muchly. The officers amused themselves coming back by firing their revolvers at ducks and other fouls in the water. We have guard mountings and dress parades every day, reviews, inspections, drills, etc. Although there are two other bands here, we have to furnish the music for almost every occasion, keeping us pretty busy.

May 5th. Heard rumbling of guns in the distance, supposed to be a battle. A few days after, we heard that it was the battle of Chancellorsville and the repulse of our army. [21]

May 10th. Our old Colonel arrived here on his way to the front. He stopped one day, then started off to take command of our division, General Averill having been arrested for disobeying orders. Serenaded him in the evening. He sat in front of his tent smoking a cigar, evidently feeling very happy on his promotion.

May 13th. Early this morning we got the order to report to our regiment, at Potomac Creek Station. We got all ready and were off by nine. Our luggage was conveyed in a team while we had to foot it five miles to the Potomac. We met the mail carrier on the way and all sat down under a tree while he picked out our letters. We arrived at the wharf pretty tuckered out, not being used to playing infantry. Got on board a tugboat and were waiting for our baggage to get along. But as soon as the captain found out that our team had got stuck in the mud he let the lines go and we were soon afloat on the broad Potomac, steaming down the Acqua Creek about twenty miles. Before we arrived at the wharf, we struck up a lively air and soon had a large crowd to see what was coming.

This was the depot for all government goods arriving from Washington. All size and shape buildings could be seen, from the large government warehouse down to the two-cent sutler's shop, great piles of hardtack boxes, barrels of pork by the thousands, stacks of arms, saddles, horse equipment of all kinds, ammunition, tents, and everything pertaining to warfare. The streets were crowded with blue uniforms, some patronizing sutler's, others dining saloons and photographers. By the prices they charge, I should judge they made money.

The harbor is full of all kinds of craft from a miniature representation of Noah's Ark to an ocean steamer. As the train did not leave until 3:00, I went into one of the numerous dining saloons for dinner, sat down to a table with a white cloth and crockery ware. The principal dish on the bill of fare was baked beans, so I regaled myself with a plate, together with a piece of pie, all for fifty cents. Left at 3:00 on the top of the baggage car, had to hold on tight to keep from being shook off, the roughest road I ever travelled on. The distance was ten miles. We found our regiment encamped beside the railroad a short distance from the station. All our baggage was behind, and we had to rely on the generosity of our brother soldiers for grub and sleeping accommodations.

May 14th. Our baggage arrived all right, and we got our horses back.

May 15th. Our regiment moved camp about a mile into a beautiful oak grove. In front of my tent is a large honeysuckle bush full of blossoms.

May 16th. Went to serenade our old Colonel, now commander of the division. On our way back we stopped at the hospitals where there are between three and four thousand men who were wounded in the last battle, and we soon had a crowd of cripples around us. It was a sad sight to see them, some hobbling on one leg, others with an arm gone or wounded in different parts of the body. Behind the house used for the surgeon's head-quarters there was a stack of fine coffins, all ready for the first poor fellow who gave up the Ghost.

May 18th. Two of us started off at half past two to find the 13th Massachu-setts. Got on the wrong road, went five or six miles out of the way, and found them at five. Nearly all the old acquaintances are gone—either killed, wounded, or discharged.

May 20th. Went and played for the wounded soldiers again. One of the doctors told us that when we played there before, some of the men left their beds for the first time since the battle and have not taken to them since. He said it done them more good than all the medicine he could give them. So you see we are doing something for our beloved country.

May 31st. Went to Warrenton Junction and stopped near our first camp-ground (Camp Mud). We lay here about a week, nothing of any note happening.

June 7th. Heard that the Reb cavalry was near Culpeper. Marched until eleven at night, and lay down to get some sleep at half past twelve near Morrisville. Seemed as though I had slept about five minutes when we were rousted up at two and resumed the march. We approached the river shortly after daylight and could hear skirmishing plainly on the other side. We stopped at a place called Mount Holly Church where our hospital headquarters were to be. The regiment kept on to join in the fight. Shortly after, the wounded began to arrive, and the surgeons commenced their operations by binding up wounds and amputating legs and arms. In the afternoon about seventy-five wounded Rebs arrived, a large part of them had sabre cuts on the head, showing they had been in close action.

One poor fellow had his leg shattered close up to his thigh. As he lay on the amputating board, he begged the doctor to save his leg. The doc told him it was impossible to do so and save his life, so he administered chloroform and commenced his bloody work. He cut the flesh all around the leg to the bone with a large carving knife, then slipped up the skin a little ways so as to allow enough to cover the stump and saw it, then finished the job with a saw resembling very much a butcher's. As soon as the man came to his senses, he asked the doc if he thought he could live. The doc thought there was a good prospect of it, as he looked to be a strong and healthy man. I had seen enough of this horrible and sickening work and left.

This was mostly a cavalry and artillery fight called the Battle of Beverly's Ford. [22]

June 16th. Heard rumors about the Rebs trying to make their way into Pennsylvania. [23] Crossed the battlefield of Bull Run, and it was still strewn with knapsacks, muskets, cartridge boxes, pieces of shell, round shot, carcasses of horses, and other warlike material. The bones of many a poor soldier were exposed to view. One I noticed in particular whose skull and feet could be seen. At the head of his grave was a bayonet stuck into the ground with his cap, belt, and cartridge box on it. Stopped for the night a few miles from Aldie.

June 17th. Reached Aldie about noon. This morning Kilpatrick's men had a fight in the vicinity and were repulsed. As soon as our regiment arrived we were sent to find out the whereabouts of the enemy. We soon found out to our satisfaction. In this fight we lost nearly the whole of our regiment. [24]

June 21st. What there was left of the regiment was ordered to report to the commanding officer at Alexandria. Camped for the night at Fairfax Court House. Reached the city about noon, and camped within the city limits in a field near the bank of the Potomac. I take a walk through the streets of the city every day to see the fashions, etc., but after I arrive back to camp I generally feel pretty blue when I look at my four-by-six tenement with the ground for a bed, then think of the comforts the inhabitants are enjoying all around us. But it's glorious to have a country that's worth suffering for. We play every evening at sundown, and many of the residents turn out to listen to us. The young secesh bring the gals round to hear a Yankee band.

June 29th. Left Alexandria, crossed long bridge, passed through Washington, and camped in the suburbs near the President's summer residence.

July 2nd. Was lying in my tent meditating on the future when one of the boys came along with a box on his shoulder and says "Here's a 4th of July present for you, Sargent." I jump up and see my box that I had given up for lost, a most welcome stranger. The boys did not like the idea of being shut up in camp when so near the city after so long an absence, and they thought there was too much ceremony in getting a pass every time they wanted to go off a little ways, so a great many took the liberty of leaving without one. This did not suit the officers; they thought it was not according to tactics, so the next day, the third, we had to pack up and move to the other side of the river on the Virginia shore, camping on the side of the road between Washington and Alexandria.

July 4th. We (that is, the band) got an order to report to General Winder's headquarters in Washington. This, though entirely unexpected, was received with pleasure, because we were wishing we could spend the day in the city. We put our horses up at a stable. The same day all our regiment who were equipped and mounted were sent to the scene of conflict in Pennsylvania near Hagerstown. (There they saw our songman hanging by the neck to the limb of a tree.) We played a few pieces in the morning and then were dismissed until evening. This fourth made me feel more like being at home than the last one—to hear the ringing of bells, salutes, popping of firecrackers and cracking of pistols. At noon we all sat down to a good dinner by ourselves and wound up with music and singing. Stopped in a hotel at night, sleeping in a bed the first time for fifteen months.

July 5th. Went back to camp this afternoon and had just got our tents up when it commenced raining. Forgot to dig a ditch round it and before morning was all afloat. One night sleeping in a feather bed, the next in a mud puddle. I thought this was going from the sublime to the ridiculous. Great uproar by cannonading from the navy yard and different fort. Soon learnt it was for the victories at Vicksburg and Gettysburg.[25]

July 6th. Went into Washington again this evening to serenade General Duffie at the National, our old Colonel, he having got the star on his shoulder. Put our horses in a livery stable, and stopped at the same hotel as before. Between every piece, the crowd would sing out for Hooker, old Hooker, fighting Joe Hooker, etc., to make his appearance, they thinking we were serenading him, but we did not know until then that he was there.[26] General Duffie showed himself but did not make any speech.

July 9th. Moved camp again nearer the river, so as to be handier to water our horses. The advantages for bathing are excellent, and we improve them every day.

July 11th. This afternoon we had the severest thundershower and gale that I've experienced since being in the army. The lightning struck a tree back of our tents, and the rain came down in torrents. George and I sat at each end of the tent holding on to the poles to keep our frail tenement from capsizing, but pretty soon a young hurricane came along and down she went in the hardest of the storm. The best that we could do was to grin and bear it. It did not last a great while but long enough to make us look like drowned rats, besides soaking our blankets, spoiling our writing material and rations.

This camp is called a dismounted camp and is a rendezvous for all cavalry men coming from hospitals, exchanged prisoners, or men who lose their horses in battle. They come here to get equipped and mounted, and every few weeks a squad goes to the front to find their different regiments. There are two or three thousand here now, representing over fifty regiments.

Toward the last of the month, great preparations were made for a grand military ball which was to come off at headquarters on the first of next month. The two bands, ours and the 1st Massachusetts, were to furnish the music. String instruments were procured, and a stand erected for the musicians. The night was a lovely one. Chinese lanterns hung in the different trees, flags were displayed in conspicuous places, and altogether it looked splendid. The fair sex began to arrive at an early hour in carriages, rigged out in silks and satins, adding much to the brilliancy of the scene.

Early in the evening a crowd of the boys gathered round at a respectable distance to see the sport, but were ordered to their quarters by the officer of the day. They went away for the time being, but were back again some time afterwards. They were ordered away again and a guard placed around so they could not see anything that was going on. This did not suit the boys very well, so they determined to have revenge and some fun on their own hook. They formed themselves into a storming party and made a desperate charge on a sutler's establishment where the officers procured their meals, tore down the shanty, broke the crockery ware, set fire to the remains, fired their revolvers into the air, and had a gay time generally. About this time the dancing stopped, the officers tore round half-crazy, ordering their orderlies to saddle their horses, bring them their revolvers, etc. The ladies turned pale with fright, wanting to know if there was any danger, and I am not sure but some fainted. The officer of the day got the guard together and proceeded to the scene of conflict. He didn't get quite there, for, owing to the darkness and his hurry, he fell into a sink hole in the ground where the eating house folks threw their swill and slops. When he got out, the appearance of his white breeches was not much improved. The tracks he made towards his tent were not slow, the crowd yelling and hooting at him all the way. Dancing was ended for that night, so we started for our humble dwellings feeling well pleased with the night's sport.

August 2nd. All the men who were mounted and equipt had orders to pack up and be ready to start for the front to their respective regiments.

We left about five in the afternoon, passed through Alexandria, and halted for the night at Fairfax Court House about midnight, having marched seventeen miles. I slept on the soft side of a board (side which is down) until daylight, when we were off again, passing through Centreville and halting beside Bull Run stream at 10:00, through the heat of the day.

Cooked our dinner, went in bathing and started again at five, marching until midnight when we reached Cattlett's Station, where we stopped all the next day.

August 5th. To Warrenton where we stop four days. The New Jersey Brigade are camped near us. They have a fine band. Hearing that the rest of our regiment were at Thoroughfare Gap, we started for there on the ninth, it being only eight miles, and found them there. The weather lately has been terribly hot and the roads dusty, the sweat pouring off both ourselves and horses.

August 10th. Two men from each company start for Rhode Island after conscripts, and our leader after musicians. This is a gap in the Blue Ridge Mountains and is a noted place for guerillas to hide; it is not safe to go out of sight of camp alone; squads go out scouting and bring in two or three most every day.

August 13th. Left the Gap, passed through Warrenton, Sulfur Springs, crossed the Rappahannock, and camped about two miles on the south side. As the prospect for stopping here a little while was good, George and I thought we would make a bed raised from the ground a couple of feet and cover the rails with dry leaves. We worked hard all the afternoon and had the pleasure of sleeping on it one night.

August 14th. This morning very unexpectedly we heard the bugler blow "Boots and Saddles." We knew very well what that meant, and acted accordingly. We recrossed the river, passed over the same road, and camped near Warrenton.

Sulfur Springs might have been a handsome and fashionable place before the war, a sort of Saratoga of the South. There were two very large hotels; one was in ruins, the other used as a hospital by our troops. Warrenton, as I've said before, is a pretty place containing three or four hotels, four or five churches, and whole blocks of brick stores. There are also a number of pretty girls here, but they will not even look at a Yank, although they are dependent on Uncle Samuel for rations.

August 18th. A squad of conscripts arrived for a Pennsylvania regiment. They are guarded night and day and watched as close as a flock of sheep: one of them cannot even go to the spring after water without a guard going with him.

August 30th. . . . Where there is no money, tobacco is scarce. The next best thing we could do was to smoke dry coffee, a very good substitute.

September 12th. Broke camp and just after getting our tents down we were treated to a thundershower, getting a ducking to start with. Camped in the woods for the night on the south side of the river, nearly blew my brains out over a smoky fire trying to create a blaze, gave it up as a bad job, rolled myself up in a wet blanket and went to sleep without my usual cup of coffee.

September 13th. Started at 4:30 this morning in a cold, drizzling rain, passed through Jefferson, and came to the Reb pickets four miles this side of Culpeper, driving them in. Got within sight of the town, where we halted for half an hour for a reconnaissance. When everything was ready, the whole corps charged, and our division at the centre, passed through the town. We went through the streets on the jump, and from a window of one of the houses I saw a woman shaking her fist at us and muttering something. I was in a hurry and did not stop to hear what she had to say.

The Rebs made a stand about half a mile the other side of the town on a knoll where they planted their artillery. The shells began to fly over in our direction, some of them coming uncomfortably near. One of them took a man's leg off a little ways in front of us. The Colonel then ordered us out of the ranks, we went to a house where the hospital was established and where we could see everything that was going on. Guns were brought to the front, a dismounted skirmish line was thrown (not far from the guns), and preparations made for a fight. I sat on my horse, watching our skirmish line crawling up the brow of the hill to pick off their gunners. When they limbered up and started off on the skedaddle, our boys followed at their heels.

The doctors were kept busy all night, attending to the wounded. That night part of us slept on the floor in the garret of a deserted nigger hut. The articles in the room looked as though they had not been disturbed for half a century, there being about a quarter inch of dust on everything, but we were glad to get anywhere under cover from the rain.

September 14th. Started off this morning in search of our regiment, passing through the old Cedar Mountain battlefield. We found our division drawn up in line of battle within two miles of the Rapidan, but our regiment was up to the front skirmishing. In the afternoon I was ordered back to the hospital to take care of the wounded by the brigade surgeon. We took possession of a neat little church near the foot of the mountain, threw the pews out of the window, brought water, laid straw on the floor and made everything as comfortable as possible for the wounded. Presently a couple of ambulances drove up in front of the door, the crippled were helped out, and the surgeons looked at their wounds. If amputation was necessary, they were laid on the board, the surgeon rolled up his sleeve and commenced operations with the carving knife and saw. I helped carry one of my company up to have his arm taken off. Two others from our regiment had their arms taken off, one being amputated at the shoulder. Stayed up all night, making beef tea, bringing them water, wetting their wounds or doing any little job that we could.

September 15th. More wounded brought in. Tonight we took turns sitting, relieving each other every two hours.

September 16th. The infantry arrived and camped at the foot of the mountain.

September 17th. They passed by here on the way to the front. Prospect of having a big fight. The wounded were placed in ambulances and carried to the cars on their way to Washington.

September 18th. Our brigade was ordered back to Culpeper. We had been away from the regiment five days and were all out of rations. Lived on green corn and string beans for the last two or three days. It rained that afternoon, and I went to bed feeling rather blue, being wet, tired, cold, and hungry. I had been there about half an hour when someone sang, "Here's the mail." I listened for my name. I heard it. One letter and papers. Spirits rose a few degrees, but, having no candle, had to postpone reading them until morning.

September 29th. A sergeant in the headquarters guard (6th Reg) was stabbed by one of his own regiment and died an hour afterwards.

October 10th. Had orders last night to be ready and march at daylight. Next morning was up early getting my breakfast in the dark, and started on the retreat. Crossed the Rap about noon on a pontoon bridge, the weight swaying the bridge to and fro, making the horses walk as though they were drunk.

October 20th. Passed through New Baltimore and camped at Warrenton. Here the general had his tents pitched in the front yard of the mansion of Extra Billy Smith, Reb Governor of Virginia. The mornings and evenings are pretty cold, and when we stop at night there is a grand rush made for rail fences. While here, a sad accident happened to one of our band boys. In every camp we are greatly troubled with loose horses that have either slipped or broke their halter, or from some old plug that has been turned loose to forage his own rations. When loose, they will always take a straight line for someone's tent and try to steal his grain bags. That morning an old played-out horse hobbling on his legs had bothered us considerable. One of the boys who was writing got tired of throwing sticks and stones at him, so he took up a rail and charged with a bayonet on him in the rear. This didn't suit the horse, for he stood on one foreleg and let the two hind ones fly up behind, and the fellow got the full force of the blow from one leg, hitting him on the side of the head, breaking the bone between the eye and temple. He was insensible the rest of the day and night and next day was sent to the hospital. The doctor was afraid it would stick to the brain and prove fatal.

October 27th. Broke camp and went to Auburn Mills, where we stopped three days. Rail fences here were plentiful, and as soon as we arrived a grand charge was made for them. The one getting the biggest pile was the best "feller." The old farmer stood with his hands in his pockets looking on, not daring to say a word, having on a doleful looking face and probably thinking to himself "Goodbye rails."

November 9th. Crossed the Rappahannock River and camped a mile and a half from Brandy Station, where we stopped a little over two weeks, on the same ground that the Rebs occupied a few days before.

November 11th. Was pretty cold, the brooks being froze over for the first time.

November 14th. We had a severe thunderstorm towards night, the rain coming down in such torrents as to flood part of our camp. Myself and blankets got pretty wet, and, to keep from freezing, had to stand shivering over a smoky log fire all night. Towards midnight, I got so sleepy that I couldn't stand, and lay down on the wet ground to rest but could hardly get to sleep before getting chilled through, then I would go to the fire and thaw out again. How would you like that, all ye individuals who have never slept outside of a featherbed?

November 17th. The 6th Corps were reviewed near our camp. It was a grand sight. Afterwards, two men were publicly branded on the back with the letter "D" for deserting.

November 25th. Had orders to be ready to march the next morning (Thanksgiving). Was up before daylight, poking round in the dark, picking up frosty chips to start a fire with to cook my breakfast before starting. Started off at an early hour and passed through Stevensburg at noon, eating my Thanksgiving dinner on horseback, consisting of boiled beef, hardtack and cold coffee. The weather was so cold that I did not take any comfort of eating even that. Stopped for the night in the woods beside the plank road leading to Chancellorsville.

November 30th. . . . As the day was very cold, we laid in a good stock of rails for night, and long into the evening we sat round the blazing wood smoking our pipes, talking of home and telling stories, then rolled up in our blankets we slept in a circle with our feet to the fire.

December 1st. For some reason that I'm not aware of, the troops started back on the retreat; perhaps the Rebs held too strong a position, or perhaps the generals could not agree on the mode of attack. Anyway, General Meade ordered the army to fall back. We did not start until after sundown, then started on the double quick over that worn-out, broken-down and dilapidated plank road, holding my breath for fear that my horse would stumble and some of those behind would run over me in the dark. This road, I understand, was built some years ago by several wealthy gentlemen of Culpeper and Richmond for a pleasant carriage drive. But after having a few wagon trains pass over it, it was pretty well used up. Recrossed the river and camped near midnight.

December 10th. Started early and reached Catlett's Station about noon, our leader got no musicians, nor the men any conscripts, they concluding in Rhode Island to fill up the infantry regiments first. We found that our regiment was divided into detachments stationed along the railroad to guard it, and scout round after guerillas which are very thick here.

Sometime in the fall the order was issued from the War Department allowing all veteran regiments to re-enlist, no man was entitled to the privilege unless he had been two years in the service. Stump speakers went round to the different camps, stirring up with a long pole in the shape of speeches the patriotism of the soldiers, on the same principle as they do just before a political election at home. One evening about the middle of the month, a cavalry regiment passed by our camp talking, laughing, singing, etc. I thought they felt uncommonly happy, so I sang out, "Where you going boys?" "Going home, re-enlisted." Bully for you. That was enough to make any soldier happy—the idea of seeing home after two years' absence—but the prospect of three years more service which lay behind the furlough was not very encouraging to look ahead to.

Towards the last of the month, the reenlisting committee got round to our camp and we were drawn up in line to learn the propositions and listen to speeches. While they were collecting a sufficient quantity of wind, the band played several soul-stirring and patriotic airs. Then several speakers made short remarks telling us what a righteous, holy and noble cause we were fighting in, how sweet it was to die for one's country, etc., but I was not particularly fond of sweet things about that time. How the Rebs were getting discouraged, their food was giving out, they were deserting by thousands, and the backbone of the rebellion was already broken (once more). The war would end in about a year, etc. Then the band struck up. After giving three cheers, the men went to their tents. "Going to re-enlist, Lang?" "No, I don't see it! Three years are enough for me."

Next day an officer went to each company to take down the names of those who were willing. About half of our crowd were in favor of it, the other half against it. We were given several days to think the matter over, and during that time many more signed their names including my bunky, then I began to look at it with a sober thought, lying awake nights thinking of both sides of the questions. I had got one year more to serve anyhow, and I thought if the war should last three years longer I would stand a chance of being drafted during the other two years, and if it did not last but a year I would have the bounty and furlough both. The officers promised to keep the band going, and, as the position was an easy one, we thought it would be wise to hold on to it. The inducements held out were as follows: $400 from the government, $300 from the state and thirty-days furlough. The bait was so good that a great many were caught, and the desire to see home again after a two-year absence was so great that I at last yielded, and, on the 4th day of January, 1864, I signed my name to the roll to serve three years from that date.[27] The rest soon followed, making the whole band, except three who had not been in the service two years.

The New Hampshire Battalion was detached from our regiment and was to form the nucleus of a regiment from its own state, and the commanding officer said that I could be transferred to one of the Rhode Island companies, so I signed my name as one of the quota of a Rhode Island town and drew the state bounty.

February 2nd. Had a pretty heavy thundershower—something uncommon for this time of year. We now learnt, much to our disappointment, that the regiment, for some reason or other, could not go home together. The first detachment left on the fourth, and we went down to the depot and played "Sweet Home" as they started off in the cars. Serenaded General Ayers in the evening by request, as they had a party of ladies from the North.

February 8th. Went to Beatton Station where one of our companies was stationed. They were situated about a mile from the depot, and they were greatly troubled by guerillas. They had a midnight attack from them a few nights before, wounding two of our boys. To protect themselves, they had made a barricade around the camp with tops of trees, and at night stretched pieces of telegraph wires across the entrance.

February 9th. While here, some of the boys came pretty near getting into a trap. A few of the young ladies in town were to have a dance with some Yanks and engaged a fiddler from our regiment. Some of the officers heard of it, and there was a double guard put on that night, which frustrated the arrangements. One of our boys managed to run guard, and, while he was waiting in the house for the rest to make their appearance, he heard horses' hoofs. Thinking all was not right, he made a rush for the door and escaped in time to see about fifteen guerillas surround the house. This was a shrewd game which was probably laid out beforehand, as the young ladies were not to be found next day. Probably they felt patriotic and wanted to do something for their country.

February 13th. Furloughs arrived. In the afternoon we started for Warrenton to turn over our horses and equipment to the division quartermaster. It came rather hard to part with my horse after having her in my possession eighteen months; it was like losing an old friend. I had got greatly attached to her; she knew my voice and would mind better than half the children, was gentle as a lamb, but let a strange horse come round while she was eating and she would strike out behind with amazing rapidity. She was one of the fastest in the regiment, could jump a fence or ditch, and was not afraid of anything. Although I had a number of others afterwards, there was none that could compare with my grey mare. The only fault about her was once in a great while she would stumble and throw me over her head. I never saw her afterwards.

February 14th. Sunday. Started from Warrenton in freight cars, stopped at the junction where we met the rest of the regiment. The officers and band had a passenger car, while the others had to content themselves in baggage cars clear to Washington. We arrived in the city in the afternoon, marching up Pennsylvania Avenue in all our glory covered with Virginia mud, while the inhabitants dressed up in their fine clothes were on their way to church. A soldier without a discharge or furlough to show, was not allowed to travel on the railroad, and would be liable to be arrested as a deserter unless with his company or regiment under charge of officers.

The band put up at a hotel, and, as it was supposed we should start early next morning, we were anxious to procure for ourselves new uniforms, but how were we to do it on Sunday? We at last found someone connected with the hotel who knew where one of the clothing dealers lived, and went with one of our boys and found him. He was one of those Jew clothing dealers (which Washington is full of) and was very willing to open his store on the sly at the prospect of selling about sixteen full suits. After considerable talk and threatening to wait until the morrow and trade somewhere else, he came down in his price and we got the suits for $30.

February 15th. Those who had their furlough started for home on their own hook, while we should have to wait a day or two to get the transportation papers made out. The band agreed to wait and go home with the New Hampshire Battalion. This morning we came out in gay colors, new uniforms, yellow stripes down the legs (which are allowed to bands), and veteran's insignia on the arm.[28] We visited the barbers, and those having yellow mustaches came out in deep mourning, for they had them dyed,

154

and altogether looked so different that we hardly knew each other. We felt so good that it was proposed to go over and play in front of the National for the benefit of the public generally, and it was a unanimous vote. In the evening went to the theatre and saw Laura Keene. [29]

February 16th. We paraded round town during the day seeing the sights, and were feeling as happy as Major Generals when we learnt that we should start at seven this evening. We were at the depot but did not leave till some time afterwards; arrived in Baltimore about midnight, where it was expected that a train would be waiting to take us to Philadelphia. Were told to find accommodations for the night and report to the depot in the morning at 8:00. The night was stinging cold, the thermometer below zero. The boys started in search for lodgings, and at every house that had the least resemblance to a hotel, someone would give the bell a jerk and wait for a head to pop out of the window. "Is this a hotel?" "No." "Can you tell me where I can find lodg–" The window came down with a slam and the person probably went back to bed cursing us for disturbing his rest. Presently we saw a policeman, and he told us to turn to the second right. We did so, but when we arrived at the hotel there were but four of us, the rest having taken different directions. We told the desk we would like accommodations for the night. "All full," says he. One of the boys had the impudence to tell him he didn't believe it. "Here we are in a strange city in the middle of the night, cold and tired. A bed we want and a bed we must have." After looking over the book for some time, he called one of the porters and told him to show these men to such and such a room. We found all the materials for a fire in the grate all ready to be touched off. After getting warmed through, we retired.

February 20th. Started for South Boston. Saw the 24th Massachusetts, they having arrived the same day on their veteran furlough. It is impossible for me to express the happy sensation I felt at the prospect of seeing relatives, friends and old familiar faces again after two years absence. I wanted to say "How are you?" to everybody I met. I thought the city would look different after three years of war; I thought the streets would look deserted (by the male portion especially), business partially suspended, and I thought possibly grass might be growing in some of the streets, but the thoroughfares seemed to be as crowded with about as many people as before the war. Business appeared to be thriving, and not more than half the people seemed to be aware that there was any war.

April 8th. Left Providence this evening in the cars and took the steamer *Corinth* from Groton about midnight for New York.

April 9th. Arrived at the wharf about six and marched to the barracks for breakfast. We expected to start off immediately afterwards for Washington, but, owing to some trouble about transportation, we stopped in the city four days. I was glad of this, for I always had a desire to see the city. Spent most of the remainder of the day looking at the curiosities in Barnum's Museum, and in the evening went there and saw the performance. Stopped at a hotel opposite the park during my stay.

April 11th. Visited that celebrated and highly perfumed part of the city called Five Points. Went to the theatre in the evening.

April 12th. Four of us crossed the ferry into Brooklyn and visited the Navy Yard. I saw a *Monitor* for the first time; an officer kindly gave us permission to go all over her. [30] This was the *Tecumseh* which was afterwards sunk (I believe) in Mobile harbor. [31] In the evening went to a place of amusement called a Hippotheatre.

April 13th. Left New York at nine this morning, crossing the ferry to Jersey City. Left in the cars at 11:00, the officers and band occupying our car. We played as we were passing through each city on the route, much to the delight of the small fry. Reached Philadelphia early in the evening and marched direct to the Cooper Shop. This is no government concern, as the victuals on the table will show, no hardtack and salt junk, but bread and butter, cheese, cold meats, hot coffee. It is carried on by private subscription from its citizens. They have men in New York and Washington to telegraph when a regiment is coming, and when the troops arrive in the city, guides are at the cars or boat to escort them to the saloon, where the tables are all spread with hot coffee and other substantials. Any soldier who has ever passed through Philadelphia can testify to the kind treatment received by their *friends* in the Quaker city. [32] Left at 9:30 and travelled all night.

April 15th. Was at the barracks at 8:00 but did not get off until noon, when we started on foot for dismounted camp, called Camp Stowneau, about four miles from the Capitol. We got "A" tents that afternoon and got them all pitched before dark. Our blankets, cooking utensils, etc., where were they? We left them with some of the boys who did not reenlist, and here we are without a blanket, or anything to cook our rations in. Consequently, we had to lie on the ground that night without any covering, but we got something next day. We began to feel pretty blue when we came to think how lovely everything had been the last two months, and then looked ahead at the prospect of three years more service. It also came pretty hard to fall back on government rations again. In the evening, we serenaded Colonel McIntosh, commander of the camp. Our camp is situated on a high piece of ground near the bank of the Potomac, overlooking Washington, Alexandria, and the country for miles around. We watch the steamers as they ply up and down the river, some freighted with troops, others with cattle, and others government goods. There are two forts near us which are each garrisoned by a company of the 9th N.Y.H.A., the regiment being 2,200 strong. [33] They practice firing every Tuesday and Friday. There are some three or four thousand men here waiting for horses.

April 25th. Burnside's corps passed over the same route and camped opposite us on the other side of the river; their campfires showed up splendidly at night, looking like an illuminated city.

April 27th. Went fishing in the Potomac, had the same luck as I usually do on such trips: didn't catch nary a fish.

May 8th. Sunday. Had church services, as we do every sabbath when we are in camp. The services consist of a short sermon, generally containing some good advice by Parson Clark, a few psalm tunes by the band, and singing by the choir.

May 9th. Was greatly surprised this morning to hear the call blow to pack up. We were expecting to stay here until we had got our horses. We got breakfast as soon as possible, packed up our duds, and had them taken off in a team. Where we were going was a mystery to all of us. We started off on foot about six, and after a hot and dusty march, reached the city. Found a train of baggage cars waiting for us on Maryland Avenue and learnt that we were going to Fairfax Station. The general commanding the post was at the station and furnished us with two teams to take ourselves and baggage up to his headquarters about three miles distant. We took possession of some huts that were occupied by the 4th Delaware for their winter quarters. The next camp to us was occupied by a regiment of the Invalid Corps, more commonly called the Diarrhea Corps, or "Condensed Yankees" as the Rebs called them. Serenaded General Tyler in the evening, commander of the post.

May 13th. At five this afternoon we left in baggage cars for Alexandria and although the distance was not sixteen miles, we did not get there until about nine. Marched to the soldier's rest where about midnight we had a government collation. As our baggage was left in the cars, we did not have even a blanket to lie on. I stretched myself out on one of the tables, with a haversack of rations for a pillow, and slept about ten minutes at a time until morning.

May 14th. We loafed around the premises all day, some of the boys amusing themselves by catching fish from the end of the wharf with bent pins, others by watching the government steamers loaded with wounded soldiers and other government property. After partaking of another of those excellent meals at the restaurant carried on by the extensive firm of U.S., etc., we marched through the city at five to the wharf, where we were to embark for Belle Plain. Had to stop here two hours, and, while waiting, about forty of Corcoran's Irish Legion came along under guard. I suppose they were tight, although they walked very loose. And on behind were others so extremely tired that they had to be brought down in the carts. Their brigade had passed through the city early that day on the way to the front, behind these were stray sheep (who had been led from the right path) on their way to join the flock. When we got on board, we found them lying on deck, packed in like so many sardines in a box, and smelling not much like the last rose of summer. I went down below and laid myself on a pile of baggage (consisting of old tents, camp kettles, sabres, shovels, pickaxes, etc.) for a night's rest. I woke up in the middle of the night feeling rather lame and wanted to curse the situation, but then I found some consolation in thinking that I was undergoing all this for my beloved country.

We came to a halt at three, and it was two hours after daylight before we could get up to the wharf. Steamers and vessels without steam of all sizes and shapes were discharging troops, provisions, ammunition, etc. Canal barges were loaded with hay and grain, and queer looking floating cattle pens were filled with beeves. We piled our baggage on the wharf, and had a guard placed over it, calculating to send teams after it when a camping ground is found. On our way we passed nine thousand Johnnies who were captured in the wilderness. Thinking they might want to hear "Yankee Doodle," we gave it to them free, but it did not evidently set well on their crops, for they made wry faces. When we finished, some of them sang out asking for "Dixie" and "Bonnie Blue Flag." Instead they got "Johnnie Stole the Ham" and "Arn't You Glad to Get Out of the Wilderness." I thought they were very appropriate to the occasion. We camped about a mile from the landing, and teams were sent after our baggage. In the meantime a thundershower came along, and, having no shelter tent to crawl into, we got a ducking.

As this was our base of supplies at that time, there was a great uproar, bustle, and excitement. Many days, long wagon trains would arrive from the front and go back laden with provisions, forage, ammunition, etc. Prisoners were on their way to Washington and troops to the front. These regiments were mostly heavy artillery that had been doing duty in the different forts in the North and around Washington but were now on their way where they could smell the powder of battle, by order of General Grant.[34] Some regiments numbered as high as 2,400. About fifty rods from my tent was an old barn containing forty Rebs, and such a set of long-legged, lantern-jawed, knocked-kneed, pocked-faced, long-haired specimens of humanity I never saw before. They all seemed to be in good spirits. Said that Lee knew what he was about, and he would fight to the last man. To a question put to one of them asking what they were fighting for, he said he didn't know, but reckoned their leaders knew.

May 20th. Today I sent a personal advertisement in the *Waverly Magazine* for a number of lady correspondents. Object: fun, improvement, and to pass off many idle hours. Half of our horses arrive.

May 23rd. The rest of the horses arrived, and the band was given grey and white ones. The one I got acted as though he never has been saddled. I had to strap up his foreleg, then two men held him before I could get on him. He went every way but ahead, and when I spurred him he turned round his head and tried to bite my foot. Then he would back under a tree among the branches and try to rub me off. After trying him on the music question, we found his taste didn't run that way. He was either awful stubborn, or had never been thoroughly broke, so I traded with one of the regiment and got one of the more docile kind.

May 24th. Left Belle Plain in the afternoon and were caught in a severe thunder and hail storm. The hail stones were actually as large as shell barks. Camped late at night, crawling under the blankets about midnight.

May 28th. While cooking his breakfast, one of the band boys had a fit. Before starting, we attempted to play on our new horses, and as soon as we struck up there was considerable scattering of horse flesh, they shooting off in all directions. Some of them were pretty wild, but with a little time and patience they will behave like old veterans. Started off at 8:00 and reached Port Conway (on the Rappahannock) in the afternoon and camped in a clover field beside a brick church. In this church was a one-horse organ which the boys amused themselves by playing on, and singing some good old Psalm tunes.

May 31st. Started off at 5:00 and reached Bowling Green about noon, where we halted three hours, making ourselves comfortable as possible under the shade of the trees. This was quite a neat little town, the houses being built mostly on one street which was wide and well shaded, but the inhabitants were intensely secesh. One woman told me that the South would never be conquered; they would fight to the last man, and, when they were gone, the women would take the field. Spunky, war'nt she? We found a barn here filled with dry-leaf tobacco which proved very accept-able.[35] Camped at night near the Matrapony river.

June 1st. Was up at 3:30 and started shortly after, halted till afternoon for the men to build a bridge across the river, the banks being too steep and the river too deep to ford. Camped at night at a place called White Chimneys. This town consisted of one large white house and outbuildings and was kind of a headquarters for guerilla bands operating in the vicinity, twenty-five having left in a hurry as our advance guard entered. The colonel commanding our squad tried to buy some butter and other eatables at the house, but they wouldn't sell to Yankees, although they had plenty. After we got unsaddled there was pretty lively skirmishing among the pigs, chickens, geese.

June 4th. Reached White House about noon, (camping near the bank of the river), very glad to get to the end of our journey, for the weather has been terrible hot and the roads exceedingly dusty. The base of supplies has been changed from Belle Plain to here. The river is full of craft all the time, since it is navigable up to here.

June 5th. Went in bathing for the first time this year, having an excellent opportunity in the river. Serenaded General Abercrombie in the evening.

June 6th. Visited a squad of Rebs just arrived from the front; among them was a woman, an orderly sergeant of a battery.

June 8th. Witnessed the burial of a large number of our troops who had died in the hospitals. [36]

June 11th. Our regiment went out scouting towards West Point; they got fired into by guerillas, wounding one of the boys as he wasn't able to ride his horse. They found an old family carriage (about a century old) in a barn, with an old harness, hitched a couple of their horses in, and they drove him into camp. This team created considerable sport for the next few days and was driven around the camp by one of the boys, who could always find plenty of room for passengers inside and out.

June 17th. Back of our camp is a smooth level road for about half a mile, which is used for a race course. Today a race took place between a captain and a private for $250. The private won. The regiment went out scouting every few days after horses, bringing in thirteen in one day.

June 20th. Very foggy. Was cooking our breakfast this morning as usual, when we were somewhat startled on hearing a discharge of artillery from the battery occupying the rifle pits next to our camp, and were wondering what it could mean, but were not kept in wonderment long, for a battery on a hill a short distance off replied, sending us their compliments in the shape of shells. We came to a hasty conclusion that we were being attacked by Rebs, packed up our goods, and saddled in a hurry. Presently the gunboats commenced throwing shells from their big guns (48 lb.). The band and teams were ordered across the bridge to the other side of the river. To get to the bridge, we had to go between the two lines of fire, the shells came thick and rapid, so we went under the bank of the river where we halted half an hour. The shells from the gunboats (which were not forty rods from us) went directly over our heads. We then started for the bridge, and when we got there, found that nobody was allowed to go across until a wagon train five or six miles long could get over. This train from the front is after supplies and is probably what the Rebs are after. Meantime, the shelling continues playing havoc among the mules, horses and teams. One Sanitary Commission team lost three horses by one shell. The fog cleared off and we watched fire and smoke from the Reb guns. Two or three of our regiment started off with a dispatch for Sheridan, who is fifteen miles off with his cavalry. About noon the firing ceased. While the Rebs were changing position, the wagons all got over, and we followed on behind. Sheridan arrived towards night, but went into camp for the night, not crossing the river, as his men and horses were tired out, having just returned from a long raid. [37]

June 21st. The Rebs held their position all night. Sheridan crossed the river, and, after a little skirmishing, the Rebs skedaddled, and the cavalry went into camp. We went back to our old position and pitched our tents. Our force was very small (before Sheridan came up), consisting of two or three veteran regiments—67th Pennsylvania Infantry, 1st Rhode Island Cavalry, and two batteries. The Rebs had the whole of Fitzhugh Lee's cavalry, besides infantry. If it had not been for the gunboats, I think we should have all been taken prisoners. Their shells exploded two of the Reb's caissons, sending great volume of smoke into the air.

June 24th. Marched about 8:00, crossing the Chickahominy. The ground in this vicinity is low and marshy, and it is no wonder that McClellan lost so many men by disease. [38] Passed through Charles City Court House and stopped for the night near Harrison's Landing. We had got to bed and comfortably fixed for a good night's rest when "Boots and Saddles" blew, so we had to saddle up and hold our horses all night, the Rebs being in the vicinity, the 2nd Division having had a fight that afternoon.

June 29th. As the troops have all got across, we start off this afternoon and march until midnight halting near Prince George's Court House at midnight. We filed into a field, formed in lines, and were ordered not to unsaddle. I was tired and lay down, tying the reins to my leg. Would get to sleep when my horse (nibbling after grass) would give my leg a jerk and wake me up. Not much rest that night.

June 30th. Off at daylight, marching as far south as Reim's Station, about fifteen miles below Petersburg in rear of the enemy. [39] We found some of our infantry there, who had been tearing up the track; the station and ties were burning when we arrived. Fell back about eight miles and went into camp about midnight.

July 1st. Took a southeasterly direction towards Suffolk and went into camp after dark.

July 2nd. Took a different direction and, after marching all day, reached the James, camped in a field where corn was planted the year before, the soil loose and exceeding dusty.

July 3rd. The troops were moved into the woods, cool and shady retreats picked out for the different headquarters, and camps laid out. Indications showed that we were to stop here some little time to rest, and much we needed it, the men and horses being about used up. During the last week we have had the toughest marching I've seen since being in the service. Travelling day and night, very little sleep, and little or nothing to eat. Some days would not stop long enough to cook a cup of coffee, living on hardtack and raw fat pork. The horses went three days with nothing to eat except what they could pick off the ground. Hundreds of them played out and were left by the side of the road to die. Others whose backs would get so sore by having the saddle on constantly would also have to be left. Those men who had to abandon their horses in this way would take their blankets and rations and leave the rest. Consequently, they had to go afoot, and, not being used to this, would get tired, and stop to rest. Not able to keep up with the horses, they would fall behind and often get taken prisoners. This is the way we lost a great many men.

The weather was intensely hot. I saw in a Washington paper a few days afterwards that those days were the hottest known for years, the thermometer ranging over 100 in the shade, the sun pouring down on our heads, blistering the bare skin, and not a breath of air. Several men had sunstrokes, and to say that the roads were dusty would be an understatement, since there has not been any rain for a month. Just imagine a substance as fine as flour, three inches deep, travelled through by seven or eight thousand horses, constantly kicking it up, then you can see what kind of condition the roads were in. [40] The sweat would pour off ourselves and horses in streams, *yes, in streams.* Our eyes would smart, and we rubbed them with our hands and got them filled with dust, and got so choked up that it would be difficult to speak. We traveled miles not able to see but a few rods ahead, and often could not see the horse ahead of us. Imagine this, all ye home guards, and then think how gay it is to be a soldier.

July 4th. Glorious Fourth. Got up at daylight and played patriotic airs. The regiment was drawn up in line, speeches made by officers and men, mixed up with music by the band. I must confess I felt a little homesick and blue, tired and about played out, ragged and dirty. Here I am lying on the dirt under an old dirty piece of canvas, depressed about even having to think how the people are enjoying themselves in Boston. I thought patriotism a humbug, but a very good thing to have in the North where everything was quiet. [41]

July 7th. We serenaded General Merriott, our Brigade Commander this evening. The Rebs tried to bother our gunboats in the river occasionally, but it didn't amount to much. They had the impudence to throw a shell from the opposite side towards our camp, but a gunboat steamed after them and made them skedaddle. Uncle Sam, besides raising our wages, has given us better grub lately, getting fresh beef, soft bread, and vegetables (in small quantities) occasionally. I saw in a Northern paper lately that a vessel load of onions were on their way to the army. I suppose it has arrived, for we have received three in our crowd, to be divided among sixteen men. There was about enough for a smell apiece, but even that was good. It shows their good intentions, and perhaps they'll do better by & by. Small favors thankfully received. The cry of the soldiers is "Onions and Union forever!"

We get Washington papers occasionally and learn what is going on in the North. In one of them we saw the columns headed in large type, "Great excitement in the North, the people fully aroused, the Rebels capture two trains of cars between Washington & Baltimore, telegraph wires cut, bridges burnt, five hundred thousand troops called for, etc." I was glad of this account. It would stir up the people to their sense of duty, and help fill up the army, and hasten to crush this cussed rebellion. And some of those *ducks* that have the pleasure of reading the *handbills* every day will have a chance to travel with the show itself.

Two out of the dismounted men from our regiment who were ordered to Washington were killed while fighting with muskets in the entrenchments around Washington. Hear cannonading from the front most every day, and occasionally in the night. Grant & Lee City Point & Petersburg Express, although not in partnership, are carrying on an extensive business in the express line, sending packages back and forth by the airline. [42] The water here is strongly impregnated with sulfur, making most of the boys sick. Consequently, we do not play much. The only piece we are obliged to play is Quickstep, which does not require much practice before we can play our parts to perfection.

July 26th. After a rest of over three weeks, we were recruited up to the marching standard again, and broke camp this afternoon and crossed the Appomattox at nine. The route we took led mostly through the woods along a narrow road, tall southern pines on each side, the night dark as pitch. Boys are sleepy, they nod in their saddles, the 1st Regimental Band strikes up "Lanegan's Ball," the audience coming in on the chorus. Fine effect. The boys enjoy another nap, wake up, wonder if they are going to run this machine all night, finally come to a halt at 2:00 in the morning, ordered not to unsaddle, lie down in the dirt to rest, either holding or tying the reins to our leg, sleep until daylight.

July 27th. Off at daylight, we heard that the infantry have been fighting this morning. Presently, we meet four dogs of war in the shape of 20-lb. parrot guns. These are what some folks call the dogs of war, but the real ones are, I think, West Pointers. We crossed the James Deep Bottom on pontoons muffled with leaves and branches of trees so as not to make a noise. We got within a few miles of Mahern Hill, where the enemy were met and quite a little skirmish ensued, slept that night within pistol shot of each other.

July 28th. We (the band) start off to water our horses, we arrive at pickets, no water unless we go beyond them. The butternuts[43] are in plain sight, posted along the edge of a cornfield, some of our pickets go with us and have their guns all cocked, ready to use them while our horses are drinking, if the Rebs should offer to shoot.

Shortly afterwards, the engagement commenced, Hill Corps advancing; they attempted to take one of our batteries, got close up when we gave them a double ration of grape and cannister, which threw them into confusion; the cavalry charged and captured a number of battle flags and prisoners.

We were ordered to fill our canteens for the wounded, and, while we were finding water, the cavalry was ordered to fall back, as the ground was not suitable to operate on, being mostly thick woods. The 2nd Corps arrived and will take care of them. Our regiment's loss was slight, but the 2nd Division lost heavy. We halted until midnight, when we stole back across the river and slept till daylight.

July 29th. The cavalry had orders to prepare to fight on foot, every number four to hold the horses.[44] Four of the band (myself included) were ordered to stay behind to take care of the horses and instruments, the rest proceeding to the front with the regiment to take care of the wounded. In the afternoon, word came back for men to carry rations up to the front. Two of us collected the haversacks belonging to the band, slung them across our shoulders, and started. When we arrived there, we found our regiment enjoying themselves under the shade of the trees, not having had any fighting nor any signs of it.

When I left, the troops were drawn up in line of battle, General Custer and staff riding up and down the line waving those flags that were captured the day before from the enemy, trying to entice the Rebs out of the woods they occupied onto the field (Strawberry Plains), but it was no go. The cavalry recrossed the river and went into camp. This movement, as I afterwards found out, was to draw the enemy troops away from Petersburg so as to weaken their lines.

July 30th. Started off at 2:00 this morning, marching along our lines, arriving in front of Petersburg at noon, seeing the city for the first time. Heard of the mine explosion which took place this morning,[45] saw large numbers of wounded, mostly colored troops. On questioning them how they made out, most of them would say I guess we killed as many of them as they did of us. I was told afterwards by one of my friends who was there that if the niggers had been properly supported by the white troops we would have carried their works.

As we were marching along the front in plain view of the Reb's works, they would occasionally throw a shell right over our troops occupying the breastworks towards us, but they couldn't quite reach us. The lines are so near together in some places that you could throw a hardtack into their works. It must be fun living in that neighborhood under fire night and day, and, as soon as anybody attempts to show his head, to have those songbirds singing about your ears. Very pleasant indeed.

July 31st. Started early and after considerable marching arrived near City Point. Our division was to embark for Maryland; I hailed this as glad news, for I had seen enough of this part of Virginia.

August 1st. Our brigade is the first to embark. While we were halted near the wharf we witnessed one of the benefits that the poor soldier deserves from the Sanitary Corps. Our officers paid a visit to that benevolent institution and came back loaded with canned fruit, meat, preserves, wine, crackers, underclothing, etc., which they spread out on the ground and enjoyed—a good feast—while we poor devils looking on had to content ourselves with the bitter cud of reflection or tobacco, just as it happened to be. Some of us tried the same game, but not a mouthful could we get. We were told that these delicacies were sent out here for the sick and wounded in hospitals. . . . These Sanitary Corps fellows may do a great deal of good in the hospitals around Washington, but I've never seen much benefit from them in the hospitals at the front. [46]

It took all day for our brigade to embark; our regiment getting all aboard about midnight. The boat we occupied was the *Thomas Powell,* formerly a riverboat. It seemed a shame to use such a handsome boat for such a purpose. The horses were put into the lower saloons or cabins, where temporary stalls were made, while the men occupied the upper cabins and deck. There was no elegant furniture or carpets aboard to be sure, but the carved and gilt work, stained glass, etc., showed off its former splendor.

August 3rd. The morning weather fine, a cool breeze fanning the decks, and I sit in an arm chair with my feet on the railing, smoking my pipe, enjoying the fine scenery on both banks of the river. This is another bright spot in the life of a soldier. The water is full of craft going and coming to and from the army. At noon we pass Mount Vernon playing the "Dead March," "Plays Hymn," and "Star Spangled Banner," the bell on the boat tolling in the meantime. As has become the custom, we pass by Alexandria and land of Geesboro Point at three. We stop near our old camping ground of April and May last.

August 5th. We break camp late this afternoon and pass through Washington by gaslight, bands playing, flags flying, and sidewalks crowded. Camp at midnight near Fentztown.

August 6th. Started at daylight, passed through Urbana, Jefferson, Buckeyetown, Knoxville, and arrived at the foot of Maryland Heights a little before dark. Some of these towns are very pretty and also contain a number of pretty girls. I've seen more good looking females in these two days than I saw in all Virginia. I don't know but what there are good looking females in Virginia, but I never saw many. Whenever we would pass through a Virginia town, we would find the houses all shut up tight and the inmates would peek out through the closed blinds as we went by, but here the houses are thrown open, smiling faces on the doorsteps and in windows, waving the stars and stripes and their handkerchiefs. They seem glad to see the Union troops. Jefferson is quite a pretty place, passing through it just as the people were coming out of church. I guess that there have not been many troops through here before, because they seemed to be very much surprised and pleased to see a band on horseback, and all white horses, too. The conduct of the inhabitants of the two states was so different that it actually took us by surprise; the whole population (except for the secesh portion, which was very feeble) would flock to the main street.

> *The men did cheer, the boys did shout*
> *The ladies they did all turn out*
> *And we all felt gay, as*
> *We went marching on.* (Then the band struck up.)

Camped that night at the foot of Maryland Heights, the Potomac in front of us and Harper's Ferry to the left.

August 8th. Marched about noon, we passed through Harper's Ferry. This is an odd and ancient looking place situated on the Potomac, and surrounded on all sides by mountains and hills. It will occupy a place in history as the base of operations for the John Brown party, besides war incidents. We saw the ruins of the arsenal where he figured so conspicuously, [47] which was burnt in the first part of the war by Lieutenant Jones on the approach of the Rebs.

August 10th. Marched at daylight, passed through Charlestown, saw the jail where John Brown was confined and the courthouse where he was tried. Passed through Berryville in the afternoon, and, towards night, had a skirmish, capturing a few prisoners. One of the prisoners captured was a deserter from our regiment. After jumping several bounties, he deserted to the enemy. [48] I believe he was hanged a few days after.

August 14th. Our regiment got back after being gone nearly a week; they got cut off by Rebs, and we had given them up for lost.

It was while staying here that our forage and supply train was captured and burned by Moseby; consequently we had to live off the country.

Ten of the Michigan Brigade were caught by him and hanged near Yueskerville, with sheep's legs stuck in their mouths. Our regiment was sent to ascertain the fact, and had orders to take no prisoners. On arriving there, they found ten new-made graves. We went out foraging every day, bringing in sheep, turkeys, chickens, geese, and forage for our horses, but it was dangerous business.

August 16th. My bunky went to the hospital, making the third member of the band in that institution. A few days later, the bass tuba player had his instrument (costing $110) stepped on by a horse, squashing it so that it had to be sent to Boston to be repaired. But we never saw it afterwards, and this reduced the band down considerable, but we managed to keep in playing condition.

August 18th. Commenced to retreat. Sheridan issued an order:[49] We are to burn all hay and grain and drive off the cattle except milk cows. It does seem kind of cruel to destroy so much property and deprive the inhabitants of all their stock, but it has to be done. It will probably help end the war, because it will leave nothing for an army to live on in the valley. This is a great farming region and the Reb government relies on it greatly for supplies. This order was entrusted to our brigade to carry out.

As we marched along, smoke could be seen rolling up from all quarters, filling the atmosphere and obstructing the rays of the sun. In some cases, the women and children would run from their houses with pails of water to extinguish the flames, but if they succeeded, they worked in vain, for the match would be applied again. When the horses and cattle were driven off, the women would beg of the men to save them a favorite horse, lamb, or other animal, but in vain. The order was strict and had to be carried out. It was a sad duty, and I'm glad that I had nothing to do with it.

In the night, the sky was lit up by hundreds of fires from burning barns, hay and grain stacks, making a grand but awful sight. To think what suffering it will cause. What kind of feelings do you suppose those men had towards us who were hovering around the army, when they saw their property in flames and their farms pillaged. Do you think they will feel like acting like brothers towards us? But it showed them that we were in earnest, that the rebellion should be put down, no matter what means were adopted to do it, and taught them a lesson dearly bought that to rebel against the government was not boy's play.

August 21st. Our regiment was ordered to corps headquarters (General Forbert) which were at Charlestown, to act as bodyguard and orderlies, we acting as headquarter's band. This is what the boys called a soft job, because they do not have to engage in any fighting. Sheridan issued the order a few days before for all male citizens between the ages of sixteen and sixty to leave our lines, [50] and we found about twenty wagons in the town filled with these men all ready to start. Our regiment guarded them as far as Charlestown. This order was a good one, if they only stay put; but, as they probably most all belonged to Moseby's gang—who would be farmers in the daytime and guerillas by night—they will be back again after enjoying an excursion trip by way of Washington at the expense of our government. It looked strange to me that after so rigid a conscription law—which the Rebs had to resort to in order to replenish their armies—that a body of two or three hundred able-bodied men should be found within a circuit of a few miles who did not belong to the army.

August 25th. The whole corps went out on a reconnaissance in force towards Martinsburg, but before reaching there we drove in the Reb pickets, and soon came to the main force, where skirmishers were sent out and a line of battle formed. The General advanced up the skirmish line, and we followed behind, expecting that he would set us a-playing. Both lines were in the woods out of sight. We were in an open field at the edge. Presently, the Rebs made a charge, the balls humming uncomfortably close about our ears, great cheering, uproar, smoke and dust. I saw men and horses fall, officers shouting for the men to keep cool and steady, and presently one of our batteries opened from a small hill but a stone's throw behind us, throwing the shells over our heads; we fell back and took a position behind the battery and struck up "Star Spangled Banner," while the battery boys were dealing death and destruction among the Reb's ranks. Great excitement, noise and confusion. The Rebs were flanking us, we fell back to a new position, the Rebs following. Headquarters moved two miles to the rear to await new developments, and we went into a field and hitched our horses to the fence. We had been here about an hour, some of the boys were boiling coffee, others roasting a piece of pork on a stick, when the Reb skirmishers came out of a cornfield at the opposite side of the road and fired into us.

There was a very rapid movement towards the horses, leaving coffee kettles, etc., behind. Although the balls whizzed over our heads and under our horses, none of our crowd got hurt, but some from another regiment got killed in a barnyard next to us. Custer's Michigan Brigade, which had just passed along the road towards the front, wheeled around and gave them the contents of their seven-shooters, [51] but they got cut off from the road and had to ford the Potomac into Maryland. The New Hampshire regiment lost pretty heavy, and altogether I guess our loss was greater than the Rebs, for they had the advantage, being on foot (we were fighting infantry), while the cavalry could not take such good aim.

This was the first time the band ever played on the battlefield and I don't care about repeating it very often. Although I liked the excitement, I didn't like the music of those lead pills that were flying about so carelessly. We camped near Harper's Ferry. They put us into an open field where there was not a rail or stick within miles to hitch to. Some of the boys tied the halters to their saddles and used them for pillows. About the middle of the night, one of the horses gets scared of something and off goes horse, saddle and all. He awoke with a start at the sudden departure of his pillow, crawled out from under the blankets, and commenced the search for a lost horse, travelling over stones and wet grass in deshabille. We remain here all the next day.

August 27th. We crossed the Potomac on pontoons near the old arsenal, travelled up the tow path of the canal, through Antietam and Sharpsburg to Hagerstown. We were met by a delegation of young ragged urchins, who escorted us through the streets to the Principle Hotel; on route they frequently gave vent to their enthusiasm by yelling and much throwing of caps in the air. The town is strong Union, the ladies exhibiting their loyalty by waving the flag and their handkerchiefs and smiling sweetly. Their bright smiles haunt me still.

The General put up at the Washington House, but we, having none of the needful in our pockets, had to put up with accommodations in the back yard. In the evening, we took our stand in front of the hotel and gave

the Hagerstowners a free concert, much to the delight of the younger portion of humanity, and I guess to the older portion too, for when we got
through some of those "angels without wings" presented us with some
huge watermelons. We thanked them in *melon-choly* tones and repaired to
our humble lodgings to divide the spoils. During the night some of the
boys dreamt that they were coming to a *watery* grave. If anyone thinks this
a *seedy* joke, they must lay it those melons.

August 28th. Left the good people of Hagerstown with sorrow at 8:00 this
morning, halting at Sharpsburg for about three hours. An old lady with a
whole soul and Christian sentiments made me the happy recipient of a
homemade pie. Probably she took me to be a youth with *pieus* ideas. What
made this gift more welcome was the fact that I had no loose change in any
pocket. Long may she live. In the afternoon, we forded the Potomac,
passed through Shepherdstown, and arrived at Charlestown near midnight, camping in the field where John Brown's body was left dangling in
the air.

August 30th. Marched to Berryville camping near that place where we remained nearly three weeks. For some cause or other, I neglected writing in
my diary for nearly three weeks but can recollect nearly all that transpired.[52] We camped on a rich old former plantation, on a flat adjoining a
cornfield. The General had his tents pitched in the yard in front of this
mansion. The old man had several pretty daughters, which the officers
liked to chat with, and, to keep on the right side of the old man, the General had a guard placed on his cornfield; but the boys were not to be
cheated out of extras so easily. Between sundown and midnight, I noticed
we generally had a supply laid in for the next day. The old man soon began
to miss it, and would walk through the camp during the day with a long
face, trying to discover some trace of it, but we managed to find a place to
put the cobs and husks out of his sight. Every evening we would play in
front of the house, and several times, by special request, would play
"Dixie," which tickled the ladies muchly, but when we struck up any of the
national airs you would think by the looks of their faces that they had just
lost their last and dearest friend.

The 3rd Division (Wilson's) went off on a scout; in the afternoon we heard guns in the distance, indicating that they had run into something. Next day, a whole South Carolina regiment, colonel and all, came marching into camp under guard, being part of the spoils of that expedition.

Back of our camp was a storehouse, and on the steps of this house our chaplain would hold forth every Sunday. The regiment formed in a circle around him. Some of the boys, I am afraid, were looking more to their bodily welfare than to their spiritual, for I noticed that the old lady's sliced peaches, which she had left on the back window seat to dry, had disappeared before the sermon did. The main topic of conversation just now is the Presidential election; the McClellan crowd is small but make a great noise; most believe in reappointing Uncle Abe as captain of our ship. Although she has met with a number of storms, we have not been ship-wrecked yet. [53]

September 19th. We break camp at 2:00 this morning, marching shortly afterwards in the direction of Winchester. We met the enemy posted on the opposite side of Opequan Creek. Two pieces of artillery were placed in position, but, as they were behind breastworks, they were well protected. Presently some of our cavalry crossed the stream farther down and drove the Reb cavalry up the hill, our guns throwing a few shells after them, one bursting so close to one cavalryman that both he and his horse dropped instantly. We advanced, crossed the creek, and the Reb cavalry fell back slowly, their sharpshooters firing at our advance from trees, until they came to their main body, then our corps was sent to the right and left, and fighting commenced in earnest. Headquarters were established a short distance to the rear. Owing to the nature of the ground—hilly woodland—we could not see much that was going on from our position, but from the noise judged that they were having lively times, while the infantry, which was some distance to our left nearer Winchester, were also having warm work. Every little while, small squads of Johnnies would arrive at headquarters and were taken care of by our regiment. Towards night, the Reb lines began to give way, and they broke and commenced to retreat, our cavalry following them several miles beyond Winchester, capturing prisoners, guns, wagons, colors, etc. We crossed the battlefield late in the afternoon. The General and staff stopped for the night in town, and we camped at the edge of it.

This is my freedom birthday, twenty-one years.

September 20th. Started at 5:00 this morning, passing through Winchester, Newtown, Middletown, and halting near Strasburg. By the looks of the road to the south, the Rebs were in somewhat of a hurry the day before; muskets, knapsacks, canteens, etc., were thrown away in the flight, and the teams that had broken down were left, the teamsters cutting the harnesses and escaping on horseback. We camped on the north side of the town while the Rebs occupied a strong position on Fisher's Hill on the south side.

September 21st. This morning Sheridan received a commission from Washington, promoting him to Brigadier General in the regular army as a reward for the victory at Winchester. No doubt this made him feel very happy. We went and congratulated him on his success with a few remarks appropriate to the occasion, through our instruments. Preparations were made to dislodge the enemy from their strong position. The whole cavalry corps were ordered up the other valley to our left, I suppose to get in rear of the enemy.

September 22nd. Marched early, in the afternoon coming to a body of the enemy who occupied a very strong position, fighting them all the afternoon, but could not dislodge them. They could not very easily be flanked, so we fell back a few miles and camped for the night. [54]

September 23rd. Continued to fall, passing through Front Royal. Here we found that several of our men who straggled behind while passing through here two days before had been murdered by guerillas, who are always hanging around the rear and flanks of our army. One was found stripped naked in a church, another—an officer—was found in the woods; after stealing his money, watch, they stripped him of most of his clothing and killed him. Several more were found in like manner.

Passing through here today, we found the town occupied by a band of guerillas who little expected us back so soon, and after a short chase, a few of them were captured outside of the town. The whole corps was drawn up into squadrons, and a consultation of the General Officers was held to consider what was best to be done to those captured cutthroats. They came to a quick decision, for pretty soon I heard the popping of carbines, and saw men running wildly about for their lives. All but two were let loose and shot down like dogs without any ceremony. The other two were saved for a worse fate, to be hanged.

I made one of the crowd who gathered around them to see how they would receive their sentence. One was a meek, innocent looking man with rather a feminine look about his face, who did not look as though he was vicious enough to commit any crime. I really felt sorry for him, for he had a wife and children at home. He was white as death and did not speak unless to answer some question put to him, probably thinking of his family. The other was a large broad-shouldered six-footer with an ugly looking countenance, with a sabre cut across it, a memento of a former skirmish. He talked without reserve and even smiled, not seeming to realize the awful fate awaiting him.

Two pieces of rope were procured, and the men were led to a small hill a short distance off, the ropes thrown across the limb of a tree with a noose at one end. They were asked if they were ready. The smaller one asked for a bible, which was furnished him. After reading a few moments, he made a short prayer, the other one looking on with indifference. The nooses were placed about their necks, placards pinned to them on which was the following, "Hung in retaliation for the murders of U.S. soldiers." They were then told if they would lead a party to Moseby's headquarters their lives would be spared and they would be treated as prisoners of war. They considered this a few moments. What do you suppose their thoughts were? It was a trying question to decide whether to turn traitor to their cause and play the spy, with perhaps a bright prospect in the future, or to meet their death like a hero and forfeit all that was near and dear to them in this world. Their decision was made quickly, their answer was NO. Does anyone dispute that they were not brave men to their cause? Their hands were fastened behind them, and then their bodies were pulled up, their souls launched into eternity.

On a hill, too great a distance off to distinguish who they were with the naked eye, was a group of men, who our officers said were Rebels (by looking through a field glass). They were there during the whole proceeding, probably swearing vengeance.

We then recrossed the Shenandoah and went into camp on the other side, with the intention to wait for wagons to come along with rations. We unsaddled, cooked our dinner, and had just eaten when a dispatch was received from Sheridan announcing another great victory and ordering us to push on rapidly, cross the mountains, and head off the enemy if possible. Notwithstanding we were out of rations and tired, the boys started off cheerfully and hailed with delight the announcement of another victory. We crossed the river again and saw those two bodies hanging just as they were left, passed through Front Royal, and marched till midnight.

September 24th. Got about three hours sleep this morning, and we were in the saddle again by daylight, and ran into the Reb cavalry again this forenoon. A skirmish line was thrown out and the troops placed into position. Headquarters was established in a field a little to the rear. We went in search of hay for our horses, which we soon found. I left my horse eating it off of the porch of a house without hitching, while I went after some plums I had eyed a few minutes before. Two of us got into the tree and were enjoying ourselves hugely, partaking of that delicious fruit, when crack, pop, pop, crack, crack, went some muskets but a plaguey short distance off. We dropped from that tree like dead ducks, all in a heap, and the way we made for our horses wasn't slow. When we heard "To Horse" blow double quick we put on more steam. I thought to myself I'll be in a pretty fix if my horse has strayed away, but when I got there, I found him quietly eating his hay, just as contented as if nothing was going on.

Our regiment rushed back with the General at the head in the direction of the firing. After exchanging a few shots, the Rebs left in a hurry.

September 25th. Started early to cross the mountains. There is a splendid road, wide and smooth, which winds round and round, making it easy travelling for the horses, and we arrived at the top shortly after sunrise. The wind was very strong and seemed to pierce right through our bodies. Oh what a sight for an artist! The level country below is unobstructed to our view for miles and miles, both to the right and left, taking in several towns and villages, the rivers in their winding course and farm houses mere specks. The view was about the best I ever had the pleasure of seeing. We found our teams parked when we came to a halt to draw rations. After partaking of a good square meal (after three or four days fast), we resumed the march, camping for the night near Harrisburg.

September 26th. Passed through the town playing "Star Spangled Banner," it being full of sick and wounded Johnnies. When within six miles of Staunton my horse played out and was shot according to orders. I transferred my baggage to another, which one of our boys had captured that day on the road, and resumed my journey. This is a large and handsome town containing many large, pretty, and substantial public buildings such as the Deaf and Dumb and Insane Asylums, young ladies seminary, etc. It is kind of headquarters or base of supplies for the Reb army operating in the Valley.

While halted in the town, some of the boys made a raid on a government bakery which was in full blast. They brought out sheets of bread a yard long, and when it was all gone they waited patiently for the next batch to come out of the oven. The Knights of Dough looked on with open mouths, considering whether it was best to remonstrate or not. No doubt they worked hard for it and *kneaded* it much for their army, but we considered it as one of the trophies of war and confiscated it as such.

"Halloe!" Here comes an Irish woman acting as though she was crazy. "Where's the Ginral? Where's the Ginral? The boys are staling all me hay, and the only blessed thing I've got to kape one poor cow on through the winther." Her cow must learn to live on short rations while the Yanks are around. Camped at the edge of the town.

September 27th. Today all the government warehouses in town were thoroughly cleared out. Our teams were employed carting the goods to camp, and, if there was anything we wanted, we took it, and the rest was destroyed. Those whose bump of destructiveness was large had the pleasure of gratifying that propensity to its fullest intent. [55] Millions-worth of property was destroyed—arms, ammunition, clothing, rations, saddles, horse equipage, and government goods of every description; the railroad was torn up, sleepers burnt, rails twisted, bridges burnt, telegraph wires cut, and poles chopped down. The fire demon reigned supreme during the rest of the day.

September 28th. This afternoon we were returning from the river after watering our horses, when we heard firing in the direction that we just came from. We were ordered to saddle up, and the General and our regiment went down to ascertain the cause. The fatigue party came rushing back after their horses and arms; the Rebs threw shells at us over the town; what few guns we had with us were placed in position and returned the compliment; they tried to flank us; we fell back a little distance. By this time it was dark, and we could see the flash from their guns every time they fired the shell, sometimes screaming over our heads and other times falling short. As there were too many for our one division of cavalry, we commenced to retreat between nine and ten, passing through Staunton at midnight in silence. Nothing but the clatter of horses' feet on the pavement and the jingling of sabres could be heard. We travelled till sunrise the next morning without halting. That was one of the most tedious and tiresome nights I ever spent. There was a wagon ahead of us, which when going up a hill would go very slow, giving us a chance to enjoy a little nap, but on the down grade it would go on the run, our horses starting off to keep up, and allowing us but a short notice to wake up. So it was all night long.

October 5th. Today our engineer on Sheridan's staff was shot by guerillas, and the General ordered all the houses burnt in the vicinity. [56]

October 6th. Broke camp and marched at 6:00 this morning, travelling all day. Camped at night in a barnyard five miles south of New Market, four of us sleeping on the top of a stack of wheat.

October 8th. Left early, travelling all day, camping near Strasburg. Today the Reb cavalry (which has been following us all the way) troubled us considerable, skirmishing with the rear guard most of the way and capturing some teams and ambulances.

October 9th. Today both cavalry divisions went back to give the Reb cavalry a chastising for being so neighborly the day before, and they found them near Fisher's Hill. Skirmishing commenced and continued for about two hours. Headquarters were established on a hill where we could see part of both lines. Presently, the Rebs showed signs of retreating. Both of our divisions charged the enemy and they were routed and skedaddled, followed closely by our boys for over fifteen miles. Captured all their artillery but one piece, all their teams and ambulances and about seven hundred prisoners. [57]

October 11th. I am pleased as well as surprised to see my bunky back so soon from the hospital. After spending two months among the good people of the Quaker City, he comes back as good as new.

October 19th. Was woke this morning by a punch in the ribs from my bunky. "Do you hear that musketry?" says he. "Yes, I guess the pickets have got into a row." "Pickets? There's something more than pickets there." I began to think so, too, when I heard the big guns speak, so I jumped up, crawled out of the tent, rubbed my eyes, and found there was considerable commotion through the different camps. Rebs were coming close on to us, "Boots and Saddles" blew double quick, tents came down in a hurry, saddles went up onto our horses, and our goods were packed in an amazingly short time. It is a good thing to have the Rebs after you once in a while just to see how spry you can work if you are put to the test. In ten or fifteen minutes we had our house, furniture, dry goods, cooking utensils, etc., on the horses, but not until the bullets were coming zip, zip over our heads and striking the dust around us. The 18th and 19th Corps, which were surprised, were retreating in confusion, and the Rebs, flushed with success, were marching inward. Men and mules were shot while taking down the General's tents and putting them in teams. We mounted, formed in line, and marched to the rear, where we met the 6th Corps marching up in two lines of battle. They met the enemy and checked their onward career.

The cavalry were stretched across the country in a close line and ordered to let no man pass by with a musket, the General was rising up and down the lines trying to rally the infantry. We followed on behind, the shells flying round uncomfortably close; had to fall back farther, heard that we had lost twenty guns; affairs began to look squally, serious apprehensions of a big defeat.

We went into a field, side of the road, dismounted, stacked our instruments, and started building breastworks. The infantry were lying down in a line on the opposite side of the road, ready to give them a volley should they make their appearance, but they came not; they had been checked. Presently someone cried out "Here comes little Phil Sheridan." We looked down the road, and, sure enough, we saw him coming on the gallop with a very small escort behind him. He turned into the field we were in, we dropped our rails and gave him three hearty cheers, which he returned with a bow and smile so much as to say, "You wait a little while, I'll fix those Rebs." As he passed along, a cheer went up from the whole line. [58]

The shells now began to come so thick and fast that we had to lie down on our bellies behind our breastworks, and for two hours we hugged the ground pretty close, then we changed our position to the other side of the road. Just as we were mounting, a shell burst seemingly not more than ten feet above us, and how we all escaped being hurt is a mystery to me.

Affairs now began to look a little brighter. Stragglers and those who had got discouraged at the first turned around when they saw Sheridan and swelled the ranks at the front, taking new courage. In the afternoon, preparations were made for a grand charge, the cavalry were sent on the flanks. Towards night, everything being ready, the word was given and the whole line advanced. They fought desperately for a few minutes. When our troops charged and broke their lines, our cavalry rushed in and made the retreat a complete rout. They ran past the panic-stricken infantry, who was retreating, each man for himself, and made for the creek to get there before their artillery.

In their hurry to get across the stream, they got blocked up and a large number of guns and caissons fell into our hands. They recaptured all those we had lost this morning and about forty more, together with the wagons by the hundred and prisoners by the thousand, chasing them far into the night.

The troops were ordered into the same camps that they left in such a hurry in the morning. On our way there, we had to keep a sharp lookout on the ground to keep from stepping on the bodies. We arrived there, pitched our tents, and made preparations to cook some coffee, not having had a chance to cook anything since the day before. Going to the spring after water, I came very near tumbling over a dead man who lay across the path, stripped of his clothing. Around our tents, within a stone's throw, lay over twenty-five bodies, most of them belonging to the 30th Massachusetts, this being the neighborhood where the hardest fighting took place.

After supper we gathered around the fire and talked over the incidents of the day. How it was that the Rebs got so close on to us before we found out, I have never ascertained. Some say that a part of them dressed in our clothes and having the countersign, relieved our pickets at midnight, representing themselves as Union soldiers. For the truth of it, I cannot swear. Anyway, they came upon us so sudden that they captured about eight hundred of the 8th Corps before they got out of bed. In the morning they had it all their own way, but in the afternoon the scales turned. This was the battle of Cedar Creek.

October 20th. Cold and pleasant. I go take a view of the dead by daylight. They lie just as they fell, presenting a horrible spectacle. The impression made on my mind seeing so many ghastly faces will never be rubbed out. I see one whose face looks familiar but cannot tell who it is or where I've seen it before. Presently, a burial party arrives, they dig a shallow grave beside each body, then carefully lift him in, throw the dirt, and place at the head of each grave a slab of wood with the name, regiment, and date of death. On one headboard I read the name of one of my old school mates, belonging to the 3rd Massachusetts Cavalry.

This morning the General and our regiment go on a reconnaissance, travelling about fifteen miles on the road over which the Rebs retreated. By the looks, you would think that the Rebs had just flown over the road: muskets, knapsacks, haversacks, canteens, clothing, etc., were strewn all along, and teams tipped over in the eagerness to get out of the way of our cavalry. Others were left standing in the road, the teamsters having cut their harnesses and fled on horseback. At a small bridge where a stream crossed the road were three medical wagons tipped over, the medicines scattered all over the ground.

October 21st. Today the generals, by invitation of Sheridan, inspected the guns and other captured property which were parked in front of his headquarters. We furnished the music for the occasion. There were two lines, one of guns and behind them were caissons. In the rear of these were wagons by the hundred, containing all sorts of quartermaster's goods. No doubt they felt well pleased while viewing the fruits of their victory. General Custer and his 3rd Cavalry Division had the honor of capturing the greater part of these spoils. The prisoners were also near headquarters, and a motley-looking crowd they were, dressed in all sorts of uniforms, no two alike, and every shade of grey and butternut color. After the inspection, part of them were sent off to Washington under guard.

November 4th. This evening we serenaded General Custer and were very well treated. The night was cold and blustery, and he ordered a large rail fire to be built in front of his tent. We formed in a circle around it, furnishing us with both heat and light to play by, and his servants were then set to work getting us up a good supper. When it was ready, we went into a large tent, sat down to a long table and did ample justice to the things there— hot oysters, cold meats, fruits, sardines, hot coffee, etc. After our quartette club sang a few songs, we started for camp, and the officers thanked us for the compliment and invited us to come again.

Now I'll relate another incident just to let you see the difference in officers. About a year ago we serenaded a general in the 5th Corps. He sat in front of his tent reading the newspaper when we arrived. We played a few pieces, and he sat there still and didn't even look up from his paper. We came to the conclusion that he was not fond of music and we left.

November 8th. Today is the presidential election. McClellan's stock is below zero. The 19th Corps pack up and have orders to leave, the rumor is for Petersburg.

November 10th. As soon as the first rays of daylight appeared, the pickets commenced popping at each other. We fell back shortly afterwards, the Reb cavalry following in our rear all the way. The General had his tents pitched in front of a large brick house two or three miles from Winchester, while our regiment occupied a field in the rear, enclosed by a hard fence. We amused ourselves the rest of the afternoon pulling down this fence to supply us with material for building some comfortable huts, as it was supposed we should stop here all winter.

November 11th. Busied ourselves all day in erecting our hut, and, when completed, were very comfortably situated: had bunks filled with hay and a chimney made of stones and mud.

November 13th. The Reb cavalry which had followed us up began to make themselves neighborly, so one of our division had to be sent out to drive them off, which they did after some fighting, our boys bringing in two hundred prisoners and two guns.

While here, we made arrangements with a woman, being but a short distance from our camp, to cook our rations, each man paying so much a week. She was to have the spare rations that were left at the end of the week. It seemed like getting into civilized life again to sit down to a table with a clean cloth, and use crockery ware, knives, forks, etc. She hung a white handkerchief out of the window to let us know when she was ready for us, and about meal time there would be many anxious eyes turned towards that window to see if that rag hung out. The first one who saw it would sing out "Handkerchief" or "The rag's out," and you can't imagine what a magic effect it produced. But after a week our arrangement came to a sudden termination. The officers got jealous, thinking that we were enjoying too great a privilege for common soldiers. They talked to the woman, offered her more pay, and the consequence was that they took our place, cutting us out completely.

November 22nd. Woke up very early with the cold, finding my clothes and blankets froze stiff, and feeling rather uncomfortable. Made up a good fire, replenishing it with wood from the neighboring fences, and thawed ourselves out. Started off at daylight, the weather very cold, having to dismount and walk every few miles to keep from freezing. Passed through Edenburg and Mt. Jackson. Passing through town, I asked one of the young Southern sympathizers if there were any Rebs in the neighborhood. "I reckon you'll find right smart heaps of 'em out cheer a little ways." In the centre of the town the column came to a halt for a few moments. A woman stuck her head out of a window and sang out "I reckon you'll go back a little faster than that."

Two miles beyond the town, we found their forces, and the General and staff occupied a hill, side of the road. Beyond is a level plain for nearly a mile, until it comes to another slight elevation, where the enemy have got six guns planted. Our forces were formed in two lines on this plain to await further orders. The shells from the Reb guns fell in their ranks in the meantime. Presently, an orderly came riding up to us and told our band master that the General wanted the band up where he was. We went there, dismounted, had men hold our horses, and got ready to strike up as soon as ordered. General Custer, who always has his eyes on the guns and is ever ready to capture some, rode up to General Torbett and asked permission to charge his division and take them; the General did not feel willing, thinking there was something behind them. It is fortunate he didn't give the order, for, shortly after, we saw ten lines of infantry advancing.

Our boys fell back slowly, two rifled guns were planted on the hill beside us and commenced shelling. We struck up "Star Spangled Banner," the guns played bass, coming in on the explosives. For excitement, it far exceeds the concert on Boston Common that takes place on 4th of July mornings. The Reb cavalry tried to flank us on the right, our reserve was sent to check them, our boys kept falling back slowly, but they were not idle. They made their seven-shooters do their duty. We kept on playing until our skirmish line got up nearly to the foot of the hill, when we were ordered to mount, an order we were perfectly willing to obey. On the right, the firing was pretty lively. They were trying to cut us off from a bridge that was in our rear, and they partially succeeded, for some of the regiments in the rear of the column had to fight their way across and others swam the river. I guess the loss on either side did not amount to a great deal, and, as the object of our expedition was accomplished (to ascertain their whereabouts and strengths), we started back for camp.

November 24th. Started at daylight. The wind that blew from the snow-covered mountains was very cold, and we had to walk part of the way to keep the blood circulating. Arrived in camp in the afternoon, where we found some turkeys awaiting us which the good citizens of Philadelphia had sent, reminding us that it was Thanksgiving day, a fact which I was not aware of before.

November 25th. Grand preparations for a Thanksgiving dinner. After much discussion as to how they should be cooked, it was decided to have a genuine roast. Half a bushel of potatoes and onions were obtained from the commissary to serve as side dishes. A little after noon the welcome cry of "Dinner's ready" was heard. On the table was a tin plate for each man and beside was a knife and fork if he possessed one. If not, a jackknife, or wooden fork supplied its place. The turkeys were brought on, all carved up and served out for sixteen hungry mouths, together with sundry black kettles containing potatoes and onions. We took our positions around the festive board, and, for want of chairs, sat on large stones and sticks of wood, and commenced a vigorous assault on Turkey and its surroundings, and for a few moments were kept busy attending to the wants of the inner man.

November 26th. We stopped in this camp about a month altogether and enjoyed ourselves much. Rations were good. Adjoining our camp was a cow yard and sheds, and in that yard and under the sheds dwelt eight cows by night, which proved a great temptation for the boys to go foraging after milk, having been deprived of that beverage for so long a time. The consequence was several midnight excursions, and, when morning came, bitter complaints made by the old man because his cows were all dry. We laid it to the boys in the regiment, and they laid it to the band because we were nearest the yard. Our regiment, by this time, had got reduced down to pretty small figures. Only about one hundred men were fit for duty, hardly enough to perform the duties at headquarters, and the probability is we shall be relieved from here in a short time. Several rumors are flying camp that we are to go home and recruit, and others that we are to be consolidated with the 3rd Rhode Island Cavalry, but nothing is known for a certainty.

November 30th. Three years ago I enlisted.

December 8th. Today we were ordered to pack up and leave headquarters, after being with it nearly four months, and take our old place in the regiment brigade. It came kind of hard to pull down our rude but comfortable huts, with the prospect of sleeping on the cold ground until we could get them built again, but it had to be done. We had our boards and other building materials carried over to our new camp in teams (about a mile distant), saving us much trouble in chopping up trees for that purpose.

December 11th. Blew a gale all day and night, so cold that we had to knock off work and stand around a log fire to keep from freezing. In the night the roof of our shanty blew off, the ridge pole striking my bunky across the head, making him see stars for a few moments, but I could see them the rest of the night, as there was nothing there to obstruct the view. Tonight one of our cavalry pickets froze to death on his post.

December 12th. This afternoon it commenced snowing and continued all night.

December 16th. Got our shanty completed after nearly a week's work, having had to make the chimney all of wood since there is no stone in the vicinity. The inside was plastered with mud and began to crumble when we made a fire the first time, but a few applications of Virginia soil made it all right. This afternoon I was busily engaged in felling a tree behind my domicile when I was greatly surprised to hear the roaring of artillery at our front. The Johnnies, I guess, came after another thrashing, "Boots and Saddles" blew from brigade headquarters, the regiments following suit. We were ordered to saddle in light marching order and wait for further orders. A short time after, the news came that it was a salute in honor of the victorious march of Sherman to the sea.[59] We unsaddled, and the camp resumed its former quietness.

December 17th. Another grand salute this afternoon, and we thought that Richmond had gone up this time sure, but it proved to be in honor of Thomas's great victory in Tennessee. We got none of the particulars, merely that it was one of the greatest victories of the war, that the Reb army had been wiped almost out of existence and that the Reb command had been turned into a *worsted Hood.* [60]

December 18th. This afternoon heard of the order for the cavalry to start the next morning on a raid to Gordonsville. The very thought of it made me shudder, the thermometer somewhere in the vicinity of zero, and snow on the ground, but at night the band got the order from General Sheridan to report to his headquarters in Winchester.

December 19th. The cavalry started on the raid, and we for Winchester. On arriving there, the leader reported to the officer of the day, who told us that we could find a camping place at the edge of the town, but we had no idea of sleeping on the ground these cold nights, so he went and made the Provost Marshall a visit to see if we could have an unoccupied house. After hunting considerable time, they found one that suited on Piccadilly Street. It was a two-and-a-half-story brick, containing two large rooms on the lower floor, and was formerly used as a cabinetmaker's shop. The tools we put down into a cellar, borrowed a broom of our next-door neighbor, and prepared for housekeeping. As it would be inconvenient for sixteen men to cook round the fire at once, it was proposed and finally agreed that two men at a time take their turns to cook for the whole, and bring water from the corner pump. We borrowed a five-gallon copper kettle from one of the neighbors to make coffee and soups in, and from another neighbor a large fry pan. Then we were all ready to commence operations.

We get along with few family quarrels, and everything goes on like clockwork. At the appointed hours, the cook rings a bell and the boys come flocking in with their tin plates and dippers for their grub; they sit down in some corner and quietly dispose of it, then resume their reading, writing, card playing, clothes mending, or promenade the streets, just as it suits their fancy. The room upstairs we use as a sleeping apartment, also for reading, writing, etc. It has a large stove, about a dozen cane-seat chairs, a table, writing desk, etc. Our horses we keep in a yard on the opposite side of the street where there is a pump, have our wood, grain and hay brought to us in teams, so you see we have every convenience. All the duty we do is to play two hours a day in front of Sheridan's headquarters between 9:00 & 10:00 in the morning and 4:00 & 5:00 in the afternoon. The rest of the day we have to ourselves. The old lady who lives next door furnishes those who bring the necessary stamps with fresh bread every morning.

December 22nd. Today being cold, the valves of the instruments froze up before we got to headquarters and consequently we did not play. We went back, sat round the fire with our feet on the stove, smoking our pipes, discussing the weather, fashions, etc., and pitied the unfortunate that are out on the raid.

December 25th. Christmas. Although our chimney is wide, Santa Claus made us no visit, but Mrs. Fletcher did, our next-door neighbor and landlady, who brought with her some pies as a Christmas gift. She was very much opposed to our occupying the house at first, but, when she found out that we had the order from the Provost Marshall, she had to deliver to us the keys. She thought we would be noisy, destructive, etc., but now says, "You are a very quiet and orderly set of young men. I shouldn't know there was anyone in the house, you keep so still. How long do you expect to stay?" (She had eyes on that wood pile in the back yard.) We expect to leave in a few days. "Oh! I'm so sorry, etc. etc. etc." At 12:00 noon the bell rings, announcing that our chicken soup is ready, a rush is made for tin plates and dippers, then we march up to the big kettle and receive our rations, which are devoured with a relish.

In the afternoon after our usual serenade, we were invited by a resident of the town to his house, as he was to have a social gathering.

After supper, we started for there and, after playing a few pieces outside, were invited in. In the room were about a dozen of our scouts dressed in their disguise as Confederates. Had just got to bed when a loud knocking at the front door was heard; it proved to be Sheridan's orderly, the General wants the band up to headquarters immediately. We wondered what could be up this time of night, and we soon found out: it was Savannah that had gone up, and we were called on to participate in the glorification.

The house used for headquarters was illuminated from cellar to garret with candles, the 1st Regiment band was already there pumping wind, and as soon as they got through, we struck up and continued to alternate till midnight, then the staff officers took our crowd and started on a journey round town to wake up the secesh, to impress on their minds that something big had transpired. The first thing on the programme was a solo on the snare and bass drum, performed while marching through the middle of the principal street. Numbers of the inhabitants heard it and ran their heads out of the windows to see what in the world was the matter. "Put in the big licks now," says the Adjutant General, "Here's where a double-distilled Reb lives." We gave three cheers and passed on, and where we knew they felt very bitter towards us we would stop and give them "Yankee Doodle" or "Star Spangled Banner." After travelling round until 3:00 making the night perfectly hideous with our noises, the officers arouse one of the keepers of a restaurant from the arms of Morpheus and ordered a hot oyster supper for the crowd. While it was in preparation, they had dancing, singing and a gay time generally—about a dozen in number of all ranks, from the Colonel down. After waiting some time, the bivalves were brought on smoking hot with the fixings. We got to bed about 5:00 A.M., pretty well played out, but were excused from duty the rest of the day.

During the remainder of our stop in town, nothing of any great importance happened. We played regularly twice a day in front of headquarters, little Phil often standing on the porch smoking his cigar listening to the music. The boys borrowed a couple of fiddles and a guitar and banjo from some of the townsmen, and together with a flute and piccolo which we had ourselves, we made quite a good quadrille band, and had music most every night. We played once to a ball at headquarters and twice to private parties, the long evenings would be spent pleasantly in playing euchre, whist, etc., often sitting up till midnight.

January 2nd, 1865. Today our leader started for home, being fortunate enough to get a furlough for fifteen days. Late this afternoon, we received the order to join our regiment.

January 5th. We packed up bag and baggage and left our abode of civilization, after a two-week residence, with much sorrow, and the incidents during that time will always be remembered with pleasure. On arriving at our camp, we found the ground where our huts stood level—not a log or even a stick left, and not a tree left standing within half a mile to build another, so we had the pleasing prospect of sleeping on the ground. We cleared a space of the snow and pitched our shelter tent, which we lived in for the next three or four days, being nearly frozen during that time. We came to the conclusion we would stand it no longer, so George and I started off on a tour of observation after building material. After travelling nearly a mile, we came to a farm house with barns and outbuildings. On one of these barns were some loose boards. How to get them off without attracting the attention of the guard at the house was the next question, but it was finally done.

We erected a hut after a few days labor, got comfortably situated, and had the pleasure of sleeping in it just one night when, on the twelfth, the order came for myself and three others of the band to report to the 1st New Hampshire Cavalry for duty, and from that day forth my connection with the band ceased. This was not entirely unexpected, because I knew that the business of transferring us, promised at the time of our reenlisting, had never been attended to, and the officer who made that promise had left the service, and it puzzled me to see how they could hold me in this regiment when I reenlisted as one of the quota of a Rhode Island town and drew the state bounty. The commanding officer of the 1st Rhode Island thought so, too, and said he would have it investigated. The affair soon blew over, I suppose, because we never heard anything about it afterwards.

January 13th. We took our leave of the band today, and it came rather hard to part company after being together every day for nearly three years, and to think of the many pleasant times spent together, the very idea made me feel homesick. This left the band in a bad fix, taking four members away, it being small in numbers already. For the next three or four days we were kept busy building huts once more, which made the fourth time that we built winter quarters within three months.

I took my old position as bugler, which I had almost forgotten after so long a rest, but after a little practice was good as new. I had to go on duty once in three days, that is, to blow all the calls during the day. The last half of the month the weather was very cold, almost equal to that of New England.

February 10th. Today helped dig a grave for one of company who died in the hospital after a week's illness. I afterward made a headboard from a cracker box, put his name, company, regiment, and date of death, and placed it at the head of his grave. About the middle of the month, the whole Corps was reviewed by General Sheridan, and it made a splendid show to see about twelve thousand cavalry on parade—a sight not often seen on this continent.

February 21st. Was sitting dreaming over the fire when I heard the orderly sergeant sing out for Troop L to fall in to him. We did so, likewise the rest of the companies, and marched up in front of the officers quarters. The adjutant read us the great and glorious news, the capture of Charleston. When he got through, we gave three rousing cheers with a will. [61] Shortly after, cheering from the other camps could be heard, as it was an official order to be read to every regiment. The prospect of affairs began to look bright, the breaking of the rebellion's back, which has been accomplished so many times on paper, will, by the looks of things, take place at no distant day. The biggest part of both armies will be concentrated around Richmond and Petersburg where a grand death struggle will occur, resulting in the caving in of the Southern Confederacy.

February 26th. This morning our division was reviewed by its commander, General Custer. In afternoon we got the order to be ready to march at six in the morning, so we commenced packing up articles. Where we were going nobody knew, but, as we were told to destroy everything we could not carry, we probably shall leave the valley either to join Grant or Sherman.

February 27th. Was up at 5:00, flew round like a parched pig to get ready in time. My company together with J and K, were detached from the rest of the regiment and ordered to brigade headquarters to perform the duty of provost guard and orderlies. The column began to move about seven, starting with five days' rations for the men and three days' grain for horses, together with the rest of our goods making the lead for our horses pretty heavy—and when those give out we shall probably have to depend on the country for subsistence.

Travelled all day, reaching Woodstock at night where we camped. Distance travelled thirty miles; passed through Newtown, Middletown, crossed Cedar Creek, and Strasburg. Crossing the stream occupied some time, as it was considerably swollen and the current swift, and I here met with a loss which was not slight, considering place and circumstance. While fording the stream, my haversack, which hung over the bundle on the front of my saddle, was liable to get wet, so I had to hold it up for protection. My horse stumbled and came pretty near falling and I dropped it. I made a grab for it, nearly losing my equilibrium; instead of getting it, I had the pleasure of seeing it float downstream, with my five days' ration of hardtack. I came out little better than my friend Brown, who together with his horse went in, losing his carbine in the scrape.

February 28th. Passed through Woodstock, Edenburg, Mt. Jackson, New Market, and camped at Lacy's Springs. In crossing the north fork of the Shenandoah, the pontoons had to be brought in use, one regiment attempted to ford it but had several horses swept downstream, drowning one or two men.

February 29th. Passed through Harrisonburg, Mt. Crawford, and camped at a place called Klein's Mills a few miles north of Staunton. On the route, we passed over a bridge that was partially burnt. Near there, I saw two or three dead Rebs and came to the conclusion that the head of the column had had a slight skirmish. We entered Mt. Crawford at just sundown; I asked an old man standing at a gate when our advance had entered, and he said 11:00 this morning, and they went through on a dead run at the heels of the Southern cavalry. I thought the column must be a pretty long one, there being still another brigade in the rear of us. That afternoon we passed on the road several ambulances and sutlers' wagons with C.S.A. on them, having been captured by the advance. Some of them were still burning, and the sutlers' teams were cleaned out long before we got there.

March 1st. A drizzling rain. As General Early had evacuated Staunton, which he occupied the day before, the provost guard was sent into the town before the main column to destroy what abandoned property was left and search for concealed arms: considerable tobacco and a few arms were found, but not in any great quantities. The town had a Sunday appearance, nearly all the stores closed and the streets deserted.

In one of the stores I thought they were doing considerable trading by the number of customers, so I entered and found the proprietor and his daughter dealing out cider and apples without regard for the necessary stamps. On the counter was a keg of cider and a row of tumblers which he was kept pretty busy keeping full, while his daughter was filling the men's haversacks with apples. Most of the men went off without even offering to pay, while others were kind enough to tell him to charge it to Uncle Sam's account. He seemed perfectly satisfied. We had no right to complain. On a placard on the wall was the following: "Cider $2.00 a glass." I thought that at $18 a month the Reb soldiers could not enjoy many luxuries. I was told afterwards by a prisoner that it took a whole month's pay to get a decent dinner in Richmond and to get respectably drunk it cost about $50. [62] As no one but the provost guard was allowed out of there, we loaded ourselves with plug tobacco and dealt it out to the boys as they passed through town, until our brigade came along, then we took our position in the line and resumed our journey towards Waynesboro.

A short distance outside the town, we passed the huts that the Rebs had occupied lately, and they probably cussed us for making them leave them at so short a notice. The whole distance (thirteen miles) between these two towns, the road was in the worse condition I ever saw or dreamt before. The mud was of a clayey substance and very sticky, varying in depth from twelve to twenty-four inches. Because of constant travelling through, this surface resembled waves. Instead of the hole closing up after the horse's feet left, it would stay open, making it tolerably easy travelling when they followed in each other's footsteps, but if they happened to mis-step and get out of these tracks, they would get stuck, especially if they were near played out. The afternoon was cold, the rain freezing on the trees, and we were wet and chilled through. When we got near the town, we found the Rebs behind breastworks ready to dispute the passage. Our division, which was in the advance, filed into the woods, side of the road, and a strong skirmish line was thrown out.

They commenced the fray by throwing shells at us, most of them passing over our heads, knocking off limbs from the trees. Presently the small arms began to talk. Part of our brigade were dismounted and sent in a roundabout way to their left flank and rear. Shortly after, we hear the cracking of their seven-shooters. They weren't expecting the Yanks in that quarter; it threw them into considerable confusion, and they commenced to retreat. Our skirmish line charged over their breastworks, followed close by the rest of the division. In the town, I saw several dead Rebs lying in the street. We went through here like a streak (the women were running around, scared half to death), and came to a halt at the river. Here is where they were mostly captured, there being a bridge wide enough for only one man to cross at a time. They were sent to the rear under guard.

The rest of us forded the river, and what few Rebs managed to get across were soon taken, for they had to cross a long level plain before reaching the mountains, which they were putting for. We continued the chase after their wagon train, a part of which was found at the foot of the mountain, the rest scattered over it all along the road. Before we stopped, the whole train was in our possession. In these wagons were all kinds of camp equipage, command and guard goods, officers' baggage, ammuni-tion, etc. I found a number of relics, which I intended to keep but some rascal stole from me. One of the boys found a pair of pants with Jubal Early on them, which he intends to send home, others found prizes of more or less value.

Some four or five regiments were ordered to start the next day for Winchester with prisoners, among them was the 1st New York and 1st Rhode Island, under command of Colonel Thornton. We halted long enough to make coffee, and then resumed our journey over the mountains via Rockfish Gap. The night was dark as Egypt and raining still, the road was perfectly awful, being full of large rocks, and in some places just wide enough for a wagon to pass, while at our side would be a steep precipice, which would make one dizzy to look down into its dark depths, the wind strong and cold. I was wet and chilled through, my hands got so benumbed that there was no feeling in them for three or four days afterwards. Altogether it was a gloomy and wearisome night, but I couldn't think of being discouraged after the glorious events of the day. We have captured 1,600 prisoners, 11 guns, 17 battle flags and 200 wagons, and our division (3rd) did the whole of it, the 1st not arriving until it was all over.

About midnight we got on to the level country again and camped at a place called Brookfield, although I saw but one house with out buildings and a blacksmith's shop. All that it takes to constitute a town here in Virginia is one house, barn, corn crib, pigsty, and a few nigger huts. Headquarters were established at the house, the escort occupying the outbuildings. I was fortunate enough to get into a deserted shanty, together with about twenty others. It had a fireplace, we made up a rousing fire to take some of the chill out of us, mixed up some meal and water which we found here, cooked us a hoe cake, then lay down for a few hours rest. It rained all night and every place that afforded shelter had an occupant, even to the hen coop and pig sty. If one was lucky enough to find a barn with hay or straw to sleep on, he would consider he had got into first-class lodgings.

March 3rd. Weather pleasant and considerable warmer than yesterday. About noon, came to a railroad depot that was full of barrels of flour, wheat, and tobacco. These were destroyed and the structures burnt. At a large house near the depot was the scene of great confusion, men rushing in and out of the door, feather beds, furniture, etc., coming out of the windows, and the house finally burnt, all this because the occupant's name was Moseby and a relation of the celebrated guerilla. In the afternoon, we destroyed a large bridge over some river. In the evening it commenced raining again for a change, and between 9:00 & 10:00 we entered Charlottesville. Headquarters were established at a large mansion outside the town, myself with others occupying one of the outbuildings. We learnt from the negroes that their master had fled on hearing of our approach, taking with him a number of valuable horses. He was a wealthy and prominent Rebel, owning large tracts of land, great numbers of slaves, and holding some civil office under government. The negroes were all pleased to see us, this being the first time our troops were in this section of the country.

Three or four of us went into one of their log huts, and a conversation something like the following ensued. "Well Aunty, are you glad to see the Yanks?" "Lor Bless yer chile, I es neber so glad in all my life. I knowd you'd come some time rudder, I'se prayed and prayed for yer, and now you've got here at last. Glory to God, I told the childerns that the Lord had his eye on us and would not forget us in the hour truble, Glory Hallelyah, etc." She kept on in this style for about quarter of an hour, going through the motions as if she was preaching a sermon. After she got through, she baked us some biscuits, which we ate with some sorghum going right to the spot. We retired about midnight, well pleased with our evening's entertainment.

March 4th & 5th. We remained here waiting for our trains to come along, which had got stuck in the mud a number of miles back, and destroying the railroad and bridges. On a hill a short distance from us (in sight) is the Monticello mansion once the residence of Thomas Jefferson. Every day, we go out foraging in parties after feed for our horses and food for ourselves and always come back well loaded. A dozen of us went out five or six miles and on the way were fired into by bushwhackers, but no damage done.

We rode up to a large mansion, the residence of a wealthy planter. Half of the men stood guard while the rest of us went in. On the porch in front was assembled the whole family, looking at us with fear and wonderment. We told the old man that we didn't intend to disturb his house, but were after food, and requested him to tell us where we could find it. He said he had got but very little, just enough for his family to live on, and begged us to spare him. "There's Squire's . . . over there a short distance, who is rich and has got plenty." But we thought we could get enough here, so we commenced to reconnoiter. From one of the negroes we learnt that there were a number of hams in the smoke house. One of the boys requested the old man to lend him the keys, which he refused to do until we started prying it open, then he gave them up. Suspended from the beams overhead were as many as one hundred hams; each of us selected one apiece of the largest. After getting some flour and apples from other outbuildings, we took our turn standing guard while the rest supplied themselves, then started for camp, stopping on the way at a haystack and corn crib to tie up bundles for our horses to eat. The flour we gave to Aunty (as the boys called her) to bake into biscuits, and she kept one-half for her trouble. During our stop here, we got well rested and supplied with rations for the next three or four days.

March 6th. All the public property for miles each way was destroyed, and we resumed the march, the greater part of the negroes on this plantation accompanying us, old and young, males and females, truding along beside us on foot through mud and water, with their packs on their backs, bouyed up by the thought of freedom. The two divisions took different routes, ours towards Lynchburg. Went within sixteen miles of the city, where we destroyed several bridges.

March 9th. Started early, striking the Richmond and Lynchburg canal in the forenoon. We travelled down the tow path a number of miles, passing through the villages of Howardville and Warren. The 1st Division, which had passed over this route the day before, left a trail of destruction behind them, locks destroyed, canal boats burnt, the banks cut in several places letting the water out. This was a great blow to the Rebels, as this and the Southside Railroad was one of the only thoroughfares left open for them to receive supplies by.

March 10th. This afternoon about 4:00 we reached Columbia, where we camped. The negroes who find us every day have by this time swelled in numbers to thousands. They would hear of our coming a day or two in advance, and, by the time we get there, have a few valuables packed up and be bidding adieu to their masters, who stand by looking on with surprise as they join their brothers, freed men, for the land of milk and honey (as they think). They march by the sides of the column, talking, laughing, asking and answering questions, seemingly happy at the prospect before them, often travelling twenty and twenty-five miles a day through mud and water, fording streams, and at night huddling around a fire.

March 11th. The command stopped at Columbia all day, we drew five days' rations of coffee and sugar, the first government food of any kind since leaving Winchester. Went foraging, bringing back chickens, potatoes, sorghum, hay, and grain. On the way passed the reserve brigade headquarters, where the 1st Rhode Island Band are. I made them a visit in the afternoon and found they were enjoying the luxury of butter, which was captured on a canal boat. It seemed good to get back among my old friends even for an hour or two.

March 12th. Started off early, striking the Virginia Central Railroad at Frederickshall Station about noon, entering very sudden and not giving the postmaster/ferry operator notice to quit, but he did without any orders, and left behind all the letters, dispatches, etc. I got a pile of letters and amused myself the rest of the day reading them, some were red hot in their language and very bitter, having no idea of being subjugated—would fight to the last ditch—others were calmer and looked at things in the true light, and thought their cause was on its last legs. Some of the letters I sent home as curiosities. Meanwhile the troops were kept busy ripping up rails and twisting them over, burning ties, destroying water tanks, bridges, etc. Near the station was a large wooden warehouse filled with leaf, plug, pigtail, and fine-cut tobacco; after the boys got all they wanted, it was set afire, sending immense volumes of black smoke high into the air, and throwing the heat a great distance. Stopped here all night. [63]

March 13th. Left here in the afternoon. Towards evening, heard skirmishing but guess it did not amount to much, stopped at night at Beaverdam Station.

March 14th. Went within seventeen miles of Richmond, some of the troops going nearer, where they destroyed a wagon train.

March 15th. Reveille at 1:00 a.m. Reports that ten thousand infantry and cavalry are near at hand, endeavoring to cut us off. We halted near Ashland, the troops put into position and preparations made for an attack. Skirmishing commenced and continued at intervals during the forenoon, and in the afternoon we left suddenly, I suppose this being merely a feint. Marched until nearly midnight, when we camped. Rained all night.

March 16th. Marched at daylight and learnt from some darkeys that the road led to White House Landing, which we supposed we were making for.

March 17th. Marched all day and camped near Prince William Court-house. For the last three or four days, food has been very scarce, as this part of the country has been cleaned out before.

March 18th. Reached Indiantown near our destination, where we camped for the night, having nothing to eat during the day. At night I pounded up some corn, to soak overnight in water, then boiled for my breakfast.

March 19th. At an early hour the troops commenced crossing the Pamunkey, our turn not coming until late in the day, then crossed on a long rickety bridge. Dismounted and two abreast we marched to White House Landing. Here we found the army of negroes who followed us had collected together. Some were listening to remarks made by some of our chaplains, while others were in small groups, praying, singing, or hearing some colored brother preach. It was a huge camp meeting, and all seemed to think that the day of jubilee had come. No doubt, they felt happy at their safe deliverance from slavery. A day or two afterwards, they were sent to Washington in steamers. We camped about half a mile from the landing, and very glad we were to reach here, as we were about played out, our horses as well as ourselves needing rest. We have been over twenty days from Winchester and travelled about five hundred miles; fifteen of these days we had to live on the country, sometimes having plenty to eat, other days nothing. Reveille blew at 4:00 every morning, the head of the column starting about 6:00, and at 4:00 in the afternoon the head of the column went into camp, the different brigades getting as near together as possible.

Our force consisted of two divisions of three brigades each, numbering about ten thousand. Our position in the line was different every day, our division being the advance every other day. When we were near the head of the column, we got into camp in good season and had a good night's rest, and did not have to start off before eight the next morning, because we would be somewhere to the rear that day. The next night, it would be about 10:00. Every turn in the road, we looked anxiously ahead to see if campfires were in sight. The head of the column got into camp, had their supper eaten, and half of the men were in bed before the rear arrived. Every night we had to see that our horses had enough feed for night and morning. Late in the afternoon, if we passed a corn crib, barn, or hay stack, we carried enough along for two feeds. If we hadn't found one by the time we reached camp, we emptied our saddles of the bundles and trudged off perhaps five or six miles after it, arriving at a place where there would be about half enough for the party, then a great pushing and scrambling would take place for it, the unfortunate ones having to look farther.

In camp at night I've been without my supper after getting back from these trips, and too tired to hunt after water. There's no aqueduct or pump to run to; you have to trudge off in the dark hunting, sometimes for an hour or two, for enough to make bitter coffee, and you are not always particular about its being clear as crystal either. One night I thought it tasted uncommonly good, and came to find out the next morning a dead horse lay in the brook just above the place where I'd dipped mine. Sometimes all the sleep we got would be three or four hours out of the twenty-four. In the morning the boys are so sleepy that had Gabriel been there to blow reveille, it would have no effect on the weary slumberers. The guard, who was detailed every night to guard the camp and tie up loose horses, had to wake up the orderlies of the different companies, then the orderlies wake up the men of their companies, by going round shaking each man and sometimes rolling him over three or four times before he would get his eyes open. Many's the morning I've been off without anything but a cup of coffee to last me through the day, thinking the sleep would do me more good than food.

After getting all ready to start, I put a pot of coffee on the fire and sleep till the order to move comes, then I pour it into my canteen and drink it on the road. During all the time I've been in this army, I don't believe I've missed my coffee a dozen times in the morning, and as sure as I did I would have the headache the rest of the day. We have the pure article, and it is the mainstay of the soldiers: a quart of it, hot and strong, drunk just before a long day's march, puts new strength and vigor into the men. At different times during the day, the men enjoy short naps; the horses get so accustomed to following each other that they needed no guiding. I generally had my nap about 10:00 or 11:00 in the forenoon.

Because all the men are so tired, there was always plenty of fun going on in the line, and playing of practical jokes. Whenever a man was caught asleep, he was pretty sure to have some trick played on him by those awake, the man travelling in front of the sleeper would turn his horse out of the road into the woods, and, of course, the horse behind would follow. Then he would dismount, tie the sleeper's horse to a tree, then go off a little ways and shout his name till he awoke. "Halloa Jim, you going into camp this time aday?" Or the rider in front of another found asleep would guide his horse out one side of the road, where a branch of a tree hung just low enough to knock off the cap of the sleeper, and he'd have to dismount to get it. We always march by fours, and the length of the column, together with the packtrain and what few wagons we have, stretches out probably eight or ten miles. We leave a large number of horses on the march from sore backs, and hoof rot or "greased hell," as the boys call it. There are about four or five hundred men who have to play infantry part of the way.

March 27th. Crossed the Appomattox River and shortly afterwards got within Grant's lines. As they have heard of our exploits in the Valley, they turned out to greet us as we went by, and there was great enquiry regarding whether they had seen anything of Early down this way. We caught a peep of Petersburg and went into camp at Hancock's Station.

March 30th. Lay still until noon for the wagon trains to come up, travelled but a few miles today, the roads in an awful condition. It had to be corduroyed[64] as fast as they went along. Every little distance, a team would get stuck, and then would commence halloaing, snapping of whips, lifting, prying, the driver shouting "Yea hoo, Pete" or "Gee up there, Sal," and swearing until the very air looked blue.

March 31st. Lay in the woods nearly all day, heard heavy cannonading in the direction of Petersburg. Our brigade was rear guard, consequently we advanced but a few miles, as the wagons got stuck every little ways. While we were halted side of the road watching the troops march past, along came the Rhode Island Cavalry Band, and a more comical looking sight I never witnessed. About half of them were mounted on lame, blind, broken-down, played-out mules. They had done the U.S. good service in teams and, no longer able to pull, had been seized upon by the boys in preference to hoofing it.

April 1st. We were travelling along the road as usual when cannonading greeted our ears in front, showing pretty evidently that we had run against the Reb force that had been sent to oppose us. The infantry were hurried up, and we started off on the double quick. As we neared the front, the musketry was rattling away pretty lively. Our division was sent to the extreme left, passing through woods, open fields, over fences and ditches, where we formed brigade at the foot of a gentle slope, where we were somewhat protected from the shells that were coming thick and fast, knocking off limbs of trees and in some cases felling whole trees in their flight. [65] We halted here about half an hour within short range of the enemy guns, listening to the horrid music of their shells, expecting every minute to heave one down through our ranks and be blown into atoms. Meanwhile, the infantry at our right were kept busy, judging from the amount of noise. Presently we got the order to get ready to charge.

Can you imagine a fellow's feelings about that time, to have to face thousands of muskets with a prospect of having a bullet put through you? If you can, all right; I can't describe it. I've heard some say that they were not scared on going into a fight, but I think it's all nonsense. I don't believe there was ever a man who went into battle but was scared, more or less. Some will turn pale as a sheet, look wild and ferocious, some will be so excited that they don't know what they are about while others will be as cool and collected as on other occasions. The men unsling their carbines, with reins in one hand and carbine in the other, the butt resting on their hips. They charge in solid ranks, spreading out to the right and left as they advance. Just as we start, the band of our division strikes up "Yankee Doodle," which puts new life into the men, and off they go with a shout.

The Rebs were found to be posted behind fences and hastily constructed breastworks of rails; we stood and gave them the contents of our sevenshooters, and then fell back to our old position, somewhat hurried by a shower of bullets after us. After waiting some time for our lines to be reformed, we were ordered to charge again, this time with the sabre. Part of the cavalry were sent to the Rebs right and rear to cut them off, in case we were successful. When the infantry were ready, we charged simultaneously. We'd gotten the lay of the land before and knew where to strike for, their lines began to waver, and soon were in full retreat, with part of the cavalry following them up capturing guns, prisoners, colors, etc. This was a short but sharp engagement, both sides losing pretty heavy, and was called the battle of Five Forks (today heard of the capture of Petersburg). [66]

Camped for the night in a pine forest. We guarded the prisoners captured by our brigade, who belonged mostly to North Carolina cavalry regiments. We gave them some of our coffee and they were much pleased, saying it was the first they had had for some time. Their rations consisted of corn meal and fat bacon. In conversation with them, I learnt that their system of carrying on the cavalry department was different from ours. Each man owned his own horse, and, when killed in battle or captured, they were made good the loss by their government at a price set upon them by certain officers: $2,000. Their cavalrymen as a general rule are a more intelligent set of men than their infantry. They consider it a grade higher than the infantry branch of the service. Whenever a cavalryman commits a petty crime, they put him into the infantry as a punishment, and put some deserving man from the infantry to fill his place.

April 2nd. This morning the prisoners were all sent to army headquarters, and we resumed the march, the infantry going in one direction, the cavalry travelling alone. In the afternoon we struck the Southside Railroad, the object of so much fighting. No enemy being in sight, we halted a short time, but since Petersburg is captured, the road is not destroyed. Probably we shall have occasion to use it ourselves before long. [67]

April 3rd. Came up with the enemy this afternoon, but they kept falling back, gradually skirmishing all the way until after dark, when we went into camp in an open field. In front of us was a narrow strip of woods and beyond that was another open space which was occupied by the enemy. The skirmish lines of both sides stationed at the edge.

Tonight we received the first mail since leaving White House Landing. I got six letters and numerous papers, and while I was reading by the light of the fire, the Rebs commenced a vigorous shelling. We were ordered to put out those fires and consequently had to postpone reading until morning. We were ordered to saddle up, but shortly afterwards unsaddled again, as they ceased firing, but the skirmish lines were popping at each other all night, and several charges were made by each side to get position of the woods. We slept on our arms all night.

April 4th. We rise at an early hour, our brigade have the advance of the whole corps, with the prospect of a fight before noon. Our turn in the advance comes once in about six days, and it makes some difference in the minds of the men whether the road is clear or an enemy ahead of us. Most of the men preferred to be the rear brigade on such occasions, for, unless the enemy make a decided stand, the head of the column will have to do most of the fighting.

We found the ground occupied by the enemy the night before vacated, and learnt from a negro that they left silently about midnight. We travel along about a couple of miles farther; when we are fired upon from a thicket on the opposite side of a small stream. We are halted and form in line on the side of the road, and a party is sent ahead to reconnoiter. Presently, a shell comes screeching over our heads, a heavy line of skirmishers are sent forward, and an order sent to the rear for artillery, which shortly after arrives. After skirmishing about an hour, they leave; we ford the stream and follow them up double quick. We find it is only their rear guard who are trying to detain us long enough to let their infantry and trains get out of the way. [68] They were fighting dismounted behind breast-works, but a flank maneuver on our part puts them to flight.

We passed the place occupied by them the night before; they had vacated it but a short time when we arrived, for their log fires are still burning. Our brigade keeps following them close in their rear, and when we come too close they halt, form a hasty line, and attempt to stop our onward career, but a regiment sent to their flank and a charge in front sends them arunning again. Once in a while a dead or wounded man can be seen lying by the side of the road or in the fields, and every little ways we overtake a Reb who had got thrown from his horse or whose horse played out. Some would try to escape by taking to the woods, or jumping a fence and scooting across an open lot, but, as we have flankers each side of the road following the column, they most generally get caught. Presently they adopt a novel plan by which they can gain on us. They leave one of their caissons in the middle of the road, filled full of shells, and set it on fire. Each side of the road is a thick piece of woods which we have some difficulty in getting through. When we pass the caisson, the shells are bursting, pretty lively, one piece passing but a few feet above my head.

We strike the road again and continue the chase, passing now and then a broken-down team or a gun that had got stuck in the mud and had to be abandoned. They make another stand and prepare to form a line to show resistance, but one of our regiments gets in their rear, and a charge in front makes them break in confusion, and we capture most of them; only those having the best horses escape. We halted here for the main column to come up but soon learnt from a courier that the main body halted about six miles back. We then started with about two hundred Reb cavalry to join them, our squad guarding them with drawn sabres, they having to travel on foot. We found the main body occupying the fields on each side of the road, waiting for our brigade to arrive.

Instead of turning to the right where their main column went, the Reb cavalry kept on the straight road, probably in order to deceive us, but the General found out the direction to take, and, after a few hours rest, resumed the march. This was the most exciting race I was ever on, chasing them for about twelve miles, through mud and water, up hill and down, across brooks, through villages, etc. It is not bad fun when you have a good horse under you and plenty of ammunition. Hear that Richmond is gone up.

April 5th. Our brigade was sent off on an expedition by itself, probably on a reconnaissance after information. At Amelia Courthouse on the Danville Railroad we halted for a couple of hours. From a negro we learnt that General Lee, Langston Ewell, and other prominent officers held a consultation in the room over the depot last night, and that part of their army passed through here this morning. On the road in the afternoon we pick up a number of Rebs that straggled behind their column, most of them being about played out with sore feet. Towards night we strike across the country for our division. On the way we passed through a swamp where some of our horses got so mired that they had to be left. After hunting around two or three hours in the dark, we find our division and learn that during our absence they had had a hard fight but with glorious results: thirty-three battle flags, seven generals, guns, and prisoners by the thousands.

April 6th. As we start off this morning, we pass the long lines of prisoners, certainly numbering five thousand, as they are preparing to go to the rear. As General Custer's headquarters march by with those thirty-seven captured battle flags fluttering in the breeze, the Rebs look on in utter dismay. To capture a battle flag is considered a big thing because a regiment is always supposed to rally around it, and it is most always placed in those men's hands who will fight until the last. When thirty-seven are captured in one fight, you must naturally think that there was some tough fighting. Most of the prisoners look tired and discouraged and think the Confederacy about played out, although some say that they would give us a good licking yet. Most of them seem to be half-starved, having had nothing to eat for two days. We tossed hardtack as we marched by, and such a pushing and scrambling to get them I never witnessed before or since.

We came upon the enemy this morning, who were behind hastily constructed breastwork of dirt and rails, but after a short fight they were driven from them. Throughout this day and next there was fighting pretty much all the time, the Rebs still retreating but, when closely pressed, they stopped and showed battle, to allow their artillery and wagon trains to get out of the way. Part of their force engaged us, while the rest hurried on to build breastworks so as to be all ready for occupation by the time our forces arrived, but they would soon be vacated. They retreated so rapidly that they had to leave the dead and wounded behind. [69] Dead men became so common as hardly to attract attention. They would be scattered along the road every little distance or lying in groups in a field, behind a pile of rails used for protection.

This morning, I had to leave my horse behind: his back had got so sore that he wouldn't let me saddle him, and the skin on his withers had worn off to the bone, making an ugly looking sore. I was sorry to leave him because he was a good horse, high spirited, a fast and easy traveller and he kept in good condition on small rations, kind and gentle. I got him the day before leaving Winchester and rode him every day since, while others have had three or four during that time. I took one that one of our boys had been riding, he having captured one from the Rebs the day before, he didn't have much spare flesh on his frame but was tough. He answered to the name of Bones.

April 8th. We leave the infantry behind and strike off on another road and travel most of the day in peace until about 4:00 in the afternoon, when a steam whistle was heard. We hear cheering ahead, a staff officer rushes down the road and orders each brigade commander to move his men ahead on the gallop. We pass by a station on the Southside Railroad, shells flying over our heads, but where from I can't tell, because I can see nothing but woods ahead. We cross the track, ascend a hill, and form in line in an open field. In front of us is a thick growth of young trees, and behind that is another open space occupied by a Reb battery, who are dealing us grape and canister in double charges, which come rattling through the young saplings like hail stones. Can see the flash of every gun and hold our breath until they pass over our heads or strike the ground in front. Expecting every minute to be our last—not a very pleasant sensation.

Our brigade is ordered to advance through the wood, which is done with some difficulty, the men losing their cups, tearing their clothes and scratching their faces. A charge is then ordered, the men dash off with a shout and uplifted sabres, and soon the battery is ours. It proved to be the Washington Artillery of New Orleans, said to be the best in their service. During this time, the other two brigades were not idle, the spoils captured by our division that night and afternoon were between thirty & forty pieces of artillery, over two hundred wagons, three trains of cars, and numbers of prisoners. Our brigade lost pretty heavy, and a large number of horses, but our small crowd (the provost guard) got wonderfully lucky: one man had his arm blown off, my bunkmate was hit in the wrist, and the colonel commanding the brigade who we were with had several grape shot through his clothes, one smashing his watch, and two through his horse (but didn't kill him)–not hurting himself. We went back a couple of miles and went into camp in the woods for the night. I asked one of the captured artillery men where their infantry were, he said they considered this to be their rear and had parked their artillery and wagons for safety, not expecting us on this road. [70]

April 9th. We saddled up at daylight and waited, side of the road, about two hours for orders. The Rebs commenced the attack, thinking that they had nothing but the cavalry to contend with, but soon found their mistake. Presently, the colored of these corps passed down the road, followed by more white troops who had travelled most of the night. White boys lined the sides of the road, cheering and encouraging them on, "Give it to them, boys, we've got them in a tight place! Show them what the colored soldiers can do, etc.," which they received with shouts and waving of caps. The firing came closer, and we learnt that part of the cavalry had been driven back. The infantry were hurried ahead on the double quick, and soon after they got into position, the cavalry were withdrawn, and the whole corps sent to the left flank. We were kept moving from one position to another all the afternoon all the forenoon without being engaged. About noon, our division was formed, ready to charge on their wagon train, which was in plain sight, when a flag of truce came in, and firing ceased. Shortly after, General Grant was sent for, he and General Lee met at a small white house in a village of a few houses called Appomattox Courthouse, within rifle shot of where our division was. About 4:00 P.M. the news of the surrender was heralded through the different bodies of troops, Lee having agreed to accept the terms offered by General Grant.[71] Salutes were fired, bands played, and such cheering was probably never heard before on this continent.

Great was the rejoicing. Everyone was good natured and happy at the thought that the object we have been fighting and suffering so long for was accomplished. The men gathered in small groups talking and discussing the prospects of the future: what would be done with us, whether we should be sent to North Carolina to help Sherman clean out Johnston or whether we should be sent home. All agreed that the wonderful backbone of the Confederacy was at last broken, this time sure, so as not to grow together again, but we could hardly realize that the event we had all looked forward to with so much anxiety had actually taken place. Men were full of enthusiasm, it often running over, and they would give it vent by cheering, shouting, etc. Take it all together, we were a happy crowd.

For the last three or four days we have been so busy that we had no time to forage, consequently our horses fared rather slim, living on what little grass they could pick off the grounds. Late this afternoon, parties were sent out, and after travelling four or five miles, we came to a barn with some corn in it, but a party of some two or three hundred who had arrived before us were scrabbling for it. Thinking our portion would be small if we waited, we pushed on further, and made out to get a couple of feeds apiece. Each man started back for camp as soon as supplied, and I got almost to camp, when, by some mistake, I got on the wrong track (it being very dark) and struck the army in a very different place from where I left. I made several enquiries where the 2nd brigade, 3rd division lay, hardly anyone knew. After trailing around in the dark two or three hours, I saw some general headquarters. Representing myself as a messenger, I made inquiries, and found the direction, and arrived there about midnight, finding the rest of the boys abed and asleep.

April 14th. Rations very low, our last five days' issue having had to be stretched out to eight. We hear of a large quantity of potatoes buried in a barn some six or eight miles distant. A party of us start for them, and come back well loaded, together with plenty of leaf tobacco.

April 15th. This evening while sitting around the campfire talking over the events of the past week and the prospects of the future, one of our boys steps up and says President Lincoln is assassinated. "How did you hear?" "Up at headquarters," says he. We placed but little confidence in this rumor, as there are always as many flying around camp as you have mind to open your ears to. Also heard that Johnston had surrendered, and that all the troops were to leave Virginia within thirty days and report to our respective states. Half a dozen Rebs pass through our camp on their way home, having been paroled. It seemed strange to see them walking around loose, unmolested, when a few days before a sight of them would have brought powder and ball into requisition.

April 16th. The rumor about the President's death has unfortunately proved true, official news having been received and read before the troops. It was received with profound sorrow, the soldiers feeling as though they had lost a dear friend. The country loses a great, good, and honorable man, the colored men a firm protector. Flags were draped in mourning, and the officers wore the emblems of death on their arms.

April 17th. Marched this morning and stopped for the night at a place called Black & White, where we found a station and a few dilapidated old houses. A train of cars with grain had arrived the night before from City Point, the first we had drawn from the government for some time.

April 19th. Reached Petersburg and went into camp at the edge of the city near the breastworks lately occupied by the Rebs; the huts occupied by them all winter were still standing and were very good ones.

April 21st. Three of us got passes to visit the city to see the place that had been within sight and rifle shot of our troops so long. I found the city much larger than I expected, and before the war it must have been quite a flourishing business place. It probably contained twenty-five or thirty thousand inhabitants. About every other house had a sign out: "Pies for

Sale," and a miserable composition of dried apples and dough they were. No one but a soldier could eat them. In one place where we went in to make a few purchases, we asked the woman if she wasn't scared the day the Yanks rushed in here. "I reckon I was a heap," says she. "Our soldiers had told us that you Yanks were awful looking critters, had horns on your heads, and long tails, but you'uns look just like we'uns, only you'uns wear better clothes." I actually think she had believed this nonsense. Stores of all kinds were open and seemed to be well patronized, the streets were full of Confederate officers and soldiers who strutted about with as much dignity as though they had accomplished all they had been fighting for, but I guess by this time they have found out what northern mechanics and mudsills are made of. Several of the large buildings show the effect of our bombarding, chimneys and signs knocked to pieces, holes through brick fronts and roofs, or a corner missing on some granite building. What an eventful month this has been, what a prominent place it will occupy in history.

April 22nd. Got orders tonight to be ready to march early the next morning, as we all supposed, for Washington.

April 23rd. Started off early with five days rations and three grain, and we were headed in the opposite direction from Washington. Soon learnt that we were going to North Carolina to join Sherman, much to our disappointment. The weather was very hot, and roads dusty making marching very disagreeable. [72] When we found out where our destination was, all those who had horses that were nearly played out and could not stand a two-hundred-mile march had permission to turn back and proceed to City Point and report to the dismounted camp situated there. My bunk mate and several others went back and advised me that my horse couldn't stand it, but I had more confidence in old Bones than anyone else, and determined to stick by him as long as he could travel, I had never been away from my command a day and was bound not to commence now that the war was about over. We travelled on what is called the Boydton Plank Road.

April 25th. This afternoon reached Boydton seventy-three miles distance from Petersburg. This is an ancient and pleasant looking little town, most of the houses being situated on the main street, which was wide. Passed two or three antique looking taverns, with faded swinging signs and low porticoes, on which were several of the solid men of the town, smoking their pipes and reviewing us as we passed by. Camped for the night near the town, our headquarters being established at a large farm house, while we were scattered promiscuously about on the grass spots. Hay and grain were found here in abundance, our horses getting as much as they could eat for a rarity.

April 28th. Continued the march the next three days, averaging about twenty-five miles a day, and got nearly to the North Carolina line. I asked a negro we met on the road what the next town was, and he answered Boston. I had a great desire to see it and wished myself as near the genuine Boston in the old Commonwealth, but presently the column came to a halt, and we saw the head of column coming back shortly afterwards and supposed we had got on the wrong road. But when General Custer[73] got opposite us, I heard him tell my commander that Johnston had surrendered[74] and we were going back to Petersburg. The good news spread down the line like wildfire, the men receiving it with rounds of cheers, and all felt gay at the prospect of having no more fighting. What an eventful month.

Notes

1. Fort Sumter had fallen to Confederate bombardment the previous April.

2. The first Massachusetts regiment marching to Washington had been attacked by a mob on its way through Baltimore. Anti-Union sentiment was so strong in and around Washington, D.C., that Southern newspapers speculated that a popular uprising would unseat the government.

3. The first battle of Bull Run had occurred in midsummer. It was a defeat for the Union that ended in a rout, although casualties were about the same on both sides.

4. Federal General Nathaniel P. Banks was being sent in pursuit of Stonewall Jackson through the Shenandoah Valley, but Jackson's movements over the next couple of months were to be so brilliant that they would earn a place in the textbooks. Jackson's primary goal was to prevent further Union reinforcements from being sent to the Richmond front, where Union forces were threatening the Southern capital. When Banks was ordered to Richmond, Jackson moved to engage him.

5. Confederate Turner Ashby's cavalry was one of Jackson's most valuable assets, screening his movements and making his already mysterious tactics even more difficult to predict.

6. There is a break in the diary at this point, with at least one missing page; also, the penmanship becomes more cramped and difficult to read, and remains so throughout the rest of the diary. The missing battle description concerns one of the engagements in the Shenandoah Valley near the end of May, probably Jackson's surprise attack at Front Royal on May 23. The outcome was that Banks retreated out of the Valley, and there were wild reports in the Northern newspapers of total defeat and confusion. Stonewall Jackson was feared to be at the Potomac, ready to hit Washington. In fact, Jackson's seventeen thousand troops were completely worn out from marching over three hundred miles and fighting and winning several battles within one month. George Sargent's regiment was kept in the Valley briefly following the retreat.

7. President Lincoln had sent Generals Irvin McDowell and John C. Fremont into the Valley to engage Jackson, but the effort failed; Jackson escaped through the Blue Ridge on June 9.

8. General John Pope, U.S.A., had fought successfully in the West, and Lincoln had called him back to be in charge of the new Army of Virginia. Compared to Federal General George B. McClellan, Pope was a radical. He ordered his troops to confiscate property where necessary, execute guerillas, and hold citizens responsible for aiding the rebel cause. Troops living off the land and destroying civilian property were, however, an evolving fact of the war, irrespective of Pope's infamous orders.

9. At the battle of Cedar Mountain, again the opponent was Jackson, this time with twenty-four thousand men, and again Federal General Banks was in charge of the advance Union divisions. The Union soldiers were outnumbered here, and in the early stages of the battle fought well, routing the famous Stonewall Brigade, but Jackson brought in more men and battered the Federals. Contrary to Sargent's statement, historians have declared the battle a Confederate victory.

10. Lee had come with an additional thirty thousand troops, who had been entrenched against McClellan's army near Yorktown since April.

11. The surprise of the Federals is due to the fact that they were in the rear of the large army under General Pope. The Confederates seemed to have come out of nowhere. General Lee had sent Stonewall Jackson to flank them and cut their supply line, and both Jackson's foot soldiers and his cavalry under Confederate General James Ewell Stuart succeeded in making surprise raids, destroying and taking supplies.

12. This was the opening of the second battle at Bull Run. Federal General Pope, with sixty thousand men, had been thrashing around ineffectually looking for Jackson, and when he finally found him, Jackson attacked. Sargent describes the aftermath of the savage initial encounter along the Warrenton Turnpike, in which Union soldiers managed to fend off twice their numbers until after dark.

13. General Fitz-John Porter, U.S.A., had not taken part in the fight, despite being ordered by Pope to attack Jackson's flank. Pope, however, was not aware of the fact that Lee and Confederate General James Longstreet had just appeared out of nowhere (through Thoroughfare Gap) with thirty thousand more men; Porter felt that to move on them would be suicidal. The left wing of the Union line crumbled when Longstreet made an all-out attack with his entire corps. Porter was later court-martialled for disobeying Pope's order, and not until the 1880s did Confederate records and testimony win him a reversal.

14. Colonel Duffie's "high encomiums" may seem like a case of searching the bottom of the barrel for something good to say to the regiment, considering the disastrous outcome of the second Bull Run, but it is an old military truism that good marching discipline is harder to accomplish than good battlefield discipline. Colonel Duffie wanted to encourage it for the future.

15. There had been a small battle at Ball's Bluff early in the war, which resulted in a Congressional Commission on the Conduct of the War.

16. President Lincoln officially removed McClellan on November 7, hoping to find a commander who would press the enemy more vigorously. McClellan would unsuccessfully run against Lincoln for President in the upcoming election.

17. Federal General Ambrose Burnside, the new commander of the Army of the Potomac, had been massing troops across the Rappahannock from Fredericksburg for the previous four days. For once, the Federals had outfoxed Lee, who had briefly lost touch with their movements. Burnside wanted to attack Fredericksburg quickly, but while he waited for pontoon bridges to arrive, the rebels were building up their lines across the river; within a few days, his 113,000 Union troops would face 74,000 troops under Lee, Jackson, and Longstreet.

18. Rebel sharpshooters were picking off the engineers who were trying to lay the pontoon bridges; three volunteer regiments went across in boats and drove them from the streets, but the entire Rebel force was behind Fredericksburg along a series of hills, in nearly perfect defensive positions.

19. Across the river, the Federals made several charges, but, despite Burnside's repeated orders, Federal General Franklin was not able to get more than half of the nearly fifty thousand men under his command into action on the left flank. At the end of this day, the Union Army had suffered nearly thirteen thousand casualties and accomplished nothing. Burnside was in a rage over the losses, and had to be talked out of leading a suicide attack the next day. Fredericksburg, and the events leading up to it, resulted in a breakdown of morale in the North.

20. The winter of 1862–1863 had been "the Valley Forge of the War," according to one officer. Morale in the Union Army had reached a nadir after the defeat at Fredericksburg. General Burnside was unpopular and a poor administrator, and General Joseph Hooker was appointed to take his place. Hooker was very active, at first, in cleaning up corruption, upgrading food, improving hospitals, and instituting more liberal furlough policy.

21. By May 5, the Union forces at Chancellorsville were in full retreat. The battle has been called "Lee's greatest masterpiece," but that is partly because Hooker's generalship here was his poorest of the war. Chancellorsville left seventeen thousand Union casualties, thirteen thousand Confederate.

22. The Confederate Army had begun to make its move into Pennsylvania. The Union Army, in turn, tried to penetrate Stuart's cavalry screen to find out what they were up to. The subsequent battle at Brandy Station, near Culpeper, on June 9, was the largest cavalry engagement of the war.

23. The rumors were true. Lee decided that now was the time for an invasion of the North. It proved to be one of the major errors of the war, since its effect was

opposite what he had intended, resulting in an outburst of sentiment that temporarily quelled the Northern Copperheads and others who were against the war.

24. Advance Confederate units, primarily Jackson's old corps, were devastating at the start of the Northern invasion; on June 28th, Lincoln relieved Hooker of command, appointing General George Gordon Meade.

25. By July 5, Lee was retreating from Gettysburg where he lost twenty-five thousand to twenty-eight thousand men; seventeen of his fifty-two generals were casualties. Lincoln prodded Meade to counterattack before Lee could cross the Potomac, but, having a total casualty figure of over twenty-three thousand men, Meade was personally exhausted and reluctant to attack. Vicksburg surrendered on July 4; now the Mississippi River was a Union highway and Lincoln settled on Grant as Commander.

26. Federal General Hooker had always been popular with soldiers and civilians alike. (The term "hooker" is said to derive from his habits as a womanizer.) Lincoln would soon reactivate Hooker for the war in Tennessee.

27. The reliance on persuasion and inducement in the form of bounties was a key factor in the North's maintenance of fighting quality through 1864, when the majority of their veterans' three-year terms ended. More than half reenlisted.

28. The veteran's chevron was a meaningful insignia in any army that was undergoing the huge changes of 1864. Many veterans regarded the mass of new recruits as bums and vagabonds, as many were.

29. Laura Keene was a successful theatrical manager and melodramatic actress. Her troupe was playing at Ford's Theatre fourteen months hence, the night Lincoln was assassinated.

30. The Union navy built or began fifty-eight ironclad or *Monitor*-class ships during the course of the war. Two years before this diary entry, the "tin can on a shingle" *Monitor* and the ironclad ram *Virginia* (previously called the *Merrimack*) fought the first battle of ironclad ships to a draw at Hampton Roads.

31. In late summer, 1864, Admiral David Farragut attacked Mobile, which was protected by four gunboats, including a huge ironclad, three forts, and a minefield. The leading Union ship struck a mine and sank. At that point, Admiral Farragut placed his wooden flagship *Hartford* at the head of the line and reportedly gave the order: "Damn the torpedoes! Full speed ahead!"

32. There are many references in soldiers' diaries, in this and other wars, to the generosity of Philadelphians toward soldiers.

33. The official size of a regiment was one thousand men; by the second year of the war, however, veteran regiments averaged less than five hundred men, and by 1863, many had fewer than two hundred. The 9th N.Y.H.A. is a huge regiment.

34. Ulysses S. Grant, General in Chief of the Union armies since March, was making coordinated movements on several fronts; during the first half of May, he led a direct assault on Lee's troops in the Wilderness and fought the horrible trench warfare of Spotsylvania. In the North, press reports of those battles were far more positive than the facts allowed: the Union Army suffered thirty-five thousand casualties within a one-week period.

35. Tobacco was rare and precious among Union soldiers, as coffee was among Confederates; it was not uncommon for soldiers to trade these and other commodities under flags of truce.

36. Grant's aggressive tactics were quickly being tested to the limits. In the trench fighting at Spotsylvania he suffered eighteen thousand casualties. After that, during the latter part of May, he continued to try to flank Lee's left, moving generally southward toward Richmond, hoping to cut off his supply line. Lee kept moving with him and entrenching his men. At Cold Harbor, a few days before this entry, Grant had once again ordered an attack on the Rebel trenches and lost seven thousand men (to the Confederates' one thousand five hundred), most within a few minutes. Before assaults on trenches at Cold Harbor, many men were said to be scrambling around looking for a way to write their names either on their tunic or a slip of paper so that their bodies could be identified. Grant did not intend to initiate a war of attrition but of maneuvering and open battle. Out of necessity, because of dwindling numbers of men and resources, Lee settled into a relentlessly defensive posture.

37. Federal General Sheridan had been extremely busy for the past month, having been sent by Grant on long raids to the rear of the Confederate lines, even attacking the outskirts of Richmond, where at a place called Yellow Tavern he killed General Stuart in a cavalry clash. Nine days before this entry he fought to a draw Wade Hampton's cavalry near Trevilian Station.

38. Sargent is referring to McClellan's Peninsula campaign in this vicinity in the summer of 1862, which got bogged down in a month's rain and a great deal of troop illness.

39. After Cold Harbor, Grant decided to assault Petersburg, and so continued flanking in the same direction, southeastward across the James River, then back westward toward Petersburg. He managed to get men into position very quickly there, but his generals and soldiers were worn out. Meade, whom he trusted to handle tactics, wrote irritated notes to his generals telling them just to attack, since he found it "useless to appoint an hour at which to affect cooperation." Veteran units of men actually refused attack orders, having recently had their fill of attacking trenches. Petersburg settled into a siege.

40. The constant troop movement in certain areas created "hardpan" soil, which is still being reclaimed today—at great expense and effort.

41. Overall, spirits were low in the North in July and August, 1864. Grant's armies had lost over sixty thousand men in a relatively brief period. Lincoln's prospects for re-election seemed dim.

42. City Point was eight miles northeast of Petersburg on the south side of the James River. It was at the north end of the Union lines. "Airline" is Sargent's term for the trajectory of artillery shells.

43. "Butternuts" were poor white Southern troops or Southern sympathizers. The term apparently derives from the natural dye of the white walnut tree, used to color the brown homespun overalls worn by many troops.

44. Cavalry normally fought on foot, for purposes of better marksmanship.

45. The battle for Petersburg had been going on for a month and a half. If Petersburg fell, Richmond would have to be evacuated. The "mine explosion" resulted from a mine consisting of four tons of gunpowder laid by Northern sappers under the Confederate lines. The explosion blew up 300 Confederate troops and created a crater 170 feet long and 60 feet wide. The division of black troops that was originally to be the vanguard of the Union attack was at the last moment held back, and unprepared white troops sent instead, because Meade and Grant feared being accused of using blacks as cannon fodder. When the black division arrived, white troops were already struggling to the rear in panic; hundreds of Union troops were shot like fish in a bowl in the crater itself. The black division fought well, losing more men than any other division. After the "Battle of the Crater," the siege of Petersburg went on as before, unresolved.

46. The Sanitary Corps was a volunteer organization with seven thousand local auxiliaries, which held benefits, collected supplies, and supervised such things as latrines and water supplies in the northern hospitals and camps. Sanitary Corps volunteers, mostly women, helped provide such things as vegetables, bandages, and other medical supplies. It was the model for the American Public Health Association, founded in 1872, which played an important role in postwar philanthropy.

47. John Brown was a fiery Calvinist who in the 1850s hatched a scheme to capture weapons from the U.S. arsenal at Harper's Ferry, hoping to arm slaves and foment a slave revolt. With the financial aid of the "Secret Six," prominent Northern abolitionists, he carried out the plan in 1859. A detachment of U.S. Marines commanded by Robert E. Lee stormed the building and captured Brown. The scheme was not practical in any sense, but Brown met death on the gallows with great dignity and became a hero to abolitionists—an example of unbending rectitude and courage.

48. The Union Army was plagued by soldiers who collected their bounty, deserted, then often signed up again elsewhere, collecting further bounties. The same problem had occurred during the Revolution.

49. Grant sent General Sheridan into the Shenandoah Valley to find and destroy Confederate General Jubal Early's cavalry, which in early July had undertaken a successful raid on the outskirts of Washington. Sheridan's other job was to destroy crops and public property in the region so that it could not again be used as a corridor for troops. Grant is reported to have told Sheridan to destroy things so thoroughly that "crows flying over it for the balance of the season will have to carry their provender for them." Grant had practiced this policy once before, when he ordered crops to be destroyed during his own siege of Vicksburg.

50. The Shenandoah Valley was thick with guerillas.

51. The "seven-shooter" is probably a seven-shot breech-loading Spencer rifle. In the later stages of the war breechloading rifles like this and the Sharp's single-shot gave the Union a powerful advantage over troops still carrying muzzleloaders.

52. Sargent is writing the entry for August 30 in late September.

53. After being relieved of his command, George McClellan lived as a civilian, then let it be known he was available for the Democrats. He opposed Lincoln's plan for emancipation and favored restoration of the Union by military victory.

54. This battle at first went poorly for Federal General Sheridan, but he managed to recover; well-organized counterattacks by cavalry on the flank and infantry in the center pushed back Confederate General Early.

55. The allusion is to phrenology, which was popular in the nineteenth century.

56. The event here described was only one of many whereby Grant's original order to destroy all property of military value escalated into a scorched-earth campaign. Rebel guerillas followed in the rear of Sheridan's army capturing and killing couriers, stragglers, teamsters, and hangers-on, and acts of vengeance and destructiveness increased on both sides. Ninety-two miles of valley land, from Winchester to Staunton were razed, and thousands of innocent people were left with nothing.

57. The battle of Fisher's Hill was a Union victory, although both sides lost about 5,500 men here and at Winchester three days before. This victory over Early strengthened Lincoln's re-election bid.

58. The Battle of Cedar Creek, here described, was one of the most dramatic surprise attacks of the entire war. General Sheridan had gone to Washington to confer about the future of his army, but was now on his way back, in Winchester. Jubal Early, C.S.A., who had been thought defeated, had in fact been reinforced, and he successfully overran the 8th Corps at dawn with three divisions of men. Sheridan, hearing the sounds of battle fifteen miles away, saddled up and made his famous ride, later recounted in song and myth, rallying the troops down the line.

59. After occupying Atlanta in September, William Tecumseh Sherman convinced Grant that he could march to Savannah. It was a risky, unorthodox plan. In the company of thousands of bummers, freed slaves, and camp followers of all sorts, Sherman's army made a fifty-mile-wide path of destruction to the sea. The Confederate forces evacuated Savannah on December 21.

60. The diarist's information was accurate: The battle of Nashville was one of the most crushing Union victories of the war. For all practical purposes, it obliterated the Army of Tennessee. Confederate General John Hood retreated clear to Tupelo, where he resigned his commission.

61. Sherman carried total war through the Carolinas. Over a month and a half, during which it rained much of the time, he marched sixty thousand men over four hundred miles through swamps and across swollen rivers, on a path declared "impossible" by knowledgeable authorities in the Confederate government. During this leg of his Southern march, the destructiveness of his troops exceeded Sherman's orders, with private homes being set afire, ordered put out by officers, then set afire again by other troops. This may partly have been a result of the fact that South Carolina was one of the most radical states—the "seat of the rebellion." Charleston surrendered on February 18.

62. By the spring of 1864, forty-six Confederate dollars were required to buy what one had bought in 1861. Many areas in the South had moved back to a barter economy. The Confederate Congress already realized that of the various methods of financing a war, merely printing money was the most destructive; they passed a comprehensive tax bill a year before, but there was no effective method of enforcement.

63. The policy of total war had resulted in massive destruction of the South. Sherman had rolled through South Carolina, burning everything in sight. Railroads, farm machinery, industries—much of the assessed value of the South was worn out or destroyed, while Northern wealth increased by fifty percent because of the war-stimulated economy.

64. Corduroying was the process of cutting and laying logs across otherwise impassable roads.

65. Grant now held Lee's army at bay in Petersburg. He feared that Lee might escape and join Johnston's army in North Carolina. On this day, he sent Sheridan's cavalry and the Fifth Corps to attack ten thousand Confederates near a road junction called Five Forks. The Federals lost a thousand men but inflicted five times that many losses on the Confederates.

66. Hearing of the success at Five Forks, Grant ordered a total assault up and down the lines at Petersburg at dawn. Four thousand Union soldiers were killed in the attack, as the Confederate soldiers continued to fall back and eventually escaped across the Appomattox River.

67. Richmond was also evacuated that afternoon and during the night, the Confederates burning or blowing up arsenals, factories, and bridges as they left. By dawn the next day the industrial sector of town was destroyed.

68. Sheridan's cavalry, along with two infantry corps, were running along beside Lee's thirty-five thousand men at this point, trying to keep them from turning south. There were other Federal units to Lee's rear.

69. On this day, the Union troops captured seven thousand men.

70. The railroad station where this engagement occurred was the Appomattox Station, one hundred miles west of Petersburg. Sheridan had maneuvered into a position in front of Lee's remaining forces. The trains that were captured were loaded with rations.

71. One of Lee's officers suggested that the army disperse and go on fighting as guerillas, but Lee decided that it would result in further, now fruitless destruction. The house where the generals met belonged to Wilmer McClean, who, through an odd coincidence, had owned a house near Manassas, Virginia, that had been used as Confederate headquarters at the first battle of Bull Run. Grant's terms were generous. He paroled Lee's entire army, allowing them to take home their horses or mules "to put in a crop." Grant later described his own feelings, as they shook hands, as "sad and depressed" at "the downfall of a foe who had fought so long and valiantly."

72. Although Lee had surrendered, Confederate General Joseph Johnston hadn't yet, nor had Confederate General Edmund Kirby Smith. Jefferson Davis and the Confederate cabinet were escaping by rail, exhorting Southerners to carry on as guerillas.

73. Federal Generals Custer, Sherman, and Sheridan played key roles in the Indian wars over the next ten years, all of them taking a more or less hawkish stance. As an Indian fighter, Custer became more eccentric and less likable to the soldiers under his command, a fact that can be demonstrated by their desertion and suicide rates. At Little Big Horn he led the entire 7th Cavalry to its death against the Cheyenne and Sioux.

74. Sherman got into a political imbroglio because the surrender he negotiated with Johnston exceeded his authority. It offered to recognize existing state governments, allowed arms to be deposited in state arsenals, and various other elements that the cabinet interpreted as items of a peace treaty rather than a surrender, far too "soft" in nature. Grant conveyed the cabinet's disapproval, and Sherman renegotiated the terms. Secretary of War Stanton continued to distrust Sherman and released to the newspapers a version of these events that put him in a particularly bad light, resulting in continuing enmity between them.

3

The Spanish-American War

Although the Spanish-American War was both brief and relatively blood-less, it was accompanied by major changes in the way Americans thought about themselves and it established the United States as a power in world politics. The immediate spark that ignited the war was the public outcry following the sinking of the *Maine,* and the rallying cause was to secure freedom for tyrannized Cuban nationals. But this conflict surely had as much to do with changing ideas about America's destiny and a belief that the nation was "coming of age" on the eve of a new century. It marked the beginning of U.S. imperialism and became an important symbol of post–Civil War national unity. In many ways, the war with Spain was similar to the Gulf War nearly a century later.

Because of a great economic boom spurred in no small part by Re-construction, the United States had already become an economic power, if not yet a military one, by virtue of its huge industrial growth in the thirty years following the Civil War. A generation of young men who had never experienced the horrors of war and who were determined to play a larger role in world affairs was on the verge of taking over leadership from the old generation. It was a time when many Americans began to hold firmly the contradictory beliefs in freedom and self-determination and, simulta-neously, in the "divine right" of the United States to expand its boundaries. The disappearance of the American frontier left us looking for new mar-kets and new worlds to conquer. Social Darwinism was one of the popular philosophies of the day, preaching the survival of the strongest nations in a world of inevitable and natural international competition.

America's pride had been damaged by incidents such as the boarding

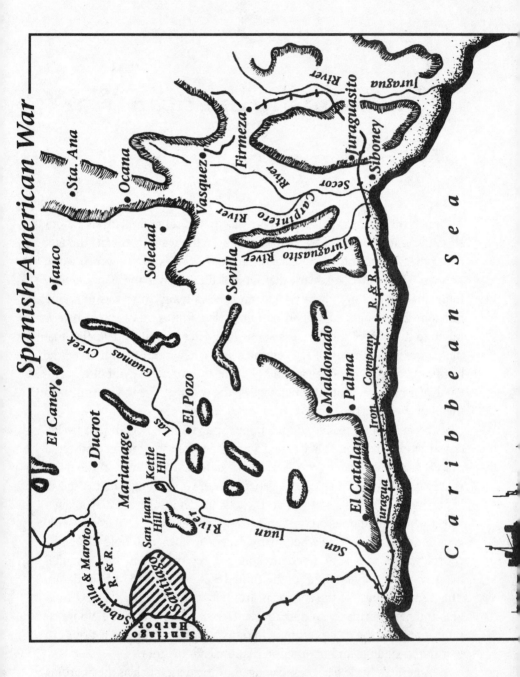

Spanish-American War

of an American steamer, *Alliança,* by Spanish gunboats in 1895—a reminder of the treatment the United States had always gotten on the seas by the European powers. Newspapers had a field day with the theme of Spanish arrogance. William Randolph Hearst and other purveyors of yellow journalism fanned the war fever with incendiary headlines and stories that were exaggerated or in some cases completely fabricated. In his unending quest to sell still more newspapers, Hearst was determined to foment a war, and he even took credit for it in the headline "How Do You Like the Journal's War." When Frederick Remington, who had been sent down to sketch scenes of the Cuban insurrection, asked to come home because he could find no such scenes, Hearst cabled back, "You furnish the pictures, I'll furnish the war."

A real turning point in the intensity of the newspapers' war with Spain came when the military governor imposed strict censorship on the press in Cuba and imprisoned several American newspapermen. Headlines began screaming for American intervention to protect its citizens. When soon after, Remington erroneously depicted a young maiden being strip searched on an American ship by a group of leering Spanish ghouls, the effect of the front-page illustration on public opinion was immediate and dramatic.

Yet the war with Spain was not merely the work of a single interest, nor was it something that happened out of the blue. The mid-1890s had been a time of domestic unrest in the United States, and there was almost certainly a connection between the economic downturn that had begun in 1893 and lasted several years and the country's embrace of "jingoism" in foreign affairs. By this time, as well, the United States had considerable business interests in the area. American investments in Cuba amounted to $50 million, and the annual trade figure exceeded $100 million. By 1895, the United States was buying 83 percent of Cuba's exports while only 6 percent went to Spain.

During this period, the United States was absorbing thousands of refugees who had fled the tyrannies of the Old World, and they were naturally sympathetic to the plight of the Cubans under the clumsy thumb of the Spanish. Once again, freedom became a charged word. Cuban revolutionaries were well represented in the United States. In New York the Cuban poet, José Martí, organized attempts to invade and liberate Cuba, and later he served as a very effective public relations point man for fanning war fever in the United States.

The Cuban Revolution in 1895 was set off by a depression brought on by the imposition of high sugar tariffs by the United States and a resulting decline in sugar purchases. Maximo Gomez, a hero of the earlier Ten Years War in Cuba and now Commander-in-Chief of the Revolutionary Army, instituted a scorched-earth campaign to burn the entire island's sugar crop, hoping to force affluent planters and merchants to join him. Gambling that he could make the expense of holding the island for Spain much greater than the economic benefit, Gomez proved to be a ruthless revolutionary leader. In three years of fighting, sugar production declined by 85 percent, mostly because of burning of cane fields by both sides, but especially the insurgents.

In response, Spain first sent the famous victor of the Ten Years War, General Arsenio Martinez de Campos, and then continued to add troops until by 1898 the force in Cuba had reached 150,000 regular Spanish troops and 80,000 loyalist Cubans. But General de Campos's heart was not in the war, and over time Spanish morale declined. Although not many perished in combat, thousands of young Spaniards were dying of tropical disease.

General Valeriano Weylar y Nicolau was sent to replace de Campos, and he implemented a "reconcentration" strategy, which he believed would sap the morale of the insurgents by putting their civilian loved ones in great jeopardy. He also ordered that whatever sugarcane fields had not been burned by insurgents be burned by Spanish troops. The reconcentration centers soon became breeding grounds for disease and famine, with many thousands dying. There was a passionate response in the United States, and Weylar would later have to defend himself against charges of violating human rights.

In 1897 the inauguration of McKinley—who had campaigned by sitting on his front porch in Ohio and giving speeches to the thousands of people who flocked to him via the railroads—marked the beginning of a period of relative domestic tranquillity. Prosperity was returning after the depression of the mid-nineties. The agrarian uprising led by William Jennings Bryan had been turned back. McKinley was the last of the presidents to have fought in the Civil War and remained deeply disturbed by memories of the war. As newly elected President, he tried to continue Grover

Cleveland's Cuban policy of restraint and patience. He continued a flurry of secret negotiations through his envoy General Stewart Woodford, trying to wring concessions from Spain that would avoid war. Meanwhile, U.S. business interests, hoping that the Philippines could serve as a base for great Far Eastern trade, pressured McKinley to force Spain to sell it. The United States had already offered many times to purchase Cuba.

But the more the United States pressured Spain, the more the insurgents were encouraged to demand total independence, something that the ego of Spain simply could not sanction. There was enough domestic unrest and intrigue in Spain that the government felt that it could not afford to relinquish the last remaining symbols of Spain's glorious heritage in the New World. Spain might fight and lose that heritage with honor, but they could not simply bargain the possession away. The constitutional monarchy was only a few years old at the time and many in Spain were convinced that war with the United States was, ironically, the only way to save the political system in Spain.

All the while, public pressure in the United States was building for war. The condition of the people in the reconcentration camps was deteriorating alarmingly. At one camp alone it was reliably reported that an average of forty-six people, mostly women and children, were dying each day. Starvation and disease were rampant. McKinley was so moved by their plight that he privately donated $5,000 of his own money toward a relief effort.

Unfortunately, McKinley scuttled his chances for peace by appointing to his cabinet a group of over-the-hill political cronies who were effectively preempted by younger, hawkish assistants, such as Teddy Roosevelt, the Assistant Secretary of the Navy. As Assistant Secretary, Roosevelt worked behind the scenes to build up the navy and involve it in war with Spain. He usurped much of the power of the aging and ill Secretary Long. He conspired with Henry Cabot Lodge to have Dewey named commander of the Asiatic fleet and even went so far as to send him confidential instructions to be ready to attack the Spanish in the Philippines.

Then in January of 1898 the U.S.S. *Maine,* under the command of Captain Charles Sigsbee, entered Havana Harbor to show the colors as an awkward gesture of friendship to Spain. On February 15, the *Maine* exploded without warning in the harbor and sank.

The Spanish government immediately expressed shock and regret over the event, offering to cooperate in an inquiry to determine the cause. But the public outcry, spurred on by the yellow journalists, swept across the country with demands for intervention in Cuba. The likelihood that it was an accidental explosion, which was apparently believed from the start, was made irrelevant by the newspapers and public opinion. Spain had surely done the deed. War fever reached its height.

Events swirled out of control. On March 7, 1898, three weeks after the explosion of the *Maine,* McKinley asked congress for a $50 million appropriation "to get ready for war." Spain was given an ultimatum to put an end to reconcentration, call an immediate truce with Cuban revolutionaries, and grant Cuba independence. Congress was pressuring the White House so intensely that there was a real threat that they would declare war with or without a request. One common feeling was that McKinley was holding out because the business community generally opposed the war. There were, in fact, contradictory feelings within the business community. Many indeed opposed war in Cuba, while others felt the United States must intervene to protect their investments. However, business interests were more united on the secondary issue of the Philippines, which they thought would offer a foothold for the Eastern trade.

McKinley extended the ultimatum to Spain until April 23, but the navy had already received orders to blockade Cuba when the Spanish answer arrived in the form of a declaration of war on the United States.

During the 1870s after the horrors of the Civil War, a belief had arisen that Americans would never fight another war. We had no strong enemies and, more important, the random destructive power of modern weaponry had proven so awesome that surely no one would ever risk unleashing it again. The army was significantly downsized. As sentiment for disarmament took hold, the military began thinking harder than ever before about what they were and what they should do. An unfinished work by Emory Upton, *The Military Policy of the United States,* began to circulate among military thinkers during this time. Known as the "Uptonian unpreparedness theory," it became one of the most influential documents in U.S. military history, postulating that the United States was never prepared for military challenges. Inadequate budgets, lack of modern weapons, and political appointments that hampered professional training found us unprepared in every war, with the result that the country squandered the lives of its citizens and wasted vast amounts of money to achieve its victories.

The result of all this self-evaluation was that military professionalism flourished. War games were begun for the first time in American history. Eventually the professionals who had served during the Indian wars, and a new generation that had missed "their war" turned their attention to innovation. Weapons were modernized—including breech-loading artillery, smokeless powder, cartridge belts, armor plated steamships—specialization was encouraged, and schools for engineering, medicine, and artillery were established.

The 1890s saw the building of a modern navy of steel ships. Legislation passed in 1886 prohibiting the use of foreign materials, making it profitable for American shipbuilders to develop state-of-the-art technology and to create a world-class navy. The Navy Act of 1890 opened the way for a new strategic naval plan, provided by Alfred Thayer Mahan, whose book *The Influence of Sea Power Upon History* equated control of the Caribbean with the Royal Navy's control of the English Channel as the key to U.S. domination of the sea.

It became popular to argue that our future national security and greatness depended upon a large navy supported by bases throughout the world. Sea power was seen as the key to future respect among nations and the best way to ensure the safety of the United States and its trade.

This was the situation at the outbreak of what was to become Teddy Roosevelt's "splendid little war." The navy performed well; the army was confused, disorganized, and unprepared. The original plan called for a blockade and a land offensive only after September when the threat of yellow fever was gone. But the blockade was perceived as too slow, and it was argued that one couldn't take and hold ground without ground troops. The country, the press, and the politicians did not want to wait until fall. Adding to the problems were the tremendous logistical difficulties of bringing an army together for the first time since the Civil War and then keeping them in one place at Tampa Bay. The chaos became unimaginable, as Teddy Roosevelt was quick to point out, and General Shafter found himself under tremendous pressure, even from McKinley, to launch an invasion.

Finally, Admiral Sampson—a Navy man—sent a cable that ten thousand troops could take Santiago in two weeks and end the war. That did it; the army had to move. No more patience, no more waiting until fever season was over, no more waiting until supply lines had been organized. After several humiliating misadventures trying to land supplies for the insurgents, a force of marines landed at Guantanamo Bay on June 10. After four days of fierce fighting, they were able to seize the harbor for the Americans in the first actual troop combat of the war.

Shafter's main force began landing on June 20 at Siboney and Daiquiri to begin the major offensive to Santiago. Fighting broke out at Las Guasimas, but soon the landing area was secured. Ten days later, in spite of massive confusion, critical supply problems, and troops already coming down with fever, Shafter launched his attack on the village of El Caney, and then San Juan and Kettle Hills. On the 4th of July, Admiral Sampson destroyed the entire Spanish Fleet under Admiral Cervera and by July 17th, the Spanish General Toral, who realized he was at the mercy of the Navy's big guns, surrendered Santiago without forcing a final full-scale assault on the city.

While the fighting was over, the most potent danger to the troops, disease, was in full attack. In all, fewer than four hundred soldiers would be killed as a result of the actual fighting, but more than five thousand would succumb to various fevers, primarily yellow fever. The initial staging area in Siboney had early on been converted into a hospital camp where conditions could not have been more appalling. Besides blundering in the matter of ammunition and food, the army apparently had managed to bring little or no medical supplies, and few if any blankets or tents. The Americans were completely unprepared to care for their sick and dying soldiers. At the moment of victory on the field, the army faced the terrifying prospect of being wiped out by disease. The symptoms of yellow fever came on rapidly, beginning with headaches, weakness, and nausea, followed by rapidly rising fever and jaundice. In a matter of hours, many men were too weak to walk. Its final stages produced bloody vomiting and diarrhea. The cause of the disease was as yet unknown, and the only treatment was rest and good nursing care to reduce fever.

Since the Crimean War of the 1850s, the work performed by women in wartime had a tremendous influence not just on the health of soldiers but on the more general development of basic health services and the health professions. Florence Nightingale, the English nurse who in 1853 went to Crimea as a volunteer, had employed sanitation and rigorous cleanliness to dramatically lower mortality rates from cholera, typhus, and dysentery, and her accomplishments helped light the way for nursing as a full-fledged profession. During the Civil War, mortality rates from illness were still twice as high as from wounds, but they would have been far higher if not for voluntary organizations like the Sanitary Commission, staffed almost entirely by volunteer women.

In 1898, faced with an epidemic of typhoid and yellow fever in army camps and unable to recruit enough men to fill the need, congress authorized the army for the first time ever to appoint women as nurses—to pay them for their services, but under civilian contract, not as enlisted military personnel. Amy Wingreen, who lived in Chicago and had been trained as a nurse in Cook County Hospital, was among this first group of women to be actually recruited by the army for service.

The women nurses were paid half of what the men were paid. In spite of this, more than 1,500 of them served between 1898 and 1901, most in the United States as nurses or aids. The experiment was highly successful. Women like Wingreen performed so well under very tough circumstances that the military was convinced of the need for permanent appointment of women as nurses. As a result, Congress established the Nurse Corps in 1901. It was considered an auxiliary of the army and held rather ambiguous, quasi-military status. Women nurses still did not receive rank or equal pay, nor were they entitled to retirement or veterans' benefits. Yet the Nurse Corp opened the way for women in the military and at long last led to the debate ninety years later over the role of women in combat.

The Spanish-American War was also the first time that black troops were commanded by black officers. In the Civil War they had fought under white officers. By the Gulf War, several of the ranking officers, including the Deputy Commander in the field, Lieutenant General Calvin Waller, were black Americans, and of course they all served under the first black Army Chief of Staff, Colin Powell.

Amy Wingreen participated in a victory with more widespread significance than the victory over the Spanish. For hundreds of years, yellow fever had been a recurring plague all over the world, particularly in tropical and seaport towns. It regularly visited places like Philadelphia and

Charleston with horrendous death tolls. During the war Walter Reed was placed in charge of studying typhoid and yellow fever. At the time it was widely thought that yellow fever was spread by contact with infected bedding or clothing, although a Cuban epidemiologist had suggested insects as the source as early as 1881, and in 1896 an Italian doctor had isolated a yellow fever bacilli. It was this bacilli that Reed investigated. By 1901 he successfully proved that mosquitoes, not bed clothes, were the transmitters and within ninety days American health workers were able to nearly eradicate the fever from Havana.

The New York Times described Amy Wingreen "as an expert in yellow fever cases." She obviously saw the chance to go to Cuba as an opportunity for romantic adventure as well as a patriotic act. If the romantic idealism she displays at the beginning of her journey strikes one as naive, it was this same quality that seemed to lend her strength during the darkest moments and in the ugliest of circumstances, when surrounded by death and coming down herself with fever, she refused to give up. She lay in her tent unattended until finally able to get up and make it to the commissary. "Four days I had fever, two more days I lounged around, then went back to work. The poor men were so glad to see me back, though I could hardly drag myself about." Her bravery and spirit of responsibility, and the victory to which she contributed, are one of the positive legacies of the war against Spain.

The Diary of Amy Wingreen

Western Union Telegraph Co.,
July 14, 1898
Washington, D.C.
Miss Amy Eleanor Wingreen,
If willing nurse yellow fever in Cuba come here immediately transportation
refunded answer.

(Signed) Ass't Surgeon Gen. U.S.A.

We are moving, en route Washington D.C. to Cuba. Left Chicago 9:00 P.M. Friday, July 15, 1898, via Pennsylvania Limited.

I must confess that I felt lonely when sister left me. A strong desire came to call loudly that I would go home with her, but it soon passed and next week I may be in Cuba.

Washington! and on time. Met by members of the D.A.R.[1] The War Department is alive with orders, and the streets surge with military men, hurrying. The Surgeon-General is in New York on the momentous errand of inspecting warships to be sent to the scene of action with supplies for our sick men. Chief Clerk Jones has made out our contract and has sworn us into the service. So now I have promised to defend my country, to fight her enemies and be loyal under every circumstance, for $30 per month, and one ration in kind per day,[2] i.e. hardtack. A nurse is looked upon in the same light as is a soldier, to share his perils and hardships.

July 19, New York. Major Arthur is to make out our transportation to Cuba at Army Headquarters, Chapel Street, but our ferry brought us over before the building opens, so we have a few moments to stroll down Broadway. We note these inscriptions being written on the bulletin-boards: "800 new cases of yellow fever in Cuba." We hold our breath, look at each other, never-flinching! We are soldiers now, to go to Cuba's fever camp and save Uncle Sam's men. We are eight in number, and attract much attention as we go in a group down the street. We are the first body of women to go out in the time of war under the Government of the United States. [3] What we go to face we do not know.

Tuesday, July 19, 3:30 P.M. On Board the U.S.S. Resolute, New York Harbor. We are preparing to leave the shore. Enthusiastic crowds wave hats, umbrellas and handkerchiefs on the dock. "All Aboard!" and the gangplank is removed. We are going—going—the boat pulls out—salutes reach us, "Hurrah! Cuba Libre!" shout the crowd on shore. Ah, yes, Cuba libre. But our hearts are filled with this desire: that it is our noble lads lives we seek to save.

Bellows Island and the arches of Brooklyn Bridge are fading from sight, the hoarse cheering is lost and the mainland grows to a tiny strip. We are steaming out into the salt water and the ocean stretches before us a field of greyish-green. The *Ann Eliza,* a small craft, is the first to salute us.

8:00 P.M. Scarcely a ripple on the surface of the water but the breeze is very invigorating and we are delighted to find the Old Sea Man so agreeable. We see many of the passengers engaged in studying Spanish. Some of the nurses and myself have had lessons and I like it, it is not so difficult to one acquainted with Latin. The Government has furnished us hand-books.

July 20, 2:45 P.M. on Mid-Atlantic. We are below Cape Henry. Some of us went into the cabin to study the map and see the course we are sailing. The Captain of the *Resolute,* Mr. Eaton, is an agreeable host, having traveled in many lands he furnishes much intelligence. Our fare is "par excellence" and we will think of it when we eat our hard tack. Our *Resolute* is owned by the Government, having been purchased from the Old Dominion Line. [4] She is a beautiful boat, 350 feet long, draws 20 feet water and speed 15 knots an hour. We have on board 5,000 tents, hospital supplies, ammunition, nurses, physicians, surgeons and soldiers from New York. This ship carried to New York 500 prisoners, and we have on board one prisoner who boarded as one of the hospital corps, but when asked for credentials failed to produce them. Major Summers, an army physician in charge of the company, has had everything done for the comfort and need of the people. Dr. McGill is also a fine nature. When I learned he was not going to Siboney [5] with us, I could not get over my disappointment. I have been promised beautiful sights in the tropics and I begin to look for them.

July 21, 10:00 A.M. At eleven last night we saw lights from Cape Hatteras after which I went down to my state room. It was growing quite rough on account of the approaching Gulf Stream. The water in the stream is a cobalt blue. We are about halfway on our sea journey. I am told from New York to Santiago is a greater mileage than from New York to Liverpool. It is so much warmer here that the men have put on white duck suits. The porpoises are quite lively in the water and the warmer strata of air tells me that we have left the temperate zone. It rains every little while and the clouds are very gorgeous.

July 21. Our Captain shouted, "All hands forward!" In a remarkably short time, every man of the crew was in his place, the soldiers at the ship's bow, the gunners at the guns. The *Resolute* is a protected steamer.[6] It is war time and excitement prevailed when it became known that the Captain had sighted a ship, through his glass, coming straight toward us, who would not strike her colors. The order came to clear the deck for action. Some were a bit nervous, but the men liked it as they stood with their hands on their guns, responding with the signal "Ready." It was, after all, only a Norwegian cruiser, a neutral nation. "I let her go," said the Captain, but he promised the mounted guard, who looked a bit disappointed as they wiped their heated faces, that they should have target practice after dinner.

4:00 p.m. We are nearing Haiti. The clouds which arise from the sea are multi-colored. They seem like painted scenery. The horizon looks like a piece of molten gold, edged with sapphire and emerald with dashes of vermillion, green and purple. This is the region of hurricanes and tropical glories. At noon there was a most beautiful phenomenon on the water, a huge rain-bow arose and spanned the ocean from zone to zone. The crimson, vermillion and blue were indescribably lovely.

July 24. In Cuban waters. At 12:30 noon we steamed into Guantanamo Bay, being saluted as we approached. I looked for the town but discovered only a few white spots and supposed the houses were in the lowlands, hidden by the plantations. The American soldiers' tents dot the hillside, but no life is visible. Night has crept down on land and sea, the moon and stars shine in the tropic sky, the lights from the battleships gleam and reflect through the waters of the bay, the boatmen ply between and salute as they pass. It is a dream of Venice in loveliness. Music floats out over the waters, American National airs, and who fears for a prowling enemy![7]

July 25. At 7:30 A.M. we steamed out of Guantanamo Bay, bade adieu to Admirals Sampson's, Schley's, and Watson's fleets. Admiral Sampson's fleet lies in one squadron, Admiral Schley's in one squadron, and Watson's in another, forming a crescent in a crescent-shaped bay. From the *New York*, Admiral Sampson's flag-ship, comes sounds of music over the water. Captain Evans's ship, the *Iowa* (the first to salute us), really interested me the most because he is a Chicago man and a hero. He did his little part in the battle and won a laurel.[8]

The banks of Cuba, as we pass, are barren, the hills and mountains are sandstone formation and vegetation does not gain a very strong hold. We turn at this moment, 9:30 by my watch, into Santiago Bay. Morro Castle[9] is deserted. It lies on our right and is built on a high rock and steps are cut into the cliff leading up to the castle. Marks show where it has been shelled. The *Virginias'*[10] crew here met their death, but then, Hobson here also was released.[11] The forts around on the shore are deserted. The *Maria Theresa*, a Spanish gun-boat, lies on her side on the bank in the mud embedded where she sunk. Two guns are noticeable, and abandoned sailors' clothing is strewn on the deck side which is not under water. Here a pace inside the *Maria Theresa* lies our own *Merrimac*. She is submerged so that only the top of the masts and smokestack are visible. Ah! It is a glorious moment to note this place where Cervera's fleet was bottled up and where our noble Hobson sunk his boat, a privilege I can hardly realize as yet, however, when I stop to think I am such a distance from the shores of the U.S. and my Illinois home. I feel indeed in a distant clime.

Boats bearing Spanish prisoners are steaming up ready to leave. The transports which carried our soldier boys from Tampa lie about the Bay. The *New York Herald* boat[12] salutes us. We have had our pictures taken on board the *Resolute,* first the nurses, then the Surgeons and Physicians. I have ordered one sent home, but you may not know me because I have had my hair cut. But down into imperishable history we go as the first band of enlisted women sent from the government of the United States of America.[13] I feel glad that I am one of that number. It is a moment to live for, that some life may be saved by us, some father, son, or husband will be returned to his own by our skill of nursing. I have taken the oath. I feel that

I shall have strength to bear privations, toil, and whatever may come up in our army life.

Santiago de Cuba is the most fertile of any place we have seen of Cuban soil. The hills are covered with trees and old sand forts loom up before us, all the places are situated on the cliffy shore. Beyond the mouth of the bay is an old Cuban town lying high on a plateau. Here waves the American flag, for the town is garrisoned by our troops. The bay is shallow and a Cuban pilot has taken charge of the *Resolute* to lead her up into the bay. Now the sailors are unloading tents which must be taken on boats. We have had no storm but it rains often. I am provided with raincoat, rain-hat and boots so that in going from tent to tent I shall have no fear of the rain. We are anxious to land. There is work to be done and we are ready to begin.

Siboney, July. Here we are situated on the shore of the Caribbean Sea, two hundred rods [14] from the water's edge, and about nine miles from Santiago. A lazy railroad runs along the shore between Santiago and Siboney, over which we came, on up to the hill across the river where there is a mine. But now our dead are buried there. A suspension bridge spans the river which is shallow but has a current flowing rapidly to the ocean. Our boys often wash their clothes there, standing on a rock which rises out of the riverbed. The country of eastern Cuba is just a rich wilderness of uncultivated forest, damp, overgrown, and so dense no sunbeam or gleam of light ever reaches vast portions of it, and so rank that for ages apparently nothing has disturbed it. The mahogany and ebony grow everywhere, the richest, most charming green I have ever seen. All the tropical vegetation has a peculiar texture and brilliancy never seen in our northern woods. The leaves are larger, heavier and waxy-looking.

There are mountains on every side enclosing the land. Everywhere the eye rests it is one blue haze of summits, and from these mountains come breezes that are heavenly. I love these peaks. Some of them tower very high but their names are not generally known. You do not know what flowers are like in America, for nothing half so brilliant is grown in hothouses there. The sun colors and draws out everything. On the slope back of our tents is a Grecian honey-suckle vine. The flowers are odorless, but so beautiful and of such a pure white they seem like angel wings.

There have been private gardens here, some of the shrubbery and bushes are still lovely. One exquisite tree whose flowers I have not seen, has a seed now ripe, coral-like, and worn by some as jewelry. To me, the most charming tree, however, is the Spanish Magnolia, with its clusters of scarlet bloom covering the center of the tree, of such dazzling luster in the sunshine as to be never forgotten. It seems only the well-to-do have grown them. These deserted gardens still grow herbs, squash, Spanish vegetables unlike anything American. The cucumbers are like baby gourds, one could drink from them. Of course, now it is all being overgrown with weeds, and overrun with reptiles.

The Governor lived in this spot before it was bombarded by our forces. The only thing left where his house stood is a deep hole. The town which formerly stood here on the hill was destroyed only fifteen days ago, so it is no wonder spots still have a fresh, cultivated look. [15] Here many of the higher class lived. The wind sweeps more freely and it is cooler. But on our portion, about the old town, nothing grows, not even grass. Charred coals cover the ground from the burned houses. It had not been large, encompassed in a stone's throw, a residence town and suburb of Santiago. On the edge of the town are freshly made Spanish graves. They are buried in a strange manner, I should never have known they were graves.

So far the climate is luxurious and dreamy, productive of indolence and torpor, and the better part of valor is discretion to keep out of the sun. But nurses cannot obey any such injunction considering what we are here for. We only wish many times our number were here. I have also gone into the entrenchments made by the Spanish, from which they fired back on our forces. This is back of the place where the Governor's house stood. The heavy plate shows riddled marks of shell, and the entrenchments into which they fell when expecting our charge are deep, like underground caves. We came and have taken possession, although we know not but that the enemy is pretty well conquered or I pity our forces so prostrate with fever. Ours has been a most marvelous victory on land and sea. I give a mental hurrah, but will add an audible one when I am sure the Spanish are on their way out of here. [16]

The Caribbean Sea which washes the coast here is lovely, of the deepest blue and scarcely ever a ripple on it, but the bluffs on the shore are ugly-looking. At a distance it looks as if the foundations are crumbling and that the whole land would fall into the sea. As I sit up on the slope and view the lines and lines of white tents on the beach and well up onto the hill, glittering and gleaming in the broiling sun and on the hot sultry rocks, and not one house anywhere to be seen, the feeling could easily be one of great loneliness. This, then, is our army and our country's pride, that here is dying. Siboney is isolated and gives one the sensation of captivity. What has impressed me most, however, is the lack of preparation for any army or body of people sent away to an untried zone. No clothing, lack of food, and boxes unopened, even our own supplies from the boat had difficulty in landing, and as yet have not been received. General Shafter, they tell me, is ill and assuredly knows no more of the needs of these boys here than he did before the charge of San Juan. [17]

Major LeGarde who is in charge of the 5th Division Hospital Corps, received us with great gratitude, and in as hospitable a way as the meagerness of the place afforded. The enlisting of trained nurses in the army is as yet an untried measure and we are anxious to know as to its success. But where brave men are, there brave women should be, and here we found no women nurses, not one. We inquired of Major LeGarde if Clara Barton was here. "She was here a day or two after the battle. Where she has gone I do not know," he replied. Clara Barton of the Red Cross did but little nursing in Cuba. Her work was her endeavor to distribute all she could in needed supplies here and there. [18] But at Siboney, the American Yellow Fever camp of the tropics, was not a woman to care for all these sick, and our Major signified his joy that we had come, assuring us that we were both welcome and greatly needed.

We found officers and doctors discouraged almost to despair. Singly and in squads, weak and ill soldiers sat about on the rocks, and we saw nothing but feverish and wounded wherever the eye might look. Being compelled to wait for orders we learned our first army lesson of obedience. We chaffed nevertheless, under the inactivity and knowing the stern necessity for our work. But it seems even an army nurse must have orders, so we were compelled the first two days to simply wait. It was not easy. At the closing of the second day, however, seeing the scores of sick men, I appealed to Dr. Newkirk. "Put me to work. I cannot wait for red tape, let me do something." To which he responded, "I'll do it; wait here." Later he returned, saying, "I want you to come with me," and oh! I found work enough. Sick men being brought in continuously, on stretchers, in all forms of fevers and exhaustion. The sick have two bearers, and the dead have four. There is no ice, but am promised some for tomorrow, and then, hurrah, for a cool old time while it lasts. My small supply of alcohol I have diluted with water for bathing. My ward book is also in good shape. Add to this that I am my own orderly and go to the Commissary's tent for my own supply, my first few days' work has been most strenuous. But how glorious to be at work among these needy.

July 31. Ah! you northern people! You cannot appreciate my situation, but I can yours. Here we bake on the rocks, and even army officials walk about like recruits in white canvas shoes, pajamas, palm-leaf hats. If we have time to glance up, we are, of course, in sight of orange blossoms and limes. On one side lies the blue spreading Caribbean, and on the other, mountains rising in blue mist, peak on peak. Only a stone's throw from the outer tents is a waving coconut valley where the sun and shadows lie and cool vapors arise, and there the boys, if able, can gather such luscious fruit as never was exported, for eaten fresh you learn its deliciousness. We drink our coffee and eat our hard tack to the accompaniment of parrots chattering in the woods, mocking birds and red birds caroling their melody over crimson and white flowers such as were never painted in a temperate zone.

Spanish, Cubans and Americans are almost the same in dress and complexion, for the sun dyes us all a rich brown. Baring what the Spanish may be at heart, they are certainly a far more agreeable people than the poor Cubans, for they have a quick intuition and a high sense of appreciation for the smallest favor. They possibly imagined the American nurses a set of "vendetta" come to torture any non-American by their apparent surprise and reluctant manner to believe in our impartiality in caring for the sick and wounded. I have seen fever-wasted faces light up with gratitude when I have dressed their gun-shot wound or given them a cup of water. If they are as consistent in their life as in their manner, they must be a charming race, these Spanish foes of ours. They tell you they will be honest *Americanas,* which of course you are never to believe for one moment, though they acknowledge in deed and in look that they are the vanquished. We try to be a generous victor, what with the conquering of Santiago, the bombardment of Morro Castle. We have opened up friendly negotiations to all, but have endless complexity involving our peace which is not yet declared.

The people of this Island are a languid, dreamy sort for whom procrastination is no thief of time. Nothing moves them. They go on in the wretched grooves worn by their forefathers. Say or do what you will for the poor Cubans, no emotion moves them or stirs them from their sodden ways. I had such glorious hopes for them until I have seen the actual doggedness of these eastern Cubans. Nevertheless, I am still hopeful that the ugly duckling may turn out a swan, that under the reign of American influence, these natives may become as glorious as their climate. "With faith's finger on the latch" I will hope it.

August 2nd, Siboney. When I remember how I wanted to go to Cuba to be valiant in this cause, I think our fervent wishes sometimes had better not be granted by a loving and wise Providence. Think not that I would shirk when Duty calls, that I truly would not. It may be, in after years when a grey-haired woman, I may be able to shine around some eager circle of friends. My experience in a land of desolation and misery may find a response outside my own self. For oh! We have no ice, or at best only a small piece. The facilities for hospital work are so meager and the odds of climate so against us that we work like soldiers sent to the front without ammunition. We have fevers and heat prostrations. Thermic fever predominates. [19] We work on hopefully for the fortunate ones who have the constitution, and strive hard for those who have not. This work, of course, could never be described along the lines of real hospital nursing. The historic block-house from its Cuban summit, seems to say truly, "Conquerors, but conquered." [20]

My life is indeed a most busy one. I have attended some prisoners on a far-off tent on the hill. They were to be taken to Santiago for transportation back to Spain. They were a wretched lot, convalescing from yellow fever, and only one able to walk at all and he not yet fifteen he told me. He was a brave lad. I gave them clean clothing and made them comfortable. They were so grateful, they thanked me with tears. One man, older than the rest, looked as if he had not the breath of life left. To him I gave a cluster of beautiful white flowers that grew on a tree outside the tent. He smiled faintly and folding his hands wearily over the spray of flowers, he slept, no more to waken.

It was at evening time yesterday, on my ward where I have fourteen men in all sorts of fevers—thermic, malarial, yellow and typhoid—that one very sick fellow was afraid he would die. I came back to him as the sun was setting, and as cheerfully as I could, I told him he was better. It was desolate enough casting one's eyes over the grounds of Siboney with the hospital tents spread out over the shore like a mighty encampment. But he wept, and weeping said, "I am not ready to die, pray I may not." "God have mercy on this man," I prayed, and hurried to another waiting sufferer. The stars were shining where the sun had disappeared, and a silver bow was on the edge of the horizon. It threw a hush over the moans of the sick and shed a calm and an assurance of forgiveness in the doubtful soul. He was praying "Our Father." I think the Father heard him, for he has been quiet since. One man who seemed better said smilingly, "I am waiting to go home to my family." "Yes John, be courageous, you will get home. Get strong for those who need you." But alas, he will not get home.

Last night some crabs chose to have a reception in my tent. They take a special delight in walking about at night and have greatly molested some of the nurses. This is my only experience of them, as I sleep finely. I roll up in my blanket and raincoat and know nothing until the sun dances on the rim of the horizon. The Cuban crab is such a funny thing, at once repulsive and fascinating. Sometimes you think you see a gorgeous tropical flower and pause, when suddenly out dart these enormous claws, four of them, which they stretch nearly a mile and run with astonishing rapidity. Some are the color of the ground and grass, while others have, as I said, bright orange and red stripes on their shell. They are cowardly as well as inquisitive. With their stalked eyes, no matter in which direction they go from you, they can look at you and a most irresistible feeling comes over you to chase them. At any rate, my fellow nurse a foot from me called as these crabs pattering over the matting were most disturbing to her, and we emerged, armed, from our beds to face the advancing enemy which scampered at once, but not before one had lost a weapon, i.e. a claw.

We have reptiles here, and scorpions, gnats and fleas, and those horrible things called buzzards, waiting for the dead and dying. Armies of red ants also invade your lodging. This fertile soil produces much in the vegetable and animal world, and the beauty of the scenery may sometimes cause you to imagine yourself in Eden when you are forcibly reminded that the trail of the serpent is not yet exterminated, and that your foes are legion.

I have seen so many sick and wounded soldiers, and so many die! I have worked with hope and faith, but such deadly elements against me—

the burning sun, rains that would wet some of the men through the tents and the chilling night winds—all would undo what had been done. Yet with a remnant of life left I toil on for these men. It is difficult to be patient, to swelter, to toil endless hours when we lack so much. It is one of each day's problems how we shall feed our sick, and what we, too, shall have. Oft-times, we yearn for a Daniel who would arise, act quickly, or that some cheering transport would come with white wings to our aid. Was Cuba, I wonder, the last place the Lord created, and could He have forgotten to bless it? Such one feels with the misery about, and when one sees the condition of the natives which is indeed squalid. How one is born should make no difference, nor where, and yet it matters much when a country is so hopelessly ignorant. Surely this land washed by the seas of the tropics is one few would care to own as their own in the year of our Lord 1898. The very insects seem to cry out, "Yellow Fever, Oh, Nurse!" I cannot, and shall not, allow discouragement to creep in when so many lives hang in the balance of our work. And then, when some one says, "You saved my life, I owe my life to you," hope dawns brighter. Some one's life! Ah, that is what I came for, to return to a mother, sister or dear one.

I have been in Dr. Newkirk's ward, and am well but very tired. It makes me happy, however, to be of service. The boys, bless their noble hearts, tell me it is due to my efforts that they are better. Dr. Newkirk has given me many tributes and I have made many friends among the lads of Chicago and elsewhere.

I am now transferred to Dr. A. A. Snyder's ward. It is a yellow fever ward almost exclusively, and I have seventy-two patients. I am so busy taking temperature and pulse, I have only a bit of time to write by candle in my tent. I labor hard to save the boys.

We hear and see things to make the stoniest heart quail. I told Dr. Snyder one day that I had nearly concluded men were better than women in this capacity. He said, "No, you must not be discouraged, for the sight of a woman is a good thing." The upper part of my ward is pleasant, with an unbroken view of the ocean, the lower is hot and stifling. My heart aches for the boys who must lie there, and yet they are so brave, and oft-times, such sudden fun. Some are so young. There are those who are only sixteen and seventeen. Here lies Illinois, there New York, Vermont, Michigan, Ohio and so on, with representatives from the states of the west. Truly Spartan-like they are. The regulars and volunteers all show the same heroic metal. One regular came into the ward sick with yellow fever convulsions and died within three hours. During the intense suffering he listened to the words spoken to him, tried to smile and to express his thanks as he took his medicine. There lies a fair-haired, blue-eyed lad who has fought bravely, the curls fall over a singularly noble face. Every effort was made to reclaim him from the scourge but he fell asleep like a child and the damp curls cling like a girl's over his finely molded brow. Close by lies one whose smile lights up his brown eyes, the anxious hours for him are relaxed. He is growing better. Oh, joy, that some one lives. Among my convalescing, I sometimes hear lively discussions, but they, almost to a man, seem to regard Miles[21] as their saving grace, and Theodore Roosevelt is their hero. He with Wood[22] went on the field sharing the perils and daring the enemy's bullets, and this fact—that he has been one with the boys—they can not forget.

Happily the band master has recovered from his illness and is drilling the colored band from New Orleans.[23] The music has a magic thrill and changes many of the set faces of the weary, sick men. Out of the wards come those who are able, limping and crutched. One soldier wears a bonnet a nurse has loaned him. Others wrap their blankets around them for the hour is near sunset when the chill sets in. Music hath charms even in a yellow fever camp.

Now a young soldier with a Bible in his hand begs between feverish gasps, "Read to me, will you read to me from that?" "Tomorrow I will read to you, then you will be stronger, you must rest now," said the nurse looking over the vast ward of closely fitted tents silently calling for aid. Ah, yes, one could only wish for many more pairs of hands, and many more nurses with so much urgent need.

"Jack! tell them to hold the transport! Tell them I'm coming. Hie there, Jack!" a poor fellow who had begged to be taken home, gasped out, as he was brought back from a mad rush into the Caribbean Sea in hopes to get away from Siboney. He fell back and died in his delirium.

August 6th. This morning the ever-glorious and hot sun shone out on the peaks when I was up betimes and had my laundry out. You see this is army life, and at present we have our own washing to do, which is nearly always done in the morning. When we have our larger pieces, such as nursing costumes, we borrow a pail from an old colored woman who carried it all the way from New Orleans. Otherwise one of our pieces of furniture (besides a chair and cot), is a tin handled basin, and we nurses stand about quite as the soldiers with their mess pans. Plans for a laundry are under way, with Cuban women to do the washing. This will be a great relief for overworked nurses. But all plans for an ice-plant have seemingly failed and we have lost hope of ever securing it.

2:00 P.M. It rains again, for the second time today. It beats and lashes the rigging of our tents until it seems they could not possibly stand another lash. I came to my tent for raincoat and boots on my way to the Commissary's for supplies, but the rain beats so hard I shall wait a few seconds, and as my pockets contain pencil and paper, I write a few lines for I am never sure of a future. I stand on an isle of rock, all the rest of the ground in my tent is swimming. America doesn't know what rain is! Here the drops seem to us about the size of tea cups, and each rain, not aqueous vapor, but a precipitous gravity of torrents. It grows cold while raining, so that one shivers. Such a contrast from a few moments ago. Everything here in the tropics is intense, from sun, flower, to rain. But I cannot wait for the rain to stop and am pretty well soaked. I am often so, but it is not so harmful, I am sure, as in northern climes. At any rate it is the sun that one minds most. Nothing native minds the rain. Sometime when I have leisure, I mean to analyze the flowers and see if they have rubber rods for stems!

So far not a moment of homesickness, there is not time for that. I do ofttimes wonder what you, in Uncle Sam's country, are doing this August weather. To exert one's self day after day to the point of fatigue is difficult. We work on coffee and hard tack eaten three times a day. At first I could not soak my hard tack, but have learned to soak it in the cold instead of the hot. I am becoming seasoned as to color, fare and experience.

Nature lulls one if we could but have the time to listen to her. We have musicals with the moon and stars as limelights. The blue sea plays a rhythm on the shore, and when I can find a moment to lend an ear, it sings to me the softest lullaby. The harmonious voices of Nature are an antidote for hurt nerves.

August 15th. Yesterday the lads who were well enough went home. They formed a line and roll-call, and then gave three cheers of joy. And they were soul-felt, all the energy of home—longing pent up for weary months found vent, and they rang down on the water and back over the hills, until Siboney re-echoed the glad cry. I was not one of them, not yet. I have more work to do. God speed the day when peace shall cover the earth as waters the sea. And oh, tyrannous Spain, thou hast done with thy yoke,[24] and thou shalt no more hold in chains this isle. Every act which has brought the world higher in the scale of civilization has cost human lives, so here is our enormous sacrifice that Cuba may be free.

"Mañana" is a word fitting for this place. The prospects are barren and wearied mortals find only a mañana indefinitely ahead. The essential thing is faith. If that has been religiously bred into one's being there may be some comfort where at present there is none in sight. What an experience these days of our lives will be to those of us who survive. Never in the history has there been such a death rate in modern civilization as this.[25] The blackened and charred spots of ground where the Siboney dwellings used to be and the heaps of stones speak out of a past that lie Sodom-like in its grave. Nothing in this place is half so dear as a letter or paper from home.

I have had some time off. I just overworked and went out in the sun a bit more than I should and have felt ill. I did not realize how far away eastern Cuba is until I was ill and lay without anyone coming into my tent for twenty-four hours, then indeed I did realize I was far from home. For the first time the full force of army life came upon me and I arose and walked to the Commissary for some remedies. I was given — grains of quinine at once, and — grains every two hours.[26] I never could take quinine and it lurches in the air yet. Four days I had fever, two more days I lounged around, then went back to work. The poor men were so glad to see me back, though I could hardly drag myself about. Some of my noble boys have died while I was off duty. One Alfred Stevenson, of Flint, Michigan, aged eighteen, brave, gentle in manner and exhibited a marvelous fortitude. Also one John S. Lee who was most manly and intelligent. I have missed his smile which he always wore as I passed by. Thus it is that one has the heart wrung, and it is hard work holding on to one's feelings. Several of the doctors are ill and many of the nurses. We have all worked too hard, but when men are dying one thinks not of oneself.

Of course, we remember we are pioneers. Such a plague must never be again. Another time we go this way to an unknown land we must be prepared in the way of food, medicine, clothing and the proper way of conducting an army. Often we feel if only we had not rushed this war, or we had been prepared, what lives might have been saved.[27] And yet the men are grandly silent in their suffering. They fight even more gloriously here than they did under baptism of fire at San Juan Hill. Again and again we turn to the half-ill doctors for more supplies. They try to encourage us that things are moving and even better, from which it is to be inferred that bad as conditons now are, there had been a sterner fact of men dying without care. And then we say, oh why our nation's sudden mad rush into the very jaws of death? But even with the unnecessary loss of life, America's motive of quick action was that the heel of oppression may be lifted from the western hemisphere forever by our magnificent army and navy.

I have seen one of the Battle Fields. I visited the graves of the Rough Riders buried where they fell at San Juan Hill. Those boys were brave as only American boys can be to dash up such a hill of wild undergrowth. Over gulleys and barbed wire fences they charged on the enemy and completely routed them. It was a grand victory for our army. These graves are sacred places, and God and the angels and men hold the ground holy. It quite affected me to see the wooden slabs put up by their comrades. They were buried without a volley fired over them for fear of the enemy. They say the Spanish fought like devils but that the Cubans fled. On that battlefield, as I stood looking over the down-trodden grass and brush and saw the ruins, I felt how daring and dashing our brave lads were. Our men made a road (the one over which we came), through a dense growth of forest in the valley, and on to Siboney, they burned and cut the trees. It seemed so freshly made that I fancied someone still working the end of it. One of our party found a Spanish sword. It was very elaborately engraved and must have belonged to some officer of high degree.

I also stood at the summit of Las Guasimas, where Roosevelt's Rough Riders crashed into the rear guard of the retreating Spaniards and had a brisk engagement. As I had at San Juan, I looked over the palm and jungle grown valleys, and mountains in their blue mist, and felt that the island had been sufficiently baptized in blood to secure its redemption.

We have had such heroes. There was one Lieut. Blue of the Carolinas, who performed a daring feat in exploring many of the hills around Santiago, covering seventy miles of the enemy's territory, and doing much to locate the enemy. That was truly brave. Lieut. Blue looked every inch a hero as he boarded the *Resolute* among the first to welcome us.

Sunday. The Chaplain, a Chicago man, has been very kind to me. He has been very busy burying the dead. He, with one of the privates, took me out to George Haven's grave, after obtaining Major LeGarde's permission. George was an Oak Park, Illinois boy, a Corporal, and his Lieut. fired two volleys over his grave. I have the emblem he wore on his cap which I shall give to his mother. We had a frightful ride on a handcar, the only way to get there. It was pumped by three negroes. The cemetery was a most beautiful spot two miles up on a hill with a coconut valley opposite. In this cemetery are many Illinois, Ohio and Michigan boys. George has a palm at his head, and a wooden slab engraved by his friends. I planted a very pretty vine on his grave. Only a moment among all these noble boys who left all to fight for the honor of their country, and we returned down the hill. Coming back on the handcar was strange but I did not mind it so much. Thus it is all things can be endured, all things can be made to be possible.

I am, nevertheless, in close confinement. I have not been to the beach which is about half a mile away. Army rules, too, are strict, and one must obtain permission. All days are most interesting here, however, if only the hours were longer, or we had more help or could be in half a dozen places at once so as to give more attention to the sickest.

I have much the largest ward in the place, and my present assistant is very poor. Today I came early and stayed after hours to make a very sick fellow comfortable. Another dear boy who was semi-delirious was so worried about his mother. I have quieted him and written for him, so now he is as docile as a child and no violence on the ward since. We have such a time getting writing paper, the boys beg me constantly for a bit. They tear off can wrappers and use edges of newspapers.

There are sad heart aches when such fine lives go out, though all is done that human skill with our army supplies can do. Then again, tears of joy well up when desperate battles for life are won. Sometimes poor lads given up to die at night have smiled the next morning and said they were better as I passed through the tents. There are those of my poor delirious boys who could not be induced to take their medicine from anyone but me, and those who have been partially violent have remained quiet on my approach.

There are no words to describe the terrific sultriness of this place as the sun beats down mercilessly on these rocks, and the only word of comfort one can give is that soon we may all be taken from this place of suffering, for the skies are growing to be molten brass, and more men are sick and we are asking every day, how soon will the transports come for us! God speed the day and save the flower of the American Army, before the Santiago campaign becomes a tragic page and Siboney has devoured every American son. [28] I am fairly well, thank God, but everyone seems to be succumbing. We have rice and condensed milk for the sick, but no ice. Major LeGarde has been telegraphing and nobly performed his duty and now he has been stricken with fever. Behold your army, and act quickly in the name of American love for human life!

Saturday, August 27. On the Caribbean Sea. Oh! The sea! The coolness! And the 350 soldiers on board, all to behold again the shores of our own land America!

We are ploughing our way through the deep ocean homeward bound. Farewell old Siboney, and hail, ye land of the Stars and Stripes! I come back as brown as the suns and rains of the tropics can dye me, a veteran of hard tack and yellow fever, and nearly as hollow as a crab's claw—a bit of rest and food will do wonders.

We left Siboney on the twenty-fifth, traveled by rail to Santiago, which is about nine miles, the speed being little more than an army mule. Capt. Leverall of the 24th Inf. presented me with a huge bouquet of roses as I left. Though unknown to me, he had often seen me pass on my way after things for my boys. Thus we find so much courtesy among military men.

The camp at Siboney is being disbanded and the hospital ship sails with all the sick from Santiago to Long Island and the convalescent also will be removed from that awful scene of woe forever. Those who have experienced its perils and found deliverance therefrom will praise God evermore. Someone blundered, and my poor Illinois boys had to lie waiting for the transport. Why these hitches must occur to our poor, brave, worn lads I do not see. [29]

I have come to care for the sick on the transport and also have in my charge a very sick nurse. She was ill on the boat going to Cuba and has been ever since, and if she ever gets home alive she will do well. I have not been on deck at all, and not a tinge of seasickness, though the boat has tossed a good deal. The things in our state room slip and slide around, and

I after them. I look out now and then and catch a glimpse of the sweeping sea and smell the ocean air and long for a billow to spray me. My prayer was, when I was so ill at Siboney, that I might rather be buried at sea, but better still, that I might be privileged to land on American soil again.

Two of our men have died. If only I could take that gaunt hungry look out of the eyes of our men—it wrings my heart to see them. We are on the *Berkshire*. It does not ride the waves as easily as the *Resolute*. Also the management is sadly in arrears. How soon I will be at home, I do not know. In spite of small fare I hold my own, though with what experience I had at Siboney, I have grown very thin indeed. Ah! Siboney! I cannot get the sight of you out of my mind, you are so impressed in my memory and so burned in my brain. I can see those white tents glaring in the sun on the coast of Cuba wherever I turn. There, indeed, as a nurse, I felt how pitiful it was to be a human instead of a God and superior to all disease when responsibility was so great. It is said we will be held in quarantine fifteen days. Whether our things will be buried or burned I do not know. [30] In four days we land on American soil. I believe I shall never want to leave it again. I do think, now, that I was brave to go, but God and His host of delivering angels were with me and never once did I feel fear. Nothing seemed too great an obstacle to be overcome. We who went did not really give up anything, for everyone who sacrificed a little of self, gained elsewhere much more. Some life saved is the sweet thought, the noblest mission. It is a thought that alone can bring rest to wearied, aching hearts and hands. I have no relic of Cuba other than this.

September. I am having time off to go over to the General Hospital and am seated in the Ambulance waiting for the driver to start. Our Camp Wikoff Detention Hospital [31] is three miles or more from the General Hospital. There, everything is in good order, with nurses immaculate in white caps and aprons. We, at the Detention, did not have time for caps. The work was of a different sort, rather more difficult and unpleasant. We landed about two weeks ago, and a couple of days after that the doctor said several of the boys would undoubtedly die that night. I had been told to rest, and still had charge of the sick nurse. But I could not fold my hands when I heard so many of these boys were so sick but went in quest of our doctor asking him what I might do. "Go ahead with whatever you think best," he said in his rush, so I did. It was 11 at night, but I went to the kitchen for

supplies and found the men very respectful, then back to the tent for remedies. The night nurse assisted me. I am much indebted to Dr. J. R. Pen-
nington of Chicago for my success, for the suggestions given by him in
lectures to us. The nursing at Montauk Point has been a pleasure compared to our Siboney experiences. There we had no floors in the sick tents,
or in any tents, a limited supply of remedies, no ice scarcely, no proper
amount of food and clothing, and rains several times a day soaking many
of the sick ones. No, Montauk will not compare with that Cuban town.
There is no use trying to create ill conditions here, for the conditions were
ill with the men before Montauk was sighted. It was the fare on the transports coming back that gave our men their relapses as well. Canned navy
beans and canned beef—none too good—are not for sick men. We could
not understand, men who had but scarcely recovered from wasting fevers,
some luckily with their bare life, in a land of resource and plenty. There
were loaded ships sent to Cuba from New York that returned again to
American shores unloaded. Two thousand tons of ice to be taken to Cuba
melted before they started. To whom does such neglect apply! Surely not
to McKinley. It was stated that our beloved President wept at the sight of
our emaciated men as they landed from the *Berkshire*. This red tape in
army life is the most difficult to bear, though I never could assail my good
Uncle Sam for the delays and blunders of some of his representatives. Putting a big country into war on short notice is no small undertaking, and if
the future will but profit by our sad experience, this suffering will not have
been in vain.

Many of my Siboney boys whom I have nursed here at Montauk have
gone home. God bless their bright faces. This dwells with me like a jewel
that cannot be taken away.

Mrs. ——, a prominent New York woman, works here among the
sick and dead. She heads the National Relief Association, and has been
busy marking the graves. The noble American woman, Helen Gould, gives
of her wealth, and she and Mrs. Walworth visit in our camps. [32] Even here
one sees military discipline. I like it.

A tearful elderly man, who had been looking for his son but failed to
find him, said as he came to me; "O, see how our men look, so miserable
and emaciated! I was through the Civil War but it was nothing like this."
"Sir," I said, "it is sad, but our boys are on the threshold of home. It is not
Cuba, thank God. Here green grass grows, and the boys can get ice cream.

People come every day it is true, looking for their own and must go away without them, but I am glad to remember army nursing something else than the Siboney pest-camp. I trust you may be successful in your search for your son. Good day, sir." "God bless you, I am sure you will be rewarded for all you have done for our boys," and with tears rolling fast the old gentleman went again in search for his boy.

This large yellow flag floating near the Stars and Stripes, the yellow fever flag of quarantine, tells what the tropics will do. Even the natives take care not to expose themselves at certain seasons, while we unacclimated, coddled and petted at home, have waded through it all. Is it any wonder we resemble something like smoked or dried fish? But the kindness here and the hospitality where these big-hearted folk have flung wide the door of their hearts to feed, nurse or caress us, is good for wistful, home-longing hearts and eyes. Columbia has opened her arms to her returned people. We have the finest dining room put up of rough boards. Meal time is one of the biggest hours and we have the luxuries—all we can eat. From the Diet Kitchen where we go to get supplies for the sick men, we can have pop or champagne, porter or sherry wines, as the case may be. So they mean to make us forget Siboney, if they can.

Ah! Some day we shall have peace congresses, instead of war congresses. Never again must there be such a pest-camp as our yellow fever camp at Siboney, to cut short life and sadden, to rob fathers and mothers of the stay of their declining years. But the driver has come and we are off! The mules dump us in and out of the hollows in great sport!

September, 1898. Montauk Point, Long Island Depot. Leaving Camp Wikoff. I have just succeeded in getting my baggage checked. If it had not been for Dr. Hamilton of Washington, D.C. of whose ward I had charge, I should not have gotten it through. Every one of the officials has shown me great courtesy and when I thanked Major Eberts in charge of Camp Wikoff, he said, "Well, a girl who has been in Siboney taking care of our boys deserves everything." I could not reply to so gallant a remark, but shook hands good-bye, adding to my list of military men, one more courtly gentleman. But for the great suffering, I have enjoyed my stay at Camp Wikoff, for it has exalted my ideas of military life and work and somewhat banished Siboney to the farforgetfulness. I shall have pleasanter remembrances of army nursing. When I think of Siboney, it all comes over me with such a rush of pain that I must choke it down—away down into my boots, leaving an aching lump in and about the region where physiologists say the heart is located. And yet, here to Montauk have come broken-hearted mothers and fathers—some old, bent and grey-haired—for their boys. Alas! So many must needs go away without them, buried, it may be at sea, or some unmarked spot in Cuba. One learns how intensely the human heart can ache.

I am on the train en route to New York, my transportation entitles me to a ten-day stay. I have worked to the last strenuous nerve and am glad to get away for rest and recuperation. As we pass, people shout themselves hoarse, and banners of welcome float on the breeze. It is the Homeland and the heart swells at the word. We pass an orchard. I had almost forgotten how to spell the word, or that such a thing existed, and the apples are ripe for my return. I shall need to have someone watch over me as I did over the soldiers when they became convalescent, to see that I do not overeat.

New York. I have worn my nurse's stripes, old weather-beaten and Cuban-sun-faded blue stripes, because I had not gotten down to the shops to secure a more civilized habiliment. I protested at being in such attire, but was greeted with, "All the silks and laces could never be half so choice as the least remnant of that faded blue stripe that you nursed our soldiers in." And thus I have found such patriotism vying in making me forget "the Cuban heart-ache." But rest I could not, that was out of the question. I had not relaxed since I landed in Cuba. I might gradually come to it, but it was a boon of the gods that I might work. It seems as if I must go and bathe some fevered brow or fold some hands across his breast. To break off so abruptly seems unnatural. Letters from mothers, wives and sweethearts of those gone in Cuba are pouring in upon me, and there is much to do to answer them. Here in New York I have also been with a mother whose son I had nursed at Siboney. He died at his home in New York, and the inconsolable mother would not let me go. The Rough Riders and 71st New York have been mustered out, yet many of the volunteer soldiers will be retained in case of need.

Two amusing incidents in connection with the 71st I must not forget to add. In their parade down Fifth Avenue, they had a goat with them, who, like the soldiers, was conspicuous for leanness. When going to Cuba they adopted a goat giving him the name of Dewey,[33] painted on his sides. The poor animal fell sick but recovered, and returned with the men and was in the front of the parade. He has since been presented to the park, having his name changed to "Billy-Bedam." One soldier carried a parrot which he had bought in Cuba. One wing had been shot off by the Spaniards, and when the salute of cannon was given, this parrot invariably would flap that one wing, and scream, "Oh! that's a peach! Give them another!"[34]

Washington, D.C. I am here a guest of the D.A.R. and have about concluded my work and experience in the Spanish-American war. I go to the War Department tomorrow to receive my contract annulled with Uncle Sam. As eager as I was to go, so glad am I to get back to the home retreat. My energies have been pretty well expended for my Uncle Sam. Perhaps, on the whole, had I known of the conditions and trials, how we would be handicapped in our work, I might have hesitated. But there is no regret, for my experience is more to me than gold and I feel it has been glorious. I have found that the trying out of Government women nurses in war-time has been successful, and I have met in every stranger a friend. My bronzed face and short hair has been more than a coronet to me. Everywhere there has been such loyal big-hearted souls ready to welcome anyone who had served in Cuba, and especially those who sacrificed themselves to go to the "horrible Yellow Fever Hospital." The Easterners are such a gentle folk that they rest one. There is a whole-souled spirit about them which multiplied words do not give. Here at Washington I have found a courtesy impossible to describe and will not try, but to say it shone down into my tired soul high above all else, even as the Washington Monument towers above all about it.

Notes

1. The Daughters of the American Revolution, the patriotic society open to women with one or more ancestors who aided the cause of the American Revolution, had just been founded a few years earlier, in 1890.

2. The *New York Times* of July 20, 1898, reported that male nurses received $60 per month and three rations per day. "When the women heard of this it did not tend to mollify them, incensed as they already were because of the lack of bedding and dishes. A protest has been filed." Miss Wingreen does not complain of this disparity in her journal however.

3. The *New York Times* reported seven women nurses, two of whom were "colored immunes." Of these nurses, the "most prominent" was Mrs. Florence Applegate Patello from the New Orleans Training School for nurses. Amy Wingreen is noted as an expert in yellow fever from Cook County Hospital.

4. In spite of the fact that the United States shipyards were building a state-of-the-art navy with the world's fastest and most modern warships, they were very short of supply vessels and bought and refitted a number of private ships such as the *Resolute* for use during the war.

5. Siboney was located about sixteen miles from the outskirts of Santiago de Cuba. It and Daiquiri, five miles away, were chosen as a main landing area for the original invasion force and Siboney was later used as a staging area during the battles of El Caney and San Juan Heights. The largest buildings in American control, those of the Spanish-American Iron Company in Siboney, were turned into a general field hospital. Their zinc roofs offered the first protection from the elements that the sick and wounded had, but also produced grueling heat for soldiers who were often already out of their minds with fever before they arrived.

6. A protected steamer was a ship with an armor-plated deck. The *Resolute* was also fitted with four six-pound guns, two on the starboard and two on the port side of the forward deck. Later it would be involved in one of the great misinformation muddles of the war, the supposed sighting of what came to be known as the Spanish "ghost fleet" supposedly on its way to attack the American shipping ports along the East Coast.

7. The navy established a base (which the U.S. still uses today) at Guantanamo Bay on June 7, about six weeks before Wingreen left for Cuba. Unlike Santiago de Cuba and Siboney, Wingreen's destination, Guantanamo Bay remained relatively free from the scourges of yellow fever.

8. The battleship *Iowa* was part of the squadron blockading the channel entrance to the harbor of Santiago de Cuba. Captain "Fighting Bob" Evans was in command of the *Iowa* during the decisive July 3 battle during which four armored Spanish vessels were sunk or beached.

9. Morro Castle was the Spanish stronghold at the mouth of the harbor. Its guns were trained on the American fleet.

10. Wingreen is referring to the ship *Virginius,* an itinerant steamship engaged in gun-running and arms-selling in the late 1870s to all sides involved in the Cuban-Spanish struggle. The crew was captured by Spaniards and executed in the Plaza de Santiago. Their executions spawned calls from many Congressmen for naval action but none was taken. The Americans wouldn't become militarily involved for another twenty years.

11. Lieutenant Richard P. Hobson was assigned to carry out the first attack on the entrance to the bay. He did so by taking the *Merrimac* into the mouth of the bay with the intention of sinking it and creating a navigational obstacle for the enemy. The mission went awry, the *Merrimac* drifted too far up the channel to post any real threat to the enemy, and Hobson and seven men were captured. They were later freed in a prisoner exchange.

12. The yellow journalists, led by Joseph Pulitzer's *New York Herald* and the young William Randolph Hearst's first paper, the *New York Morning Journal,* had their heyday during the Spanish-American War. Newspaper competition was fierce and the results were splashy, wildly sensationalistic news accounts of life at the front. Reporters accompanied troops into battle and artists rendered lurid and often inaccurate battle and hospital scenes.

13. They were actually "contract" employees without military title or rank, though their position was in fact unprecedented for the U.S. military.

14. A little over a thousand yards.

15. Wingreen arrived shortly after a particularly large naval build-up and bombardment of the city of Santiago de Cuba that began on July 10. After considerable bickering and disagreement between the navy and the army, the Americans secured a Spanish surrender of Santiago on July 17. The Americans were left to bear the costs of repatriation and clean-up.

16. By the end of July the war with Spain was more or less over. Commodore W.S. Schley and Rear Admiral Sampson had destroyed the Spanish fleet as the Spanish attempted to break through the U.S. blockade and escape the harbor of Santiago de Cuba. W.R. Shafter had led seventeen thousand U.S. land troops to capture Santiago and shortly thereafter, General Miles led troops into Puerto Rico. Though fighting continued on the other side of the world in the Philippines, the armistice was signed August 12. In Cuba, by July the military was primarily preoc-

cupied with the battle aftermath and with the enormous problems of yellow fever, for which they were extremely ill-prepared.

17. General Shafter was a fairly ridiculous figure who weighed over three-hundred pounds and whose uniform reportedly was always way too tight. He had been ill and nearly prostrate from the heat since early July. McKinley had appointed him field commander on the basis of seniority not competence. Although he was in fact a detailed planner and much of the confusion and lack of supplies during the campaign were not entirely his fault, he was an easy target for the press, whose wrath he invited by imposing strict censorship regulations after a particularly embarrassing fiasco known as the "Gussie expedition," his first attempt at landing guns and ammunition in Cuba. His more tragic mistake was his failure to support his troops' frontal assault on San Juan and Kettle Hills with any sort of naval artillery bombardment.

18. Clara Barton, who in 1898 was seventy-seven years old, was primarily aboard the *State of Texas,* a passenger ship chartered by the Red Cross as a floating hospital. She came to Siboney to tend the influx of wounded that arrived after the Rough Riders' battles at San Juan and Kettle Hills on July 1. Though the *State of Texas* had been loaded with supplies for Cuban refugees, Barton found the army without hospital supplies of any kind and in a desperate situation, so she turned over the supplies to the military. In addition, the Red Cross managed to furnish seventeen tons of ice, obtained in Jamaica—something the army was also unable to accomplish.

19. Sunstroke.

20. The Spanish Forces had taken up positions in well-fortified stone and masonry-walled blockhouses.

21. Nelson Appleton Miles fought in the Union Army during the Civil War and rose up through the ranks by participating in battles with Indians in Minnesota and the Dakotas. In 1895 he was made Commander-in-Chief of the Army. While General William Shafter was given command of the expedition against Santiago de Cuba, Miles brought in the land forces and accepted the Spanish surrender. He later commanded in Puerto Rico.

22. Leonard Wood, Commander of the Rough Riders and Teddy Roosevelt's nominal superior. After the war, Wood took over from John Brooke as military governor of Cuba and helped to elect a Cuban president. He also built and repaired schools, roads and bridges, and dredged Havana Harbor.

23. Black infantry soldiers—as well as black army bands—played an important part in the Spanish-American War. Four black regiments, largely dormant since the Civil War, were called up. Their members came from the 24th and 25th Infantries and the 9th and 10th Cavalries. One thousand one hundred ninety-five men

served and for the first time were commanded by black officers (during the Civil War, black troops were commanded by white officers). The legendary Rough Riders, under the command of Leonard Wood and Theodore Roosevelt, followed *behind* the 9th and 10th Cavalry in charges up both Kettle and San Juan hills. The press, however, giving no credit to the black troops, reported that the Rough Riders bore the brunt of the fighting and portrayed them as the heroes of the day. In fact, no fewer than eight black soldiers received the Medal of Honor for actions during this campaign. Chaplain T.G. Steward, member of the 25th Infantry and black historian, wrote in 1904 in his book, *The Colored Regulars in the United States Army,* "The Cuban campaign has forced the nation to recognize the completion of the Negro's evolution as a soldier in the Army of the United States." Unfortunately, the newspapers of the time promoted a different story.

24. This entry was written three days after the preliminary Peace Treaty was signed in Washington, D.C., signaling the end of hostilities, although the final Treaty of Paris was not completed until December 10.

25. While only 379 servicemen were killed or died of actual battle wounds, 5,049 died of disease, primarily yellow fever. Wingreen is referring to the death rate in the fever camps.

26. For some reason, Wingreen decided not to reveal the dosages of her treatment for fever.

27. When war was formally declared on April 25, 1898, a vast majority of Americans viewed it as a noble crusade to halt oppression and aid the struggling, revolutionary Cubans. McKinley was sympathetic to the Cubans' plight, making a personal $5,000 donation to a Cuban relief agency, but he became haggard and depressed as war approached. Naval blockades of Havana were the first step and an invasion was to be held off until fall—*after* the yellow fever season had passed. Instead, due to overzealousness, the significance of the plan's timing was apparently forgotten. The invasion took place in July at the height of the hot, rainy fever season, and the shortage of proper rations, lack of ice, poor supply lines, and heavy wool uniforms, soon took their toll on the Americans.

28. It was quite common for ships carrying supplies to get "lost" for a week or lie outside of the harbor for several days before being ordered on to Siboney. General confusion over command and geographic routes only aggravated the situation already plagued by a woeful lack of basic supplies.

29. She may be referring to a last-minute hitch, or to the general situation which kept so many there so long. The first ship with fever-stricken soldiers, the *Seneca,* had left Siboney and reached New York on July 20, the day after Wingreen left for Cuba. The journey usually took eight days.

30. At this time it was still believed that yellow fever was transmitted through dirty clothing and bed linens.

31. Camp Wikoff, located at Montauk Point on Long Island, was a quickly and crudely constructed hospital built in early August to accommodate the influx of sick soldiers who began arriving in numbers on August 14. Though it appeared luxuriously supplied and staffed compared to the Siboney fever camps, Montauk was accessible by just one railroad line. It was located in a sparsely populated and underdeveloped region and terrible confusion ensued as additional transports came in. Many Americans—their fears fueled by dramatic newspaper accounts— were afraid the fever would sweep the entire nation, and great pains were taken to quarantine and detain all soldiers. Supply lines and organization eventually improved as private benefactors and charitable organizations came to the military's aid.

32. Ellen Harding Walworth and Helen M. Gould were Director General and Assistant Director General, respectively, of the National Women's Relief Association. The Association is perhaps best known for establishing Camp Walworth, a soldiers' hospice located in a house on East 15th Street near Stuyvesant Park in New York. Gould gave $25,000 to start the camp and it was named after Ellen Walworth.

33. Commodore George Dewey, whose squadron defeated the Spanish in the Philippines at the Battle of Manila Bay.

34. Many cities planned homecomings and parades for soldiers, but crowds were often quieted by the sight of them. The men were emaciated and pale, many of them still too weak to walk very far.

World War I

Strait of Dover

Rotterdam

NETHERLANDS

Zeebrugge

Ostend

Antwerp

Dunkirk

BELGIUM

Calais

Ypres

Brussels

Boulogne

Lille

Charleroi

Meuse River

Liege

Arras

Cambrai

Namur

Dieppe

Amiens

Somme River

St. Quentin

Sombre R.

GERMANY

Laon

Mezieres

Sedan

LUX

Compiegne

Aisne

Luxembourg

Oise

Soissons

Virton

Thionville

Seine R.

Eure

Chateau-Thierry

Marne

Reims

Verdun

Metz

Epernay

Chalons-sur-Marne

Ruffey

Etamps

Provins

Meuse River

Toul

Nancy

Melun

Seine

Fontainebleau

Epinal

Montargis

Seine River

Gien

Auxerre

Chatillon

Langres

Belfort

Battle of Verdun

Ogeville

Douaumont

Fort Douaumont

Dieppe

Bras

Vaux

Fort Vaux

Fleury

Eix

Thierville

Fort Tavannes

Verdun

Fort Belrupt

Chatillon

Belrupt

Haudainville

Meuse River

Fort Rozellier

Fort Haudainville

Dieue

4

World War I

How the world fell into war in 1914 will always be something of a mystery. It was a war with neither clear issues nor simple villains. Perhaps the final cause of the Great War was the rulers themselves, and their greed and vanity as quaintly ludicrous as the gilded eagle sprouting from the top of the war-helmet crown of Kaiser Wilhelm II. Whatever or whoever the instigators were, it was soon obvious that Europe had launched into a terrible mistake.

The ambitious Kaiser and his German government were more to blame than others, but Kaiser Wilhelm was no Hitler and the German government was not in a class by itself. The leadership cultures of Europe, and European governments, had much in common with each other in 1914. The twentieth century had dawned upon a fully industrial but only tentatively democratized Western world. Relatively small percentages of citizens (excluding women) could vote. The governments of Europe were still overseen by a small class of aristocrats, who felt threatened from below by democratic and socialist movements. Kaiser Wilhelm, Queen Victoria of England, and Czar Nicholas of Russia were all related to each other (Kaiser Wilhelm apparently held Queen Victoria, his grandmother, at the moment of her death), and the governments they headed were in many ways similarly "run from the top" by aristocrats, plutocrats, and the military.

The turn of the century saw a heating up of the imperialistic free-for-all among industrial powers. Under Kaiser Wilhelm II, Germany competed with other European nations for African colonies. The United States entered the imperialistic fray in its war against Spain, netting offshore territories in the Caribbean and Pacific; England had an imperialistic war, her first in some time, against the Dutch settlers in South Africa who refused to accept British control; in the east, the Ottoman Turks occupied the Balkans. All over the globe, the major powers, covetous for new avenues of commerce, elbowed each other for world position.

The assassination in Sarajevo, Bosnia, of the Archduke Ferdinand and his wife Sophia Chotek of Austria-Hungary by a rogue pack of Serbian nationalists who called themselves "the Black Hand" appeared at first to be a manageable event. Sir Edward Grey, the British Foreign Secretary, was confident that it could be settled by a conference in London. Before the assassination, relations between Britain and Germany had been improving. While the fear of war had haunted Europe for some time, there had been little immediate expectation of it. When Austria-Hungary sent an ultimatum to Serbia, however, Russia, as the self-designated defender of Slav nationalism, began to mobilize against Austria-Hungary.

In the atmosphere of greed, blustering, and militarism, the mutual alliances of Europe that originally had been created to avoid war became a house of cards ready to tumble. Germany had allied with Austria-Hungary and the old Ottoman Empire, and Russia had made a pact with France, which was later joined by Britain.

In 1905 the German Count Alfred von Schlieffen had devised a plan to fight a European war on two fronts that called for Germany to make a lightning strike westward, capturing Paris and thereby immediately neutralizing the more potent enemy. When Russia mobilized against Austria-Hungary, the Schlieffen plan, revised in the nine years since it had originally been conceived, was the grand scheme by which Germany suddenly unleashed three-quarters of her army in a gigantic westward march across Belgium and northern France. According to the minutely detailed plan, it would take Germany exactly forty-two days to capture Paris.

The illusion that the war would be over soon was shared by the countries on both sides. "BERLIN ANXIOUS. VIENNA IN A PANIC" said a headline in *Le Matin* in early September, 1914. The ascendant military theories in 1914 were based on movement and offensive strategies, an approach that played well with ambitious politicians like Kaiser Wilhelm. But as is often the case, the preconceptions about a major war and the actual circumstances and technology of it radically diverged. The forty-two-day adventure of conquest turned into a drawn-out and, on the Western Front, profoundly static bloodbath, in which the lines that were soon drawn in

1914 were basically unchanged after four years of carnage. The war, inspired by illusion and greed, turned out to be an unmitigated disaster from start to conclusion and, perhaps even more significantly, after its conclusion.

Some have said that the United States won World War I and everybody else lost it. The war did hasten advancement of the economic and geopolitical power of the United States, but a poorly conceived peace and huge national debts incurred by all the nations that had been involved also contributed to the economic instability from which issued a worldwide depression, the rise of fascism, and an even more terrible war. The immediate effects of World War I for the United States included the deaths of 112,000 Americans (half from disease), expenditures of about 112 billion dollars, and an expansion by 1919 of the gross national debt by twenty times what it had been in 1914.

The United States did not intend to enter the war, and it managed to avoid doing so until Germany was about to run out of steam, although that was not apparent at the time. By far the most important contribution of the United States to the Allied victory was as a supplier of money and foodstuffs while the Central and Allied powers smashed away at each other in what by 1917 had become a war of attrition. Even without U.S. help, the Allies had a natural advantage over the Central Powers in resources, and U.S. food and money tipped the balance further.

Before America's entry, throughout 1916, the two warring sides had conducted hesitant peace negotiations; however, the Germans refused to retreat to their prewar boundaries. Millions had died for a dream of total victory, and politicians were afraid to present their nations with compromise solutions. The inertia of war, the self-prolonging trajectory, lasted beyond the time that it became apparent who would win.

The United States would probably have succeeded in staying uninvolved militarily if the Germans hadn't tried to cut off U.S. shipments to Britain by unrestricted submarine warfare. In 1916, bad harvests and the success of the British North Sea blockade worsened Germany's problem of diminishing resources, and they took the calculated risk of declaring open war on all shipping coming into Europe. The second immediate reason for the United States' entry into the war was the Zimmerman telegram, Germany's proposal to Mexico that she join in war against the United States.

The telegram was intercepted, Wilson was enraged, and the United States soon declared war.

Despite the fact that all of the original combatants were sick and tired of war by the end of 1917, Germany was producing more arms than ever. Russia's revolution and her capitulation to Germany in the Treaty of Brest-Litovsk allowed Germany to withdraw from the Eastern Front and launch a major offensive in the West.

Up to that time, offensive strategies had failed to a degree that would have been inconceivable to the generals in early 1914. Neither side could move the other, primarily because of outdated military tactics operating with imperfectly understood new tools and weaponry. The principal tactic of the war was massive frontal assaults, sent out after long artillery barrages. The dominant weapons were quick-firing bolt-action rifles, accurate field artillery with rifled barrels, and the unbelievably deadly machine gun. Tanks, airplanes, and field telephones were all introduced in World War I, but none of these innovations was of decisive importance. Nothing was as important as the machine gun. Artillery barrages were seldom as effective as officers at general headquarters continued to imagine them to be, and they served to thoroughly warn defending lines that an attack was coming. The infantry attacks themselves, in which hoardes of men were sent out to run across barbed-wire-lined landscapes against machine-gun and rapid-fire rifles, were massively suicidal, and the solution that the generals on both sides continued to resort to throughout the war was to merely use more stunning artillery barrages and more men.

When a large enough force was hurled across no-man's land, they might succeed in capturing the defenders' trenches, but then soldiers found themselves in extended positions, with extremely poor communications—wireless radios were not yet effective—subject to counterattacks from reserve trenches. When assaults did succeed in moving lines into bulging "salients," they were often later flattened back out because of the difficulty of defending a salient. Therefore when territory was taken, it had a way of later being lost. The war that was to be characterized by lightning offense had become a gigantic, largely unmoving factory of attrition.

In 1916, at the first Battle of the Somme, the British had sent out wave after wave of men after five days of artillery bombardment. Many of the British were new to the war, and the Germans, amazed to see them walking with their officers in front, mowed them down by the hundreds.

More than thirty thousand British soldiers were killed or wounded within the first hour of fighting. Headquarters didn't understand what was happening. Tanks were used for the first time at the Somme, but there weren't enough of the lumbering, still awkward machines to make a difference. There were sixty thousand casualties in one day—the worst day of carnage of any army during the war and the bloodiest day in the history of the British. By the end of the months-long battle, the lines had moved about five miles, the British had lost 420,000 men, the Germans 450,000, and the French 200,000. What happened at the Somme was to be of immense importance. The twentieth century was stamped inalterably by that day, and in battles like it that continued to follow.

In spite of indisputable evidence that mass frontal assaults didn't work, plenty more were to be ordered by both sides. By the spring of 1918, the French were exhausted and the British had recently suffered immense losses at Passchendaele. At this very late point, the Germans began to employ new tactics using briefer artillery barrages and "saturation" attacks at certain points rather than frontal assaults, and the new tactics at first worked. The Germans came within thirty-seven miles of Paris. For the first time during the war panic engulfed the French capital. In April nearly a million people fled the city. There were already more than three hundred thousand Americans in France and more pouring in by the week, but the German High Command was confident that it would take some time for them to be ready to fight.

It was during this fairly brief period, of the spring through the summer of 1918, with the Germans attacking in several places along the front, that U.S. soldiers fought in the war. By August 8, the Germans had exhausted themselves, and three months later, on the eleventh hour of the eleventh day of the eleventh month, the armistice was signed.

Charles Ponton, a teacher in the commercial department of Kalamazoo High School, was among the earliest Americans to sign up for service and he was to be among the earliest to arrive in France. At the beginning of mobilization, Ponton joined an American ambulance corp, along with his brother Joe, who was younger by six years and had only recently graduated from high school in Ypsilanti, Michigan. The 591 Army Ambulance Unit consisted mostly of students from the University of Michigan, and it was assigned to the French army. Like many Americans, Ponton felt that the United States "could have kept away from these fighting nations," but at the same time he felt an obligation to serve. Ponton was of half-French and half-German descent, his mother a second-generation German American.

In his diary Ponton describes how eager the boys were for their uniforms, which they regarded as having magic powers over young women. Joining up was something of a lark. Indeed at several places along the way during training and while being shipped out, young army volunteers were greeted generously and openly by young women. There are moments of spontaneous warmth, instant friendships, photographs exchanged, even kisses between strangers. After the eerie sleeplessness of a submarine-haunted crossing, the 591 arrived in France and was soon put to work assembling and preparing Ford ambulances. They traveled north across the beautiful countryside of southern France, which had not been directly touched by war, through Paris to the front in the north.

Only three months before, in early spring, the French army, wasted from nearly three years of carnage, had cracked and undergone a widespread mutiny. The leadership had changed for the third time, with General Henri Pétain taking command of an army that had given up hope. French soldiers marching to the front had bleated like sheep and posted signs everywhere saying "Down with the War!" The mood had spread from troops to factories, where during May and June there had been nearly two hundred major work stoppages in war plants. By June, half of the divisions of the French army were insubordinate. But Pétain listened to grievances, upgraded food and conditions, and during the summer the mutinies subsided.

The horror of the war was finally being appreciated by politicians. Near the time of Ponton's arrival, David Lloyd George, British prime minister, privately remarked to a friend, "If people really knew, the war would be stopped tomorrow. But of course they don't know and can't know." Information coming out of the war, both by individual soldiers and by news correspondents, was rigorously censored, and it was out of this cloud of unknowing that Ponton and the rest of the 591 arrived at the front.

The battle line, before the last great offensive of the Germans, ran almost exactly where it had for most of the war, from near Ostend on the North Sea all the way across northern France to the Swiss frontier. The trenches themselves were elaborate systems consisting of front-line trenches, usually dug in zigzags to avoid enfilading fire when they were partially overrun, with narrow communications trenches leading back to second-line and support trenches. Enemy trenches were typically about a quarter of a mile away but could be as close as fifty yards. The bottoms of trenches were usually laid with duckboards, and there was a "firestep" at the front to bring men up to ground level. The fighting between the two sides essentially never ceased. In the mornings after breakfast and inspection, the men were ordered to step up for the quarter of an hour of "morning hate," in which they fired at each other, some being hit despite the cover. Snipers were active at any time, night or day, and artillery fire was seemingly endless.

The most persistent facts of life in the war were mud, body lice, rats, and the continuous presence of the dead. In no other war in history were such masses of men forced to live for such long periods of time literally among the dead. Rats, too numerous to try to exterminate, could typically be heard feeding in the night. Because of the unprecedented stress of the front lines, men simply could not stand much more than a week at the front at a time. After eight-day stints at the front, they were regularly evacuated to the rear of the lines for a three-week recovery.

In the rear they were able to take hot baths, their clothes were cleaned and deloused, and they could partake of Red Cross or the YMCA canteens, which offered canned food, some fresh foods, and occasional social and cultural events. Houses of prostitution thrived behind the lines.

Existentialism was born in the trenches. The trenches fostered fatalism, superstitiousness, and alienation from "normal" life. Soldiers going on leave sometimes felt cut off from civilian life. One of the weirdest effects of the war was that soldiers sometimes developed almost an addiction to the camaraderie and emotional edge of the front, where the small problems and anxieties of "normal" life were neutralized by the fact that at any moment one could be extinguished. Death was always imminent. Newly arriving soldiers were told not to worry about ducking sniper fire, since "you won't hear the one that gets you."

In addition to the wounds of artillery and small-arms fire, soldiers were subject to mustard gas, which caused skin blistering, blinding, and partial asphyxiation due to constricted throats and burned lungs. Men who had been gassed suffered gummed-up eyes, either couldn't talk or could barely talk, and were often in the throes of asphyxiation. There was no cure for gas inhalation. Wound infection was high; the well manured fields of France caused a form of gangrene. Shell shock, often character-ized by a kind of goofy grin on the soldier's face, made soldiers hysterical, disoriented, or paralyzed. In addition to wounding, soldiers were sub-jected to a complex of illnesses characteristic of trench life: flu viruses, tetanus, and "trench foot," a form of frostbite caused by feet being continu-ously wet.

The ambulance men had to do a good deal of stretcher bearing as well as driving, and both of these jobs had mortality rates a little higher than that of front-line infantry. Many of the roads that Ponton and the others in the 591 drove were under frequent shellfire and continuously busy with con-fused, frenetic traffic. A division of about fifteen thousand men required fifty railroad cars of supplies per day, and the roads and rear areas became vast, busy suburbs. A road that Ponton traveled often, the *Voie Sacree* be-tween Verdun and Bar-le-Duc, at times had traffic of trucks stretching as far as the eye could see across the low rolling hills. These roads were often surrounded by the dead and dying—unburied corpses and braying wounded horses and trench burros.

For much of its tour of duty, the 591 remained in the general vicinity of Verdun. Verdun had been the scene of a ten-month battle in 1916 in which virtually the entire French army (4.4 million men, in all) had fought to contain the Germans. Defense of Verdun became a symbol of French military power, due more to the historical significance of the city in the Franco-Prussian War forty-five years before than to its immediate strategic importance. At Verdun, the German Commander Falkenhayn decided to wear the French down by attrition—as he put it, "to bleed the French army white." It turned into a slaughterhouse for both armies, ending with no strategic gain being made by either side.

The area continued to be the scene of intense trench warfare after the 591 arrived. The unit worked in and out of posts at places like Fleury and Bras, one or two kilometers from Fort Douaumont—the epicenter of the war on the Western Front—and at nearby Avocourt, which was a few hun-dred yards from the current front line. Later the 591 was moved westward on the front, as part of the effort to stop the German offensives in the spring and summer of 1918.

Like most of those in the 591, Charles Ponton was strongly moti- vated. Ambulance driving provided him and other men with the chance to contribute to the effort without being combatants. Ponton felt that the United States could have avoided this war, but at the same time he regret- ted that he had not personally joined earlier for ambulance service. After more than a year of sleeping with rats, however, of driving roads like "Di- arrhea Crossroads," and dealing first hand with the hatred, lies, atrocities, and confusion of war, he shouts out in his diary, "When—will—this— war—ever—end!!!" Ponton came to question the war in the same terms that the great novels and films of the 1930s later did. *All Quiet on the West- ern Front, The Grand Illusion, The Road to Glory*—all of which saw the sol- diers of both sides as common victims of its horror. As the child of parents representing the two great enemies in this war, Ponton came to see it as a tragedy within the human family.

The government and military "managed" information in World War I by means of universal censorship. Censorship was blunt and indiscrimi- nate, the principal reason why the letters home of World War I were so generally informationless. Written under fear of reprisal, most of the field diaries are as bland as the letters. The censors peeked over the shoulder of every man with a pencil. But Ponton wrote his diary in shorthand and thereby feared the censors less.

After nearly two years of dangerous duty, by which time he had more than earned his spurs in the field, and one stripe, Ponton openly ques- tioned the nature of war in a letter home to his mother. He wrote to her that war was a "butchering hell game" and that "Power could enforce but not engender." For these dangerous statements he was pounced upon by a censor, court-martialled in the field for "pacifistic writing," convicted and punished by being demoted back to private.

It testifies to Ponton's character that while this angered him, and while he did not emotionally accede to it, at the same time he didn't let it get to him. He remained expansive and curious to learn more about the people and landscape of France, and at the end of the war he fell into a romance that he took far more seriously than he took his court-martial.

When he returned, Charles Ponton continued to teach in Detroit high schools and later at the University of Tampa. He died in 1971 at the age of eighty-one. He was survived by a second wife, four daughters, and fifteen grandchildren. He told his daughters that his shorthand "squiggles" would never be translated. But Phyllis C. Bryant spent months doing just that, making possible the presentation of this diary.

The Diary of Charles Ponton

June 1, 1917. When war was declared, April 6th, I was teaching in Kalamazoo in the Commercial Department. Personally, I had been asleep to the horrors of this great world's war that had been going on since the first days of August in 1914. I had read the reports of the thousands of men who were daily giving up their lives, as I had read of the French Rebellion or the Hundred Years' War. It was not at all real to me, but way off. After war was declared, however, I began to think and for one month I thought night and day. Now of what service I would go into, now of how I could stay home, but also of the justification of throwing a great country into such a hell of slaughter, of fighting a foe on his own ground three thousand miles from home, of the practicality, etc. The greatest question with me, however, was what and how much our grievance was. Had we invited trouble? Was it a war of self-defense, of independence or for humanity? These were questions that must be settled before I could decide just how reckless I would be with my life in their defense.

At last I said to myself, "Life is too sweet to throw it away in a war of self-defense against a foe who is engaged by all Europe." We could have easily laid an embargo and kept away from these fighting nations. [1] But the strong plea to me was the abuse of right to my fellow men. Then the question came, "But why didn't this occur to me when the Germans crossed Belgium?" From the moment that that came to me I deeply regretted not enlisting in 1914. I was ashamed of myself from that time on for sleeping for two long years. I saw here so vivid a cause that I should give all I had, so the 28th of May, I signed up with Dr. Case to go to France as an ambulance man in the French army.

After I had once made the decision, I couldn't get away too quick. I returned to Kazoo and finished my school, while the boys waited orders at Battle Creek. My brother surprised me with the news June 7th that he had been promised a place in the section and was to go with me. We were told now that we had best pay our parents goodbye at once, as we might be called at any minute and would not have time to go to our homes. Accordingly, we took a train to Sherman, Michigan, on June 8th and paid a hurried farewell.

There was something about this parting for war that when it was over and you turned to go, you knew if he or she was your real friend, and just how much he cared. It really takes something like this to find people out. There are times when you can deceive and camouflage. But in those parting moments, one couldn't stammer something he didn't feel. If he tried it, he made a bad mess.

Most of us took the physical exams the nineteenth and twentieth. It was a very serious matter with most of us, for a number were turned down the first couple of hours. [2] You could tell by the look on a chap's face if he has passed. Some of the boys drank over two quarts of water to raise their weight, some were memorizing the eye chart, etc. Anything to get by, for we felt if once we got by we could make good. At last this great suspense was over, but we were soon to learn that it wasn't the end, for the soldier's life is a life of suspense, uncertainty and waiting. Question #2 was, "When shall we be called to the Allentown ambulance camp?"

The next few days we were sworn in, given our equipment, taught some of the simple formations necessary to marching, while men from the front in France endeavored to picture to us the life we were suddenly to be plunged into. They succeeded so thoroughly in convincing me that I would not return that I placed my ring, fob and watch in a box and sent it home, and I disposed of all my personal property.

While we were being warned of these dangers and hardships, Dr. Martin was giving us stereopticon lectures on the great "Battle of Paris." He said little of the battle itself, but he sure gave us some wonderful pointers on the results, and it's my opinion that Dr. Martin did a far greater service to the soldiers than he ever shall realize.

We were marched to the depot about 8:00 just before train time. Just before we arrived we were halted, and mothers, sweethearts and friends were allowed to pass among us to say a last farewell. That was a sad sight and I saw few after that that affected me so deeply. I had plenty of time to watch and reflect on the scene for in that sea of heads I didn't see a familiar face. As the mothers, sweethearts and sisters kissed the boys at my side, my brother who stood at my side, said, "I guess we will have to kiss each other." Many mothers searched among us for their boy but could not find him, and in some cases were never to find him again. Fathers shook their boys goodbye and never twitched a muscle, but large tears followed one after another down their cheeks. Sisters wept on their brothers' necks, and sweethearts had that far-off look that seemed to say "I am always with you." Suddenly the train whistled and we were off. Tears were wiped away, and the past was left behind. All life from here was new and in the present. We were hurled among strangers to whom we were all the same, and the thing that made us so much alike was that we were all machinery in the great cause for which we were assembled.

Of course we were gay for a time, for we were now on our way to the other side. Two by two we stowed ourselves away for the night. All became still, apparently we were sleeping, but most of us spent a few hours thinking before sleep overcame us, for this was our first real break from home.

We arrived in Allentown about 7:00 of the twenty-sixth, tired and hungry. We had about two and a half miles to walk to camp. We met many boys along the road, some already in uniform, but most of them were still in civilian clothes. They all told us the same story—that we had a beefsteak supper waiting for us. Our mouths were all set, but in a few minutes we were to learn a great lesson. "You're in the army now."

Manners were to be left behind with your sweethearts, and if you liked black molasses and bread, macaroni, etc., you often had to beat the others to it.

The issue now that began to give us all alarm was when are we going to get our outfits? And will they fit! This was a very important question with us for many reasons. In the first place as long as we were soldiers we wanted to look like soldiers, and I think some of us really hankered for them. I never wished to dress up in any garb as I did the uniform. Without it the girls couldn't see you *at all,* but once you have it on, you have to become diplomatic to keep them from fighting.

The next weeks that followed this shall *always* mark an epoch in my life. "Nothing to worry over." "A neat and attractive outfit" and "A town full of the most congenial girls I ever met." We had a 9:00 pass every night and could get two late passes a week. To make a long story short, we got hog fat on this program. Girls visited Allentown from all the surrounding burgs: Catasanky, Phillipsburg, Reading, etc. Well, a number of girls lost their life of single blessedness here, and the boys lost their hearts and all of their dollars. Central and Dory Park were the chief centers of sunshine. Here were large dancing pavilions, swimming pools, etc.

While at camp we spent most of our time drilling, learning how to make up our packs neatly and quickly, how to carry wounded, how to maneuver stretchers, etc. This was all more or less as interesting as it was new. Even sleeping on your army cot the first night was some fun, as we knew we had to learn to like it.

Meal time was an interesting event also. Our dining room was in the Fair Ground Building and it was located underneath the grandstand. Five thousand of us had to eat in this great room. Only a portion of us could eat at one time and the remainder waited in line. The people showed a wonderful spirit of friendliness toward us, inviting us to dinner, church, boating parties, lawn suppers, etc. These people were probably 90 percent German but they were certainly 100 percent Americans.

When we were not drilling we could do about what our wishes of a leisure time might be. You could see boys playing ball, cards, crap, etc., or fellows walking about the park within the grounds. And, in the large YMCA, some would be playing checkers, some the piano, the phonograph, while others would be reading or writing. Many of the boys were bright serious fellows with high aspirations and ideals. About 90 percent of them were college men, the various units scattered about the grounds represented such heads of learning as N.Y. University, Columbia, Harvard, Princeton, Leland Stanford, U. of Call., Tuskegee Institute, U. of Tennessee, U. of Pennsylvania, U. of Michigan. Each college stuck together pretty much, and you knew the unit better than the man individually.[3] Some were more democratic, some indifferent, some dignified, others very civil, some very studious, while others went more to class spirit. All of us were probably at our best because we knew the other fellow was always getting our measure.

About August 1st rumors began to be spread that twenty sections were soon to be picked for overseas. From this time on the foremost question in our life was, will we be picked among the twenty sections?

At last the twenty sections were known, but Battle Creek was not among them. Section 591 from Ann Arbor was chosen to go. They were not complete, so Van Boyd, Spart Bilon and my brother and I joined them. I have often been grateful for this move, for had I not been transferred I should have never seen action with the French.

The 21st of August, just as the day was beginning (1:00 A.M.), we crept silently forth from our beds, hastily ate a light breakfast, hurried to some covered trucks, and were taken to the depot, to embark for—none of us knew where.

We were put on the *Baltic* and at noon ate our first meal on the ship. It was quite a novelty at first, but it wore off very soon. About noon of the twenty-second we steamed out of the harbor. As the boat was about to draw anchor—in fact, for some time before—we were making the best of our last minutes with the girls of the USA. They never seemed so attractive and loveable. They wrote their names and addresses hastily on scraps of paper, wadded them up and threw them to the boys who most appealed to them, and the boys did the same. I shall never forget one girl. She received more notes than all the rest combined. She could not begin to answer them, for it kept her busy just collecting them. She was surely a good mental picture for a fellow to take to France.

We thought we were bound for France but we were sadly disappointed when on the third day we came into Halifax Harbor.

We lay there in the harbor for eleven days and were forbidden to leave the ship. The only events to break the monotony of the long day was the meal hour and the visit paid us in the evening by the girls who would come out with row boats and hand up kisses on their paddles through the lower loop holes. This was all the introduction we received, yet, in some cases, it was the beginning of a great romance.

At last one pretty day about noon it was reported that our convoy was complete and we were ready to face the sea and the subs. While we were eating supper the engines began to pound, the tables began to sway and we knew once more we were on our way. That ended all thoughts of supper, we all arose and ran to the deck to view the harbor as we went out, and to watch the last speck of land fade from view. There were no card or crap games that evening. Now that we were really on our way the joy of starting gradually turned to the contemplation of what was to follow this happy beginning. Most of the boys watched the water and as it became dark, paired off with their pals, discussed their past and prophesied on their future. We were now to sleep below decks, as we were in danger of subs. This was severe punishment. The nights were very warm and it appeared that the air never got down to the bottom of that boat. Many of us hid the first few nights in the life boats, under the dining room tables and so forth, but one by one our hiding places were found by the guards and we were chased to the hole below. I seldom slept in my bed, for the want of sleep was never quite sufficient to overcome my want of air.

The air was terrible below but they were insistent on us being in our room as we were in dangerous waters. I was first chased from one of the life boats that was hanging high up over the deck. While I was descending I spied a bench, and as the guard was occupied with many others, I succeeded. I escaped, however, only long enough to get to sleep. We were soon discovered and all driven out. As we were all being shoved below, I saw a pile of hatchway covers piled up about eight feet high. I crawled to the top and lay exactly in the center. At last I lost the guards and lay undisturbed until morning. I certainly appreciated it for the air was suffocating below.

During the day we could pass our time as we desired. We might sit on the railing and gaze on the angry waters, watch the waves as they depart from the boat and gradually disappear into nothing, we might watch the horizon for subs, or content ourselves watching the porpoises as they leaped so gracefully from the water.

Sometimes hundreds of us would rush to the center of the deck and form a ring around a couple of boxers or wrestlers. Most of the contests were between the medical bunch from the North and the signal corps from Texas. All the scraps were carried out in the best spirits and good sportsmanship prevailed.

When we were three days out of Liverpool, we were met by fourteen destroyers. This made in all thirteen boats of the convoy and fourteen destroyers. From this time on the keenest watch was kept, for we were in the zone of the U-boat proper. [4] We were all kept below from dark on and we had our life preservers strapped on us at all times, and some of the boys did not remove their clothes these last three nights. During the day we kept a close watch for the U-boats.

All went well until the evening of the night we landed. We were in sight of the Irish Coast. It was about 7:00 P.M. when a "U" showed her periscope right in our midst. Three of our boats were running in the form of a triangle and she popped up in the center about equal distance from all of us. She squared away and directed a torpedo at our broad side. The pilot quickly swung our stern to her and the Captain reported to the wireless station at Liverpool that we had been hit a glancing blow but that the torpedo had not exploded. This sounds fishy, but nevertheless was the story of the crew.[5]

While this was going on, the other boats were firing at her and our boat shot once. The destroyers were charging at her from all directions. Three of our destroyers were English and one, #38, was American. She ran very close to her just as she was in the act of submerging. #38 dropped a mine and wheeled as if on a pivot and ran with the speed of the wind. Then there was one great splash of water, some black smoke and suddenly such a shock to the surrounding water that those below who were not aware of the fight fell from their seats to the floor. The boom of the exploding mine and the shock to the boat, along with the fact that one side was gradually lowering, convinced us all that the boat was hit—not only that we were hit but that we were going down. We all rushed to our places as we had been taught in boat drills. Some of the boys unfortunately did not have their life preservers and rushed wildly to the bottom of the boat. One fellow was so excited that he knocked the steward down and tried to take his life preserver away from him.

The boat crew rushed madly about and were so excited I believe the boat could have sunk ten times before they could have gotten the boats down. About the time we had all resigned ourselves to a watery grave, report was spread that the boat was still safe and that the U-boat had gone up with the smoke. These were the most welcome words I ever drank, for in the past ten minutes many things had flashed through my mind as I stood looking into those cold blue waves as they whipped and drove about the boat. I stood next to my brother. I tried to think of some last word of cheer, and we talked some about what we should do if the boat continued to sink, and they didn't get the boats down. We were going to try and get hold of some piece of wreckage and hang together if possible. We could hardly believe the report that the boat was O.K., it was so nearly turned over. This was later explained as being due to turning it so suddenly to avoid a direct hit. The chasers watched carefully for ripples or trails in the water that would be made by the departing sub but could see nothing, and we were well satisfied that the bomb was the sub's finish.

That night few went to sleep until we landed, about 2:00 A.M., in the Liverpool harbor. After twenty-four days on that packed boat, it seemed as if we would never get the stretch out of our legs. I felt as if I had been bound hand and foot and suddenly released. After descending we lined up along the dock, unslung packs and waited for our train which was to take us to Southampton. A snappy young chap hurried among us taking cablegrams from us to our parents; each one coming to $3.50. We boarded a first-class train and arrived in Southampton in the early morning, about 2:00, worn out, only to find we had three miles to lug our packs to camp.

This was a tough hike and we lay down with our packs as pillows and rested several times before we reached the camp. It was so dark that we could see nothing of the city and the only thing that disturbed the silence of the night was the tramp, tramp, tramp that echoed up and down the streets for blocks. We were taken to barracks, where we found about six inches of straw strewn on the ground on which we lay our blankets, and very soon we were dreaming of what lay ahead.

Our stay here was short. At noon we started for the station. It was a very pleasant day and people came to give us a smile of appreciation and wish us good luck. Many walked by our side and one pretty girl walked up to Griesey and reached out for his hand. We were walking at attention so Griesey reached out rather reluctantly and she said, "Don't be shy, lad." One fellow in his enthusiasm forgot his national pride and shouted, "Hurrah for the Yanks—you whipped us in '76, now go get Hiney." From here we took the boat across the English Channel to LeHavre. It was a warm September night and the boat was so crowded it looked like a Detroit streetcar in working hours. If we should have been hit, without question all would have gone down with the boat.

I stayed on top and enjoyed the sights along shore until dark. An Australian I had fallen in with and I sought a place of shelter from the wind. We stayed there and talked the forepart of the night. The Australian had been a stockbroker. He gave me the first straight-from-the-front dope I ever heard. [6] He told of the hand-to-hand conflicts with the Boche and of their cruelties, some of which could scarce be credited. He told also of a Scotchman who was given twenty prisoners to take back and how he put them all to bayonet on his way back. He made war more vivid than it had ever been made before, and I decided that if I lasted a few months I should owe Providence a deep debt.

At last I got cold and sleepy where I lay and went below, but I was too late, for every place that a man could lie was full. I went on down and down from deck to deck. The sights I saw there horrified me. There were thousands of men crossing and recrossing one another, all using each other for pillows. Many did not have room for their arms and legs and were supported by the other fellows. Many were in heavy sleep, snoring. And the air—there wasn't any.

Fortune was with us, we escaped the subs and early the next morning pulled into LeHavre. I was much relieved when I put my feet on earth once more.

It was here that I saw the first Boche prisoners, and we scrutinized them as we would have the Kaiser himself. There were great numbers working on the docks taking care of freight. The prisoners were certainly deliberate in their movements.

The camp here consisted of hundreds of wigwam tents. We would lie with our heads around the outer edge and our feet in the center. We saw many English soldiers here, and every button on their uniforms was a curiosity. We heard stories of the front from them and I don't think they left out any of the blood and thunder. As we saw these Englishmen march down to the depots with full marching equipment and entrain for the front, the war came nearer and nearer to us.

After a couple days rest, we were marched to the station to entrain for St.-Nazaire. [7] We were lucky enough to draw second-class passage. Three times a day as the meal hour rolled around the sergeants would pass the length of the train and throw canned bully beef[8] through the door to the animals within. Sometimes sardines or cheese were substituted. This with bread was our meal.

We arrived in St.-Nazaire just in time to miss our dinner. The way from the depot led along the bay. On our left were the ships landed with thousands of Ford ambulances crated up. We were informed that we were to assemble them before we left for the front. Our hearts fell at that, for we were anxious to get to the front.

Our barracks were pointed out to us, and we were soon making our new home comfortable by putting in straw, shelves and so forth. There was about an acre of grapes in front of our barracks, but every evening the vines were stripped.

We soon became cogs in the machinery of that great camp: guarding, doing KP, garbage detail, assembling cars.

St.-Nazaire

Monday, September 24, 1917. A large Zeppelin is passing over my head now.[9] This is my first day of assembling cars. And I am to go on guard duty now for twenty-four hours. I was just talking with a German prisoner (officer) and he claims that Germany has fifteen million men yet. He was working at latrine duty and said he would rather be in the trenches.

Thursday, September 26. Went downtown for the first time. Found the streets very narrow, many wine and fruit shops. I saw a great many fast women and very few of any poise at all. I visited the slum district and was impressed with the children and women who begged for pennies. Depressed and sorry for the lot of some people. We heard of the first two boys from Allentown being shot at the front. Officers who are unpopular with their men are shot in the back in the first charge by their own men.[10]

Sunday, September 30. There is a strong feeling between the marines and engineers. A couple have been killed in their fights. I went to Church twice today. I go on guard tonight. Yesterday, I met the Misses Maude and Louise Lounette of 51 Nantes St., St.-Nazaire. We had a dictionary conversation; she with her English book and I with my French dictionary. Our progress was slow. Friday, Sections 85, 39, 94 and 35 left for the front. We expect to go within a week.

Friday, October 2. I was put on permanent detail today, inspecting cars. Worked all day and must go on watch at 10:00 P.M.

The section received their cars today and the drivers were selected.

October 3, 1917. I was appointed associate driver with Bauman. Joe was appointed to drive with Deyo.

October 6 to October 9. Saturday morning at 7:00 A.M. we started across France. We started at St.-Nazaire to Sandricourt, passing through the following towns: Nantes, Angers, La Flèche, Chartres, Rombouillet, Versailles, Sandricourt.

The beautiful country impressed me as we came that three hundred miles across France. We saw ruined castles and estates and beautiful valleys and hills. All we saw in the cities were old women and children. This is a fact all over France—you see no men, and the young women are at work in factories and hospitals.

The first night we stopped at Angers within the large barracks of the French, and I went out with Kelsey to dinner. I had some time with my "French," both finding the place and getting what I wanted after I got there. Two ladies at last took us to the place. We met two very nice young men and I gave one my picture and address. They were both students and their father was a professor in the army. Most of the land along the road was fine pasture but there were few cattle to pasture. On our first day we passed a wonderful large castle, partly destroyed; at Chartres we saw a wonderful cathedral. I met two English women at Chartres. Sunday night we stopped at Nogent. I saw a girl who looked just like Florence.

Monday morning, when Siggins [11] and I came out of the hotel, we saw the train of ambulances already going past. By running hard, we got there before it was our turn to start our cars. At Versailles, we stopped two hours and visited the palace of Louis XIV who reigned seventy-two years, during which time he ruined the nation. I saw the stables where he kept his three thousand horses and the place where his hostlers and pages roomed, his palace with the thousand painted pictures covering its ceilings, and the white hardwood floor, so slippery that you could hardly walk on it. His chapel was very swell also. His summer grounds were beyond description; beautiful swimming pools, courts for games, parks, gardens, etc. After the war, I plan to see Versailles to a finish.

When we left Versailles with four other cars who were delayed, we got lost and later found we were on the road to Paris and only ten miles distant. We finally found the road through my little French, but darkness soon overtook us. I shall not soon forget the thrill of trying to keep up or in sight of the tail light of the car ahead. We had no lights on either end, and it was as dark as could be. Near Versailles I was eating a hunk of dry bread and a civilian came up and asked for half of it. We had no stops for meals during our trip but ate anything we could get when we could get time to eat it.

The percentage of French girls who are beautiful is high. The French girl has a way of looking at you that indicates her friendliness or even fondness for you, at the same time retaining her self-respect. Everybody in the country builds back from the road, their house reached by a private road leading from the main road. We stayed at St. Germaine at night and left at 5:30 A.M. Arrived in camp at 8:30 Friday, A.M. Thursday, eleventh, a rumor was circulated that Sections 58 and 91 were to leave on the morrow for Italy.

Friday, October 12. We left for Bar-Le-Duc, [12] after eating supper in Paris at the American Hospital. It was very interesting to note on the doors the various American cities and individuals who kept up the ward. The up-keep (ten in a ward) was $6,000 yearly. I saw a great many wounded in Paris and we saw many in mourning. Paris is a busy city. We had little time to visit it. We arrived in Bar-Le-Duc at 2:00 A.M. The French soldiers shared their breakfast with us. They will even give you their hat. I am impressed with the selfishness of our own boys, in contrast with the generous nature of the French.

Thursday, October 18. We reached Jubicourt October 13th, 7:00 P.M. [13] We took quarters in an old barn. We ate what little we had in the dark and made our beds on straw. The rats ran all over our beds, our shoes and so on. [14] I went on guard at 2:00 A.M., and very soon had a semicircle of little eyes gathered around me.

Tuesday, sixteenth, I made my first trip with wounded. I carried Tuesday and Wednesday five coucheys and sixteen assis. [15] I was relieved Thursday. I went on duty at B.1 P.J. à gauche. I saw a Boche airplane surrender and land near me. He lit and threw a match in his tank then threw up his hands. [16] In an air fight, a German pilot was shot through the neck. He was still breathing, but the lieutenant flying with him was dead. They fell within forty rods of my ambulance. I saw him fall to the ground.

I have my little finger cut almost off; hence, my bad writing. Wednesday, five Frenchmen on their way home on a twelve-day leave came into camp about 1:00 A.M. I put them all to bed and begged breakfast for them, for which they were thankful. Thursday noon, I lost my dinner in the dirt and the French cook would not give me a "re," but Artie Cook swiped two pieces for me.

Friday, October 19. I carried two coucheys and two assis. Saturday, one couchey and three assis. Tuesday, I carried eight blessés [17] and two assis. Wednesday, two blessés and one assis.

I received my first letter in French. I went to Avocourt and starshells were falling very close around us. [18]

When not driving, which is nerve racking, an ambulance driver is either standing or sitting around a smoky stove. If he is not wiping the tears out of his eyes, he fights for a place by the stove where the smoke soon overcomes him. When we have no wood, we hug the stove just the same. Occasionally one tries to read by the dim light of a black lantern globe, but soon gives up and contents himself to listen or talk to the other boys. He is called on to go on a trip, returns too late for supper, finds that there is no bed with blankets and the fire has gone out.

He goes again back to his ambulance and finds a few blankets, damp with the blood and mud from the wounded, returns with them and makes his bed and sleeps. But he kicks and jerks from the cold. After all this, he is fortunate if he is not called out in the night or just before breakfast. He sleeps with his cap, mittens and, many times, boots.

He eats without washing, as he hasn't a place or articles to wash with. His hands are greasy from the machine and his dishes are dirty from want of warm water or soap, his clothes are wet and muddy, his hair is un-combed and altogether he is a forlorn object to look upon. But his face, through all this, carries a look which says my lot is a happy one for I am administering to the suffering, and I am contented, for how much better is my life than that poor devil in the trenches. Thus goes his life.

Mail comes so seldom that he ceases even to look forward to it. He has no daily news and hasn't time to read a book, and thus his life passes on without attaining any new knowledge and forgetting what he has. He takes a bath now and then, but it does little good, for he goes back to a lousey little bed the very same night. Of course it is lousey. We are all lousey for the rats are all over us at night and lice are as familiar to a rat as his hair. Notwithstanding all these drawbacks, we like the life, not because of the work itself, but the cause which it represents.

October 26th. A joke: An Englishman in the French service meets Spartalis and Kiefer [ambulance drivers], takes them for two Frenchmen and tries to inquire his way. Kiefer listens, gets disgusted, and says, "Come on, he doesn't know any more now than when you started." The Englishman says, "I say, any of you speak English?"

I drove a machine across to Oseyville and met A. "Poullier" P.P.F. Convois, Aulourobelos Echclor C.G.O. Par B.C.M. Paris. I received a letter from Albert Pinard, 36 Foubourg St., Michel Hotel, Notre Dame, Angers.

Since the twenty-sixth, I carried two malades [19] and one very bad couchey. I thought he would die, but he lived.

Monday, November 5. Carried thirteen assis and one couchey. My first attempt to drive wounded.

November 6. Carried three assis. A great German victory in Italy. Sixty thousand prisoners. Took the soldiers from the Russian front and surprised the Italians. [20]

November 14. Was at P.1 during a bombardment. My closest experience of shell fire as yet. One fell within 120 feet of our car. Dirt and brush hit the car and fell in the road in front of the car. I was also exposed to gas the first time on route to and from P-1 by P-2. In the evening, Spiller and Coe found two wounded men and carried them to the ambulance. They died very soon.

November 15. In the morning, I saw them buried. They were put side by side with everything on. They lay there, very natural, and were covered with five feet of earth.

November 21. Carried one couchey. A German officer was taken prisoner, shot through the thigh. The first question he asked us was why we were at war with him.

November 29th. We had a wonderful Thanksgiving dinner. Chicken, peas, dates, olives, figs, chocolate pudding and beer, cabbage salad and apple salad. A few toasts and many songs were given.

November 30. I visited the first-line trenches. It was very interesting: blood-soaked banks, water, mud, etc. Places were gouged out of the banks by hand grenades, machine guns, places for observers, for shooters of star-shells, for tenders of signal lights for the artillery miles back. I put my head over the trench and saw two Germans outside of their abris.[21] The first-line trenches here were only about three hundred yards apart. The communicating trenches led from B-1 to Avocourt and there we took the third-line trenches to the first lines. There was nothing left of Avocourt, not a single wall. The only thing left in the town square was the big cross. Its foundation was mostly torn away but still it stands. Five big shells went over our heads and hit a nearby hill. A piece of éclot[22] struck ten feet from me.

December 1st and 2nd. I carried twenty-three assis and two coucheys. Two fellows I had, the life was fast ebbing out of, very bad head wounds.

December 8. U.S. declares war on Austria. Also, the great explosion at Halifax.

I did not see the Boche plane fall, but reached the plane soon after. It had two in it, one fell out over Dombasle, a descent of about five hundred feet. He was killed. The pilot fell at P-4. He came to the ground very fast, breaking the whole top of a tree, tearing the plane to bits. He had two bullets through his head, but he still lived. His face was badly bruised. I ran a quarter mile back to P.4 for a Joe and G. car and took them to the scene. I handled his legs in placing him on the stretcher and he appeared conscious in trying to help, but he did not open his eyes. He thanked us for putting a blanket under his head. He died at Ville-Sur-Cousances at 8:00 P.M.

December 14. I carried twenty assis from Ville.

December 15. At 11:00 A.M. I was frightened by a very peculiar sound overhead. I ran out and directly over our heads, a plane was falling rapidly through the air about one thousand feet up. It exploded probably two thousand feet up and divided into three parts and the two men were blown out also, but there were so many pieces falling that we could not follow them in their rapid descent. I saw the big black cross at once and decided that it was a German plane. We tried for several minutes to find the pilot in the burning mass. I found the plates and decided it was an observation plane. Many watched the plane burn but about one hundred of us went in all directions in search of the Boche. At last, a quarter mile off, one was found and brought in on a stretcher. Crowds followed him and crowded around as in a fight on Cadillac Square, Detroit. He was put on the ground and stripped of all possessions with pockets turned out. He was put in our sleeping quarters (a partition in between). Many went to see him and many took souvenirs (belts, helmet, shoes, collar). Later, I looked at him and he was naked with a sheet wrapped around him inside a very narrow wooden box. I could have had his belt or helmet but after seeing his pale ghostly face could not do it. Taking a look at this Boche I discovered that both his legs were broken above his knees and his arms were broken in many places. Otherwise, you would never have suspected that he fell all of five thousand feet. With his comrade, it was different. The whole side of his head was caved in. He was not found until 4:00, a half mile off, and brought in in a wagon.

December 31. I went on duty, had a malade, arrived late and watched old year out. Many rats watched it with me (at my elbow). All but a few of the boys at Jubicourt got drunk. [23]

Huss coming in from the country after running the guard and sleeping at a farmer's house all night: *I didn't get a chance to wash out there.*

January 4, 1918. A shell shot at a plane by an anti-aircraft gun—was not timed right and fell only one hundred feet from the barn while we were all in front watching the fight.

January 10. Carried six assis and one couchey. Our car was the only one that would run in the snow and we took care of all the posts. A poor sleep. I awoke with a rat chewing my head. Awoke again, and one was within six inches of my nose looking at me.

January 16. I began to evacuate from Raricourt. The rats like my pillow of sheepskin and insist on sleeping with me. Just asked a Frenchman if he knew where I could get some water to drink and he said no. Though he works hard, a Frenchman does not use water.

January 20. 5:30 P.M. left Raricourt on permission. Reached Paris at Gare de L'est.

January 21. 7:30 A.M. found YMCA about 9:00 A.M. Ate breakfast and immediately after rented a sightseeing car for the balance of the forenoon. On way, stopped at Provost Marshal's. Among the things we visited were the guillotine and the Notre Dame. After dinner we hunted up ambulance headquarters and reported and got our tickets for Nice for the twenty-sixth. In the evening, we went to the Folies Bergères. That night I slept between two white sheets for the first time since June 15th at Ypsilanti at Mrs. Yerkes. It was very unnatural at first but easy to get used to.

January 22. Rode a streetcar much of the day. Just before supper I met a clerk in the Louvre who was very genteel and attentive to me. In the evening went to Casino Paris.[24]

January 24. Visited Napoleon's Tomb and went to the Grand Opera in the evening and saw *La Favorite.* Had seats in the orchestra.

January 25. Visited the guillotine, the tower that Napoleon brought from Egypt and the tower that he built from the brass off the cannon he captured. In the evening went to the Casino de Paris where a very pretty young girl came over where I was and told us all she had to sleep alone tonight, but she congratulated two of her friends who had captured two Australians and said she hoped they would sleep warm.

January 28. I reached Nice at 7:00 P.M. Ate for the first time in twenty-six hours and started to look for the boys. The next morning, I went to the Bureau de Police and found that the boys were at the Franc Hotel. I found them in bed. They slept on until noon and I went to look about.

January 29. I met a woman who asked to be my "God Mother." She was a very wealthy lady, English, a "Miss" with much importance and a dog tied to her. She spoke seven languages. She gained permission for me to go through the home and grounds of Queen Victoria. I never visited a place where nature was so beautiful; many beautiful cedar and pine trees, many walks, all hidden in the foliage, and several caves. I climbed a tower and at the very top is a glass ball, beside which I scratched my name with a knife. After dinner I went promenading along the beach where I saw the most beautiful girl I have yet seen.

January 30. 7:00 A.M., took a car to Monte Carlo. Visited the "Great Casino." More luxurious rooms I have never seen. The paintings on the walls, pictures, rugs, the library, theatre and furniture were très rich. In the afternoon we visited the Italian border. I tried to talk French to an Italian, but he didn't compré. Went to a vaudeville in the evening which was très amateur.

February 2, 1918. Arrived at 7:30 in Paris. Never saw such a crowd. Took twenty minutes to wait our turn for tickets for the subway.

February 3. We reported at American Headquarters and they told us to take a train the following day at 8:00 A.M. In the afternoon, I visited the Louvre. In the evening, the boys went to Feminin and I went to call on Miss Richard. A young lawyer. She, her sister and father entertained me until 10:00 P.M. I drank my *first ale.* I was held up by several women on my way to the "Y" but was très stubborn.

February 5. Got home at 9:30 and find many letters and anxious friends.
     Pronounce the trip a great success. Found the French a very hospitable people. They were very genteel and a most handsome race. They know no sex difference as we do. They have no feeling of shyness or modesty as to these differences. Sexual intercourse is accepted by them in a matter-of-fact way and spoken of and joked about as we would speak of holding hands, etc. They treat their children as companions and are very polite to them which makes them so wonderfully well behaved. The Parisian whore differs from ours in that she is genteel. I believe a very great percent of French women have no sex scruples and I know the men haven't. Paris is a clean city. It has many poor and many rich. Not much of a well-to-do class. I was charmed with the climate of Nice and its pretty women.

February 5. Stayed around Jubicourt in forenoon, got to post in afternoon.

February 6. Aroused at 1:00 A.M. to go to P.2. Carried four assis. Bunk at ten.

February 7. Carried six assis.

February 18. Left Jubicourt to go on our "Grand Repos."[25] Reached there in the evening at 6:00 P.M. Went on guard at 1:00 P.M. and guarded until 7:00 A.M. all alone, as Ranft didn't wake up. It sure was cold. The most we did at Ligney was to have a little drinking party with the Frenchmen. It was a very poor place for a good time.

February 26. Left Ligney and went to Villers-Le-Sec. It's a real small place here but we are rooming out in families. I am with Rathert and Poriea. We sure have some nice fires in our fireplace. Spend most of my time reading and studying French, and we drink altogether more beer than I approve of. Night of March three was our big night. We were all happy with beer but Rath was very happy. Puts the quietus to the Frenchman and Poriea. Knocks Poriea down three times where he stands. "Rath" and I were made prisoners to do all detail work for a week for missing roll call: a good illustration of justice in the army.

March 5.[26] Spent a few minutes in the Club Room with the boys. The conversation ran thus: "I wish they'd quit writing this crap about a Father watching over you. If they would see this work over here, they would change their minds." From another: "If there is a Father, He's either gone to sleep or drunk on the job." Another: "Now don't try to reason if you're going to talk religion, for religion is faith." Another: "If you fellows don't believe there is a God, just wait until I read you an extract from my mother's letter." Another: "Yes, they all say at least save your soul, but I'm for my body. A bird in the hand is worth two in the bush." Another: "Well, God has helped me duck all the obies so far." Another: "If there is any God, why in hell doesn't he stop this." Another: "Well, boys, I think there is a God all right, but I think he's with the guy who has the longest gun." Another: "This war is certainly knocking my faith all to hell." Another: "Well, when I came over here (pointing to his left breast) I carried a testament here. You see what I carry now—a dictionary!" And thus the conversation runs. As to me, my faith remains the same. To me, man is a part of God.

March 14. Today is my birthday and I expect a quiet one for no one knows it but me, and there's nothing to do to celebrate it. As I reflect today, I feel that my progress in life has been considerably retarded. I am not nearly so far advanced educationally as I should be. I will at least lose two years from this war. If I lose a third, I shall hardly attempt to finish in medicine, but take a Master of Arts and continue in the educational world. My future at this writing seems rather blighted.

March 15. Went to Revigny with Hauser on a bicycle. We visited the Boche prisoners at work in a sawmill and again in a locomotive repair shop. They regarded me with such a strong curiosity that it was hard to see another feeling behind that. They carried an air of respect toward me in almost every case. Now and then I could read even a sign of fellowship. However, I saw a few sparks of disgust and envy, some of indifference, and again some carried a distinct look of subjection. On the whole, they were large and looked well kept. The French said they were good workmen but had to be pushed in some cases.

March 17. At noon we departed for Glorieux,[27] one kilometer from Verdun. I reached Glorieux at 5:00 P.M. From there I went to Verdun to deliver some things to the general, thereby getting me one chance to see Verdun, being the first of our cars to enter the gates. I never saw such a sight of destruction. Not a civilian was in the city. All that is left of the great establishments are the signs, now and then a wall, and occasionally, a tall chimney holding its head up over the surrounding ruins. I got lost on my way home and went to another town three kilometers from Glorieux. I reached the place too late to find a house to sleep in. I slept outside on my cot. The Germans bombarded the town. Between the cold and the obies, I was awake most of the night. Two houses were hit, two Frenchmen and six horses were killed and a Ford with one of Section 504's drivers blown off the road.

March 18. A shell came very close to me on the road in the morning. I visited the front-line post at Verdun, or Fort Douaumont.[28] The hardest hit point in the war! While I was going up Death Valley to get there, several shells hit near me and I ran through three hundred yards of gas. The Poste de Secour at Carrière de Haudramont[29] was the best I had seen yet (electrically lighted, wide tunnels, operating rooms, etc., all under forty feet of rock). I wandered around the hill keeping close to the rock bank, where I could get a view that took in the thousands of batteries that were then being besieged. You could also see the spit of fire from our cannons, scattered helter-skelter over that mountain ash heap that was once a vast forest. [30]

March 19. Section 504 leaves for repos. They go to Villers-Le-Sec. They leave twelve men behind who had been gassed the last three days. The last night they were on duty, a shell hit an ammunition train in the "Valley of Death" killing five horses, four Frenchmen, and blowing over the car of one of 504's men with him in it. When he was pulled out and saw what lay around him, he shook hands with himself and beat it for an abri. The week previous to this, an explosion frightened an officer's horse so that he tried to get inside of Red's Ford. He jumped right in the seat and put his foot through the steering wheel.

March 20. Find my name boarded for the front the morning of the twenty-second. Such heavy firing on both sides all night that I could not sleep.

Poierer: *If you fellows think that was a close call you should have been with me.*

Boyd: *This is the damndest life.*

March 21. [31] Awoke with acute pains of rheumatism in knees, back and hips. Symptoms first appeared ten days back. Answered an extra call to the front. Found more horses along the road, dead, which I expected, as Huss had told us in the morning that there were several "new dead horses" on the road. Had a new sensation. Saw two shells burst in the road ahead about a minute apart, but fortunately we hit the place just about one hundred feet before the shell burst and got part way up the steep hill to the post before the next one came. We covered our faces with our helmets against the flying éclot.

The Germans interfered with an early dinner today. They made it so hot, all flew for the abris. We are twelve kilometers from the first-line trenches. Two Germans were brought in badly wounded today. Asked one what he thought of the Kaiser. He said he was a "big shit" and that the Crown Prince was worse. It was amusing how they referred to the French often as their comrades. Two of our boys gave them cigarettes and lit them for them. I often argue with the boys for showing the Germans so much interest and attention. I regard them as an enemy in captivity, as well as when they are loose and killing my friends. It would be very unfortunate for me to be taken prisoner, for I could not show them respect.

I carried twenty-four assis, mostly gassed, and two coucheys, one gassed. Total for Verdun, thirty-four assis and two coucheys. When evening came, I explored my new home (the dugout), which was really long tunnels, running far into the side of a small mountain of rock (Carrière de Haudramont). These tunnels were about seven feet high and ten feet wide, and, in turn, are crossed by numerous tunnels at right angles. In different parts of the tunnels, broncards (stretchers) are stretched three deep on either side. Here and there is a stove with benches by it. Here a room for bandages and there a room for chemicals. An operating room is also equipped to take care of emergencies. The most that is done, usually, is to clean off the wound well and fish out the éclot, after which it is well bandaged. First, though, comes the tetanus shot. The doctors have good light, as the whole thing is lit up with electricity. At intervals of twenty feet, blankets are stretched across the tunnel and kept wet to keep out gas. I had a 3:00 A.M. call. It was very foggy and we passed a division going down and one going up. We almost crashed head-on three times.

March 23. Shells came in, wounding many outside the abri near me and killing one in Ninth Company. I watched them dressing the wound. He died while they were working on him. His life went out and none of us knew it, he was so quiet.

March 24. Germany has begun an attack on an 80 km. front in the north against the English. At 8:00 P.M. Germany sends over a balloon and again at 1:00 A.M. I am wondering what was in them. Rathert was just held up by a French major for not saluting and taken to the bureau. He had saluted him several times, but the major did not think Rathert saluted properly. We salute very differently.

March 25. Watched three German planes try to get a sausage. After they failed, we saw the man in our sausage send out a dove. It flew straight to the front lines. [32]

I attended the operations at the hospital. First case, two holes, one through each foot and one through the leg. Second case, arm all shot to pieces. Third case, a big hole through the hip. This hip had a long white worm in it. Fourth case had a gash in the back six inches long, two inches deep by two inches wide, a terrible gash! The fifth case was very serious. A big hole in the right breast. Two ribs were cut out, a hole five inches square. The lung was pulled out, where éclot had penetrated it was cut out and three stitches put in. Then it was sewed up and a big hole put in his back with two tubes for drains. He died one hour after the operation.

March 26. England and France are coming back strong at the Germans. Witnessed two more serious operations. First, a big hole four-by-four inches in the back. The second, a big hole clear through the body missing the heart by one-half inch. Cut big hole in back and wash out the whole thorax. Much clotted blood comes out.

March 29. See two more serious operations. One was a big hole in lower part of thorax. It was washed out by pumping in about three quarts of water. Several bunches of clotted blood came out. I assisted by lifting the patients about and holding them. Had they known how little I knew about operations, I wouldn't even have gotten into the room, saying nothing of helping the surgeon. I got by with the bluff, however, and the surgeons took my name and address, thinking perhaps I suppose that later they would read of my greatness in the medical journal.

April 1, 1918. Spent twenty-four hours at Bras on duty. Called out 1:00 A.M. It was very dark and rainy. We carried fifteen assis. There was a grave-yard forty feet from the kitchen and bureau. I think it was filled with men buried while the place was under shelling, and that was most of the time since 1915. I am sure that when the owners come back, they will never be able to find their homes, for the place is one heap without a chimney or a corner of a house or any streets left. When the people left Glorieux, they left some furniture. We lugged this from house to house wherever we happened to be. I am wondering if the owners will scrap over it as much as we did, and if it will ever occur to them how their neighbor came by their chairs, etc.

April 2. Big news hit the section today with the announcement that Sergeant Paley and Gus Bauman had been cited and given Croix de Guerres for bringing down a wounded major from Fort Douaumont. Both were warmly congratulated.

Every fellow there had experienced the road—hills, ravines, and valleys from Fort Douaumont and the nearby Haudramont Quarries—down through the valley toward Bras with its gas and acrid smell of high explosives,[33] constantly exposed to heavy Boche shelling, the stench from dead rotting horses, but, worst of all, the pathetic cries of many wounded horses, still struggling off the road, in ditches, under tipped-over wagons or against tangled harness; or the cries of countless wounded trench burros,[34] many lying there bleeding, with packs or bundles of duck boards still strapped to their back, waiting to die, helpless in their struggles—and no one able to shoot them or put them out of their misery.

Other news, the poorest driver in the section was given a car. A car was taken away from a fellow for showing shyness of shellfire. This story was told the lieutenant by one more nervous than the fellow he squealed on. Three of the boys go to Paris tomorrow to act as witnesses against one of the boys held in Paris for court martial. He, Swindell, attempted to build a fire. Huss told him to take the pieces out, for they would never burn. He would not. Huss attempted to take them out. Swindell is much the smaller, but he fell on top and grabbed a stick of wood and hit Huss. He also said he would shoot Huss later. He is very unpopular with the men in power. A guard was placed over him with a loaded revolver until he could be hurried to Paris under the guard of two men.

Next to me sits a very efficient college man, son of a general, who is only a buck private. He is a very likeable fellow and the only one who has really won a medal from merit, but he isn't "in" with the powers that be. Joe is twenty-two years old today. He must surely have missed his birthday cake, for all days are the same here. He was given a car today.

April 4. We are taken from the Fourth Division and attached to a "Shock Army" and left Glorieux today. I don't know where we are now, but near Ippicourt, on a short repos. We are not so far from the front and I could hear a fearful barrage.

April 6. We celebrate the first year of war by all lying in bed and having our breakfast served us. The finger bowl is passed, cigarettes are passed and then the ash tray. We had royal service.

Swindell: *Oh boys, jest wait til I get back ter old Allentown with that little girl. I'll have one hell of a time. I'll get me a Ford and dress suit and lay off for three months.*

Clint: *If I could only get back to some hospital, man, this place would kill a well man.*

My idea of hard luck: A Frenchman was disqualified for the infantry because one leg was three centimeters short; the other leg was broken and when it healed, it was the same length as the other, so he passed the next exam and had to go.

A bunch of aviators arrived at Souilly. They left the States March 4th. They had a hard time. A car with their provisions and five of their fellows was lost and they were without food for three days. They listened to our tales with mouths wide open. The front was about fifteen miles off, but the guns gave them some alarm. They were very green to France and the French lingo. They had fourteen medals, but they had not been in barrages where shells came in every seven minutes. They asked us what an Austrian 77 sounded like, etc., all of which was a joke to us.

When you first land, you observe many strange things. The people are so polite that before you know it, you are exchanging greetings by facial expressions and you invariably start talking English to them. They in the same spirit, talk French to you. You speak slowly and emphasize each word and, if they can't understand you, become disgusted with them, because they can't comprendre. The Frenchmen, however, seldom become discouraged, but continue to repeat, each time faster, and louder! At last, you feign intelligence with a faint "oui," after which the Frenchmen feel repaid many times. It really is a funny feeling when you get in the center of a group of eager, inquiring Frenchmen and you gaze at them and they at you, but you can't exchange a word with them. You may be among hundreds and still not find one who can talk English. You may want something to eat or drink or wish to know where you can sleep, or to know the city you are in, the road to so and so. I once went in a cafe and attempted to tell them I was very hungry but instead told them I had many wives. On another occasion, I wanted "coiffured" and called for covers. Again, I tried for twenty minutes to get some jam and finally entered the kitchen and searched every shelf, but couldn't find it, for its French name had no resemblance to jam. I finally left without it. The lady felt very sorry for me. She never learned what the American wanted.

April 17. Nothing of importance has happened lately. Last night a company of signal men came over to see us. It was a surprise. They all came in the barracks and found seats on our cots. We gave them music. (Two fiddlers, a mandolin and banjo) and then we sang them some funny songs, gave them a glad hand on every side, and, for our thrilling tales of the front, they told us of their trip over here. Through poor management, lack of any plan or knowledge, they had run all over France. Slept in open box cars sitting up, for there was no room to even sit comfortably. They had gone without food, etc. And now, they are all eating good food and lying around, not a thing to do and won't be for at least six months. It is the same throughout France. We have several thousand men here who have nothing to train with. They have much undue exposure, irregular eating and no exercise. And yet, Taft is hollering for seven million more men in France when we haven't the leaders, plans, etc., to utilize what we have here. [35]

May 4. The British are holding at Amiens. [36]

May 9. Went up to the post with Spartalis. It was his first time out with a car. I recall more hair-raisers those two days than in any two days from shells. We carried eight assis and one couchey. I went to Post Alsace. I never saw such a picture of destruction. For miles the hills and valleys have been made over. Not a square inch remains untouched. The shells have uncovered and recovered many of the dead, but many they fail to recover and you find the dead lying about. Again, you will find bones in helmets and in shoes, showing that they lie where they fell, untouched. This land is as barren as a desert and the town of Fleury is so totally destroyed that you can't find a brick as a souvenir. The solitude of the barren land is broken now and then by a shell, trying to locate a hidden battery, or by the rats that run about. As you wander about this waste, your progress is often interrupted by the horrible fumes coming from dead horses and human bodies. Yet among all this you find the artillery men and brancardiers living for days. [37]

May 13. Went up to the front for two days with Bill Botruba. We carried 14 assis.

Rath: *Say, have you tried that road yet? It's shorter and better.*

Section 591

Section 591 is a sad mixture ranging anywhere from a German to a Russian Jew and our names and maps have given the Frenchies many hair raisers on first sight.

We come from Michigan, New York, Ohio, Indiana, Illinois and California but with the exception of eight, we come from the University of Michigan. We have eleven taking law, one medic, one journalist, five or six teachers, three chemists, two actors, three bankers, a couple in the mercantile business, two mechanics, two engineers and the rest are lits. When you get this bunch to arguing, each reasoning in terms of his own profession, you surely get a variety of viewpoints and you hear everything hashed over, from why did you join the ambulance [corps] to when will the war be over.

We have spent eight months now and not one of us has been wounded with the exception of a few gassed. Nevertheless, during these eight months, we have seen some real stuff and five of us have been awarded Croix de Guerres.

A visit to the first line at Port Auvergne and from there to Fleury, we got to the observatory N.E. of Post Auvergne. From here you could look far into the German lines. We were stopped by a French lieutenant and taken up to the general. He would not let us go farther. They started us for Verdun but we soon turned in our course and made for LaLouvre. We found one leg in a shoe that had been shot off. Later we reached the place that was once called Fleury. You can hardly find a brick for a souvenir. The road leads through it, but unless you are shown the exact spot, you would never know it. I found several remains of dead Germans. I took a picture of a skeleton lying directly on a French grave and his shoes were not in place, so I took hold of one to arrange it. I was much shocked when I found the feet inside. The skull was the best one I have seen. It was very dry and shiny, but I couldn't take it. Several of the boys have them and even pay for them. If I get a chance to take something from a live Boche I shall, but after he is dead, he is the same to me as a comrade.

May 22. Been to the front again and carried three coucheys and nine assis. I rode inside with one fellow shot all to pieces. It was a hard position to keep him quiet for I couldn't talk to him and was afraid to touch him because of his wounds.

I carried a French officer today. He was wounded in the hand and in each leg by éclot. His story: "Forty of us went over to and into the German first line. We found it. Nine got away. The fellow who was caught knew he would be killed but he wouldn't come. He threw the grenade that wounded the lieutenant. They gave him the bayonet and returned."

Notwithstanding this stubbornness and hate, Wilson protests we are not fighting the German people.

May 27. Shall use shorthand from now on that I may not forget it.

Entered hospital because of sore throat. I was under a doctor's direction for two days. A Boche prisoner was brought in while I was there. He was unconscious. They were too busy to give him attention. Later he was taken to Gloria Hospital. While sitting there a Moroccan came in, saw him, looked up and cut his throat.

Read a story, *Get Up and Fight,* in which all were killed. The Germans were coming at him; he prayed aloud to the dead comrades to get up and help him, and they rose and saved the place. The Germans were awed by this from Soissons to Reims. [38]

June 1. About 11:00 in the morning a Boche plane hovered over the place for nearly five minutes. We thought surely he'd drop a bomb. I read *A Week's Work* by Henry Griffin in less than a week.

June 3. I read *Julie, the Unconquerable,* by Howard Markle Hokie. Also, *Chances of Getting Killed or Hurt in This War* by Mary B. Mullett. I hurt my hand while trying to stop a wagon loaded with explosives from going over the bank.

June 10. The Germans are slowly advancing south of Soissons. We held on. The French took one thousand prisoners and Americans took three hundred. [39] Our French headquarters were moved from Verdun back to Souilly. I read *This Bud of Love* by Merwin.

June 15. Hauser and I walked up to the front. We spent much time looking over that devastated land over which the French fought with the Germans in February of 1916. This land now was then no-man's land. Thousands who fought in that area were never buried. When the French took the land, much later, they buried the French bones, but the Germans were left on top of the ground. This was a terrible place in hot weather, and I can't understand how they ever stood the fumes. There is no smell now. Nothing is left but the rotted clothing and the bleached bones. I saw one French skull which was still lodged in its helmet. You find hundreds of shoes, and in all you find their owners' feet. I brought back a German helmet which still had some of its owners hair in it. I think I shall send it to East Avenue School. After leaving these past scenes of hell, I advance to the present hell. I follow a Frenchy through the communication trench to the second line.

While I was traversing this trench, the Germans shelled it. 105s fell all around me; some within fifteen feet of me. One fell right in the trench I was in, about sixty feet ahead of me. I never was so scared in my life. I lay flat until it was over, making my helmet cover all of me it could. The trench ahead and behind was filled with shrapnel and éclot for one hundred yards. I don't know why that particular spot was not blown into pieces. Pieces hit within three feet of me. When the last shell hit and we heard no more coming, we jumped and ran through a quarter mile of this trench, sprinkled with iron and full of smoke. When we reached the abris, we were completely fagged. We soon had to return over this same trench, however, for we were seven miles from quarters.

I wanted to take a picture on my way back of a large part of the German front that was in full view, but I was afraid to expose myself. An incoming shell reminded me that I was in no place to take pictures. I ran most of the way to Post Alsace and from there to Post Normandy, dropping in shell holes for shelter from falling shrapnel. I decided this was the last time I would expose myself needlessly.

June 28. The Italians have been doing fine work for three weeks. They have taken nineteen thousand prisoners after the Austrians' retreating. I was sick the twenty-sixth and twenty-seventh with a fever. Our front has been comparatively quiet since May 2nd.

Hank: *Yes, but the Boche aren't as near whipped as you think.*

July 4. Helped decorate our dining room. We had a wonderful dinner and a good program. We made a canopy of our pup tents and lined it with flowers of red, white and blue. Most of the boys were drunk. They couldn't see the small ball so had a game with the indoor ball. I was sick with a headache most of the day. It took us three hours to eat our dinner.

Coe: *I am always misunderstood. When I am joking, you take me seriously and when I am serious, you think I am joking.*

July 7. The German ambassador to Russia is greeted by the Russians.

July 11. The balloon which hangs directly over our heads here at Ferme Dix-Huit was attacked by a Boche plane.[40] He was pulled instantly to the ground. Our man took to his parachute.

July 20. Finished reading *David Copperfield*. I like the characters of Dora and Agnes. Steerforth also, but I think many of the others were droll.

Had a trip to the front. Carried nine assis and four coucheys. I had a wonderful experience trying to find Post Beville. I lost my way. We were from 10:00 P.M. to 1:30 A.M. At Mares, trying to find my way, I walked right into a battery before I knew where I was. I was looking into the mouth of a cannon. I went back toward the Boche, three kilometers, within one kilometer of the Boche lines.

July 21. I had cramps after supper so started out bare-headed to walk it off. I strolled in the long gardens south of Verdun, where I had walked many times. The strawberries were gone and through very much trouble I found a pretty red rose. There used to be thousands, but near the hill what was left were a few raspberries. I walked these gardens much more than anyone else and usually went alone. I love flowers to the point of femininity. Wistrand goes on permission and I take his car.

The Amex are fast driving the Germans way into their pocket between Soissons and Reims. From July 18 to 25 they took twenty-five thousand prisoners.

August 9.[41] I left for Paris on my second permission. Carried four assis and one couchey since July 21. Visited No. 10 in Bar-Le-Duc. Left as usual with sorrow for the girls and general disgust for the human kind. We had a long hard ride to Paris and arrived three hours late. Lost Rathert going through the gate in Paris. I spent much of my time alone. I went to the Folies with a Canadian (Winters) from Windsor. An actress came down into the crowd and teased an American lieutenant. A dough boy hollered out, pinch my balls (uproar of laughter). The girl regards him and answers back, pinch my bottom. I met two girls on my way to Chambrey[42] with whom three of us had some time. Arrived in Chambrey and checked in August 13. Yesterday I was at the station and met a very pretty girl on the train for Paris. (A Miss A. Detrez). I was very much taken with her and haven't gotten over it since.

I visited the largest lake in France where I ran a nail in my foot. I was taken to a chateau of the Duchess of Bordeaux where her daughter bandaged my foot and showed me through the home. It was luxurious. They had two very pretty Russian greyhounds. The daughter was peculiar looking but pretty. The Duchess picnicked with and smoked cigarettes while the boys gave her a light. This country is a grand place for one wishing to isolate himself.

August 18. I took the morning train at 9:30 and came back that night at 11:00 P.M. We spent the day boating, playing croquet and singing and taking long walks. We took many pictures. I had three wonderful meals. Among the people I met there was: Madame C. Spileman, Madame Henri Gauget and Monsieur M. René Japhet. They had lived in the states ten years. They said they loved the Americans, and every one from the oldest (75) to the little girls came to the depot to see us off and warned us never to come to Paris or Nice without staying with them. Nice is their winter home.

August 21. I went to the park at Bar-Le-Duc and found there that the section was at Vavincourt. We remained two days and at 4:30 A.M. on the twenty-second arose, took a hurried lunch and started for the Somme. We went through Villers-Le-Sec. We stopped for ten minutes to visit with our old friends. It was like getting home. When I started to leave I thought I had a flat tire. The convoy left me, but I overtook them at Vitry-La-Francoise where we had dinner. I picked up a seventeen-year-old lad in the country. He rode into town and waited on me as a servant until we parted at supper time. The second night we spent at Chaumont near Meaux. I slept in an orchard. In the morning my clothes were wet with dew. The next night we stopped at St. Maxisum near Senlis.[43] We arose at 4:00 A.M. and followed a cannon convoy to Hartennes et Faux. At 8:30 P.M. two of us were sent to Vierzy. I saw there the most wonderful abris I had ever been in. The cars all drove inside. They cared for the wounded just to the right of the entrance. As you went on through you found several gassed, sleeping on either side of the passage. Later, you came to another class of blessés. The Boche prisoners during the day slept to one side, while in still another group you would see civilians stretched out by men, women and children. I never saw a darker night and I was the first out. I was soon called to go to Villers Cottérêts with one couchey and three assis to St. Rémy.

I stopped several times thinking I was about to go over a cliff. It was over fifty kilometers and I had to stop many times to inquire the right route. I was two and a half hours getting to the hospital. In passing through the Villers-Cottérêts Bois[44] I saw a jackal or coyote. While I was waiting at the hospital a group of German prisoners gathered around me. One guy gave me a congenial look, and I sidled up to him and began to crab about there being no way to tell where to enter with a blessé at night. I then realized that he was a Boche and the conversation stopped there. I found my way back much easier—among many cannon drivers, etc., with broken cars along the road, I found Birch. I hated to leave him, but I could do him no good, so I pulled on, leaving him to sleep in his car until the morrow or to try and repair it in the dark. He got it started three hours later. I awoke at 5:00 A.M. just in time to prepare to move again, as a motorcycle man came in saying our division was advancing and we must move at once. Tonight!

August 30. I find myself in sight of the fighting at Soissons, with our troops slowly advancing.[45] I am called to Ecuary where I stay two days without getting a call. At 2:00 they send me back to my section telling me my section moves again tonight.

August 31. We started at 8:00 P.M. for Fontenay. I never hope to go so fast in a convoy again. Several times I thought I would run over the car ahead. I had as many as twenty close calls in running close to traffic in the opposite direction. We went to Nouvillon Vimey but there wasn't enough there to camouflage our cars, so we returned to Fontenay. The next morning, September one, we were told a thrilling story by an excited Frenchman about a company of U.S. troops volunteering to rescue a regiment of

French who were cut off by the enemy. They made a dash with knives in their mouths and frightened the Germans to the extent that they brought back the French. They found three Americans crucified on trees with bayonets for spikes and fifteen Germans were gathered around with mocking faces on them; when they saw the Americans coming at them they put up their hands and hollered *"Kamerad!"*

September 2. We rest all day and at night 12:00 to 2:00 A.M. I go on guard and rise at 4:30 to go to Hartens. September 3rd at 11:00 A.M. I was taken to Chavigny, then to Maison Blanc, then our advance post. I can never forget my impressions on that trip. I saw dead Frenchmen and dead Germans on either side of the road, but the worst sight of all was a dead Frenchman, standing up in the trench, elbow against the mud and head bent over, resting on his hand, just as in life he might have stood when completely exhausted. His head was facing the road and at his feet lay his comrade, dead also. They had been here since the Germans were driven back perhaps eight or nine days ago. Later, I carried a French soldier over this road and he was constantly pointing out the spot where his friends had fallen. I drove this day and continued into the next night until 11:00 P.M., when I met another car head on. I had two coucheys and didn't see him until we were twenty feet apart. I think he was running fast and he was on the wrong side of the road. Both cars were broken, but a third car soon came along and we transferred my coucheys to it. Bauman went along and I stayed with the cars. It was a lonesome, dark night to spend there on a battlefield with dead Frenchmen and Germans on either side of me and the wind in whatever direction was bound to bring to me the scent of these decaying bodies. Up to this time, September 3, I had carried twenty-two coucheys and thirty-three assis blessés.

September 4. I carried three coucheys and thirteen assis blessés. One couchey I had was a German who had been lost in the woods. One Frenchman said to him that the Americans are "pas bon, n'est pas?" but he answered they are the best of the allies. He asked me if I wanted his gas mask and I took it. During the past two days our division has been advancing rapidly and we are continually advancing our posts, following them over such roads as I never saw. We go over one place where the road has such a slant that we expect to slide sideways down the hill or tip over. Two cars have already slid down the hill with the wounded. The other night, I lifted one front wheel out of a deep shell hole and the car was full of wounded.

September 5. Last night was one of the darkest drives I have had. The brancardiers put a man in my car. I noticed his glassy stare when they brought him up and I felt for his pulse, but he had none. Other men were dying on a row of stretchers by my car. I told them to take him out and put in a live man. They did so without a word and carried him off to the side and lay him with the dead without even examining him. I never have had a man die in my car yet, which is very extraordinary as the other boys have had so many. Yesterday, I worked for two hours under heavy shelling, fixing my car. One hit a Frenchman within 150 feet of me. His comrades started to get him when another came right in the bunch. Some ran but a couple crouched by, then beat it with this wounded man.

Many Frenchmen lay near and one wounded American. They started to load a Frenchy, but suddenly thought and asked me if I preferred to take the American, but the life of one nation is no dearer to me than another. We are all God's children.

The cave men have nothing on me, as I eat and sleep very often far under the ground, in an immense hole in a rock. Where they cook, the smoke gathers about the ceiling. I sometimes eat with prisoners, Negroes and Arabians, all assembled together.[46]

September 7. Carried ten assis and two coucheys.

The lieutenant: *There's time you just simply eat éclot before you leave here.*

September 8. I walked over to Tartiers. On my way back, I examined some dead Boche. I never saw such sights. I found that the story of the Boche turning absolutely black was true. They are left there to rot with face to the sky. In one place, a Boche lay dead on his seat of a wagon within four feet of the road.

September 11. We moved our base from Chavigney to Clamexcey. We can run all of our cars in the cave. I have a part of the cave next to the front. It was full of German grenades and ammunition. We had a prisoner come up and carry most of it out. Last night a cave was blown up by a German mine. It killed thirty men. I expect to be called to evacuate tonight over roads that I know not. On the seventh, Joe's car was blown to bits, and part of it was in the trees. Rigy drove it and had just gotten out of it. Carroll's was also blown up and the night before Bauman's, Dink's and Kammerer's were blown up.

I relieved Dink at noon. That night Joe, Warren, Poirier and I were at Villery when they began to shell the place. They were coming very close when all of a sudden we heard a crash and found ourselves enveloped in smoke and fire. We could not see each other, though we were all very close to each other. We crawled around like moles feeling for each other, excited and at the same time, half wondering where to go, for the shells kept coming in. I was reading a book which was blown from my hand, which I first started to look for. When I found it, my helmet occurred to me, and I found it by my side. Three Frenchies soon made a dash for an abris and we followed, but shells kept coming so close that we bolted for another safer spot where we stayed until it was over.

When—will—this—war—ever—end!!! Several Boche planes are near me now firing *mitrailleuse* [machine gun fire] into the trenches.

September 12. I stayed at quarters. The Americans begin an attack at Someille.

Clint: *The next war I see will be in the movies.*

September 13. I saw a very pretty barrage. 10:00 P.M. It was a continual play of flashes of fire all along the valley. I carried four men, one couchey and three assis.

Cummings: *I was reading the Lord's Prayer in French. Say, I want to learn that in French. He never hears me when I talk English.*

September 14. I carried one assis, one couchey and three Boche assis. Deyo steered a car home whose top was blown off. It would not go of its own power so we had some Boche prisoners going our way push it. Official communiqué stating the Americans had advanced twenty kilometers and taken 135,000 prisoners.

September 15. I finished reading *Great Expectations* some time ago. Two characters, Pipi Herbert and Mrs. Haversham and her adopted daughter, who liked men, and Joe. One section of the story is that without the practice of love you lose the recipient power also. The degree of feeling and understanding have grown proportionally as you practice it on others. It also showed how an act of sympathy touched the hardened villain of the story.

September 16. I carried two coucheys and nineteen assis.
    Griesey: *Say, was that a dead horse I ran through back there?*

September 18. I took the post at LaFaux. I had a shell land in the road in front of me. I went that much the faster charging through the smoke for I knew one would soon follow. I was struck this morning with the eagerness of the Boche prisoners to please. They jump around like the most humble servant at the motion of a finger. One just came in and pleaded with the adjutant to do something for his back. It hurt him very much to carry the wounded. If I am ever to be a prisoner, I should choose to be a prisoner of the French. On this trip, I carried ten assis and three coucheys.

September 20. Spent today in camp and had a fine rest last night.
    Poirer: *I heard that all the girls smoke back home. Why don't you like a girl who smokes? For the same reason I don't like a girl who chews.*

September 21. Tonight I am at R.1 and have a mighty dangerous road to travel. I had a close call after supper. Was taking a crap when one came within forty feet. I had some close calls and a bum machine all night. I had to go in low in some of the most dangerous places. I carried eleven assis and one couchey.

September 23. I stayed at LaFaux all night. I thought when I should go out in the morning I would be minus a car, for shells fell all over the abris. I found it covered with dirt but unharmed. I went down in the morning and I found three big shell holes in the road. I carried ten assis and two coucheys.

September 25. I went on evacuation for the first time. I evacuated twenty-eight gas cases. My first trip I never can forget. I hoped to get Rathert to go with me to show me the way through Soissons; I could not get him; hence took a very bad route leading by the cave. It was very dark. I slipped over a bank of two and a half feet and could not climb back into the road, nor could I back down off from the road. I asked two men to get out (best two). Each insisted in crying accents that he was worse than the other. I shut the door up, only now realizing what a plight I was in, for I'd thought they could push. I could not start the engine now because I could not turn the crank around, so here I was with men so bad and on a road dangerous from shelling and never frequented. I now made the men get out or lugged them out, as one by one they sat down in the road unwilling to stand. I now attempted to lift the car over this ridge. I got on the under side to keep it from tipping over. When I finally lifted the hind wheel by a lunge, it nearly went over on me. I now straightened it parallel with the road, and backed it up to a point where I could mount the road. Only to find Boche over my head bombing the place and the guard under cover. I beat it and eventually found the way. Any place was better than standing still.

September 28. Evacuated six gassed.

September 29.[47] Spent my first night at post 165 and at crossroads of Chemin des Dames. I never went over such a road. It was just lined with dead horses of the Germans. The twenty-eighth the Germans retreated for six kilometers, giving up the Chemin des Dames and falling clear back to the canal. One company of the Marines crossed the canal but the company on either side failed to advance. They surrendered but were all shot down. I had one hard trip in the night with a couchey. My door came down and I tried to get it up. The shells came so close, I had to hurry on down the road. Of a sudden, I came on one of our cars standing on its head in a great hole made by a .240. During the night I carried four coucheys, twelve assis, and immediately after supper I took three coucheys and one assis to St. Rémy. It was a terrible trip to make at night. I had no lights to read the signs on the road. I took the wrong road four times and at last hit the Soissons, Paris road, which I didn't mean to use. Through all the towns I passed, I couldn't find a soul. The polar star was my only guide and that is a poor guide for an automobile with coucheys.

October 1. I went directly to R.1 but spent the night at the crossroads. The Boche made some powerfully close shots during the night. I had many trips, but there was no room to sleep unless I went clear down in the bottom of the abri where the smell was too strong. I let a sick Frenchy have my blankets, so it left me too cold to sleep on a bench where I lay. My totoes [lice] were especially active in the region of my neck.

October 2. Now I am sitting in a cave by a fine fire. Some are washing, some reading, and a couple are cleaning their horses. There we are, all assembled together, horses and men alike. I could not get here with my car but left it on the other side of the valley and walked around the end. It is narrow and full of dead horses and human refuse. It was the most stinking hole I ever got into. [48] While picking my way among these rotting horses, the Boche were sending them in very close, but I preferred the chance of getting hit to flopping on this rot. The marines fed me when I arrived and I was much in need of it. Now I await dinner. Three men are sitting here by me, one with a ball in the sole of his shoe, another with a ball in his overcoat, another with a hole just through the top of his instep, but he is going to be evacuated. I carried four gassed.

Was relieved at 5:00 P.M., but while eating supper, I was informed that I had to go to St. Rémy with three coucheys and one assis to Pont Tarché. It's about 40 km. I had never been over the road, had no flash nor even a bricay [brancardier]. I got off from the road four different times, going in all about 15 km. out of my way. And when I got to Villers Cottérêts I couldn't find St. Rémy. At last, at 11:30 I arrived, after five hours, tired clear out. I had decided to pull to the roadside and sleep until morning, but while unloading I found that the ambulance in front of me was going back to Pont Tarché at once, and he had lights. I decided to follow him as I could get back much quicker and easier through the long woods of Villers Cottérêts. I judged the road in front of me from what it looked like fifty yards ahead. He hit a terrible pace and several times I lost control, coming to a stand crossways of the road.

I reached the cave at Clamexcy at 2:00 P.M., tired out. I stole quietly into the first cave where I heard Joe's bed was, but Dorf was in that. I felt a still form in each bed, and after being cussed by some and pitied by others, I decided I had no place to sleep. I now go to cave two and find Birch's bed empty and after picking Kelsey up and putting him on his side so he won't snore, I lay down too.

October 4. I carry one assis. We start for repos and make one first stop at Soissons.

October 6. We leave Soissons for Ivors.

October 7. I go to Boursonne for two assis and taking them to St. Rémy.

October 8. I was court-martialled for a letter I wrote and fined $10. The charge was pacifistic writing. I said power could enforce but could not engender. I said the force to will an act comes from within, not without. I also called war a "butchering hell game." On the seventh Germany, Austria and Turkey ask for an armistice. [49]

October 11. We received news that Van Boyd was dead in the hospital. We have eight men left in the hospital. On the first, I evacuated him to R.1. I said goodbye Boyd, good luck, and he answered, "Merci, don't let em get you." I went down to Villers Cottérêts to see if Boyd had been put in a box. I also went to see his grave. I couldn't think poor Van was under that dirt. [50]

A Buck Private
From the private's point of view:

1. *The man who won the war.*
2. *The fellow who gets crapped on, always.*
3. *The one who does all the dirty work.*
4. *The guy who gets the poorest pay.*
5. *The guy who can't write about his living.*
6. *One who never gets a writeup in the papers.*
7. *A man physically fit, brains not considered.*
8. *Fellow who never gets a permission.*
9. *Fellow who never gets enough to eat.*
10. *The fellow who is going to knock hell out of his lieutenant when he gets back home.*

October 13. We celebrated our anniversary at the front. Everyone here was forced to sing his favorite song. The spirit of the evening ran high and so did the pinard.

October 19. We took Ostend and Bruges and the fifteenth we took Lille, liberating 120 civilians.

October 20. We took Zeebruge. All German subs are called into their base the eighteenth.[51] Wilson's reply to Austria is that he cannot talk peace until she liberates the Czechs. His first reply to Germany is that he couldn't talk peace with them until all invaded soil is evacuated. She agrees to this and calls for a committee to make ready for evacuating. But Wilson answers that he cannot talk to the present government.[52]

October 22. Carried five assis to Villers Cottérêts.

October 24. She reached our camp just before we left at noon and asked for a doctor as she had walked 15 km. and was very tired. After supper, I went to Hartens to stay for the night and wait a call. Three women had moved into the chateau. They asked me in for coffee and provided a fine place to sleep. The girl was very pretty. She gave me her address: Madilene Brismantier, 23 Rue Des Cordeliers. At 1:00 A.M. I went on a long trip for a malade. When I returned to Soissons, I saw an English ambulance at the square, and supposing that he could tell me where the hospital was, I stopped. I found him in the ambulance asleep. I shook him only to find I had a woman in my grasp. She was so glad to be awakened that she apologized for being asleep. Her car was broke. I left her—I could find no hospital so I went to Pont Tarché.[53] Reached Hartens 5:30 A.M.

October 25. Was called 7:30 to get seven assis at Noyant and take them to Pont Tarché.

October 26. Austria asked for an armistice without contest.

October 29. These days we are traveling over land that was just evacuated by the Germans. The road we are near was held by the Germans for four years. We get many stories direct. A man of forty-five was telling me how, when he left Annecy, they had taken his mother, age seventy-two, with them. They were taking all men from fourteen to sixty with them. At or near Ivors a mother and daughter three miles apart were kept from seeing each other for three years. When the Germans left Láon, they left everything in good condition in the cathedral but took the organ, and it was a very good one.

November 2. Austria has signed an armistice, the Kaiser abdicated, and the Americans took 3,000 prisoners. I took my first trip to Láon. It has a very pretty location. It is a town of 22,000 before the war, but the Germans only left 6,500. They are a cheerful bunch. Their soul comes right out in their face.

Incidental Stuff

Some of the prisoners came around our quarters and picked up crusts that had been thrown on the dung pile. I went into the kitchen and found several ends for them. I can't hate them or anybody I know, but I feel sorry over many things of this war. These are very critical times in the history of the war. The Allied Council of all nations has been sitting now for four days.

November 4. We could see for miles and could see where the Germans were. They shot at our abri all day, and we had a very hard time. Either shit or get out of the pot, for they shot so close that they put the lights out. They hit one abri nearby and wounded a fellow. He was the only blessé I got until the next morning.

November 5. There were so many in the abri and so little room that I had to stand up all day the fourth, and until I went to bed at 9:00 P.M. At 8:00 P.M. the night of the fourth I ate my first bite and first drink since 4:30 P.M. the third. The men came with the supper at 8:00. The infantry hadn't eaten for one day and night and the trenches were very wet. I finally took three assis to Crepy and got a good dinner at 11:00 A.M. In the morning when I first went out, the whole front at some distance was on fire.

November 6. Peace or an armistice was signed with Austria at 3:00 P.M. and all firing was to cease by 5:00 P.M.

We moved to Erlon. We stayed until 3:00 P.M. and are moving to Marle. I was on kitchen detail there next morning and used the wood the Boche had split. The houses are all just as if the people had left yesterday.

We used their beds, stoves, chairs, tables, glasses, etc. It was remarkable that we could make ourselves at home.

November 7. While going to Vervins where the Boche had left but twelve hours before, Carroll heard civilians saying that all boys over twelve should salute and pay the German officers, going by in groups, special notice. All the civilians of this region are to be helped by the American Relief Commission. There was an order forbidding any Boche soldiers from getting any of the food from our section.

The Boche here took the upper part of the houses and let the owners sleep in the cellars, then when the town was shelled they changed places with them. We were the first Americans these people had seen. Many girls rushed out and kissed us on both cheeks. The men stopped me many times to shake my hand, and they all took their hats off to us. There were many young women with little babes. The people here are all wild with joy. A very common scene is a number of civilians coming along the road, just set free, with several French soldiers feeding them from their rations, and drinking pinard and shouting, laughing and crying with joy.

November 9. I took three assis and a couchey to Láon. In coming back, I picked up some women who had walked thirty km. and had hardly anything to eat. They were dead tired. It certainly is a sight to see the people flocking back to their homes. The kids vent their joy by kicking and stoning Boche things left behind. Many little fellows are wearing Boche shoes. Some boys playing about the place found a Boche hiding and took him prisoner. Some of these mean fellows are certainly tough. Little boys, two and a half feet high blow smoke through their noses and call each other "Mon Vieux."

November 11. We received the news that the Kaiser had abdicated and that Germany had signed the armistice, making this the greatest day ever known in history. No one has any control of Americans. We moved back to Vervins this morning, and now we are located in a Boche whore house.

November 12. We moved to Plomion. As the horsemen came into the town they yelled, "Where are the Boche?" A young boy of twelve, without thinking, said, "There they are." Two Germans near him, back out of sight, put a bullet through his head and escaped through some crowds. This was only an hour before hostilities ceased.

General Boulloye, a horseman Afric, demanded that a Boche fleeing on a bicycle be caught. He took his head off with a sword.

November 17. Read a very fine story in the *Atlantic* about the one-legged Italian hero who fell only after the third bullet hit him. As he fell, he threw his crutch at the enemy and died laughing.

November 22. I can hardly say which I prefer, the girls of France or the girls of America. In general, I think I like the French girls the best. They are more polite, kinder, have more sympathy, more smiles and a sweeter disposition in general. They are not nearly so important, indifferent or independent as the American girls. Whether this is in their favor or against them I am not prepared to say. The French girls are gifted with more life. They love with a passion. They are frank and very natural. But with all this to the credit of the French girls, I don't believe that they have the staying qualities of the American girls. I think the American girls have much higher attributes, and I think they are not so fickle as the French girls. As for natural beauty, I think our American girls have anything beat in this world. They may not be so dainty looking as the French girls but they have more character in the face. They are very different but both possessing good qualities and I love them both.

November 26. We moved to Fourmies. I got fine quarters with Joe at a private house. We asked the lady what it would be and she said nothing as the Boche officers who stayed never gave her money. Many of the younger kids here talk Boche as well as French. One of the 165th French Division fellows got permission to go to his home, only to find that the Boche had shot both of his sisters.

December 6. I took a Boche soldier and a Boche sergeant, both wounded prisoners, to Láon. I got a ring from one of the Boche. We had a fine talk with the sergeant. When I left later he came up and wished me good luck. There were a couple hundred soldiers and officers, French and many Boche lined up just across the road, and, before I thought, I shook hands with him, bid him goodbye. I found in talking with him that he fought exactly opposite where I was carrying French wounded.

December 19. Went to Paris to get glasses. Met Ralph Passley from Princeton, Ohio.

December 26. I met a wonderful girl by the name of Luce Burband. I had a fine Christmas with Andrée. I got better acquainted with Andrée and liked her very much. I saw her the twenty-fourth with her hair down ready for bed and wasn't disappointed.

January 15. I left the section for Paris. I had some sad thoughts when I said goodbye to the boys. I knew for a certainty it was the last I would ever see many of them. This was a very sad thought. Eating together, sleeping together, suffering together and sharing dangers and the thought of victory and of the uneasiness at home from a feeling between success and remorse. The feeling brought some of us much closer than brothers. I regretted leaving Rush, Rigy, Ray, Dink, Birch, Dorf, Kiefer and Jones. I'm meeting Mlle. the fourteenth. She made a very strong impression on me.

January 18. Went last night to hear 77th Division. The play was fine. I am going to the Louvre this afternoon. This bunch here at the show sure wanted to go home. It was all they talked about.

January 19. I saw a great football game Sunday: Eddy Mehan, Tulber, Brown, Captain Whitney, Am. End., Sptiz Clark and Indian Meesee, etc. I sleep here in a large garage, the roof is glass. It's great to lie there nights and look up at the sky. Had a fine chicken dinner with Andrée.

January 21. Went to boxing match at Palace de Glace. Seven bouts of four rounds each. The French won two bouts. An American broke his hand. He kept looking at his hand and the Frenchy hit him many times in the face. Lerder announced that the American Chief of Secret Service ordered the fight stopped. One fellow hollered, "Tell us when we are going home, that is the secret!"

    P.S. The section received citations and nine Croix des Guerres, Jan. 15. General kissed the lieutenant on both cheeks.

March 5. I was to see Andrée and in fact, I had just proposed when I heard a guttural noise as though two dogs were growling in a fight. I recognized the human voice, and my first thought was that two men were having a death struggle with knives and one was wounded. I tried to get out but Mrs. Detrey held me while Andrée ran to the window and saw three civilians and a French lieutenant about forty years old. The light fell on them and they ran. Andrée was so excited that she could not continue the discussion. She was to give me an answer the following night but she said she would write me at Lyon. I love her and hope she will say yes.

March 18. Joe arrived the night before from Germany. Met him at the University. We had some time deciding whether to obey orders and go to room at the convent or get a room downtown. Many reasons for the latter.

The American easily acclimates himself. They often surpass the French in their own customs. I saw one today who did not get his pants buttoned up within twenty yards of the latrine on Main Street walking among many people. I learned that if you want your mail brought regularly in France you must tip the postman or he will not deliver your mail.

March 21. I was making a way for a room today when all was settled. She told me in the same tone that I couldn't have women in the room. I and a young Frenchy of twenty was visiting a very fine young lady and she put a white garment in front of us on the tip and said voyez vois le lace on my pretty pantaloons. Received a very sad letter from Andrée which was almost an acceptance to my offer.

March 27. Received letter from Andrée getting the answer yes. She also said she would come to the U.S. and live with me. I paid Mrs. Reniere to March 24th. I slept at the convent twenty-four and twenty-seven. I am having a hard time finding a course I can understand here. I try everything once. They have a funny show here for all Americans, four times a week. You see a very great deal of misery on the streets, many disfigured, some starving, some victims of the war, and now and then a grafter.

April 19. Andrée arrived from Paris on the 5:40 P.M. train. The depot had two sorties, so Mrs. Reniere stood at one and I at the other. Andrée came her way. Mrs. Reniere knew her from my description. Andrée grabbed me from the back. I embarrassed her on the spot—American style! It caused some curiosity and some jealous looks from the men. They hate above all things to have the American getting a pretty French girl. Andrée took my room at Reniere's. We spent all the night in this room, which I enjoyed very much more than any theatre or house party. The first time I ever really hugged or kissed her was in this room. How many dozen times I kissed her these nights I didn't count. I went to heaven the first night she came and never awoke until the train puffed slowly out of the station. As far as I could see, I could see the white gloved hand of Andrée waving adieu. We spent Sunday forenoon on the hill about the church, ate dinner on the bank of the Seine.

Monday, we ate dinner in a fine restaurant. My spirits were rather rough. I felt like eating about a dozen Frenchmen. They regarded Andrée on the street, and said that she was an ordinary chicken that anyone could go with. I made a vow that the first Frenchman I heard make a remark about a girl with an unchaperoned American, I would pound him to a jelly. Monday P.M. we went to the park. Joe, Andrée, Mr. Thevillon and I went for a boat ride.

Monday, the twenty-first at 10:30 A.M., I presented Andrée with her diamond. I think she liked it. Tuesday morning, I arrived from the convent before she had her toilet arranged. But Andrée looks as good to me un-dolled as dolled.

She is going to England to teach until December, at least, at which time she will go to join me in America.

April 23. Day following departure of Andrée I knew it had to work. From April twenty-three to May, I received a couple of nice letters from her. She decided that she could not live away from me, so she wrote to England telling them she was to be married. Then she wrote for me to come to Paris at once, as I had but little time left to get married. With much trouble I received a pass for this for May eleven.

The family was fine to me. That evening and the next day we never really kissed. Andrée sat on my lap all the time. We even fed each other. Lovers were never more satisfied. But there, Andrée complained to me! Said that in truth, I was a bore. She made so many suggestions, especially as to my manner of dress and more, that I began to think that perhaps she made too much of material things. I felt that she began to change from then on, but not outwardly. She was very demonstrative, and loved me constantly.

That night I did not sleep well. I went to Andrée at 10:00 in the morning. We went to the depot to inquire about our train, and from there to a park by the Gare de Lyon. Andrée wanted to buy some cards. She talked to our friends.

On Friday she said she was not quite so in love today, and that evening she did not kiss me with the same zeal. I was very depressed in the evening, but slept well that night. Telepathy was working strong on me from Tuesday evening on. I felt that something ominous was about to happen. She spoke very sharply to me of my quiet ways, and showed me how rigid my face always was, and how tightly shut my mouth. She insisted on my taking off my glasses. This showed me how material was her feeling for me. On our way to the station, she said it didn't matter. She liked our moments together very much. I asked her if she had enjoyed the last three days in Paris as much as the three days in Lyon. She said she didn't know. She seemed dejected when we parted but smiled and gave me a kiss. I can never forget that, though I was suffering within my thoughts. I never batted an eye.

I thought much on the train, and did not rest when I got to Lyon until I heard from her, for I was wild with a fear that something had come between me and the girl I loved.

When I received the letter, all I had ever thought was there and more. It was the most unhuman act I ever saw put into words.

I was crazy that night, and for three days I did not sleep or eat. Joe was in Paris and he called to see her mother. Her mother could offer no cause for the change. She said, "It was simply a sudden turn in her nature." Said she had never said a word against it, but had wondered why we should fancy each other when I was so serious, quiet and reflective, and she was so gay.

Andrée said she would give my pictures to Joe while he was in Paris, but she kept the one in her locket. Joe took her my picture of her, except for the one she took out of my book. She must have left about the twentieth for Italy. [54]

Notes

1. American neutrality had been widely agreed upon for much of the war. President Wilson tried to maintain a neutral stance throughout his first term and was reelected in 1916. Serving in the ambulance service was a popular alternative to fighting, particularly on university campuses.

2. There were no widely accepted standards of medical fitness in the war. However, a surprising number of volunteers were rejected. In Britain, over the course of the war, 40 percent of the total number of men examined for service were rejected.

3. This was generally true about the ambulance services. The American Field Service, ambulance branch, had about 1,200 volunteers, about a fourth of whom were from Harvard alone. Stanford University had sent the first Field Service ambulance unit overseas two months before the U.S. declared war. England, Russia and other nations also contributed volunteer ambulance units that were connected with the French army.

4. The convoy system had only recently developed after the large losses to submarines of 1916–17. Total Allied losses had been averaging 630,000 tons per month to the one hundred submarines on the prowl, and it had peaked three months before the 591 Ambulance Unit sailed for France. The convoy system was already resulting in a drop in losses.

5. Defective and unexploded torpedoes were common in both world wars.

6. Australian troops had recently fought at Messines, near Ypres, where Anzac and other British troops made one of the most successful and well planned attacks of the war.

7. St.-Nazaire is on the south Atlantic coast of France, safely away from the front.

8. Bully beef was canned corned beef, an omnipresent item in the diet of American soldiers.

9. This "Zeppelin" is probably an Allied observation balloon. Zeppelins sent out of bases in Belgium inaugurated the era of strategic bombing, in which civilian communications, production, and populations were bombed, but their principal importance by this point in the war was in mapping, photography, and observation. Zeppelins as bombers rapidly declined after 1916, when the introduction of incendiary bullets made the hydrogen-filled "zeps" more danger to their crews

than those below. By 1917, the Allies and Germans were using large two-engined aircraft for strategic bombing.

10. For three or four months the French had been heartily sick of the war. The disastrous Chemin des Dames Offensive, in April 1917, resulted in negligible gains, the loss of 270,000 French, the sacking of Nievelle as commander, and mutinies and in discipline in a majority of the 112 French divisions.

11. The man Ponton is traveling with toward the front, "Icy" Siggins, was one of the men of the 591 who would not return from France.

12. Bar-le-Duc is about 180 km. west of Paris, on the Ornain, a tributary of the Marne. Verdun was one of the three fortified cities in western France, and it had been the site of intense fighting in the Franco-Prussian war of 1870. Because of its historical and mythic significance, in 1916, Verdun was fought over until nothing was left of the city and more than seven hundred thousand men, German and French, had been killed. Bar-le-Duc, 45 km. south of Verdun, was the principal staging area and depot to Verdun and the front lines in that area. The battle of Verdun had been effectively ended by the Allied assaults that opened the battle of the Marne, but sharp front-line sparring continued there.

13. Jubicourt was to remain the base of the 591 for four months, and this barn was later remembered by the men as their principal "home" in the war, partly because of the French family who lived there.

14. Rats in and around the Western Front were so numerous that any attempts to exterminate them were superfluous. The huge number of unburied corpses of men and horses provided them with plenty of food.

15. *Assis,* sitting or seated, became the term ambulance men generally used for those who did not have to be put on stretchers. "Couchey" is an Americanization of *couché,* reclining or lying down.

16. Pilots were instructed to destroy their machines if they survived downing. Aerial warfare increased during the last half of the war. At the front, planes were used for bombing, harassment, and, most important, air reconnaissance. About 50,000 airmen, all sides, were killed in the war.

17. *Blessé,* wounded, often Americanized to "blessie."

18. Starshells were for lighting up an area at night.

19. *Malade* means sick or ill, as opposed to the "blessies" or wounded.

20. The Italians joined with the Allies in May, 1915, when Italy declared war on Austria-Hungary. Most of the fighting was in northern Italy. The "surprise" that Ponton refers to occurred at Caporetto, where a German-Austrian attack broke the Italian line, taking a stunning three hundred thousand Italian prisoners and three

thousand heavy guns. With British and French troops, the Italians would later regroup along the Piave River, from Asiago to the Gulf of Venice.

21. *Abris*, shelters or covers, may refer either to a covered place in the trenches or to true bunkers of the sort that the Germans had more of than the Allies. Some of the better engineered German bunkers went as deep as thirty feet in the ground and could protect men from even the most intense artillery barrage.

22. *Éclat:* fragment, piece, chip, explosion; Ponton Americanizes the spelling but retains the dual meaning of the French *éclat,* referring either to the explosion of artillery shells or to pieces of shrapnel.

23. Alcohol was often available just behind the front, in cafés, bars and canteens.

24. While there were commercial entertainments for soldiers, life in Paris during the war was generally gray, dull and depressing, with sporadic bombing, soup lines in the streets and, by 1917, a pervasive desperation.

25. "Grand Repos": furlough.

26. On March 3, 1917, the new revolutionary government of Russia signed the Treaty of Brest-Litovsk, withdrawing from the war and offering Germany a huge satellite empire in the east.

27. The 591 Ambulance Unit would remain at Glorieux, on the front, for two weeks.

28. Fort Douaumont, 6 km. northeast of Verdun, was the largest of the three forts surrounding the city. It and Fort Vaux were taken early in the German offensive and then retaken by a counteroffensive in October. Douaumont was militarily insignificant but it became symbolically important to the French in the bitter mythology of Verdun.

29. The *poste de secour* was the casualty clearing station, which was almost on the front lines at Verdun because the quarry *(carrière)* at Haudramont allowed for a secure underground location. Casualty clearing stations were an innovation of World War I, and they provided a great improvement to the haphazard methods of emergency treatment in previous wars. Alternating teams of surgeons worked around the clock in active times, separating the approximately one in ten men who required immediate treatment or who could not be moved. However, the clearing stations were hampered by the fact that surgeons still did not have a good grasp of the nature and treatment of shock. Hospitals were located farther to the rear, and the majority of sick and wounded men were sent by ambulance or rail to them.

30. The Germans used 1,200 guns at Verdun, including the gigantic Krupps 38 cm. "Big Bertha," which could shoot twenty miles. In nine months of intense barrages, the Germans and French had lobbed almost forty million artillery shells, atomizing the town and landscape.

31. On this day, the Germans launched a massive attack at several places along the Western Front, made possible by the withdrawal of Russia from the war and consequent closing of the Eastern Front.

32. The "sausage" is probably a "kite balloon" anchored behind the lines for observation. Invented by the Germans, they were used by both sides all along the front. The "dove" or carrier pigeon demonstrates a general fact about field communications in World War I: While portable wire communication existed, it was generally too clumsy and unreliable in the muck and destruction of trench warfare, leaving front-line communications to the old standbys of signalling, dogs, runners, and pigeons.

33. Bras, which was about one kilometer from the front line at this time, is directly west of Fort Douaumont and 6 km. north of Verdun. Some ambulance men called this road "Hell's Corner." The men of the 591 called it "Diarrhea Crossroads." All trips between Verdun and Bras had to be made at night, between 9 P.M. and 2 A.M.

34. Burros were used at the front because they were surefooted and small enough to stay below the trench line. They hauled supplies through the mazes of communications tunnels from the rear to the front lines.

35. Former President William Howard Taft, an active speechmaker, had made an abrupt reversal from being a proponent of international disarmament to supporting universal conscription. There were more than three hundred thousand Americans in Europe at this time, and there would be over 1,760,000 by October.

36. The last German offensives had been underway since March 21, and the British, who occupied the western salient of the front, suffered mightily. Amiens was the British communications center, and Germans had advanced to a point 16 km. away, and taken nearly one hundred thousand British prisoners in the area.

37. Brancardiers are stretcher bearers, who had one of the most dangerous jobs in the trenches because they constantly had to get around in exposed, sometimes unfamiliar territory.

38. Meanwhile the real Germans on this day launched a major offensive between these same two cities, smashing the French Sixth Army, capturing four hundred guns, forty thousand prisoners, and bringing heavy artillery within the range of Paris, where panic reigned through the spring.

39. This is an optimistic view at the moment. Militarily, the situation on the front wasn't particularly good for the Allies in mid-June. The Germans had created three great bulges on the Western Front, Allied lines had been cut and their communications severed. However, the intensity and speed of the offensive left German troops fatigued; thousands of soldiers now were coming down with a virulent strain of the flu, which would ultimately cause a great epidemic killing

twenty million people worldwide. A few historians have seriously offered the opinion that the flu beat the Germans in World War I.

40. The 591 remained at the post at Ferme-Dix-Huit from May 2 through August 22. Gus Bauman, one of the men in the unit, later remembered this station as a relatively pleasant one despite the action. Men who weren't on duty played baseball and swam in the Marne. Another of the drivers, Ken Easlick, remembered Ferme-Dix-Huit as the place where on July 8 he broke his hand in several places when an ambulance motor he was trying to crank backfired. (From letters by each man in their annual collection of letters, which each year was bound with the title "Le Jubecourt Matin.")

41. The day Ponton began his second leave was the "black day for the German army," according to Ludendorff. The second battle of the Marne was followed, to the north and west, by an 8 km. advance by British, American, and Australian troops. Many German soldiers had finally lost morale due to sickness, semi-starvation and the seeming endlessness of the war.

42. Ponton is traveling by rail from Paris into southwestern France.

43. Senlis is just north of Paris, west of Chateau-Thierre, where Americans had fought with distinction in June.

44. Halfway between Senlis and Soissons.

45. Allied troops were driving the Germans northward, rolling back the lines. The 591 was located at Tartiers for a week, then moved to Chavigny.

46. There had been ten thousand blacks in the prewar army. Conscription expanded the U.S. army to four million men, and the two hundred thousand of them who were black were kept in segregated regiments. Many American blacks were treated as equals for the first time not by the U.S. army but by the French.

47. Three days before this entry, the Allied Commander Marshal Foch had started attacks at several places along the front, including this point in Champagne. Foch hoped to prevent German buildups at one location, and he hoped to sever communication and rail contact running behind German lines. This road overlooking the Aisne had been the site in the spring of 1917 of the disastrous Chemin des Dames Offensive.

48. The French alone lost 270,000 men here in spring, 1917.

49. Ponton was stripped of his single stripe in this field "court-martial" over a letter written to his mother and disapproved by the censors. At the time it happened, he did not dwell on it, but according to his family he never forgot it.

50. Van Boyd was one of the three men in this forty-two-man unit who would not come home. This is close to the overall casualty rate of all soldiers who served in

World War I, all nations, and it is about twice the overall rate of all Americans who served during the war (about 4 percent). An ambulance unit was lucky to have a mortality rate this low.

51. Zeebruge, Belgium, on the North Sea, had been the entry and exit point for German U-boats coming down the canal from Bruges, where one of their principal submarine bases was located.

52. Wilson demanded the resignation of Ludendorff.

53. Some women served in various ambulance services during World War I, including the American Field Service's.

54. The 591 returned to New York in April, 1919.

World War II: Pacific

China

Korea

Japan

Tokyo

Okinawa

Chichi Jima

Iwo Jima

Marcus

Taiwan
(Formosa)

Philippine
Sea

Saipan

Roth

Tinian

Guam

Thailand

Indo China

Manila

Mindoro

Philippine
Islands

Yap

Ulithi

Eniwetok

Mindanao

Davao

Pecelio

Anguar

Majuro

Borneo

Celebes

New
Guinea

Australia

5

World War II—The War in the Pacific

World War II brought an end to the Great Depression as the United States embarked on the most prodigious manufacturing, logistical and military endeavor the world had yet seen. If the First World War had vaulted America into position as the world's leading power, by the end of World War II the United States emerged as the most powerful nation in history—a superpower, based on a manufacturing capability dwarfing that of the entire rest of the world combined, and in sole possession of the atomic bomb. Americans remained solidly united throughout the course of this war as they had never been before. Everyone pitched in to support the war effort. The attack on Pearl Harbor saw to that. Harry Truman often afterwards complained that if only Americans could pull together in peace as they had during the crisis of this war, there was no limit to what the nation might accomplish.

Although he campaigned on the promise to keep America out of the conflict in Europe, President Franklin Roosevelt was already increasing production of warplanes as early as 1939, with the secret aim of making them available to England and Europe for the fight against Hitler. He also authorized the design and development of new fighters and bombers. During the next few years, orders from England and France created an economic boom that began to revitalize the American economy in a way that the New Deal never could. The United States was seriously rearming and, as factories were built in record numbers, the manufacturing program beginning to take shape would change the world. By 1944, a year of high production in Germany despite the relentless bombing, the United States produced over 50 percent more munitions than the combined enemy, and almost half of the total arms of all belligerents on both sides. In the years immediately following the war, President Truman would claim that the United States was responsible for 75 percent of the world's manufacturing output. This manufacturing boom also helped make this war the only one not followed by a recession.

Even though the isolationist mood across the country remained strong, Congress passed a draft law to replenish the army that had been decimated by budget cuts in the demilitarization that followed World War I. Between 1939 and the end of 1941, the army more than quadrupled in size to over one and a half million men. The navy commissioned a fleet of new carriers designed to be part of a new mobile air-sea strategy of aggressively carrying a war to the enemy by first gaining air superiority. At the height of production in 1943, a new battleship was being completed every two months and a new carrier almost every month, with escort ships being turned out even faster.

In the meantime, in July of 1941, President Roosevelt cut off shipments of crude oil and scrap metal to the Japanese in an attempt to pressure Japan to halt its decade-long aggression in China, a conflict which had recently broadened and escalated. This embargo may have influenced the outcome of the war with Japan as much as any of the early preparations; throughout the Pacific campaigns, the Japanese navy found itself continuously hampered, both in overall strategy and in fighting tactics, by fuel problems. Japan's manufacturing capacity suffered even sooner, making adequate resupply of crucial machinery and equipment difficult if not, by the end, impossible.

As is so often the case with the beginnings of wars, the conflict with Japan was rooted in misunderstandings and miscalculations. America at first believed that sanctions would discourage the Japanese in their expansionist ambitions against East Asia. The Japanese, for their part, were convinced of American weakness. They also believed the United States would never turn its full attention to the Pacific so long as they had the war in Europe to worry about. In the end, they were unwilling to "lose face" and give up their dreams of hegemony by withdrawing from China, the American condition for ending its embargo of Japan. Instead, they determined on the bold course of war with the United States.

As negotiations with Japan continued, the United States became increasingly convinced the Japanese planned to attack, though they expected the attack to occur somewhere in the Philippines or Asia. The strike on Pearl Harbor on December 7 hit the nation—and the world—as an enormous shock. Because U.S. codebreakers had cracked the Japanese cypher and were listening to all embassy traffic, a warning message was intercepted. But, just as so many battles are lost for want of timely communications, this message was not decoded until the day after the attack. Roosevelt was caught by surprise at the audacity of the Japanese attack, and he was genuinely shaken by the fact that they had so easily destroyed much of the Pacific fleet in half a day's work.

The declaration of war against Japan was passed with one dissenting vote. Days later, Germany and Italy, with whom Japan had signed the Tripartite Pact, entered the war against the United States, setting the stage for a truly worldwide conflict with fronts thousands of miles apart. Unique among American wars, this was no *rage militaire* that soon slipped into doubt and uncertainty. Debate ceased. We were in it for the duration.

Although Pearl Harbor was a devastating blow, the American carrier fleet did not get caught as completely as the Japanese had hoped. Due more to luck than good planning, much of the fleet was away from Pearl Harbor and survived. More important, the Japanese neglected to blow up the American fuel supply, a puzzling omission given their own preoccupation about lack of fuel. During the remainder of the war, Japan's strategy would be based on attempting to strike that one decisive blow that would neutralize the American naval force.

The Japanese navy sped through the islands of the Pacific in a feeding frenzy of victories. Guam was captured on December 10, just a few days after the attack on Pearl Harbor. On December 22, the Japanese army made the first of several landings a short distance above Manila, and by February 22, MacArthur was ordered out, escaping in March to bases in Australia from where he could try to regroup. Bataan fell, and on May 6, so did Corregidor.

As resistance crumbled, the Japanese recklessly overextended their forces. Though they originally had planned to take only enough territory to set up a solid defensive perimeter from which they could launch powerful air sorties, gain more access to oil, and keep the Americans from regaining staging areas from which they might reach Japan, the ease of their initial victories seduced them into abandoning their defensive strategy.

In May, Admiral Nimitz caught up with the Japanese fleet in the Coral Sea in the first major naval engagement in history to be fought entirely in the air without a single ship either sighting or directly firing on another. Though the battle of Coral Sea was a standoff, it was the Japanese who broke off the engagement, and the next great battle a month later at Midway—a brutal air-sea battle between carrier fleets that inflicted heavy damage on both sides—resulted in a major American victory and the first of several turning points in the war.

After nearly a year and a half of prolonged and sometimes rancorous debate, American military planners decided on a bold strategy to retake control of the crucial Philippines. MacArthur had proposed starting from Australia and New Guinea and working up island by island in what was sure to be a long, bloody campaign that might take years. Instead it was decided to adopt the plan of Admirals Nimitz and King to strike directly at the Central Pacific island groups, beginning with the Marianas, selecting significant targets often several hundred miles apart, thereby isolating large numbers of Japanese troops and greatly shortening the length of time needed to regain control of the Pacific. The navy used its air power to control the skies while its ships blocked any Japanese attempt at reinforcement of the targeted islands. Navy fliers could then fly close air support for the marines as they hit the beaches, or leapfrog ahead to the next target. Heavily defended islands were to be cut off and "mopped up" later as circumstances allowed. Although the "mopping up" operations would prove to be some of the most hellish and bloody fighting in history, the strategy caught the Japanese by surprise, playing a significant role in their ultimate defeat.

The American decision to invade Saipan forced the Japanese out of their anchorage at the southern end of Mindanao. Because the Japanese remained determined to strike a decisive blow that would halt the invasion of Saipan at any cost, the First Mobile Fleet was sent through the San Bernardino Strait to attack the American Fifth Fleet, under Admiral Raymond Spruance, in the Philippine Sea. With three carrier divisions and a full complement of supporting destroyers and cruisers, on June 19 Admiral Jisaburo Ozawa launched a long range aircraft strike in conjunction with a planned attack of land-based aircraft from the Bonin Islands and Guam. His expectation of land-based support was bolstered by false information Ozawa continued to receive from the Japanese commander at Guam, who reported nothing but victories to Ozawa, while in fact he had sustained such extensive damage that he was unable to send up any kind of force or even to provide landing facilities for the carrier-based planes to refuel and rearm.

By 1944, the Japanese already were sending many poorly trained pilots into combat. Because of their lack of experience, these pilots were forced to circle about seventy miles out from their targets while receiving target assignments from their flight leaders. The Americans, who had the benefit of radar, were able to send out interceptors to shoot them down before they got within threatening distance. The Japanese planes that survived during the battle of the Philippine Sea flew on to Guam for fuel and bombs as planned, but the runways there had been so badly torn up by previous U.S. air raids that most of them either crashed or were shot down while waiting for the runways to be cleared.

During the afternoon of June 20, the second day of the battle, an American Avenger scout plane located the enemy fleet some three hundred miles away from the American carrier force. Admiral Marc Mitscher ordered a full attack by all available American planes from his Carrier Task Force 58 even though the distance was almost certainly beyond the planes' range and they would have to return in the dark that night. The American planes caught the Japanese fleet at sunset and inflicted serious damage. On the same day, the American submarines *Albacore* and *Cavalla* sank two Japanese carriers.

As the first of the returning planes approached the American carrier force, Rear Admiral J.J. Clark on the *Hornet* ordered lights turned on, ignoring the danger of discovery by any Japanese force still in the vicinity. Permission was also given for fliers to land on any available deck. In spite of this, many American planes ran out of fuel and were ditched in the ocean, their pilots to be picked up later by submarines, or by the fleet as it resumed steaming toward the enemy. Many other planes were simply dumped over the side once landing had been made on a carrier deck so that the next plane, running out of fuel, could be cleared to land.

The Battle of the Philippine Sea was a victory for the United States that secured the invasion and broke the back of Japanese carrier aviation. In all, the Japanese lost more than 470 aircraft and 450 pilots. Three carriers, including their flagship *Taiho,* were sunk along with close to a dozen destroyers and supply ships. The Americans lost 130 planes, but more than eighty of these were ditched in the water when they ran out of fuel and virtually all those pilots were rescued. No American ships were lost.

Though they would continue to fight ferociously a battle of attrition on the ground, making the marines pay a horrific price for retaking the islands, and its navy still possessed a formidable battleship group, the Japanese would never again be able to mount a serious carrier attack. By November, at the battle of Leyte Gulf, Admiral Ozawa was forced to use his carriers only as bait, rather than as the main attack force, to lure the American fleet north. The battle of Leyte Gulf inflicted real damage on the Fifth Fleet, but in the end that battle as well went to the Americans.

The Japanese fleet was the most powerful in the world, having been built up since the end of World War I for the purpose of controlling the Pacific. But from the outset, it suffered from shortages of fuel. One of the primary goals of the early American strategy was to cut the Japanese navy off from their refineries, and by 1944 they were forced to burn unrefined Borneo crude oil which fouled engines and was also highly explosive. Japan did not have the manufacturing capacity to match the American ability to replace aircraft and other equipment, nor did they have an adequate training program to replace their experienced pilots. Because of this, they had pursued a strategy of quick strikes, hoping to score a decisive victory in a single battle and cause the United States to lose heart.

Victory in the Pacific also represented a victory of logistics on the part of the American military. It required a level of organization that had never been contemplated before. The problems of maintaining supply lines across thousands of miles of ocean were enormous. Nevertheless, the American forces were relatively well supplied and, at least on board ship, its personnel were well fed and cared for, even while staying at sea for as much as a year at a time. The situation for the marines on the ground was often quite different. All over the Pacific, they faced repeated shortages and deprivation. Even so, they fared better than the Japanese soldier.

There remain intriguing questions about key moments before the war in the long standoff between the United States and Japan. Pearl Harbor did not occur in a vacuum. The Japanese invasion of China was inspired in part by the same motive that would later drive the United States for nearly fifty years—the fear and hatred of Communism. Pearl Harbor, which shocked the Japanese public as well as the American, was to some degree the product of attempted and failed rapprochements between Japan and the United States, and motives and intentions on both sides that continue to be reinterpreted a half-century later. Yet despite whatever extenuating factors there were, or whatever uncertainties remain about the causes of this war, World War II quickly became—and remained—the least uncertain of all U.S. wars. There has never been anything like it in American history.

Looking at the entire spectacle of World War II, one is struck by the immensity of it. This war covered nearly the entire globe, with active battlefronts at one time or another throughout the southern, central, and northern Pacific, from New Guinea to the Aleutian Islands, with major action over all of Europe, from the Balkans to England, through much of Asia, including China, Burma, and India, and across the entire zone of the Mediterranean, including North Africa—in fact just about everywhere except the Western Hemisphere. World War II killed over thirty million people and wreaked mass destruction everywhere it went.

The war was fought by a generation raised in austerity during the Great Depression. Their opportunities were limited. Because of economic hard times, few young men like Everett Fulton had the money to go to college, travel, or own a car. World War II was their chance to break out of this kind of life. These men were practical, used to relying on their own ingenuity, and willing to see tough times through to the end.

Everett Fulton was born the son of Ben Fulton and Kate Parker Fulton in Gatesville, Texas, on September 3, 1917. He was the middle sibling among five brothers and one older sister. The family moved to San Angelo, Texas, where Everett graduated from high school in 1936. He soloed his first aircraft at age sixteen, flying a Curtiss-Wright Junior, a high-wing plane sporting a 45-horsepower 3-cylinder radial engine. He earned the thirty dollars that he paid his flight instructor, Luther Reed, by washing milk cans in a creamery for a dollar per day. Luther Reed would later become chief pilot for Braniff Airlines.

Having no money for college, Fulton joined the navy as an apprentice seaman in 1936. After boot camp in San Diego, he was selected to attend machinists school in Norfolk, Virginia, and in late 1937 he reported for duty on the light cruiser *Cincinnati*. When he passed exams to be trained as a naval aviation cadet after reenlisting in 1942, the navy sent him to Abilene Christian University for specialized courses and civilian pilot training, and then to the University of Georgia for courses in math, navigation, aerodynamics, and physics. He reported to Naval Air School in Dallas for primary flight training. While there, he married his high-school sweetheart, Lora Magill. He graduated from advanced flight training at the Naval Air School in Corpus Christi in June of 1943, in the same class with George Bush, whom he remembers as a "young skinny kid."

Bombing Squadron Fourteen, Fulton's squadron, was formed at Wildwood, N.J., in the fall of 1943 and assigned to the newly commissioned Carrier *Wasp*. The *Wasp* made her shakedown cruise off the coast of South America, then squeezed through the Panama Canal and sailed to San Diego to take on four hundred marines for the trip to Hawaii.

Fulton was one of the lowest ranking officers in the squadron and often flew "Tail-End-Charlie," which on occasion afforded him a better view of the action than if he had been in the middle of the formation. Fulton believes he had one other advantage over most of his fellow fliers— his four years' previous experience as a seaman on the *Cincinnati*. This acquaintance with the sea helped him survive long flights over open water when it was necessary for a pilot to accurately read the sea's state. Each shift in wind direction and force had to be taken into account if a pilot expected to find his carrier when returning from a long mission. At times, inaccurate navigation was more to be feared by a carrier pilot than the enemy. Fulton's ability to read the sea no doubt helped him on the evening of June 20, 1944, when he was the only member of his squadron to land safely back on a carrier deck.

In action from May, 1944, through November, Air Group Fourteen pilots averaged forty-two combat missions, a fleet record at the time. The squadron flew sorties against targets from Marcus and Wake islands to Leyte and Luzon. They began with the opening salvo of America's push through the Marianas to retake Saipan on their way to rolling up the Philippines—Saipan, Guam, Mindanao—and were relieved not long after participating in the Battle of Leyte Gulf and flying sorties against Luzon, by which time the Japanese Mobile Fleet and naval aviation was effectively destroyed. Nearly half of the original squadron pilots were lost and even more of the replacement pilots, who arrived after being in transit for four to six weeks without flying practice and were almost immediately launched into combat. Fulton lost seven roommates in as many months.

He earned seven operation and engagement stars and was awarded the Distinguished Flying Cross for "heroism and extraordinary achievement" during the battle of the Philippine Sea.

Upon returning from combat, Fulton was sent to Florida to train fighter pilots in carrier landings. At the end of the war, he took a discharge into the reserves. He was recalled to active duty during the Korean War in 1951, serving as an instructor on the U.S.S. *Monterey* for thirty-three months. He was then ordered to Pearl Harbor where he had responsibility for four hangars and a crew of about two hundred men, providing maintenance to all fleet aircraft transiting the area bounded by Hawaii and Midway Island. He also served on the Admiral's staff and flew with the carrier squadrons. During this tour, he was checked out to fly jet aircraft, including the F9F-8 Cougar Fighter, in which he broke the sound barrier diving from 35,000 feet.

Fulton had begun flying from a west Texas cow pasture in a plane whose top speed was 60 mph and he retired from the navy flying high performance jets faster than the speed of sound. He is now retired and living again in Texas hill country on five acres with a large orchard, a garden, and his wife of fifty years. He builds stringed musical instruments.

Though Fulton doesn't mention it much in his diary, many of his missions served directly as close air support for various marine landings, especially as deterrents to Japanese fighters that attacked the marine beachheads. Planes from the *Wasp* provided either direct air support, or more often, bombed landing facilities and enemy planes caught on the ground. This includes the last action which Fulton participated in during the days following the Battle of Leyte Gulf. The two days of bombing airfields on Luzon, from which the Japanese were flying sorties against marines on Leyte, resulted in the destruction of more than four hundred Japanese aircraft, most of them on the ground. By the end of 1944, the actions from Marianas to Leyte brought the Americans inside the rim of Japan's inner defenses, in command of the air and the sea, and within range of Tokyo.

The Diary of Everett Fulton

May 14, 1944. Aboard the *Wasp* riding at anchor in Majuro lagoon, Marshal Islands. We left Pearl Harbor on May 3rd, anchored here since. Received word today that we will get underway tomorrow for a strike on the Jap held islands of Marcus and Wake. This will be my first combat mission—also the first mission of VB-14[1] and the new *Wasp*.[2]

May 15th. At sea en route to Marcus Island having left Majuro yesterday for an aerial strike on Marcus and Wake islands. This task force will strike the first blow against the Japs holding these islands since September 1943.[3]

May 16th. (At sea.) We had several accidents aboard today with aircraft. An F6F[4] nosed over while being taxied, a TBF[5] and F6F damaged due to contact while turning up the engines. One SB2C[6] dribbled off the bow and into the water, Bob Ohm was the pilot. He experienced a power loss which I believe was due to the long period of operating the engines at low rpm, which fouled the plugs, while we were testing our VHF radios.

May 17th. I flew number two spot[7] on Lt. Cdr. Downing's[8] wing in a mock attack on the task force—our last practice before the strike. We were airborne three hours. An F6F making a strafing run on a sled towed by a ship tore off pieces of his tail assembly in the high speed dive. He apparently forgot to lower his landing gear to the "trail" position which acts as dive brakes. He landed aboard alright.

May 18th. Briefed on target Marcus Island[9] today. We have received information that there are no enemy aircraft on the island. Hope this is true.

May 19th. Our F6Fs held reveille on the Japs at Marcus early this morning with a strafing attack. No enemy planes were seen. Our squadron sent in four waves of dive bombers. One Jap twin engine "Betty"[10] was seen in a revetment. All raids were opposed by A.A. fire of all calibres. The fire was moderate to intense. Three of our bombers were damaged. Ens. Hunicke received a 40-mm hit in the right wing which blew a hole two-by-three feet and set fire to the hydraulic fluid leaking from the broken lines. The fire lasted about five minutes and went out. The heat caused the 20-mm ammunition in his wing guns to explode. It was a miracle he wasn't hurt. He brought the plane aboard without flaps. Lieutenant Walls had two small holes in his tail surfaces and damage to his engine. Lcdr. Downing also received hits in his plane. No personnel were hurt or lost.

One pilot on our sister ship, *Essex*, [11] received a leg wound and returned aboard his ship. The *Essex* lost one plane near the island and the pilot was picked up by our rescue submarine. A TBF pilot from the *Essex* had a radioman to bail out about five miles from the island. He apparently thought the plane had been hit. He was also picked up by the submarine. About 15:00 hours Lcdr. Biros, our fighter squadron skipper and his section sighted a Jap Betty heading for the ships. They shot it down thirty miles from the formation of ships.

We had heavy rain squalls over the target area that hampered the late P.M. strikes. Several fires were started and photographs showed some direct hits. After the day's operation we received a "Well done!" from Admiral Montgomery. [12] He is the same Admiral which I served under at Corpus Christi when I was a cadet there in training. I had the anti-submarine patrol about the task force today.

May 20th. During the night we steamed from the south side of Marcus to the north side and launched dawn attacks. A second wave was sent in at 08:15 hours. I was scheduled to go on this one, but my plane was not loaded in time for the launch. These carriers hate to stay on the same steady course for long as they are easier for the submarines to shoot a torpedo into. The ship must hold a steady course into the wind when launching planes. I ended up staying aboard for the anti-submarine patrol. Ens. Berg took a hit in the windshield portion of his canopy and caused it to craze so badly he could not see through it. He had to hang his head out into the wind coming aboard in order to see the LSO's [13] signals. He came into the ready room and discovered that a sliver of the plexiglass had stuck into his cheek. He asked the flight surgeon to put him down for the Purple Heart. The Doc laughed at him, and so did we.

The *Essex* had a fighter pilot land in the water near the ship as his plane was so badly shot up that it was not stable at approach speeds. The pilot was O.K. The bombing today was more accurate due to better visibility over the target. The Jap's water works was blown up, several gun emplacements were put out of action and an underground hangar and storage was opened up. The Japs put everything of importance underground except their water works. Since they must rely on collected rain water this will give them a long thirst. . . .

And so was Marcus Island. We are now steaming toward Wake Island for the same treatment, but we do expect a "warmer" welcome there.

May 21st. Underway for Wake Island. Learned today the *Essex* had a dive bomber go straight in on the target. The pilot, Ens. Nixon, never pulled out of his dive. He and I were cadets in the same class at dive-bomber training in Kingsville, Texas. That makes a loss of two lives and three aircraft at Marcus. Tokyo Radio claimed to have shot down thirty-two of our planes. . . . We are being briefed on target Wake.

May 22nd. Received target assignment today. Making final preparations for the attack tomorrow.

May 23rd. We made five strikes on Wake Island today. I was on the second raid. We dived from 14,000 feet at targets on Peacock Point. I carried two 500-lb and two 100-lb bombs. I saw very little A.A. fire and no small-arms fire at all. It seemed they were short of ammunition and would not open up unless our planes came very low. After the dive we made two strafing runs with our 20-mm guns. Ens. Heath had his windshield shattered by two bullets. Lieutenant (j.g.) Skaggs got hit in the left wing by an explosive shell which tore a large hole in the leading edge. All our planes returned aboard. The *Essex* with air group fifteen was less fortunate. One fighter plane in on the target; one TBF went down on the way back from the target with the three-man crew, and one dive bomber made it back inside the destroyer screen before ditching—crew was saved. Many buildings, water storages and fuel storages were blown up by bombs and strafing. Many guns were put out of action by strafing. . . . We are leaving Wake Island for our anchorage at Majuro. [14]

May 25 to June 6th. Each day during our anchorage in Majuro lagoon, new ships arrive until the harbor is bulging with hundreds of ships of every class. We are gathering our great armada for the invasion of the Marianas Islands. We have had many briefings on the operation by the U.S. Marine General in command of the landings. These islands of the Mariana chain, except for Guam, have been under Japanese control for many years and they are expected to be our toughest fight so far. . . .

We pulled out this P.M. (June 6) for the Marianas. We are to strike Tinian, Saipan and Guam.[15] After the air assaults and shipboard gunfire have mauled the Japanese defenses, we will make the landings. We have with us the largest fleet of men-o-war the world has ever seen. Around us are more major naval ships than are at present invading the continent of Europe.[16]

Today, June 6th, we received our first word of the invasion in France. We know that the show we are about to stage cannot compare in men and the number of small craft involved in Europe, but I think of the thousands of miles we have traveled to reach our beachhead. All of our supplies of every description must be carried with us as our nearest supply bases are several thousand miles away. We stand to come to grips with the Jap fleet, engaging them in waters they have controlled for years. I believe we are well prepared to meet all possibilities. This operation will be a great blow to the Japs as it will neutralize all her South Pacific bases, especially the naval bastion of Truk.[17] More than one hundred thousand troops, mostly veteran marines, will hit the beaches. Their average age is thirty-eight and the toughest men alive—anywhere.

June 7, 1944. Aboard the U.S.S. *Wasp* heading for the occupation of the Jap-held Marianas Islands. We spend our days en route to battle in various ways. We go over our battle plans and emergency procedures and play cards. Every morning before daybreak and every evening at sundown we have general quarters. All the ship's compartments are sealed as single units because the hours of twilight are the most critical for submarine attack.[18] At night the ships run without visible lights on the weather decks and maintain their position in the formation by using radar. Every fifteen minutes the whole fleet changes course, zig zagging toward the west.

June 8th. Steaming westward. This large fleet is broken into smaller Task Groups. Our group has two carriers of the Essex class, two light carriers, two Iowa-class battle ships, three light cruisers and twelve destroyers.

June 9th. We rendezvoused with our fleet oilers to replenish our fuel oil [19] and aviation gasoline supply aboard. Ships of all classes may be seen in all directions as far as the eye can see. Steaming westward.

June 10th. We launched search patrols today to the north of our task force. We maintained anti-submarine patrols yesterday while the oiling was in progress as the oil tanker and ship being oiled must steam a steady course and are vulnerable to submarine attack. Our carriers are surrounded by battleships. Outside of the battleships are a ring of cruisers, and on the outer rim are the destroyers. A submarine would have to penetrate the three screens to get to the carriers. On the searches, aircraft search each 20-degree [20] sector around the ship for a specified distance. Our planes are armed with depth charges and would attack any submarine sighted. Each of us carry a chart showing the "sanctuaries" assigned to our own submarines and since a submarine running submerged is next to impossible to identify, we do not attack any submarine in the sanctuary.

June 11th. (Sunday) Nearing enemy territory. One of our fighter pilots, Ens. Red Stokes, shot down a twin engine medium bomber "Helen" [21] while on CAP [22] about noon. We are about 150 miles from the target. We sent in a fighter sweep this P.M. which caught some thirty Jap bombers on the ground on Tinian Island. They were strafed and set afire. Very few enemy fighters were encountered. Our sister carrier lost one F6F near the target. It is highly possible the pilot will be picked up as he was last seen in his life raft. Our group lost no planes.

Tomorrow is our big day. We start our attacks and do not stop until the islands of Saipan and Tinian are captured by our ground forces. Rota and Guam come a few days later.

June 12th. The fighter sweep of yesterday afternoon reported all enemy aircraft sighted on the ground were destroyed, but the Japs must have had some in underground hangars—or they could have flown them in from Rota or Guam—as we were hunted by a sizable formation of Jap planes from midnight to dawn. They were trying to locate us by dropping flares, but most of them floated down miles from the force. About 04:00 hours a Jap plane sneaked through our screen and got within two thousand yards of our ship where the battleship *New Jersey* shot it down. About 05:30 hours a fighter from the light carrier *Cabot* shot down a Jap dive bomber (Judy).[23] Our first strike was launched at 05:30 to bomb and strafe Tinian's airfields.

Our second strike was launched at 07:15. I flew on this mission and we met moderate but inaccurate A.A. fire. Our group took no damage and got in some good hits on gun emplacements and made a second dive for strafing. One of our fighter pilots and my very good roommate, Ens. Lowry of Houston, Texas, was hit by A.A. fire and went in on the target. There is no chance he survived the crash. A fine man lost. . . .

I saw many fires on Tinian Island. It is very pretty—grows mostly sugar cane and will make us a very good base. Saipan, close by, is a little larger, but with rough terrain features. There are approximately fifty thousand Japanese civilians on the two islands. Our latest count is forty-two Jap aircraft destroyed and only five of these were in the air. This indicates we had the element of surprise. Barracks, oil storages and warehouses have been blown apart. There are about twenty small boats in the area. Some TBFs from another carrier sank an oil tanker twenty miles northwest of here.

I was scheduled to make the last strike, but my plane developed a fuel leak and I remained aboard. The bombing was made on air strips to prevent the Japs from bringing in planes during the night. The runways and hangars were pulverized. Planes from this ship dropped napalm on Titian Town [24] and left it burning fiercely. One fighter pilot reported he made a strafing run right down Main Street. Many delayed action bombs were dropped to explode every half hour throughout the night. We laid-off to the northwest of the island and bombs were heard exploding all night.

June 13th. Only patrol planes took to the air today. Our big battleships and heavy cruisers moved in close and poured shells into Saipan and Tinian for five hours. Many fires were started. Yesterday, Radio Tokyo reported that a "small" U.S. task force was making a "nuisance" raid on the Marianas Islands. It is a "nuisance" that will cost them four of their major island bases and several thousand citizens. One of our destroyers picked up about fifty Jap seamen from the oil tanker sunk yesterday. We have seen a lot of wreckage on the sea surface. One of our F6F fighters, Ens. Malarski, was forced to land in the water near a destroyer due to damage from A.A. fire over the target this morning. He was quickly rescued. No Japanese planes have been sighted in the past forty hours. Tonight the surface forces are bombarding the islands. We are about twenty miles out and the gun flashes and fires are plainly visible. From air observer reports, the shore line of the island has literally been plowed up by shipboard gunfire. This will be the second night of no sleep for the Japs.

The population of Garapan and Saran-Kanoa towns were warned to evacuate before the shelling began by air leaflet drop this morning. One spotter for the shipboard gunfire saw a suspicious looking building with a big red cross painted on it. A salvo was fired into it and the building blew sky high. It was an ammunition dump marked as a hospital. They are doomed and cut off from all possible aid. I have the anti-submarine patrol around the bombarding ships tomorrow morning. I am somewhat eager to get a look at what has been done the past two days.[25]

June 14th. I had the ASP[26] today and got to see little of the action for I drew the sector that ran down by Rota Island. Our bombers continued attacks against the Japanese shore gun positions. The surface ships bombarded the shoreline again today, starting new fires. The frogmen, underwater demolition crews, were busy setting explosive charges to either clear underwater obstructions or to blast a channel through the coral for the landing barges tomorrow, the day of the invasion. The Japs had placed sharpened steel beams in the water at an angle to rip open the bottoms of the landing craft. Our demolition crews placed the charges during the day and waited until after dark to explode them so the Japs could not see where the channels had been blasted as they would train their shore guns on them when the invasion begins.

June 15th, 1944. Our air group gave air support to the troops landing on Saipan. Reports are coming in that our landing troops are meeting stiff resistance. By sundown our Marines had captured the airbase north of Sharan-Kanoa[27] and penetrated two thousand yards inland. This P.M. I flew a raid on Rota. My target was a group of barracks near the airfield. I strafed them with my 20-mm guns during the dive and dropped a thousand-pound bomb. My strike leader gave me credit for a hit. We also made strafing runs on two small cargo vessels anchored near Rota town. We left them smoking. Very little A.A. fire was seen on this hop. We had our first Jap planes in days over our task group last night. They apparently came from one of their carriers west of here. Five of the Japs were shot down and the others fled. . . .

I heard today that spotters for the shipboard guns saw a group of Jap civilians on a cliff north of Garapan and they were throwing their children over then jumping after them to their death below. It was a mass suicide. Late yesterday afternoon small boats were sent in near the beach with loud speakers and a Japanese linguist to try and discourage the mass suicide. It is estimated that about two thousand persons chose this method of escape from being captured by our troops. The Jap military must have told them they would be horribly tortured if captured by us. If the people are judging how we would treat them by the conduct of the Jap army toward prisoners they capture, it is not hard to understand how they arrived at the decision to jump off the cliff.[28]

Tokyo Radio has dropped the nuisance raid term and is now saying they are sending the Imperial Fleet to put us to flight. We have seen nothing of it yet. Perhaps these are statements to bolster the morale of the Saipan defenders. . . .[29]

June 16th. The ground forces have met with rather stiff Jap resistance on Saipan. Our air group gave air support in knocking out gun emplacements and troop concentrations.[30] Tonight we will head west and search about four hundred miles for the Jap fleet. Indications are that they are launching some planes from somewhere west of here as one Jap plane was shot down at sunset. We refueled today and there is a feeling the Jap fleet just might try to interfere with our Saipan landing.

June 17th. Last night we launched a pair of night fighters to investigate an unidentified airborne radar contact. They were vectored in close enough to pick up the target plane on their aircraft on-board radar and closed in for the kill without ever seeing the plane knocked down. On returning to our task force the night fighters were fired on by our destroyer screen gun crews. They got back aboard after a slight delay. Today our search planes scouted 350 miles west, but found no Jap ships. A fighter and a dive bomber on patrol shot down a Jap medium bomber. We are about 200 miles west of the Marianas. After sunset the Jap planes visited us again. One Jap dive bomber (Judy) was shot down by shipboard gun fire and the others fled. Tokyo Radio announced tonight that a high ranking Jap admiral had been killed in aerial battle southwest of the Marianas. We assume that he was in the transport our night fighters got two nights ago. Mel Mor and Brown made a long search today with no results. John Magee and fighter pilot Keefer shot down a Betty while on a search mission. A longer range search using TBFs will be launched about 01:00 in the morning. The TBFs can carry more fuel and go farther.

June 18th. Early this A.M. we launched VT-14[31] pilots Poole, Weeks, Williams, Drake, McKeever, and Yarbrough on a long night search for the Jap fleet. We are seeing carrier based Jap planes and the fleet must be out there somewhere. One Judy was shot down by our fighter CAP.

June 19th. We were west of Guam by this morning. Our search planes have not yet found the Jap fleet. We were attacked by about one hundred Jap fighters and bombers at 11:00 hours. Our defending fighters were launched about 10:30 to intercept them. One of our fighter pilots said his flight was heading west when they ran head on into about sixty Jap planes. Our fighters got most of these and the ones who got through were downed by our ships. Jap planes were literally falling like flies. It was like seeing an exaggerated Hollywood production of an air battle—for real. A small number of Jap pilots bailed out which is a rare act for them and did little good for they were many hundreds of miles from land with no raft. The Jap pilots are noted for machine-gunning our pilots who bail out and perhaps they think we will do the same thing. They have little chance to survive out here as they do not use submarines to rescue their downed pilots.

While our fighter planes were fully engaged, a few of the Nip dive bombers sneaked through. They began shallow runs on us and the sky was instantly filled with heavy A.A. fire from all the ships. More Jap planes began falling into the sea. As we watched a diving plane it suddenly turned into a blob of falling debris. Wings floated crazily down, detached from the aircraft. Jap bombers got through and dropped a heavy bomb just off our port bow. Fragments from the bomb killed a ship's gunner and wounded four others. I had been standing on the flight deck taking in the show and after the bomb hit, I went down to the ready room for a bracing cup of coffee and found our mess steward had locked himself in the pantry and refused to open up. That made two of us who were scared.

One of our light cruisers took a bomb hit which started a fire but it was quickly controlled. Our ship shot down five dive bombers that were so close that parts from the exploding plane landed on our flight deck. One of them had a load of incendiary bombs and pieces of this magnesium material started small fires about the wooden flight deck. The only damage from this material was to the shoe of the ship's executive office, CDR. Slattery, who attempted to extinguish a fragment by stepping on it. His shoe began to burn and he quickly removed it.

All the attacking planes are carrier-based and we have scouted 350 miles to the west without finding the enemy carriers. Evidently they are even farther away which is beyond our scout range. Even the Japanese pilots could not cover that distance and return to their carriers if they survived the attack on us. The probable answer is that the survivors are going on to Guam which is still held by them.[32] The Guam airfields were bombed several days ago, but they can easily fill the holes with crushed coral. The Guam airfields were bombed again this P.M. Returning from the Guam raid our bombers shot down a Judy. Haggerty and Coari teamed up to shoot down a Betty while on a 325-mile search. We were raided by dive bombers again this afternoon. They were intercepted by our fighters and the sky was thick with falling Japanese planes. Our fighters followed some of the Jap planes into Guam and many were shot down while attempting to land there. The best estimates are that the enemy lost 250 aircraft and crews on this single day. Our ship lost only one fighter plane and one bomber plane when Bingham landed in the sea beside a destroyer after his plane was severely damaged by A.A. fire over Guam. It was an exciting day and a tense one. I had the standby to hit the Jap fleet had our scouts found them. Not one of our ships suffered any real damage.

June 20, 1944 (June 19th. in the U.S.). A few Japanese snooper planes were trying to spot us throughout the night. No attacks were attempted by them. I am convinced that our very good radar system saved the fleet considerable damage yesterday. The Jap planes were being picked up over eighty miles away which gave us plenty of time to launch intercepts and cut their flights to bits before they could reach our ships. We received word that one of our submarines had sunk a large Jap carrier west of here yesterday. Also, one Jap heavy cruiser was damaged. We are steaming west and have not been attacked since yesterday. We held a burial at sea today for gunner Bridges who was killed by the near miss of the Jap bomb yesterday.

Our skipper's division and Lieutenant Kane's division (the one I'm in) had the standby for strike duty. At 15:30 hours contact was at last made with the Jap fleet. Our scout planes reported the main body of the fleet 275 miles west (we had closed a lot of distance during the night). Still, this was too far for us to go and return without auxiliary fuel tanks.[33] Our planes had been loaded and ready all day, but there were bombs where the fuel tanks should be. There was no time to change if we expected to hit the enemy before sunset. By morning they could be long gone.

We were launched at 16:00 (4 P.M.), and as soon as I got airborne, the fuel mixture was leaned out as far as I dared. We joined up in formation and headed west, climbing to 15,000 feet. We had twelve dive bombers from our squadron plus torpedo and fighters from our air group. The other carriers in the task force had a like number of planes heading west for a showdown with the Imperial fleet. We knew they had lost a lot of aircraft and would have a greatly reduced air group to defend against our attack. This was our golden opportunity to break the back of the Jap fleet. I flew the "tail-end-charlie" position loosely to keep throttle changes to a fuel-saving minimum. Quinlan[34] and I wasted no energy in conversation on the flight west. This was our most serious challenge and we met it with serious silence.

At 18:15 hours we spotted a group of ships consisting of six oil tankers, large freighters and escorted by six destroyers. We knew this force was the supply train for the main Japanese fleet. We were looking for larger game, so we headed south and searched for forty miles but sighted nothing. At this point we were as close to the Philippine Islands as we were to our own ship (approx. 300 miles). The Skipper headed us back north again. We had used over half our fuel at this time and the sun was about gone. Upon sighting the Jap supply train for the second time, the Skipper gave the attack signal. The other air groups had found the main fleet northwest of our position. Next to enemy aircraft carriers, supply ships have priority over all other ships as targets and we were going in on these. The

Skipper, Jack Blitch, must have been very excited for he forgot to open his bomb bay doors and therefore did not drop his bombs. Since I was the last to dive, my section leader, Scatourchio, had passed the vertical position for a downwind dive and I had to fly far enough past the vertical and dive upwind. All this time I was passing over the Jap ships, they were shooting at me and I was changing course constantly.

At 15,000 feet the A.A. shell bursts looked so harmless, more like someone throwing oranges at me, but the large puffs of black smoke near my plane told me otherwise. I finally got into my dive but was not steep enough, so I took a step forward.[35] The ship I was going after was a large fleet oil tanker. The wind aloft from the east was so strong I had to take two more steps as I kept shallowing up in my dive. Just before I released my bomb, I saw a torpedo plane coming in low on the tanker from the east. I worried my bomb might hit him, but had to release it. I was grateful the TBF had drawn away some of the A.A. fire from me. I was too busy jinking[36] to look back until I was several miles to the east. Quinlan said my bombs had hit near the port side of the ship and shortly TBF's fish had blown the ship apart from the starboard side. When I did get a chance to look back, a huge mountain of flames covered the tanker. The sun was already down and the flames showed brightly in the dusk.

Blitch had set the rendezvous point as ten miles east of the target and when I got there only one of our planes was waiting. Pethic of our squadron was circling and I joined on him. I checked my plotting board and my fuel gauges and the sickening realization of our hopeless lack of fuel to return to our ship hit me. The time was 19:45 (7:45 P.M.) and the dusk suddenly turned to dark as we were in the lower latitudes where twilight is short-lived. Shortly a TBF from the *Essex* and two F6Fs joined our group. Pethic was circling, waiting for other planes, when we overheard Blitch report his position as forty miles east of the target and heading for home. Pethic turned us east and we all turned on our navigation lights so we could keep formation in the dark.

Our fuel was very low. It took 200 gallons to get us out here and we had only about 120 gallons to get us back. We had about 255 miles to go when I checked my plotting board. Pethic took up the right course until we started hitting some heavy rain squalls, then he started veering left and climbing. I had Quinlan to pass him a blinker light message questioning his course. His answer was that he was turning the lead over to the TBF because he had better search radar. The TBF changed course still farther left of the course I wanted to fly and continued to climb to get out of the lousy weather. I rechecked my plotting board and was convinced we were heading thirty degrees too far left and I did not want to climb because that takes extra fuel which we did not have. My best judgment caused me to break away from the small group, stay low and take up the heading I believed to be correct.

I stayed on instruments in the foul weather and was half blinded by the lightning flashes. In the SB2C the pilot and radio gunner are in separate cockpits and cannot see each other, but I knew Larry would do the praying for us as he was a devout Irish Catholic and the Southern Baptist in me was happy to have him aboard. The fuel tank I was on ran dry and the engine quit. I switched to another tank, the engine caught and on we went. I did some serious thinking about every way I could cut my fuel consumption. I placed my left thumb back of the mixture control and with my right hand I moved the mixture control back notch by notch until the engine stopped. I left my left thumb on the notched quadrant, moved the control forward to start the engine with my right hand and then moved my left thumb forward two notches from the idle-cut-off position. I brought the mixture control back to my left thumb and ran the engine in that very lean position. I pulled the engine rpm back to 1800 which caused a very high manifold pressure. I also remembered that the right wing tank was the vapor return tank which collected several gallons of fuel condensate from the induction ring of the engine per hour of running. I would leave this tank for last.

Quinlan reported our radar was being jammed. I turned up the volume on my VHF radio but heard nothing. My radio homing ZBX[37] gave me nothing but static. . . . My engine quit again and I switched to my last tank of seventy-five gallons. There was still a long way to go. . . .

Soon radio reports could be heard on my VHF from other planes. Some were calling for a vector (course and distance to the ship), but that was futile for we were not close enough to raise the ship. We were not allowed to open up on our LF radio[38] as it carried too far and the Japs could get a fix on us. Some of the pilots reported that they had only minutes of fuel left and were going to bail out. Others said they were going to make a hazardous night water landing. Some gave their positions and some did not. The frequency of these calls increased as time passed—some bordered on panic and those who stayed airborne long enough to get within radio range of the ship were heard and their positions plotted for later rescue. I decided we would try a water landing rather than bail out and lose our large raft in the plane. I had a small seat-pack raft on my parachute, but Quinlan had none and would surely be lost if I bailed out on him. We still had over an hour's fuel remaining and a long way to go. We planned to make an instrument let down to where my altimeter read fifty feet. Larry would fire a Verys pistol flare and we hoped we would be able to determine our true height above the water for the landing. This way we could save all our emergency food and water and other equipment.

We continued on our course and the distress calls mounted. All this was the result of our eagerness to destroy the Jap fleet. The Imperial fleet had paid its price and now each of us had to face our part of the bill.

In our planes we have a very useful gadget called a relief tube. It is a urinal made from a small plastic funnel with a tube attached and leading to the outside of the aircraft. We had been airborne for quite a while and I needed to use the gadget, but it would not come free from its mounting bracket under the seat. I had to zip up and forget it. As the minutes and miles passed I checked my radio ZBX and my plotting board. My best hope was my navigation, as the radio was not good at low altitude and we did not have the fuel to climb. At 21:00 (9 P.M.) my fuel gauge read forty gallons remaining. According to my navigation we should be close to home. At 21:10 I sighted a small searchlight through the clouds. What a beautiful sight. This was most unusual for a ship to turn on a visible light at night in enemy waters, but considering what we had come through I guess the command decided this was "Be kind to pilots night." Actually, only the outer destroyer screen was showing lights and the carriers were still running dark except for the shielded masthead light which could only be seen from the air. The clouds were not so thick around the ship formation.

I headed for what looked like a carrier and arrived at the ship at 21:30 and entered the landing pattern. I had never landed on a carrier at night, but I was eager to try. The first carrier I made an approach on waved me off early and as I went by it I saw the small CVL[39] had a deck full of planes. There was another a few miles east and I headed for it. My fuel gauge was near ZERO. I would estimate there were more than fifteen planes in the landing pattern when six planes is normal. I took my interval on a plane upwind and entered the pattern. The night was so dark I could not make out what carrier it was, nor did I care with so little fuel left. While in the upwind portion of my approach, I noticed a plane with a large blinking red light on my level, heading in the opposite direction. I had to shove the stick forward to avoid a collision. We nearly hit the water. Gaining back our approach altitude we continued our approach. Coming into the final part of the approach near the ramp I was having trouble seeing the LSO's signals when I realized that my green hook-down light was reflecting off my oil-smeared windshield. Most dive bombers are gum chewers to keep their ears clear and I planted my well worn cud on that green light. At the ramp I got the cut signal and felt the wheels hit the deck, then that best-of-all-feelings of the hook picking up the wire with the rapid deceleration that follows.

As I taxied forward there was this huge outline of the stack on the right side and I knew I was aboard the *Enterprise,* the BIG "E." I was very, very glad to be aboard. Quinlan climbed out of the rear cockpit and stood on the wing beside me. Putting one arm across my shoulder, he extended his hand and said, "I want to shake your hand." He was no happier than I. I looked back in the landing area on the flight deck and saw two planes hit the deck at the same time. One was an F6F who landed long and the other was an SBD[40] without approach lights and he landed short. The LSO worked the F6F which had lights and did not see the SBD below him. Shortly after witnessing this unreal incident, an SBD in final approach ran out of fuel about 150 feet short of the ramp and landed in the wake of the ship. His running lights stayed on as the plane sank. Moments later another plane took a wave-off to the right and ran out of gas abeam of the island. . . .

I felt unsafe standing just forward of the landing area under these adverse conditions as a plane can bounce off the deck on a hard landing and leap the barriers and crash among the planes parked forward. A plane handler had checked our fuel tanks at my request and reported them dry and perhaps a gallon or two left in the fuel strainers. Quinlan and I left the flight deck. Looking back on our "Helldiver" with gratitude, I read her nickname painted on her cowling, "Incredible Lady," a most fitting name.

Descending the ladder to the pilot's ready room, my joints felt stiff after the long (five and a half hours) tense flight. I learned from the LSO that brought me aboard that he thought he was working an F4U (Marine fighter) and wondered where it had come from. Mine was the first SB2C he had landed aboard. I also learned that the plane with the flashing red light was a Jap plane, apparently from Guam. [41] Several observers reported seeing the large "meatball" on it. It is thought some of the ships had shot it down. The LSO said the carriers on the west side of Task Force 58 were getting all the business tonight because the planes did not have enough fuel to reach those farther east. In fact, the light carrier I made my first approach on had filled up real quick and started landing one aboard, removing the crew then pushing the plane over the side to make room for landing another. Normally, after a day of combat missions the flight surgeon issues each of the airmen a small brandy, but only one. Tonight in the *Enterprise* ready room there were open cases of brandies—help yourself. . . . After three brandies I tried to get some sleep in a ready room bunk, but those frantic radio calls kept ringing in my ears and all night I wondered about my shipmates on the flight. [42] I felt real bad that I had not made it back to my own ship, the *Wasp*. . . . I felt I had forgotten how to sleep. . . .

June 21, 1944. I had breakfast aboard the *Enterprise* this morning and felt alone as I did not know anyone aboard. I still felt embarrassed that I had not made it back to my own ship last night. After breakfast Quinlan and I launched and flew back to the *Wasp*.

Upon landing, we were besieged with handshakes and congratulations as we learned that we were the only one from our squadron to make it back. On our sister ship, the *Essex*, none of the dive bombers made it back. My division leader, Lieutenant Joe Kane, had made it to the outer destroyer screen and ran out of gas. He left his sinking plane and when a nearby destroyer gave no sign they had seen him and were passing him by, he pulled his .38-calibre pistol and began firing tracers at the bridge. A destroyer farther back in the formation picked him up.

June 22, 1944. We got word this morning that our Skipper, Blitch, had been picked up from his life raft by a patrol plane. He had hit the water at high speed some distance from the Task Force. He said he was flying along and the next thing he knew he was in the water trying to inflate his small raft. His chief radio gunner went down with the plane. Yesterday I was called up to see Admiral Baker and he questioned me about the possible positions of downed aircraft. I had copied down a few though the radio was so jammed with frantic calls for vectors that I could not make out most of them. I gave him the course of the group led by Pethic which I had left near the target. None of this group have been accounted for to this date. Amussen and Berg were picked out of the water by destroyers and returned to the ship today. The ones unaccounted for are Browne, Stanley, Walraven, Haff, Connett, Scatourchio and Pethic. Our hopes are high they will be found as we have destroyers, patrol planes, carrier-based aircraft and submarines searching for them.

Our damage to the Jap fleet was fair considering the great distance we had to go to hit them. We sank one of their large carriers, seriously damaged two small carriers, left one battleship burning, one cruiser hit, one destroyer believed sunk, two large fleet oilers exploded, three large supply ships believed sunk, plus many Jap aircraft shot down. Our torpedo squadron, VT-14, was credited with the sinking of the large fleet oilers.

Before this action our Task Force had destroyed about six hundred Jap planes and we had lost only twenty-five planes and twelve flight personnel. This remarkable average will be lessened by our losses in the Philippine Sea Battle for at present our missing pilots number forty-nine and we lost over one hundred aircraft in the night engagement. No doubt many of these pilots will be found and returned as only a small percentage of these were lost to enemy action over the target. . . . Our CAP shot down two large Jap flying boats trying to scout our position. We lost contact with the Jap fleet yesterday just east of the Philippines. They are running back to Tojo beaten and less some seven hundred aircraft and pilots that cannot be easily replaced. [43]

June 23, 1944. Admiral Nimitz sent our Task Force the following message, "Well done! You have written another glorious page in naval history. The damage you have inflicted upon the enemy's fleet cannot be easily repaired. You have made our occupation of Saipan secure." Scatourchio and Blitch were returned to our ship by a destroyer. Blitch told of losing his gunner, Runyon, and spending forty hours in his small raft before being rescued by an OS2U. [44] Scat and his gunner had made a controlled water landing while they still had fuel and saved all their survival gear. A destroyer picked them up thirty-five hours later.

Yesterday, G. Kellogg of our VT-14, found a Jap seaplane while on ASP. His guns jammed and he put his plane in a position where his crewman Hathaway and Lucas could fire on it. They set one engine afire before our fighters arrived and splashed it. Kellogg had even tried to drop his load of depth charges on the seaplane without luck.

June 24, 1944. Since it was possible for the Japs to stage-in aircraft to the northern islands of the Marianas group, we raided Pagan Island[45] today. We bombed and strafed the airfield until it looked like a plowed field. We met no air opposition and very little A.A. fire. We set fire to and sank four small island freighters and sampans. Our group suffered no losses or damage. The radio news stated that our victory over the Jap fleet was highly praised by our officials and that it was a great victory marking the beginning of a new phase of the Pacific war.

Our troops on Saipan have everything under control and have destroyed all reinforcements sent in by the enemy before the barges could land. The large Aslito airfield has been captured and two squadrons of Army Air Force fighters are using it. Soon B-29s will launch from there to bomb Japan. Scatourchio reported seeing Stanley land in the water and thinks Walraven did the same a short time later.[46] We are heading for Eniwetok[47] for fuel, bombs, replacement aircraft and, most important of all, MAIL.

June 25, 1944. Steaming for Eniwetok anchorage. We had word that additional survivors from our Philippine Sea battle have been picked up by our submarines. It is now estimated that the Japs have lost over one thousand planes and pilots in the actions of the past three weeks. Also, some of our submarines were able to sink some of the Jap cripples that were trying to make it to the Philippines for repair. We now know they lost two large carriers plus two more damaged. At least two large fleet oilers and four large supply ships were sent to the bottom.

June 26th. Underway for Eniwetok anchorage.

June 27th–30th. Anchored in Eniwetok during this period. We went ashore on this island, but outside of cold beer there is not much there. Only a few palm trees remain after the battle for the island. The Navy and Marines have built a nice base here, but coral dust is everywhere. Nearly every pup tent has a hand-made clothes washing machine in front of it.

These are made from scrap metal, wood and a bucket of about five-gallon capacity. A crankshaft is attached to the fan and a rod is attached to the crank throw. At the bottom end of the rod is a funnel attached by the spout to the rod so that the open end of the funnel faces down. The G.I. puts in some salt water, salt water soap and his dirty clothes, then leaves it to the wind to churn it up and down all day long. A very ingenious gadget—very useful, too.

June 30, 1944. Pulled anchor this A.M. and headed out to sea for more strike duty. This time we will hit only six hundred miles from Japan proper. We know there are large concentrations of aircraft in the Bonin Islands [48] and we intend to make them into a junk heap.

July 1, 1944. Steaming for the Bonin Islands. Our target in that group of islands is Iwo Jima. We expect a warm reception.

July 2–3, 1944. Steaming north. We strike Iwo Jima tomorrow.

July 4, 1944. Our planes made a dawn attack against Iwo Jima [49] and planes from another group hit Chichi Jima and Haha Jima all in the Bonin Island group. We sent our patrols within 250 miles of the coast of Japan. One patrol found a group of ships 300 miles south of Tokyo and called for support. There were three destroyers, one large AK [50] and one light cruiser. My division made the strike against these ships. We could not find the cruiser and suppose that the bombs dropped on it by the patrol sank it. We hit the AK and the remaining destroyer and left both dead in the water. The DD [51] was being abandoned by its crew. The AK burned. We flew back by Haha Jima and Chichi Jima where we observed many burning ships in the harbors. These islands seem to be volcanic in origin as they are very rough and peaked. After the pilots had knocked out the enemy aircraft, our cruisers moved in and shelled the islands. Our total losses in planes and personnel are not known yet. [52] Our fighters bagged a good score in Jap planes. Gordon Bjornson shot down one Zero. John Drake of VT-14 was shot down over Iwo Jima. He made it off shore before landing in the water. During his eight-hour stay in the water the Japs mistook him for one of them and dropped him a life raft and a dye packet. He was picked up by a cruiser OS2U. We lost two F6Fs and pilots, one TBF and our VB squadron lost two planes and one pilot, Ens. Brady. These two were lost near the ship due to engine failure.

When we were diving on the ships just south of Japan, my section leader, Scatourchio forgot to open his dive flaps and he went down like a rock, passed up everybody in the dive and made a spectacular pull-out ending up on his back at 3,000 feet. He had blacked out during the recovery and had not come around until he had climbed very steeply back to the inverted position.

While in this area I thought of my younger brother, Ben, being held prisoner somewhere not too far away.[53] I wished I had a way to let him know we are getting closer every day. He was part of the submarine crew *Grenadier* lost to Jap depth charges and bombs off the island of Penang, Malaysia, over a year ago. On my way back to the ship, I lost my generator and did not realize it until the electric prop on my SB2C-3 had lost considerable rpm and I was held last for coming aboard. I had to make a gliding approach as I could not have gone around if I missed. In that case there would be only one choice, land in the water. Everything went well until just a few feet above the deck and I caught some air turbulence (stack and island wash), my right wing dropped and I was heading for a gun turret. I felt the hook catch a wire and it stopped me inches from the turret. Tonight we had a fine dinner of roast turkey with all the trimmings from soup to nuts. For dessert—pie a-la-mode.

July 5th. We are steaming south to the Marianas. Guam[54] will probably be our next target. To date, I have lost four roommates. I have to inventory their personal effects and pull out anything that might be embarrassing to their family. I have accumulated quite a liquor stock. Most of the others have depleted their private stocks brought out from Pearl Harbor and some visit me often after hard days of combat flying for a glass of tension reliever.

On many nights I find a half of a glass of whiskey and water is the only way I can relax and get a sound night's sleep. "Sleep that mends the ravelled sleeve of care," and "Sleep, beloved from pole to pole, blessed be to Mary queen that sent the sleep that slid into my soul."[55]

July 6th. A small group of our planes hit the island of Pagan today just to be sure there was no build up of planes by the Japs. Our Air Group Commander (I will not use his name) got his fourth plane today. The trouble with that is, all four were our F6Fs. He insists on taking a combat flight now and then,[56] but he has not flown enough in recent months to keep proficient in carrier landings, if he ever was. He flies an F6F with the numeral "ONE," painted on the side. After a strike he is the first to make a landing approach on the ship, but is always the last to get aboard because he makes bad approaches and does not answer the LSO's signals. LSO Simpson finally cuts him in desperation and CAG[57] floats up the deck and into the cable barriers, wrecking the plane. Today was his fifth hop and his fourth crash into the barrier. Today Simpson lost his patience and turned his paddles over to his assistant LSO and headed for the bridge mumbling, "Let the s.o.b. land in the water." The assistant LSO finally gave him a "cut" and CAG ended up in the barrier.[58] Tonight some joker painted four American flags on the side of CAG's wrecked plane. He was trying, and I felt this was an unnecessary jest. I hope when I get his age and am tied down with administrative duties that I will have the good sense to stay out of carrier aviation.

July 7th. We are nearing the Marianas Islands.

July 8th. Our CAP knocked down three Zekes and three Judys early this morning trying to sneak a punch at us. I made an air strike on Guam. We bombed airfields and selected Jap buildings. Two Jap Zeros were shot down by our fighters. Our fighter squadron Skipper was hit while strafing. A large A.A. shell tore off one of his wings and he crashed. He was our only loss for the day. Our bombing results were good. After the air strikes, our ships moved in and bombarded the island with shipboard gun fire. It is confirmed that Lcdr. Biros, VF-14 C.O. was killed today.

July 9–15th. During this period we made strikes on Guam, Rota, and I made one ASP. A navy radioman was rescued from Guam by a destroyer. The radioman had sent a flashing light signal to the ships while they were bombarding the island, they returned and picked him up. He had been on the island for several years hiding out in the hills with the natives since the

Japs invaded Guam. We experienced some bad weather during this period.

July 18th. Our squadron bombed Guam four times today. I made two of the strikes. It rained on us all day, but we continued our raids. Minesweepers were busy clearing the harbor of mines in preparation for the invasion. One of our LSTs [59] got stuck on a reef about three hundred yards offshore. The battleships, cruisers and destroyers kept the Jap shore batteries silent while other small craft went in and towed the LST clear. If a Jap shore gun opened up it would be his last round fired as his flash would give his position away and the ships and aircraft would pounce on it with savage fury—bomb and shell.

July 19th. I made two of four strikes on Guam today. The island is beginning to look as if it has small pox. [60]

July 20th. Struck Guam twice again today. The island has been shelled and bombed from dawn to dusk since the eighteenth. The air over the island stinks of burned gun powder and debris. The invasion starts tomorrow. [61] Ens. Godman was returned to us today.

July 21st. I had the first strike on Guam at 05:00. The invasion forces were preparing for the landing. During the night the large troop ships moved in and launched the hundreds of small craft that make the final run into the beach. From the air the small craft looked like drunk, little water beetles making their tight circles in the water—ever moving and waiting their turn to load up with Marines. We dive-bombed coastal gun positions. I got a direct hit on a large one—on the pullout I looked back and saw it do a flip, end-over-end. Ens. Hunicke crashed on take-off this A.M. and went down with his plane. His gunner survived. . . . The troops made the landing as scheduled and acquired a beach head without too much opposition.

July 22nd. We bombed Guam again today. Our troops are advancing and meeting mild resistance. After the day's operation we steamed north and anchored in Tanapag Harbor at Saipan. From our deck we watched our troops' field artillery bombard some pockets of resistance on Tinian Island a mile and a half away. The gunfire lasted throughout the night. We reprovisioned here from our AKs and got our mail. We are off now to strike Yap, Palau. [62]

July 26th. We launched strikes against the Jap-held Palau islands. Very few Jap planes were found here, the A.A. fire was heavy and fairly accurate. We lost two fighters over the target with one of the pilots being rescued. The other, our second fighter squadron Skipper, was lost. We lost the first one over Guam. Several dive bombers and other fighters were hit but all returned aboard. The Japs have some rather elaborate facilities here. Large warehouses, oil storage tanks, government buildings as well as gun positions and small cargo ships were hit. Ens. Wrzesinski, of our squadron, had to make a water landing shortly after take-off—engine lost power.

July 27th. We continued our attacks on Koror Town and nearby facilities. I went rather low over the target area after my dive and saw much damage had been done by us. The A.A. fire was intense and I had to fly like a snake crawls to keep from getting hit. Large fires were started and heavy smoke boiled up from Koror Island. On the way home we found an inter-island freighter and sank it by strafing with our 20 mm guns.

Ens. Smith, VF-14 pilot, had to bail out due to bad damage to his F6F. He did not have his chest strap fastened and when the chute opened he slipped out of the harness and only a leg strap took the full shock with a half hitch around his knee. He tried to pull himself up to reenter his harness and the half hitch slipped off his knee but caught around his ankle. He was afraid to move and remained hanging head down until he hit the water. Smith is my roommate. His leg is badly bruised with torn flesh.

We are heading back to Saipan to reload.

July 28–29th. We did not stop at Saipan, but instead are going on to Eniwetok. We will get a rest period badly needed by all hands, also mail.

July 30–31st. Underway for Eniwetok.

August 1–28th. These inclusive dates were spent anchored in Eniwetok lagoon. We have had a lot of mail and a few beer parties on the beach. I ferried one of our old planes down to Majuro atoll (609 miles) and arrived there at night during a foul thunder storm. One of our pilots, Davis, got lost and nearly ran out of gas before finding the island. Our new planes were not ready and the weather was bad, so we were stuck on Majuro for three days. The first night we slept aboard an abandoned LST and then moved into what had been a small hotel. We had Spam for breakfast, dinner and lunch all three days. It seems their supply ship was way overdue and that was all they had to eat. I learned the great great discomfort of shaving with salt water soap rinsed with cold salt water.

The night we landed here in the rain, the coral strip was lighted by very dim smudge pots. The air seemed very turbulent on the landing, and on the rollout, I found out why. Mike Reardon was ahead of me and had no lights. I taxied into his rudder near the parking spot as I could not see him in the dark and rain.

On the flight back to Eniwetok we passed over many small islands still occupied by the Japs which we had bypassed and were starving into submission. I checked out in an F6F fighter plane while in Eniwetok because we are going to be using some of these on special missions. We also received some replacement pilots to bring our squadron back up to a full complement. We have lost almost one-third of the original group of thirty-six. Al Walraven came back aboard here. He went down on the night of June 20th, and was rescued by the submarine *Seawolf*. [63]

August 29th. We are underway for strike operations against Yap, Palau, and the first raids on the Philippines. During practice carrier landing for our replacement pilots today one of them made the very bad mistake of taking a "cut" for a landing and then added back the power to his engine. He settled into the deck and his tail hook caught a wire as he was attempting a left turn away from the ship. The wire held and slammed him into the side of the ship. The wire had to be cut and the plane dropped into the water where the pilot swam free and was picked up by a D.D. We have Vice-Admiral "Joc" McCain [64] aboard for this operation.

September 6th. We launched a fighter sweep of the Palau Islands. No enemy planes were found in the air and very few on the ground.

September 7th. I made the dawn dive-bombing attack against Ngesebus Island. [65] There seems to be very little left on this island. The air strip was well bombed and we only received meager A.A. fire. At noon I made another attack on Anguar Island. We hit buildings and industrial installations. This island has a large phosphate mine and it is doubtful if the production the past two months has been very good due to our interruptions. I saw little A.A. fire. I flew seven combat hours today and I am totally exhausted tonight.

September 8th. I bombed Anguar Island today. The Jap military shows no activity whatsoever against us. Other flights bombed this and Koror Island. WE DEPART THIS P.M. FOR OUR FIRST CARRIER-BASED AIR STRIKE ON MINDANAO OF THE PHILIPPINES. [66] Tomorrow we will knock out their airfields of which there are about forty. We expect a warm welcome.

September 9th. Bombed airfields and shipping in Davao Gulf, Philippine Islands. Only two enemy planes were found in this vicinity. Our planes roamed the area at will. A small convoy of forty island freighters and luggers were sighted at the entrance of Davao Gulf. Our destroyers and light cruisers moved in and destroyed them to the last vessel. Three larger ships were sunk by our planes. The only sign of the Japs' presence was the moderate A.A. over the airfields. On our approach to the airfields we swung wide to the west of Davao Gulf, over the forest-covered mountains. The tops of the mountains were close under us and the few spots of erosion showed the soil to be dark red. Just west of here is where the Moros live, the savage Mohammedan tribes that raid their neighbors to capture slaves. If I should go down here, I don't know who I would want my captors to be—the Japs or Moros.

September 10, 1944. We bombed Digos airfield today, near Davao Gulf. Still no Jap planes oppose us. I had the pleasure of blowing up a large building on the airfield. Mindanao is truly a beautiful island. No doubt it had a most violent birth, as it is very rough and jaggered. We were over it just at sunup and veils of early morning fog lay dammed in the valley waiting for the sun to devour it. The tops of the peaks stood as bright as polished daggers. We are pulling back from the Philippines tonight for refueling and then to take a swing somewhere else. We lost no planes today.

September 12, 1944. I flew the first strike on Cebu Island airfields in the Philippines. We had much more opposition here than in Davao Gulf. We set off large oil fires, blew up storage buildings, bombed some cargo ships, and the fighters downed several Jap planes. I also flew the last strike today. We bombed ships and set them afire along the coast of Cebu. We would hit a ship with bombs and the Japs would head them into shore and beach them to keep them from sinking. Coming back to the ship we hit a violent storm over the mountains along the east side. We had made our dive in rain. Sam Walls was leading us and we entered the storm too low (5,500 feet) as there were mountain peaks up to 5,000 feet. The rain was so hard I could not see the plane I was flying formation on with my goggles down and when I raised them the rain felt like steel balls hitting my eyes. I closed my canopy and could not see through it. Since close formation flying is dangerous when you cannot see, I went on instruments and slid away from the group. The farther we got into the storm the more violent it became. My gyro horizon and compass "tumbled" due to the rough ride and I had to go to my primary needle and ball to keep upright.

In such violent air a magnetic compass is useless as it swings so erratically. I had little knowledge of my true heading. After a few minutes I broke out into a fairly calm area and found I was back on the west side of the storm and mountains. In level flight I "caged and uncaged"[67] my gyros and bored into the storm again on an easterly heading. The violent air currents tumbled my gyros again and I entered a screaming, spiraling dive. I recovered on needle and ball again back on the west side of the storm. I made a few practice turns with my gyro instruments and found they would tumble even in a slight turn. Faulty gyros forced me to go back into the storm on very closely watched needle and ball. It was several minutes of a hard fight to maintain level flight and Quinlan called that he could see blue water below and I knew we were over the water east of the mountains.

On landing aboard, many gallons of water flew out of my wings when my hook caught the wire. Quinlan and I both were soaking wet and about two inches of water sloshed in the bilge of the plane. I have never fought so hard to maintain control of a plane before. We had twelve SB2Cs when we entered the storm on the west side, but only eleven came out on the east side. Ens. Workman was lost and I am sure he could be found on the side of one of those jagged peaks. Thank God for my instrument flight training! Our score tonight stands at sixty-two Jap planes destroyed, six probables, twenty-two damaged. We lost two planes and pilots and crew. We sank three oil tankers, five cargo ships, two destroyers, one small steamer, three patrol boats and one torpedo boat. We inflicted damage on twelve cargo ships, two large oil tankers, two destroyers, one submarine, one light cruiser, three luggars, two barges, one trawler, one minesweeper and five small craft. It was a satisfying sight to see so much damage done to the enemy in one day.

September 13, 1944. We bombed and strafed an airfield on Negros Island which had many two-engine bombers on it. I set one Nick[68] afire by strafing and dropped my bomb in the plane dispersal area. We counted more than twenty planes destroyed on the ground and there was no airborne opposition. Lieutenant Moramski, flying one of our F6F fighter bombers, was about five planes ahead of me in the dive. We were strafing the Jap aircraft on the ground. When he pulled out of his dive he went through the .50-caliber fire of one of our own planes. He crashed in flames on the airfield. What a lousy way to get shot down. These things happen in battle, and also to a lesser degree back in the States during training. A VT-14 pilot, Ens. Quick, had to make a water landing and was knocked out on the landing. His crewman, Donaldson, managed to pull him from the cockpit and inflate his Mae West, saving his life. Another VT-14 pilot, George Kellogg, was shot up over Negros and had to make a water landing. He apparently was knocked out and drowned before his crewmen could get to him. They were picked up out of the water by an SOC[69] float plane. Another TBF crew spent the night with Filipinos after a water landing and signalled our planes the next morning. A float plane went in for them. They reported that the Filipinos were out of salt and the food they ate was very "flat." A large bag of salt was delivered to the natives by float plane.

September 14, 1944. Steaming south. I was on a strike on Mindanao this P.M. We dive-bombed strong A.A. positions on Digos airfield. Two of our bomber pilots, Mike Reardon and G.C. Davis, were hit and forced to land in Davao Gulf about one mile from the beach. The pilots and crewmen got into their rafts. The Japs launched a boat to take them prisoners but our fighters strafed the boat and a shore gun that started shooting at the rafts. After only one and a half hours in the water, float planes from the battleships came in and picked up the men from under the Japs' noses. EXCEL-LENT WORK! This gave tired pilots' morale a boost. Bill Shawcross of VT-14 got revenge on the Digos A.A. battery for shooting down Reardon and Davis. Bill took his bombing run real low and unloaded all he had on them.

September 20th. We replenished our supplies and are headed north to bomb the Japanese installations at Manila, capital of the Philippines and the Jap strongpoint for the whole area. It will be the first raid by American carrier-based planes on Manila in history.[70] We expect to find much Japanese shipping in the harbor and a hot reception. For protection and cover our Task Force is moving up the east coast of the Philippines in a large storm system, rain and low visibility.

September 21, 1944, Manila, P.I. I went in with the first wave of dive bombers early this A.M. Our targets were ships anchored in Manila Bay. Fifteen minutes before our attack, our fighters paid a call on the Japanese airfields (about 30). They did such a thorough job of destroying the enemy on the ground that we met little resistance in the air. Our bomber formation crossed the rugged Sierra Madre mountains and beyond, at the end of a broad valley, lay Manila. Still beyond in the morning mist and veil-like clouds stood Bataan Peninsula. At its tip, low and tadpole-shaped, was Corregidor. The foremost thought in my mind was the effect the sight of American planes with big white stars on the wings would have on the minds of those men and women who had served there and had suffered Jap imprisonment now for two years. Also, I thought of the Filipinos cheering and waving as they had done on the central and southern islands.

Nearing Manila Bay we started our high-speed run in and there were so many ships at anchor it was hard to pick a target. Up to this point there were no planes opposing us and Manila radio was playing a popular Guy Lombardo number. Suddenly the music stopped and a voice announced in English that this was an air raid and to take cover. Then, silence. Two Jap fighters appeared and they were being chased by our fighters. I saw both go down in flames into Manila Bay, just as I was pushing over into my dive. We dived on a large dry dock in the former Cavite American Naval Base. There was a Jap D.D. in the dry dock. The flak was intense and accurate. We destroyed the dry dock and the ship in it. Our VT-14 sent their torpedoes into the anchored ships. Many ships were afire and there were some explosions. We rendezvoused at a low altitude over Manila Bay and two Jap fighters hopped us. Our fighters and fire from our rear cockpit gunners drove them off. They ran! I still can't see how we lived through the crossfire from the city docks, Cavite Naval Base, the anchored ships and Jap fighters. We had twisted the tiger's tail and he was fighting back. Even the small craft in the bay popped away at us with small calibre guns.

A fighter section flying close cover for us saw a stream of orange juice (tracers) being squirted up past their wings and they peeled off and went in on the small boat doing the firing. For a moment I could not see the boat for the water splashed by the hail of bullets. After the water settled the boat had been cut in half and each part sank separately. We wiggled our way through the A.A. fire past Manila and made it back to the ship in heavy rain. The weather was good over the target but we had to use ZBX to find our ship. This is a tough way to operate, but good for hiding our ships. The air crews get soaking wet going to their planes on the flight deck, but they operate real good in such adverse conditions. Other strikes hit the docks, ships and airfields all day long.

I had a second hop late in the afternoon. We met no air opposition but the raid before this one we lost one of our VBF pilots, Cy Grubin, who was hit by a Jap fighter who made a run from high above, fired and then ran away. Lieutenant Heath was shot up and had to land in the water outside the bay where we had a rescue submarine standing by. On this last strike our bombers did a remarkable job of accurate bombing. We set fire to nine ships. I chose a large oil tanker and got a good hit on the stern followed by a secondary explosion. It settled quickly by the stern into the mud near Cavite.

Still there were plenty of Jap ships left, for we had caught them with a great merchant fleet at anchor in Manila Bay, so we'll be back tomorrow. The flak over Manila is murderous. Lieutenant Laz landed aboard with a two-foot hole in his right wing. Tonight I am very tired, having spent eight very tense hours in the air.

Sept. 22, 1944. Apparently the Japs repaired their airfields during the night, for our task force had an early morning raid by Jap planes. About six were sighted over our ship. Two dropped bombs far astern with no damage. The ship shot down two of the planes and the others fled. We launched two strikes against ships in Manila Bay this A.M. I was to go on the third but a typhoon was swiftly moving in[71] and we were forced to cease operations and leave the area. It is estimated we sank twenty-two large ships in Manila Bay and severely damaged twenty-five others. We lost no planes this morning, even though some were shot up badly. Our total losses for the entire task force was believed to be fifteen. We destroyed 501 Jap planes, 140 of these were shot down by our pilots in aerial combat. Walt O'Brien, of VT-14, got a bomb hit on a ship this morning. Bjornson, on landing aboard today, in his F6F had his hook bounce and stick up. He hit the barrier.

Sept. 24th. We had a pre-dawn launch today and flew 340 miles across the central Philippines to the west side and dive-bombed ships in Corran Bay.[72] We had reports from our scout submarines that a number of Japanese ships had slipped out of Manila Bay during the night and headed for the Jap fleet anchorage in Corran Bay. In order for us to make this long flight and return, we installed droppable fuel tanks on the wings.

When we arrived over Corran Bay, not a single Jap ship could be seen. While we circled one of our pilots spotted a wisp of smoke coming from under the thick trees. The Japs had tied up to a dock or pilings next to a wooded area and had cut tree branches and covered their decks as camouflage. I was half way down in my dive before I could make out the outline of a cruiser under the tree branches. We got our cruiser and two destroyers good. Other squadrons sank oil tankers and merchantmen. The total was ten sunk and twelve damaged. We lost no planes and no Japanese planes were seen.

On the way back across the Philippines we ran into a Jap patrol boat. We formed a round-robin, single-file strafing circle. Before I could get around for my second run, someone hit the boiler and blew it in half. The Japs were swimming in the water when we left for home. Tonight we are heading south to the Admiralty Islands to reprovision and rearm.

September 25th to October 1st. We arrived and anchored in Sea-Addler Harbor, Manus Island[73] on Sept. 28th. I went ashore to see if I could still walk on land. It felt good—the land. The men stationed here have developed quite a business in exotic sea shells. The shallow reefs here produce some unusual cowrie and cats-eye pearl shells. The men bury the fresh shell in the sand and let the ants eat out the meat from inside. Then, they dig them up and polish the shells to a high lustre. If there is an extra buck to be made, the American G.I. will find a way.

October 3–4–5–6–7–8–9th. We are steaming north on the heels of a large typhoon. The weather makes the seas very rough and the wind is over gale force. Some of the ship's crew have been injured by the mountainous waves breaking over the sixty-foot flight deck. One of our escort destroyers had a man washed overboard. He was found and picked out of the water. This large carrier *(Wasp)* shakes and quivers as if it was a toy in the hands of an angry giant. We had to use guard rails on our bunks last night to keep from rolling out on the deck.

October 10, 1944, Okinawa. Today we struck Okinawa [74] at the lower end of the Japanese empire. Their airfields are well built here and many planes were caught and destroyed on the ground. We bombed several ship docks and storage facilities on the airfields. Naha town was set afire. A huge cloud of smoke from the ground to ten thousand feet soon covered the town. On the last strike of the day many of the fires were still burning fiercely.

We lost Ens. Gates on the target. He was one of our replacement pilots we picked up on our last visit to Eniwetok. Another of our replacement pilots, Ens. Edwards, had an explosive shell come into the cockpit and explode just below his handgrip on the control stick. It blew off the small and ring fingers of his right hand and shortened the stick by at least six inches. His right thigh was also cut by the shrapnel. He tied his right hand very tightly with a handkerchief to stop the bleeding and flew the plane back to the ship. He elected to land aboard rather than in the water even though his plane was badly damaged and of questionable approach-speed stability. It is a tough enough job to bring these planes around just above stall speed, on altitude, and line up with a pitching deck with two healthy hands—he did it with his left hand only and a very short control stick. Also, he had no flaps and his bomb bay doors were stuck open. The flight surgeon said the fingers and attaching hand joints were severed so cleanly by the shell, all he had to do was a little cleanup work and sew. It was only Edwards' second hop.

Another one of our pilots, Asmussen, was shot down just off the beach and when the rescue submarine tried to go in for him, the Jap shore batteries opened fire. The sub had to back out. Our squadron executive officer, Lcdr. Art Downing, sent the flight back to the ship and he remained to strafe the shore batteries. The ship ordered him back by radio as it was getting near sunset and the fleet wanted to get some distance away before night. Art pretended he did not hear the message and stayed and strafed until the sub rescued Asmussen. Art landed aboard after dark and was restricted to his room (put in hack). We did not like the penalty placed on him, as he is our best pilot and often takes extra hops when others do not feel like going. Besides, this is his second combat tour—he volunteered for it.

October 11th. We refueled today and our fighters paid a call on the Jap airfields on northern Luzon, P.I. We are steaming for an early dawn strike on Formosa.

October 12th. We hit Formosa today.[75] I made the first attack on Takao airfield. No Japanese planes were airborne but we got plenty burning on the ground. I dropped my bomb on a plane assembly plant. It was so big I could not miss it. I also flew the third strike against the harbor installations. Our group blew up oil storage dumps, three ships and I got credit for a direct hit on a concrete storage building. The flak was intense and accurate over the harbor area. My "jinking" was not up to par I guess for I got hit for the first time. Nothing serious though—a few holes in the wing and one through the cockpit between Larry Quinlan and me.

Tonight we are being attacked by many Jap torpedo planes. Our night fighters are very busy meeting them at a distance and those that get through are fired on by our ships.

October 13, 1944, off Formosa. The attack by enemy planes last night lasted until 04:00 hours. None of our ships were damaged. The Japs lost a total of fourteen twin-engine bombers during the night. We made three strikes against Formosa today. I had the last one and got credit for three two-engine bombers on the ground. Again, my evasive action after the dive was less than perfect as Quinlan and I shared two holes in the cockpit between us and two more in the tail.

Large formations of torpedo planes attacked us at sunset. I found out tonight that Gordon Bjornson of VF-14 shot down two Jap "Zekes" yesterday. Also learned that Bill Davidson of our VT-14 squadron failed to return from a strike on Formosa. By 19:30 tonight our task force had shot down fifteen two-engine bombers and four single-engine planes. One of our heavy cruisers, U.S.S. *Canberra,* [76] was hit by an aerial torpedo and put out of action. It is being towed by another ship to clear the area.

October 14, 1944. We hit Formosa again today—one strike this morning and then started our withdrawal from the area. We have to go slow to provide air cover for our damaged cruiser. Another of our replacement pilots, Ens. Wallacek, went down in the China Sea and was lost.

About 17:00 large formations of enemy planes came after us. Our fighter planes met them half way and shot down eighteen, the others withdrew. At dusk they came back for another try. Five of these were shot down by our ships, but one got through and put a "fish" into the cruiser *Houston.* [77] She was hit forward and badly hurt. Most of the crew were taken off by the destroyers. She is in tow also. The Japs tried another attack but the A.A. fire was too much for them. We are in some very rough weather and cannot operate our night fighters, as the deck is pitching too much for carrier landings. If their attacks had been more determined we no doubt would have suffered more damage. Our ship suffered only a broken radio antenna which was hit by an exploding Jap plane—Kamikaze!

October 15th. Throughout today small groups of Japanese dive bombers tried to reach our formation. Our fighters met them thirty miles out and shot down some and forced the remainder to withdraw. Gordon Bjornson of our fighter group intercepted a Betty, and splashed it. One lone dive bomber sneaked through and dropped his bomb for a miss on our sister carrier. He was hit by our A.A. and was last seen going low over the water and smoking badly. Fighters from the *Wasp* alone shot down forty-six planes. We lost one. Our sister carrier and two light carriers brought the total for the day to seventy-five Japanese planes downed. Our sister carrier did not fare so well as they lost seven of their planes. The *Canberra* is now steaming partially under her own power, assisting her tow to make about fourteen knots. The *Houston* is still under tow and I understand that a historic effort by her crew was all that has kept her afloat up to now. Our smaller task group broke off from the main force and stayed behind to guard the cripples and we will soon be out of air-raid range of the Japs.

Tonight Tokyo Radio claimed ten U.S. carriers were sunk and two damaged, along with other ships of all classes sunk and crippled. They boasted the Imperial Fleet was steaming south to finish the crippled American task force. We are hoping that their pilots made such claims and they make the fatal mistake of sending their fleet down our way. Tomorrow we will make 450-mile searches to the north for their supposedly approaching fleet. I have one of the searches. I expect to find nothing except that the Japs are liars.

October 16–17th. The last statement above was correct, for we searched for two days trying to find the Jap fleet. The truth is they never left the safety of the Sea of Japan.[78]

October 18–19th. All our planes have spent the last three days striking airfields. We have destroyed hundreds of Jap planes in the air and on the ground. Pretty good performance for a task force that was supposed to be crippled.

Tomorrow G. Douglas MacArthur and forces invade Leyte of the central Philippines.

October 20th. Gen. MacArthur's troops landed on Leyte today.[79] The Navy gave air support with carrier-based planes. Tokyo Radio calls it a nuisance raid. This landing cuts off all the Japs in the south Philippines.

October 21–22–23rd. We are steaming for Ulithi Island for re-provisioning. We received a message that units of the Jap fleet are converging on the Philippines.[80] We still have the major part of Task Force 38 there, but we reversed course and will join the fight.

October 24th. Steaming west. Got word the *Princeton*[81] was sunk.

October 25th. The CVE *Princeton* was sunk at Leyte Gulf by units of the Jap fleet. Our submarines have sunk and damaged various units of the enemy fleet. I was catapulted off about 04:00 this morning with all the fuel

I could get aboard to make the longest carrier-based search in naval history, over one thousand miles. I had all the regular fuel tanks full, wing tanks full and a large bombay tank full. They allowed Quinlan only fifty rounds of .30 cal. for our defense. I searched the 20-degree sector due north of the ship and there was a searcher on each side of me.

After flying for about two hours it got daylight and I saw a sub on the surface, but it also saw me and crash dived. It was in a sub sanctuary zone and I could not have attacked it anyway. Over seven hours of looking at a lot of water and no trace of the Japs. The searcher in the sector west of me found the Japs. By the time I returned to the ship all our planes had been launched for the attack. About one hundred miles out before I got back to the ship, one of the search teams west of me (one SB2C and one F6F) came crossing my stern on a course a good 20 degrees to the left of mine. A blinker message from the SB2C questioned my course. I had Quinlan to signal that we were holding our course. The other search team held their course until nearly out of sight, then changed course and joined on us. We flew together about twenty minutes and broke through a cloud and there was the *Wasp* directly below. I imagine the other pilot had missed a drastic change in the wind direction observed by me on our cross leg segment of the search. I find few aviators know how to read a sea state.

I landed aboard and as soon as it was refueled and armed, Lcdr. Art Downing took my plane for a lone plane attack on the Jap battleship *Yamato*[82] which had been detected coming through the San Bernardino Strait. He got a hit on a forward gun turret and his gunner got a picture to prove it. On his pull out his plane was holed many times, but he was able to shoot down a Jap float plane taking off. Our group did a lot of damage to the northern group of Jap ships and they withdrew. There is another group farther south which we will hit tomorrow. Our VT-14 pilots had a busy day off Leyte Gulf. Bill Shawcross, Tom Campion, Jack Coffey and Bob Davis glide bombed a Jap heavy cruiser and inflicted heavy damage. Peter Gray laid his bombs on a Jap battleship.

October 26th. We steamed closer to the Philippines and attacked a formation of enemy battleships and cruisers. Several hits were scored. Another roommate of mine, Lieutenant Hank Welker, was hit by flak in his dive and crashed into the target. Hank was my seventh roommate to go down. We were up at 3 A.M. and he was irritable. I had picked up some coconuts on the last island and when I opened one I put the uneaten portion of it under my desk light so the heat would dry it out and make the meat shrink away from the hull. This makes the meat sweeter, too. Hank had helped me eat the coconuts. My desk light bulb had been out for several days and I had put a large piece under his desk light. This morning he threw the piece of coconut on the deck and muttered something. I left him in a bad mood as I was catapulted early. I am told he never pulled out of his dive on a Jap battleship. We lost Jud Doane on a search mission this morning. This ceaseless strike after strike is beginning to show on everybody—tired beyond normal recovery. As usual Tokyo Radio made wild claims of great damage to the American fleet, but the truth is we lost only the small carrier *Princeton* and saved most of her crew. What was left of the Jap fleet fled the area.

Again our torpedo squadron, VT-14, had a very good day delivering torpedoes into the sides of a Jap battle group in Sibuyan Sea. William House led the group consisting of Wiley Williams, Arlo Ford, Graydon Wright, Walt Fitzgerald, Jack Cochran and Charlie Hoffman in a torpedo run on Jap battleships. John Drake put his torpedo into the side of a Jap CL.[83] Walt O'Brien put his fish into a Jap destroyer in Tablas Straits forcing the DD to beach rather than sink. Ralph Cole was the unlucky one of this group as he was shot down in flames by a Jap DD. This group really punished the heaviest ships the Japs have.

October 30–31, November 1–2nd. We were anchored in Ulithi Lagoon, expecting to get relieved by another air group. The aviators and air crewmen were having a beer party on the beach when a jeep came by with a loud speaker telling all hands to return to their ships. So, here we are on our way back to the Philippines. The Japs have ferried in so many planes that we have to go back and relieve some of the pressure on our troops by knocking out the airfields again.

November 5, 1944, OFF THE PHILIPPINES Again. I was on the first hop today. We dive-bombed an airfield north of Clark Field on Luzon. I put my bomb into the shop area and set one plane afire with strafing on the pullout. Our fighter cover engaged some Zeros over the field before we dived. During my dive I went through this dog fight and barely missed a collision with a Zero. We were rendezvousing after the dive when a Zero came out of a cloud and shot Burnham off my left wing. He and his gunner bailed out okay and a fighter covered them all the way to the ground. They hit and ran for the woods.

I was flying wing on the Skipper. Our bombing was good and many planes were burning when we left the target area. Our fighters shot fifteen Japs out of the air and we lost one of our fighters, Lieutenant Knight. On the second hop our planes bombed and strafed an airfield in the Clark area. Many planes were destroyed. This has been a costly day for the Nips. Jap suicide planes tried unsuccessfully to dive into our carriers this P.M. They were all shot down very near the CVs.[84] There has been an increasing number of suicide attempts since our landing on Leyte and the defeat of the Jap fleet.

November 6th. We launched three strikes against airfields on Luzon today. I flew the first one against Mabalacat Field, and we shot up too many planes to count. I would estimate we have destroyed over 400 planes in the past two days. About 150 of these were shot out of the air yesterday. No Jap planes attempted to hit our ships last night and none have been seen airborne today. We received another "Well Done" from the Secretary of the Navy and Admiral Halsey. Our final score (official) for the past two days is: 720 aircraft destroyed, one cruiser sunk, one destroyer sunk, and five DDs damaged and several large AKs and AOs[85] either sunk or severely damaged.

November 7, 1944. Underway for Guam to be relieved by a replacement air group. GREAT NEWS!!! We are very tired and weary after nearly seven months of almost continuous fighting. Our squadron by itself has shot down over 150 planes, sunk 75 large ships and damaged 130 more. We average forty-two combat missions per pilot (not counting many searches and patrols). This is a fleet record up to this date. We have fought major elements of the Jap Fleet twice and won, covered five invasions, bombed eighteen enemy-held islands. We received congratulations from the Commanders of the Third Fleet and the Fifth Fleet and Fleet Admiral Nimitz, on our excellent record. We lost seventeen of the original group of thirty-six pilots we left Pearl Harbor with, plus two replacement pilots. (Three of the original group were later returned from the Philippine guerillas.) Seven of these pilots were my roommates. I was awarded a Distinguished Flying

Cross for my part in the Battle of the Philippine Sea, and an Air Medal for the strikes on Formosa. I got a promotion to Lieutenant (j.g.) so I will no longer be "Tail-end-Charlie." . . . Larry Quinlan, my radio/gunner will always have my kindest thoughts for keeping the Japs off my tail. We must have been a good team as the Japs only nicked us twice with small A.A. fire. Whatever we did, right or wrong, we beat almost 50-50 odds we would get shot down.

There is no way one person could observe or report every act of heroism by so many dedicated men in Air Group Fourteen.

November 14, 1944. We got relieved at Guam as scheduled. The Nips finally gave up and let us go home. We spent one night on Guam as the jeep carrier we were to ride back to the States on was late in arriving. Al Lewis and I had no place to sleep. We tried the cold deck of an LST. It started to rain and all we had was a poncho to huddle under, but it leaked through the neck hole. We wandered down toward the airfield, found a sentry shack with hot coffee and moved in with him for the night.

January, 1945, Jacksonville, Fla. I am instructing new fighter pilots in carrier landings at the Navy's Fighter Operational Training Command, Green Cove Springs, Fla.

Notes

1. Bombing Squadron fourteen. "V" designates a fixed-wing aircraft, heavier-than-air. "B" designates a dive bomber. These planes also flew scouting missions.

2. The seventh U.S.S. *Wasp* was an Essex Class aircraft carrier christened in November 1943, by Eleanor Roosevelt, whose son was in the ship's company. It had recently completed its shakedown cruise to Trinidad with the same crew. *Wasp's* keel was originally scheduled to be a cruiser named U.S.S. *Oriskany;* plans changed when the previous *Wasp* was sunk by the Japanese in the Coral Sea in September of 1942. In the 1960s, the *Wasp* would become the recovery ship for astronauts splashing down in the Atlantic during the Gemini program. The first *Wasp* was a sailing ship that saw action during the Revolutionary War.

3. In September 1943, the U.S. Army Aircorp had made ineffective high altitude bombing raids against Wake and Marcus islands.

4. Fighter aircraft by Grumman, nicknamed "Hell Cat."

5. Torpedo bomber built by Grumman, nicknamed "Turkey."

6. Dive bomber built by Curtiss-Wright, nicknamed "Beast" or "Helldiver." This was the type of plane flown by Fulton.

7. Right wing position in a three plane section. Two "sections" equals a "division" of six.

8. Lcdr. Arthur Latimer Downing, the squadron executive officer. He later became commanding officer of VB-14.

9. One thousand miles east of Japan, Marcus Island contained an airbase that staged scout patrols crucial to the Japanese defense system.

10. Japanese medium bomber, the Mitsubishi G4M.

11. The *Essex* was the carrier for which the new class of heavy aircraft carriers were named. These carriers were built on the same keel as heavy cruisers. Light carriers were built on the same keel as light cruisers.

12. Admiral A.E. Montgomery, the Task Group Commander of 58.2 which included *Wasp,* the *Bunker Hill,* the *Monterey* and the *Cabot.*

13. Landing Signal Officer. A pilot trained to signal corrective information to other pilots approaching the ship for a carrier landing of their aircraft. His word is

final whether an approaching aircraft is "cut" for the landing or waved-off for another try.

14. Majuro Island, in the Marshall Group, was an early staging area in 1944.

15. Guam, on the lower end of the Marianas Islands, had been under the control of the United States at the beginning of the war. It was a key strategic and symbolic target in driving the Japanese out of the Philippines.

16. The invasion of Europe did not require a large fleet of men-of-war ships, but rather transports and supply ships. In all, 535 ships were used in the Marianas invasion, and a high percentage of these were classified as men-of-war, or fighting ships. The Normandy invasion was able to make use of land-based air cover support while the Marianas invasion was forced to rely only on sea-borne aircraft carrier support. Fifteen aircraft carriers, and a total of 58,902 aircraft, comprised Task Force 58.

17. In the central Caroline Island group, Truk was a major, long-time Japanese naval base.

18. In fact, Japanese submarine operations never posed a serious problem for the U.S. forces, though American submarines were to take a terrible toll on the Japanese fleet. At least twenty-five Japanese subs were in the area of operations during the time leading up to the Philippine Sea offensive and at least seventeen of those were quickly sunk. The destroyer escort *England* alone sank six subs in thirteen days, with the result that the Japanese had no submarine support for battle operations or scout missions. On the other hand, U.S. submarine patrols were highly successful in tracking Japanese movements, in disrupting fuel supplies and in sinking Japanese destroyers.

19. Oil was transferred while underway through a large flexible hose. The ships were required to hold a steady course for a long period of time during this procedure and were especially vulnerable to attack. Fueling problems plagued the Japanese Mobile Fleet throughout this campaign. American submarines were very successful in blowing up Japanese oil tankers and in catching their fighting ships in the process of fueling. At times the Japanese fleet was without enough fuel to steam from their home islands to fight battles in the Philippines. They were finally forced to use unprocessed Borneo oil that was both highly volatile and tended to foul their engines. The situation became so severe that at times Japanese battleships were ordered to transfer most of their oil in order to resupply their carriers.

20. The search procedure in enemy waters called for four aircraft to search ahead of the task force, flying a 20-degree sector pattern for two- to three-hundred miles.

21. Allied code name for the Japanese land-based medium bomber.

22. Combat Air Patrol. Fighter protection for the fleet from enemy aircraft.

23. Japanese carrier-based dive bomber with fixed landing gear.

24. A village on the northwest coast of Saipan.

25. Ray Heiden, Fulton's friend and fellow pilot, described the scene in his diary (unpublished) as well: "Battleships shelled Saipan all day long. Tonight you can see a glow in the sky over the island, so apparently it is burning fiercely." These actions prepared the way for the Marine landings on Saipan.

26. Anti-submarine patrol or anti-snooper patrol, providing airborne protection for the fleet from enemy submarines.

27. A town on southern Saipan. This was the beginning of Operation Forager, during which more than 127,500 troops were carried over 3,500 miles to begin the assault on Saipan. This was one of the largest and most important invasions of the war, coming just a few days after the Normandy invasion on the other side of the world.

28. The National Archives in Washington, D.C., apparently contain motion pictures of this event.

29. Admiral Ozawa with the Japanese Mobile Fleet was in fact underway with orders to strike the Americans in one decisive battle named Operation A-GO on which he was told depended "the rise and fall of Imperial Japan." However, Ozawa was outnumbered and already short of fuel. Worse, he was depending on significant land-based support from Guam which would never materialize.

30. Heiden June 15 excerpt: "Had one canned strike on Saipan today. Practically every building had red crosses painted on them. . . . I dove on the biggest building I could find. . . . The next thing I saw was a plane in the distance heading due west. After a time I began to think it was a Jap snooper high-tailing it for home. So, with a cry of glee and great zeal I poured the coal on and started chasing it. About that time Elway joined me and then Berg. Before I knew it about nine other planes began following us. After almost burning out my engine the bogie turned out to be an SBD from the Lex. As it turned out I had led eleven out of sixteen planes about seventy miles from where they were supposed to be. It made the Skipper a bit peeved, especially since our fighter cover followed us instead of the Skipper. Ah well, it's things like this that adds a little zest to life."

31. Torpedo Bomber Squadron.

32. The Japanese already were relying on many poorly trained and inexperienced pilots who would orbit out about eighty miles while getting target assignments from their flight leader, who was often the only experienced pilot in the group. Meanwhile, the American force had them on radar and could send out fighters to intercept and shoot them down. The surviving planes apparently made for Guam for refueling and bombs, but the runways were so pockmarked from American

bombing that most of them crashed on landing. A critical problem for the Japanese was that the commander on Guam, Vice-Admiral Kakuta, seriously misled the fleet about the state of his runways and the numbers of airworthy aircraft he could send in support of this battle.

33. This day brought the completion of the greatest naval air battle ever fought, a battle that began two days earlier and resulted in a decisive victory for the United States. It secured the Marianas invasion, gained control of the Philippine Sea and broke the back of Japan's carrier aviation. The night of the twentieth, after the battle was over and the enemy in retreat, eighty aircraft were lost because the planes had been sent too far. The error was Admiral Raymond Spruance's, Commander of the Fifth Fleet and overall commander of Operation Forager, for not closing the distance on June 18–19. He feared the Japanese fleet would make an end run around the U.S. fleet and disrupt the Saipan invasion. Also, the planes had been readied with small bombs rather than dropable auxiliary fuel tanks under the wings, and by the time the launch was ordered, it was too late to change them. American planes had to either go or risk losing the chance to strike the Japanese fleet in the dark. Despite such foul-ups, this battle cost Japan three-fourths of its trained airmen.

34. Lawrence Quinlan was Fulton's rear-seat radioman and gunner. He shot twin 30-caliber machine guns from the rear cockpit.

35. Slight pull out and reenter the dive. A normal dive is made downwind. In a large formation with strong winds, the last man to dive was sometimes forced to dive upwind, causing the dive angle to shallow out into more of a glide. A brief pullout to a level flight position enabled the pilot to reenter in a steeper dive over the target.

36. Flying an erratic course with abrupt changes in altitude and direction to confuse the enemy gunners.

37. Homing radio signal which broadcast a letter of the alphabet, assigned at random and changed daily, every 20 degrees around a ship.

38. Low frequency radio was used only on long searches to report enemy positions. Otherwise short range VHF transmissions were used.

39. A light aircraft carrier.

40. An older dive bomber built by Douglas. It was being replaced by the newer SB2C, but some squadrons that had been deployed earlier still used these older planes.

41. There were several reported stories about Japanese planes lost and trying to land on American carriers. None were really confirmed, though it is certainly possible that Japanese planes lost while trying to reach Guam could have done this

during the confusion. There was much panic in trying to recover hundreds of aircraft out of fuel in the darkness.

42. Heiden, who had remained on board *Wasp* that day, provides a vivid glimpse of the intensity and chaos of this operation: "MOTHER OF GOD. WHAT A DAY! A call came over the speaker for all pilots to man their ready rooms on-the-double. I learned the Jap fleet had been sighted and it was larger than they had thought. At 16:20 the Captain's and Joe Kane's divisions took off. At 16:50 we were informed that the *Bunker Hill* would not be ready to launch until 17:20. Consequently the second wave was cancelled. That delay probably saved more Naval Aviator's lives than any previously planned action. Needless to say when the second attack was cancelled, all the pilots were pretty disappointed. However, as events unreeled we became very glad that circumstances prevented our taking off.

"All told they would have to fly at least 630 miles beside the rendezvous. And on top of all this it would be extremely dark when and if they returned. All this made us very grateful toward the person who fouled-up the launch on the mighty *Bunker Hill*.

"Nothing was heard until about 20:15. We were given the word to standby to receive aircraft and we all rushed out on the flight deck catwalks. The first thing we saw was plane lights milling around in the pitch-black sky. There seemed to be no semblance of order. It was then we knew it was going to be a rather sordid affair. The next thing was a plane which crashed into the water and exploded. A few minutes later we heard a plane land. It was a barrier crash, an SB2C from the *Yorktown*. About fifteen minutes later there was a terrific crash on deck. An F6F took a cut on a wave-off and came up the deck at one hundred knots with his wheels not even touching. His wheels hit the barrier cables, which threw him over on his back, knocking off the engine. Amazingly enough the pilot crawled out and walked away. Some of us went out to see what had happened and we saw a plane go in the water on the starboard side and another hit the water on the port side and explode. They were pushing the wrecked F6F over the side when a man fell overboard. I have never seen such terrific confusion in all my life. All this time planes were making passes and being frantically waved off. We could see deck crashes on other carriers resulting in tremendous fires. In all this time, we hadn't heard from any of our boys. We really worried about them when we hit the sack that night. There was little sleep for any of us."

43. The Japanese had no way to match the manufacturing capabilities of the United States, but even more of a problem was their lack of an effective training program for replacement pilots. The Japanese strategy had depended on quick victories using a small, elite force of highly trained and experienced pilots. Their lack of well-trained replacement pilots would lead to increasing disadvantages in the air over the months to come.

44. A single-engine scout and observation float plane, built by Vaught, commonly deployed from a cruiser or battleship.

45. Located in the northern Marianas Islands, about three hundred miles north of Saipan. The Japanese used it as a staging base to fly in replacement aircraft from Japan.

46. Al Walraven was still missing from the night battle of the twentieth. The submarine *Seawolf* rescued him and returned him to the *Wasp* in August. The next patrol the *Seawolf* made it was mysteriously lost with all hands.

47. The most northwest atoll of the Marshall Islands, Eniwetok was captured from the Japanese and used as the U.S. naval staging base for the invasion of Saipan, Tinian and Guam. It had a large harbor surrounded by coral reefs for safety.

48. Located about halfway between Tokyo and Saipan, the Bonin Islands were a major staging area for Japanese planes and for picket sampans.

49. The small island of Iwo Jima, located about six hundred miles south of Tokyo, served as a base for Japanese fighters. It would not be invaded by Americans until February, 1945, when it would be the site of a flag-raising victory that captured the imaginations of the American public back home.

50. Large cargo ship.

51. Destroyer or "tin can" or just "can."

52. Due to the very rugged landscape and the fact that the Japanese were turning to a posture of defending to the last man, the invasion of the islands in the northern Pacific exacted higher losses on the ground than the atoll fighting of the central Pacific.

53. Fulton's brother was captured off Penang, Malaysia, sent to Singapore and later Japan where he was held in a POW camp near Nagasaki and forced to work in a large steel mill. He heard the first atomic bomb explosion in Hiroshima. The day Nagasaki was bombed, the steel mill was the primary target, but fog covered it so the bomb was dropped on Nagasaki itself. Except for the fog, he and his fellow POWs would have been "nuked" by his own government. Weighing 150 pounds at the time of his capture, he was down to 92 pounds by the time he was freed and suffered poor health thereafter.

54. They had been delayed in invading Guam by the Battle of the Philippine Sea.

55. S.T. Coleridge, "Rime of the Ancient Mariner."

56. Commander Walter C. Wingard, Jr., USN. He was later transferred to other duty and replaced by Commander Jack Blitch. Heiden notes on July 26 that "the

Air Group Commander bounced over all the barriers, hit the crane, kept going and hit one of our mechanics and killed him." After this incident, Wingard apparently gave up flying from the *Wasp*.

57. Carrier Air Group composed of a squadron of each, bombers, torpedo and fighters plus night fighters. Fulton here, though, is actually still referring to the Group Commander Wingard.

58. A carrier-based plane must approach for a deck landing at near stalling speed.

59. Landing ship for troops.

60. The two-week bombardment was the longest of the entire war.

61. Guam is a large island that contained the best harbor in the Marianas Group. The United States controlled this island before the war and the natives were friendly to the U.S. and hated the Japanese invaders who treated them with exceptional harshness. Guam was to provide a key base in the planned retaking of the Philippines. From Guam, the Japanese could be cut off from re-supplying their islands that the U.S. naval forces had bypassed to the south. The ruggedness of the thirty-mile long island allowed Japanese soldiers to hide long after the end of the war. The last Japanese soldier on Guam did not surrender until 1972, nearly thirty years later.

62. Yap and Palau islands are about five hundred miles east of Mindinao, Philippines.

63. Al Walraven had this to say in his unpublished diary about life on a submarine: "It would naturally be impossible from here on to record what happened but there was one incident that will always stand out. We were patrolling an enemy held island when a plane was suddenly sighted heading our way. The captain thought our periscope had been spotted and set off that blood curdling alarm from which I'll never recover. The sub's tanks were all flooded immediately and down we went until I thought the depth indicator would never slow down. It was then when things really began to happen. I didn't mind being knocked down by a toolbox that came sliding down the deck, nor listening to all those plates crashing in the galley but when I heard someone say that our stern plane controls had gone out, that was the last straw. The only thing to do was to blow out some of the tanks and maintain a nice steady altitude, but in doing so some joker blew too much water which caused us to reverse our course and start ascending even more rapidly than we had descended. I thought for sure everything was lost and frankly so did everyone else on the sub when it surfaced with a Jap plane up over us and ready to drop a bomb—we thought. Evidently though, that Jap must not have been looking for subs that day and they finally got the sub back under control. After that Banner and I both decided those contraptions weren't safe."

64. Vice-Admiral John J. "Joc" McCain was Commander of the Fast Carrier Task Group One.

65. One of the Palau group, which are the westernmost group of the Caroline Islands, about three hundred miles from Mindanao.

66. The largest of the Philippine islands, it was also the most southern and least defended. Mindanao contained a large harbor, Davao Gulf. U.S. forces were testing the Japanese defenses as the first step in the historic retaking of the Philippines, so publicly promised by MacArthur, before venturing north.

67. A gyroscope, or gyro, is a free-floating instrument which indicates the banking and pitch of a plane with respect to the horizon. "Caging" refers to forcing the gyro to a level position as related to the horizon. "Uncaged," the gyro horizon maintains this relationship on its own, producing an artificial horizon, but extremely rough air or drastic maneuvering can cause it to tumble out of balance and fail to accurately indicate position. Needle and ball, which works like a carpenter's level, is the primary blind flying instrument. Because it is not a gyro it doesn't tumble.

68. A two-seat Kawasaki fighter.

69. A scout/observation float plane built by Curtiss-Wright.

70. The pilots were briefed not to bomb any part of the city of Manila itself. Liberating the Philippine capital without destroying it was of considerable symbolic and propaganda importance. The Philippines had been a U.S. possession since the Spanish-American War.

71. There was a lot of bad weather during the final stages of retaking the Philippines. While typhoons forced a stop to all carrier operations, the U.S. fleet would often hide in the bad weather of lesser storms and launch strikes on targets that were clear.

72. Corran Bay on the South China Sea side of the Philippines was used as a Japanese anchorage.

73. In the Admiralty Group off the east coast of New Guinea, in the Bismarck Sea.

74. Located in the Ryukyu Islands off the lower part of Japan. The colossal invasion of Okinawa was still five months away, but the Joint Chiefs of Staff were already thinking about it, rather than the Philippines or Formosa, as the best springboard for an invasion of the main home islands of Japan.

75. Now called Taiwan, located seventy miles off the China Coast between Japan and the Philippines, was an industrially important target.

76. A new heavy cruiser, next in size to a battleship. The *Canberra* was attacked by eight torpedo bombers about ninety miles south of Formosa. One bomber slipped through to blow a large hole that flooded both engine rooms and firerooms, leaving her dead in the water. The story of rigging her to be towed by the

Wichita, something that had never before been accomplished, rather than having her scuttled, under cover of a hastily organized additional airstrike, provides one of the more remarkable examples of Yankee ingenuity of the war.

77. A light cruiser in McCain's Group, *Houston* was damaged even more severely than the *Canberra* when a torpedo struck amidships. Engineering spaces were completely flooded and all power was lost. The *Houston* was struck again while under tow two days later, but in spite of taking on more than 6,300 tons of water, this ship, too, was eventually towed to safety and overhauled.

78. Part of the Japanese fleet actually sailed on the eighteenth. At the time the Japanese fleet was split into two forces, trying to overhaul and rearm for one last desperate battle, to be called Operation Sho. Their problems included lack of fuel, confused communications and self-delusionary reports of successes coming from the Imperial High Command, along with a stunning lack of airplanes and trained pilots for aerial support. Admiral Ozawa, "in a spirit of self-sacrifice," was to come down from the Inland Sea with his entire carrier force of perhaps one hundred planes and engage the entire Third Fleet while Admiral Kurita steamed from Brunei to attack the American landing and surface forces.

79. Leyte is an island on the east side of the central Philippines. This landing truly marked the beginning of MacArthur's triumphant return to the Philippines and a major turning point in the war. After failing to stop the landing, the Japanese themselves realized the war could not be won, except by attrition.

80. This was Admiral Kurita's force, too late to stop the landing, but still able to cause serious damage to the American force. In fact, the American fleet was in real danger, but Kurita hesitated and withdrew rather than pressing his attack to the fullest. Both sides suffered from confused and garbled communications and faulty intelligence throughout the upcoming engagement.

81. The *Princeton* was a light aircraft carrier giving air cover and support to MacArthur's landing on Leyte. Remnants of the Japanese fleet came through the water passages in the central Philippines to strike the American force in this action that came to be known as the battle of Leyte Gulf, during October 24–26. A bomb from a lone Judy bomber struck the *Princeton*'s flight deck, dropped through three decks and exploded, setting off chain explosions from loaded torpedo planes below and engulfing the ship in flames. Valiant attempts by the *Birmingham* to fight the fire and take the crippled ship under tow failed when *Princeton*'s torpedo storage blew, causing tremendous damage to its stern and a great many casualties aboard the *Birmingham* as sailors were hit by the flying debris.

82. The superbattleship *Yamato* and its sister ship the *Musashi*, completed in 1942, were the world's largest, fastest, and most powerful fighting vessels. The Japanese counted heavily on them to make the difference in sea battles against the American forces. The picture snapped by Lcdr. Downing that Fulton refers to was

apparently the first look the Americans had of the *Yamato,* which until then had remained a mystery ship even though it had been involved in numerous engagements including the Battle of Midway.

83. Light cruiser.

84. Large aircraft carrier such as *Essex* class, *Enterprise, Hornet,* etc.

85. Large oil tanker or "Oiler."

Vietnam War

NORTH VIETNAM

LAOS

GULF OF TONKIN

SOUTH CHINA SEA

Mekong River

THAILAND

Khe Sanh Quang Tri
Hue
Phu Bai
Da Nang

Bong Son
Pleiku
An Khe
Qui Nhon

CAMBODIA

SOUTH VIETNAM

An Loc

Bien Hoa

Saigon

Vung Tau

Cam Ranh Bay

6

The Vietnam War

The war in Vietnam was both the longest and the least popular war ever fought by the United States. With 58,000 dead and more than 150,000 wounded, it was also the fourth costliest in American history. Sometimes referred to as the Ten Thousand Day War, fighting in Vietnam had been going on since the end of World War II to throw off the colonial yoke of the French who had controlled the country since the later half of the nineteenth century until their defeat at Dien Bien Phu in 1954. In that year the country was divided along the 17th parallel into the communist North and non-communist South. Fighting soon broke out again as the communists, who had successfully driven out the French, launched a second "war of liberation" to unify Vietnam under their leadership.

American advisors appeared in Vietnam during the Eisenhower administration, but the first massive buildup of American troops did not occur until 1965. By March of 1973 the last ground troops finally left Vietnam, though the United States maintained some presence up until the final hours of the fall of Saigon two years later. In between, America was entangled in a bloody, futile conflict that polarized the country. During that time, more than two million American soldiers served in Vietnam. But it was the pivotal year of the Tet Offensive and the siege of Khe Sanh, 1968, that first brought the war into vivid focus for many Americans.

If the American cause in World War II was clear-cut and unifying, the ambiguities of Vietnam were, and remain, legion. That so many people can continue asking questions about every aspect of our involvement— our purposes and strategies, the rules of engagement, the absence of sound military objectives, the nature of the enemy and of Vietnam itself, perhaps our self-delusions that winning the battles would necessarily lead to winning the war—speaks directly to the main characteristic of this most unpopular and ambiguous of all American military ventures. The United States was schizophrenic about its commitment in Vietnam, constantly worrying about whether to escalate or get out, coming up with different answers at different times. Sometimes we seemed to be doing both things at once. It was a place of many paradoxes, deceptions, and self-defeating strategies.

The fact is the Vietnam war was not lost on the battlefield; it did not represent a failure of the soldiers. It did, on the other hand, represent a failure of both political and military leadership. Having gotten in by gradual and confused stages, we lacked the political commitment and popular support to do what was necessary to win. Military planners were frustrated because they were given no clear military objective and the political expediencies kept changing. The Johnson administration, in particular, simply did not want to tell Congress or the country the extent of U.S. involvement or its massive cost. One hard lesson we learned was about the inherent limitations of American military power. Without support of its citizens, a democratic government had better not go to war.

The "police action" in Korea was a precursor to Vietnam, the first example of the post–World War II nuclear age concept of limited war, one fought with less than full commitment or with even the formal approval of the citizenry. Because a nuclear confrontation was unthinkable, it was argued that in order to stop the spread of communism, the United States must establish "credibility" by a willingness to fight small, conventional wars in out-of-the-way corners of the world. The "domino theory" was embraced by almost all the political thinkers of both parties in the fifties and early sixties. If history has shown us that communism might inevitably fall of its own weight, this was in no way apparent during the war in Vietnam. It was certainly not clear to President Lyndon Johnson who apparently felt he had little choice but to prosecute the war even at the risk of his domestic agenda and, ultimately, his own popularity.

As the Korean conflict dragged on, it had become an increasingly unpopular war. Vietnam upped the ante. It tore the country apart emotionally and eventually discredited and effectively drove from office two presidents.

The hundreds of billions of dollars that it cost to keep this war going also sabotaged Johnson's promised Great Society. Guns and butter were simply not possible. Civil rights leaders began to feel betrayed, and then felt doubly so when it seemed that blacks were disproportionally carrying the burden in Vietnam. Not only was the war draining resources promised to them to end poverty and raise up their people; it was also responsible for killing and maiming them at higher and higher rates. And by 1967, mortality rates in many units were comparable to what the British had experienced in the dark days of the trench warfare of World War I.

Although handfuls of U.S. "advisors" had operated in Vietnam for years, it was not until 1965 that the first major American buildup began. In March of that year, the U.S. initiated "Operation Rolling Thunder," a campaign of sustained aerial bombing of North Vietnam. From then on, the United States was continually announcing bombing campaigns and then suspending them. At the same time, the first marine and army battalions reached the country, setting up at Da Nang, while President Johnson was already proposing negotiations to end the war. In the fall of 1965, the first major U.S. operations were taking place at Ia Drang.

For the next two years the war escalated and the United States became more and more drawn into the quagmire of fighting for a South Vietnamese regime that it was simultaneously having to prop up. The difference between public posturing by American officials and the private reality were blatantly at odds. The United States was forced to publicly support an independent regime that was in fact inept, corrupt, incapable of ruling through its own authority, and without financial resources separate from largess. At the height of the war, the U.S. was providing up to 90 percent of the resources of the South Vietnamese government.

General James Westmoreland was continuously baffled and exasperated by President Johnson's inability to give him a clear objective. Johnson and his group of advisors, primarily Robert McNamara and Dean Rusk, mistrusted the military and believed in the policy of initiating a gradual escalation of power in order to pressure the communists to give up. What Johnson and his advisors managed to signal to the North Vietnamese was that under no circumstances would America invade North Vietnam. This gave North Vietnam a free sanctuary. They ignored contrary advice from their own military planners who could see that the North Vietnamese were not going to just quit. The NVA Commander General Giap had demonstrated that even hundreds of thousands of deaths were of little consequence to him in the larger scheme of the war. Time was on the side of the North Vietnamese and they realized it. They understood the struggle as a question of political will.

By 1967 Westmoreland finally implemented a strategy designed to take the country section by section, clearing the enemy forces and then turning the captured ground over to the South Vietnamese to hold while American forces pursued and destroyed the enemy, until eventually all the sections could be connected. This strategy, which Westmoreland called "the spreading oil spot," ultimately led to two misguided concepts that perhaps best symbolize the problems of Vietnam—pacification and body count.

Territory could not be taken and held in Vietnam, partly due to the terrain and guerilla nature of the fighting, and partly due to the constraints of limited war. American troops were not allowed to pursue targets into enemy-held territory. Rather, the enemy was allowed sanctuary zones where they could retreat, only to return when American forces had left an area. As a result, Westmoreland began to rely on a war of attrition, attempting to wear down the enemy. He introduced the concept of "body count" as a measure of the success of a mission. Despite the fact that in both world wars and more recently in Korea, the desperate strategies of attrition, like saturation bombing, had proven to be unsuccessful, Westmoreland nevertheless argued that we could reach a hypothetical "crossover point" at which North Vietnam was losing troops faster than they could be replaced. In fact, there were far more fighting-age men in North Vietnam than were needed to replace any losses inflicted by U.S. fighting.

To reduce its own casualties, the United States introduced the tactic of plastering a suspected enemy area with massive artillery—a tactic called "harassment and interdiction" fire. Along with the enemy, these massive bombing strikes destroyed the countryside, leveled the villages, napalmed the crops, and killed civilian women, children, and old men. It led to the often quoted, apocryphal principle that "in order to save the village we had to destroy it." The tactic undoubtedly saved many American lives, but obliterated any chance for pacification.

Pacification, and its corollary "Vietnamization" during the Nixon administration, was the paradoxical attempt to win the hearts and minds of the Vietnamese by protecting the peasant population while securing the rural areas through the tactic of massive bombing. Pacification was a failure partly because of the distrust between American soldiers and the Vietnamese. It was often difficult to recognize whether someone was friendly or hostile. Villagers in the countryside often played both sides—collaborator during the day, VC at night. American troops were in a country with weird rules of war and surrounded by people who they were theoretically protecting, but whom they couldn't trust. Even women and children would sometimes be carrying bombs or machine guns, a circumstance that added greatly to the distress of American soldiers.

Though the United States continually won battles on the field, the enemy was allowed to simply retreat to a safe haven, from where it could regroup and strike at any time. The Viet Cong and the NVA became experts at the hit-and-run tactics of jungle ambush. Mines and booby traps accounted for a fifth of U.S. casualties. The NVA learned to fight mainly at night to neutralize the Americans' main weapon—air mobility. Choppers rarely flew at night. They also learned that they could avoid artillery by aggressively closing with Americans and attacking. American troops became the ones who dug in and the NVA were the ones to initiate and break off contact.

Historians agree that the Tet Offensive of 1968 was a humiliating military defeat for North Vietnam, but that distorted press coverage turned the battlefield victory of U.S. troops into a propaganda and public relations defeat for the United States. There is no doubt that the offensive marked a crucial turning point in the war, as Americans for the first time really woke up to the reality of American policy and its consequences. While the war had been going on for years, this would spark the beginning of a tremendous vituperative wave of dissent.

Tet in most ways came as an even bigger surprise than did Pearl Harbor, though Westmoreland had ample warnings about Tet and ignored them. Fortunately, General Ford Weyand became worried about reports of massive hostile movements and convinced Westmoreland at the last minute to pull troops in to form a defense of Saigon that saved the city from being overrun. But Westmoreland believed Tet was simply a diversion for the main attack at Khe Sanh, an isolated marine fire base in the northwest corner of South Vietnam, near the Laotian border and the Ho Chi Minh trail. It lay along the route that the NVA naturally would take to invade Hue and Quang Tri on the coast.

The NVA originally considered Tet to be a horrible failure. After the first rather desperate blows, they were defeated thoroughly in the field, suffering 60,000 dead and perhaps a quarter million men wounded. In contrast, combined American and ARVN forces suffered 2,600 killed and fewer than 13,000 wounded. Further, the populous did not rise up in spontaneous support for the revolution as the NVA had fully expected they would. Worse, the carefully placed Viet Cong saboteurs who had long awaited this moment to show themselves were nearly annihilated as a fighting force.

The American press, however, sensationalized the story that the U.S. embassy in the heart of Saigon had been captured. In fact, a few desperate Viet Cong saboteurs had blown a hole in an outer wall and were trapped and killed in the embassy courtyard. When eventually the report was corrected, the correction had none of the impact of the original reports. Of twenty-one assaults mounted in provinces throughout the country during the course of three days, only in the ancient city stronghold of Hue were the NVA not driven back. Instead, they took the city and held it for twenty-five days. It required intense house-to-house fighting to retake the city, and in the end two thirds of the buildings in the historic provincial capital were destroyed. By almost any measure this action was a tremendous victory for the American and ARVN forces. But the media managed to portray the Tet Offensive convincingly as an American defeat. For the NVA, although the battle was lost, perhaps, here the war began to be won.

This distrust on the part of the reporters and the American public probably was due to the fact that by now everyone was beginning to realize that they were being lied to by both the administration and by the military, who were taking their lead from the White House. The effect back home is easy to understand when one considers that this was the first "television" war. Almost surely, a visceral reaction against the blood and horror entering American living rooms every night was inevitable. The question of whether it is possible to conduct a war with the television cameras running was one that followed the American military all the way to the Gulf War, resulting paradoxically in a high degree of censorship during the most televised war in history.

Meanwhile, Westmoreland was at least publicly still saying that he did not believe Hanoi was up to waging a long war. He argued that we had crossed the point at which we were inflicting more casualties than North Vietnam could absorb. This, of course, was either a delusion or a deliberate attempt to mislead the American public about the war. Either way, tactics and overall strategy in the war were predicated upon a mistaken assumption—thus pacification, body count, search and destroy.

The siege of Khe Sanh began on January 20, 1968, and lasted for seventy-seven days, capturing the attention of the American public as the war in Vietnam had never done before. Although the battle changed the direction and momentum of the war, it represented a heroic effort in which a few thousand marines held out against three elite NVA divisions. There were many dire predictions and comparisons to the disastrous defeat suffered by the French at nearby Dien Bien Phu in 1954, when ten thousand French troops had been forced to surrender to the Viet Minh, ending France's involvement in Vietnam. This time, however, American marines managed to hold the high ground surrounding the fire base. The marines were otherwise entirely cut off except through very dangerous air-resupply. They lived in heavily sandbagged bunkers for three months and withstood incessant bombardments from NVA heavy artillery. Attempts to overrun their position were nearly successful, as fighting in the outer trenches inside the marines barb-wire perimeter was hand to hand, with men sometimes fighting with shovels and entrenching tools.

B-52 bombers and other air power was brought to bear, blasting the enemy-held area around the fire base in an operation referred to as Arc-light, for the white light that sometimes seemed to bounce along the ridges like lightning from the massive explosions of saturation bombing. In all, some 100,000 tons of bombs were dropped during this operation, making it the most heavily bombed target in the history of warfare to that point, and according to Westmoreland, American forces "effectively shattered two crack NVA divisions."

The marines were finally rescued by the First Air Cavalry, McNamara's "sky cavalry," in a division-sized leapfrogging movement known as Operation Pegasus that ultimately cleared Highway 9 into the firebase. In this action the First Air Cavalry proved once again the value of the new air mobile concept that could mass troops quickly where they would be most effective. A few weeks after the army opened the highway to Khe Sanh, the NVA broke off the siege and, ironically, not long after that the marines abandoned the fortification altogether.

In spite of the eventual success in breaking the siege, Khe Sanh was an enormous psychological defeat for the United States back home. Johnson was stunned by it and by the audacity of the Tet Offensive, which came at a time when he was trying to convince himself that the NVA were ready to come to the peace table. Johnson swung from an overly optimistic point of view to an overly negative one. He had his own minutely detailed situation relief map and photomural of Khe Sanh constructed in a basement war room of the White House and had it updated several times a day. In that room, he began brooding, trying to direct the action, playing general and making unreasonable demands of the Joint Chiefs, even having them sign a paper promising not to let Khe Sanh fall.

Most of the soldiers sent to Vietnam after 1968 were draftees, although by far the majority of Americans reaching draft age managed to avoid induction or were given exemptions. Among the myths of the Vietnam War is that the average draftee came from a poverty-stricken background and was more poorly educated than the typical young American of the 1960s. It has long been accepted as an article of faith that blacks were disproportionately represented among the casualties.

It is true that McNamara used the draft as a social program with his "100,000 men program" which mandated accepting that number of men a year who would in the past have been disqualified because they did not meet the minimum aptitude standards. Also, later in the war draft boards often made pointed efforts to induct antiwar protestors, even at times ignoring physical disabilities that would normally have kept them out. All of this represented the opposite policy from earlier wars, when the military was looking for the best educated and most reliable soldier it could find, and it no doubt hastened worsening morale and efficiency problems in Vietnam. While the average World War II soldier had been twenty-seven years old with a family and at least the hope of a job to come home to, the soldiers in Vietnam represented the youngest group ever to be sent into combat by the United States. They were on average nineteen, rootless, and especially from 1969 on, often unhappy about being in the army.

The twelve-month tour of duty further hindered morale and fighting efficiency because it kept a unit from developing a tradition of continuity or leadership. As soon as the troops learned to fight and survive, they were redeployed home, to be replaced by inexperienced soldiers and officers. Perhaps an indication of this is that while Joe Abodeely was in charge of his platoon for the first six months of 1968, during the second six months, the platoon had six different leaders, an average of one a month. Not surprisingly, they began taking higher casualties.

On the other hand, a recent study of the names of the dead on the Vietnam Memorial Wall, based on Department of Defense records, suggests a somewhat different profile. Almost 70 percent of the 58,000 casualties were volunteers rather than draftees. While at different times, blacks did suffer disproportionately high casualties, over the entire course of the war the rate was only slightly higher than the percentage of the population. Surprisingly, the same holds true for the economic homes of these soldiers. By no means did they come from predominantly poverty-striken backgrounds. And a higher percentage of Vietnam veterans took advantage of the G.I. Bill than did any other veteran group before them. Overall, American soldiers in Vietnam were not misfits or victims of a class war as is too often depicted. Rather, they represented a roughly accurate cross-section of American society with all its strengths and flaws.

The year of the Tet Offensive, 1968, was especially one of turmoil and unrest at home, leaving Americans polarized and intensely political. This was the year Robert Kennedy was shot while running for the Democratic presidential nomination. Martin Luther King was assassinated in Memphis, sparking riots and burnings throughout the country, including the nation's capital. The Democratic Convention in Chicago in August broke out in riots and televised battles between Vietnam protestors and Chicago police. Such protests were by no means limited to this country. Students in France, for example, were even more violent and successful in disrupting the establishment. This same year, Soviet tanks rolled in to occupy Czechoslovakia. In the one ray of hope, perhaps, Apollo 8, the first lunar orbiting manned flight, sent down its disturbingly beautiful color photos of the planet earth. This was named by the press as the most significant news event of the year.

Originally from Tucson, Arizona, Joseph Abodeely was born in 1943 and graduated from the University of Arizona, where he joined the ROTC, in 1965. As a college graduate and ROTC officer, his decision to volunteer for

Vietnam came after reading an article in *Life* magazine about the death of an American advisor in the field. He was idealistic about protecting the people of South Vietnam from communist aggression. At the suggestion of his father, he kept this diary through his entire tour of Vietnam, beginning deliberately on January 1 of 1968 "to start things at the beginning."

A rifle platoon leader of Company D, 2nd Battalion, 7th Cavalry, 1st Air Cavalry Division, his platoon spearheaded Operation Pegasus, the drive that broke through to relieve the marines at Khe Sanh, and they were the first to enter the Khe Sanh firebase. Abodeely entered blowing a captured bugle he had found on the dirt road, Highway 9, leading into the compound. The incident was highly reported back home, with a reporter filing this wire service account of the moment: "Troops of the U.S. 1st Cavalry Division, sounding charge on a captured North Vietnamese bugle, walked the last two miles into Khe Sanh fortress yesterday and joined marine defenders who had weathered the heaviest siege of the war. . . . Lt. Joe Abodeely, 24, of Tucson, Ariz, reached through the wire, grabbed [a marine's] hand and said, 'We're glad to be here.' "

Abodeely led his platoon through some of the bloodiest campaigns of the war, during a turning point in the conduct of the war and in the American public's attitudes toward it. Following the relief of Khe Sanh, they were sent on an extensive sweep of the infamous A Shau Valley, an NVA stronghold for several years. During this time he received, among other awards, the Air Medal and the Bronze Star for action leading up to the relief of Khe Sanh. He also served for a time as a service platoon leader and officer in charge of the 3rd Brigade VIP Center, an R&R center of Headquarters and Headquarters Company at Camp Evans. He finished his tour as a Liaison Officer holding down a perimeter at Quan Loi near An Loc, not far from Saigon, a place that was later overrun in the final communist push to Saigon in 1975.

Abodeely's outfit, the 1st Air Cavalry, established the efficacy of the then unproven concept of "air mobility." The Division was created at Fort Benning, Georgia, in 1965 and sent to Vietnam by Robert McNamara, against the military's advice, to test and develop an air-mobile version of classic cavalry roles. The troops often referred to their role at the time as "real-fire training" or "on the job fighting." Their assignment was to move quickly, provide deep reconnaissance, and fight ambush and delaying skirmishes. As a fighting and tactical force they proved to be highly useful.

After returning stateside, Abodeely received his law degree from the University of Arizona Law School in Tucson then attended the Judge Advocate General's school. He spent nearly fifteen years as a prosecuting attorney, and now practices criminal, administrative, and military law out of his own office in Phoenix. Through the 1970s he served in the Arizona National Guard. He is currently a Colonel in the Judge Advocate General's Corp of the Army Reserve assigned as Chief of the Law Branch (IMA), U.S. Army Military Police Operations Agency.

The Diary of Joseph Abodeely

Monday, January 1. Today I will start to keep this diary. I'm sleepy now as it is 12:30 A.M. of 2 January, but it seems proper to make an entry for 1 January to start things at the beginning. I have a lot to do tomorrow for preparation for my trip.

Tuesday, January 2. I bought a pocket flashlight. Tonight, Mat, Fred, our dates, and I are going to see *Camelot*. I'm anxious to get under way on my new adventure. At times I feel apprehensive realizing the situation I am heading toward, but most of the time I feel excitement and anxiety for this new and I hope profitable experience.

Saturday, January 6. Today is 6 January 1968. I am now in RVN.[1] We landed at Bien Hoa and took buses to Long Binh[2] where I am now. It is hot and humid. I've seen a lot of guys who were in my CPLC at Ft. Benning.[3] I've got a bad cold from San Francisco, but that's the least of my worries. The area reminds me of Nogales with beat up houses and poor people walking the streets. Right now I'm in a base camp at Long Binh. I'll know my assignment by tomorrow.

1615 hours. I slept awhile and then attended an orientation. We are waiting for our assignments to be confirmed. My buddies are playing cards and listening to my transistor radio. I'm going to sleep some more.

Sunday, January 7. Waited all day for confirmation of assignment. I checked with operations and the Sgt. said I'm assigned to the 1st Cavalry Division.[4] That means I fly north after midnight tonight or tomorrow night. I'm a little scared at the change of assignment[5] and the thought of flying north. I slept and listened to my transistor radio today. It's humid so I'll take a shower and be ready to move out tonight.

Monday, January 8. It's midnight and most of my buddies from my CPLC have left for their units or are waiting to leave in an hour or so. I'll leave tonight. Everyone tells me that the 1st Cav. Div. sees a lot of action and this scares me somewhat to think that I may not come back. This abstract word "death" now has some meaning, but I feel I'm doing something worthwhile. Two Vietnamese maids are here and I think I'll talk to them to kill time. I sure wish people in the U.S.A. really could appreciate what's happening in this country but our nation has grown soft and selfish.

Tuesday, January 9. It is 0300. I got up one hour ago and am now at the air field at Bien Hoa waiting for the plane to An Khe.[6] I met another Lt. from Cedar Rapids, Iowa. He knows the Abodeely family. In a few hours I should be at An Khe and at my new assignment. I keep experiencing alternating feelings of anxiety, apprehension, excitement, and boredom. It's hard to believe I'm on the other side of the world in a combat zone, but the armed jeep escort of the busses to the airfield helped to remind me.

(1515 hours) I'm at Adm. station in An Khe. We packed on to a cargo plane like sardines and had a roller coaster flight here. Now I'm just waiting to find out where I go for my assignment. They were impressed with my education and adjutant experience, but I'm still ready to be a platoon leader. It's rainy and muddy here. A lot of helicopters keep circling this base.

Friday, January 12. 2030 hours. Another Lt. (Richard Vincent) and I just came back from an Officers Club. Yesterday we attended class, which involved our going outside the perimeter. The VC[7] could have attacked us at any time. Last night I slept on the perimeter. I surely like the M-16, if it just won't ever jam on me. Here's hoping. I'm listening to my transistor radio now. Tomorrow is a free day. I think I'll go into the city of An Khe. Constantly I hear "choppers" and artillery fire searching the outside area. When our artillery fires (175 mm.), it rocks this room.

Saturday, January 13. 0820. I was awakened this morning by artillery fire. The guns usually fire a few rounds to scare the VC out of the brush, but apparently this morning some VC were spotted by a patrol or by the two choppers circling the area. The artillery had a fire mission and just kept pumping rounds off for about 10 to 15 minutes.

Sunday, January 14. 2028. I attended classes for my four-day orientation again today. Tomorrow I fly to Qui Nhon[8] to have my eyes checked. We had a lot of artillery and machine gun fire on the perimeter early this morning. It was routine searching fire into the boonies looking for VC.

Monday, January 15. 0925. I've just boarded an Army Caribou.[9] It's taking off now heading to Qui Nhon where I'll have my eyes checked. The plane is shaking while I'm writing. It's a troop transport plane and I'm loaded on with other troops sitting across from each other. We're taking off now. We're in the air now and it's a rough flight—we're dipping and fish-tailing as we go.

1315. I've had my eyes checked. I'm now on a C-130[10] heading back to An Khe. This is going to be a rough ride.

Tuesday, January 16. 0807 hours. I'm in the battalion orderly room with Lt. Vincent and the Adjutant. All three of us are flying to Phan Thiet[11] today. It's drizzling outside now. In Phan Thiet it's supposed to be hot. I'll find out soon.

1530 hours. False alarm! I'm back at 2/7 Cav BOQ.[12] We got to the airfield at 0900 and waited 'til 1500. Many planes came in and departed carrying troops but none to Phan Thiet. I'm going to have to get a camera to record the many sights I've seen already and will see. Tomorrow we'll try and get another flight to Phan Thiet. It's cool outside and in here as this wooden room has screens for windows. Thank goodness for my sleeping bag which I have on the bunk. It's really warm at night even though I'm sleeping completely naked except for my dogtags. I haven't been wearing underwear either as is customary with many of the field troops.

Wednesday, January 17. 1030. I'm finally on a C-130. Flights keep getting delayed or cancelled. The weather's bad in Phan Thiet, but here goes.

1550 hours. We got to Phan Thiet at 1300. I'm with 1st Lt. Lutchindorf, who is Executive Officer of the company. The 2d of the 7th (my unit) is moving up north of the Pershing AO (Area of Operation). It's a lot of action up there. Tonight I fly to LZ Bartlett.[13]

Thursday, January 18. Last night I slept on LZ Bartlett. I took my first ride in a chopper; it's great as the side doors are open and I can see for miles. I met my plt. sgt., Sgt. Stacey, who has twenty-three years' service, is a very capable man, but drinks literally all the time. He was high when I met him. He somewhat resents me taking over his platoon, but I think we'll do all right. Phan Thiet is near the South China Sea which is beautiful, but our battalion is going up north to Bong Son [14] where the action is hot. My men and I will carry just what we can carry on our backs. I'm ready to go to a hot area—many VC and regular army troops of North Vietnam.

Friday, January 19. 1925. I cleaned my M-16 this morning. We're supposed to get new weapons up north, but I'm counting on this one at present. The officers and NCO's got drunk last night. Lt. Gayheart and I each put in $10 to buy beer as we'll both make 1st Lt. in the field—he will about two weeks before me. It's scary listening to all these war stories of these guy's men getting wounded and killed. About two-thirds of my platoon are new, going to a new area with a new platoon leader, so it will be a challenge to all of us.

Saturday, January 20. 0835. The planes won't come in until 1600 today, so we'll sit on our butts all morning and part of the afternoon. Sgt. Stacey got drunk again last night and he's sleeping on his duffel bag. The rest of the platoon is standing around or eating their C-rations. We should be at LZ English sometime this evening. Capt. Roper, who was wounded by a punji stake, is back with the company and I met him yesterday. Lt. Linde and I slept outside on some plywood sheets last night.

Sunday, January 21. 1250. Last night we got to LZ English. We spent the night sleeping on the ground in the open. It rained and the whole company was drenched. I slept on an air mattress under a poncho and all of us were muddy and wet just like in a war movie. Today we took Chinooks [15] to LZ Two Bits where we are now. My platoon has six bunkers to occupy. Right now I'm in a wooden "hootch" drying off while everyone else is doing the same.

Monday, January 22. 2324. I fixed my hootch up today at my platoon CP. My bunkers are well secured and I hope we don't have any trouble.

Snyder is playing his harmonica in the room next door. Today I took a nine-man patrol about fifteen meters outside our perimeter to check for breaks in the protective wire in front of my platoon's seven bunkers. There were breaks where kids would come up, but we fixed them all except one which we'll use as an exit through the wire for patrols. There is a machine gun and claymore mine on it so there's no problem. I got a letter from home today. I'm sleeping on the floor in a sleeping bag which my RTO [16] found. My M-16 is right by my side.

Tuesday, January 23. 1410. Last night 3d Plt. saw two VC in the wire in front of their bunker. I went out and sat radio watch awhile. I didn't get much sleep last night. Today, the CO told us three platoon leaders that there is a Division of NVA [17] in the area. I sleep with my M-16 right beside me. Today, we policed up extra ammo from our bunkers. We stored it all in a room next to mine. There are M-16 rounds by the boxes, M-60 rounds by the cases, a case of M-79 grenade launcher rounds, and 50-caliber MC rounds there. If a mortar round lands nearby or if spontaneous combustion starts a fire, the ammo will go off like an ammo dump.

Wednesday, January 24. 0815. It's nice and cool outside my hootch. The scenery off this mountain is beautiful. I can see the green rice paddies, jungles, and mountains off in the distance. The ground is damp, but my plt. HQ and I are very comfortable in our hootches.

1920. Rose, Snyder, Pee Wee, and I went to the outskirts of Bong Son today. All four of us got a woman and got satisfaction. We have to be careful here as the VD rate is very high. Bulldozers started levelling the area around my bunkers so that just bunkers and my CP [18] are left. Tomorrow we'll move to the middle giving up the bunkers to be destroyed. We'll probably leave this area in a couple days. I haven't had a shower or a change of clothes in about five days.

2331. Bunker 48 (3d plt.) saw, through the starlight scope, four VC on the other side of the wire walking along with children. The 3d plt. ldr. said it looked as though the kids had hand grenades. I hope we don't have any problems tonight.

Thursday, January 25. 2120. I am in a fortification—sandbags, 50-gallon drums and wooden rocket ammo boxes filled with dirt. I am writing by candlelight. I only have four bunkers manned. We moved across the air strip and I'm with my two RTOs. I got on the radio and called the CO and he said that we could fire only when we checked in first at the CP. He says the VC must be inside the wires before we can fire.[19] This war stinks with rules like that. We were told today that the NVA are planning a major attack on one of five major LZs before their lunar new year.[20] Because we are not well defended, it could be us.

Saturday, January 27. Last night I went about 250 meters forward. It was scary. Beginning at about 2400, I called Lt. Steelman, our artillery FO;[21] and he called to the guns on LZ English to fire illuminating rounds. I didn't get much sleep last night. Today, I just cleaned my M-16 and now I think I'll sleep after I read some mail I just got.

Sunday, January 28. Maintained perimeter. We are still shrinking the perimeter.

I had a discipline problem with Sgt. Stacey and the CO backed me 100 percent. I think it will be all right now. I know that my brother has a birthday, but I haven't been anywhere to get him something.

Monday, January 29. 0740 hours. We have shrunk the perimeter. There is only one company and an ARVN company in its compound on this LZ. The dozers have destroyed most of the bunkers. All of my platoon are on the east side of the runway and we have three bunkers on the other side of the ARVN[22] compound. We still have problems chasing the civilians off the old perimeter because they are such scavengers. I checked my perimeter (which is almost a straight line of defense) at 0630 this morning.

Tuesday, January 30. 1155. Last night we had an intelligence report of five hundred NVA forming around Bong Son. It was a cloudy dark night last night. The Vietnamese celebrated their lunar new year last night at midnight by shooting off flares and rifles and automatic weapons. I moved my RTO and myself right next to the concertina wire of the ARVN compound. One of my bunkers said they received incoming fire. It could have been just the ARVNs celebrating. At about 0100 or 0130 all positions on our company perimeter were put on 100 percent alert. I was up all night. At LZ English, a bunker was hit by a rocket. Anyway, the truce we were on yesterday is broken. Today we get the brand new modified M-16s.

1950. Another sleepless night coming up. We got a report that a NVA company was spotted about one thousand meters from here. Tomorrow, the company goes on an operation. We'll walk from here for about seven thousand meters. There are NVA all over. I hope all goes well tomorrow on my first combat operation. I've only slept forty-five minutes today, with almost no sleep last night.

Wednesday, January 31. 1215. We moved out on a company operation. Right now, I'm sitting on a two-foot wide trail. The jungle is so thick that the whole company is moving in a single file. We stopped about forty-five minutes ago to eat C-rations. We've already crossed a couple of rice paddies. We all got new M-16s yesterday; I haven't fired mine yet.

Thursday, February 1. 1605. Yesterday, we moved over some hills after we went through the thick stuff. We returned to our positions by way of a large village. The people seemed wealthier than most with more cattle, water buffalo, and chickens. The edge of the village was along the river. We got a few sniper rounds, but nothing of any consequence. At 0600 this morning the whole company walked through the town of Bong Son to where we are now—the Bong Son Bridges. These bridges are of very high strategic value as they link a vital supply line. [23] I'm in my CP bunker at the south end of one of the bridges. I took a bath in the river after thirteen days of no bath.

Friday, February 2. 1850. I led a nine-man patrol about one thousand meters from the bridge today. At dark I'll take eight of us to set up an LPOP [24] on a sand bar to observe any VC crossing the river. I'm very scared and everyone says the job is dangerous, but I think it's important and to use the cliché—it's a challenge.

Saturday, February 3. 1330. My patrol left after dark last night. We walked in the river close to the bank for cover and silent movement. At one point, part of the bank fell on my RTO knocking him down into the river. The radio got wet and we had no radio contact back to the company CP. We could hear them but we couldn't talk to them. We had to break squelch on the radio to signal them. We made positions along the bank with our backs to the river, but we got sniped at from the other side. We slept in a garden between the irrigation furrows. I thought for sure we had it.

Monday, February 5. 1635 hours. I played touch football on the sand in the river bed for one and a half hours. I found out that we'll go on an operation Thursday. Snyder told me that two men in Company C got killed while walking point.

Tuesday, February 6. 1655. I went to one of the huts outside my bunker perimeter and got a haircut. The barber used hand clippers. He also shaved the hair on my forehead and ears. He also shaved my face and gave me a head, neck, shoulders, and forearm massage. I gave him $2.30 American money which was too much, but I felt it was worth it. I bathed in the river today. It's cool and windy now.

Wednesday, February 7. Tomorrow we air assault at 0900. We'll go about four thousand meters from here on a search and destroy mission.[25] We should be on this operation for ten days or so. We got another starlight scope for the platoon. I took the grenadiers and one machine gunner down the road to fire their .45 pistols which they carry along with their main weapon. I coached them on their firing and they shoot pretty well. We may not go to Hue for a while because of guarding these bridges and the need to operate around this area. Tomorrow will be my first air assault. I'm ready to go to bed now on these wooden boards. I wonder if I'll ever be able to sleep in a bed again. Snyder and Powell (1st sqd) are sitting here bullshitting.

Thursday, February 8. 1910. We walked from the bridges instead of being air assaulted. We are now in an open field with two platoons in a perimeter defense. We are in VC Valley.[26] How appropriate. We did a lot of walking today.

Friday, February 9. 1910. I had lead platoon today for the company and we moved through many huts in villages. We checked them out as we moved. We have a perimeter in a grave yard. It's dangerous here because of mountains nearby where VC can sneak up and fire down on us. I'm going to sleep on the ground near a big mound (grave). We have a mortar tube set up about twenty meters away and it just fired a couple of spotting rounds in a nearby mountain. I hope we don't get hit tonight as we are vulnerable. I already checked my positions.

Saturday, February 10. 1300. We're just relaxing right now. We'll move out, each platoon in a different area, to set up "goats."[27] We'll leave at 1400. We already went on a patrol this morning. We got on a hill where I could see for miles. I could even see the South China Sea about 4,500 meters away. My RTO heard a call on the radio last night that two VC battalions are formed in the area. In the past few days I've done a lot of walking and searching of villages, but no VC. We may hit some soon. I'm not so scared anymore, but I still try to be cautious.

Monday, February 12. 1620. We set up our ambush perimeter site at a graveyard in the middle of the rice paddies. We walked to the site on dykes so we didn't get wet. The graveyard was a grassy area with mounds for graves. We positioned ourselves behind the mounds. Nothing happened last night except it rained early in the morning and my whole platoon and I got soaked. We walked back to where the company CP was and we were picked up by Chinook helicopters (carries a whole platoon) and brought here—LZ Mustang. We'll be running patrols from here. I'm still drying off as my clothes and gear are wet. I haven't slept on a bed in a long time and I miss it.

Tuesday, February 13. 2030. I went on a patrol today and we waded several streams and forded a river. A year ago today, I entered active duty in the Army. I should be a 1st Lieutenant today, but apparently the paper work hasn't gone through yet.

My feet are still cold from being wet.

Thursday, February 15. 2100. We really travelled today. We spotted many old bunkers and fighting positions and we destroyed them with concussion grenades. We blew the hell out of them. About fifteen minutes ago we had a 100 percent alert. A grenade exploded inside the perimeter. We fired flares and the quad 50-caliber MG[28] and mortars and artillery, but we couldn't see the VC who threw the grenades.

Saturday, February 17. 2037. We got the news today that we're moving north to Hue[29] or close to it. There's a lot of action there. I've packed for tomorrow. 1st plt. set off hand poppers[30] from the LZ just one click[31] away. We are firing 50-caliber ammo to get rid of it as we're moving. The CO said the paper work is in for my being 1st Lt. When it reaches the colonel, he'll come out and pin the silver bar on me—so I'm told.

Monday, February 19. 2110. I'm sitting in a foxhole at Quang Tri.[32] Doc, Pee Wee, Snyder and I are huddled together. Sgt. Stacey and one other man from my platoon were on the other plane from LZ English and they haven't come in yet. In fact only 1st and 2d plt. are here. It's drizzling, but we put ponchos over us. We are nearer to Hue and this whole area is bad. We are listening to my portable radio. We have a little light bulb hooked up to a PRC-25 battery. Snyder and I are playing crazy eights.

Tuesday, February 20. 2210. I'm writing by my pocket flashlight. We left Quang Tri by convoy today and came here to Camp Evans.[33] It was wet, cold, and miserable last night. We're going out on an operation tomorrow. I believe it will drizzle all the time here. We are now north of Hue about four miles. I'm afraid we'll see a lot of action here. I'm going to sleep on top of my duffel bag as the floor of this bunker is wet and muddy.

Wednesday, February 21. 1909. At 0600 this morning we "saddled up" to move to where we are now. Along with our full field gear, we have been wearing flak vests as VC (NVA) here have artillery. Today we flew from Camp Evans to where we are now which is between Hue and the DMZ. The choppers buzzed very low over the rice paddies and it's almost like flying without a machine as I sit next to the open door. We landed here near a bridge and a village. Just our company and some ARVNs on the bridge are defending two artillery batteries—six 155-millimeter guns and six 8-inch guns.[34] My platoon made bunkers all day from scraps of this old French compound we are in. Today another building was dynamited to clear for artillery fire.[35] Sgt. Stacey went to see a doctor today about a swollen leg. Sgt. Blank from 3d plt. is with me now. He's a fine NCO.

Thursday, February 22. 2140. I moved into one of the old French buildings where the Company CP is because one of the 175-millimeter guns is blasting away right outside my bunker and the shock wave is too great. We got sniper rounds last night and some already tonight.

Friday, February 23. 1015. My third squad built this latrine where I'm sitting now. My platoon has built some outstanding bunkers. In fact, some of the people started bunkers and tore them down again to improve them, and I didn't tell them to do so. Sgt. Stacey came back on a log ship this morning. The howitzer just fired and shook the hell out of this shit house. Sgt. Blank went in today as he cut his shin on an engineer stake. Today we'll probably repair our defensive wire.

Saturday, February 24. 1040. At about 0600 we received mortar fire on the bridge. Three ARVNs were wounded, one mortally. I got out of this one man hole which my men built for me and checked two bunkers where we were firing M-79 for searching fire. It's drizzling again and everything is muddy and slushing and wet. Right now my people are repairing the wire, which they didn't get done yesterday.

The battalion commander flew in by chopper and pinned my first lieutenant bar on me.

Sunday, February 25. 1636. This morning the company HZ, 1st plt. and 2d plt. (mine) swept the area. My platoon was sniped at about four times. I'm wet and muddy and cold and miserable. My feet are shriveled up from being wet.

Monday, February 26. 0705. I moved from my grave-like fox hole to one of the old buildings. There is tin on the roof and I made a secondary roof of tin. The CO and I took a bath in the river. It was freezing, but I felt better afterwards. My plt. HQ is making a bunker. It's going to be a good one. It's still overcast and drizzling. I hope the monsoon season ends soon. I got radio batteries from home and a letter from Carolyn McCain in Louisiana. Third platoon brought in a VC suspect. My new hootch is good except no adequate overhead cover from mortar fire.

Tuesday, February 27. 1735. I haven't much time. We just got back from an operation. My platoon went on a patrol north along the river. We were pinned down and surrounded by sniper fire by what seems to be a company or possibly a battalion. The CO brought the rest of the platoons. Five of my men were wounded. I thought several times today that I was going to die. Thank God we're back. Now we have to move by 1815 somewhere else.

Wednesday, February 28. We came by chopper yesterday evening to Camp Evans where I am now. We walked to an area which we were supposed to man, but it was the wrong place so we walked to another area. After we got settled, my CO and two other captains came by to show me another sector of the perimeter which I am manning now with fifteen men until a company comes in to replace us. Snyder is fixing his radio. I'm tired.

Thursday, February 29. 1935. It's dark and I can hardly see. We are set up in the boonies on an operation. I took a combat patrol out last night. I slept in a foxhole with no blanket or cover and lay there as it rained on me.

Saturday, March 2. 0935. Snyder and Pee Wee (my RTOs) are in a tent made of two ponchos with me. It's raining like a son-of-a-bitch outside. My men are on the perimeter getting drenched. My platoon is supposed to go on an ambush patrol today, but I hope we don't. Yesterday 3d plt. ambushed some rice carriers but their machine gun jammed after the first shot and the gooks dropped the rice and fled. I hope to go back to Camp Evans today.

Sunday, March 3. 1722. I sent out two "goats" (ambushes) last night. I was miserable all day yesterday as it rained all day and we all were soaked. Today we air assaulted and now we're camped on a sandy beach two to three thousand meters from the South China Sea. Thank God it hasn't rained yet today.

Monday, March 4. 2100. It's dark. I'm writing by moonlight. We're on the beach again. My platoon led a drive up the coast through villages. Artillery is booming around us, as we were fired on tonight. I dug a foxhole in the sand in the dark.

Tuesday, March 5. 1044. We're still in the same place, on this beach with a brush that looks like pine. I'm sitting on the sand on my poncho liner. It's slightly overcast, but it's a nice day. I can tell the sun will come out. We'll be air assaulted today or tomorrow to act as a blocking force on this battalion operation. The ARVNs who worked with us yesterday moved on. They are good at searching and finding booby traps and VC.

2025. We're set up for tonight. We can hear another company in the distance firing on VC.

Wednesday, March 6. 1200. We walked about three clicks (3,000 meters) to an old Catholic Church. My platoon is on line on a trail waiting to ambush about twenty-five NVA seen moving this way. Artillery is about to fire behind the NVA to flush them this way. The sun is shining brightly.

1353. Artillery fell near us. We couldn't see the NVA, so we headed back to the church. I didn't even get to eat lunch when we had to saddle up ASAP and move to where we are now—on the hot white sand waiting for NVA to come out of the tree line.

Friday, March 8. 0945. Last night we set up on a road along the river. At about 2100 last night, one of my positions opened up on a boat sneaking across the river. We killed three women, captured one man, captured two weapons and one grenade. We feel bad about killing women, but they sneaked up on us. One of the women had her brains hanging out of her head. They all were VC.

1921. We air assaulted back to the sandy beach again. We are right out in the open. Flying here, we were sniped at in the air. We will sleep on the beach tomorrow.

Saturday, March 9. 1055. We moved off the sand into the village. My 2d sqd found a great deal of stored rice which choppers came in and picked up. We are resting and checking the immediate area.

Steelman is hacked off about something, but he laughed as I recounted old experiences in my diary.

Sunday, March 10. 0740. We went out on a plt.-size ambush last night. We are here at the site now, at a school house where two paths intersect. Children and women crossed the path, but no men with weapons. We'll be walking back to the company perimeter soon. We are in the middle of the village now. We set up the ambush site in the middle of a VC village.

Monday, March 11. 1325. Right now I'm sitting along the river on the grass and sand while I am stark naked. We're on a patrol and we've stopped to wash ourselves and our clothes. A bunch of children are around me but I "shooed" them away.

2215. It's night time and I'm writing by moonlight through the hazy sky. I'm sitting on the sand. There are supposed to be about forty VC in the area. Artillery is hitting off in the distance to our south. Otherwise all is quiet except for crickets and frogs and mosquitoes which I hear buzzing. Shrapnel zinged through my poncho tent. We'll probably be mortared tonight.

Wednesday, March 13. 0940. Yesterday evening we were air assaulted to Camp Evans. We ate hot chow last night and this morning. We all got a good night's sleep last night, except for when we were rocketed. I got several new men which helps a lot. Today we're supposed to go to some more bridges.

1530. We were picked up by Chinooks and half the company went to one bridge while the other half went to another bridge. Then we walked toward each other along Highway 1 [36] leaving some men at each bridge. We're on a grassy hill with Highway 1 just to our front and a river right to our rear. We all dug in, and now we're fixing tents and relaxing.

Thursday, March 14. 1855. Today my platoon walked security guard for some engineers on a mine sweep operation on Highway 1. When we got to the end of our sweep, I let my men rest and relax in a village. They bought cokes and got haircuts. Now we're resting at our company perimeter. Tomorrow we'll sweep along the road again in the other direction, but we'll go off the road to look for VC who threw rockets in Camp Evans today.

Sunday, March 17. 0827. My platoon is waiting along a road at the entrance to Camp Evans to go on a road clearing operation. We're waiting for the engineers. This morning my platoon and 3d platoon were getting C-rations when two mortar rounds dropped in on us.

Wednesday, March 20. 1333. My men are laying concertina wire with the engineers in the NW sector of Camp Evans perimeter. We are expanding the perimeter. I'm sitting on a gassy hill overlooking other hills and mountains and streams. It is very hot. Today I borrowed a three-quarter-ton truck to go get water for my platoon. It rained last night. The 2d plt. will probably have to go out on a goat tonight when we get back.

1700. I got use of another truck and found a way to buy four cases of beer for my platoon. They really enjoyed it. As I suspected, we do have a plt.-size goat tonight. The sky is very cloudy.

Friday, March 22. 1507. It's hot. I'm sitting under a poncho liner tied to four stakes for a sun shelter. Tonight my platoon is to go out to set up a goat on Highway 1 to catch any VC setting up mines on the road. We're supposed to be air assaulted but we could go by truck or walk. We turned in one of our M-60 MGs today to get a new one. Rumor still is that we'll go to Khe Sanh. [37] During the evenings, it's been raining.

Saturday, March 23. 0637. My platoon and I are sitting on top of a hill overlooking Highway 1. It's dawn now and I just went to my positions to check if the men were awake. As we moved in last night, three of my men saw two people across the highway on the other side. I thought for sure we'd be sniped at, but we weren't. Today, we'll probably act as a blocking force.

2310. We hit some NVA today. Several of 1st plt. got wounded; one medic killed. My plt. and I moved under fire to get the wounded out. Tomorrow we go back to recover the dead body.

Sunday, March 24. 1635. We air assaulted to find the body. The medic had been shot in the eye. Tonight we go out on a goat here from Camp Evans.

Monday, March 25. 1700. Last night on our goat, it rained. VC started mortaring Camp Evans, but I called artillery in on the mortar positions in the dark. Today, my platoon found the mortar site and brought back mortar rounds and other equipment. The battalion commander and CO were pleased. Now we are at a bridge in an old French bunker. An ARVN Sgt. is in here; we made friends as I talked to him from my translation book.

Tuesday, March 26. 1655. Today I coordinated with a Major at the ARVN compound down the road. On the way back, Sgt. Blank, Pvt. Osman and I stopped and had a beer in the village. We got in trouble with some MPs who passed by and said we were "off limits." A "mamason" who sells stuff nearby came to the bunker. I got "laid" today. My men are filling sandbags now. Some ARVNs are helping them. We are setting claymores and trip flares all around our positions—more than usual. Last night, a VC turned two claymores around. It was good we did not set them off.

Wednesday, March 27. 1115. Last night we spotted some VC moving around and shot at them. I called some artillery illuminations. The "mamason" came today and we bought fourteen more hats. She left some "pot" with me for safe keeping because the ARVNs will kill her if they find out she has it. Since I don't even smoke cigarettes, much less pot, I buried the marijuana by the bunker just in case "mamason" was trying to set me up.

Thursday, March 28. 1130. Some of my men and I are here at the river. I'm sitting here nude on the grassy bank. Some Vietnamese children are washing my pants and socks. We got the word yesterday—we move north. Some of the children are sitting next to me. My men are swimming. We will probably leave the bridge today or tomorrow.

Friday, March 29. 0940. The sun is getting bright now. I'm in the tower bunker. There are a lot of flies. The ARVNs got in a firefight this morning to our south. We could hear the shooting. I've been practicing speaking Vietnamese and I can get by O.K. now. One of the ARVNs told me this morning that four VC slept in the village last night and left in the early morning. My company will probably go back to Camp Evans today.

Saturday, March 30. 1435. My half of the platoon moved to the company site along the road between the bridges. It was relaxing being at the bridge. The kids who sold the cokes and beer were cute. Now, we'll go to Camp Evans to move north near Khe Sanh.

Tuesday, April 2. 0645. We air assaulted to the top of this mountain surrounded by a river on three sides. It's jungle and grassy. I jumped from the chopper and hurt my arm. I could see bomb strikes off in the distance as the sky lit up and the ground shook.

1000. The sun is out. We're on a high mountain top. Today my company is to air assault to a new location to set up there. We just got a log ship[38] with food and water. It was nice sleeping last night.

1720. D Company[39] led the air assault to where we are now. My platoon led a ground movement. We found an NVA site for a 50-caliber anti-aircraft gun. Also some of my plt. found some ammo and grenades. Now we are waiting to see where we'll set up. We're hot and tired.

Wednesday, April 3. 0953. We are sitting in the jungle right now. 3d plt. hit some NVA a little while ago. They got one of their men KIA. The S-3 [40] carried him back on his shoulders and then three of my men took the KIA to the rear. We're waiting for artillery to come in. There are huge bomb craters all around. I can hear the choppers circling the area now. There are trees, high grass, and ferns all around.

1808. We moved to Hill 242. [41] The NVA mortared us; we had ten or eleven wounded. NVA have us surrounded now. One platoon from another company tried to bring us food and water, but got pinned down. I hope we make it through the night. We dug in and made overhead cover.

Thursday, April 4. 1540. Last night we received more mortar and artillery fire. We are now back at the guns. I have my platoon in position on the perimeter. As we came back today, we picked up a couple of the dead and wounded who tried to get us supplies yesterday. When we got back here we saw more dead and wounded. The 2d plt. ldr. of C Company was killed. One medevac chopper was shot up. The NVA here are dangerous. I don't like this area. I hope we all get out alive. I got a card from Colleen today which cheered me up. We didn't have any food or water all day yesterday and for most of today. Everyone is tired.

Friday, April 5. 1550. I got the word today that our battalion may walk to Khe Sanh tomorrow. This could be disastrous. We've incurred a lot of dead and wounded since we've been here. I hope to God we make it alive. I've had a lot of close calls and I'm getting scared again. Everyone is scared of this area. The NVA are near us and good fighters. We're digging in again for tonight.

Jets keep circling the hill. There are also a lot of choppers in the air. Artillery keeps pounding the surrounding areas also. I hope the NVA move out. They ambush a lot here.

Saturday, April 6. 1400. Well, we tried to walk from this LZ to Khe Sanh, but we had to come back as the two forward companies received effective fire. Now our company is supposed to air assault to five hundred meters east of Khe Sanh. I hope we make it; we have many reporters with us.

Sunday, April 7. 1045. We air assaulted to an open area on a mountain top and received light sniper fire. We found an NVA complex with rockets, mortar-tubes and ammo, AK-47s, and all sorts of material. I have a sharp AK-47 which I hope to keep. We are to go to Khe Sanh.

1700. We are at Khe Sanh camped outside the east entrance on Highway 9.

Monday, April 8. 1130. Today, D Company was the first to walk into Khe Sanh on Highway 9 in over two months.[42] The marines had been pinned in, but now they can move. My platoon was the first in. This place is bunkers and trenches. The incoming artillery is deadly. I sent my AK-47 in with Sp. 4 Sanders who I hope will take care of it for me. My men sent in their captured weapons yesterday and they've been distributed out as trading material. This pisses me off, but I talked to the CO and maybe we can do something about it.

2345. I'm writing by moonlight. I'm sitting on guard at a bunker. I can see to the west (Laos) where flares are shot over the mountains. A plane is shooting red streams of tracer bullets into the mountains.

Tuesday, April 9. 1055. Our company is waiting along the air strips to get air lifted back to LZ Mark (named after CO's son—also called LZ Thor) to the fire base there. I've still got a VC bugle that I blow for the company. I blew it when we came to Khe Sanh. There is rumor we'll go back to Evans soon. I hope so.

Thursday, April 11. 0730. Yesterday afternoon my plt. took a bulldozer west down Highway 9 to fill in bomb holes and clear away trees. We found two dead NVA. They smelled and flies and maggots covered the distorted bodies.

Today we moved from LZ Thor to a mountain top overlooking a bridge below. The rest of the company is at another bridge. I'm pissed off because we didn't get food and water because we weren't on the right radio frequency to call the log ship in. The CO didn't even act concerned.

Friday, April 12. 1405. Today my plt. hitched a ride with a Marine convoy (trucks and tanks) to LZ Thor. We're waiting here to go to Khe Sanh and later to Camp Evans. It appears that our work is done here. I hope so. Last night it was cold on the mountain top. The sky looks like rain.

Sunday, April 14. 1102. My plt. and 1st plt. got here to Evans yesterday. The rest of the company isn't here yet. Today I went to PMO to see about getting captured weapons home.

Monday, April 15. 1405. The HQ and mortar (4th plt.) came in today. We're supposed to have an awards presentation sometime today. I'm afraid we may go into the A Shau Valley.[43] Today I wrote several letters.

Tuesday, April 16. 1100. Lt. Lutchendorf and I had a spat about my AK-47. I'm not going to turn it in as he wants. The CO sides with me. My old medic moved to mortars, and I got a new one. I hope I get out of the field soon.

Wednesday, April 17. 0900. Again, we're sitting around waiting to make an air assault. Last night I scrounged some steaks and my men got everything else and we had a good time. Now we're "saddling up" to move out. We're going near the A Shau Valley.

1815. We air assaulted about six clicks west of Camp Evans. We moved out today company minus[44] (1st & 2d plts.) and now we'll set up here for the night. 3d plt. is going out on a goat about two hundred meters away. Another log bird (chopper) is coming in now.

Thursday, April 18. 1100. I took my plt. on a patrol down to the river this morning. There were three destroyed houses, some old punji pits and spider holes,[45] and some old trails. A chopper just brought some water in. It's hot already.

Friday, April 19. 0700. We air assaulted to a large assembly area for the battalion near a river. Many of us went swimming yesterday. Today we have one of two missions—secure a radio relay station or create a battalion fire base—both missions in A Shau Valley. Last night one of our plts. air assaulted in the dark. It's weird to see the choppers fly in the dark.

Saturday, April 20. We're getting all kinds of extra supplies we have to carry as we may have supply problems. I heard four ships were shot down in the A Shau area. This will be the worst area yet. We're going to the top of a mountain to set up a fire base.

1115. I'm listening on the radio; the 1st ship of one of our companies is on the mountain at A Shau; another ship hit a tree and is burning. We'll go in later.

Monday, April 22. 0710. Here we go again. We're going to try to get to that mountain top. One company has been stranded there without food and water for three days. The weather has been too bad to fly. The B-52 strike on the mountain missed and there is no artillery support and the forest is thick, so everything is bad. Also the weather still doesn't permit much chopper flying. NVA have mortared the company at the mountain already—two KIA, one WIA.

Tuesday, April 23. 0755. Part of another company and our 1st and 2d plt. are on the PZ[46] waiting to go to LZ Pepper. The sky is still a little cloudy but we may make it today. The terrain there is supposed to be very thick. Some flying cranes with bulldozers were shot down a couple of days ago.

1145. We finally made it. We flew high above the mountains and clouds. This is the place where the two helicopters crashed and burned. The terrain is thick except for a few bomb craters. We're trying to clear the area. Not three hundred meters away we can hear a firefight. There's a lot of automatic weapons' fire. I don't like this place.

Wednesday, April 24. 1025. Yesterday we worked on clearing an LZ. A Chinook crash landed right over our company's location. Several of our people were hurt. One of my men was injured badly. A man in 3d plt. had a leg severed. The Chinook kept exploding near my platoons' positions as it had fuel and artillery and 90-mm ammo. I had to move my platoon to a different location in the woods in a ravine and set up in the dark. It was somewhat of a problem. I pulled a muscle or something in my left leg.

Thursday, April 25. 1055. We've continued to improve the LZ. The artillery has four guns on this hill. We are still set up in the woods. My men built outstanding positions with overhead cover and camouflage. Eventually we'll probably operate off this mountain. The forest is amazingly thick and difficult to move through. The area around here is high and mountainous and heavily vegetated. It's very cold at night. We're only about three clicks from Laos. I went to the field aid station and the doctor said I pulled a tendon.

Friday, April 26. 1345. I'm sitting by some log bunkers my men made overlooking the valley far below. It's almost eerie as the fog rolls in through the forest and the skeleton trees with the limbs and leaves blown off from bangalor torpedoes.[47] The Catholic chaplain gave Mass which I attended. I had a dream last night that my mother and father got killed in a car accident when my dad missed a turn on the freeway. I hope nothing like that happens. The fog has rolled in again so I can't see the valley below anymore. There's rumor that we'll air assault to the valley tomorrow if the weather is good.

Sunday, April 28. 0810. Music to the ears—choppers are coming in landing on both log pads with food and water. Because we weren't resupplied before, we couldn't move out, but with food and water we are supposed to walk to the valley floor. The mountain we are on has a 45-degree slope and is very thickly wooded. It will be a challenge to get off this mountain.

Monday, April 29. 0715. Our whole company climbed out of a ravine last night to the top of this hill. We stayed here as we hadn't reached the valley. One of the other companies was in heavy contact on the adjacent ridge. We all slept on the hill's slanted slope. Today we should reach the valley. I don't like the area. The NVA have too much here.

2025. My platoon led today. We got off the ridge we were on, got to a hill, went down to the valley, and we're now on another hill. It's pitch black out with fog in the sky and on the mountains. This hill was bombed before, so the trees are without leaves and the place looks desolate and spooky. Our company's mission is to walk around to the NW over a lot of mountains to the A Shau Valley side. It's an impossible task. I'm sitting on the ground near a big tree writing by my flashlight with the red lens.

Wednesday, May 1. 1230. We got a change of missions. We are to go around this high ridge. We got resupply today, which improved our morale. I believe that this company is doing all the hiking out of harassment. It's very hot now. I'm sitting on a trail cut in bamboo twenty-feet high. The land leeches and ants are numerous. I had a disciplinary problem with a new guy. He didn't pull guard and I'm going to court martial him. I hope we don't run into any contact. We're the only company in our battalion who has walked off the mountain.

Friday, May 3. 0920. We're moving out again. Yesterday we got completely soaked in rain. We are still on our same mission. We can't move too far at any time because the terrain is so mountainous and heavily vegetated. Fortunately, we've had no contact yet, but we're due. I hope we don't hit the shit tomorrow. Today ends our sixth day in the boonies. We've been humping a lot of mountains. Right now we are only a click and a half from Laos.

Saturday, May 4. 0945. We got an early start today. We are rounding Hill 900 and heading N by NE. We all have heavy beards. The sky is cloudy. We are up high in the jungle forest. I can see ants walking on leaves and I can hear the jungle birds and insects making noises.

Sunday, May 5. 0835. We are on the "road" again. My platoon is point today. Yesterday I got stung by a bee on my left hand forefinger. My finger and hand are swollen, but I don't dare go in as my "shamming" platoon sergeant hasn't come back from Camp Evans. Last night I fired artillery on a hill where my men saw tracers being fired from. I got a large secondary explosion which means I hit an ammo dump or p.o.l. location.[48]

Monday, May 6. 0735. We are moving out again. We won't go too far right away as we'll make an LZ for resupply. I'll go in today to have my hand checked as it is swollen. Sgt. Rose will go in today, too. This operation should end soon.

1915. Here I am back at LZ Pepper. The company comes in tomorrow. I came in today because of my swollen hand. We'll be here for a few days. I finally shaved today after nine days in the field.

Thursday, May 9. 1240. Last night one of the other companies accidentally shot an artillery round into our perimeter. Nobody was injured. "A" Company, who took our places, ran into some NVA. We were lucky we didn't stay out one day longer. They had three KIA and several WIA. There's an estimated NVA battalion where we were. Air strikes have been called in. Luckily the artillery round hurt no one, but on 5 May our FO was shooting and he accidentally landed a "105" round only ten meters from my plt. and me. It's a miracle nobody was hurt as its killing radius is fifty meters.

Sunday, May 12. 0807. We got here to Camp Evans yesterday. It was exciting flying high over the A Shau Valley which was pock marked with artillery, mortar, and bomb shells. Last night the officers had a get-together. There's a good chance I'll get a staff job soon. Later today or tomorrow, we'll go out on another operation around here.

Tuesday, May 14. 0735. It's a cloudy overcast day. Yesterday we air assaulted on the sands again. We walked the white sands and then cut into the villages. Yesterday evening we walked from one village to this location on the sand. We got mortared; I knew it'd happen. My HQ and I were sitting around and we heard the mortar tubes go "thump." We were down in holes before the rounds hit. Then Hale and Sanders helped me adjust our mortar fire on the VC mortars. Last night we got sniped at several times. My men have found rice caches buried in the ground at this location.

Wednesday, May 15. 1030. We got more sniper fire. My plt. sgt.—Sgt. Blank—took PFC Brown and the 90 mm and shot a cement building where some gooks were. The CO called in air strikes up ahead. Our mortar plt. fired at the villages. Last night we set up here and found punji pits, a booby trap which 2-5 blew, and we found some more rice caches. Today our FO called in naval gun fire to the area ahead of us.

Thursday, May 16. 1040. We're at the same place as yesterday in the sands. We're calling in an air strike to our front on a village from which we've been receiving sniper fire. I can hear the roar of the jets diving and then the blast of the exploding bombs. We'll have to check the village out later. Sgt. Rose went in yesterday. It's hot again already.

1618. We've moved into the village area. It's very green and fertile. There are bombed out hootches and pagodas. Right now we're stopped on a large green grassy field while the FO shoots artillery up ahead. We've found booby traps, but we haven't been sniped at yet. I hear roosters off in the distance, so people (VC)[49] are around somewhere. It's overcast now and not so hot; just humid.

Friday, May 17. 1600. We got sniped at some more. Some of the rounds came very close. Today, SP4 Brown fired the 90 mm into some hootches, and blew the shit out of them. I'm tired of getting shot at. I feel like a moving target. We air lifted a little while ago to a fire base on the sand just north of Camp Evans. We have sand bag bunkers and it's like being on the Sahara Desert here. I hope we can rest here for awhile.

Sunday, May 19. 0900. I got a new platoon sergeant and squad leader yesterday. I came in yesterday by chopper to check on the asst. S-4 job. It looks good.

1600. I flew here to Da Nang [50] where I am getting my toe x-rayed and checked.

1745. I'm sitting in the sand looking at the beautiful South China Sea. I'm talking to a pretty blonde haired, blue eyed nurse—Sharon Frank.

Monday, May 20. 0845. I'm in the hospital mess hall having a cup of coffee. I'll see the Doctor in about 15 minutes. Last night, a couple of the doctors, the supply sergeant, some special forces men, and I all got drunk. Later, one of the special forces men (Griffen) and I took a jeep and drove around Da Nang at night, which is off limits. The special forces team rented a house and keep it stocked with prostitutes. We visited them last night.

1705. My plane to Phu Bai [51] is to leave tomorrow. I'm with three other officers who are in transit. The doctor said I'd have to wait to get my toe operated on.

2030. Four of us just left one officers' club which had the Tokyo Dollies for entertainment. They were great. Now we're at another club.

Tuesday, May 21. 0705. I'm in an air terminal to catch a plane to Phu Bai, then to Camp Evans. I've just finished a book *Courtroom* by Quentin Reynolds. It's about Sam Leibowitz, a famous criminal lawyer, later judge. More than ever I want to be a lawyer—probably a criminal lawyer. Meanwhile, I guess I'll just worry about staying alive. I'll probably make it back to my platoon tonight if I don't have any flight problems.

Friday, May 24. 0915. I'm with the company again. We set up a perimeter here on this road near a bombed-out village. I sent a squad-size ambush on a trail and the road across the bridge last night. Last night we got a report of a VC convoy moving toward us, so Lt. Ron Little and I jumped into a foxhole and pulled guard for awhile. I had Brown on the road with the 90-mm RR. [52] The convoy never came.

1915. Our platoon made a recon to the East today. 1st and 3d plts. captured some VC. The interrogators beat the hell out of the VC who confessed.

Sunday, May 26. 1137. Last night my plt. went out on an ambush near a church. We were discovered, received automatic weapons fire and mortars. We moved out at night and were ambushed. No one was hurt. Today 1st and 3d plt. are making sweeps. 1st plt. killed a VC woman w/carbine and binoculars. 3d plt. had two men wounded by a booby trap. They called in medevac; then thirty minutes later another man was wounded by booby trap. Another medevac called in.

Monday, May 27. 1150. Yesterday, one of the injured men died. One of my men was his close friend and I tried to comfort him. I almost cried myself seeing the anguish this man had. We were mortared today, about three or four rounds. We fired back and some villagers (old men, women, and children) came to us for medical aid. To hell with them. They hide the VC; let him shoot at us; we return fire; they want aid. I sent 1st sqd. to look for a better PZ.

Tuesday, May 28. 1715. I had another disciplinary problem with Sgt. Blank yesterday, so I had him transferred to 3d plt. Today is Dad's birthday and I can't even say Happy Birthday. I am in an old French twin steeple church. My platoon found some refugees. It rained very hard as we moved. Some ARVNs are working with us. I had the interpreter with me, so he helped talk to the refugees and the ARVNs. We'll camp around this church area tonight.

Wednesday, May 29. 1925. It's getting dark. We got ambushed crossing a rice paddy. One of the ARVNs with my plt. got hit in the head. It was just a graze and he was medevaced. We captured three POWs. One is a confirmed VC. We put the 90 mm and called in aerial rocket artillery (ARA) on the treeline to the front where we received fire. Rifle grenades landed close and so did small-arms automatic weapon fire. We checked the area later and found that it was well shot up. We evacuated the refugees we sent to this church from here to a refugee camp. We'll move out tomorrow.

Thursday, May 30. 0730. Some ARVNs are cooking some rice and meat here. I like working with them and using the interpreter and speaking my little Vietnamese. I surely hope I get that staff job soon.

Friday, May 31. 1530. It just poured monsoon rain. We saw five VC last night and my squad flushed some onto the sands today. The CO did not pay any attention to my advice and info. Today the ARVNs beat and kicked the hell out of a young VC mother (suckling her baby). We had thirty-eight refugees when the CO made us sweep a village. I'm waiting to go in to see about another job.

Saturday, June 1. 1412. I went in last night and saw the colonel (Bn CO). He told me I'm tops for consideration for the Asst. 4 job. I'll go in approximately two weeks. We're still working with the ARVNs. 3d plt. got some more prisoners and weapons. The CO and some others are giving me a bad time for some reason. My plt. sgt., Sgt. Lucas, says it's because of my education and the others are envious. It's not my fault and I never mention my education. I've got a good plt.

Sunday, June 2. 0912. Last night my plt. had to go back to the same area we were at a few days ago. We spotted three VC in the goat site and five VC on the sands. I called artillery in on the five VC. I disobeyed an order to set out a squad in the village. The CO is "messing" with my plt. and me. I told him the area was no good for an ambush, but he ignored my on-the-spot observation.

Monday, June 3. 1140. Last night the CO had my plt. go almost three clicks back to the twin steepled church for a goat. None of the other plts. have been going as far at night. We saw about eight VC and the CO would not give me an artillery fire mission. I talked to him today. He's trying to undermine everything I do. I'm going to have to talk to the Bn CO.

Tuesday, June 4. 1237. I told the Protestant Chaplain about my problem with the CO. He said he'd keep it confidential.

Wednesday, June 5. 1830. It's a cloudy, breezy day. Most of my platoon are just lying around writing letters, sleeping or listening to a radio. I have one squad patrolling the firebase perimeter. I got a letter from Marge yesterday. I got one package from Colleen and two packages from Mom and Dad today. I hope we stay here a few more days so I don't have to carry this stuff.

I heard on the radio that Kennedy was shot in the head.[53] He is still in critical condition. The sky has heavy clouds and it looks like rain. The word is that our company will be in the field until 15 June. I can hardly believe that it is June already.

Saturday, June 8. 0900. The CO came out yesterday. I finished a book— *The Challenge of Abundance* by Robert Theobald. I just sent a squad out on a patrol around the perimeter of the LZ. The rumor about going to An Khe sounds better all the time.

Sunday, June 9. 0800. Today we're supposed to go work the coastal villages again. Jim Coan wrote me and told me that Jim Muir was KIA. Colleen wrote and said her husband is leaving her.

1422. We're along the road further east than we were before. We are at an old bombed out school house. A temple is nearby which has a life-size Buddha made of gold. If I could steal that it would be worth a fortune. One of my squads is up the road. We're trying to get a medevac for an old woman with a partially amputated finger with gangrene.

Monday, June 10. 0755. The CO told me they wanted me in for the S-4A job today. I'll go in this evening. It's difficult to believe I'll be getting out of the field. I'll miss my platoon. Several of them came up to talk to me last night. Right now some of the men are cooking ducks they found.

2030. I finally made it out of the field. I'll be working with the battalion supply. I'm at my company supply now. I'll sleep here for a few days. I hated to leave my platoon because I really grew attached to them, but then again I'm glad I have this job.

Well, I did it. I went through my tour in the field and never lost a man. None killed.

Thursday, June 13. 1235. I'm in the S-4 office. I'm still checking things. I've got a meeting to attend at 1320 at Brigade HQ. I detect a cold atmosphere toward me by some of my fellow officers. I've neither said nor done anything offensive to anyone. I believe it's the education bit again.

Friday, June 14. 1710. I signed for Lt. Jones property today. Now I own all of the battalion's property. Lt. Lutchendorf is my HQ CO. He's a lot more friendly than he used to be. I got another 30-round magazine for my AK-47 today. The weapon is really sharp. I hope to get it back home.

Saturday, June 15. 1330. I've been working with the books in S-4. I've signed for everything, and I'm now discovering the discrepancies. My problems lie in that I am signed for the warrant officer and service platoon leader.[54] I am assuming two jobs rather than one. I think I can straighten out everything.

Sunday, June 16. 1530. It's hot again today. I believe I am finally getting the hand receipts squared away. The warrant officer leaves tomorrow, so I'll move in then. I believe I'll build my own hootch. Building materials are hard to get, but one of my men says he has ways.

Monday, June 17. 1250. I moved into the large S-4 bunker today. Captain Roper said he and I can build another bunker. One of my men got the materials. Last night I found a contact where I believe I'll be able to buy beer and Coca-Cola in large quantities.

Wednesday, June 19. 1600. I can see that this job is going to give me much spare time. At times, I'm very busy in spurts and if the battalion has to move, I'll be real busy; but so far this is a real fun section. The S-4 section reminds me of *McHale's Navy* on TV where everyone is a loafer and schemer. That's us.

Thursday, June 20. 1840. The new Bn CO came in today. I went to G-4 and got a briefing and some equipment. Then Lt. Gayheart (D Company) had an ammo problem which I solved since I'm also battalion ammo officer. Also I've been writing up a skit today for Col. Robinson's going away.

Friday, June 21. 1800. I just got done playing volleyball. Today, I took two of my men and the jeep and went outside the camp to the bridge my plt. used to man. We had the jeep washed there. I saw Lin, a girl I met when my platoon was on the bridges, and she gave me a free coke. The Vietnamese are money hungry and can make as much as $1 off cokes.

Then we took Lin back to the village and bought ice. A large block costs $10, but I traded two "C" ration cases for it. The Colonel is having a going-away party tonight.

Saturday, June 22. 1215. The party was good last night. We had very good steaks. After the party, Capt. Roper and I took a jeep to the MARS station where he called his wife. I got assigned a LOD investigation to do.

Monday, June 24. 1940. Today Lt. Jones, Spec. 4 Laird and I went to the river. An MP gave Lt. Jones a bad time for not having a flak jacket on. I saw Lin at the river. She fascinates me by her Oriental shyness. Today I had a four-hour class on supply procedures. It was informative. I'm going to try to learn the job right rather than just get by.

Tuesday, June 25. 2107. I came through today. A two-and-a-half-ton truck rolled up in front of S-4 and delivered one pallet (80 cases) of beer. Beer is hard to get around here, but all went well.

Friday, June 28. 2020. It was another busy day. I'll be glad when Captain Roper gets back from Da Nang. I went to a G-4 meeting today for all the supply honchos in the Division. It was a three-hour meeting. I learned a lot about supply—problems, etc. From info I gathered, I believe we'll be here awhile. We'll be getting ice machines and other installation equipment.

Saturday, June 29. 2210. I just attended a meeting for Captain Roper. It was a staff briefing on an operation. We'll be working with combat engineers clearing the area along the "street" as we call it.

Sunday, June 30. 1500. I am now at Phu Bai (outside Hue) sitting on a cardboard box waiting for Sgt. Dix to get the supplies we need. We stopped in Hue on the way up and we took turns patronizing the prostitute facilities there. I walked on to a boat and the girl came up in a little sampan. Then we drove here to Phu Bai where I bought some beer and cokes for Major Monville. Hue is a pretty city with many reminders of war—bullet riddled and bombed buildings.

Tuesday, July 2. 2111. We are escorting bulldozers and road plows to level the village along the road where we've been receiving fire. One of the dozers hit an eight-inch shell booby trap. It killed a man on the dozer.

Monday, July 8. 1635. Here I am in An Khe. Lt. Little is here too as he is getting a MACV[55] assignment. We've been through Khe Sanh and A Shau together. I just checked on my luggage. I brought too much to RVN.

2137. Lt. Little, Lt. Lukenbil, myself and two other lieutenants are here at the *Can Do* officers' club drinking. They have MACV assignments. I'm on a refrigerator mission.

Tuesday, July 9. 1527. I'm sitting here at R&R BOQ. Lt. Little and I just came back from the city of An Khe. We got hair cuts, boot shines, steambaths, massages, and lays. I checked on a refrigerator at the PX today. The last shipment was sold out, so I'll go back empty-handed.

Thursday, July 11. 1650. I'm on our log pad waiting to go to LZ Jeanne to see what building materials they need. They say they need more PSP[56] but I don't think so. It's cloudy and windy now. The breeze feels good. I'm sitting on top of some 81-millimeter ammo boxes now. A Chinook just was lumbering into the sky.

Friday, July 12. 2220. I worked on a movement transportation requirement plan all day today. It's good experience to work on projects like that. It rained today. The monsoon season will be coming in soon. I miss being in the U.S. and having little comforts I once took for granted.

Sunday, July 14. 1934. Today I'm twenty-five years old. Laird (my driver), Sgt. Williams, and I went to Utah or Wonder Beach.[57] We took a jeep and a low boy (truck). We got four pallets (80 bags) of cement.

Monday, July 15. 1910. I'm pay officer for HHC[58] this month. I drew about $8,000 and paid most of it today. Tomorrow I'll go to LZ Jeanne to pay some troops there. We've been improving the area around S-4. We also leveled the ground for a messhall. It should be nice when completed.

Tuesday, July 16. 2135. We just had another going-away party for officers. We had barbecued chicken which was delicious. Our two-and-a-half-ton truck made a run to Phu Bai and came back with a two-and-a-half-ton water trailer. I went to LZ Jeanne to pay some troops. I'll probably go there again tomorrow.

Wednesday, July 17. 1010. I'm on the sand north of Camp Evans at A company's location. I came out to pay the medics. On the way here I saw an air strike from the air. It was fantastic. I wish I had a movie camera to record it.

Sunday, July 21. 2155. Sgt. Dix and I went to the 14th Engineers area and saw a show consisting of a band and some exotic dancers. I've been building a hootch which should be done tomorrow. We got more lumber in today. I believe we'll build a supply room which at present is a tent.

Tuesday, July 23. 2055. I flew to Wonder Beach today and scrounged some more cement. Baize and I swam in the Gulf of Tonkin. There were jelly fish in the water. The water was an aqua color. We moved the supply tent today. We're flooring it. We got a typhoon warning for tomorrow.

Wednesday, July 24. 2135. We had another officer's going-away party. Capt. Roper was honored tonight. He got the Bronze Star and Air medal, but I believe he should have gotten more. The awards system is political also.

Thursday, July 25. 1605. I'm here in An Khe sitting on a bunk at the DEROS[59] center. I want to get to the PX to buy a stereo tuner-amplifier. I got the payroll turned in without any problems. I hope to get a jeep tomorrow. I believe I'll buy the stereo set I want tomorrow. I saw Capt. Cate and Lt. Grant here. They're DEROSing.

Saturday, July 27. 0936. I've been waiting here since 0630 to get a flight back to Camp Evans. Replacements have priority so I'm still waiting for a plane to come in. Last night Lt. Kendall and I went to the Officers Club which had a floor show—a band with two go-go dancers. It was great.

Friday, August 2. 1735. It's cloudy today. I got the asphalt machine to work on the log pad. A fork lift picked up extra concertina wire in the area. The monsoon season is coming on. I'm somewhat disappointed that the Colonel wouldn't let me leave the battalion to take a General's aid job in Saigon. I was the only man eligible in the brigade, but we're already short of officers. My job here makes the time go fast.

Sunday, August 4. 1415. We're on the road to Da Nang. The view is beautiful as we get up high at the passes and look out at the South China Sea. The road is narrow and winding and mountainous.

Monday, August 5. 1835. I'm in Lt. Donahue's (CO of HHC, 15 Transportation Corp at Da Nang) tent having a beer. Today I went around Da Nang to various places. I patronized a girl near the 15 TC area. My Vietnamese is passable. It's hot and humid. I should have my business taken care of tomorrow.

Tuesday, August 6. 0850. Today I'm going to try to get a great deal of lumber. We need it to build sleeping quarters. Last night the 15 TCO club had a good floor show.

Thursday, August 8. 2055. I moved into my hootch last night. It's pretty comfortable. I have a fan in here, too. I was selected a few days back to represent the 1st Air Cavalry to compete for the job of general's aid in Saigon. I was honest to certain people and told them I was planning to get out of the Army. Now I hear the interview with the general is off. I believe it to be because of my not being career. Now I'm determined to ETS. I'll serve my time and get out.

Tuesday, August 13. 1943. It rained most of the day. We are using 8-by-12-inch timbers for our maintenance area and they are too big. We'll have to saw them. I think the XO is pissed off because I let the motor pool have plywood to build pretty nice living quarters.

Wednesday, August 14. 0730. I finished reading *Poems of Francois Vilos* translated by Norman Cameron. They were poems from a man who lived in France during the 15th Century.

2045. I traded the 8-by-12-inch timbers for 4-by-4-inch lumber for the motor pool shed. The motor pool area is coming along fine. I also picked up the payroll.

Tuesday, August 20. 1150. I'm sitting in my jeep with Sp4 Laird here in Da Nang at the 95th Evac Hospital. I'm waiting for a nurse (Joan) to take her to lunch and have a few drinks.

1830. Lt. Joan Burridge and I had dinner at the Stone Elephant.[60] We had a few drinks in the lounge, and I took her back to the hospital.

Wednesday, August 21. 1900. It's hot and humid. I'm back here at Red Beach (15th TC). Today I swung a deal for eight bundles of three-quarter-inch plywood. I've now got the problem of getting it back to Camp Evans. Also I've got to fly to An Khe to turn in the payroll. I've been driving all around Da Nang observing the people, the historic and sometimes beautiful buildings, the peasants, the ARVNs, our own troops, everything in general.

2145. I just finished reading *Management Uses of the Computer* by Irving I. Solomon and Laurence O. Weingart. It's an interesting book about computers and their uses.

Thursday, August 22. 2140. I'm sitting in an Armed Forces Police station in downtown Da Nang. I'm trying to retrieve an M-2 carbine (sawed-off stock) that was confiscated from one of my men. I hope I can get the weapon as the trucks will leave by convoy tomorrow. I haven't decided whether or not to stay downtown for awhile. An attack is expected.

Friday, August 23. 0830. Last night I got the weapon back. Then the two warrant officers and I went to the Stone Elephant Club. Then we walked around the block to the MACV club. We came back last night while the 15th TC compound was on alert. At about 0300 I woke up to an explosion and a flash of light I saw through the tent flap. We got mortared heavily (103 rounds total). Lt. Donahue and I hit the floor of our cots and then went outside near some sandbags. The rounds just kept dropping all around us. I hugged the ground where I was rather than run to the bunker another thirty meters away. The 15th TC Battalion Commander's office, only fifty meters away, was hit.

Saturday, August 24. 0650. I'm sitting on a chopper landing pad facing the ocean. The sun just came up and I can see some U.S. ships in the ocean. This early in the morning all is quiet, and it seems as though there is no war. Sp.4 Norman and I tried to get back to Evans, but we got bumped from the choppers by some brass. The lumber and self-service supplies got back to Evans O.K.

Friday, August 30. 1955. I'm listening to Humphrey speak on the radio.[61] He sounds so phony—a typical political speech. Today we had a meeting with the motor pool to iron out some difficulties. I'm getting tired of this place. I need a change.

Saturday, August 31. 2130. I just got a call from our S-1. He said to report to G-1 tomorrow for a mission involving sixty-days temporary duty. It sounded so mysterious. I won't know what I'll be doing until tomorrow.

Sunday, September 1. 1525. I took an LOH[62] here to Hue MACV compound. I was informed I was getting a liaison officer job, but I see that I'm to go back to the field with an ARVN unit. I made calls to try and straighten it out.

Monday, September 2. 1125. I am sitting waiting for a confirmation that I do or do not have to be an ARVN advisor. I am really getting screwed.

Tuesday, September 3. 1115. I got a ride from the MACV compound to the hospital log pad inside the "old" walled city of Hue. A marine chopper just brought in a dead woman. I'm waiting for a chopper going to Dong Ha[63] to drop me off at Camp Evans. Major Monville, battalion XO, told me all was taken care of. I'm sitting on a table near the log pad looking at a pond on one side and a canal on the other. Vietnam is really beautiful in some places, but the filth and the scars of war detract from the beauty. Some of the Vietnamese women are really beautiful.

Wednesday, September 4. 1040. It's rained all morning. All is rectified reference the assignment problem I had. I'm back at Camp Evans in the S-4 shop. Lt. Barger will go on the advisory team job.

Friday, September 6. 1335. We've been in the midst of the edge of a typhoon. It's been raining constantly. The winds have been strong. My hootch leaks. Everything is wet. The rain is just a drizzle now.

2035. Things are drying out. It's stopped raining. I'm drying clothes in my hootch. I hope I get some letters from home soon. Planes haven't been taking off and landing for the past few days because of the weather. Tomorrow I'll try to repair my hootch (fix the leaks).

Monday, September 9. 1150. I took a Caribou here to An Khe. I'm at the air terminal waiting for the bus to the R&R center. The sky is cloudy and there's a gentle cool breeze blowing. I'm finally going to Singapore on R&R.

Tuesday, September 10. 1445. Last night I saw a movie at the Can Do Club. It was *How to Save a Marriage* with Dean Martin and Stella Stevens. I believe there's a floor show tonight. Today I went to the city of An Khe. I looked for this girl I would always visit, but I couldn't find her. I found another girl who was cute soliciting outside. When I told her I wanted her, she acted surprised. She stepped to the back of the shop looking for someone and then motioned to me to go to her. Her room was neat and clean and very orderly, not at all like a prostitute's room one finds in Vietnam. While I was with her in her room she would signal for me not to make noise. She was nineteen years old, cute, clean, and well built.

Wednesday, September 11. 0920. The club had a floor show last night. They were Koreans and were good. I'm sitting on a bunk at the DEROS center listening to some tapes being played in the building next door.

Thursday, September 12. 1255. I'm at Cam Rahn Bay R&R processing area.[64] I saw Paul Middleton at An Khe. He was a crew chief—1/9 Cav. He DEROSs in about thirty days. I'm waiting to process now.

Saturday, September 14. 2130. I'm in my room now. I had a girl yesterday and I have a different one tonight. She's in the lounge now. The girls are called "hostesses." There's a girl, June, who is assistant manager. She's Chinese and a real entrepreneur. She's intelligent and orientally beautiful. I called home yesterday and talked to Ma.

Sunday, September 15. Capt. Bill Luther, our girls and I went downtown to Chinatown area and ate authentic Chinese food. We ate shark fin soup, crab claws, fried rice, octopus, and sweet and sour pork. Everything was absolutely delicious. I have a Malaysian girl who waits on me hand and foot.

Tuesday, September 17. 1650. We go back to Cam Rahn Bay tomorrow. It's been interesting. I've been able to buy gifts and clothes at very low prices. I bought gems and pearls and ivory and silk, etc. I've been entertained by girls whose job it was to please me in any way possible. I've been on two tours—the one today we went on a boat. I've taken films which I hope are all right. I've called home twice since I left the U.S.A. nine months ago.

Wednesday, September 18. 0850. Today we go back to Vietnam. We're to assemble at the hotel here at 1000. We'll get to Cam Rahn Bay today and maybe An Khe, too. I hate to go back to Camp Evans. I wonder if my hootch got flooded while I was gone.

Friday, September 20. 0920. I'm at the dispensary here at An Khe. I'm checking on my foot (toe) again. Lt. Joy is also here at An Khe. We'll go to the PX later and then to the city of An Khe. I don't believe I'll extend after all. I saw Capt. Steelman, Bob Steelman—my first FO, last night at the Can Do Officers' Club. I really like him. He and I took that small day time patrol out at the bridges. He was also with me on Feb. 27 when we hit the big shit.

1535. I went to Sin City (An Khe). I made love to a pretty Vietnamese girl whose family has a shop on the main street. She's really pretty. I went to the bar section and a cute Chinese-looking girl caught my eye and cost me another $5. What a life!

Sunday, September 22. 1930. It rained all day today. I feel sick. I have what feels like a chest cold and the flu combined. My hootch still leaks. I wrote a letter to Lt. Ron Jones, my predecessor here as Service Platoon Leader. I've got to write Margi and Colleen, Aunt Lorraine, and Aunt Jay. The Colonel seems to have so many projects for the motor pool. We have a CMMI[65] day after tomorrow. This is a big inspection. We have the IG next month, so everyone is hopping.

Monday, September 23. 1015. I went to the aid station today as I felt sick. I vomited twice last night and today my temperature was 103.4 degrees. It's out at the 15th Med Bn ward where I'll be overnight. The Doc thinks I have bronchitis. I feel lousy all over.

Tuesday, September 24. 1445. I'm still at 15th Med. I feel lousy. My temperature hit 104 degrees last night. I haven't eaten anything yesterday or today. I don't have malaria; just a bad chest cold. I called the S-4 shop to see how the CMMI came out. Capt. Grubb wasn't around. I may go back to work tomorrow but I don't really see how. I feel so lousy.

Thursday, September 26. I returned to the 2/7 Cav area today. I feel better. I went to brigade today and was accepted as the brigade R&R officer. This is an outstanding idea for morale, and I'll be the officer in charge.

Friday, September 27. 2145. I saw the R&R center site. It's right on the other side of the log pad. It's going to really be outstanding. The buildings are being built now. This job will be interesting and a challenge and a good way to spend the time. I've got about ninety-seven days left in country.

Monday, September 30. 1745. The R&R site is still improving. All the billets' roofs have tin on them. I'll move my hootch down to the R&R area tomorrow. I tried to get a detail to move it today, but they couldn't handle it. Right now I'm sitting in the briefing tent at the Brigade Tactical Operations Center. I'm waiting for the briefing and then chow. Capt. Grubb was pissed that I was taking my hootch, but that's too bad. Chief Stephans tried to get into the act, but the XO already okayed my taking the hootch. How petty people can be.

Wednesday, October 2. (Late entry, 0740 3 Oct.) On 2 Oct. I got a fork lift and moved my hootch to the R&R center area. I wrote a letter to Aunt Lorraine and a letter to Aunt Jamelia.

Thursday, October 3. 1740. I got orders today to serve as a defense counsel on a court-martial. The defendant is charged with three different counts, and his case looks bleak. It'll be good experience for me as I'll try to give him the best possible defense. I got a dozer at the R&R center area today, and the area was cleared nicely. The place is shaping up. I've been walking a lot lately as I don't have a vehicle. I'm still waiting to sign over my property at the 2/7 CAV.

Saturday, October 5. 1307. I'm in Da Nang at the USO waiting for a ride. I came here with a Lt. John Dorsey who is to help me get the funds to start the PX at the R&R Center. Yesterday, I told Major Womack, the Bde S-1, that I didn't want the case because the man had gone AWOL from *my* platoon. But I talked to Sp. 4 Goins and I now believe he is innocent, so I will defend him.

Sunday, October 6. 0945. Lt. Dorsey and I got civilian clothes and stayed in a hotel last night in Da Nang. I had a girl all night. It's a real morale booster to have female companionship once in a while. We'll go back to Evans today. I have $3,000 in cash in a suitcase.

Tuesday, October 8. 1730. I got a letter from Colleen and one from home. Everyone got the gifts I sent. Col. Curtis, Col. Gorval, Col. Hardesty, and Major Schiano all checked out the R&R center today. Everyone is impressed. Col. Hardesty commented on the police of the area though. Hell! My people have been doing an outstanding job.

I've been working on the defense for Sp. 4 Goins. It's going to be tough. The trial counsel is evasive on many things. I called Long Binh to get a statement from a witness. The guy is in jail there. It's hot and humid.

Thursday, October 10. 0716. I'm at the air terminal now waiting to manifest to An Khe. I've got to get records to clear my defendant.

1530. I got to An Khe, got medical statements and missed the flight to Qui Nhon. I believe I can prove Sp. 4 Goins's innocence.

Friday, October 11. 0650. I'm waiting in an MP jeep here in Qui Nhon to shuttle back to An Khe. Last night I got some info at the 504th MP station in reference to Sp. 4 Goins's marijuana charge. I rode shotgun this morning as we patrolled the streets in the dark to get to this MP station. The court-martial is tomorrow and the trial counsel has not done anything to get evidence or witnesses.

0915. I got to the top of An Khe Pass when we had to turn around and chase ten speeding two-and-a-half-ton trucks in convoy. The MPs are citing the drivers now. The sky is cloudy and it's starting to get hot already.

Saturday, October 12. 1737. Today I bought some items for the PX. While I was gone, the CG inspected the Gary Owen VIP Center[66] as it is now called. I've been extremely busy the past few days. Colonel Gorval, Bde XO, told me that the CG was pleased. I'll buy some electronic equipment from the main PX for my PX tomorrow.

Monday, October 14. 2222. We opened the VIP Center today. It rained all day; I'm soaked. There were little problems with the company, but we'll iron them out. We had hot coffee, dry clothes, and good chow for the troops when they came in. General Forsythe visited us twice today.

Tuesday, October 15. 1900. Today Sp. 4 Goins had his court martial. He was charged with: (1) AWOL (2) marijuana (3) sleeping on guard. The last charge was dropped. I got the second charge thrown out because the MP statements were hearsay. The first charge was reduced to a lesser offense—failure to repair to place of duty. Goins was lucky. Well, the VIP Center is running okay. The PX sold out of items.

Wednesday, October 16. 1755. I bought more electronic equipment for the PX today. It sells fast. I'm having problems balancing my sales, purchases, and inventory figures. I guess it will come out O.K. The first company we had at the Gary Owen VIP Center left today. We get another one tomorrow.

Thursday, October 17. 2126. Today Col. Gorval told me that Lt. Kendall would take my place as OIC of the VIP Center. I will take his place as the liaison officer for 2/7 Cav at Phon Dien[67] just outside of Camp Evans. I think I'll like that job. Apparently Col. Gorval was pissed off at me because the bunkers weren't being built as fast as he wanted. He checked on our area all the time, making comments on what he didn't know about. Anyway, I talked to Col. Curtis tonight, Bde CO, and he said not to worry about it. He told me that I did an outstanding job and that Col. Gorval probably preferred someone else. Well, such is life.

Friday, October 18. 1400. I'm in a chopper on the way to Da Nang. We are flying low over the rough ocean along the beach. I can see boats lined up on the sand. The waves are rough. It's cloudy and visibility is limited for the pilots. Lt. Kendall is with me.

1715. I transferred the PX account to Lt. Kendall. We're sitting in the chopper at Da Nang. It's raining and the sky is heavily clouded. I believe we'll be stranded here tonight.

Saturday, October 19. 2030. I'm at an ARVN compound at Phong Dien. I'm working with a MACV team. I'm the 2/7 liaison officer. I'll be around a lot more Vietnamese now. A Vietnamese 1/Lt. invited three of us lieutenants to his house tomorrow night for a Vietnamese dinner. I think this will be an outstanding job. I like working with the people.

Monday, October 21. 2110. "Tunwi" [68] had us over at his area in the compound this evening for another Vietnamese dinner. We always take our interpreter with us. I speak a little Vietnamese and he speaks a little English. Capt. Blanchette speaks French to Tungwi and I catch a few of the words from my Spanish training. I test fired my .45 pistol and AK-47 today.

Wednesday, October 23. 1902. Lt. Waldron and I checked out an accident in front of the refugee village between Camp Evans and here. A five-year-old boy was hit by a truck and killed.

Friday, October 25. 2030. Lt. Evans, Lt. Davidson, and I played Scrabble this evening. I lost. It's starting to get cooler. Tungwi Kung left today for Quang Tri. A new ARVN artillery unit is in. I went to the village today and got a haircut. I need to buy a foot locker.

Sunday, October 27. 1240. I'm back at the 2/7 Cav TOC. I'll work with Major McDonald in the S-3 shop. We're going near Saigon. There are four NVA divisions and the situation is extremely dangerous. This will be an extremely dangerous area.

2130. I'll get up early tomorrow. We should get to our new AO tomorrow. This is my 4th big move with the Cav. Fate is so unpredictable.

Tuesday, October 29. 1010. We are at our new AO location. The area is really set up. We have clubs and nice buildings to live and work in. I'm at the airport acting as liaison to get the troops to their new area. PFC Connell, my RTO at Phong Dien, is with me with a radio. Yesterday, I got here at 2000. There are a lot of trees, rubber plantations, and dust.

1935. I'm on a perimeter defense now with about 55 men positioned hastily on the perimeter. The only commo I have is with the CP (radio) and the whole defense is inadequate. I don't know whether I'll be on base defense for a while or if I'll go to a jump CP.

Wednesday, October 30. 1845. I'm on this perimeter again tonight. We're supposed to be hit hard sometime before 7 November. Doc Halvorson, my old plt. medic, is with me tonight. The dust around here is really bad. I'm really dirty. I wrote a letter home today.

Friday, November 1. 0847. Last night there was a lot of scare shooting on the perimeter. My sector only fired once, and that was because there was a trip flare ignited in the concertina wire. The battalion is sending out a forward CP today. The dust here is atrocious.

Saturday, November 2. 0800. I had perimeter defense last night. There was a lot more scare shooting around the perimeter except in my sector. I told my men not to shoot unless they could produce a body the next day. Yesterday morning after I made my diary entry, I heard on the radio Johnson's bombing halt declaration.[69] I hope we don't suffer. Also yesterday, the battalion sent out a forward CP to operate the companies closer to Cambodia.

Sunday, November 3. 0730. Capt. Mira, CO B Co., was killed yesterday. One of the captains at LZ Billie may have to take his place, and I may go out to LZ Billie. The LZ is near Cambodia. There are many NVA. The 2/7 Cav just began LZ Billie yesterday.

Monday, November 4. 1330. I'm at the S-3 operations hootch here at Quan Loc, monitoring the radio. So far our battalion has set up a fire base five clicks south of the Cambodian border. I'm still waiting to be sent forward to act as liaison between the battalion and brigade. Our companies are sweeping the surrounding area. Brigade has put many exterior and interior guard commitments which we must keep.

Tuesday, November 5. 0800. Yesterday I met a really cute Vietnamese girl named Khan who lives at An Loc[70] down the rode. She rode a Honda here and we talked for a while. She said she'd take me to the village to see the area, but it's OFF LIMITS to us now.

2045. I flew to LZ Billie and stayed there all day. It's on an open field surrounded by woodlines all the way around. I'll work as the liaison officer in the operations section, assisting in coordinating air strikes, medevacs, artillery & ARA support, and anything which aids our operations. I'll fly to LZ Billie in the mornings and return in the evenings unless something develops. Col. Davis got a silver star for rescuing Captain Mira's body.

Wednesday, November 6. 1637. I'm at LZ Billie now. A Chinook is hovering about thirty meters away, blowing a strong wind. Jets are conducting an air strike about three clicks away as D Company got into contact to the North of LZ Billie. I've been monitoring the radios. I just heard the humming sound of the jets' guns. The ground shakes as the bombs hit. I can see the smoke from the bombs' impact rise above the trees. Trees surround this LZ which looks like a round huge football field with guns and bunkers.

1900. D Co. hit many NVA today. Captain Siders got killed. Many of D Co. are wounded. I guess I won't go in tonight. Most of the battalion, including leaders, are inexperienced, and they all want glory.

Thursday, November 7. 0755. I'm in the CC with Major McDonald and Cpt. Opheus. We have two companies, and Col. Davis, on the ground near where D Co. got hit yesterday. We still want to recover Capt. Siders's and the medic's bodies. We are flying high and I can see the FAC[71] plane marking the spot on the ground for an air strike. I slept on the ground last night at LZ Billie.

2103. I'm back at Quan Loi[72] now. All the companies are on LZ Billie. B-52 strikes will hit the objective and our companies will check it out tomorrow. I heard that an NVA set up a claymore beside Capt. Siders's body and blew him to kingdom come. His body and the medic's body were never found. Col. Davis made a good move pulling back and putting in B-52 strikes.

Friday, November 8. 1330. We had four NVA artillery rounds impact outside of our LZ. I hope I get a leave to Hong Kong.

1455. Pony teams[73] from C Company just made contact. We got some incoming stray small-arms fire. The contact is not far outside our perimeter. One end of the runway took a barrage of enemy mortars.

My mail is finally catching up with me. I got several letters yesterday and today. I got a Snoopy "stuffed dog" from Colleen and a book *Ben Franklin's Wit and Wisdom* from Margi.

Sunday, November 10. 1315. Yesterday, Capt. Siders's and the medic's bodies were recovered. They were decayed and putrid. Their dental plates will have to be checked for official identification. Three of our companies are going to recon the area of contact today. The Colonel and S-3 will stay out overnight with the companies and come back tomorrow.

2050. I moved into a BOQ hootch. I hear we may move again. I hope I go on leave soon. I have fifty-six days left in RVN. I hope all goes well.

Monday, November 11. 1120. I've already been to LZ Billie and back this morning. I'm in a "hook" to go back now. Our companies found some dead NVA and some bicycles. I wrote to Colleen this morning.

1822. I just saw five bursts of anti-aircraft fire about five clicks north of here near the Cambodian border. The NVA were shooting at one of our jets. That jet made two more passes and got fired on both times about six rounds each. It's getting dark now and there's a whistling sound of the approaching night—the sounds of insects.

Tuesday, November 12. 1230. My leave was disapproved by the Colonel because of a shortage of officers. I'm waiting to take a log bird to LZ Billie.

1845. I flew in on a LOH. They are fun to ride in as I ride up front next to the pilot. It had a mini-gun on it. I got a letter from home that my AK-47 I mailed home was found by the postal authorities. I hope I don't get into too much trouble. I wanted to get it to the VFW, but I didn't have time to send it through S-2 channels. What a life!

Wednesday, November 13. 1407. I'm at Than Le Chan. It is a special forces compound with an air strip outside of it. There is also an artillery battery outside of it. I came by Chinook this morning bringing demolitions which the engineers are using to blow down trees. We will move our own 105-howitzer battery and our battalion here in a few days. I've come to coordinate the movement.

Thursday, November 14. 0905. Last night I slept on the ground with my poncho liner. It rained and I got soaked as I used to when I was in the field. Also last night, LZ Dot, which is six clicks to the NW of here, got hit heavily by an NVA attack. I could hear them calling for artillery on the radio. Today they are still being hit by rockets. Our choppers have also spotted a lot of 50-cal. MGs on the ground. Our engineers are still blowing down trees, to clean an area for our 105 howitzers. I'm still trying to get a dozer.

Friday, November 15. 1817. Im here at Quan Loi. I'm on the perimeter now with Sp. 4 Jamison who used to be in my old rifle plt., and Sgt. Garcia, a medic. I'll be in charge of base defense. The sun is almost down now. I hope I don't get into too much trouble over the AK-47.

Saturday, November 16. 1100. I'm sitting on the runway waiting for a Chinook to LZ Billie to go pay the troops and talk to the Colonel about my AK-47 problem. The S-1 told me that the Colonel told the XO to court-martial me. If I can't get support from the Colonel, I'm in trouble.

1645. I talked to the Colonel and he said he wouldn't court-martial me, but that everything is out of his hands anyway. He said I'd probably get a fine.

Wednesday, November 20. 1347. We have intelligence reports that Quan Loi is highly subject to attack during the next four days. Col. Gorval, Bde XO, wants us to improve our perimeter sectors of defense. He came to my CP last night and asked me many questions about my sector. There was a base defense meeting today and as usual there are many requirements and little support.

Friday, November 22. 2022. I'm going to Long Binh to check my toe again. It is very dark and quiet outside except for the crickets and occasional thunderous "boom" of the 155 howitzers. We've been on alert for an attack for the past few days. Everyone is worried. Since the French houses are in my sector, I'm not too worried as they have never been hit, and I believe that they are paying a bribe to the VC and NVA not to hit this sector. We'll see.

Sunday, November 24. 0745. Being commander of the 2/7 Orange Sector[74] means I work at night and can rest during the day, but usually I still work during the day. Last night I drove up and down the perimeter road checking my bunkers. It's dangerous but necessary.

Monday, November 25. 0730. I'm waiting at my CP for Sgt. Tate to bring the tower guards back. I sent most of the men back to garrison while I'm waiting around. I put in for a leave to Hong Kong again. I'm curious to see what happens.

Tuesday, November 26. 0900. I bought two Seiko watches yesterday— one for Dad and one for me. Lt. Taveneau is stalling around on my leave. It's supposed to go to the field today for the Colonel's approval. I may get to Hong Kong yet. Still no word about the AK-47 incident.

1235. Lt. Taveneau told me that Colonel Davis disapproved my leave due to "job requirements."

Thursday, November 28. 1430. Today we had a fantastic Thanksgiving dinner. Shortly thereafter, I got word to man our defense sector because of a report of 750 VC three clicks NE of here—LZ Andy. This morning, Lt. Rodriguez and I went to An Loc to get paper to decorate the mess hall. I bought some Vietnamese Christmas cards there.

Friday, November 29. 1820. I got a package from Mom today with candy, sardines in tomato sauce, and assorted cheeses. I also got some popcorn which I have here at my CP now. Today Sgt. Tate and Sp. 4 Reeves (Major O'Brien's driver) and I test fired a 50-cal. machine gun, which we have now mounted here at tower 4.[75] It's an impressive weapon. Well, I'm getting closer to home.

Sunday, December 1. 1415. We had the change of command ceremony this morning. I wished Colonel Davis "farewell and good luck." Colonel Hardesty is my new battalion commander. Still no word about the AK-47 incident. Lt. Rodriguez is teasing me about going to jail. That's not funny.

Monday, December 2. 1750. I'm at my base defense CP. The guards are in and I'm waiting for the sun to go down. I got letters from Margi and Colleen. I wrote each one a Christmas card. I started reading a novel today. I guess I'll try again for a leave to Hong Kong.

Tuesday, December 3. 0940. I'm in my room at the BOQ. Chief Stephans just gave me a statement for a report of survey I'm doing. Last night tower 4 (next to my CP) saw an object inside the fence which looked like a person. I saw it too through the starlight scope after climbing up into the tower at 0300. I fired three M-79 rounds at it and the third shot set off a trip flare which showed sandbags or something only looking like a person. I put in another leave request to see Colonel Hardesty's policy on leave for officers. If it's "no" this time—that's it.

1355. I got word from Major O'Brien that I'm flagged for investigation on the AK-47 incident.

Wednesday, December 4. 1740. I got four brand new radios from Brigade which I gave to our battalion commo for five old radios for base defense. I also called a CID[76] man to come over and I told him about my problem. He said he will check on it ASAP and then get a statement from me. Lt. Rodriguez told me that HHC had to cut my flagging orders on me today. I've got so damn many problems—being here on the perimeter all night; wondering about the outcome of the AK-47 incident; and hoping to get home for my normal DEROS. I got a delicious fruit cake from Marjorie today. Sgt. Tate and the driver are checking our land line commo right now. The end of the day is nigh.

Thursday, December 5. 1705. I mailed a night gown type dress (Vietnamese) to Colleen today. I bought a Vietnamese smoking jacket for Bob. I'll mail it later. I've still got to get something for Mom. I already sent Dad the watch. Sgt. Keen is assigning the guards their bunkers now. Sgt. Keen and Sgt. Tate rotate each night as my NCOIC.

Friday, December 6. 0942. Last night tower 3 took three mortar rounds to its rear. Enemy mortar rounds impacted at other points in the perimeter. D Company's contact a few days ago caused the company about 50 percent casualties. Twenty-two men were KIA, a couple from my old platoon. They were damn good men, too. One hundred dead NVA or VC aren't worth one dead G.I. as far as I'm concerned.

1755. I'm at my CP again. Bernie (Lt. Joy) and I played "crazy eight" today. I talked to the girls who work at the Vietnamese laundry in our battalion area. I read to them the expressions I learned in my Vietnamese phrase book and they think I speak well.

Saturday, December 7. 0730. My sector of the perimeter got hit twice last night by rockets. The first time about eight to ten rounds landed about one click from tower 3's front; the second time about three rounds landed about three hundred meters to tower 3's front. Both tower 3 and 4 called in artillery and ARA on the origin of fire. I didn't get much sleep last night.

1550. I went to Mass today. I bought a pearl broach for Mom.

Monday, December 9. 1126. I'm at Phuoc Vinh at the JAGC office[77] getting legal assistance on this AK-47 problem. I'll make a statement to my attorney and we'll save it if anything develops. I've got two concerns—(1) getting off with nothing, or only a verbal reprimand (2) making my DEROS date on time.

1743. I talked to both JAGC officers at Phuoc Vinh and they said to wait a while longer, and someone should come to get a statement from me. They also said that I could get an Article 15 with a small fine or just a verbal reprimand. They don't believe a court-martial will arise, but I'm still worried. I hope all is resolved well soon and that I can go home on time. Ma wrote and said that the items from Singapore arrived.

Tuesday, December 10. 1028. I'm at the Battalion aid station waiting to soak my left foot big toe—ingrown toenail. Last night tower 3's location took several rockets. We found the blown up rockets today and I took two of them to Brigade S-2. Last night my tower 4 saw the origin of rocket fire and we called in ARA on it. I called on base defense push and had to cut in and tell them to quit "bullshitting" on the radio when a target location is being sent in. Later a Captain chewed me out as he was on the radio at the time. He was still "bullshitting."

Wednesday, December 11. 1808. I drove to An Loc with Lt. Charlie West. We went by a cat house to see a girl I met here at Quan Loi. Co Khan is her name and she's good looking even if she is a Vietnamese whore. I plan to patronize her in the near future. Some of these people are so poor; it's really pathetic. I hope someday I'll be able to visit this country under different circumstances.

Thursday, December 12. 1236. All was quiet on the CP last night, but Colonel Gorval told me that today begins the VC/NVA offensive on all military reservations and cities. Ben, Larry and I went to An Loc. Co Khan and I made love. She is really attractive and intelligent for an eighteen-year-old Vietnamese prostitute. She has short black hair and she speaks pretty fair English. She has a very nicely developed body. As we were leaving, a school girl came into the house. She had silk black long flowing hair and she demurely went upstairs. I could smell pork cooking in another room.

Saturday, December 14. 1315. Capt. Lacey, the new HQ Commandant, inspected my guard sector last night. He seemed quite satisfied. All was quiet on guard last night. I still have not received word on the AK-47 problem or my flagging action. This waiting and not knowing is a punishment in itself.

Sunday, December 15. 1321. I went to Mass again today. Our battalion is supposed to be prepared to move; but there is also a rumor we may not.

Monday, December 16. 1238. All was quiet on guard last night. The bipod on one of the M-60 machine guns broke and I replaced it today. I'm reading *The Graduate* by Charles Webb. It's great.

1521. I'm sitting in the front room of this whore house in An Loc. Another lieutenant is getting laid; I've just been. An old woman, head shaved, is singing to a baby and rocking the baby to sleep in a hammock. This house is old with cracked cement for a floor. There are wooden stairs. Co Khan was not here. The ceiling is tin.

Tuesday, December 17. 0942. Last night I called An Khe to check my records to see if I was flagged, and I'm not. Lt. Taveneau, the S-1, is playing games with me, as he and I hold each other in contempt. I called SJA [78] to check with USARV CID [79] to see if they initiated a flagging action. SJA will call me back.

1720. I'm at my CP now. Colonel Hardesty told me today he'd help me and he'd give me an Article 15 if I wanted to have action taken so no one will mess with me later. He told me he held me in high regard, and right now I don't care if he court-martialled me because I have the greatest respect for him. He's a West Pointer and in the top 5 percent for promotion to full colonel. I just want to go home.

Wednesday, December 18. 1242. I'm reading while Chief Stephens, Chief Rosey and Lt. Rainier are playing cards. Today about twenty-five armored personnel carriers rumbled by to go on an operation. The nights are getting colder and shorter. I hope some mail comes in.

Thursday, December 19. 1536. Colonel Gorval had a base defense meeting today. General Forsythe has intelligence info of sapper attacks at various bases. Our guard is to be increased tonight, and I'm to send out an LP about two hundred meters outside our perimeter. Our C Company had four KIA today as they made contact where D company had their twenty-two KIA.

Friday, December 20. 1835. Capt. Fields said that CID and USARV have no record of a flagging action on me, except initiated by here. Lt. Taveneau deliberately flagged me to prevent my taking leave. I'm waiting until the Colonel comes in to tell him. Today Lt. Rodriguez and I went to An Loc. We went to a whore house, but we just drank beer. We're on another big alert tonight. I've got every bunker manned. I'll send out another LP tonight.

Saturday, December 21. 1500. I flew to LZ Sue today to see Colonel Hardesty. I told him that SJA informed me that I was flagged by the battalion and not USARV. The Colonel was unhappy that someone took it upon himself (Lt. Taveneau, the S-1) to flag me other than the Colonel. I hope all turns out O.K. I believe that the S-1 will get what he deserves. I believe all will be all right.

Sunday, December 22. 1300. I went to Mass this morning. Some of the officers are writing up awards for the move from Camp Evans to here. A lot of the awards are bull shit.

Monday, December 23. 1420. Capt. Lacy, HQ CO, said he called Division to lift my flag. I never was flagged by any USARV or higher HQ, only here at Major O'Brien's and Lt. Taveneau's orders. I could go to the IG and raise a stink about the unauthorized flagging action, but Colonel Hardesty has been more than fair and understanding, and I believe he'll take care of any injustices. I don't believe any repercussions will follow me. The year here is almost over, and I've learned a great deal about life and people. I've made some real friends and worked with some outstanding people.

Tuesday, December 24. 1410. Today is the day before Christmas and the only things reminding me of it are cards on the wall and decorations at the An Loc Chieu Hoi [80] compound. Chief Posey and I went there and I played with some of the Vietnamese kids. They are cute. I'll have base defense tonight, too. I hope no problems, as it's Christmas Eve. Capt. Lacey told me the Colonel definitely doesn't want me flagged and he will give me the necessary papers to assist my DEROS. I wrote Sgt. Tate a letter of commendation today. Even though it's almost over, danger still lurks. Two days ago I had to disarm a damaged hand grenade, and last night I put a small fire out near one of my ammo bunkers, which had hand grenades, ammunition (M-16, M-60), and 90-mm RR ammo. What a life!

Wednesday, December 25. 1800. Today is Christmas. We had another great meal today. Colonel Hardesty awarded me my Bronze Star and Air medal. [81] I go back to An Khe in three days. I hear that An Khe has been penetrated by VC several times who threw sachel charges in the R&R and DEROS center. I guess I'm never safe over here, even going home for DEROS. I briefed Lt. Schields on the defensive sector, and he has it tonight. I got my movie camera and field jacket today. Chief Stephans, Lt. West, and Lt. Francourty are playing cards. I'm drinking beer and writing. Lt. Granger is reading. I can hardly wait to get home, but in a way I'll miss the battalion.

Thursday, December 26. 1810. I went to An Loc today and took some movies of An Loc and Quan Loi (here). I patronized another brothel and drank beer with two EM and Lt. Rodriguez. The girl I had was named Tu Hong, an attractive, intelligent Vietnamese. I'm short (time in country), as the expression goes, and I'm killing time. Yesterday, Sp. 4 Oslin, one of my best men in my old platoon, gave me the highest compliment. There have been six platoon leaders since I left, and Oslin said I was the best. That means more to me than any medal or award. I've learned a lot about my fellow man this year, and a lot about myself. I believe I'll have to work for myself—be my own boss. I've got to really work hard to get through law school.

Friday, December 27. 1047. Capt. Lacey showed me a copy of the CID report which came down on my AK-47. He said it's a late Christmas present and that he won't "have received it" until I've gone, but nothing should follow.

2210. A bunch of us drank beer and BSed tonight. I'm a little high. Ben is falling asleep on his cot. Tonight is my last night with 2/7 Cav. In a way I am sad to leave. This year has been exciting and interesting. I've got to worry about An Khe now, and then to home.

Saturday, December 28. 0733. I can hardly believe it. I'm in the process of going home. Last night I drank a lot of beer and went to sleep. Around 2330, Chuck West woke me up and said some guys came over to see me off. I'm at the Quan Loi airstrip now.

Sunday, December 29. 1007. I got here to An Khe yesterday. I'll just kill time until my name is called to manifest to Cam Rahn Bay.

1851. I'm at the Can Do Club having a few drinks with a guy named Jim Tornillo. He will DEROS soon, too. He's been telling me about his wife and how he really misses her. I guess being married can really be great, but it just isn't for me right now. I believe a wife would hinder my endeavors now. I hope I can attend law school at ASU, but I'm not counting on it. I really want to be an attorney.

Monday, December 30. 1819. Jim and I went to Sin City today. I took some movies. I met a cute girl who I just made out with. I may make love to her tomorrow. I bought some ivory figurines at the PX.

Tuesday, December 31. 1607. Today, the last day of an extremely exciting year, Lt. Dick Vincent and I went to An Khe village. I patronized a pretty Vietnamese girl. It's a shame to see poverty drive people to do the things they do, especially here. We Americans are so lucky. Tonight the Can Do Club will have a floor show. I cleared finance and AG records today. I'm just waiting to board the plane to Cam Rahn Bay.

I hope this war ends soon. Peace really means a lot to me now. It sounds trite, but I really appreciate life and peace after seeing what I've seen. I've learned my strong points and my drawbacks. I guess I'll always be a free soul and independent. I believe law is for me as I can express myself through it and serve my fellow man (and myself). I'm thankful that God or Someone has watched over me and allowed me to accomplish the missions I've done and still keep my men alive.

Notes

1. The Republic of Vietnam.

2. Bien Hoa was an entry point city for incoming American troops. Long Binh was where replacements were assigned to units as needed. Here many new soldiers first glimpsed the carnage of war as dead and wounded were staged out at the area, as well.

3. Combat platoon leaders course. Infantry officers' basic training course at the Army's Infantry School at Fort Benning, Georgia.

4. The 1st Cavalry Division was the unit, organized at Secretary of Defense McNamara's insistence at Fort Benning, Georgia, to develop and test the concept of an air mobile assault force. It originally deployed to Vietnam in 1965, without having finished its scheduled testing maneuvers, and almost immediately was involved in the brunt of the fighting. The Air Cavalry, with about fifteen thousand men, featured its own helicopter component, which made it the force that was often choppered into firefights on short notice.

5. Abodeely had originally been assigned to the 199th light infantry brigade, but the 1st Cavalry was in need of platoon officers when he arrived, so the assignment was changed.

6. The division headquarters location for the 1st Air Cavalry. Later on the headquarters was moved to Camp Evans.

7. Viet Cong. The guerilla fighters, usually South Vietnamese, who were well trained and armed. Many of them had fought the French before they fought the United States. They knew the villages and the people in the villages, and how to convince them to cooperate. While U.S. forces usually controlled the day, the Viet Cong controlled the night.

8. A city near the coast, located about midway between Da Nang and Phan Thiet.

9. A twin-engine aircraft that could land and take off on a short runway, it was used to carry either troops or supplies.

10. An Air Force workhorse aircraft that could carry a large number of troops or large vehicles that could be rolled off through a rear door. During the siege of Khe Sanh, the C-130's often never stopped on the landing strip, but touched down and continued to roll toward take-off, as men and equipment were loaded and unloaded on the run.

11. A coastal city with a beach that served as a rest and recreation (R&R) center in Vietnam.

12. Bachelor Officers' Quarters.

13. Bartlett was a small cleared area on a mountaintop surrounded by jungle. Most LZs, or landing zones, were small temporary clearings, sometimes with a defense perimeter, sometimes not. There are many LZs referred to throughout the diary because the Air Cavalry was constantly air assaulting to one area or another. Only some of these are referenced by notes.

14. A city north of Qui Nhon. They actually assembled for a movement north in a staging and operations center outside the city.

15. CH-47 was a large helicopter with double rotors that could be used to transport an entire platoon and howitzers into combat areas.

16. Radio-telephone operator. A rifleman who carried the radio on his back and was responsible for maintaining communications.

17. North Vietnamese Army. The regular army was well trained and armed with Chinese Communist weapons, AK-47 assault rifles, SKS rifles, rocket-propelled grenade launchers, light machine guns, hand grenades and sachels carrying high explosives for suicide missions.

18. Command Post. Platoon headquarters consisting of RTOs, medic, platoon sergeant, and platoon leader. Abodeely's platoon was divided into three large squads, two of them with M-60 machine guns, and a third with a 90-millimeter recoiless rifle. His platoon also had five radios, which was highly unusual, since some entire companies only had two. Delta Company had been a reconnaissance unit, with several radios assigned to jeeps, and when they were converted to line infantry, the platoon kept the radios. Abodeely believes that the extra communications capability of the platoon made a critical difference in helping them do their job and stay alive.

19. Much has been said about the Rules of Engagement during the Vietnam war. The rules as written were meant to ensure the protection of innocent civilians and recognized that "the enemy in Vietnam is frequently intermixed with non-combatants." In a guerilla and civil war that was often fought in areas surrounding villages and hamlets, with women and children often participants, many troops felt frustrated and threatened by what seemed to be dangerous restrictions on their ability to defend themselves in the field. They often felt that by the time an enemy had been identified according to the rules of engagement, it was too late. These rules acknowledged "the nature of the war in Vietnam has placed an unusual requirement on small unit leaders to carry out sensitive combat operations, often in an environment where large numbers of civilians are present. Due to the extensive firepower available to U.S. forces, the degrees and type of force

must be carefully considered. This decision, often in the heat of battle, is usually made by individuals with limited experience such as squad leaders, patrol leaders and platoon leaders. Therefore, all leaders must be aware of the rules of engagement and of their individual responsibilities in applying the rules."

20. In fact U.S. forces had reliable intelligence to expect a major NVA attack during the upcoming Tet new year. This comment by Abodeely lends credence to the assertions that command should have been more prepared for the Tet Offensive.

21. Forward Observer. Artillery personnel would be assigned to infantry units to help direct artillery fire.

22. Army of the Republic of Vietnam. These were the South Vietnamese regulars who fought alongside American troops. In theory, American forces were assisting the ARVN.

23. The Bong Son bridges spanned a wide river. They were steel bridges, supporting railroad tracks and were considered an important transportation route. Abodeely's platoon was assigned to ensure that the bridge was not blown up by the NVA or Viet Cong.

24. Listening Post—Observation Post. Two to four men with a radio set up in a forward observation position.

25. This term describes the typical tactics of airmobile operations. The mission was to close with and kill or capture the enemy by means of fire and movement. Later, as the term took on negative connotations, especially in the press, the army changed the term to "search and clear," which was supposed to sound less offensive.

26. So nicknamed because of the high concentration of Viet Cong in the area.

27. An ambush. A small patrol would go out away from a larger unit and set up a small perimeter defense as bait, hoping to get attacked to bring the enemy out of hiding.

28. A tracks vehicle, or "duster," with four 50-calibre machine guns mounted on it for heavy firepower.

29. Hue was the only provincial capital that the NVA managed to hold for any significant time during the Tet Offensive. During the three weeks that the marines fought to retake the city, it became one of the most filmed and documented battles in history.

30. A hand-held flare about a foot long and one-and-a-half inches in diameter. It was struck by the palm of the hand at one end to shoot out a flare for temporary illumination at night.

31. One kilometer or one thousand meters.

32. A city just south of Dong Ha, the northernmost city before the DMZ.

33. Previously a marine base camp, it became the headquarters and main base from which the First Cavalry operated.

34. The basic artillery used by U.S. forces included 105-millimeter howitzers which could be transported by helicopter as the infantry leapfrogged to their objectives. 155-and 175-guns were heavier calibre artillery with long barrels which increased their range. Eight-inch guns were self-propelled on tracks like a tank. They were very heavy artillery that could be fired with exceptional accuracy.

35. This was to provide fire support for the units engaged in combat at Hue.

36. The main highway running along the east coast of Vietnam connecting many of the major cities from North Vietnam through Saigon and further south.

37. Some of the heaviest and most desperate fighting of the war was taking place at Khe Sanh. On this day, the Command Post at Khe Sanh took a direct hit, as did at least one of the platoon bunkers, and the NVA were believed to be tunneling under the perimeter. According to the Command Chronology, the base received 1,049 rounds of "incoming" that day.

38. Logistics ship, sometimes referred to simply as LS.

39. Abodeely's platoon was the 2nd platoon of Delta Company of the 2nd Battalion, 7th Cavalry regiment of the 1st Air Cavalry Division.

40. The battalion operation's officer. These designate different staff positions: S-1 is personnel; S-2, intelligence; S-3, operations; S-4, supply; S-5, civil affairs. For a general officer's command, the terms begin with the designation G rather than S.

41. Hills were given designations corresponding to their elevation.

42. Highway Nine, the main route into the marine base at Khe Sanh, had been cut off during the whole time of the siege. Abodeely's platoon was the first to clear the road and walk into the base. As they walked in, Abodeely played "charge" on a captured bugle they had found along the way. Several reporters wrote stories for the newspapers back home about this incident with the bugle.

43. A densely vegetated mountainous area near the Laotian border and an NVA stronghold. The North Vietnamese had long operated with impunity in this Valley, and it was an extremely dangerous place to patrol.

44. Indicates less than the full company of three rifle and one mortar platoons.

45. Punji pits were camouflaged or covered holes with sharpened bamboo stakes in them. Spider holes were small foxholes with a camouflaged cover so that an NVA soldier could pop out and spring an ambush.

46. Pickup Zone. An assembly area for men to be picked up in helicopters, usually in small groups of four to seven men.

47. Narrow cylinders several feet long filled with explosives which could be assembled end to end and detonated to destroy obstacles or fortifications.

48. Petroleum, oil, lubricants.

49. The Viet Cong were known to carry live fowl with them to eat, and the birds' crowing could sometimes be overheard.

50. A large coastal city along Highway 1 where marine and cavalry units were stationed. It also had a hospital and served as a main resupply area.

51. A town adjacent to Hue. It later became Headquarters area and base of operations for 101st Airborn.

52. 90-millimeter recoilless rifle. A large anti-tank weapon, shoulder fired by one person.

53. Bobby Kennedy was assassinated while challenging Vice-President Hubert Humphrey for the Democratic nomination for President after Lyndon Johnson had dramatically announced that he would not run for reelection.

54. The warrant officer is the property book officer who serves as an accountant for his unit. The service platoon leader is the assistant supply officer.

55. Military Assistance Command Vietnam. An infantry officer would usually work as an advisor to ARVN units.

56. Perforated steel planking. Originally designed to make airplane runways, it was also in great demand for overhead cover for bunkers.

57. The navy had supply ships there and it was a major center for trading among the services.

58. Headquarters and headquarters company. The administrative headquarters company for the battalion.

59. Date of estimated return from overseas.

60. An old, fancy restaurant that was a carry-over from the French occupation.

61. Hubert Humphrey was nominated at the Chicago Convention that turned into televised clashes in the streets between Vietnam protestors and the Chicago police. He was narrowly defeated by Republican Richard Nixon for the presidency because he had been tainted by association with Lyndon Johnson's Vietnam policy and because Nixon promised to end the war.

62. Light observation helicopter.

63. A city north of Quang Tri.

64. Cam Ranh Bay on the coast was a main point of departure for soldiers leaving Vietnam either for the United States or to R & R elsewhere.

65. Command Maintenance Inspection and Inspector General.

66. Gary Owen comes from Irish folklore. Early Irish cavalry troopers used the expression, which referred to a famous Irish drinking establishment. It was passed on in tradition to the American Cavalry and incorporated as part of the crest for Custer's old 7th Cavalry.

67. A city between Quang Tri and Hue, northeast of Camp Evans.

68. A phonetic spelling of the Vietnamese word for 1st lieutenant, more correctly "Trungsi."

69. On October 31, President Johnson announced a halt to all bombing of North Vietnam, and the next day Hanoi agreed to expand the Paris Peace talks, although the talks immediately bogged down. Johnson also probably hoped his announcement would help Hubert Humphrey's presidential campaign.

70. A city near Quan Loi, about one hundred kilometers north of Saigon.

71. Forward Air Controller. This refers to a light aircraft that would shoot white phosphorous rockets to mark targets for the jets to strike.

72. A small city with an airstrip from where the Americans operated and launched air strikes in the area.

73. Small splintered-off teams from larger Cavalry units.

74. The airstrip at Quan Loi had three sectors on its perimeter to defend. Abodeely's company was given responsibility for the "orange" sector.

75. The towers were about twenty feet high with wooden, roofed platforms that were heavily sandbagged for protection.

76. Criminal Investigations Detachment—military investigators.

77. A city near Quan Loi where the Judge Advocate General's Corp, the army lawyers' office, was located.

78. Staff Judge Advocate—the legal office.

79. United States Army Republic of Vietnam Criminal Investigations Detachment.

80. The Chieu Hoi, or "open arms," program was the propaganda campaign to get the Viet Cong and NVA to defect. Some Chieu Hoi's became scouts for U.S. troops.

81. Abodeely received the Air Medal for "meritorious achievement while participating in aerial flight" while a platoon leader. The bronze star was awarded for his participation in "ground operations against hostile forces."

PERSIAN GULF WAR

SYRIA

Mosul

Tigris

İrbil

IRAQ

Euphrates

Damascus

Baghdad

Bakhtaran

IRAN

River

River

Al-Kut

Dezful

JORDAN

SYRIAN DESERT

As-Samawah

Ahvaz

As-Salman

Basra

Safwan

KUWAIT

Kuwait
City

Neutral Zone

AN-NAFUD
DESERT

Hafar
al-Batin

Ras al-Khafji

Persian Gulf

SAUDI ARABIA

QATAR

Bahrain

Riyadh

Red Sea

7

The Gulf War

Nearly a century after the Spanish-American War, the United States fought a mirror version of its "splendid little war," this time in the desert of Kuwait and Iraq. Into the conflict America sent the most highly educated force of soldiers in all of its history in the first real test of the all-volunteer army instituted at the end of Vietnam. It was also the first test for a new generation of high-tech weapons systems. In a lesson taken from Vietnam's harassment and interdiction tactics, the U.S. military had learned to rely upon technology to do the fighting wherever possible rather than risk the lives of soldiers. In the Spanish-American War, the United States had built up the world's most modern navy, featuring steel-hulled, steam-driven warships and a naval strategy waiting to be tested; in the Gulf War, it was smart bombs and sophisticated electronic weaponry developed with the unprecedented military budgets of the Cold War.

The press fanned the flames of war fever in this conflict almost as shamelessly as they had during the Spanish-American War, portraying it in the most melodramatic and unquestioning terms. Managed by people who had presumably earned their doctorates in skepticism during Vietnam, the American news media energetically packaged the Gulf War as a sensational drama, complete with charts and graphs from the Pentagon. The war sold newspapers, and millions of Americans remained riveted to their TV sets, as well.

This was our second TV war, but unlike the gruesome scenes that invaded American living rooms during the Vietnam era, the pictures this time were practically bloodless, distant and abstract technological miracles of destruction without the mess—a computer-games simulation of war.

The military remembered Vietnam, and carefully controlled the news during this campaign. Surprisingly, the media was willing, for the most part, to go along.

Once hostilities began, the American public, as is their custom, overwhelmingly supported the troops. Dissent either disappeared or was ignored. Those who opposed the war somehow seemed hopelessly out of touch. This war remained popular because it was so short and so relatively bloodless, at least for the Allies. In all, Allied losses numbered 234 dead, 479 wounded, and 57 missing in action, far lower than most predictions. It also had a clear villain, regardless of the details of our previous relationship with Saddam Hussein. The victory came so much faster and in a more spectacular fashion than Americans had been led to believe it would. The ground conflict was over in just one hundred hours.

Historians sometimes point to the Spanish-American War as an important symbol in reunifying the country after the devastating schisms of the Civil War. For the first time former Confederate officers fought side-by-side with Union officers against a common enemy. Likewise, today's pundits were quick to see the Gulf War as a national catharsis that healed America of the psychic wounds inflicted by that earlier war. America was rising above its past and showing that it had finally dispelled the shadow of Vietnam. The public welcomed its soldiers home in a near orgy of excess, a welcome in fact that included those troops from Vietnam who had been shunned at their own homecoming years before. For many, this served as a long-postponed acknowledgment of their earlier service and sacrifice.

For a time at the end of the war, President George Bush enjoyed an unprecedented 90-percent approval rating in the opinion polls. But as the euphoria and sense of relief faded, critics of the war and the policies leading up to it began asserting themselves, convening no less than nine intragovernmental investigations. In the end, the president who had so briefly basked in approval the previous year joined the ranks of other rejected leaders after wars, garnering only 38 percent of the popular vote in the next election, nearly a record low for a sitting president.

The stated goal of the U.S.-led action in the Gulf was to liberate Kuwait from the brutal, illegal occupation of an invading army, whether the Kuwaitis themselves seemed to entirely deserve the help or not. This goal was not unlike America's rationale for intervening in Cuba against Spain ninety-some years before. The United States also wanted to prove it would respond as a reliable ally of the Saudis and other Arab countries when they asked for assistance. Again, America's credibility was at stake. At least at some level, the war served to demonstrate that we could and would fight effectively when called upon. If the Spanish-American War was fought in large part to gain respect around the world for an emerging power, this war can be said to have been fought to regain that respect which had been lost by our obsessive reaction to the Vietnam debacle.

Of course, an economic imperative was at work as well. America's most direct and important goal was to thwart Iraq's attempt to control a major percentage of the world's oil supply. Throughout July of 1990, Saddam Hussein began threatening Kuwait and the United Arab Emirates with military force unless they agreed to cut oil production to help raise oil prices. Iraq was in need of the additional income because of the vast expense of the long Iran-Iraq War, 1980–1988, which had produced a victory for neither side. Iraq also still possessed a huge army of nearly one million men, the world's fourth largest. It was by far the strongest and most ambitious military power in the region. Although an OPEC compromise was reached, on August 2nd the Iraqi army poured into Kuwait on the pretense that they had been invited in to dethrone the ruling Al Sabah family. Later, Hussein would simply annex Kuwait as a province of Iraq.

When Iraqi troops began almost immediately to take up positions threatening Saudi Arabia and the Saudi oil fields as well, King Fahd turned to the Americans for help. Whether Hussein intended to intimidate the Saudis or was truly preparing another invasion, the Saudis wanted to take no chances. President Bush declared he would not let the Iraqi aggression stand and would accept nothing short of total Iraqi withdrawal from Kuwait, and King Fahd gave his permission for a United Nations army to occupy Saudi Arabian soil.

The President announced Operation Desert Shield on August 7th, sending elements of the U.S. "rapid deployment force" to Saudi Arabia. Ships from the former Soviet Union, Britain, and France were included in the force, giving it at least a semblance of international cooperation. Meanwhile, the first of many UN resolutions was passed, this one imposing an oil and commerce embargo on Iraq. A long series of public and private positioning and chest beating followed, with a flurry of UN resolutions, while President Bush put together an international coalition of both NATO and Arab countries. For the first time since Vietnam, a U.S. president called reserves to active duty, and a massive deployment was well underway by September. Captain Duane Lee Smith arrived in Saudi Arabia on January 5 as part of a unit assigned to performing what would turn out to be the busiest duty of the Allied ground forces engagement with the Iraqi army—collecting prisoners of war.

On January 17 Operation Desert Storm, the air war, began with allied air and missile attacks on strategic targets, especially in and around Baghdad. The operation had three goals: to gain air supremacy; to destroy all possible targets that could support both Iraq's short- and long-term ability to make war; and to attack and degrade the Iraqi ground forces so that they would no longer be an effective fighting force. In a matter of a few days, Allied air forces gained air superiority, destroying the Iraqi air force and their air defense systems. They then concentrated on economic and military targets, and attacked Iraqi ground forces with an unprecedented concentration of heavy bombing, which may be one of the only examples in history of an army in the field literally being bombed into submission.

The most effective weapon the Iraqi's had in response were their Scud missiles, which could be fired from mobile launchers hidden in the desert. Finding them proved to be like looking for needles in a haystack, because they could fire and move out before Allied sorties could reach them. Although the Scuds were of limited military value because they carried a small payload and were notoriously inaccurate, they were an effective terrorist weapon. Many of them were fired toward Israel in an attempt to bait the Israelis into the war, and it was widely feared as well that they were capable of delivering chemical or biological weapons.

Operation Desert Sabre, the ground war, commenced on February 24, and was over one hundred hours later after the nearly complete collapse of the Iraqi army. The tactical key to the operation was General Norman Schwarzkopf's blitzkrieg strategy which included a two-pronged flanking attack. The largest part of this was a drive into the desert west of Kuwait and then east along the Euphrates River toward Basra. As this wave was sweeping across the desert, the second flank raced forward to meet the front of the wave, moving past Kuwait City toward Safwan. Because of their superior electronic weapons and tracking systems, the advancing U.S. forces were able to destroy large numbers of Iraqi tanks from a great distance before the Iraqi's even realized they were under attack.

The Iraqi army had been dug in solidly in anticipation of a frontal attack against Kuwait City. Their lines had been significantly degraded by the murderous pounding from the air. They were outgunned, outgeneraled, war-weary rather than battle-hardened, shell-shocked and starving conscripts, who began surrendering in such great numbers that it was difficult to even count them, much less keep close track of them. Whether the result was inevitable as some now believe, or whether the overwhelming firepower, surprise and speed of the assault reduced an otherwise powerful army so quickly will be debated for some time. In all, Allied forces collected over sixty thousand prisoners. The overwhelming majority appeared relieved to be captured. The number of Iraqi casualties is unknown because American commanders, again remembering Vietnam, refused to even estimate a body count, but the losses appear to have been staggering.

The flood of prisoners kept Captain Duane Lee Smith busy during those several chaotic days in February during and immediately following the ground offensive. During that time he served as the leader of a unit whose job it was to collect and ensure the humane treatment of the often starving and shell-shocked Iraqi prisoners of war who were surrendering in almost uncountable waves. In all, Smith's unit alone oversaw the collection of more than four thousand prisoners.

Duane Smith was born in Jackson County, Missouri, in 1960. As one of the first in his family to finish college, he enrolled in the ROTC program for a scholarship that would pay for his education. After graduating with a BA in Political Science, he volunteered for Jungle Warfare School in 1983. He spent several years in Panama, Honduras, and El Salvador serving in turn as a tactical, liaison, and training officer. In 1986 he transferred to Fort Riley, Kansas, as the Battalion Logistics officer and then as Assistant Adjutant for the 2nd Brigade of the 1st Infantry Division. It was during this assignment that he was deployed to Saudi Arabia. He kept the following diary from the time he left the states until the day he returned to Fort Riley.

Presently he is a member of the reserves, serving as Direct Support Team Chief in the 418th Civil Affairs Battalion in Belton, Missouri. He is the owner and manager of a ten-unit apartment complex, and is doing graduate work toward a Master's degree in Public Administration.

The Diary of Duane Lee Smith

5 January 1991 [C+151]. I left Fort Riley, Kansas, at 2:00 P.M. Arrived at Forbes Air Base in Topeka at 3:00 P.M. The Red Cross had hot coffee and donuts there for us while we waited for our baggage to be loaded onto the plane. I am the stick leader[1] for the soldiers from Headquarters and Headquarters Company, 2nd Brigade, 1st Infantry Division (Mechanized) (HHC 2nd BDE)[2] deploying on this flight, a United Airlines 747. The flight was supposed to take 21 hours. The stewardesses were very helpful. The in-flight movies I watched were *Ghost, Dick Tracy,* and *My Blue Heaven.* Our first refueling stop was in Philadelphia. We stayed on the plane for an hour and a half before we took off again.

6 January 1991 [C+152]. I stopped drinking coffee and Coca-Cola after we took off from Philadelphia because I read that avoiding caffeine minimizes the effects of jet lag.

When we landed in Brussels, Belgium, they wouldn't let us off the plane again. U.S. Air Force security personnel boarded the plane during the refueling stop. The head stewardess announced that all stewardesses were volunteers on this flight. They fed us chicken breast with carrots four times during the trip. It was good, but I don't think I could have eaten it one more time.

Arrived at King Fahd Airfield, Saudi Arabia, at 10:30 P.M. The temperature was in the 40s. We had to march with our carry-on baggage around a mile to a holding area. The holding area was a gravel parking lot. Each soldier received a bottle of Taiba drinking water. We waited for an hour and a half as our bags were unloaded from the belly of the aircraft. Even though it was chilly, I was happy we had arrived in the winter. The holding area would have been unbearable in the summer heat with no shade.

7 January 1991 [C+153]. They bussed us to the "MGM Grand" at Al Khobar.[3] The bus driver was an Arab and the bus was an old school bus. The ride took an hour. Many soldiers, including myself, desperately needed to

456

go to the bathroom. When we finally arrived, I ran off the bus to relieve myself in the bushes next to the bus. It took another four hours to receive briefings, unload our bags and move to our rooms.

The "MGM Grand" is a snide nickname for an apartment complex the Saudi government made available to the U.S. Army.[4] It houses around sixteen thousand soldiers waiting for their equipment to arrive from the port. The complex consists of eight-story apartment buildings that all have the same floor plan. Each apartment has six rooms. The plan was to put thirty soldiers in each apartment at around five soldiers per room. The apartments had carpet, three bathrooms and a kitchen. The bathrooms had bidets. The building was trimmed with marble. Despite this luxury, we could not use toilet paper in the toilets. We had to dispose of the used toilet paper in a trash bag next to the toilet. The toilet's waste pipe was too small for toilet paper.

Triple strands of concertina wire surround the apartment complex. Weaving roadblocks and sandbagged guard points protect the interior roads. The 1st Battalion, 16th Infantry Regiment (1/16th Infantry) is responsible for operating the "MGM Grand." They will provide a quick reaction company to respond to threats and maintain positions on top of selected buildings in order to view the whole area. An MP platoon also assists in security. Each unit provides a guard for their building. They will not let us have ammunition within the compound.

8 January 1991 [C+154]. I had breakfast at one of the dining facilities. The breakfast was good. The line was not long because I went late in the morning. As part of the support agreement between the United States and Saudi Arabia, the Saudis provide the food, which is prepared by a local catering service. Breakfast was scrambled eggs, pancakes or potatoes, a mystery meat, and fruit juice.

9 January 1991 [C+155]. A division band gave an impromptu concert for the soldiers in Al Khobar village this afternoon. Perhaps two hundred soldiers watched the band perform. It was satisfying that the band members were actually doing something to improve the morale of the soldiers.

The Japanese gave us their contribution to Operation Desert Shield: three television sets, three VCRs, and three boom boxes. The television sets do not have 110v adapters.[5] I don't see how we are going to use them in the field. Only one battalion picked up a television set. The boom boxes are much more practical because they are smaller and they have a short-wave band.

Listened to Secretary of State Baker's statement on the result of his talks with the Iraqi Foreign Minister on the Armed Forces Radio Television Service (ARFTS).[6] The ARFTS station, "107 Shield," plays a lot of good music with few interruptions. There does not seem to be many Saudi FM stations.

10 January 1991 [C+156]. The Emergency Operations Center (EOC)[7] increased the threat level to "Threatcon Charlie,"[8] which means that there is specific intelligence of a possible terrorist attack. The threat level was increased because local Arabs were spotted on overpasses observing the "MGM Grand," and some were taking photos. Due to the higher threat level, we have to wear our Kevlar[9] helmet and rucksack with chemical protective gear when outside. They still have not issued us ammunition.

I did a 3.6 mile forced march with my rucksack, weapon, Kevlar helmet and load-bearing equipment.[10] During the march, I saw six Arabs in a Toyota station wagon observing the compound from a parallel road. I mentioned it to a MP roving patrol. It had been a long time since I force marched, and my feet were sore when I finished. Luckily, water was available and I took a shower.

I finally got some mail. I received the 10 and 17 December 1990 issues of *Newsweek*. It had the old APO number, so I wrote them with my new address. The company received a giant Christmas card signed by residents from Wichita, Kansas. It is reassuring to receive that type of support from the American people.

11 January 1991 [C+157]. I had duty at 0500 at the EOC. The last plane from our brigade is due to arrive this morning. The last ship is due to arrive on 14 January 1991. The water is still out. Today is Friday, which is a holy day for the Moslems. That means the plumber will not fix the plumbing until tomorrow.

They told us that security in the Tactical Assembly Area (TAA) will be 50 percent.[11] There have been reports of infiltration into the TAA. Without the major combat units of the division, everybody up there seems to be a little nervous. The only unit north of our position is the Egyptians.

There was an incident on the northern end of the perimeter where a M249 squad automatic weapon was fired. A group of Arabs in a vehicle were shouting anti-American chants, and the squad leader loaded the machine gun. He then left to go to the bathroom and put a specialist in charge of the weapon. The specialist pulled the trigger to see if the weapon was loaded and four rounds were discharged. The soldiers in the dining facility panicked and abandoned sixteen weapons. They were Army Central (ARCENT) and VII Corps soldiers. I hope that their actions are not indicative of soldiers in the Second Brigade.

12 January 1991 [C+158]. I had duty today at 0500. I found out at 0505. Someone changed the duty roster last night and did not inform me of the change.

We get a daily supplement of fresh fruit, soda, fruit drink, and bottled mineral water with our daily lunch MRE. Some of the Pepsi-Colas bottled in Saudi have a sulfur taste and smell. The fruit drinks are good and are packaged in six-ounce cartons. My favorite is mango drink. A lot of the soldiers haven't acquired the taste for mangos, so there are usually extra mango drinks.

The compound has become more security conscious. The security company will be picking up their Bradley Infantry Fighting Vehicles (BIFV) [12] to augment perimeter security. Everybody has the Beirut Marine Barracks [13] in the back of their minds. Security procedures in the event of attack are being rehearsed by all soldiers.

The water came on for a short period today. I was able to wash clothes, but they did not dry rapidly because of the high humidity.

13 January 1991 [C+159]. I have become floor commander for my floor in my building at the "MGM Grand." I coordinate with all the soldiers on the floor (about 40) for the actions to be taken in case of an attack. We are to rehearse those actions tonight. I'm sure the rehearsal has something to do with Saddam Hussein's allowing of hostilities after midnight on the 13th of January. [14]

A soldier in 3rd Battalion, 37th Armor Regiment (3/37 AR) shot himself in the foot this morning at the port. His unit had just issued him ammunition for the convoy up to the TAA. He loaded his weapon in violation of orders. His chain of command thinks that he did it on purpose because

of his previous behavior. The bullet shattered his ankle, and he will probably be crippled for life. I told his battalion that, until they prove it was
intentional, I will need an accident report. [15]

I went to King Abdul Aziz Royal Saudi Air Base in Dhahran to coordinate with the AAFES Distribution Center. [16] There are American and some
British units stationed at the airport. They are at "Threatcon Bravo," which
means that terrorist attack is possible. I rode down with the division Trial
Defense Counselor, and we stopped in a Saudi barracks to make a telephone call. I noticed American graffiti on the walls. I didn't see any Arabic
graffiti on the walls, and it makes me angry to see this done by American
troops in a foreign country.

17 January 1991 [D-Day]. At 0145 I was awakened and told to take the
PB tablet (anti-nerve gas agent) and to go to MOPP 1 level. [17] I went downstairs to confirm this, and the Brigade Commander, Colonel Anthony
Moreno, confirmed the order. The order stated that the Nuclear, Biological, and Chemical (NBC) status was Amber, [18] which meant probable. I
informed the rest of the floor and convinced them that this was for real. At
0300 the Emergency Operations Center issued the order to go into MOPP
4. Some of the soldiers panicked when putting on their gear. We evacuated the floor, and everyone moved to an underground garage. We stayed
in MOPP 4 for around an hour. The radio announced the beginning of
Operation Desert Storm with the bombing of Baghdad. It was later confirmed that five Scud [19] missiles were actually launched against Saudi Arabian targets. By the time we moved back to the apartment, it was time for
stand-to.

18 January 1991 [D+1]. At 0430 we are told to take our PB tablets and go
to MOPP 2. Twenty minutes later we are told to go to MOPP 4. Everybody
is calmer this time. This alert was because of a Scud attack. While in MOPP
4 we leave the radio on and hear there was an explosion at Dhahran and
that a Patriot [20] missile had intercepted the Scud missile. The Scud was
intercepted over Al Khobar village. The explosion was actually the Patriot
missile firing. A Scud is reported to have hit Tel Aviv for the first time. [21]

The Saudi contractors did not serve hot breakfast that morning due
to the attempted attack. Our convoy did not take off as scheduled. The
problem was a lack of trailers to carry the armored vehicles north. The

HHC 2nd Brigade First Sergeant, Leslie Axton, told us to prepare to move out to the port of Damman when the trailers became available. [22]

They kept us in a large warehouse full of perhaps six hundred soldiers. The food at the port was better than the Saudi-catered food at Al Khobar village. The port is modern, with large cranes to unload the break-bulk ships. Military Transportation Command has contracted with foreign flag ships to carry cargo for Operation Desert Shield. Many of these ships are rust buckets.

19 January 1991 [D+2]. At 1030 we were told to go to MOPP 1, then to MOPP 0, then to MOPP 2. The radio said that a piece of a Soviet satellite had fallen out of orbit, triggering the radar systems. Scud missiles hit Tel Aviv again this morning.

I spent the rest of the day playing rummy and resting.

That night we were alerted to an attack by Iraqi frogmen on the port. The military police spotted two of them exiting the water around three hundred meters from where I was staying. One was shot by the MPs. We were kept inside as the reaction force searched the port. I was told later that two three-man rafts were found, and one frogman was killed.

20 January 1991 [D+3]. The Port Operations Center rescheduled the 1000 convoy to 0400. The HHC 2nd Brigade executive officer was supposed to wake us at 0100 so we could prepare for the move. I woke up at 0222 because I had to go to the bathroom. We woke everyone up and got them moving as fast as possible. When we were ready to board the bus, they could not find the driver. When they finally did find him, the bus that was supposed to take us would not start. We finally found another bus and left Damman at 0410.

We had to travel 260 miles to the TAA. The bus stopped every two hours for a rest break. The half-way point was a comfort station that gave out MREs, sodas, fruit, and heated Lunch Buckets. The road was normally a deserted stretch of two-lane desert highway. It was odd to see it crammed with army vehicles of many units of several different nationalities. Many vehicles were passing other convoy vehicles. I saw the results of several wrecks on the sides of the road. No one was making an effort to recover those vehicles.

I saw the first of many camels in the desert. The Bedouins were taking care of their herds. Most Bedouins had small Japanese pickups.

We arrived at the convoy release point at 1500. After we unloaded the armored vehicles, we waited five hours until a unit representative arrived to take us to our unit. While waiting, we saw British and Egyptian vehicles pass our position.

21 January, 1991 [D+4]. It rained hard in the morning. Most of our gear is wet because we were sleeping on cots outside. We were told that it usually rains in the mornings. The desert has a coarse grain of sand that does not get muddy when it rains. It is like being on a wet beach. There is very little dust.

22 January, 1991 [D+5]. My electric shaver broke. I did not drop it and it did not get wet. I can't figure out why it broke. I don't look forward to shaving the rest of the time out here with a razor. I don't like shaving with cold water in the mornings. The electric razor also came in handy for touching up before putting on my protective mask in order to have a better seal. I packaged the razor up in a Saudi map and sent it back to an appliance service center in Independence, Missouri. I hope they will fix it fast.

Sent a soldier down to division to pick up mail, but there was very little ready to be picked up. There was an enormous amount of mail waiting to be sorted. It does not look like anyone will be going back to Dhahran for a long time, now that we are preparing to attack.

23 January, 1991 [D+6]. Received a report that 3rd Armor Division (3 AD) established contact southwest of our sector with a force of sixty Iraqi dismounted soldiers. Fifty Iraqis were captured, two killed and two of our soldiers were wounded. Security was increased in our sector.

Our sleeping tents finally arrived. The Brigade Executive Officer, Lt. Colonel Donald Schenk, took our two-and-a-half-ton truck from the Administrative Logistics Operation Center (ALOC) for the Brigade Tactical Operation Center (TOC). Now we have more equipment than we can carry.

The brigade commander relieved Captain Michael Ramsgard, the Bravo Company, 4th Battalion, 37th Armor Regiment (B CO 4-37) commander for hitting one of his lieutenants. Capt. Ramsgard is a good soldier, and I hate to see him relieved, but he should not have hit the lieutenant.

25 January, 1991 [D+8]. The best way to describe the desert here is to compare it to the sea. You can see as far as the horizon in all directions, and the ground is perfectly flat. Our tents and units are like boats on the sea with nothing between units. Maps are useful only as charts to plot the relation of one unit to another. I could have as easily drawn grid lines on white paper for a map. Navigation for those who do not have Magellan Global Position Systems[23] is primarily by compass azimuth and vehicle pace count.

I can start to understand what it means to be a nomad on the desert. The desert gives me the same feeling of peacefulness as I had in the jungles of Panama.[24] The custom of Arabs driving out in air-conditioned four-wheel drive vehicles to set up a Bedouin tent for a picnic does not seem so odd to me anymore.

We were on a red alert for enemy aircraft for most of the night. Thirty Iraqi aircraft were supposed to be preparing to take off. Nothing happened.

26 January, 1991 [D+9]. I have been staying in my camouflaged Eureka Timberline tent under a camouflage net. It is nice because I can lay out my personal gear and it has a floor. It also has net pockets on the walls and hooks on the ceiling, which aid in organization. The rest of the soldiers are staying in general purpose medium and small tents. These tents have no floors, but they do have locally purchased heaters in them. I work on the night shift in the Brigade ALOC and sleep during the day, so I do not need a heater for my tent.

We have been eating two MREs per day and one Tray Ration (T-RAT), or Class B Ration (prepared canned food) per day. I eat only one MRE and the hot evening meal per day. The food is good and for the last two days they have had left-overs at night, so I end up eating three hot meals per day.

Not all soldiers have been issued the same amount of ammunition for various reasons. I have been directing the redistribution of the ammunition among our soldiers. Ammunition is a very personal matter now, and

I've met resistance in this cross-leveling of ammunition. I have to make these soldiers understand that the effectiveness of the team is more important to their survival than their own actions.

I can constantly hear jets overhead. They are so far up that they cannot be seen. I wonder what the Iraqi soldiers are feeling like about now.

27 January, 1991 [D+10]. I have been taking showers about every other day. Many soldiers have not had a shower for two weeks. I have a plastic water bag that heats the water using solar energy. It warms the water up around forty degrees centigrade in two hours if the sun is shining. They have plywood shower stalls here in the brigade support area, but the soldiers are not using them because they have to carry water to the shower and then climb up a ladder to put the water in a container. I take my sun shower and put it on top of the shower stall and have a warm shower.

An Iraqi was captured in our divisional sector. He was conducting reconnaissance of the area in a civilian Toyota pickup. A M3 Bradley Cavalry Fighting Vehicle attempted to stop him by firing over the vehicle. When the vehicle did not stop, the Bradley shot the 25-mm Bushmaster Cannon at the vehicle, hitting it in the front end. The occupant was an Iraqi in civilian clothes with three fake identification cards. We briefed our soldiers on rules of engagement and procedures for detaining local civilians in the area.

30 January, 1991 [D+13]. Found a goat cemetery on the way to the logistics support area. There were twelve goats lying on their sides and burned. A light covering of sand was blown on top of the carcasses. The skin was still on the goats. Possibly they had had a disease and the Bedouins killed the herd before it spread. There was also an old pair of shoes nearby. This is the only evidence of humans (other than military) I have found since I have been out here in the desert.

31 January, 1991 [D+14]. It has not rained for several days and is starting to become more dusty now. We have run out of bottled water and have to drink the purified water that has a strong taste. The taste disappears if the water is mixed with Kool-Aid or coffee. The Brigade Commander, Colonel Moreno, says he does not want us to dig fighting positions with overhead cover. The reason for this is that there have been several deaths in Saudi because of improperly constructed bunkers collapsing on soldiers. He has made a decision based upon the risk of enemy fire versus the risk of collapse. I feel that the soldiers should be required to build overhead cover on their bunkers in order to train them how to do it properly. Many units have plenty of time here to train the soldiers on the proper way to build fighting positions. The sand makes it easy to dig. I am afraid that the soldiers will learn bad lessons from this war that will hurt us in the future.

2 February, 1991 [D+16]. Preparations are being made to move. Major Branz tells me that I will be in charge of the brigade enemy prisoner of war (EPW) point. I make the initial coordination with the 101st Military Intelligence Battalion (101 MI) interrogation team and read the brigade operation order.

1-4 Cavalry is making contact with enemy forces and made the first confirmed kill for the 1st Infantry Division. A lost Iraqi bulldozer shot at one of the 1st Squadron, 4th Cavalry (1-4 Cav.) Cobra gunships. He was engaged by the Cobra with the 20-mm Vulcan cannon and destroyed. It says a lot for the enemy's determination when a lost bulldozer operator attacks a gunship.

3 February, 1991 [D+17]. Armed Forces Radio and Television Service has finally set up repeater stations to transmit to our units up north. [25] We are now ready to continue to move north, and they will probably not catch up for another ten days. It is important to us to find out what is going on, and the news provides more up-to-date information than we could find out through command channels.

I experienced my first Saudi dust storm. It started around 1000 and lasted until 1500. The winds were about fifty miles per hour. Some of the camouflage poles fell down, and one of them hit my tent, upsetting it enough that it started to catch the wind and tip over. I had to put a dust rag over my mouth to strain out the dust while I slept. This dust storm was not as intense as some that I experienced in the Mojave desert at the National Training Center.

Machine-gun fire was exchanged between two American units up north. No one was hurt, but it shows how edgy they are up north in the neutral zone.

4 February, 1991 [D+18]. The brigade conducted an electronic rehearsal on the radio for the attack. They stated that the following transmissions were "for training only," but they had the same effects as Orson Wells' "War of the Worlds" radio show. Several people, including myself, thought that the transmissions were actual events. I had to answer a question during the rehearsal concerning enemy prisoners of war.

5 February, 1991 [D+19]. The sound of units conducting live-fire training is constant. It serves as a good reminder that we are in a combat zone.

The time for stand-to is changed to coincide with sunrise. The soldiers do not conduct stand-to correctly; they are not in their fighting positions, do not have their proper equipment, do not man their posts for the specified time, and just do not take stand-to seriously. At the daily shift change-over briefing I talk to them about the purpose and standards of stand-to.

While I was on the telephone to the Brigade tactical operations center, a British M-109 Howitzer exploded near the TOC location. The explosion could be seen and heard from our location, thirty kilometers away. There was considerable consternation here since the soldier at the other end said, "I need to go now, a vehicle just exploded," and then hung up. I could not re-establish communications for several minutes, and we thought maybe it was one of our brigade's vehicles.

6 February, 1991 [D+20]. I fell in a foxhole last night. I was walking to the latrine, and I turned off my flashlight because of light discipline. About five seconds later, I fell in the foxhole. I remember falling through the air, then looking up, flat on my back, at the sky. Somehow I ended up scraping my knee and hyper-extending my leg. The first thing I did was turn my flashlight back on. I decided that safety was more important than light discipline.

7 February, 1991 [D+21]. The ALOC jumped in the morning to participate in the brigade rehearsal for the attack. Our main mission is to monitor the battle on the brigade command radio net. We were supposed to jump at 0400, but we don't until 0545 due to bad planning and poor interpersonal communications.

At 1300 we jumped again. I was able to get four hours sleep in the morning before we jumped. I slept outside the M577 command-post vehicle on a cot.

8 February, 1991 [D+22]. The rehearsal continues, and we jumped again at 0200. The brigade will repeat the rehearsal two times with an after action review following each rehearsal. At 0800 we jumped again. I stayed awake all morning since we were constantly on the move. The ALOC moved through the simulated breach during the rehearsal. After jumping three times and traveling twenty kilometers on each jump, we are still in the same terrain: flat. We could have run around in circles for two hours and set up in the same location, and I would not have known the difference.

10 February, 1991 [D+24]. They have started to issue meals operational ready to eat (MORE). These consist of two commercial microwaveable entrees (i.e. Lunch Buckets, Hormel Top Shelf, etc.), two candy bars, soda, fruit drink, bread, Hunt's Fruit Cup pudding, and a MRE accessory packet. The bread is the new, individually wrapped extended shelf life bread. It tastes a lot better than the stale Saudi bread. It is one of the developmental items the Army has pushed into production for Operation Desert Shield. The meal is good, filling, and satisfies the urge for snacks.

11 February, 1991 [D+25]. During stand-to in the mornings, we are conducting pre-combat inspections of the soldiers and asking them questions on basic survival skills. The soldiers appreciate this. It gives them something constructive to do during stand-to. We expect the Iraqis to use chemical agents in any assault by Allied forces. This provides real motivation to become sharp on chemical survival skills.

We had another big argument with the 201st Forward Support Battalion about human waste burning details. As a result, the HHC 2nd Brigade soldiers now have their own latrine that they are responsible for maintaining. Just another headache.

14 February, 1991 [D+28]. We jumped over 130 kilometers. The movement took twelve hours. I rode in the back of a Kevlar-armored ambulance. The Judge Advocate (JAG) lawyer attached to the brigade (Captain Wells) objected to us being in the ambulance. Ground combat troops are not supposed to be transported in ambulances with the Red Cross emblem (the red Muslim crescent was on the front and back of the ambulance also). However, we were forced to use the ambulances since they were the only available transport. The brigade surgeon (Major Leroy Graham) is upset at Capt. Wells's comment. Wells was just doing his job, which is to make the commander aware of possible violations of the Law of Land Warfare. The law was intended to prevent the use of ambulances as Trojan Horses or as a shield from enemy attack. In our case, the Iraqis did not have any assets that could target individual vehicles in the area into which we were deploying.

The ambulance ride was comfortable, although cramped, and I managed to grab a couple of hours sleep. The only irritant was the dust stirred up by the long convoy (possibly 4,000 to 5,000 vehicles). It came through the driver's compartment into the back area of the ambulance and covered everything. I wrapped my cotton scarf around my head to keep the light out of my eyes and the dust out of my lungs.

That night was a busy one. The long road march had used up the unit's basic load of petroleum products, and they wanted to get more as soon as possible. I found out that night that Delta Company, 2nd Battalion, 16th Infantry Regiment (D Co., 2-16) had suffered three casualties in an attack on a small village in the old neutral zone. [26] These casualties were the first for the brigade and probably the first for the division. The company was attached to 1-4 Cav. and the mission was to clear the village of enemy forces. We suspected the Iraqi Remotely Piloted Vehicles (RPVs) conducting reconnaissance of our new positions were being launched from that town. They were dropping flares at night to illuminate the area for the television cameras they carried.

One of the soldiers cut his hand on broken glass and the other two were wounded by a fragmentation grenade. They threw the grenade into a corrugated steel building and then put their backs against the other side of the corrugated steel. Of all the missions we practiced at Fort Riley, fighting in built-up areas was not one of them. Proper training in urban operations would have taught the soldiers what type of munitions to use on what structures and in what circumstances. It turned out there were no enemy soldiers in the town.

We were also informed that two Scud missiles were fired on the convoy and intercepted by Patriot missiles. Several soldiers in the convoy saw the intercept. That night two BLU-52 bombs were dropped out of the back of a C-130 transport plane on the Iraqi infantry division in our sector. These bombs consist of 15,000 pounds of high explosives mounted on pallets. Last used in the Vietnam War to clear trees from helipads, I am sure they create a tremendous psychological shock to the Iraqi soldiers. All I could see was the sky lighting up on the horizon.

The soldiers are more serious now about their duties as we start moving closer to Iraq. They do not complain about digging fighting positions. The guards are more serious about their work. Two guards challenged me as I was digging a cat hole to relieve myself at three in the morning.

I tried to coach the soldiers in the construction of fighting positions. They believe that bigger is better. I explained that a fighting position is like a basketball hoop. The enemy is trying to put artillery into your fighting position. The bigger the hoop, your fighting position, the easier it is for the basketball, the artillery, to enter. The fighting positions should be narrow and deep.

15 February, 1991 [D+29]. My body is sore from digging yesterday. I spent three hours along with Sergeant First Class (SFC) Pascal Morales digging a fighting position. It was only two-and-a-half-feet deep, two M-16s long and three-quarters of an M-16 wide. The first six inches was sand; the remainder was all shale. Cutting the shale is all hard pick-axe work. The position is more stable than the ones dug in sand, but it is hard work and will take many days to complete to standard. Digging is good exercise for me since I don't have an opportunity to run or lift weights. I plan on spending at least an hour improving my fighting position every day.

16 February, 1991 [D+30]. Found out this morning that 1st Battalion, 41st Infantry Regiment (1-41 Infantry), screening along our brigade's front, had two vehicles hit by fire from an Apache helicopter last night. Two enemy vehicles were reported with dismounted infantry out in front. When the helicopters arrived they saw a target array that matched the reported enemy target array. The right wing man lazed the target and reported to the flight leader that the grid location did not match the reported target grid and asked the left wing man to laze the target. [27] Before the target could be lazed, the flight leader fired two Hellfires. He hit the turret of the Bradley, knocking it off, killing the two soldiers inside the turret and wounding six others. The other Hellfire missile hit the front of the M113 and bounced off. It is ironic that the more survivable vehicle was destroyed by a sophisticated missile and the venerable M113 Armored Personnel Carrier deflected the missile.

17 February, 1991 [D+31]. My tent zipper broke. It is the same problem that I had with my other one during the last National Training Center rotation. The small nylon zipper just gets clogged up with sand and will not close properly. I ended up piling my duffel bags against the tent end and putting the vestibule on the broken end of the tent. The main disadvantage is that now I do not have total protection from bugs and rodents as I did before. I will have to start taking more time and making sure that my bags are packed each day.

18 February, 1991 [D+32]. The 1-4 Cav. Company commander is conducting an investigation of the friendly fire casualties[28] from D Co., 2-16th Infantry, and I help Major Dinnel, who is conducting the investigation, to pass information between him and the company.

All classes of supply are limited by the long distances required for transport. Water is at a premium and we no longer receive bottled water. We are still having at least one MORE or T-RAT meal per day, but the portions are reduced.

The radios are working well, but are limited by the antennas. The IBM computer keyboard is sticking after the dust storms and attempts to clean it with a vacuum cleaner have not been sufficient.

19 February, 1991 [D+33]. The temperature today was 37 degrees Fahrenheit for the low and 67 degrees Fahrenheit for the high.

The new replacements coming in from Fort Jackson and Fort Benning are coming in without desert fatigues, helmet covers, CANA injectors, M291 kits,[29] enough magazines or correct ammunition, and with the old M-16A1. The M-16A1 is a fine rifle for a combat service support soldier, but our unit has the new M-16A2 rifles. The problem is that the ammunition from the M-16A1 can be used for the M-16A2 with degraded accuracy, but the ammunition for the M-16A2 cannot be used safely in the

M-16A1. It is very difficult and dangerous to manage two different types of ammunition of the same caliber in the same unit.

20 February, 1991 [D+34]. It rained hard in the morning from midnight to 0600. My little Eureka Timberline tent was one of the few tents that did not leak. By late morning, the desert had soaked up the water and the dust was up again. A strange combination of fog and a dust storm started around 2230. The scouts along the berm initially reported there was a smoke screen. The Brigade executive officer, Lt. Col. Donald Schenk, came back over the radio and told the scouts to look outside to see that the weather conditions had changed.

At 2330 an Iraqi 120mm mortar carrier pulled up to the Iraqi-Saudi berm and fired south into our sector. They did not hit anyone. The firing was detected rapidly by the artillery section's fire-direction radar. Colonel Moreno immediately gave permission to engage the target, and from there on, everything went wrong. The artillery battalion did not fire the first rounds for six minutes because they were already firing a pre-planned mission on an artillery raid. After they fired the first rounds, the adjustments were being relayed over the brigade command net instead of an artillery fire command net. The initial adjustments were made by the 2nd Battalion, 16th Infantry Regiment (2-16 Infantry) scouts and did not include the observer-target direction necessary for the artillery fire direction control center to make adjustments. The TOC officers didn't know that this was needed. It took thirty minutes until fire-for-effect phase was reached. By the time they were through adjusting the rounds, the Iraqi mortar carrier was long gone.

The British have reconnaissance drones they are flying out here on missions for us. There has been some consternation among the units now with both friendly and enemy drones flying overhead.

The Apache attack helicopter battalion conducted a rehearsal today using field artillery in support vehicles (FISTVs) to laze the forward edge of friendly troops. This exercise was conducted to get confidence back on both sides after the friendly fire incident last week.

I had to wake up early in the afternoon to go to a meeting for the rehearsal to move out the forward support element. The enemy-prisoner-of-war team I am in charge of will be moving out right behind the last maneuver battalion. The rehearsal didn't take long and I got back in time to get some sleep.

I fixed my tent temporarily by putting camouflaged duct tape on the broken zipper. This will limit the amount of sand blowing into my tent, but I will not be able to use both exits.

23 February, 1991 [D+37]. Received spot reports on three minefields in the Iraqi security zone. All minefields were around two kilometers wide. There were two reports during the night of dismounted Iraqi infantry in the security zone between our forces and their forces.

24 February 1991 [G-Day/D+38]. The 2nd Brigade enemy-prisoner-of-war team for G-Day consisted of the 3rd platoon of the 233rd MP Company and an interrogation of prisoner-of-war team consisting of a counter-intelligence team, an interrogation team and two Kuwaiti interpreters. I was in charge of the team and responsible for executing the enemy-prisoner-of-war evacuation plan.

At 0130 Task Force 3rd Battalion, 37th Armor Regiment (3-37 Armor) captured two Iraqi enemy prisoners of war. The night before we had planned on moving out from the forward assembly area at 0630, but we decided to move our enemy-prisoner-of-war team out early to establish a holding area for the two prisoners. We arrived at a pre-designated holding area off the main supply route at 0430.

The MPs strung out a single strand of concertina wire around the area. The prisoners arrived with their hands tied behind their backs. The MP cut loose their hands, and the interrogation section split into two teams. Both enemy prisoners of war said they had not eaten for five days and had not had water for seven days. One was a squad leader who had only four soldiers in his squad. One of those soldiers deserted with him. We could not immediately pass the spot report of the interrogation to brigade because the radio was not working and the MP platoon, a National Guard platoon from Illinois, did not have secure radios. When the interrogations were completed, another platoon came to evacuate the prisoners to the corps cage because the division cage was moving forward for the breach. The military policemen hog-tied the prisoners' hands behind their backs and put sand bags over their heads. I talked to the MP platoon leader, Lt. Rakker, and explained to him that enemy prisoners of war would not be treated that way unless they were being uncooperative. I also pointed out that these prisoners had walked seventeen kilometers at night, through a minefield, in order to defect.

We went to MOPP 2, which consists of the chemical protective over garment and rubber boots, at 0600. We waited for the rest of the MP company to join us to go through the breach. We arrived at the second planned position, which only had thirteen EPW. There were reports of hundreds more farther forward, so we continued on our designated breach lane to the third planned position. As we arrived at the site, they were bringing hundreds of prisoners in on "low boys." [30]

The artillery, both M109 Howitzers and Multiple Launched Rocket System (MLRS), fired from positions one kilometer to the rear. The sound of the howitzers and MLRS firing was intense and hurt our ears. We were positioned so that we could also hear the sonic boom of the rockets as they went skyward. It was the most intense barrage I have ever seen. Some of the prisoners were crying because they knew that some of their friends who had not surrendered were dying.

The interrogation team questioned the brigade commander of one of the forward brigades of the 26th Iraqi Infantry Division. He stated that he told his soldiers to listen to the radio and when they heard that the Allied forces were attacking, to walk forward of their positions with their hands in the air to surrender. His whole brigade did surrender. One of the Iraqi lieutenants, after being interrogated, got down on his knees facing Mecca to pray. All of the interrogation reports showed that the divisions we face in the 1st ID sector were no more than 50 percent strength due to desertions and soldiers being transferred to other higher-priority units.

That night we got the okay to move out. We moved through the breach to a site where the 2-16 Infantry had collected 300 enemy prisoners. The brigade processed 267 prisoners through the collection point that day.

25 February, 1991 [G+1/D+39]. The new collection point location was eerie. There were prisoners all over the site in groups of ten to fifteen. The moon was bright, and there were sand berms all over the place. It was hard walking in the soft sand with the chemical protective boots. Everybody was tired. The military policemen built a concertina enclosure and herded the EPWs inside. The prisoners started to riot when an MP took a case of MREs into the cage, and they all mobbed to get one. The MP was pulled out, and it took a half an hour to get the cage under control.

Morning came and more prisoners arrived. I had problems with the radio. Major Branz told me the night before that the frequencies would change as normal at 0300. I could not raise anyone on the radio until around 1100 when I realized that maybe the frequencies were still frozen on day three. I could not contact the brigade ALOC because they were over thirty kilometers to the rear. I could talk to the battalion ALOCs. Later in the evening I could relay messages from the battalion ALOCs to the brigade ALOC. There was a lot of radio traffic on a normally quiet net. I spent the rest of the night constantly relaying messages and answering questions. Radio communications became key to maintaining contact with the units. Everybody was moving and it was impossible to find anyone unless there was radio contact to confirm the location and to find where and when to move next.

It started to rain, and the prisoners had no protection from the elements. They used the cardboard from the MRE boxes for shelter, and the interrogation team had a Bedouin tent that the EPWs were allowed to use. The MPs required them to remain seated. They pulled the canvas over their heads for shelter.

The 651st Medical Evacuation company commander, Captain Rice, came by our position and I talked to him about supplying an ambulance for the prisoners. He agreed, since his people have not been evacuating the numbers of casualties they expected. His medics evacuated a couple of prisoners and treated several others for hypothermia and dehydration.

The British brought over two prisoners, one injured. The other could speak English. The English speaker claims they were beaten by the British. Both have "UK" written on their faces on both cheeks. The 651st Medical Company ambulance evacuated the one prisoner and a replacement ambulance was sent.

As a group was being moved to division, we received a re-supply of MREs. We distributed the MREs to the prisoners as they were moved onto the trucks. When the prisoners in the cage saw the MREs being distributed to the prisoners on the truck, they started to riot. Shots were fired over their heads and it took a few minutes to calm them down. The military policemen came up with a plan to feed the prisoners by moving them from a full cage to an empty cage. That day we process 646 EPWs.

26 February 1991 [G+2/D+40]. The second site I was operating was finally emptied out this morning. The MP Co. was choppered back to division. The remainder of the collection-point soldiers moved out to the third site that had been constructed by the engineers. We navigated to the new site by following a compass azimuth across the desert. We found some munitions which I thought were expended flares, since they were cylindrical and had parachutes on them. I thought it was strange so many flares had been shot at the enemy and I hadn't seen the illumination. I found out later they were dual-purpose improved conventional munitions (DPICM). I found out when one of the 5-ton trucks hit one of them, and the explosion knocked a wheel off the vehicle.

We arrived at the new site. The wind was starting to pick up. The MP platoon leader, Lt. Rindal, was burned out and only provided security for the prisoners. He did not count them, nor did he tag and search them. The brigade S-4[31] arrived and wanted numbers just minutes after I arrived. I went into the cage, leaving my weapon outside, and found an Iraqi second lieutenant who could speak English. I had him form the prisoners up into a formation to count them. This goes against the policy of segregating enlisted men from officers, but I had to come up with a way to break the mob psychology that was building in this large group of tired, hungry, and thirsty prisoners. It worked well and I received a good count. I had 2nd Lt. Aziz tell his soldiers to dig a latrine trench. I then had them form up to receive a meal and water.

We continued to shuttle the prisoners to the corps cage located south of the Iraqi-Saudi Arabia berm. A fierce sandstorm came up which produced enough wind to rock the HMMWV.[32] The sandstorm was so fierce that goggles and a rag covering the face were needed to walk into the wind. Most of the prisoners were able to take cover in the Sealand van. Others put on their gas masks (Soviet made) and some put clear plastic trash bags over their heads for protection.

27 February 1991 [G+3/D+41]. We decided to stop moving when the moon went down because of limited visibility and because no one had had more than an hour of sleep in the last 48 hours. When dawn came, we started moving and came across a squadron from 1 Cav. Div. that was in pre-battle formation with companies in column and the artillery covering the move in alternating positions. We got nervous because we didn't know how close we were to the front.

We reached our destination in the middle of the desert and in half an hour, Major Lourentzos showed up and gave us the grid for the next location. We took an hour to do personal hygiene and then we move out again.

We passed through an area where there were dozens of destroyed vehicles. Most were still burning. There were T-55 tanks, BMP fighting vehicles, trucks, and Cascavel reconnaissance vehicles. One tank looked like it had melted to one side. There were bunkers all over.

We crossed an asphalt road and hooked up with 2nd Armor Cavalry Regiment. They had forty prisoners. We took them after some argument. One of the prisoners claimed later that they took 650 dinars (Iraqi currency worth $200). The EPWs were marched all day long. There was a scrawny-looking dog that had followed the prisoners all day. The saddest thing that I have had to do so far was to separate the dog from his owner; the dog would certainly die in the desert. The dog followed the convoy as we drove off into the desert.

We followed the asphalt road north until we came upon a group of twenty-eight prisoners captured by SSG McCormick of 1/A/4-37 Armor. We processed them. After the platoon drove off, we heard the sounds and saw the flashes of a tank firing. I called the brigade ALOC to update the tactical situation. While I was on the radio, the tank opened up with its .50 caliber machine gun. The tracers flew across our convoy three hundred meters ahead. I started to become nervous because I knew that the enemy must be close if the tank was using the .50-caliber machine gun. We established contact with SSG McCormick on his platoon radio net and found out that he has destroyed one T-72 tank and engaged another unidentified armored vehicle. While we were on his radio net a 1-4 Cav. platoon leader came up to argue about who actually made the kill. I made the decision that the convoy needed to move ahead, since the danger from the remaining vehicle on our flank was minimal and there would be more danger staying stationary. Going back would not have facilitated mission accomplishment, since we had reports that the brigade was already in Kuwait. I had Lt. Rindal coordinate for passage through 1-4 Cav. and 4-37 Armor.

We passed through and two mortar rounds exploded a couple of hundred meters away from the convoy.

We came upon the 210th Field Artillery Brigade S-4 which had twenty-eight trucks loaded with artillery ammunition, stuck in the sand. He requested recovery help. The major was quite excited and I did not want to make him go hysterical by telling him what we had just passed through, so I advised him to move one hundred meters over to the hard-packed sand road that we were on and to get out of there as quickly as possible. By now we had 208 enemy prisoners of war.

28 February 1991 [G+4/D+42]. The EPW team arrived at the new brigade support area (BSA) location just outside of Kuwait in Iraq at 0430. The BSA was jumping to a position on the Basra-Kuwait City highway at 0800. We transported the 208 prisoners in a convoy route.

The Basra-Kuwait City highway[33] was littered with destroyed vehicles. There was even a blue Mercedes that was destroyed. There were numerous armored vehicles on the road, all burning. All the facilities we could see had been destroyed. There were over fifty burning oil wells in the distance,[34] each with a bright orange flame and dark, black smoke pouring out of the well. Our convoy had to weave between the destroyed vehicles. We arrived at the new site at 1400. The sky was a haze with all the smoke, and I could hardly see the sun. We were given the grids for a new brigade cage. The new site was a former concrete plant. It had a ten-foot wall around the outside with barbed wire on the top. The site was square, enclosed by walls over eight hundred meters long. The scout platoon from 4th Battalion, 37th Armor Regiment (4-37 Armor) was on the outside perimeter, providing security. We built a sub-cage inside the site for the prisoners. I coordinated with the brigade engineer, Major Muscarelli, for engineer support to fill in the holes in the wall and dig a berm to contain the prisoners. When the ACE vehicle[35] arrived it filled up the holes and dug fighting positions for the Bradleys outside.

The site had been the location of an Iraqi signal platoon. They had built bunkers at various locations within the site. All were destroyed and the signal vehicles were still burning strong, putting off a strong acid stench.

Three Egyptian displaced civilians asked for shelter. The civil affairs

team had not linked back up to us, so I had the military intelligence interrogators check the Egyptians out to make sure their passports were valid.
We gave them shelter in a destroyed administrative building and told them
they could not leave it unescorted, but they could leave the camp at any
time they wished with an escort.

The brigade had two other EPW sites. 1-4 Cav. and 4-37 Armor had
1,400 prisoners; 3-37 Armor had 1,054 prisoners inside a water-bottling
plant. The original plan was to empty prisoners into the division cage as
soon as it opened at midnight. The prisoners at these two sites had not
been fed or given water due to lack of resources. Adequate shelter was a
problem. There were problems with rioting and one of the prisoners died
of starvation. [36]

1 March 1991 [G+5/D+43]. During the morning hours, the brigade was
again ordered on the offensive. This time we are headed toward Iraq to
secure the airfield at Safwan, [37] which is to be used as the cease fire negotiation site for the talks scheduled to begin 3 March 1991.

The division cage did not open as planned and the prisoners were
transferred to the brigade site. By morning, we had over 1,450 prisoners. I
tried to get the scout platoon to move four scout Bradleys inside the perimeter to provide interior security, but I could not have them because of the
brigade mission to secure the airfield. I felt I needed them inside the cage
because the soldiers at the EPW point had had less than 90 minutes rest for
the last six days. There were only thirty-three soldiers available for guard,
screening, searching, and tagging. We had to thoroughly search each prisoner after one of them, who was being brought in from the 4-37 Armor
cage and who had supposedly already been searched, gave an MP a dagger
with a six-inch blade.

Some of the prisoners were in bad shape as they arrived at the brigade cage. Some had to crawl off the truck. Others had no socks or jackets.
I went to get some space blankets to provide shelter for the prisoners suffering the most from exposure. The wall provided some shelter from the
wind, but the walled site was so large that there was only partial protection
from the wind. The prisoners built small campfires to warm themselves.
They used the cardboard from the MRE boxes for fire and shelter.

The light from the burning oil wells reflected off the low hanging
smoke clouds produced by the burning oil. This light was enough with the

full moon to make it unnecessary to use a flashlight to read. Some of the oil wells were so close together that their flames would merge in to one giant fireball. The background of the burning oil wells, combined with the small groups of enemy prisoners of war huddled around the small campfires was a memory that I will not forget.

At times I feel sorry for the enemy, but when I look at the destruction that Iraq has caused to Kuwait, I feel that they are only now reaping the seed that they had sown on 2 August 1990. The wasting of the oil is criminal in a world that is so dependent upon this resource.

By the end of the major EPW operations, the brigade had captured and processed over 4,011 prisoners. Each prisoner had received a meal and water before being transferred to higher headquarters. There were many times when I thought we wouldn't be able to make it through, but one way or another, the needed resources arrived in time.

2 March, 1991 [G+6/D+44]. The brigade is preparing the negotiation site at Safwan Airfield. We were told that the brigade support area will jump from this location today. I got the mission of leading a convoy of trucks back to the division support area (DSA) to pick up mail. The DSA has just closed to the division area and we have not made contact with them. I had to wait till mid-afternoon before all the trucks from the various units made it to the convoy site. The brigade support area jumped north to a location just southeast of the Safwan Airfield, inside Iraq.

Major Brown, the 201st Forward Support Battalion Executive Officer, requested one of my trucks to haul bodies of dead Iraqi soldiers. The 201st has the mission of burying the remains of the Iraqi soldiers who died on the Basra-Kuwait City highway, and assisting in clearing the vehicles off the highway. I see at least one forty-foot stake-and-platform truck piled with Iraqi bodies at least three high for the length of the truck. The engineers are digging mass-burial sites with bulldozers. The bodies are laid out in rows in the pit before they are buried. The Iraqi prisoners cried when they heard that their fallen comrades are being buried on Kuwaiti soil. Apparently, the Koran prohibits the disinterment of bodies. All the personal effects of the dead are being collected and 95 percent of the bodies have been identified. The bodies have to be buried this way for sanitary reasons, since we do not have the assets to return them to Iraq.

I let the 101st Military Intelligence (101 MI) team run back to Kuwait

City with the translators to check on their families. Yousif's family had fled to Saudi Arabia, and he went back to his house. The Iraqi soldiers had used his house as a barracks and it was trashed out, but the structure was intact. Abdulaziz's house was in good shape and his family was okay. They told stories of torture, rape, and vandalism. The Iraqi soldiers carried off everything they could. They also told of Iraqis kidnapping children for ransom. There were several stories of the Iraqis using electric drills to drill holes in Kuwaiti's arms until they could not take the pain, and then killing them. They even said that the tortures were videotaped by the Iraqis.[38]

3 March, 1991 [G+7/D+45]. The new brigade support area site is located at the Iraqi customs post. The place is pretty much trashed. I got my picture taken next to a picture of Saddam Hussein. The Kuwaiti translator for the 2nd Platoon, 1st Company Military Police knocked a hole in the face of the poster.

I took a shower in the afternoon. It was my first shower in perhaps ten days. I started to wash clothes, we ran out of water and there is no more in the BSA except for bottled water.

There are dogs all over the area. They run in packs and are becoming increasingly brave. Some of them are found eating the dead Iraqi bodies.

The highway is starting to carry civilian traffic again. This is the first civilian traffic I have seen in perhaps two months. There is a lack of security around the BSA. I guess the attitude is that the Iraqis would not dare attack us now and start the war over again.

4 March, 1991 [G+8/D+46]. There was a spot report that the Republican Guards are in conflict with rebel Iraqi Army forces in Basra and that they are using chemical weapons. The brigade sent out a decontamination team and a medical team to treat contaminated casualties.[39] The Kuwaiti hostages that were in Basra were released by the rebel Iraqi Army. About 1,200 passed through the brigade sector.

There were constant explosions all day long. The 1st Engineer Battalion, attached to the brigade, was blowing up Iraqi ammunition stores. One explosion I saw sent a fireball two hundred meters in the air. It was no more than one thousand meters away. The shock wave broke out all of the windows in the Iraqi customs post nearby. When the windows broke, I got down flat on the ground. Seconds later debris started raining down all around. One piece was a five-pound hunk of metal that landed twenty meters away. The whole front end of a truck landed no more than ten meters away from a sleeping tent for our headquarters company. We were extremely lucky that no one was killed. The engineers are supposed to give a warning for the explosions, but we only received a two-minute warning at the headquarters, and there was not enough time to warn all soldiers in the area. After that explosion, the brigade required the engineers to give at least a thirty-minute warning.

5 March, 1991 [G+9/D+47]. It rained in the morning and my tent got wet. A Kuwaiti brigadier general at the ALOC was trying to link-up with the hostages that were released last night. I had Abdulaziz explain that he was not permitted forward of the ALOC and that the released hostages had already been picked up.

Captain Bennie Williams, Bravo Company, 2nd Battalion, 16th Infantry (B Co., 2-16 Infantry) commander, came by with a deserter from the Republican Guards. I took him down to the Corps' EPW cage, but when I arrived they had already gone, and I went to division main (DMAIN) command post to find out where to take the prisoner. Every place I went was closed. I ended up at the 118th Military Police Battalion headquarters. They wouldn't accept the prisoner at first because they had closed their cages. They finally accepted him after some argument.

It was raining all the way down to the EPW cage. The closer we went to the burning oil wells, the thicker the smoke haze became until it was so thick we couldn't see the road. The smell of the burning oil was in the air. The rain water was draining on the graded-sand road into the 118 MP headquarters, forming a small stream on the desert floor. When we returned to the ALOC, it was flooded with five inches of water.

I was already cold and wet from trying to find the enemy-prisoner-of-war cage. When I arrived at the ALOC, my feet were soaked. I checked my tent and all of my gear was wet, including my sleeping bag, which was under water. I brought it into the ALOC to dry next to the heater. It was a futile effort. Staff Sergeant Sims loaned me his poncho liner to sleep in.

6 March, 1991 [G+10/D+48]. Two more enemy prisoners arrived. They were deserters from the Iraqi Army. One had deserted one month ago, the other eighteen months ago. They had been living in Safwan and crossed the border into Kuwait to get food from the Red Cross refugee center. The provincial Kuwaiti police arrested them. The Kuwaitis tied them up, beat them, stole 350 dinars, and burned them with cigarettes. They then turned the Iraqis over to our MPs. Our MPs accepted them without questioning the Kuwaitis. The Iraqis were not badly beaten, but they were physically abused, a serious violation of the Law of Land Warfare. I had the 101 MI interrogation team take statements from the Iraqis and gave the statements to the 233rd Military Police Company who accepted the prisoners from us.

8 March, 1991 [G+12/D+50]. Awards are the S-1 (personnel) section's priority mission now. The awards are for the 24 February to 3 March 1991 period. The standard for the Bronze Star is changing constantly, and every-body is changing their award recommendations constantly. Everyone wants their people to receive their fair share. The award criteria is subjective and depends more on what the higher headquarters will approve. Some units are setting standards for awards within their units, and their soldiers will be left out when the awards process is completed.

9 March, 1991 [G+13/D+51]. The engineers are constantly blowing up enemy equipment. The 1-4 Cav. had debris from the explosions flying within their perimeter. They frantically called for a cease fire. I am waiting for someone to die because of the engineers blowing up enemy equipment.

There was a new twist on the unexploded DPICM situation. Iraqi children are carrying these munitions up to our units, as if they are return-ing something we lost and want back.

The refugee problem continues to grow, with more and more civil-ians returning to the Safwan area and trying to get food from the American soldiers. Invariably, some soldiers will give food to the begging children, which encourages them to beg for more. It is sad to see children begging for food, but they have to be kept away from our perimeter for security reasons and for their own safety. Some of our trucks on the highway are being surrounded by refugees. Any time they see a truck with packages on it, they think it has food. The Red Cross refugee center is inundated with refugees.

10 March, 1991 [G+14/D+52]. The local provincial Kuwaiti prince came into our perimeter escorted by his bodyguard. They were wearing a mixture of clothes, from traditional Arab attire to jogging suits. All were armed with various weapons, from G-3 assault rifles to sub-machine guns. The weapons were all locked and loaded. The bodyguards formed a defensive perimeter around the prince as he talked to Major Branz. I sent Abdulaziz over to translate. Major Branz told the prince they must clear their weapons inside our perimeter. They were probably nervous since they were in Iraq. What they wanted to do was move the Red Cross refugee center closer to the border so they could return the Iraqi refugees to Iraq. We explained that we did not control the refugee center.

Two children have died. They and their mother were seriously injured today when they stepped on an unexploded DPICM. They were brought into our perimeter for medical care, but one of the children was already dead and the other died as Major Graham was operating on her. After the mother was stabilized, they were Medevaced to the evacuation hospital. Division was angry because we let them into our perimeter to provide medical care. They do not see the human agony or have to deal with dying people. Major Branz explained to them that it is the medics' duty to deal with any dying human and that we will continue to accept civilians in risk of life or limb for medical care.

Another 1st Infantry Division soldier died today from an accidental discharge. The total of 1st Infantry Division soldiers to die so far is eighteen, according to official records. The majority of the deaths are still from friendly fire or friendly unexploded munitions.

11 March, 1991 [G+15/D+53]. The Iraqis established a roadblock on the Basra-Kuwait City highway with a thirty-man infantry platoon. The position is within the demarcation line.[40] Colonel Moreno finally talked to one of their commanders, a brigadier general, and told him they needed to pull back by 1800 hours or we would remove them by force. The Iraqi general claimed that he didn't know that he was within the demarcation line. Our brigade moved 4-37 Armor up and an air troop from 1-4 Cav. The Iraqis pulled out at 1730.

Three more Iraqi civilians were brought in to the medical company for treatment of injuries sustained from accidentally setting off unexploded DPICMs.

The dogs continue to be a problem. I took a bowel movement at night and placed the waste in a plastic trash bag to put in a trash pit. When I approached the pit, two dogs would not let me approach and growled madly. I loaded my M16, but I could not see the dogs to shoot them, even though I knew they were close. I found myself in the embarrassing position of retreating from two dogs with a loaded M16.

12 March, 1991 [G+16/D+54]. The military police had six more prisoners turned into them by the local Kuwaiti police. One was belligerent and had to be flexi-cuffed. This was the first time we have had to restrain a prisoner because he was non-cooperative.

The day was darkly overcast and the sun appeared no brighter than a dim full moon. Vehicles turned on their headlights by 1400. It was colder than normal, perhaps because of the lack of sunshine.

The engineers continued to blow up vast quantities of ammunition and supplies. I was surprised that the Air Force had not already destroyed such a large concentration of fixed logistics sites during the air war.

13 March, 1991 [G+17/D+55]. We received notification to jump the brigade support area to the Safwan Airfield at 0700. We woke up early, tore down and prepared to move. We were then told that we would not move. We unpacked and set-up again on the same spot. I took this opportunity to straighten up my tent. The green duct tape had pulled off a long time ago, and I used safety pins from M16 ammunition bandoleers to close my tent door. I worry more about rats and bugs coming inside my tent now that we are in a populated area.

The entire division is being moved up to the demarcation line to conduct a screen. The Iraqis have a strong desire to recover as much munitions and equipment as possible before we destroy it or the anti-government forces recover it. The 1st Infantry Division is moving north to discourage this. With the current state of internal disarray, it is unlikely that Iraq will attempt to resume hostilities.

An exploding cluster bomb injured another Iraqi child. He was throwing rocks at the cluster bomb when it went off. His father said he told his son to leave the cluster bombs alone. I guess boys are boys no matter what the nationality.

14 March, 1991 [G+18/D+56]. Problems continue to arise with civilians. Reports are coming in that the Iraqi children will mob a truck, with one group in the front of the truck to stop it while the rest of the children go to the back of the truck to empty it of MREs and water. If the truck doesn't stop, they throw rocks at it. Our military police have been reporting that the Iraqi children have also been using unexploded cluster bombs in the road to stop vehicles.

18 March, 1991 [G+22/D+60]. The low temperature today was 54 degrees and high was 66 degrees. It felt colder because the smoke from the oil wells blocked the sun.

The military intelligence interrogators questioned five prisoners today that had been captured by 1st Engineer Battalion. Three of them were with the rebel Iraqi army. They were captured more for intelligence purposes, to find out what was happening inside Iraq. They told of chemical weapons being used in the cities of Najaf, Karbala, and Basra. [41] They told of the secret police torturing civilians in Basra after government forces had regained control. The person in charge of the secret police was Ali Hasan Majid, the Interior Minister, [42] and they said that he went into Basra after the rebel force had been defeated and strangled a child to symbolize the crushing of the resistance.

20 March, 1991 [G+24/D+62]. The BSA jumped 40 kilometers southwest into Kuwait. We stopped in the middle of the desert to allow 3rd Armor Division to assume the 1st Infantry Division mission. We only set up the minimal items needed. I slept on a cot outside and woke up with blown sand all over me. But at least we did get away from the smoke, the dogs and the refugees.

The 1st Infantry Division is moving 120 kilometers west, well inside Iraq, to conduct a show of force and convince the Iraqis that we are not leaving Iraq until the peace treaty is signed.

23 March, 1991 [G+27/D+65]. We are processing soldiers through the brigade ALOC to go on the "Love Boat" in Bahrain. They spend four nights and three days there, and two days in transit getting to Bahrain. They can wear civilian clothes in Bahrain, and they stay on a cruise ship anchored off the coast. Each company sends one soldier every nine days. One soldier told Major Branz that he took three showers every day on the ship.

24 March, 1991 [G+28/D+66]. We are starting to settle into southern-central Iraq. The division has realized that we are now more likely to go forward than back to assembly area Huebner.[43] They are moving up more division support assets. Colonel Moreno wants to take the time to reconstitute from the long road march and operations in the Safwan area. He wants every soldier to have two hot meals a day and some time off. We set up a rotation schedule to let every soldier off for a day to clean himself, organize his gear, and collect his thoughts.

31 March, 1991 [G+35/D+73]. We celebrated Easter Sunday today. Many of the soldiers had received packets with Easter bunnies and Easter chocolates. The brigade chaplain, Major Cook, conducted Easter Services in our area under a big cross.

The brigade volleyball tournament championship playoff was today. The winning team got to go on the "Love Boat" in Bahrain. Most of the teams did not find out about the prize until the playoff phase yesterday. If we had known earlier, I am sure there would have been a lot more teams practicing around the clock.

1 April, 1991 [G+36/D+74]. Major Brown, the battalion executive officer for 201st Forward Support Battalion, killed a pit viper in his tent with a sledge hammer. He put it in a plastic bag and showed it to several people. It was around two feet long, sand colored and about one-and-a-half-inches in diameter. It is starting to get scary around here with all the poisonous snakes and insects showing up. I check my tent each night to make sure it is closed. I spray it again with insecticide.

I feel lucky to be sleeping during the day. The temperature at night is in the mid-60s; during the day, the temperatures are up to 90 degrees. I sleep in my underwear on top of my sleeping bag. Around noon I have trouble sleeping for an hour or so because of the heat, but I usually go back to sleep after a while. I do not have to worry as much about the snakes and scorpions, since they are not active during the day. I can check my sleeping area out before I go to sleep in the daylight. I also can get more work done in the cooler nighttime hours.

16 April, 1991 [G+51/D+89]. We leave Iraq for redeployment assembly area (RAA) Huebner. I ride in the back of the M577, monitoring the brigade command net and assisting in the command and control of the brigade movement. The entire division moves out at the same time and everybody is happy to be finally leaving Iraq.

17 April, 1991 [G+52/D+90]. The brigade continues to move south. We covered over eighty miles yesterday. Today we passed through the same lanes that carried us north through the breach into Iraq. We stopped at Tapline Road[44] and waited for the entire division to ensure that all of the vehicles and soldiers have been recovered from Iraq.

As we waited, several local Arabs approached us offering to sell us Iraqi dinars at above the market rate. Two Arabs also approached and offered to buy weapons from us. They showed us cash, but we explained to them the best we could that we didn't have any weapons for sale.

18 April, 1991 [G+53/D+91]. At 0700, the brigade began to cross Tapline Road at six crossing points manned by the 1st Military Police Company. We reached RAA Huebner at 1100.

19 April, 1991 [G+54/D+92]. RAA Huebner is quite an extensive facility built in the middle of the desert. When the division planned its construction, I am sure they expected us to use these facilities for a longer period of time. There are concessions available, wolfburgers, a field PX, post office, telephone banks, a recreation center and a big screen television theater. I appreciate the facilities, but I think it was a waste of resources for the amount of time that they would be used by the majority of the soldiers. I feel that it contributed to a loss of focus on the mission in south-central Iraq.

29 April, 1991 [G+64/D+102]. Departed RAA Huebner at 0700. I rode back with Capt. Mark Crawford in an open-topped HMMWV. I am glad I used plenty of sunscreen and used a drive-on rag over my face. It was hot and the sun was bright. We drove down Tapline Road to Al Khobar.

3 May, 1991 [G+68/D+106]. The vehicles have all passed customs inspections and are now in the sterile area. There is not much to do. There are free magazines at the Saudi contractor dining facility. The lines are a lot shorter now than they were in January. They have opened up many more dining facilities and expanded the hours.

We all start cleaning our individual equipment for the redeployment. Normally this is a dull chore, but now it seems almost like a pleasure.

12 May, 1991 [G+77/D+115]. HHC 2nd Brigade redeployed today. We had our first flight formation at 0700 and moved off toward the airfield. After we passed the customs inspections, we boarded a Tower Air 747. We landed in Brussels that night to refuel.

13 May, 1991 [G+78/D+116]. The flight continued to New York for another refueling stop. They let us out of the plane, and we went to the USO area. They had donuts, sodas and coffee for us. I telephoned home to let my family know when I would be arriving at Fort Riley. We landed at Forbes, and there were already people waiting for us there. We all loaded up on buses and started the road journey to Fort Riley. All along the bus route there were yellow ribbons.

When we arrived in Fort Riley we turned in our weapons. We then formed up and marched into the hangar at Marshall Army Air field where our families were waiting for us. The commanding general gave a short speech and let three soldiers meet their newborn children for the first time. There were 475 soldiers on our flight and many more family dependents in the hangar. After the commanding general finished speaking, we were released for a two-day pass. I could not find my family in the crowd. After five minutes I finally found them, and I was home again.

Notes

1. A stick leader is temporarily placed in charge of all the personnel from a particular unit on an aircraft for purposes of deployment.

2. Headquarters and Headquarters Company, 2nd Mechanized Infantry Brigade (HHC 2nd BDE) is stationed at Fort Riley. Its mission is to provide command and control between a number of maneuver battalions and other combat support units as required.

3. Al Khobar is a village near Dhahran. The village had originally been built by the Saudi government to house bedouin families, but was turned over to U.S. forces to use during the war. A number of these complexes were built at places like Escan Village in Riyadh and Al Khobar, but the bedouins were reluctant to give up their nomadic life style, so these complexes were available for the U.S. troops. There was a group of bedouins living in another section of the Al Khobar complex, but they were separated by concertina wire from the American perimeter there. Whether the rest of the complex had ever been lived in or if the bedouins had simply left during the winter season when they traditionally lived in the desert is not known.

4. Housing the U.S. soldiers was a sensitive problem because the U.S. command was concerned for their safety and wanted to avoid incidents that might embarrass the Saudis. The Saudis were equally concerned with keeping the troops away from the populace as much as possible. Their first concern was with their role as the defenders of the Islamic culture and the honor of its holiest shrines. They didn't want images of shirt-sleeved American female soldiers, troops drinking alcohol, or Jewish and Christian religious ceremonies on Saudi soil to be broadcast throughout the Arab world. The self-contained housing complexes that kept the American troops largely out of sight were a perfect solution to both countries' problems.

5. This comment reflects widespread American resentment about Japan's role in the Gulf War alliance. Although deploying troops outside its borders is forbidden by the constitution imposed upon Japan following World War II, many Americans felt that because Kuwaiti oil was so essential to Japan's economic survival, they should be more committed to the war effort. The criticism ultimately led to Japan raising its financial contribution by early 1991 from its original one billion dollar pledge to almost eleven billion for U.S. expenses and three billion to the Middle East nations.

6. This meeting was considered the last real chance to avoid war. The United Nations had authorized the use of force unless the Iraqis withdrew by January 15. During a series of meetings and public exchanges, both sides had traded recriminations through the month of December, until finally Secretary James Baker and Iraqi Foreign Minister Tariq Aziz met on January 9 in Geneva. Hopes were raised when the meeting lasted an unexpected six and a half hours, but at the end of the meeting Aziz revealed his rejection of a letter from Bush to Hussein because he found the language "insulting."

7. An EOC was an all-purpose emergency center operating twenty-four-hours a day to handle everything from terrorist attacks to finding soldiers who had to go home because of family emergencies.

8. The EOCs issued three alert levels. "Threatcon Alpha" meant an attack was in progress; "Threatcon Bravo" meant an attack was expected in the near future; and "Threatcon Charlie" meant an attack was possible, but there was no immediate threat.

9. Kevlar is a DuPont trademark for a stronger-than-steel synthetic fiber used in making body armor.

10. Load bearing refers to regularly carried equipment such as pistol and pistol belt, ammunition pouch, canteen, etc.

11. A Tactical Assembly Area is a staging area used to prepare for combat operations. Security at 50 percent means that half of the soldiers are actually at their posts and half are off duty.

12. The decade-long controversy surrounding the Bradley Fighting Vehicle was one of the most contentious and public struggles over the development of a U.S. conventional weapon system, with delays, cost overruns, and multiple redesigns. The lengthy redesign process produced a heavily armed, heavily armored vehicle to be used in concert with M1 tanks and Apache helicopters to move troops quickly in front-line attacks. The Gulf War was the Bradley's first use in actual warfare and it performed very effectively.

13. On October 23, 1983, a suicide bomber drove a truck-bomb through roadblocks around the Marine Barracks at Beirut International Airport. The explosion killed 241 marines.

14. On January 13, U.N. Secretary General Perez de Cuellar was in Baghdad meeting with Saddam Hussein, and it is reported he offered a guarantee that the Allies would not attack if Saddam agreed to withdraw immediately from Kuwait. De Cuellar characterized the meeting as fruitless.

15. After returning from the Gulf War, Captain Smith was assigned to do the line of duty report on the soldier who shot himself in the foot. All evidence indicated that it was in fact intentional in order to avoid combat.

16. The Army Air Force Exchange Service runs all of the post exchanges, which are general stores known as PXs.

17. There are four levels of Mission Oriented Protection Posture (MOPP) for biological and chemical attack. MOPP 1 calls for wearing a protective overgarment and carrying protective boots, mask, and gloves. MOPP 2 calls for wearing both overgarment and boots. MOPP 3 calls for wearing the overgarment, boots, and mask. MOPP 4 calls for wearing all protective gear—overgarment, boots, mask, and gloves.

18. There are three NBC statuses: green means no threat; amber means a probable threat; and red means an NBC attack is in progress.

19. The Scud is a liquid-fueled surface-to-air missile developed by the Soviets in the mid-1960s to deliver nuclear weapons over short distances. The Iraqis bought hundreds of Scuds from the Soviets and used them to attack cities in Iran during the Iran-Iraq War. The Iraqis modified the missiles to increase their range and outfitted them to be fired from mobile launchers. Considered to be of limited military value because of their inaccuracy, the Scud created concern during the Gulf War as a weapon of terror because it could be used to deliver chemical or biological weapons and because it could reach Israel.

20. The Patriot is designed to intercept and destroy missiles with shrapnel explosions. It consists of a launcher, a control station, and a trailer with a sophisticated radar system. First used in combat in the Gulf War, the Patriot system proved to be effective against Iraqi Scuds.

21. During the first days of Allied bombing, Iraq threatened to expand the war by attacking Israel with chemical warheads from its Scud missiles. On January 18, eight Scuds were fired at the cities of Tel Aviv and Haifa, causing property damage and dozens of injuries. Later that day another Scud was fired at Saudi Arabia, but was destroyed by a Patriot. The attacks on Tel Aviv caused an outcry in Israel for retaliation against Iraq. This could have unraveled the allied coalition by putting Arabs in the position of fighting on the same side as Israel against another Arab country, but the Israelis agreed, after consultations with the United States, to refrain from retaliation.

22. Damman is a port in the vicinity of Al Khobar, Dhahran, and the bridge to Bahrain.

23. The Global Positioning System is a network of satellites used in conjunction with ground units to give exact locations. They are about four inches by ten inches and weigh about one and a half pounds. They were distributed down to the platoon level during Desert Storm and proved to be a great advantage as Allied Forces swept west of Kuwait City into the flat desert, without landmarks, to out-flank the Iraqis.

24. Duane Smith was stationed in Panama during his first assignment, from 1982–84, at Fort Clayton in what had formerly been the Canal Zone.

25. Moving hundreds of miles at a time and with transmitters limited to low wattages to keep them from interfering with Saudi broadcasting, U.S. troops were often out of reach of AFRTS stations.

26. This was a diamond-shaped area 280 kilometers west of the Persian Gulf between Iraq and Saudi Arabia.

27. Hellfire missiles are usually guided by lasers. The helicopter projects a laser spot on the target. Another laser, often manned by a soldier on the ground, also lazes the target, giving its position. The missile is then guided to the target by the laser spots.

28. *Time* magazine reported that 35 of the 145 deaths and 72 of the 467 wounded reported by the military to that time were caused by friendly fire incidents. Although military experts expect this kind of statistic in combat, civilians, and especially the media, found it shocking. Such casualties during the Gulf War seemed more tragic because the war produced the lowest casualty numbers on the allied side of any comparable war, lower even than the Spanish-American War. Overcast weather, large nighttime operations, and new technology with increased range for frontline weapons systems made target evaluation difficult. Twenty of the twenty-five Bradley Fighting Vehicles destroyed in the war were destroyed by U.S. fire. After the war, the army pledged to upgrade its IFF, or Identification of Friend or Foe, procedures.

29. The CANA injectors are used to give anti-nerve gas injections and the M291 kits are personal decontamination kits.

30. Large, flat-bed trucks used to transport heavy vehicles, such as tanks and bulldozers.

31. The staff supply officer.

32. The army's High Mobility Multi-purpose Wheeled Vehicle is the successor to the Jeep.

33. This is the infamous Highway 6, also called "The Highway of Death" and "The Highway to Hell." An Iraqi convoy of over one thousand vehicles was bombed on that highway on February 26 and completely destroyed. Broadcast of pictures of the miles of wreckage shocked the world. In his autobiography, *It Doesn't Take a Hero*, General H. Norman Schwarzkopf says that the casualties caused by the bombing have been exaggerated and most of the Iraqis abandoned their vehicles during the bombardment.

34. Iraqi troops apparently mined all of Kuwait's one thousand oil wells shortly after the invasion. They detonated the mines as they retreated, leaving six hun-

dred wells on fire. The pollution caused by this ecological warfare and the earlier Iraqi ploy of releasing crude oil into the Persian Gulf from one of Kuwait's offshore pipelines further outraged the world. The Iraqis had first adopted the tactic of destroying oil pumping facilities in 1986 following their attack on the Iranian oil fields at Tabriz during the Iran-Iraq War.

35. Armored Combat Engineer Vehicle, an armored bulldozer.

36. The plan was for the capturing unit to search the prisoners, confiscate any weapons, and tag the prisoners and their personal possessions with an invoice. The prisoners were then to be brought to the brigade cages, segregated by rank, interrogated, fed, and treated for any life-threatening injuries. They were then supposed to be moved to division cages, and then to corps cages. As the ground operation progressed, there were so many prisoners that this plan tended to break down. Toward the end of the operation, advancing units would simply toss prisoners cartons of MREs, point north, and move on.

37. This is the site in the American-held sector of southern Iraq where General Schwarzkopf and Saudi General Khalid met with Iraqi generals Ahmad and Mahmud to dictate the conditions of the cease-fire on March 3.

38. A U.S. Defense Department report submitted to the United Nations in 1993 blamed the death of 1,082 Kuwaiti civilians on Iraqi atrocities and documented the existence of at least two-dozen Iraqi torture sites in occupied Kuwait. Torture appeared to be aimed at stifling Kuwaiti resistance, however slight, by making gruesome examples of anyone behaving impolitely toward Iraqis. The report presents evidence that many prisoners were slowly hacked to death in front of their families. The use of rape and sexual mutilation as a way of further humiliating Kuwaitis was also reported.

39. Much was made of the Iraqi ability to use chemical weapons before the Gulf War began and the threat of chemical weapons had tremendous psychological impact, although in fact none were actually used against allied troops. During the rebellions that followed the allied victory expectations about the use of chemical weapons rose again, fed by stories from refugees and the fact that Iraq had previously used them on its own rebellious population, most notoriously in a 1988 attack on the Kurdish town of Halabja.

40. Generally speaking, the demarcation line agreed to at the meeting at Safwan on March 3 went north from Saudi Arabia just to the west of Al Salman until it met the Euphrates River and then traveled east along that river's southern shore, eventually dipping south of Basra, and then to the Persian Gulf.

41. By March 7, 1991, fifteen cities in Iraq were reportedly in revolt against the government of Saddam Hussein. The revolts were led mainly by Kurdish and Shiite minorities. Najaf, Karbala, and Basra were centers of Shiite rebellion. Najaf

and Karbala are areas holy to this sect. Stories of the use of chemical weapons to quell these rebellions were widespread, but never confirmed. Western correspondents were able to ascertain only that the Iraqi military dropped leaflets threatening its use and probably did disperse conventional tear gas from the air in some instances.

42. Ali Hassan Majid is believed to be the man who ordered the 1988 gassing of the Kurdish town of Halabja. He directed the occupation of Kuwait for its first three months and is a member of Hussein's innermost circle.

43. This was a holding area consisting of portable buildings and tents set up in the Saudi desert for U.S. troops who were waiting their turn to redeploy to the coast for the return home.

44. Tapline Road is a two-lane highway through desolate country from the Saudi Arabian coast near the western corner of Kuwait to Jordan. During the war, it was used to move men and supplies west. It gets its name from the Trans-Arabian pipeline, known as the "Tapline," which route it generally follows.

Bibliography

The Revolutionary War

Ernst, Joseph Albert. *Money and Politics in America, 1755–1775*. Chapel Hill: University of North Carolina Press, 1973.

Greene, Jack P., Ed. *The American Revolution: Its Character and Limits*. New York: New York University Press, 1987.

Higginbotham, Don. *The War of American Independence: Military Attitudes, Policies, and Practice, 1763–1789*. New York: Macmillan, 1971.

Higginbotham, Don, Ed. *Reconsiderations on the Revolutionary War: Selected Essays*. Westport, CT: Greenwood Press, 1978.

Martin, Joseph Plumb. *A Narrative of Some of the Adventures, Dangers and Sufferings of a Revolutionary Soldier, Interspersed with Anecdotes of Incidents That Occurred Within His Own Observation*. Hallowell, ME: 1830.

——. *Private Yankee Doodle: Being a Narrative of Some of the Adventures, Dangers and Sufferings of a Revolutionary Soldier by Joseph Plumb Martin*. Ed. George F. Scheer. Boston: Little, Brown and Co., 1962.

Rakove, Jack N. *The Beginnings of National Politics: An Interpretive History of the Continental Congress*. New York: Alfred A. Knopf, distr. by Random House, 1979.

Royster, Charles. *A Revolutionary People at War: The Continental Army and American Character, 1775–1783*. Chapel Hill: University of North Carolina Press, 1979.

Wood, Gordon S. *The Radicalism of the American Revolution*. New York: Alfred A. Knopf, 1992.

Young, Eleanor. *Forgotten Patriot: Robert Morris.* New York: The Macmillan Co., 1950.

The Civil War

Beringer, Richard E., et al. *Why the South Lost the Civil War.* Athens: University of Georgia Press, 1986.

Catton, Bruce. *The Centennial History of the Civil War,* 3 vols. Vol. I: *The Coming Fury,* vol. II: *Terrible Swift Sword,* vol. III: *Never Call Retreat.* Garden City, NY: Doubleday, 1961–65.

Farwell, Byron. *Stonewall: A Biography of General Thomas J. Jackson.* New York: Norton, 1992.

Foote, Shelby. *The Civil War: A Narrative,* 3 vols. Vol. I: *Fort Sumter to Perryville,* vol. II: *Fredericksburg to Meridian,* vol. III: *Red River to Appomattox.* New York: Random House, 1958–74.

McPherson, James M. *Ordeal by Fire.* New York: Alfred A. Knopf, 1982.

The Spanish-American War

Gatewood, Williard B., Jr. *Black Americans and the White Man's Burden, 1898–1903.* Urbana: University of Illinois Press, 1975.

Holm, Jeanne. *Women in the Military: An Unfinished Revolution.* Novato, CA: Presidio Press, 1982.

Keller, Allan. *The Spanish-American War: A Compact History.* New York: Hawthorn Books, Inc., 1969.

Perret, Geoffrey. *A Country Made by War.* New York: Vintage Books, 1990.

Roosevelt, Theodore. *The Rough Riders.* New York: Charles Scribner's, 1902.

Trask, David F. *The War with Spain in 1898.* New York: Macmillan Publishing Co., 1981.

World War I

Hoobler, Dorothy and Thomas Hoobler. *The Trenches: Fighting on the Western Front in World War I.* New York: G.P. Putnam's Sons, 1978.

Prior, Robin and Trevor Wilson. *Command on the Western Front: The Military Career of Sir Henry Rawlinson, 1914–18.* Cambridge, Mass.: Basil Blackwell Press, 1992.

Thoumin, General Richard. *The First World War*. Trans. and ed. Martin Kieffer. New York: G.P. Putnam's Sons, 1960.

Toland, John. *No Man's Land: 1918, the Last Year of the Great War*. Garden City, NY: Doubleday and Company, 1980.

Tuchman, Barbara Wertheim. *The Guns of August*. New York: Macmillan Company, 1962.

Winter, J. M. *The Experience of World War I*. New York: Oxford University Press, 1989.

World War II

Devlin, Gerard M. *Back to Corregidor: America Retakes the Rock*. New York: St. Martin's Press, 1992.

Fahey, James J. *Pacific War Diary, 1942–1945*. Boston: Houghton Mifflin Co., 1963.

Hoyt, Edwin P. *The Battle of Leyte Gulf: The Death Knell of the Japanese Fleet*. New York: Weybright & Talley, 1972.

Layton, Edwin T. with Roger Pineau and John Costello. *"And I Was There": Pearl Harbor and Midway—Breaking the Secrets*. New York: William Morrow, 1985.

Leckie, Robert. *The Wars of America*. New York: HarperCollins Publishers, 1968.

Manchester, William. *Goodbye, Darkness: A Memoir of the Pacific War*. Boston: Little, Brown, 1980.

McCullough, David. *Truman*. New York: Simon & Schuster, 1992.

Mooney, James L., Ed. *Dictionary of American Naval Fighting Ships*, vol. III: *Historical Sketches—Letters W through Z*. Washington: Naval Historical Center, Department of the Navy, 1981.

Morison, Samuel Eliot. *History of U.S. Naval Operations in WW II: Leyte, June 1944–January 1945*, vol. 12. Boston: Little, Brown and Co., 1961.

Perret, Geoffrey. *A Country Made by War*. New York, Vintage Books, 1990.

Sears, Stephen W., Ed. *Eyewitness to World War II: The Best of American Heritage*. Boston: Houghton Mifflin Co., 1991.

Vining, Donald. *American Diaries of World War II*. New York: The Pepys Press, 1982.

Wade, Betsy. *Forward Positions: The War Correspondence of Homer Bigart.* Fayetteville: University of Arkansas Press, 1992.

Y'Blood, William T. *Red Sun Setting.* Annapolis: Naval Institute Press, 1981.

The Vietnam War

Del Vecchio, John M. *The 13th Valley.* New York: Bantam Books, 1982.

Hammel, Eric. *Khe Sanh: Siege in the Clouds.* New York: Crown Publishers, Inc., 1989.

Leckie, Robert. *The Wars of America.* New York: HarperCollins Publishers, 1968.

Lifton, Robert Jay. *Home from the War.* Boston: Beacon Press, 1973.

Perret, Geoffrey. *A Country Made by War.* New York: Vintage Books, 1990.

Santoli, Al. *Everything We Had.* New York: Ballantine Books, 1981.

Schell, Jonathan. *The Real War.* New York: Pantheon Books, 1987.

Terry, Wallace. *Bloods: An Oral History of the Vietnam War by Black Veterans.* New York: Ballantine Books, 1984.

The Gulf War

Leckie, Robert. *The Wars of America.* New York: HarperCollins Publishers, 1968.

Schwarzkopf, General H. Norman with Peter Petre. *It Doesn't Take a Hero: General H. Norman Schwarzkopf, the Autobiography.* New York: Bantam Books, 1992.